Frommer's Hawai'i 2017

By Martha Cheng, Jeanne Cooper & Shannon Wianecki

FrommerMedia LLC

Published by
Frommer Media LLC

ISBN 978-1-62887-314-6 (paper), 978-1-62887-315-3 (e-book)

Editorial Director: Pauline Frommer
Editor: Alexis Lipsitz Flippin
Production Editor: Michael Brumitt
Cartographer: Roberta Stockwell
Photo Editor: Helen Stallion
Front cover photo: © Konstanttin/Shutterstock.com
Back cover photo: © KQRoy/Shutterstock.com

For information on our other products or services, see www.frommers.com. Frommer Media LLC also publishes its books in a variety of electronic formats.

Manufactured in China

5 4 3 2 1

HOW TO CONTACT US

In researching this book, we discovered many wonderful places—hotels, restaurants, shops, and more. We're sure you'll find others. Please tell us about them, so we can share the information with your fellow travelers in upcoming editions. If you were disappointed with a recommendation, we'd love to know that, too. Please write to: Support@FrommerMedia.com

FROMMER'S STAR RATINGS SYSTEM

Every hotel, restaurant and attraction listed in this guide has been ranked for quality and value. Here's what the stars mean:

★ Recommended
★★ Highly Recommended
★★★ A must! Don't miss!

AN IMPORTANT NOTE

The world is a dynamic place. Hotels change ownership, restaurants hike their prices, museums alter their opening hours, and busses and trains change their routings. And all of this can occur in the several months after our authors have visited, inspected, and written about, these hotels, restaurants, museums and transportation services. Though we have made valiant efforts to keep all our information fresh and up-to-date, some few changes can inevitably occur in the periods before a revised edition of this guidebook is published. So please bear with us if a tiny number of the details in this book have changed. Please also note that we have no responsibility or liability for any inaccuracy or errors or omissions, or for inconvenience, loss, damage, or expenses suffered by anyone as a result of assertions in this guide.

CONTENTS

LIST OF MAPS

ABOUT THE AUTHORS

Martha Cheng came to Hawai'i for a boy and stayed for its food, ocean, and people. She is the former food editor of *Honolulu Magazine* and now writes feature stories for local and national publications on everything from squash farms in Waimea to fly fishing in Maui. Originally from San Francisco, she's a former pastry chef, line cook, food-truck owner, Peace Corps volunteer, and Google techie. These days, she surfs, eats, and writes.

Jeanne Cooper fell in love with the real Hawai'i on her first visit in 1998, after growing up with enchanting stories and songs of the islands from her mother, who had lived there as a girl. The former editor of the *San Francisco Chronicle* travel section, Jeanne writes frequently about Hawai'i for the newspaper and its website, SFGate.com, home of her Aloha Friday column and Hawaii Insider blog, and for magazines such as *Sunset* and *Caviar Affair.* She has also contributed to guidebooks on her former hometowns of Boston, Washington, D.C., and San Francisco.

Shannon Wianecki grew up in Hawai'i swimming in waterfalls, jumping off of sea cliffs, and breakfasting on ripe mangoes. An award-winning writer and editor, she writes feature stories for numerous travel and lifestyle magazines. Having served 8 years as food editor for *Maui No Ka 'Oi Magazine*, she knows the island's restaurant scene as well as her own kitchen. She once won the Maui Dreams Dive Company's pumpkin-carving contest.

ACKNOWLEDGEMENTS

Thanks to Anna Harmon, for the famed staycation memory, and Kelly Tam Sing for being home base.

—Martha Cheng

I would like to thank my editor, Alexis Lipsitz Flippin, and my husband, Ian Hersey, for their support, and all those in Hawai'i who have shared their knowledge and aloha with me.

—Jeanne Cooper

Thanks to Gabe Marihugh for driving the Jeep through mudbogs in Lāna'i.

—Shannon Wianecki

1

THE BEST OF HAWAI'I

There's no place on earth quite like this handful of sun-drenched Pacific islands. Here you'll find palm-fringed blue lagoons, lush rainforests, cascading waterfalls, soaring summits (some capped with snow), a live volcano, and beaches of every hue: gold, red, black, and even green. Roadside stands offer fruits and flowers for pocket change, and award-winning chefs deliver unforgettable feasts. Each of the six main islands possesses its own unique mix of natural and cultural treasures—and the possibilities for adventure, indulgence, and relaxation are endless.

THE best BEACHES

- **Lanikai Beach** (O'ahu): Too gorgeous to be real, this stretch along the Windward Coast is one of Hawai'i's postcard-perfect beaches—a mile of golden sand as soft as powdered sugar bordering translucent turquoise waters. The waters are calm year-round and excellent for swimming, snorkeling, and kayaking. Two tiny offshore islands complete the picture, functioning both as scenic backdrops and bird sanctuaries. See p. 106.

Lanikai Beach, O'ahu. PREVIOUS PAGE: **Hawaiian beach.**

- **Hāpuna Beach** (Big Island): A half-mile of tawny sand, as wide as a football field, gently slopes down to crystalline waters that in summer are usually excellent for swimming, snorkeling, and bodysurfing; in winter, the thundering waves should be admired from the shore, where the picnicking and state camping facilities are first rate. See p. 221.
- **Wai'ānapanapa State Park** (Maui): Maui has many terrific beaches to choose from, but this one is extra special: On the dramatic Hāna coast, jet-black sand is pummeled by the azure surf, sea arches and caves dot the shoreline, and a forested path leads to a secret swimming hole, the hiding place of an ancient Hawaiian princess. Plan to picnic or camp here. See p. 330.
- **Pāpōhaku Beach Park** (Moloka'i): The currents are too strong for swimming here, but the light-blond strand of sand, nearly 300 feet wide and stretching for some 3 miles—one of Hawai'i's longest beaches—is great for picnicking, walking, and watching sunsets, with O'ahu shimmering in the distance. See p. 448.
- **Hulopo'e Beach** (Lāna'i): This large sprawl of soft golden sand is one of the prettiest in the state. Bordered by the regal Four Seasons resort on one side and lava-rock tide pools on the other, this protected marine preserve offers prime swimming, snorkeling, tide-pool exploring, picnicking, camping, and the chance to spy on resident spinner dolphins. See p. 473.
- **Po'ipū Beach** (Kaua'i): This popular beach on the sunny South Shore has something for everyone: protected swimming, snorkeling, bodyboarding, surfing, and plenty of sand for basking—with a rare Hawaiian monk seal joining sunbathers every so often. See p. 532.

THE best AUTHENTIC EXPERIENCES

- **Eat Local:** People in Hawai'i love food. Want to get a local talking? Ask for her favorite place to get poke or saimin or shave ice. The islands offer excellent fine-dining opportunities (see the examples below), but they also have plenty of respectable hole-in-the-wall joints and beloved institutions that have hung around for half a century. On O'ahu, eat poke at **Ono Seafood** (p. 145), enjoy true Hawaiian food at **Helena's Hawaiian Food** (p. 149), and join the regulars at **Liliha Bakery** (p. 150) for a loco moco. On Kaua'i, slurp saimin and shave ice at **Hamura's Saimin Stand** (p. 582).
- **Feel History Come Alive at Pearl Harbor** (O'ahu): On December 7, 1941, Japanese warplanes bombed Pearl Harbor, forcing the United States to enter World War II. Standing on the deck of the **USS**

Hula.

***Arizona* Memorial**—the eternal tomb for the 1,177 sailors trapped below when the battleship sank—is a profound experience. You can also visit the USS *Missouri* Memorial, where the Japanese signed their surrender on September 2, 1945. See p. 77.

- **Experience Hula:** Each year the city of Hilo on the Big Island hosts a prestigious competition celebrating ancient Hawaiian dance: the **Merrie Monarch Festival** (p. 175). The week after Easter, local *hālau* (hula troupes) perform **free shows** at several shopping centers. On O'ahu, check out the **Bishop Museum** (p. 71), which stages excellent performances on weekdays, or head to the Halekulani's **House Without a Key** (p. 165) at sunset to watch the enchanting Kanoelehua Miller dance beautiful hula under a century-old *kiawe* tree. On Maui, the **Old Lahaina Lū'au** (p. 427) is the real deal, showcasing Hawaiian dance and storytelling nightly on a gracious, beachfront stage.
- **Ponder Petroglyphs:** More than 23,000 ancient rock carvings decorate the lava fields at **Hawai'i Volcanoes National Park** (p. 207) on the Big Island. You can see hundreds more on a short hike through the **Puakō Petroglyph Archaeological Preserve** (p. 189), near the Fairmont Orchid on the Kohala Coast. Go early in the morning or late afternoon when the angle of the sun lets you see the forms clearly. On Lāna'i, fantastic birdmen and canoes are etched into rocks at **Luahiwa** (p. 470), **Shipwreck Beach** (p. 475), and **Kaunolu Village** (p. 472).
- **Trek to Kalaupapa** (Moloka'i): The only access to this hauntingly beautiful and remote place is by foot, mule, or nine-seater plane. Hikers can descend the 26 switchbacks on the sea cliff's narrow 3-mile

trail, but the **Kalaupapa Guided Mule Tour** (p. 442) is a once-in-a-lifetime adventure astride sure-footed mules. Once you've reached the peninsula, you'll board the **Damien Tours** bus (p. 444)—your transport back to a time when islanders with Hansen's Disease (leprosy) were exiled to Moloka'i and Father Damien devoted his life to care for them.

THE best OUTDOOR ADVENTURES

- **Surfing on O'ahu:** Whether you're learning to surf or a pro, O'ahu has waves for everyone. Few experiences are more exhilarating than standing on your first wave, and Waikīkī offers plenty of lessons, board rentals, and gentle surf. During the winter, the North Shore gets big and rough, so stay out of the water if you're not an experienced surfer. But even the view from the beach, watching the daredevils take off on waves twice their height, is thrilling. See p. 113.
- **Witness the Whales:** From December to April, humpback whales cruise Hawaiian waters. You can see these gentle giants from almost any shore; simply scan the horizon for a spout. You can hear them, too, by ducking your head below the surface and listening for their otherworldly music. Boats on every island offer whale-watching cruises, but Maui is your best bet for seeing the massive marine mammals up close. Try **Trilogy** (p. 333) for a first-class catamaran ride or, if you're adventurous, climb into an outrigger canoe with **Hawaiian Paddle Sports** (p. 334).
- **Visit Volcanoes:** The entire island chain is made of volcanoes; don't miss the opportunity to explore them. On O'ahu, the whole family can hike to the top of ancient, world-famous **Diamond Head Crater** (p. 114). At **Hawai'i Volcanoes National Park** (p. 207) on the Big Island, where Kīlauea has been erupting since 1983, acres of new black rock and billowing sulfurous steam give hints of Pele's presence even when red-hot lava isn't visible. On Maui, **Haleakalā National Park** (p. 309) provides a bird's-eye view into a long-dormant volcanic crater.

Lava flowing into the sea.

THE welcoming LEI

A lei is aloha turned tangible, communicating "hello," "goodbye," "congratulations," and "I love you" in a single strand of fragrant flowers. Leis are the perfect symbol for the islands: Their fragrance and beauty are enjoyed in the moment, but the aloha they embody lasts long after they've faded.

Traditionally, Hawaiians made leis out of flowers, shells, ferns, leaves, nuts, and even seaweed. Some were twisted, some braided, and some strung. Then, as now, they were worn to commemorate special occasions, honor a loved one, or complement a hula dancer's costume. Leis are available at all of the islands' airports, from florists, and even at supermarkets. You can find wonderful, inexpensive leis at the half-dozen lei shops on **Maunakea Street** in Honolulu's Chinatown and at **Castillo Orchids,** 73-4310 Lau'ī St., off Ka'iminani Drive in the Kona Palisades subdivision, across from the Kona Airport on the Big Island (✆ **808/329-6070**). You can also arrange in advance to have a lei-greeter meet you as you deplane. **Greeters of Hawai'i** (www.greetersofhawaii.com; ✆ **800/366-8559**) serves the major airports on O'ahu, Maui, Kaua'i, and the Big Island.

- **Get Misted by Waterfalls:** Waterfalls thundering down into sparkling pools are some of Hawai'i's most beautiful natural wonders. If you're on the Big Island, head to the spectacular 442-foot **'Akaka Falls** (p. 193), north of Hilo. On Maui, the Road to Hāna offers numerous viewing opportunities; at the end of the drive, you'll find **'Ohe'o Gulch** (p. 320), with some of the most dramatic and accessible waterfalls on the islands. Kaua'i is laced with waterfalls, especially along the North Shore and in the Wailua area, where you can drive right up to 151-foot **'Ōpaeka'a Falls** (p. 509) and 80-foot **Wailua Falls** (p. 509). On Moloka'i, the 250-foot **Mo'oula Falls** (p. 436) can be visited only via a guided cultural hike through breathtaking Hālawa Valley, but that, too, is a very special experience.
- **Peer into Waimea Canyon** (Kaua'i): It may not share the vast dimensions of Arizona's Grand Canyon, but Kaua'i's colorful gorge—a mile wide, 3,600 feet deep, and 14 miles long—has a grandeur all its own, easily viewed from several overlooks just off Kōke'e Road. Hike to Waipo'o Falls to experience its red parapets up close, or take one of the helicopter rides that swoop between its walls like the white-tailed tropicbird. See p. 521.
- **Explore the Nāpali Coast** (Kaua'i): With the exception of the Kalalau Valley Overlook, the fluted ridges and deep, primeval valleys of the island's northwest portion can't be viewed by car. You must hike the 11-mile Kalalau Trail (p. 497), kayak (p. 537), take a snorkel cruise (p. 541), or book a helicopter ride (p. 523) to experience its wild, stunning beauty.

- **Four-Wheel It on Lāna'i** (Lāna'i): Off-roading is a way of life on barely paved Lāna'i. Rugged trails lead to deserted beaches, abandoned villages, sacred sites, and valleys filled with wild game.

THE best HOTELS

- **Halekulani** (O'ahu; www.halekulani.com; © **800/367-2343**): When price is no object, this is really the only place to stay. A place of Zen amid the buzz, this beach hotel is the finest Waikīkī has to offer. Even if you don't stay here, pop by for a sunset Mai Tai at House Without a Key to hear live Hawaiian music while a lovely hula dancer sways to the music. See p. 128.
- **Royal Hawaiian** (O'ahu; www.royal-hawaiian.com; © **800/325-3535**): This flamingo-pink oasis, hidden away among blooming gardens within the concrete jungle of Waikīkī, is a stunner. It's vibrant and exotic, from the Spanish-Moorish arches in the common spaces to the pink-and-gold pineapple wallpaper in the rooms in the Historic Wing. See p. 130.
- **Kahala Hotel & Resort** (O'ahu; www.kahalaresort.com; © **800/367-2525**): Situated in one of O'ahu's most prestigious residential areas, the Kahala provides the peace and serenity of a neighbor-island vacation, but with the conveniences of Waikīkī just a 10-minute drive away. The lush, tropical grounds include an 800-foot, crescent-shaped

Four Seasons Resort Hualalai, the Big Island.

Grand Hyatt, Kauai.

beach and a 26,000-square-foot lagoon (home to two bottlenose dolphins, sea turtles, and tropical fish). See p. 134.

- **Four Seasons Resort Hualalai** (Big Island; www.fourseasons.com/hualalai; ✆ **888/340-5662**): The seven pools alone will put you in seventh heaven at this exclusive yet environmentally conscious oasis of understated luxury, which also offers a private, 18-hole golf course and an award-winning spa, exquisite dining, and impeccable service—with no resort fee. See p. 256.
- **Fairmont Orchid Hawai'i** (Big Island; www.fairmont.com/orchid; ✆ **800/845-9905**): Subtle elegance and warm service mark this recently renovated beachfront hotel in the Mauna Lani Resort, which takes pride in the area's cultural treasures—including a vast petroglyph field and a network of fish ponds—as well as its own top-notch dining and an inviting, open-air spa set amid tumbling waterfalls and leafy walkways. Just outside the Fairmont lie two 18-hole championship golf courses of equal beauty. See p. 258.
- **Hapuna Beach Prince Hotel** (Big Island; www.princeresortshawaii.com/hapuna-beach-prince-hotel; ✆ **888/977-4623**): This is the sleeper on the Kohala Coast, boasting huge rooms, an enormous beach, and an exceptional restaurant in a relaxing, low-key atmosphere. A nightly shuttle allows guests to explore the excellent dining options at the iconic Mauna Kea Beach Hotel, the property's gorgeous but pricier sister. See p. 259.

- **Andaz Maui** (Maui; www.maui.andaz.hyatt.com; © **808/573-1234**): The newest resort in Wailea offers a prime beachfront locale, chic decor, an apothecary-style spa, and two phenomenal restaurants, including one by superstar chef Masaharu Morimoto. Accommodations here ramp up the style quotient with crisp white linens, warm wood furniture, and midcentury accents. Wrap yourself in a plush robe and nosh on the complimentary minibar snacks from the sanctuary of your private lanai. Visit the 'Āwili Spa, where you can mix your own massage oil and body scrubs; yoga and fitness classes are complimentary. See p. 373.
- **Travaasa Hāna** (Maui; www.travaasa.com/hana; © **808/248-8211**): Nestled in the center of quaint Hāna town, this 66-acre resort wraps around Kau'iki Head, the dramatic point where Queen Kaahumanu was born. You'll feel like royalty in one of the Sea Ranch Cottages here. Floor-to-ceiling sliding doors open to spacious lanais, some with private hot tubs. You'll be far from shopping malls and sports bars, but exotic red-, black-, and white-sand beaches are just a short walk or shuttle ride away. This is luxury in its purest form. See p. 383.
- **Four Seasons Resort Lanai at Manele Bay** (Lāna'i, www.fourseasons.com/lanai; © **800/321-4666**): This gracious resort on Lāna'i's south

Dole Plantation, pineapple field, O'ahu.

coast overlooks Hulopo'e Beach—one of the finest stretches of sand in the state. Guest rooms are palatial, outfitted with museum-quality art and automated everything—from temperature, lighting, and sound system to fancy toilets! The suites have deep soaking Japanese cedar tubs, and views that stretch on for an eternity. The restaurants and service throughout the resort are impeccable. See p. 481.

- **Grand Hyatt Kauai Resort & Spa** (Kaua'i; www.kauai.hyatt.com; © **800/554-9288**): At this sprawling, family-embracing resort in Po'ipū, the elaborate, multitiered fantasy pool and saltwater lagoon more than compensate for the rough waters of Keoneloa (Shipwrecks) Beach. Don't fret: Calmer Po'ipū Beach is just a short drive away. Anara Spa and Poipu Bay Golf Course offer excellent adult diversions, too. See p. 570.
- **Poipu Plantation B&B Inn and Vacation Rentals** (Kaua'i; www.poipubeach.com; © **800/643-0263**): Just a short walk from Brennecke and Po'ipū beaches, a handsomely renovated 1938 cottage holds four bed-and-breakfast suites, with a half-dozen well-equipped cottage units sharing the quiet compound, managed by gracious innkeepers and their helpful staff. See p. 573.

THE best RESTAURANTS

- **Alan Wong's Restaurant** (O'ahu; www.alanwongs.com; © **808/949-2526**): Master strokes at this shrine of Hawai'i Regional Cuisine include ginger-crusted fresh *onaga* (red snapper), a whole-tomato salad dressed with *li hing ume* (plum powder) vinaigrette, and *opihi* (limpet) shooters. Alan Wong reinvents local flavors for the fine-dining table in ways that continue to surprise and delight. See p. 151.
- **Izakaya Gaku** (O'ahu; © **808/589-1329**): The city is dotted with *izakayas,* Japanese pubs serving small plates made for sharing, and Izakaya Gaku is the best of them all. You'll discover life beyond maguro and hamachi nigiri with seasonal, uncommon seafood, such as sea bass sashimi and grilled ray. Thanks to the large population of Japanese nationals living in Honolulu, the Japanese food here is some of the best outside of Japan. But it's not just straight-from-Tokyo fare at Gaku; the chefs here scour fish markets around town daily for the best local fish. See p. 152.
- **The Pig and the Lady** (O'ahu; http://thepigandthelady.com; © **808/585-8255**): This casual restaurant, with its traditional Vietnamese noodle soups and playful interpretations of Southeast Asian food, is both soulful and surprising. The soulful: the pho of the day, drawing on recipes from chef Andrew Le's mother. The surprising: hand-cut pasta with pork and *lilikoi* (passionfruit). The best of both

worlds: a pho French dip banh mi, with slices of tender brisket and a cup of pho broth for dipping. See p. 149.

- **Ka'ana Kitchen** (Maui; www.maui.andaz.hyatt.com; ✆ **808/573-1234**): Treat chef Isaac Bancaco's grid menu like a gourmet bingo card; every combo is a winner. Start off with a hand-mixed cocktail and the ahi tataki: ruby-red tuna, heirloom tomato, and fresh burratta sprinkled with black salt and nasturtium petals. The $45 breakfast buffet grants you access to the kitchen's novel chilled countertops, stocked with every delicacy and fresh juice you can imagine. See p. 406.
- **Mama's Fish House** (Maui; www.mamasfishhouse.com; ✆ **808/579-8488**): Overlooking Kū'au Cove on Maui's North Shore, this restaurant is a South Pacific fantasy. Every nook is decorated with some fanciful artifact of salt-kissed adventure. The menu lists the anglers who reeled in the day's catch; you can order ono "caught by Keith Nakamura along the 40-fathom ledge near Hāna" or deep-water ahi seared with coconut and lime. The Tahitian Pearl dessert is almost too stunning to eat. Though pricey, a meal at Mama's is a complete experience. See p. 415.
- **Merriman's** (Waimea, Big Island; www.merrimanshawaii.com; ✆ **808/885-6822;** Kapalua, Maui, ✆ **808/669-6400;** and Po'ipū,

Mama's Fish House, Maui.

Kaua'i, ✆ **808/742-8385**): Chef Peter Merriman, one of the founders of Hawai'i Regional Cuisine, oversees a locally inspired culinary empire that also includes Monkeypod Kitchen outlets on Maui, Kaua'i, and O'ahu (p. 157). His original Waimea restaurant, opened in 1988 and now under the direction of chef Eric Purugganan, still merits the drive upcountry from the coast. See p. 276.

- **Da Poke Shack** (Kailua-Kona, Big Island; www.dapokeshack.com; ✆ **808/329-7653**): Poke—pronounced *po-kay*—the islands' diced raw, marinated seafood specialty, comes in many varieties at this hole-in-the-wall takeout counter, where it's prepared so expertly that patrons make repeat visits just to try them all. A second branch opened in Captain Cook (✆ **808/328-8862**) in 2014 to equal acclaim. See p. 270.
- **Pueo's Osteria** (Waikoloa, Big Island; www.pueososteria.com; ✆ **808/339-7566**): Former Four Seasons Hualālai chef James Babian takes his inspiration from Tuscany and, as much as he can, uses ingredients from local farmers and fishermen, creating exceptionally fresh, well-priced cuisine paired with an intriguing wine list. Another reason to drive 15 minutes off the highway and up the mountain: The thoughtfully crafted bar menu is served until midnight daily. See p. 275.
- **Bar Acuda** (Hanalei, Kaua'i; www.restaurantbaracuda.com; ✆ **808/826-7081**): When the sun goes down, the surfing set freshens up for a night on the town at this stylish tapas bar. Created by Jim Moffat, a former star of San Francisco's culinary scene, Bar Acuda's fare is centered around fresh seafood and seasonal pairings inspired by Mediterranean cuisine. See p. 583.
- **The Beach House** (Po'ipū, Kaua'i; www.the-beach-house.com; ✆ **808/742-1424**): Sunset should be listed as its own course on the menu here because everyone stops to ogle it or snap pictures from the oceanfront lawn. But the food, which is just as good at lunch, stands on its own merits, from a crackerjack kitchen that was sourcing ingredients locally long before "farm-to-table" became a buzzword. See p. 587.
- **Nobu Lāna'i** (Lāna'i; www.fourseasons.com/manelebay/dining; ✆ **808/565-2290**): Lāna'i now ranks among New York, Milan, Budapest, and Mexico City as somewhere one can dine at a Nobu restaurant—a measure of how fun a place is, in the immortal words of pop star Madonna. The best way to experience this epicurean phenomenon is to order the *omakase*—the chef's tasting menu—for $120. Each dish is as delicious as it is artful. See p. 483.
- **Hale Kealoha** (Moloka'i; www.hotelmolokai.com/dining; ✆ **808/553-5347**): Siblings Kama Hoe and Tammy Smith, known for their down-home Hale Kealoha restaurant in Kailua, O'ahu, have brought

Moloka'i its first island-inspired, locally sourced menu in an ocean-front setting—the low-key Hotel Moloka'i. They've kept the Aloha Friday entertainment and moderate prices of the previous on-site restaurant but kicked everything else (including poke) up a notch.

THE best OF HAWAI'I FOR KIDS

- **Aulani, a Disney Resort & Spa, Ko Olina, Hawai'i** (O'ahu; http://resorts.disney.go.com/aulani-hawaii-resort; © **714/520-7001**): Disney built this high-rise hotel and spa (with timeshare condos) on 21 acres on the beach, about an hour's drive from Waikīkī. It's a great destination for families, with a full children's program, plus areas and activities for teens and tweens. Mickey, Minnie, Goofy, and other Disney characters walk the resort and stop to take photos with kids. See p. 136.
- **Dole Pineapple Plantation** (O'ahu; www.dole-plantation.com; © **808/621-8408**): Get the kids (and yourself!) a Dole Whip and fresh pineapple, and then take them through the main attraction: part maze, part scavenger hunt. They'll also enjoy the Pineapple Express, a short train ride on a single-engine diesel locomotive around the plantation's grounds. See p. 97.
- **Build Sandcastles on Kailua Beach** (O'ahu): This gorgeous beach is kid-friendly, with sand that slopes gently into the water. The waves vary in spots—perfect for the young ones to splash around and older kids to boogie board. The broad stretch of sand is also great for building castles. See p. 106.
- **Slumber Party at the Aquarium** (Maui): Kids can book a sleepover in the Maui Ocean Center, staying up into the wee hours to watch glowing jellyfish and other nocturnal animals. See p. 306.
- **Snorkel in Kealakekua Bay** (Big Island): Everyone can enjoy the dazzling display of marine life here on a **Fair Wind** cruise (www.fairwind.com; © **800/677-9461** or 808/322-2788), which offers inner tubes and underwater viewing boxes for little ones (or older ones) who don't want to get their faces wet. Two water slides and a spacious boat with a friendly crew also make this a treat. See p. 228.
- **Play at Lydgate Park** (Kaua'i): If kids tire of snorkeling in the protected swimming area of Lydgate Beach, a giant wooden fantasy play structure and bridge to the dunes await, along with grassy fields and several miles of biking trails. See p. 508.
- **Ride a Sugarcane Train** (Kaua'i): At **Kilohana Plantation** (p. 507), families can enjoy an inexpensive, narrated train ride through fields, forest, and orchards, with a stop to feed sheep, goats, and wild pigs.

2

SUGGESTED HAWAI'I ITINERARIES

For most people, the fetching dollops of land in the middle of the Pacific Ocean are a dream destination—but getting to this remote region can seem daunting. So once you finally arrive, you'll want to make the most of your time. In this chapter we've built five 1-week itineraries for O'ahu, Hawai'i Island, Maui, Moloka'i, Lāna'i, and Kaua'i, each designed to hit the highlights and provide a revealing window into the real Hawai'i.

You can follow these itineraries to the letter or use them to build your own personalized trip. Whatever you do, *don't max out your days.* This is Hawai'i, after all—save time to smell the perfume of plumeria, listen to wind rustling through a bamboo forest, and feel the caress of the Pacific.

A WEEK ON O'AHU

O'ahu is so stunning that the *ali'i,* the kings of Hawai'i, made it the capital of the island nation. Below, we presume that you'll be staying in Waikīkī; if your hotel is in another location, factor in extra time for traveling.

DAY 1: Arrive & Hit Waikīkī Beach ★★★

Unwind from your plane ride with a little sun and sand. Take a dip in the ocean at the most famous beach in the world: **Waikīkī Beach** (p. 102). Catch the sunset with a Mai Tai, Hawaiian music, and some of the loveliest hula you'll ever see at **House Without a Key** (p. 165).

DAY 2: Surf in Waikīkī & Visit Pearl Harbor ★★★

Thanks to jet lag, you'll be up early; take advantage with an early-morning surf session, aka dawn patrol, to take advantage of the morning glass. Waikīkī has great waves for learning, and a surf lesson (p. 113) will have you riding the waves in no time. The poke at **Ono Seafood** (p. 145) makes a great post-surf meal. In the afternoon, head to the **USS *Arizona* Memorial at Pearl Harbor** (p. 77), site of the infamous 1941 attack. For dinner, go local. Head to the **Highway Inn** (p. 147) for kālua pig, laulau, pipikaula, and poi.

DAY 3: Explore the North Shore ★★★

Fuel up on fresh fruit smoothies and chocolate banana bread at **Tucker & Bevvy** (p. 143) before heading to the **North Shore** (see "Central O'ahu & the North Shore," on p. 97). Stop in the quaint

FACING PAGE: **Surfer in Waikīkī.**

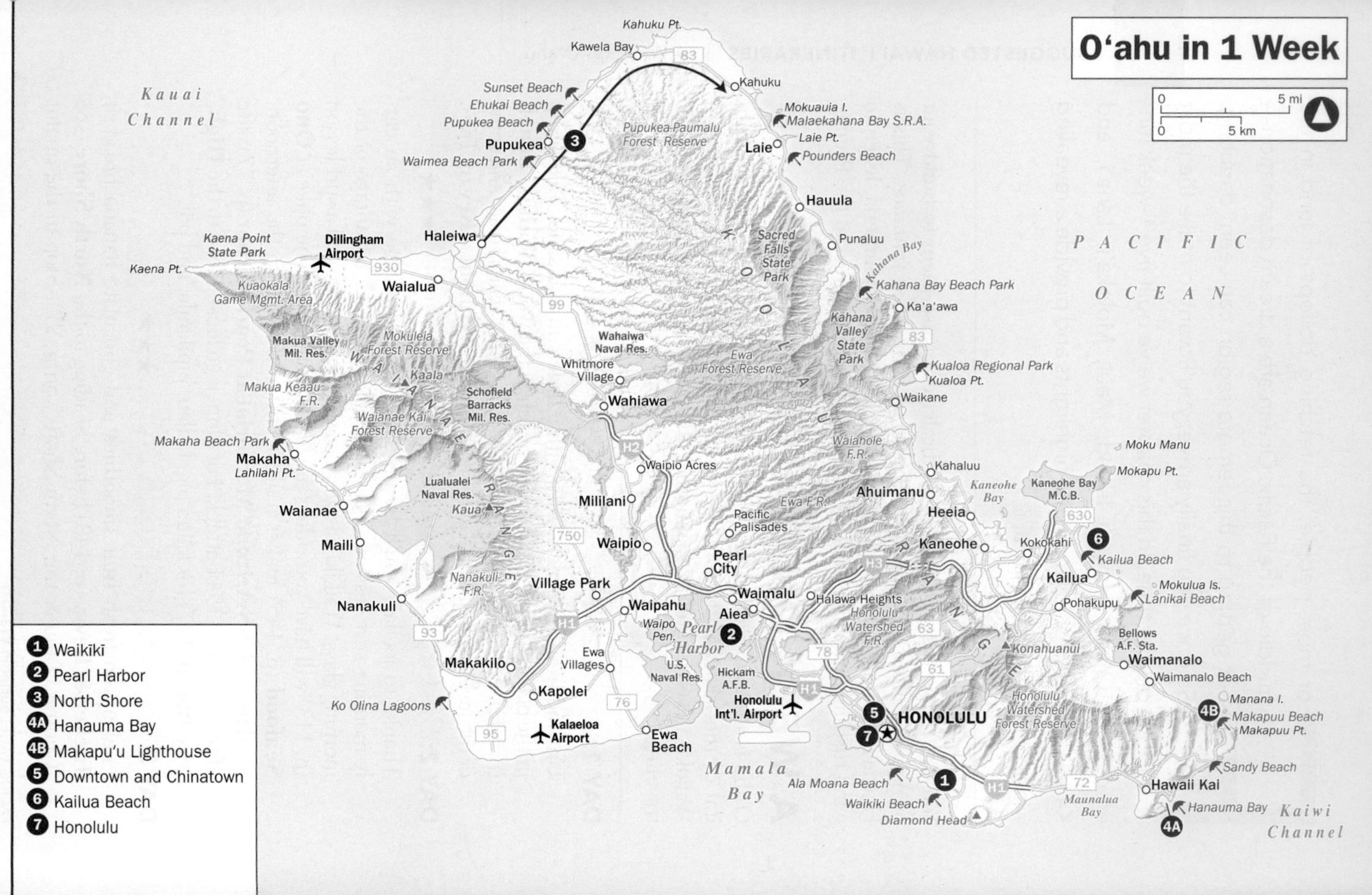
O'ahu in 1 Week
0
5 mi
0
5 km
Kauai Channel
PACIFIC OCEAN
Mamala Bay
Kaiwi Channel
Kahuku Pt.
Kawela Bay
Kahuku
Sunset Beach
Ehukai Beach
Pupukea Beach
Pupukea
Waimea Beach Park
Pupukea-Paumalu Forest Reserve
Mokuauia I.
Malaekahana Bay S.R.A.
Laie
Laie Pt.
Pounders Beach
Hauula
Haleiwa
Kaena Point State Park
Kaena Pt.
Dillingham Airport
Waialua
Kuaokala Game Mgmt. Area
Sacred Falls State Park
Punaluu
Kahana Bay
Kahana Bay Beach Park
Ka'a'awa
Kahana Valley State Park
Makua Valley Mil. Res.
Mokuleia Forest Reserve
Wahaiwa Naval Res.
Whitmore Village
Ewa Forest Reserve
Kualoa Regional Park
Kualoa Pt.
Makua Keaau F.R.
Kaala
Schofield Barracks Mil. Res.
Wahiawa
Waikane
Waianae Kai Forest Reserve
Makaha Beach Park
Makaha
Lahilahi Pt.
Waipio Acres
Waiahole F.R.
Moku Manu
Mokapu Pt.
Kahaluu
Kaneohe Bay
Kaneohe Bay M.C.B.
Lualualei Naval Res.
Kaua
Mililani
Ahuimanu
Ewa F.R.
Waianae
Heeia
Pacific Palisades
Maili
Waipio
Kaneohe
Kokokahi
Kailua Beach
Pearl City
Kailua
Nanakuli F.R.
Village Park
Waimalu
Halawa Heights
Mokulua Is.
Lanikai Beach
Nanakuli
Waipahu
Aiea
Pohakupu
Honolulu Watershed F.R.
Waipo Pen.
Pearl Harbor
Bellows A.F. Sta.
Konahuanui
Waimanalo
Makakilo
Ewa Villages
U.S. Naval Res.
Hickam A.F.B.
Waimanalo Beach
Kapolei
Honolulu Watershed Forest Reserve
Manana I.
Ko Olina Lagoons
Honolulu Int'l. Airport
HONOLULU
Makapuu Beach
Makapuu Pt.
Kalaeloa Airport
Ewa Beach
Sandy Beach
Ala Moana Beach
Hawaii Kai
Waikiki Beach
Maunalua Bay
Hanauma Bay
Diamond Head
1 Waikīkī
2 Pearl Harbor
3 North Shore
4A Hanauma Bay
4B Makapu'u Lighthouse
5 Downtown and Chinatown
6 Kailua Beach
7 Honolulu

Waikīkī Beach.

town of **Hale'iwa** for a pineapple-*lilikoi*-mango treat at **Matsumoto Shave Ice** (p. 100), and grab a picnic lunch from **Beet Box Café** (p. 156). Pick one of the gorgeous North Shore beaches for a day of swimming and sunbathing. **Waimea Beach Park** (p. 108) is a favorite, no matter the season. In winter, if the waves are pumping and conditions are right, head to **Pipeline** (p. 100) and watch pro surfers ride this tube-like wave over razor-sharp reef. Heading back south, hit the **shrimp trucks at Kahuku** (p. 155). Still daylight? Take the longer coastal road back into Honolulu. On the way back to Waikīkī, stop at **Town** (p. 153) or **12th Ave Grill** (p. 153) for dinner.

DAY 4: Snorkel in Hanauma Bay ★★ & Hike the Makapu'u Lighthouse Trail ★★

Head out early in the morning to grab a fried *malasada* (hole-less doughnut) dipped in sugar at **Leonard's Bakery** (p. 142) on your way to a snorkel at **Hanauma Bay** (p. 111). If you're a strong swimmer and the water is calm (check with the lifeguard), head out past the reef and away from the crowds, where the water's clearer and you'll see more fish and the occasional turtle. Continue beach-hopping down the coastline—watch bodysurfing daredevils at **Sandy Beach** (p. 105). Hike the easy **Makapu'u Lighthouse** (p. 116) trail, with views to Moloka'i and Lāna'i on a clear day. In winter, you may even see migrating humpback whales. Turn back to take the Pali Highway home to Waikīkī—and be sure to stop at the **Nu'uanu Pali Lookout** (p. 83).

'Iolani Palace.

DAY 5: Glimpse Historic Honolulu & Experience Hawaiian Culture

Head to downtown Honolulu to see the city's historic sites, including the **'Iolani Palace** (p. 75) and **Kawaiaha'o Church** (p. 76). Lunch at **The Pig and the Lady** (p. 149) for modern Vietnamese food, pick up some tropical fruit to enjoy later, and browse the trendy boutiques (p. 62). Spend the afternoon at the **Bishop Museum** (p. 71) to immerse yourself in Hawaiian culture. Head up to **Pu'u 'Ualaka'a State Park** (p. 83) to watch the sunset over Honolulu. For dinner, get a taste of Honolulu's spectacular Japanese cuisine at **Izakaya Gaku** (p. 152).

DAY 6: Relax at Kailua Beach ★★★

On your last full day on O'ahu, travel over the Pali Highway to the windward side of the island and spend a day at **Kailua Beach** (p. 106). It's the perfect beach to kayak or stand-up paddle to the Mokulua Islands (or, as the locals call it, "the Mokes") or simply relax. For your last dinner, splurge at **Alan Wong's Restaurant** (p. 151), with classic local-style foods reimagined for the fine-dining table.

DAY 7: Marvel at Shangri La ★★★

Head to the **Honolulu Museum of Art** for your tour of **Shangri La** (p. 75), the private palace of tobacco heiress Doris Duke. Filled with Islamic art, the interior is stunning, but so is the location, on a cliff facing Diamond Head. Pick up souvenirs at the museum's gift shop. On your way to the airport, stop at **Ala Moana Center** (p. 161) for more shopping, and grab a pre-flight meal and in-flight snacks at Shirokiya's second-floor **Yataimura** (p. 147).

A WEEK ON THE BIG ISLAND OF HAWAI'I

Because of the distances involved, a week is barely enough time to see the entire Big Island; it's best to plan for 2 weeks—or even better, a return visit. Here's how to see the highlights, changing hotels as you go.

DAY 1: Arrive & Amble Through Kailua-Kona ★★★

Since most flights arrive at lunchtime or later, check into your Kona Coast lodgings and go for a stroll through historic **Kailua-Kona** by **Hulihe'e Palace** (p. 181) and **Moku'aikaua Church** (p. 182). Wear sandals so you can dip your feet in one of the pocket coves, such as Kamakahonu Bay, within sight of **Kamehameha's historic compound,** and enjoy a sunset dinner at an ocean-view restaurant. Don't unpack—you'll be on the road early the next day.

DAY 2: A Morning Sail & Afternoon Drive ★★★

The day starts with a morning snorkel tour (plus breakfast and lunch) aboard the ***Fair Wind II*** (p. 228), sailing to the historic preserve of **Kealakekua Bay.** After returning to Keauhou Bay, head south to **Hawai'i Volcanoes National Park** (p. 207), by way of **Pu'uhonua O Hōnaunau National Historical Park** (p. 187) and the **Ka'ū Coffee Mill** (p. 211), for a pick-me-up. Check into **Volcano Village** lodgings (p. 264) or **Volcano House** (p. 266) in the park, where you'll dine in full view of Kīlauea's fiery evening glow.

DAY 3: Explore an Active Volcano ★★★

Stop at the national park's **Kīlauea Visitor Center** to learn about current lava flows (if any) and the day's free ranger-led walks. Take **Crater Rim Road** past billowing **Halema'uma'u Crater** (p. 208) to see **Nāhuku,** aka the Thurston Lava Tube (p. 209), and **Devastation Trail** (p. 246), before driving down **Chain of Craters Road,** leading to a vast petroglyph field and the 2003 lava flow that smothered the roadway. After sunset, visit the **Thomas A. Jaggar Museum** (open till 7:30pm; p. 208) and its observation deck (open all night) for yet another look at Pele's power.

DAY 4: Tour Old Hawai'i ★★★

It's just a 45-minute drive from Volcano to **Hilo** (p. 175), so after breakfast go to **'Imiloa: Astronomy Center of Hawaii** (p. 202),

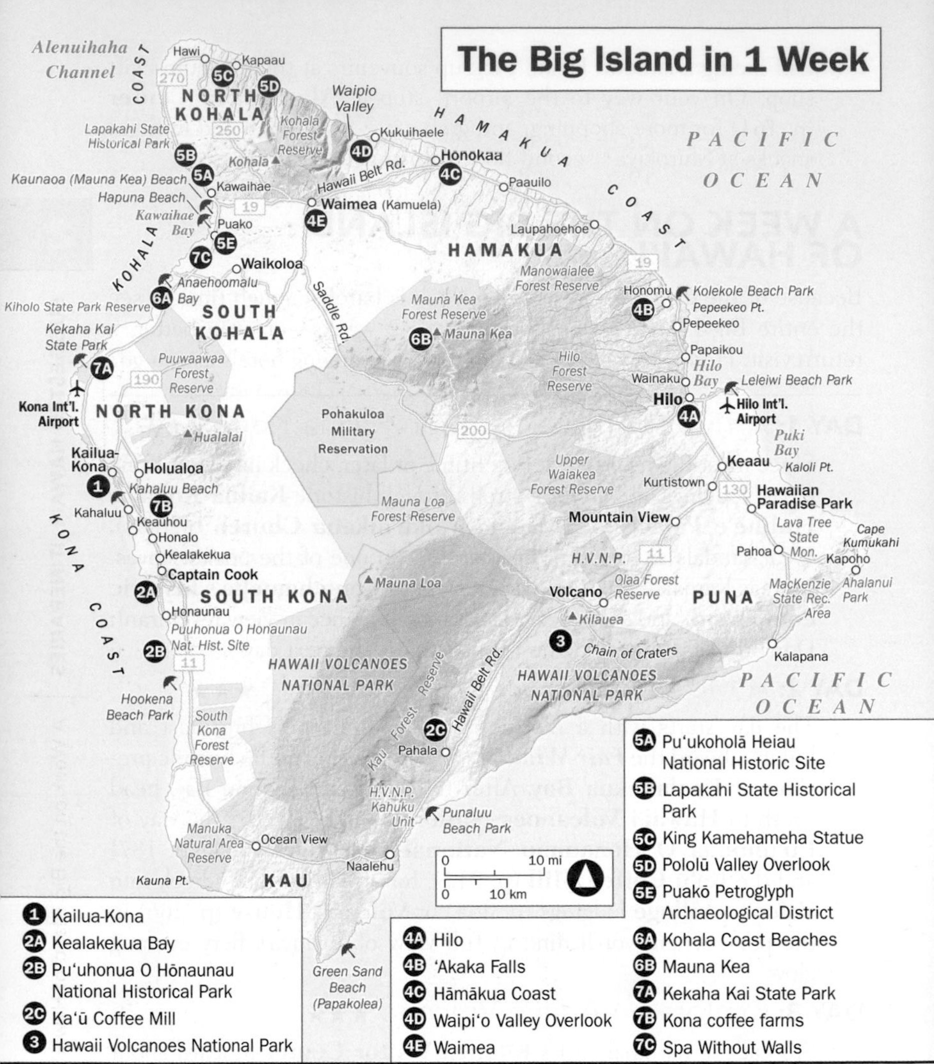

opening at 9am. Then explore **Banyan Drive** (p. 199), **Lili'uokalani Gardens** (p. 199), and one of Hilo's small but intriguing museums, such as the free **Mokupāpapa Discovery Center** (p. 203). Stroll through **Nani Mau Gardens** (p. 203) or the **Hawaii Tropical Botanical Garden** (p. 194) before driving along the pastoral **Hāmākua Coast** (p. 193), stopping at breathtaking **'Akaka Falls** (p. 193) and the similarly stunning **Waipi'o Valley Lookout** (p. 198). Dine on farm-fresh cuisine in **Waimea** (p. 276) or **Kawaihae** (p. 273) before checking into your Kohala Coast hotel.

DAY 5: Explore the Historic Kohala Coast ★★★

Start by visiting **Puʻukoholā Heiau National Historic Site** (p. 189), the massive temple Kamehameha built to the war god, Kū; it also looks impressive on an intimate cruise with **Kohala Sail & Sea** (p. 230). Continue north on Hwy. 270 to **Lapakahi State Historical Park** (p. 190) to see the outlines of a 14th-century Hawaiian village, and have lunch in Hawi or Kapaʻau; the latter is home of the original **King Kamehameha Statue** (p. 190). The final northbound stop is the picturesque **Pololū Valley Lookout** (p. 190). Heading south in the late afternoon, stop at the **Puakō Petroglyph Archaeological Preserve** (p. 189). To learn more Hawaiian lore, book one of Kohala's evening **lūʻaus** (p. 288).

DAY 6: Sand, Sea & Stars ★★★

You've earned a morning at the beach, and the Big Island's prettiest beaches are on the Kohala Coast: **ʻAnaehoʻomalu Bay (A-Bay), Hāpuna,** and **Kaunaʻoa** (see "Beaches," p. 215). Skip the scuba, though, because in the afternoon you're heading up 13,796-foot **Mauna Kea** (p. 191), revered by astronomers. Let an expert with four-wheel-drive, cold-weather gear, and telescopes for stargazing take you there; **Mauna Kea Summit Adventures** (p. 195) or **Hawaiʻi Forest & Trail** (p. 195) are recommended tour guides.

DAY 7: Spa, Beach, or Coffee Time ★★★

On your last full day, visit one of North Kona's gorgeous beaches hidden behind lava fields, such as **Kekaha Kai State Park** (p. 216) or the tranquil cove at **Kaloko-Honokōhau National Historical**

Thurston Lava Tube.

Pololū Beach.

Park (p. 182) in the morning. In the afternoon, relax with a spa treatment at the Fairmont Orchid's **Spa Without Walls** (p. 258) or another Kohala resort spa, or tour a **Kona coffee farm** (p. 185) and pick up gourmet beans as souvenirs.

A WEEK ON MAUI

You'll need at least a week to savor Maui's best experiences. We recommend splitting your vacation between East and West Maui, starting with hot and sunny beaches and ending in the rejuvenating rainforest. We've designed this itinerary assuming you'll stay in West Maui for the first 3 days, but it works just as well if you stay in Wailea or Kīhei. To minimize driving, move your headquarters to lush East Maui on day 4.

DAY 1: Arrive & Explore West Maui ★★★

After checking in to your hotel, head immediately for one of West Maui's prime beaches (p. 324). After a reviving dip in the ocean, spend a couple of hours walking around the historic old town of **Lahaina** (p. 295). As the sun sets, immerse yourself in Hawaiian culture at **Old Lahaina Lū'aū** (p. 427).

DAY 2: Sail to Lāna'i ★★★

You'll likely wake up early on your first morning here, so book an early-morning trip with **Trilogy** (p. 333), the best sailing/snorkeling operation in Hawai'i. You'll spend the day (breakfast and lunch

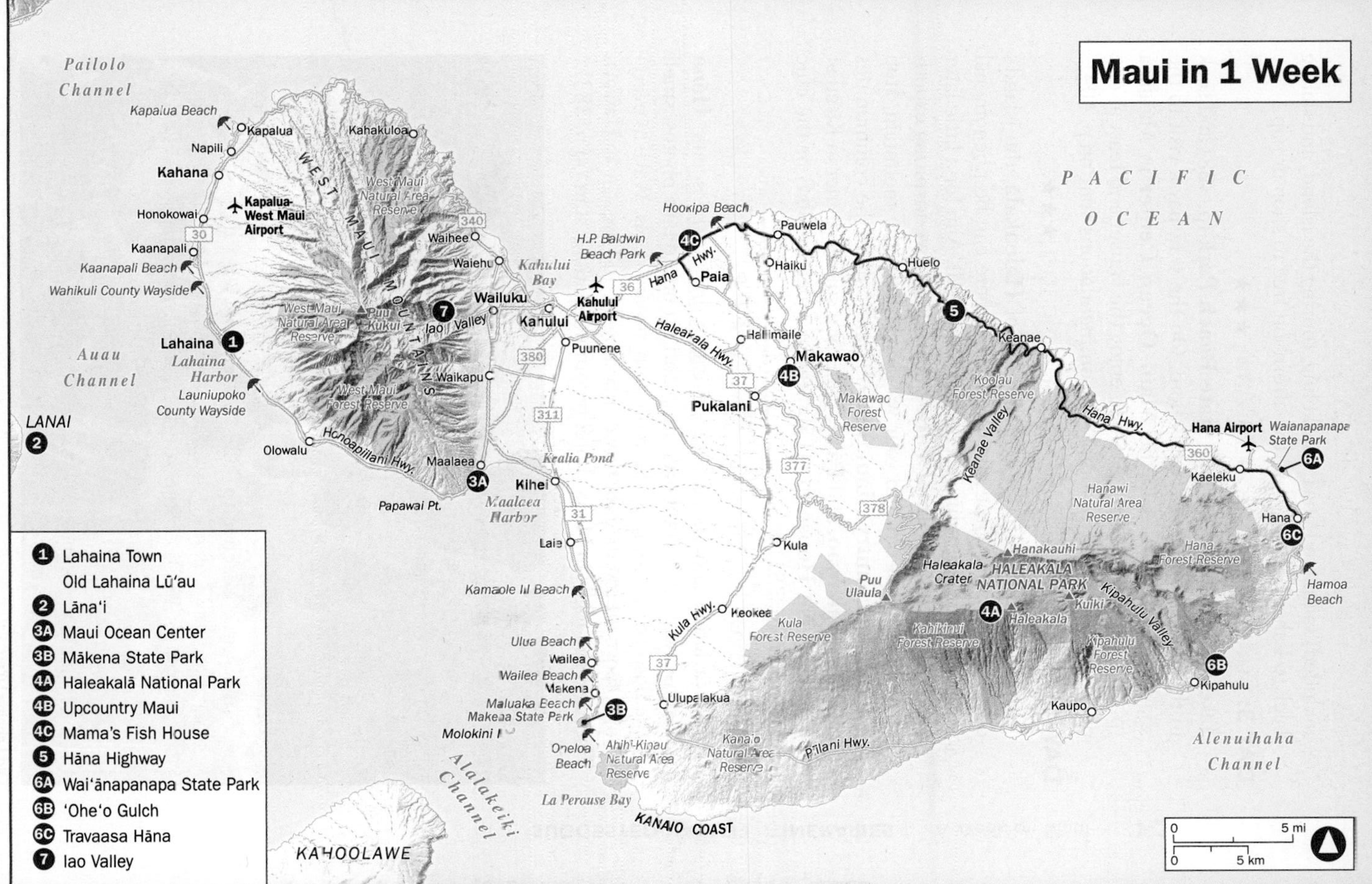

Maui in 1 Week
PACIFIC OCEAN
Pailolo Channel
Auau Channel
Alalakeiki Channel
Alenuihaha Channel
LANAI
2
KAHOOLAWE
Kapalua Beach
Kapalua
Kahakuloa
Napili
Kahana
Kapalua-West Maui Airport
Honokowai
Kaanapali
Kaanapali Beach
Wahikuli County Wayside
Lahaina
Lahaina Harbor
Launiupoko County Wayside
Olowalu
Honoapiilani Hwy.
WEST MAUI MOUNTAINS
West Maui Natural Area Reserve
West Maui Forest Reserve
Puu Kukui
Iao Valley
Waihee
Waiehu
Wailuku
Waikapu
Maalaea
Papawai Pt.
Kahului Bay
Kahului
Kahului Airport
Puunene
Maalaea Harbor
Kealia Pond
Kihei
Laie
Kamaole III Beach
Ulua Beach
Wailea
Wailea Beach
Makena
Maluaka Beach
Makena State Park
Molokini
Oneloa Beach
Ahihi-Kinau Natural Area Reserve
La Perouse Bay
KANAIO COAST
Kanaio Natural Area Reserve
Piilani Hwy.
Ulupalakua
Kula Hwy.
Keokea
Kula
Kula Forest Reserve
Puu Ulaula
H.P. Baldwin Beach Park
Hookipa Beach
Paia
Hana Hwy.
Haiku
Pauwela
Huelo
Haliimaile
Haleakala Hwy.
Makawao
Pukalani
Makawao Forest Reserve
Koolau Forest Reserve
Keanae
Keanae Valley
Hana Hwy.
Hana Airport
Waianapanapa State Park
Kaeleku
Hana
Hamoa Beach
Hanawi Natural Area Reserve
Hana Forest Reserve
Hanakauhi
Haleakala Crater
HALEAKALA NATIONAL PARK
Haleakala
Kuiki
Kipahulu Valley
Kahikinui Forest Reserve
Kipahulu Forest Reserve
Kipahulu
Kaupo
30
340
36
37
311
31
380
377
378
360
0 5 mi
0 5 km
1 Lahaina Town
Old Lahaina Lū'au
2 Lāna'i
3A Maui Ocean Center
3B Mākena State Park
4A Haleakalā National Park
4B Upcountry Maui
4C Mama's Fish House
5 Hāna Highway
6A Wai'ānapanapa State Park
6B 'Ohe'o Gulch
6C Travaasa Hāna
7 Iao Valley

included) sailing to Lāna'i, snorkeling, touring the island, and sailing back to Lahaina. You'll have the afternoon free to shop or nap.

DAY 3: Sunbathe in South Maui ★★★

Take a drive out to **Mākena State Beach Park** (p. 328) and soak in the raw beauty of this wild shore. On the way, pay a visit to the sharks and sea turtles at the **Maui Ocean Center** in Mā'alaea (p. 306). Linger in South Maui to enjoy the sunset and feast at one of the area's terrific restaurants (recommendations start on p. 404).

DAY 4: Ascend a 10,000-Foot Volcano ★★★

Venture up to the 10,023-foot summit of **Haleakalā,** the island's dormant volcano. Witnessing the sunrise here can be phenomenal (as well as mind-numbingly cold and crowded). Aim for a little later and hike in the **National Park** (p. 309), an awe-inspiring experience any time of day. On your way back down the mountain, stop and tour **Upcountry Maui** (p. 297), particularly the communities of **Kula, Makawao,** and **Pā'ia.** Plan for a sunset dinner in Kū'au at **Mama's Fish House** (p. 415). Stay at a nearby B&B or the chic **Pā'ia Inn** (p. 381).

DAY 5: Drive the Hāna Highway ★★★

Pack a lunch and spend the entire day driving the scenic **Hāna Highway** (p. 299). Pull over often and get out to take photos, smell the flowers, and jump in the mountain-stream pools. Wave to everyone, move off the road for those speeding by, and breathe in Hawai'i. Spend the night in Hāna (hotel recommendations start on p. 383).

Old Lahaina Lū'au.

Hālawa Valley, Moloka'i, as seen from the beach.

DAY 6: Explore Heavenly Hāna ★★★

Take an early-morning hike along the black sands of **Wai'anapanapa State Park** (p. 318); then explore the tiny town of **Hāna** (p. 318). Be sure to see the **Hāna Museum Cultural Center, Hasegawa General Store,** and **Hāna Coast Gallery.** Get a picnic lunch and drive out to the Kīpahulu end of Haleakalā National Park at **'Ohe'o Gulch** (p. 320). Hike to the waterfalls and swim in the pools. Splurge on dinner at the **Hotel Travaasa Hāna** (p. 416).

DAY 7: Relax & Shop ★★★

Depending on how much time you have on your final day, you can relax on the beach, get pampered in a spa, or shop for souvenirs. Spa-goers have a range of terrific spas to choose from, and fashionistas should check out the boutiques in **Makawao** and **Pā'ia** (recommendations start on p. 417). If you have time, explore the verdant gardens and waterfalls at **'Iao Valley** (p. 302).

A WEEK ON MOLOKA'I

Some visitors would quail at the thought of spending 7 whole days on Hawai'i's most low-key island, which at first glance seems to offer only a few activities and attractions. But you'll need to plan your vacation carefully—including the season and days of the week—to be able to experience everything on this itinerary, based on a Monday arrival (weekday arrival strongly recommended). If you're staying on the West End or East End, where the most desirable lodgings are, leave plenty of time to drive to Central Moloka'i attractions.

Moloka‘i in 1 Week

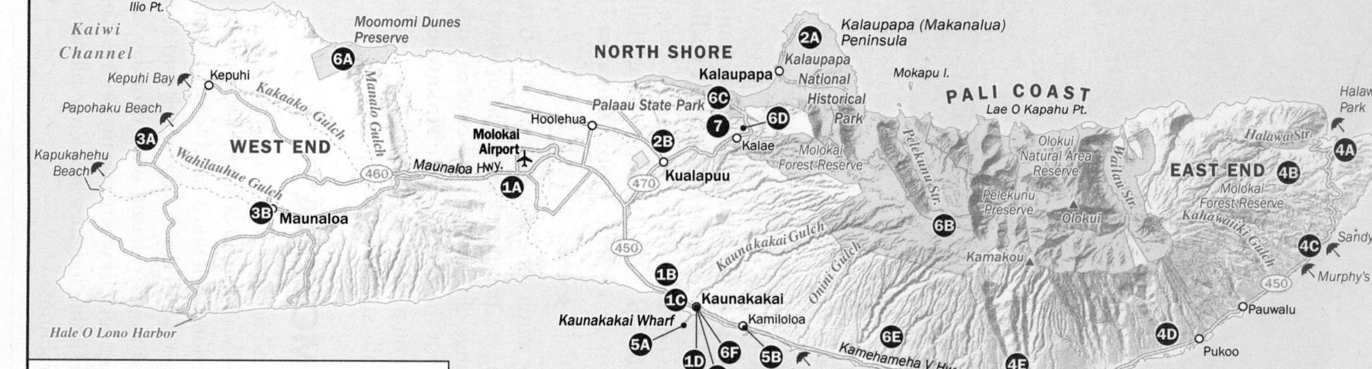

1A Kumu Farms
1B Molokai Plumerias
1C Kapuāiwa Coconut Grove
1D Kaunakakai

2A Kalaupapa National Historical Park
2B Coffees of Hawaii

3A West End Beaches
3B Maunaloa
3C Kanemitsu Bakery

4A Hālawa Beach Park
4B Hālawa Valley cultural tours
4C East End Beaches
4D Our Lady of Seven Sorrows
4E St. Joseph Church

5A South Shore boat, stand-up paddle, or kayak excursion
5B Aloha Friday at Hotel Moloka‘i

6A Mo‘omomi Preserve guided hike
6B Kamakou Preserve guided hike
6C Pālā‘au State Park (Kalaupapa Overlook and Phallic Rock)
6D Moloka‘i Museum and Cultural Center
6E Purdy's Natural Macadamia Nuts
6F Kaunakakai Saturday morning farmers' market

7 Ironwood Hills Golf Course

DAY 1: Arrive & Pick Up Edibles

Since you're most likely staying in a vacation rental, after you pick up your rental car (a must), stop by **Kumu Farms** near the airport (p. 457) for organic produce. While en route to **Kaunakakai** (p. 435) to finish your shopping, enjoy the views of the **Molokai Plumerias** orchard (p. 438), typically in bloom March to October, and the historic **Kapuāiwa Coconut Grove** (p. 441).

DAY 2: Tour Kalaupapa ★★★

Whether you're hiking, flying, or riding the mules down to **Kalaupapa National Historical Park** (p. 441), you will need to have made reservations in advance—up to a month or more for the **Kalaupapa Guided Mule Tour** (p 442). But the effort and expense are worth it to explore this otherwise inaccessible, always impressive site of natural beauty and tragic history, where two Catholic saints, **Father Damien and Mother Marianne Cope** (p. 442), helped care for the leprosy patients exiled here. After your return "topside," recharge at **Coffees of Hawaii** (p. 438), which grows its own.

DAY 3: Savor Beaches by Day, Bakery by Night ★★

Pack a picnic lunch and beach gear—stop at **Molokai Fish & Dive** (p. 448) or **Beach Break** (p. 450) to buy or rent gear—to spend a day exploring the glorious **West End beaches** (p. 447). If it's winter, don't plan on going in the water; instead, enjoy the sightings of whales (at their peak Jan–Mar) or intrepid surfers. Drive into the quiet plantation town of **Maunaloa** to restock your refreshments at the **Maunaloa General Store** (p. 457) or browse the eclectic wares at the **Big Wind Kite Factory & Plantation Gallery** (p. 460). Note that the only public restroom facilities are at the northern end of nearly 3-mile-long **Pāpōhaku Beach Park ★★★**, where you'll want to stay for sunset. At 9pm make a "hot bread run" at **Kanemitsu Bakery** in Kaunakakai (p. 448).

DAY 4: Hike to a Waterfall and into the Past ★★★

Anyone can take the incredibly scenic, sinuous, shore-hugging drive to pretty **Hālawa Beach Park** (p. 447), but you'll need reservations (book several weeks in advance) and a picnic lunch for the **Hālawa Valley cultural tours** (p. 445) offered by the Solatorio family. After the traditional Hawaiian protocol to welcome visitors and an introduction to the ancient enclave's history, you'll hike to the gorgeous, 250-foot Mo'oula Falls, where a dip is possible in calm conditions. Since you have your swim gear, stop at the East End's **Sandy** and **Kūmimi** beaches (p. 447) on the drive home. You'll also want to make a photo stop at Father Damien's picturesque churches on the eastern half of King Kamehameha V Hwy., **St. Joseph** and **Our Lady of Seven Sorrows** (p. 442).

DAY 5: Paddle, Snorkel, or Watch Whales on the South Shore ★★★

If you haven't explored the teeming marine life and tranquil waters sheltered by the South Shore's enormous fringing reef, then you haven't really seen Moloka'i at its finest. Depending on your ability, book **a stand-up paddle** or **kayak excursion** with **Moloka'i Outdoors** (p. 449), or a **snorkel/dive trip** with **Molokai Fish & Dive** (p. 448). The reef typically keeps the water calm even in winter (Dec–Mar), when several outfitters also offer **whale-watching excursions** (p. 445). Unlike on Maui, your boat may be the only one visible for miles around. If it's Friday, head to **Aloha Friday at Hotel Moloka'i** (p. 460), where resident recording artist Lono and island elders play old-school Hawaiian music and pop classics by the oceanfront pool from 4 to 6pm; stay for a fresh, island-sourced dinner at **Hale Kealoha** (p. 456)

DAY 6: Explore Nature Reserves ★★★ or a Scenic Park & Unique Shops ★★

The best (and only recommended) way to explore the windswept dunes of **Mo'omomi Preserve** and the miniature trees in the cloud forest atop the **Kamakou Preserve** is via one of the **Nature Conservancy's guided hikes** (p. 451), offered once a month March through October—book as far in advance as possible. If neither hike is available or practical, drive to **Pālā'au State Park** (p. 443) to check out the Kalaupapa Overlook and Phallic Rock, and stop by the **Molokai Museum and Cultural Center** (p. 439) and **Purdy's Macadamia Nut Farm** (p. 440). Or simply browse the **Saturday morning farmer's market** (p. 459) and quaint stores in Kaunakakai (p. 459).

DAY 7: Enjoy the Peacefulness

If this is Sunday, then there's little to do on Moloka'i—besides going to one of the many churches—and that's the way local folks like it. Now's a good day to revisit a favorite beach or drive up to rustic **Ironwood Hills Golf Course** (p. 450).

A WEEK ON LĀNA'I

The smallest of all the Hawaiian Islands, this former pineapple plantation is now home to a posh resort, hundreds of years of history, and a postage-stamp-size town with some of the friendliest people you'll ever meet. There are enough activities here to keep you busy, but you'll probably be happiest skipping a few and slowing down to Lāna'i speed.

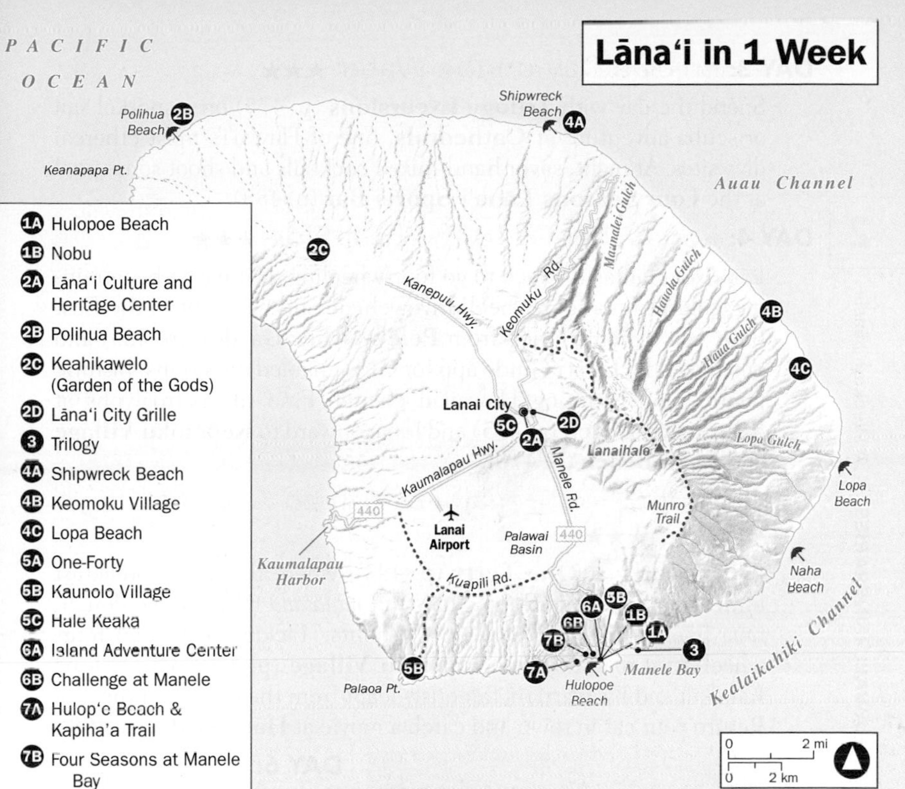

DAY 1: Arrive & Investigate Hulopo'e Bay's Tide Pools ★★★

After settling into your hotel, head for the best stretch of sand on the island (and maybe the state): **Hulopo'e Beach** (p. 473). It's generally safe for swimming, and snorkeling within this marine preserve is terrific. The fish are so friendly you practically have to shoo them away; dolphins are frequent visitors. Climb up to the Pu'u Pehe or Sweetheart Rock lookout. Dine like a celebrity at **Nobu** (p. 483).

DAY 2: Explore Lāna'i City & Garden of the Gods ★★★

Head into quaint Lāna'i City to browse the boutiques (p. 486) and get a colorful history lesson at the **Lāna'i Culture & Heritage Center** (p. 468). Buckle up for a 3½-hour tour with **Rabaca's Limousine Service.** Let your driver navigate the rough road down to **Polihua Beach** (p. 474), Lāna'i's largest white-sand beach. On the way back, linger at the **Garden of the Gods** (p. 469) to snap photos of the otherworldly landscape at sunset. Finish your day at the **Lāna'i City Grill,** listening to live music and dining by the fire pits out back (p. 484).

DAY 3: Enjoy a Day on the Water ★★★

Spend the day with **Trilogy Excursions** (p. 475) on a snorkel sail or scuba adventure at **Cathedrals,** one of Hawai'i's most ethereal dive sites. At night, savor hand-mixed cocktails and shoot some pool at the **Four Seasons Lāna'i Sports Bar** (p. 488).

DAY 4: Four-Wheel It to the East Side ★★★

Lāna'i is a fantastic place to go four-wheeling. If it hasn't been raining, splurge on a four-wheel-drive vehicle and head out to the East Side. Get a picnic lunch from **Pele's Other Garden** (p. 485) and download the Lāna'i Guide app for GPS-enabled directions, historic photos, and haunting Hawaiian chants. Find the petroglyphs at **Shipwreck Beach** (p. 475) and forge onward to **Keōmoku Village** and **Lopa Beach** (p. 470).

DAY 5: Brunch like Royalty & Visit an Ancient King's Temple ★★★

Fill your belly at **One Forty** (p. 483), where the lavish breakfast buffet's omelet station, juice bar, and *malasada* (Portuguese doughnut) fryer should fuel you up for hours. Tackle the rugged four-wheel-drive road down to **Kaunolu Village** (p. 472), where King Kahekili and his warriors famously leapt from the cliffs into the sea. Return your car in town and catch a movie at **Hale Keaka** (p. 488).

Hulopo'e Beach tide pools, Lāna'i.

DAY 6: Choose Your Adventure & Hit the Spa ★★★

Visit the **Island Adventure Center** to book your preferred activity: a horseback ride through Lāna'i's upland forests (p. 478), a rambling UTV tour through several cultural sites, or a round of golf at the award-winning **Challenge at Mānele golf course** (p. 478). Follow your adventure up with a soothing treatment at the **Four Seasons Resort Lāna'i spa** (p. 481).

Kayaking in Hanalei River.

DAY 7: Spend a Day at the Beach ★★★

Soak up the sun at **Hulopoʻe Beach** (p. 473). Grab a book and watch the kids play in the surf. If you feel inclined, follow the **Kapihaʻa Trail** (p. 480) along the rocky coast. For lunch, wander over to the **Views** (p. 484) and scan the horizon for dolphins or whales.

A WEEK ON KAUAʻI

Because much of the Garden Island, including the Nāpali Coast, is inaccessible to cars, a week will *just* suffice to view its beauty. To save driving time, split your stay between the North and South shores (detailed below) or stay on the East Side.

DAY 1: Arrival, Lunch & a Scenic Drive ★★★

From the airport, stop by **Hamura's Saimin Stand** (p. 582) or another **Līhuʻe** lunch counter (see "Plate Lunch, Bento & Poke," p. 580) for a classic taste of Kauaʻi before driving through the bustling Coconut Coast on your way to the serenity of the rural **North Shore** (p. 496). Soak in the views at the **Kīlauea Point National Wildlife Refuge & Lighthouse** (p. 511), and then poke around Kīlauea's **Kong Lung Historic Market Center** (p. 595).

DAY 2: Hike & Snorkel the North Shore ★★★

Thanks to the time difference, you'll have a head start driving across the nine one-lane bridges on the way to the end of the road and popular **Kēʻē Beach** (p. 530). If conditions permit, hike at least a

1A Hamura's Saimin Stand
1B Kīlauea Point National Wildlife Refuge & Lighthouse
1C Kong Lung Historic Market Center
2A Kē ʻē Beach
2B Kalalau Trail
2C Mākua (Tunnels) Beach
2D Limahuli Garden & Preserve
2E Tahiti Nui
3A Hanalei Bay
3B ʻAnini Beach
3C Nā ʻĀina Kai Botanical Gardens
3D St. Regis Princeville
4A Anaina Hou Community Park
4B Kapaa
4C ʻŌpaekaʻa Falls /Wailua River State Park
4D Old Kōloa Town
4E Shops at Kukuiʻula
5A Nāpali Coast helicopter or boat tour
5B Kauai Coffee
5C Wailua Falls
5D Kilohana Plantation & Luau
6A Waimea Canyon
6B Kōkeʻe State Park
6C Salt Pond Beach Park
6D Hanapēpē
7A Poʻipū Beach
7B Māhāʻulepu Heritage Trail
7C Anara Spa at Grand Hyatt Kauai
7D National Tropical Botanical Garden
7E Spouting Horn
7F The Beach House

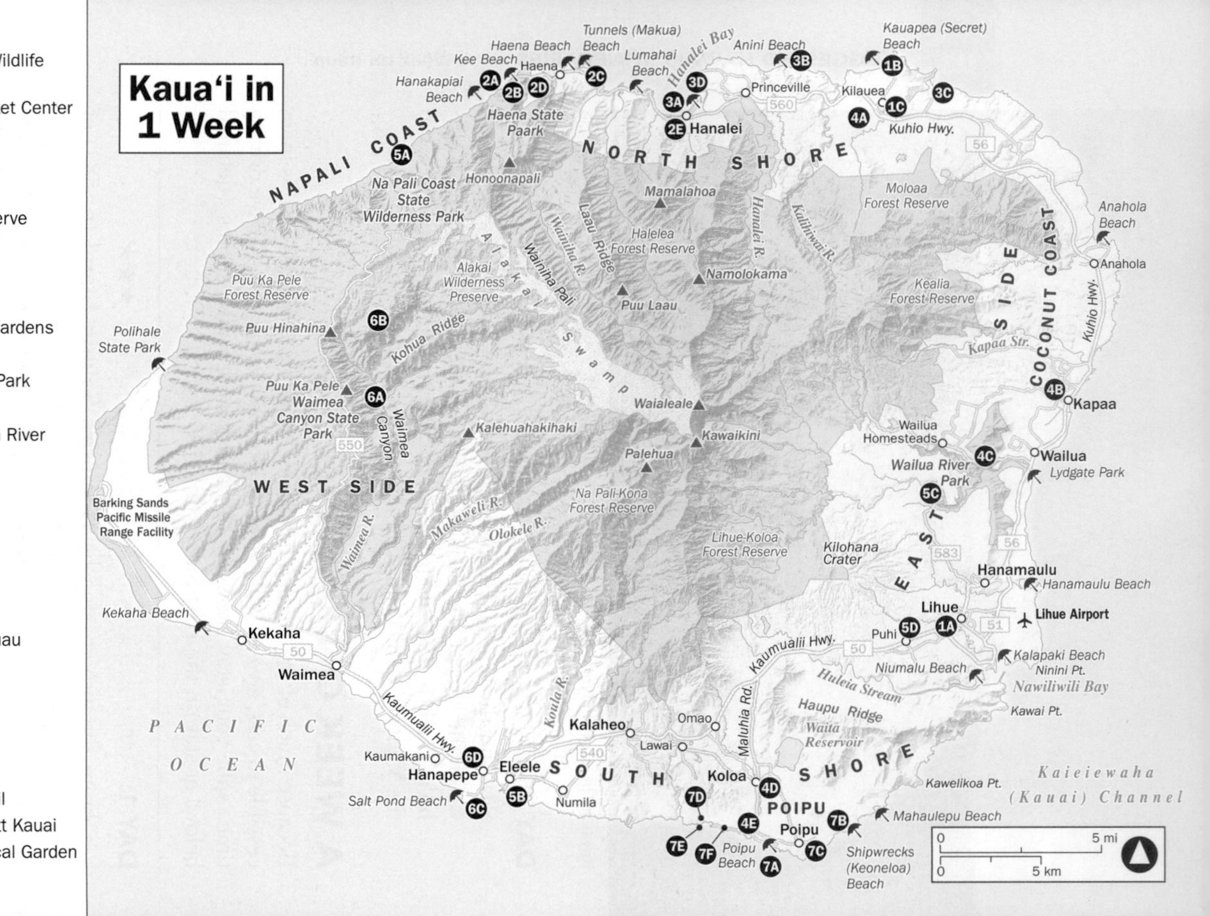

half-hour out on the challenging **Kalalau Trail** (p. 552) for glimpses of the stunning **Nāpali Coast,** or tackle the first 2 miles to **Hanakā pi'ai Beach,** 3 to 4 hours round-trip. After (or instead of) hiking, snorkel at **Kē'ē** and equally gorgeous **Mākua (Tunnels) Beach** (p. 531), accessed from **Hā'ena Beach Park** (p. 532). Eat lunch in Hā'ena and then spend time in the jewel-box setting of **Limahuli Garden and Preserve** (p. 512). Return to Hanalei to explore shops and galleries; after dinner, enjoy live Hawaiian music at the venerable **Tahiti Nui** (p. 601).

DAY 3: Adventures in Hanalei ★★★

The day begins on **Hanalei Bay, kayaking, surfing,** or **snorkeling** (see "Watersports," p. 535) or just frolicking at one of the three different beach parks (p. 530). If the waves are too rough, head instead to lagoon-like **'Anini Beach** (p. 528). In the afternoon, try **ziplining** (p. 557) or **horseback riding** (p. 555) amid waterfalls and green mountains; the less adventurous (who've booked in advance) can tour delightful **Nā 'Aina Kai Botanical Gardens** (p. 512). Savor views of Hanalei Bay and "Bali Hai" over cocktails at the **St. Regis Princeville** (p. 568) before dinner at **Bar Acuda** (p. 583).

DAY 4: Nature & Culture En Route to Po'ipū ★★

After breakfast, head south. Visit Kīlauea's **Anaina Hou Community Park** (p. 509) for Kaua'i themed mini-golf in a botanical garden or a hike or bike along the scenic Wai Koa loop trail. Stop for a bite at a funky cafe in **Kapa'a;** then drive to **'Ōpaeka'a Falls** and see the cultural sites of **Wailua River State Park** (p. 508). After crossing through busy Līhu'e, admire the scenery on the way to **Old Kōloa Town** (p. 596), where you can browse the quaint shops before checking into your Po'ipū lodgings. Pick a dinner spot from the many excellent choices in the **Shops at Kukui'ula** (p. 597).

DAY 5: Nāpali by Boat or Helicopter ★★★

Splurge on a **snorkel boat** or **Zodiac raft tour** (p. 535) to the **Nāpali Coast,** or take a **helicopter tour** (p. 523) for amazing views of Nāpali, Waimea Canyon, waterfalls, and more. After your boat returns, hoist a draft beer at **Kaua'i Island Brewery & Grill** (p. 592). For helicopter tours, most of which depart from Līhu'e, book a late-morning tour (after rush hour). Then have lunch in Līhu'e and drive to **Wailua Falls** (p. 509) before perusing the shops, tasting rum, or riding the train at **Kilohana Plantation** (p. 507).

DAY 6: Waimea Canyon & Kōke'e State Park ★★★

Start your drive early to "the Grand Canyon of the Pacific," **Waimea Canyon** (p. 521). Stay on the road through forested **Kōke'e State Park** (p. 518) to the **Kalalau Valley Lookout** (p. 497), and wait

The Nāpali Coast from helicopter.

for mists to part for a magnificent view. Stop by the **Kōke'e Museum** (p. 554) to obtain trail information for a hike after lunch at **Kōke'e Lodge** (p. 592). Or head back down to hit the waves at **Salt Pond Beach** or stroll through rustic **Hanapēpē** (p. 500), home to a **Friday night art walk** (p. 601).

DAY 7: Beach & Spa Time in Po'ipū ★★★

Spend the morning at glorious **Po'ipū Beach** (p. 532) before the crowds arrive, and then head over to **Keoneloa (Shipwrecks) Beach** (p. 533) to hike along the coastal **Māhā'ulepū Heritage Trail** (p. 554). Later, indulge in a spa treatment at Anara Spa at the **Grand Hyatt Kauai** (p. 570) or take a tour (booked in advance) at the **National Tropical Botanical Garden** (p. 517). Check out the flume of **Spouting Horn** (p. 518) before sunset cocktails at **RumFire Poipu Beach** in the **Sheraton Kauai** (p. 572) and dinner at the **Beach House** (p. 587).

HAWAI'I IN CONTEXT

by Shannon Wianecki

3

Since the Polynesians ventured across the Pacific to the Hawaiian Islands 1,000-plus years ago, these floating jewels have summoned visitors from around the globe.

Located in one of the most remote and isolated places on the planet, the Hawaiian Islands bask in the warm waters of the Pacific, where they are blessed by a tropical sun and cooled by gentle trade winds—creating what might be the most ideal climate imaginable. Mother Nature has carved out verdant valleys, hung brilliant rainbows in the sky, and trimmed the islands with sandy beaches in a spectrum of colors. The indigenous Hawaiian culture embodies the "spirit of aloha," an easy-going generosity that takes the shape of flower leis freely given, monumental feasts shared with friends and family, and hypnotic Hawaiian melodies played late into the tropical night.

Visitors are drawn to Hawai'i not only for its incredible beauty, but also for its opportunities for adventure. Go on, gaze into that fiery volcano, swim in a sea of rainbow-colored fish, tee off on a championship golf course, hike through a rainforest to hidden waterfalls, and kayak into the deep end of the ocean, where whales leap out of the water for reasons still mysterious. Looking for rest and relaxation? You'll discover that life moves at an unhurried pace here. Extra doses of sun and sea allow both body and mind to recharge.

Hawai'i is a sensory experience that will remain with you, locked in your memory, long after your tan fades. Years later, a sweet fragrance, the sun's warmth on your face, or the sound of the ocean breeze will deliver you back to the time you spent in the Hawaiian Islands.

THE FIRST HAWAIIANS

Throughout the Middle Ages, while Western sailors clung to the edges of continents for fear of falling off the earth's edge, Polynesian voyagers crisscrossed the planet's largest ocean. The first people to colonize Hawai'i were unsurpassed navigators. Using the stars, birds, and currents as guides, they sailed double-hulled canoes across thousands of miles, zeroing in on tiny islands in the center of the Pacific. They packed their vessels with food, plants, medicine, tools, and animals: everything necessary for building a new life on a distant shore. Over a span of 800 years, the great Polynesian migration connected a vast triangle of islands stretching from New Zealand to Hawai'i to Easter Island and

PREVIOUS PAGE: **Fire dancers.**

encompassing the many diverse archipelagos in between. Archaeologists surmise that Hawai'i's first wave of settlers came via the Marquesas Islands sometime after A.D. 1000, though oral histories suggest a much earlier date.

Over the ensuing centuries, a distinctly Hawaiian culture arose. Sailors became farmers and fishermen. These early Hawaiians were as skilled on land as they had been at sea; they built highly productive fish ponds, aqueducts to irrigate terraced *kalo lo'i* (taro patches), and 3-acre *heiau* (temples) with 50-foot-high rock walls. Farmers cultivated more than 400 varieties of *kalo,* their staple food; 300 types of sweet potato; and 40 different bananas. Each variety served a different need—some were drought resistant, others medicinal, and others good for babies. Hawaiian women fashioned intricately patterned *kapa* (barkcloth)—some of the finest in all of Polynesia. Each of the Hawaiian Islands was its own kingdom, governed by *ali'i* (high-ranking chiefs) who drew their authority from an established caste system and *kapu* (taboos). Those who broke the *kapu* could be sacrificed.

The ancient Hawaiian creation chant, the *Kumulipō,* depicts a universe that began when heat and light emerged out of darkness, followed by the first life form: a coral polyp. The 2,000-line epic poem is a grand genealogy, describing how all species are interrelated, from gently waving seaweeds to mighty human warriors. It is the basis for the Hawaiian concept of *kuleana,* a word that simultaneously refers to privilege and responsibility. To this day, Native Hawaiians view the care of their natural resources as a filial duty and honor.

WESTERN CONTACT

Cook's Ill-Fated Voyage

In the dawn hours of January 18, 1778, Captain James Cook of the HMS *Resolution* spotted an unfamiliar set of islands, which he later named for his benefactor, the Earl of Sandwich. The 50-year-old sea captain was already famous in Britain for "discovering" much of the South Pacific. Now on his third great voyage of exploration, Cook had set sail from Tahiti northward across uncharted waters. He was searching for the mythical Northwest Passage that was said to link the Pacific and Atlantic oceans. On his way, he stumbled upon Hawai'i (aka the Sandwich Isles) quite by chance.

With the arrival of the *Resolution,* Stone Age Hawai'i entered the age of iron. Sailors swapped nails and munitions for fresh water, pigs, and the affections of Hawaiian women. Tragically, the foreigners brought with them a terrible cargo: syphilis, measles, and other diseases that decimated the Hawaiian people. Captain Cook estimated the native population at 400,000 in 1778. (Later historians claim it could have been as high as 900,000.) By the time Christian missionaries arrived 40 years later, the number of Native Hawaiians had plummeted to just 150,000.

King Kamehameha I.

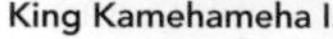

King David Kalākaua.

In a skirmish over a stolen boat, Cook was killed by a blow to the head. His British countrymen sailed home, leaving Hawai'i forever altered. The islands were now on the sea charts, and traders on the fur route between Canada and China stopped here to get fresh water. More trade—and more disastrous liaisons—ensued.

Two more sea captains left indelible marks on the islands. The first was American John Kendrick, who in 1791 filled his ship with fragrant Hawaiian sandalwood and sailed to China. By 1825, Hawai'i's sandalwood groves were gone. The second was Englishman George Vancouver, who in 1793 left behind cows and sheep, which ventured out to graze in the islands' native forest and hastened the spread of invasive species. King Kamehameha I sent for cowboys from Mexico and Spain to round up the wild livestock, thus beginning the islands' *paniolo* (cowboy) tradition.

King Kamehameha I was an ambitious *ali'i* who used western guns to unite the islands under single rule. After his death in 1819, the tightly woven Hawaiian society began to unravel. One of his successors, Queen Kaahumanu, abolished the *kapu* system, opening the door for religion of another form.

Staying to Do Well

In April 1820, missionaries bent on converting Hawaiians arrived from New England. The newcomers clothed the natives, banned them from dancing the hula, and nearly dismantled the ancient culture. The churchgoers tried to keep sailors and whalers out of the bawdy houses, where whiskey flowed and the virtue of native women was never safe. To their credit, the missionaries created a 12-letter alphabet for the Hawaiian language, taught reading and writing, started a printing press, and began recording the islands' history, which until that time had been preserved solely in memorized chants.

Children of the missionaries became business leaders and politicians. They married Hawaiians and stayed on in the islands, causing one wag to remark that the missionaries "came to do good and stayed to do well." In 1848, King Kamehameha III enacted the Great Māhele (division). Intended to guarantee Native Hawaiians rights to their land, it ultimately enabled foreigners to take ownership of vast tracts of land. Within two generations, more than 80% of all private land was in *haole* (foreign) hands. Businessmen planted acre after acre in sugarcane and imported waves of immigrants to work the fields: Chinese starting in 1852, Japanese in 1885, and Portuguese in 1878.

King David Kalākaua was elected to the throne in 1874. This popular "Merrie Monarch" built 'Iolani Palace in 1882, threw extravagant parties, and lifted the prohibitions on the hula and other native arts. For this, he was much loved. He proclaimed that "hula is the language of the heart and, therefore, the heartbeat of the Hawaiian people." He also gave Pearl Harbor to the United States; it became the westernmost bastion of the U.S. Navy. While visiting chilly San Francisco in 1891, King Kalākaua caught a cold and died in the royal suite of the Sheraton Palace. His sister, Queen Lili'uokalani, assumed the throne.

The Overthrow

For years, a group of American sugar plantation owners and missionary descendants had been machinating against the monarchy. On January 17, 1893, with the support of the U.S. minister to Hawai'i and the Marines, the conspirators imprisoned Queen Lili'uokalani in her own palace. To avoid bloodshed, she abdicated the throne, trusting that the

WHO IS Hawaiian IN HAWAI'I?

Only *kanaka maoli* (Native Hawaiians) are truly Hawaiian. The sugar and pineapple plantations brought so many different people to Hawai'i that the state is now a remarkable potpourri of ethnic groups: Native Hawaiians were joined by **Caucasians, Japanese, Chinese, Filipinos, Koreans, Portuguese, Puerto Ricans, Samoans, Tongans, Tahitians,** and other **Asian and Pacific Islanders.** Add to that a sprinkling of **Vietnamese, Canadians, African Americans, American Indians, South Americans,** and **Europeans** of every stripe. Many people retain an element of the traditions of their homeland. Some Japanese Americans in Hawai'i, generations removed from the homeland, are more traditional than the Japanese of Tokyo. The same is true of many Chinese, Koreans, and Filipinos, making Hawai'i a kind of living museum of Asian and Pacific cultures.

United States government would right the wrong. As the Queen waited in vain, she penned the sorrowful lyric "Aloha Oe," Hawai'i's song of farewell.

U.S. President Grover Cleveland's attempt to restore the monarchy was thwarted by Congress. Sanford Dole, a powerful sugar plantation owner, appointed himself president of the newly declared Republic of Hawai'i. His fellow sugarcane planters, known as the Big Five, controlled banking, shipping, hardware, and every other facet of economic life on the islands. In 1898, through annexation, Hawai'i became an American territory ruled by Dole.

O'ahu's central Ewa Plain soon filled with row crops. The Dole family planted pineapple on its sprawling acreage. Planters imported more contract laborers from Puerto Rico (1900), Korea (1903), and the Philippines (1907–31). Many of the new immigrants stayed on to establish families and become a part of the islands. Meanwhile, Native Hawaiians became a landless minority. Their language was banned in schools and their cultural practices devalued.

For nearly a century in Hawai'i, sugar was king, generously subsidized by the U.S. government. Sugar is a thirsty crop, and plantation owners oversaw the construction of flumes and aqueducts that channeled mountain streams down to parched plains, where waving fields of cane soon grew. The waters that once fed taro patches dried up. The sugar planters dominated the territory's economy, shaped its social fabric, and kept the islands in a colonial plantation era with bosses and field hands. But the workers eventually went on strike for higher wages and improved working conditions, and the planters found themselves unable to compete with cheap third-world labor costs.

Tourism Takes Hold

Tourism in Hawai'i began in the 1860s. Kīlauea volcano was one of the world's prime attractions for adventure travelers. In 1865, a grass structure known as Volcano House was built on the rim of Halema'uma'u Crater to shelter visitors; it was Hawai'i's first hotel. The visitor industry blossomed as the plantation era peaked and waned.

Volcano House, Hawai'i's first hotel.

In 1901, W. C. Peacock built the elegant Beaux Arts Moana Hotel on Waikīkī Beach, and W. C. Weedon convinced Honolulu businessmen to bankroll his plan to advertise Hawai'i in San Francisco. Armed with a

SPEAKING Hawaiian

Nearly everyone in Hawai'i speaks English, though many folks now also speak *'Ōlelo Hawai'i*, the native language of these islands. Most roads, towns, and beaches possess vowel-heavy Hawaiian names, so it will serve you well to practice pronunciation before venturing out to 'Aiea or Nu'uanu.

The Hawaiian alphabet has only 12 letters: 7 consonants (*h, k, l, m, n, p,* and *w*) and 5 vowels (*a, e, i, o,* and *u*)—but those vowels are liberally used! Usually they are "short," pronounced: *ah, ay, ee, oh,* and *oo*. For example, *wahine* (woman) is *wah-hee-nay*. Most vowels are pronounced separately, but on occasion they are sounded together with the "long" pronunciation: *ay, ee, eye, oh,* and *you*. For example, Wai'anae on O'ahu's leeward coast is *Why ah-ny*.

Two pronunciation marks can help you sound your way through Hawaiian names. The 'okina, a backwards apostrophe, indicates a glottal stop or a slight pause. The kahakō is a line over a vowel indicating stress. Observing these rules, you can tell that Pā'ia, a popular surf town on Maui's North Shore, is pronounced *pah-ee-ah*. The Likelike Highway is *lee-kay-lee-kay*.

Incorporate *aloha* (hello, goodbye, love) and *mahalo* (thank you) into your vocabulary. If you've just arrived, you're a *malihini* (newcomer). Someone who's been here a long time is a *kama'āina* (child of the land). When you finish a job or your meal, you are *pau* (finished). On Friday, it's *pau hana*, work finished. You eat *pūpū* (appetizers) when you go *pau hana*.

stereopticon and tinted photos of Waikīkī, Weedon sailed off in 1902 for 6 months of lecture tours to introduce "those remarkable people and the beautiful lands of Hawai'i." He drew packed houses. A tourism promotion bureau was formed in 1903, and about 2,000 visitors came to Hawai'i that year.

The steamship was Hawai'i's tourism lifeline. It took 4½ days to sail from San Francisco to Honolulu. Streamers, leis, and pomp welcomed each Matson liner at downtown's Aloha Tower. Well-heeled visitors brought trunks, servants, and Rolls-Royces and stayed for months. Hawaiians amused visitors with personal tours, floral parades, and hula shows.

Beginning in 1935 and running for the next 40 years, Webley Edwards's weekly live radio show, "Hawai'i Calls," planted the sounds of Waikīkī—surf, sliding steel guitar, sweet Hawaiian harmonies, drumbeats—in the hearts of millions of listeners in the United States, Australia, and Canada.

By 1936, visitors could fly to Honolulu from San Francisco on the *Hawai'i Clipper*, a seven-passenger Pan American Martin M-130 flying boat, for $360 one-way. The flight took 21 hours, 33 minutes. Modern tourism was born, with five flying boats providing daily service. The 1941 visitor count was a brisk 31,846 through December 6.

World War II & Statehood

On December 7, 1941, Japanese Zeros came out of the rising sun to bomb American warships based at Pearl Harbor. This was the "day of infamy" that plunged the United States into World War II.

The attack brought immediate changes to the islands. Martial law was declared, stripping the Big Five cartel of its absolute power in a single day. German and Japanese Americans were interned. Hawai'i was "blacked out" at night, Waikīkī Beach was strung with barbed wire, and Aloha Tower was painted in camouflage. Only young men bound for the Pacific came to Hawai'i during the war years. Many came back to graves in a cemetery called Punchbowl.

The postwar years saw the beginnings of Hawai'i's faux culture. The authentic traditions had long been suppressed, and into the void flowed a consumable brand of aloha. Harry Yee invented the Blue Hawai'i cocktail and dropped in a tiny Japanese parasol. Vic Bergeron created the Mai Tai, a drink made of rum and fresh lime juice, and opened Trader Vic's, America's first themed restaurant that featured the art, decor, and food of Polynesia. Arthur Godfrey picked up a 'ukulele and began singing *hapa-haole* tunes on early TV shows. In 1955, Henry J. Kaiser built the Hilton Hawaiian Village, and the 11-story high-rise Princess Ka'iulani Hotel opened on a site where the real princess once played. Hawai'i greeted 109,000 visitors that year.

In 1959, Hawai'i became the 50th state of the United States. That year also saw the arrival of the first jet airliners, which brought 250,000 tourists to the state. By the 1980s, Hawai'i's visitor count surpassed 6 million. Fantasy megaresorts bloomed on the neighbor islands like giant artificial flowers, swelling the luxury market with ever-swankier accommodations. Hawai'i's tourist industry—the bastion of the state's economy—has survived worldwide recessions, airline-industry hiccups, and increased competition from overseas. And yet year after year the Hawaiian Islands continue to be ranked among the top visitor destinations in the world.

HAWAI'I TODAY

A Cultural Renaissance

Despite the ever-increasing influx of foreign people and customs, the Native Hawaiian culture is experiencing a rebirth. It began in earnest in 1976, when members of the Polynesian Voyaging Society launched *Hōkū le'a,* a double-hulled canoe of the sort that hadn't been seen on these shores in centuries. The *Hōkūle'a*'s daring crew sailed her 2,500 miles to Tahiti without using modern instruments, relying instead on ancient navigational techniques. Most historians at that time discounted Polynesian wayfinding methods as rudimentary; the prevailing theory was that Pacific Islanders had discovered Hawai'i by accident, not intention. The

Hula girls.

Hōkūle'a's successful voyage sparked a fire in the hearts of indigenous islanders across the Pacific, who reclaimed their identity as a sophisticated, powerful people with unique wisdom to offer the world.

The Hawaiian language found new life, too. In 1984, a group of educators and parents recognized that, with fewer than 50 children fluent in Hawaiian, the language was dangerously close to extinction. They started a preschool where *keiki* (children) learned lessons purely in Hawaiian. They overcame numerous bureaucratic obstacles (including a law still on the books forbidding instruction in Hawaiian) to establish Hawaiian-language-immersion programs across the state that run from preschool through post-graduate education.

Hula—which never fully disappeared despite the missionaries' best efforts—is thriving. At the annual Merrie Monarch Festival commemorating King Kalākaua, hula *hālau* (troupes) from Hawai'i and beyond gather to demonstrate their skill and artistry. Fans of the ancient dance form are glued to the live broadcast of what is known as the Olympics of hula. *Kumu hula* (hula teachers) have safeguarded many Hawaiian cultural practices as part of their art: the making of *kapa,* the collection and cultivation of native herbs, and the observation of *kuleana,* an individual's responsibility to the community.

In that same spirit, in May 2014, the traditional voyaging canoe *Hōkūle'a* embarked on her most ambitious adventure yet: an international peace delegation. During the canoe's 3-year circumnavigation of the globe, the crew's mission is "to weave a lei around the world" and chart a new course toward a healthier and more sustainable horizon for all of humankind. The sailors hope to collaborate with political leaders, scientists, educators, and schoolchildren in each of the ports they visit.

The history of Hawai'i has come full circle. The ancient Polynesians traveled the seas to discover these islands. Today their descendants set sail aboard the *Hōkūle'a* to share Hawai'i with the world.

DINING IN HAWAI'I

The Gang of 12

In the early days of Hawai'i's tourism industry, the food wasn't anything to write home about. Continental cuisine ruled fine-dining kitchens. Meats and produce arrived much the same way visitors did: jet-lagged after a long journey from a far-off land. Island chefs struggled to revive limp iceberg lettuce and frozen cocktail shrimp—often letting outstanding ocean views make up for uninspired dishes. In 1991, 12 chefs staged a revolt. They partnered with local farmers, ditched the dictatorship of imported foods, and brought sun-ripened mango, crisp organic greens, and freshly caught *uku* (snapper) to the table. Coining the name Hawai'i Regional Cuisine (HRC), they gave the world a taste of what happens when passionate, classically trained cooks have their way with ripe Pacific flavors.

More than 2 decades later, the movement to unite local farms and kitchens is still bearing fruit, and the HRC heavyweights continue to

Ahi poke.

Shave ice.

keep things hot in island kitchens. But they aren't, by any means, the sole source of good eats in Hawai'i.

Shops selling fresh steaming noodles abound in O'ahu's **Chinatown.** Francophiles will delight in the classic French cooking at **La Mer** on O'ahu and **Gerard's** on Maui. You'll be hard-pressed to discover more authentic Japanese fare than can be had in the restaurants dotting Honolulu's side streets.

Plate Lunches, Shave Ice & Food Trucks

Haute cuisine is alive and well in Hawai'i, but equally important in the culinary pageant are good-value plate lunches, shave ice, and food trucks.

The **plate lunch,** which is ubiquitous throughout the islands, can be ordered from a lunch wagon or a restaurant. It usually consists of some protein—fried mahimahi, say, or teriyaki beef, shoyu chicken, or chicken or pork cutlets served katsu style: breaded, fried, and slathered in a rich gravy—accompanied by "two scoops rice," macaroni salad, and a few leaves of green, typically julienned cabbage. Chili water and soy sauce are the condiments of choice. Like **saimin**—the local version of noodles in broth topped with scrambled eggs, green onions, and sometimes pork—the plate lunch is Hawai'i's version of comfort food.

Because this is Hawai'i, at least a few fingerfuls of **poi**—steamed, pounded taro (the traditional Hawaiian staple crop)—are a must. Mix it with salty *kālua* pork (pork cooked in a Polynesian underground oven known as an *imu*) or *lomi* salmon (salted salmon with tomatoes and green onions). Other tasty Hawaiian foods include ***poke*** (pronounced *po-kay*), a popular appetizer made of cubed raw fish seasoned with onions, seaweed, and roasted *kukui* nuts); ***laulau,*** pork, chicken, or fish

ON LOCATION IN HAWAI'I

Hawai'i's iconic landscapes serve as a backdrop for numerous TV shows and films. Fans of ***Lost*** might recognize Mokulēi'a Beach on O'ahu's North Shore as the site of the fictional plane crash. Episode three was shot in O'ahu's Ka'a'awa Valley, a lush and remote spot that appears in several movies, including ***50 First Dates, Godzilla,*** and ***Pearl Harbor.*** Johnny Depp leaps into Kīlauea Falls on Kaua'i in ***Pirates of the Caribbean: On Stranger Tides.*** Adam Sandler and Jennifer Aniston luxuriate at the Grand Wailea's pool and pass through the lobby of the Mana Kai on Maui in ***Just Go With It.***

The Descendants, Alexander Payne's film about a dysfunctional Hawai'i *kama'āina* (long-time resident) family, features a wealth of island scenery and music. George Clooney (as Matt King) and the cast spent 11 weeks shooting in Hawai'i; it's easy to trace their trail. Matt King's house is on Old Pali Road in Nu'uanu. When King runs down the hill to visit a friend, he's greeted by Poppy, a pygmy goat standing beneath a 50-foot-tall lychee tree. Payne rented the plantation-style house—goat and all—from a local family and shot scenes there without changing a thing. Whether or not you're a film buff, you should definitely pick up a copy of ***The Descendants* soundtrack.** This goldmine of modern and classic Hawaiian music features the very best island voices, from Gabby Pahinui to Keola Beamer, and includes several versions of the hauntingly beautiful anthem "Hi'ilawe." You won't find a better soundtrack for your Hawaiian vacation.

George Clooney, Shailene Woodley, Amara Miller, and Nick Krause in *The Descendants.*

steamed in *ti* leaves; **squid *lū'au,*** cooked in coconut milk and taro tops; ***haupia,*** creamy coconut pudding; and ***kūlolo,*** a steamed pudding of coconut, brown sugar, and taro.

For a sweet snack, the prevailing choice is **shave ice.** Particularly on hot, humid days, long lines of shave-ice lovers gather for heaps of finely shaved ice topped with sweet tropical syrups. Sweet-sour *li hing mui* is a favorite, and gourmet flavors include calamansi lime and red velvet cupcake. Aficionados order shave ice with ice cream and sweetened adzuki beans on the bottom or sweetened condensed milk on top.

WHEN TO GO

Most visitors come to Hawai'i when the weather is lousy elsewhere. Thus, the **high season**—when prices are up and resorts are often booked to capacity—is generally from mid-December to March or mid-April. The last 2 weeks of December, in particular, are prime time for travel to Hawai'i. Spring break is also jam-packed with families taking advantage of the school holiday. If you're planning a trip during peak season, make your hotel and rental car reservations as early as possible, expect crowds, and prepare to pay top dollar.

The **off season,** when the best rates are available and the islands are less crowded, is late spring (mid-Apr to early June) and fall (Sept to mid-Dec).

If you plan to travel in **summer** (June–Aug), don't expect to see the fantastic bargains of spring and fall—this is prime time for family travel. But you'll still find much better deals on packages, airfare, and accommodations in summer than in the winter months.

Climate

Because Hawai'i lies at the edge of the tropical zone, it technically has only two seasons, both of them warm. There's a dry season that corresponds to **summer** (Apr–Oct) and a rainy season in **winter** (Nov–Mar). It rains every day somewhere in the islands at any time of the year, but the rainy season can bring enough gray weather to spoil your tanning opportunities. Fortunately, it seldom rains in one spot for more than 3 days straight.

The **year-round temperature** doesn't vary much. At the beach, the average daytime high in summer is 85°F (29°C), while the average daytime high in winter is 78°F (26°C); nighttime lows are usually about 10° cooler. But how warm it is on any given day really depends on *where* you are on the island.

Each island has a **leeward** side (the side sheltered from the wind) and a **windward** side (the side that gets the wind's full force). The leeward sides (the west and south) are usually hot and dry, while the windward sides (east and north) are generally cooler and moist. When you want arid, sunbaked, desert-like weather, go leeward. When you want lush, wet, rainforest weather, go windward.

Hawai'i also has a wide range of **microclimates,** thanks to interior valleys, coastal plains, and mountain peaks. Kaua'i's Mount Wai'ale'ale is one of the wettest spots on earth, yet Waimea Canyon, just a few miles away, is almost a desert. On the Big Island, Hilo ranks among the wettest cities in the nation, with 180 inches of rainfall a year. At Puako, only 60 miles away, it rains less than 6 inches a year. The summits of Mauna Kea on the Big Island and Haleakalā on Maui often see snow in winter—even when the sun is blazing down at the beach. The locals say if you don't like the weather, just drive a few miles down the road—it's sure to be different!

Average Temperature & Number of Rainy Days in Waikīkī

	JAN	FEB	MAR	APR	MAY	JUNE	JULY	AUG	SEPT	OCT	NOV	DEC
HIGH (°F/°C)	80/27	80/27	81/27	82/28	84/29	86/30	87/31	88/31	88/31	86/30	84/29	81/27
LOW (°F/°C)	70/21	66/19	66/19	69/21	70/21	72/22	73/23	74/23	74/23	72/22	70/21	67/19
RAINY DAYS	10	9	9	9	7	6	7	6	7	9	9	10

Average Temperature & Number of Rainy Days in Hanalei, Kaua'i

	JAN	FEB	MAR	APR	MAY	JUNE	JULY	AUG	SEPT	OCT	NOV	DEC
HIGH (°F/°C)	79/26	80/27	80/27	82/28	84/29	86/30	88/31	88/31	87/31	86/30	83/28	80/27
LOW (°F/°C)	61/17	61/16	62/17	63/17	65/18	66/19	66/19	67/19	68/20	67/19	65/18	62/17
RAINY DAYS	8	5	6	3	3	2	8	2	3	3	4	7

Holidays

When Hawai'i observes holidays (especially those over a long weekend), travel between the islands increases, interisland airline seats are fully booked, rental cars are at a premium, and hotels and restaurants are busier.

Federal, state, and county government offices are closed on all federal holidays. Federal holidays in 2017 include New Year's Day (Jan 1); Martin Luther King, Jr., Day (Jan 16); Washington's birthday (Feb 20); Memorial Day (May 29); Independence Day (July 4); Labor Day (Sept 4); Columbus Day (Oct 9); Veterans Day (Nov 11); Thanksgiving Day (Nov 23); and Christmas (Dec 25).

State and county offices are also closed on local holidays, including Prince Kūhiō Day (Mar 27), honoring the birthday of Hawai'i's first delegate to the U.S. Congress; King Kamehameha Day (June 12), a statewide holiday commemorating Kamehameha the Great, who united the islands and ruled from 1795 to 1819; and Admission Day (third Fri in Aug), which honors the admittance of Hawai'i as the 50th state on August 21, 1959.

Hey, No Smoking in Hawai'i

Well, not *totally* no smoking, but Hawai'i has one of the toughest laws against smoking in the U.S. The Hawai'i Smoke-Free Law prohibits smoking in public buildings, including airports, shopping malls, grocery stores, retail shops, buses, movie theaters, banks, convention facilities, and all government buildings and facilities. There is no smoking in restaurants, bars, and nightclubs. Most bed-and-breakfasts prohibit smoking indoors, and more and more hotels and resorts are becoming smoke-free even in public areas. Also, there is no smoking within 20 feet of a doorway, window, or ventilation intake (so no hanging around outside a bar to smoke—you must go 20 ft. away). Even some beaches have no-smoking policies.

Hawai'i Calendar of Events

Please note that, as with any schedule of upcoming events, the following information is subject to change; always confirm the details before you plan your trip around an event.

JANUARY

Waimea Ocean Film Festival, Waimea and the Kohala Coast, Big Island. Several days of films featuring the ocean, ranging from surfing and Hawaiian canoe paddling to ecological issues. Go to www.waimeaoceanfilm.org or call ✆ **808/854-6095.** First weekend after New Year's Day.

PGA Hyundai Tournament of Champions, Kapalua Resort, Maui. Top PGA golfers compete for $1.12 million purse. Go to www.pgatour.com/tournaments/hyundai-tournament-of-champions.html or call ✆ **808/665-9160.** Early January.

Pacific Islands Arts Festival, Kapi'olani Park, Honolulu, O'ahu. This Saturday and Sunday fest features more than 75 artists and crafters, entertainment, food, and demonstrations. Free admission. Go to www.icb-web.net/haa or call ✆ **808/637-5337.** Mid-January.

Ka Moloka'i Makahiki, Kaunakakai Town Baseball Park, Mitchell Pau'ole Center, Kaunakakai, Moloka'i. Makahiki, a traditional time of peace in ancient Hawai'i, is re-created with performances by Hawaiian music groups and *hālau* (hula schools), sporting competitions, crafts, and food. It's a wonderful chance to experience the Hawai'i of yesteryear. Ceremonial games start at 7:30am. Go to www.visitmolokai.com/wp/events-molokai-events-calendar or call ✆ **800/800-6367** or 808/553-3876. Late January.

Chinese New Year, most islands. In 2017, lion dancers will be snaking their way around the state on January 28, the start of the Chinese Year of the Rooster. On O'ahu, Honolulu's Chinatown rolls out the red carpet for this fiery celebration with parades, pageants, and street festivals. Visit www.chinesechamber.com or call ✆ **808/533-3181.** On Maui, lion dancers perform at the historic Wo Hing Temple on Front Street (http://visitlahaina.com). Call ✆ **888/310-1117** or 808/667-9175.

FEBRUARY

Waimea Town Celebration, Waimea, Kaua'i. This annual 2-day party on Kaua'i's west side celebrates the Hawaiian and multiethnic history of the town where Captain Cook first landed. This is the island's biggest event, drawing some 10,000 people. Top Hawaiian entertainers, sporting events, rodeo, and hat lei contests are just some of the draws of this weekend celebration. Details at www.waimeatowncelebration.com or ✆ **808/645-0996.** Weekend after Presidents' Day weekend.

Sand Castle Esquisse, Kailua Beach Park, O'ahu. Pull up a beach chair and watch University of Hawai'i School of Architecture students compete against professional architects to see who can build the best, most unusual, and most outrageous sand sculpture. The building is 9am to noon; judging is noon to 1pm. Visit www.facebook.com/AIASHawaii or call ✆ **808/956-7225.** Mid-February.

Maui Whale Festival, Kalama Park, Kīhei, Maui. A daylong celebration in the park, with a "parade of whales," entertainment, a crafts fair, games, and food. Go to www.mauiwhalefestival.org or call ✆ **808/249-8811.** Early or mid-February.

Punahou School Carnival, Punahou School, Honolulu, O'ahu. This 2-day event has everything you can imagine in a school carnival, from high-speed rides to homemade jellies. All proceeds go to scholarship funds for Hawai'i's most prestigious private high school. Go to www.punahou.edu or call ✆ **808/944-5711.** Early to mid-February.

Narcissus Festival, Honolulu, O'ahu. Taking place around the Chinese New Year, this cultural festival includes a queen pageant, cooking demonstrations, and a cultural fair. Visit www.chinesechamber.com or call ✆ **808/533-3181.**

Daylight Saving Time

Most of the United States observes daylight saving time, which lasts from 2am on the second Sunday in March to 2am on the first Sunday in November. **Hawai'i does *not* observe daylight saving time.** So when daylight saving time is in effect in most of the U.S., Hawai'i is 3 hours behind the West Coast and 6 hours behind the East Coast. When the U.S. reverts to standard time in November, Hawai'i is 2 hours behind the West Coast and 5 hours behind the East Coast.

Buffalo's Big Board Surfing Classic, Makaha Beach, O'ahu. Now in its fourth decade, this contest features classic Hawaiian-style surfing, with longboard, tandem, and canoe surfing heats. Go to www.buffalosurfingclassic.com. Mid-February or early March.

MARCH

Whale & Ocean Arts Festival, Lahaina, Maui. The entire town of Lahaina celebrates the annual migration of Pacific humpback whales with this weekend festival in Banyan Tree Park. Artists offer their best ocean-themed art for sale, while Hawaiian musicians and hula troupes entertain. Enjoy marine-related activities, games, and a touch-pool exhibit for kids. Get details at http://visitlahaina.com or call ✆ **888/310-1117** or 808/667-9175. Early March.

Kona Brewers Festival, King Kamehameha's Kona Beach Hotel Lū'au Grounds, Kailua-Kona, Big Island. This annual event features microbreweries from around the world, with beer tastings, food, and entertainment. Go to http://konabrewersfestival.com or call ✆ **808/987-9196.** Mid-March.

Kaua'i Quilt Show, Lihu'e, Kaua'i. Quilting became an important creative outlet in the islands after the arrival of Western missionaries. Learn about Hawai'i's unique style of quilting and view modern takes on this lovely art. Go to www.kauaifestivals.com or call ✆ **808/652-2261.** Mid-March.

St. Patrick's Day Parade, Waikīkī (Fort DeRussy to Kapi'olani Park), O'ahu. Bagpipers, bands, clowns, and marching groups parade through the heart of Waikīkī, with lots of Irish-style celebrating all day. Visit www.fosphawaii.ning.com/page/parade or call ✆ **808/926-1777** (Kelley O'Neil's Pub). March 17.

Prince Kūhiō Day Celebrations, all islands. On this state holiday, various festivals throughout Hawai'i celebrate the birth of Jonah Kūhiō Kalanianaole, who was born on March 26, 1871, and elected to Congress in 1902. Kaua'i, his birthplace, stages weeklong festivities at various locations around the island; visit www.kauaifestivals.com for details. Week of March 26.

Celebration of the Arts, Ritz-Carlton Kapalua, Kapalua Resort, Maui. Contemporary and traditional Hawaiian artists give free hands-on lessons during this 3-day festival, which also features song contests and rousing debates on what it means to be Hawaiian. Go to www.celebrationofthearts.org or call ✆ **808/665-7084.** End of March.

APRIL

Maui County Ag Fest, Waikapū, Maui. Maui celebrates its farmers and their fresh bounty at this well-attended event. Kids enjoy barnyard games while parents duck into the Grand Taste tent to sample top chefs' collaborations with local farmers. Go to www.mauicountyfarmbureau.org/maui-county-agricultural-festival-2 or call ✆ **808/243-2290.** First Saturday in April.

Buddha Day, Lahaina Jodo Mission, Lahaina, Maui. Each spring this historic mission holds a flower festival pageant honoring the birth of Buddha. Call

✆ **808/661-4304.** Generally the first Sunday in April.

Easter Sunrise Service, National Memorial Cemetery of the Pacific, Punchbowl Crater, Honolulu, O'ahu. For a century, people have gathered at this famous cemetery for Easter sunrise services. Call ✆ **808/532-3720.** April 16, 2017.

Merrie Monarch Hula Festival, Hilo, Big Island. Hawai'i's biggest, most prestigious hula festival features a week of modern *('auana)* and ancient *(kahiko)* dance competition in honor of King David Kalākaua, the "Merrie Monarch" who revived the dance. Tickets sell out by January, so book early. Go to www.merriemonarch.com or call ✆ **808/935-9168.** Late March through early April.

East Maui Taro Festival, Hāna, Maui. Taro, a Hawaiian staple food, is celebrated through music, hula, arts, crafts, and, of course, taro-inspired feasts. Go to www.tarofestival.org or call ✆ **808/264-1553.** Last weekend in April.

MAY

Outrigger Canoe Season, all islands. From May to September, canoe paddlers across the state participate in outrigger canoe races nearly every weekend. Go to www.ocpaddler.com for this year's schedule of events.

Big Island Chocolate Festival, Kona, Big Island. This celebration of chocolate (cacao) grown and produced in Hawai'i features symposiums, candy-making workshops, and gala tasting events. It's held in the Fairmont Orchid hotel. Go to www.bigislandchocolatefestival.com or call ✆ **808/854-6769.** First or second weekend in May.

Lei Day Celebrations, Waikīkī, O'ahu. May Day (May 1) is Lei Day in Hawai'i, celebrated with lei-making contests, pageantry, arts, and crafts. On O'ahu, the real highlight is the live concert from 9am to 5:30pm at the Queen Kapi'olani Regional Park Bandstand. Go to www.facebook.com/LeiDayCelebration or call ✆ **808/768-3041.** May 1.

World Fire-Knife Dance Championships & Samoa Festival, Polynesian Cultural Center, La'ie, O'ahu. Junior and adult fire-knife dancers from around the world converge on the center for one of the most amazing performances you'll ever see. Authentic Samoan food and cultural festivities round out the fun. Go to www.worldfireknife.com or call ✆ **800/367-7060.** Mid-May.

Lantern Floating Hawai'i, Magic Island at Ala Moana Beach Park, Honolulu, O'ahu. Some 40,000 people gather at Shinnyo-en Temple's annual Memorial Day lantern ceremony, a beautiful appeal for peace and harmony. At sunset, hundreds of glowing lanterns are set adrift. Hula and music follow. Go to www.lanternfloatinghawaii.com or call ✆ **808/947-2814.** Last Monday in May.

Memorial Day, National Memorial Cemetery of the Pacific, Punchbowl Crater, Honolulu, O'ahu. The armed forces hold a ceremony recognizing those who died for their country, beginning at 10am. Call ✆ **808/532-3720.** Last Monday in May.

Maui Windsurfing Race Series, Kanaha Beach Park, Kahului. This annual windsurfing slalom race takes place at Kanaha Beach Park, west of Kahului Airport in central Maui. Go to www.facebook.com/Maui-Race-Series-600081173346035 or call Hi-Tech Surf Sports at ✆ **808/877-2111.** Late May through June.

JUNE

Obon Season, all islands. This colorful Buddhist ceremony honoring the souls of the dead kicks off in June. Synchronized dancers circle a tower where Taiko drummers play, and food booths sell Japanese treats late into the night. Each weekend a different Buddhist temple hosts the Bon Dance. Go to www.gohawaii.com for a statewide schedule.

Molokai Ka Hula Piko Festival, Mitchell Pau'ole Center, Kaunakakai, Moloka'i. This 3-day hula celebration occurs on the island where the Hawaiian dance was born and features performances by hula schools, musicians, and singers from across Hawai'i, as well as local food and Hawaiian crafts: quilting, woodworking, featherwork, and deer-horn scrimshaw. Go to www.kahulapiko.com or call ✆ **800/800-6367** or 808/553-3876. Early June.

Honolulu Pride Parade & Celebration, Waikīkī, O'ahu. Since 1990, Hawai'i's capital has celebrated diversity. This annual rainbow-splashed parade features a gay military color guard, roller derby, and high-energy floats. Kapi'olani Park hosts daylong festivities. Go to www.honolulupride.org or follow @honolulu pride on Twitter. Early June.

King Kamehameha Celebration, all islands. This state holiday (officially June 11, but celebrated on different dates on each island) features a massive floral parade, *ho'olaule'a* (party), and much more. O'ahu: ✆ **808/586-0333.** Kaua'i: ✆ **808/651-6419.** Big Island: www.kamehamehafestival.org and www.konaparade.org. Maui: http://visitlahaina.com or ✆ **808/667-9194.** Moloka'i: ✆ **808/553-3876.**

Maui Film Festival, Wailea Resort, Maui. Five days of premiere screenings, celebrity awards, and lavish parties under the stars. Go to www.mauifilmfestival.com or call ✆ **808/579-9244.** Early or mid-June.

King Kamehameha Hula Competition, Neal S. Blaisdell Center, Honolulu, O'ahu. This daylong hula competition features dancers from as far away as Japan, Canada, and Mexico. Go to www.blaisdellcenter.com or call ✆ **808/586-0333.** Third weekend in June.

Kapalua Wine & Food Festival, Kapalua Resort, Maui. Big-time oenophiles and food experts gather at the Ritz-Carlton Kapalua for 4 days of formal tastings, panel discussions, and samplings of new releases. The seafood finale ranks among the state's best feasts. Go to http://kapaluawineandfoodfestival.com or call ✆ **800/KAPALUA** (527-2582). Mid-June.

Lāna'i Pineapple Festival, Lāna'i City, Lāna'i. The local pineapple is long gone, but this 2-day festival celebrates the island's plantation legacy, including a pineapple-eating contest, a pineapple-cooking contest, arts and crafts, food, music, and fireworks. Go to www.lanaipineapplefestival.com or call ✆ **808/565-7600.** Late June/early July.

JULY

Makawao Parade & Rodeo, Makawao, Maui. The annual parade and rodeo has been taking place in this upcountry cowboy town for 60 years. Good fun! Go to www.gohawaii.com/maui or call ✆ **808/572-9565.** July 4.

Ala Moana Fourth of July Spectacular, Ala Moana Center, Waikīkī, O'ahu. The 15-minute fireworks display is among the largest in the country. People gather on the Ewa parking deck at 4pm for the best view. A concert at 5pm is followed by fireworks at 8:30pm. Shoppers enjoy a 20% discount all week. Go to www.alamoanacenter.com/Events/4th-of-July-Celebration or call ✆ **808/955-9517.** July 3 to 6.

Molokai 2 O'ahu Paddleboard World Championships, starts on Moloka'i and finishes on O'ahu. Some 200 international participants journey to Moloka'i to compete in this 32-mile race, considered to be the world championship of long-distance paddleboarding. The race begins at Kaluakoi Beach on Moloka'i at 7:30am and finishes at Maunaloa Bay on O'ahu around 12:30pm. Go to www.molokai2oahu.com or call ✆ **760/944-3854.** Late July.

'Ukulele Festival, Kapi'olani Park Bandstand, Waikīkī, O'ahu. Now in its 47th year, this free concert features a 'ukulele orchestra of some 800 students, ages 4 to 92. Hawai'i's top musicians pitch in. Get the details at www.ukulelefestivalhawaii.org. Late July.

Queen Lili'uokalani Keiki Hula Competition, Neal S. Blaisdell Center, Honolulu, O'ahu. More than 500 *keiki* (children) representing 22 *hālau* (hula schools) from the islands compete in this dance fest. The event is broadcast a week later on KITV-TV. Go to www.kpcahawaii.com or call ✆ **808/521-6905.** Mid- to late July.

50th State Fair, Aloha Stadium, Honolulu, O'ahu. The annual state fair is a great one, with displays of Hawaiian agricultural products (including orchids), educational and cultural exhibits, entertainment, and local food. Go to www.ekfernandez.com/events/50th.asp or call ✆ **808/682-5767.** Late May through early July.

AUGUST

Neil Pryde Hawai'i State Championship, Kanaha Beach Park, Kahului, Maui. Top windsurfers compete in the final race of the series. Go to www.facebook.com/Maui-Race-Series-600081173346035 or call Hi-Tech Maui at ✆ **808/877-2111.** Late July or early August.

Pu'ukoholā Heiau National Historic Site Anniversary Celebration, Kawaihae, Big Island. This homage to authentic Hawaiian culture begins at 6am at Puukoholā Heiau. It's a rugged, beautiful site where attendees make leis, weave *lauhala* mats, pound *poi,* and dance ancient hula. Bring refreshments and sunscreen. Go to www.nps.gov/puhe or call ✆ **808/882-7218.** Mid-August.

Duke's OceanFest Ho'olaule'a, Waikīkī, O'ahu. Nine days of water-oriented competitions and festivities celebrate the life of Duke Kahanamoku. Events include longboard surfing, paddleboard racing, swimming, tandem surfing, surf polo, beach volleyball, stand-up paddling, and a lū'au. Visit www.dukesoceanfest.com. Mid- to late August.

Admission Day, all islands. Hawai'i became the 50th state on August 21, 1959. On the third Friday in August, the state takes a holiday (all state-related facilities are closed).

Hawai'i Food & Wine Festival, multiple locations on O'ahu, Hawai'i, and Maui. Cofounded by Alan Wong and Roy Yamaguchi (two of the state's most celebrated chefs), this 2-week gourmet bonanza includes wine and spirit tastings, cooking demos, field trips, and glitzy galas. See www.hawaiifoodandwinefestival.com or call ✆ **808/738-6245.** Mid-October.

SEPTEMBER

Waikīkī Roughwater Swim, Waikīkī, O'ahu. This popular 2.5-mile, open-ocean swim traces Sans Souci (Kaimana) Beach between the Natatorium and the New Otani Kaimana Beach Hotel in Waikīkī. Early registration is encouraged, but last-minute entries on race day are allowed. Go to www.wrswim.com. Saturday, Labor Day weekend.

Queen Lili'uokalani Canoe Race, Kailua-Kona to Honaunau, Big Island. Thousands of paddlers compete in the world's largest long-distance canoe race. Go to www.kaiopua.org or call ✆ **808/938-8577.** Labor Day weekend.

Parker Ranch Round-Up Rodeo, Waimea, Big Island. This hot rodeo competition takes place in the heart of cowboy country. Go to http://parkerranch.com/labor-day-weekend-rodeo or call ✆ **808/885-7311.** Weekend before Labor Day.

Kapalua Open, Kapalua, Maui. Held over Labor Day weekend, this USTA–sanctioned event features the largest tennis purse for a tournament in the state. Registration includes a tennis tourney, dinner, raffle, and T-shirt (and trophy if you're lucky!). Go to www.golfatkapalua.com/tennis-tournaments.html or call ✆ **808/662-7730.** Labor Day weekend.

Aloha Festivals, various locations on all islands. Parades and other events celebrate Hawaiian culture and friendliness throughout the state. The parades with flower-decked horses are particularly eye-catching. Go to www.alohafestivals.com or call ✆ **808/923-2030.**

OCTOBER

Emalani Festival, Koke'e State Park, Kaua'i. This culturally rich festival honors Queen Emma, an inveterate gardener and Hawai'i's first environmental queen, who made a forest trek to Koke'e with 100 friends in 1871. Go to www.kokee.org or call ✆ **808/335-9975.** Second Saturday in October.

Maui County Fair, War Memorial Complex, Wailuku, Maui. Now in its 94th year, the oldest county fair in Hawai'i features a parade, amusement rides, live entertainment, and exhibits. Go to www.mauifair.com or call ✆ **808/280-6889.** Early October.

Hawai'i Chocolate Festival, Honolulu, O'ahu. Indulge your sweet tooth at this celebration of Hawaiian-grown cacao. Dozens of local vendors share their gourmet creations—everything from truffles and crepes to chocolate-scented soap. Go to http://hawaiichocolatefestival.com. Mid-October.

Ironman Triathlon World Championship, Kailua-Kona, Big Island. Some 1,500-plus world-class athletes run a full marathon, swim 2.5 miles, and bike 112 miles on the Kona-Kohala Coast of the Big Island. Spectators watch the action along the route for free. The best place to see the 7am start is along the Ali'i Drive seawall, facing Kailua Bay; arrive before 5:30am to get a seat. (Ali'i Dr. closes to traffic; park on a side street and walk down.) To watch finishers come in, line up along Ali'i Drive from Holualoa Street to Palani Road. The first finisher can arrive as early as 2:30pm. Go to www.ironmanworldchampionship.com or call ✆ **808/329-0063.** Saturday closest to the full moon in October.

Hana Ho'ohiwahiwa O Ka'iulani, Sheraton Princess Kaiulani, Waikīkī, O'ahu. This hotel commemorates the birthday of its namesake, Princess Victoria Ka'iulani, with a week of complimentary hula lessons, lei making, 'ukulele lessons, and more. The crowning touch is the Princess Ka'iulani Keiki Hula Festival, which showcases performances by more than 200 *keiki* (children) from *hālau* (schools) on the island of O'ahu. Go to www.princess-kaiulani.com or call ✆ **808/922-5811.** Mid-October.

Xterra World Championship, Kapalua, Maui. Hundreds of gonzo athletes plunge into the Pacific, jump on mountain bikes, and race through the rainforest to be crowned Xterra world champion (and win $100,000). After the race, athletes and friends celebrate at an awards dinner and adrenaline-fueled Halloween party. Go to www.xterraplanet.com/maui or call ✆ **877/751-8880.** Late October or early November.

NOVEMBER

Hawaiian Slack Key Guitar Festival, Kaua'i Beach Resort, Lihu'e, Kaua'i. The best of Hawai'i's folk music (slack key guitar) performed by the best musicians in Hawai'i. It's 6 hours long and free. Go to www.slackkeyfestival.com or call ✆ **808/226-2697.** Mid-November.

Kona Coffee Cultural Festival, Kailua-Kona, Big Island. Celebrate the coffee harvest with a bean-picking contest, lei contests, song and dance, and the Miss Kona Coffee Pageant. Go to http://konacoffeefest.com or call ✆ **808/326-7820.** Events throughout November.

Hawai'i International Film Festival, various locations throughout the state. This cinema festival with a cross-cultural spin features filmmakers from Asia, the Pacific Islands, and the United States. Go to www.hiff.org or call ✆ **808/792-1577.** Mid-November.

Nā Mele O Maui, Maui. A traditional Hawaiian song competition for children in kindergarten through 12th grade, sponsored by the Ka'anapali Resort and held at the Maui Arts & Cultural Center. Free admission. Go to www.mauiarts.org or call ✆ **808/242-7469.** Late November or early December.

EA Sports Maui Invitational Basketball Tournament, Lahaina Civic Center, Lahaina. Elite college teams battle in this intimate annual preseason tournament. Go to www.mauiinvitational.com. Thanksgiving weekend.

Invitational Wreath Exhibit, Volcano Art Center, Hawai'i Volcanoes National Park, Big Island. Thirty-plus artists, including painters, sculptors, glass artists, fiber artists, and potters, produce both whimsical and traditional "wreaths" for this exhibit. Park entrance fees apply. Go to www.volcanoartcenter.org or call ✆ **808/967-7565.** Mid-November to early January.

Vans Triple Crown of Surfing, North Shore, O'ahu. The world's top professional surfers compete in thrilling surf events for more than $1 million in prize money. Go to www.vanstriplecrownof surfing.com or call ✆ **808/637-2245.** Held between mid-November and mid-December, depending on the surf.

DECEMBER

Kona Surf Film Festival, Courtyard Marriott King Kamehameha's Kona Beach Hotel, Big Island. An outdoor screening of independent films focusing on waves and wave riders. Go to www.konasurffilm festival.org or call ✆ **808/936-0089.** Early December.

Festival of Lights, all islands. On O'ahu, the mayor throws the switch to light up the 40-foot-tall Norfolk pine and other trees in front of Honolulu Hale, while on Maui, kids can play in a "snow zone" and make holiday crafts beneath the Lahaina Banyan tree, glowing with thousands of twinkle lights. Moloka'i celebrates with a host of activities in Kaunakakai; on Kaua'i, the lighting ceremony takes place in front of the former county building on Rice Street in Lihu'e. Call ✆ **808/768-6622** on O'ahu; ✆ **808/667-9175** on Maui; ✆ **808/553-4482** on Moloka'i; or ✆ **808/639-6571** on Kaua'i. Early December.

Honolulu Marathon, Honolulu, O'ahu. More than 30,000 racers compete in this oceanfront marathon, one of the largest in the world. Check it out at www.honolulu marathon.org or call ✆ **808/734-7200.** Mid-December.

Hawai'i Bowl, Aloha Stadium, Honolulu, O'ahu. A Pac 10 team plays a Big 12 team in this nationally televised collegiate football classic. Go to www. sheratonhawaiibowl.com or call ✆ **808/523-3688.** December 24.

First Light, Maui Arts & Cultural Center, Kahului, Maui. The Maui Film Festival screens Academy Award–contending films over the holidays. Go to www.maui filmfestival.com or call ✆ **808/579-9244.** Mid- to late December.

4

O'AHU

by Martha Cheng

O'ahu has it all: wide, sandy beaches; year-round surf; breathtaking ridge hikes; and a vibrant urban city in Honolulu. Home to Pearl Harbor and the only royal palace in the United States, Honolulu is imbued with history. Always deeply mindful of its past, it is also streaking into the future. The revitalization of old neighborhoods has sprouted trendy boutiques and attention-grabbing cuisine, and Waikīkī, the world-famous vacation playground, gets more cutting-edge luxe every day. Sure, O'ahu may be Hawai'i's most crowded island, but its rich human tapestry—locals of myriad ethnic mixes, wealthy Japanese expats, Mainland sunseekers, surfers from around the globe—makes it unlike any other place in the world.

ESSENTIALS

Arriving

Even though more and more transpacific flights are going directly to the neighbor islands these days, chances are still good that you'll touch down on O'ahu first and Honolulu will be your gateway to the Hawaiian Islands. **Honolulu International Airport** sits on the South Shore of O'ahu, west of downtown Honolulu and Waikīkī near Pearl Harbor. Many major American and international carriers fly to Honolulu from the Mainland; for a list of airlines, see chapter 10, "Planning Your Trip to Hawai'i."

LANDING AT HONOLULU INTERNATIONAL AIRPORT

You can walk or take the free airport shuttle from your arrival gate to the main terminal and baggage claim on the ground level. Unless you're connecting to an interisland flight immediately, you'll exit to the palm-lined street where uniformed attendants can either flag down a taxi or direct you to **TheBus** (www.thebus.org; see "By Bus," below). For Waikīkī shuttles and rental-car vans, cross the street to the median and wait at the designated stop.

Passengers connecting to neighbor-island flights take the free shuttle or walk to the large interisland terminal serving Hawaiian Airlines or to the more distant commuter terminal, which serves smaller carriers such as Island Air and Mokulele Airlines. (For details on interisland flights, see "Getting Around Hawai'i" on p. 604.)

FACING PAGE: **'Iolani Palace.**

GETTING TO & FROM THE AIRPORT

BY RENTAL CAR All major car-rental companies have vehicles available at the airport. Rental-agency vans will pick you up curbside at the center island outside baggage claim and take you to their off-site lots. It's about a 20-minute drive from the airport to downtown Honolulu.

BY TAXI Taxis are abundant at the airport; an attendant will be happy to flag one down for you. Taxi fare is about $25 from Honolulu International to downtown Honolulu and around $35 to $40 to Waikīkī. If you need to call a taxi, see "Getting Around," later in this chapter, for a list of cab companies.

BY AIRPORT SHUTTLE **SpeediShuttle** (www.speedishuttle.com; ✆ **877/242-5777**) offers transportation in air-conditioned vans from the airport to Waikīkī hotels; a one-way trip from the airport to Waikīkī is $15 per person and $27 round-trip. You'll find the shuttle at street level outside baggage claim on the median. You can board with two pieces of luggage and a carry-on at no extra charge. Tips are welcome. For advance purchase of group tickets, call the number above.

BY BUS **TheBus** (www.thebus.org; ✆ **808/848-5555**) is a good option if you aren't carrying a lot of luggage. TheBus nos. 19 and 20 (Waikīkī Beach and hotels) run from the airport to downtown Honolulu and Waikīkī. The first bus from Waikīkī to the airport leaves at 4:46am Monday through Friday and 5:27am Saturday and Sunday; the last bus departs the airport for Waikīkī at 1:22am Monday through Friday, 1:24am Saturday and Sunday. There are two bus stops on the main terminal's upper level; a third is on the second level of the interisland terminal. ***Note:*** You can board TheBus with a carry-on or small suitcase, as long as it fits under the seat and doesn't disrupt other passengers; otherwise, you'll have to take a shuttle or taxi. The travel time to Waikīkī is approximately 1 hour. The one-way fare is $2.50 for adults and $1.25 for children 6 to 17, exact change only. For more on TheBus, see "Getting Around," later in this chapter.

Visitor Information

The **Hawai'i Visitors & Convention Bureau (HVCB),** 2270 Kalākaua Ave., Suite 801, Honolulu, HI 96815 (www.gohawaii.com or www.hvcb.org; ✆ **800/GO-HAWAII**), supplies free brochures, maps and accommodations guides.

A number of free publications, such as ***This Week Oahu,*** are packed with money-saving coupons and good regional maps; look for them on racks at the airport and around town. ***Another tip:*** Snag one of the Japanese magazines scattered around Waikīkī. Even if you can't read Japanese, you'll find out about the latest, trendiest, or best restaurants and shops around the island.

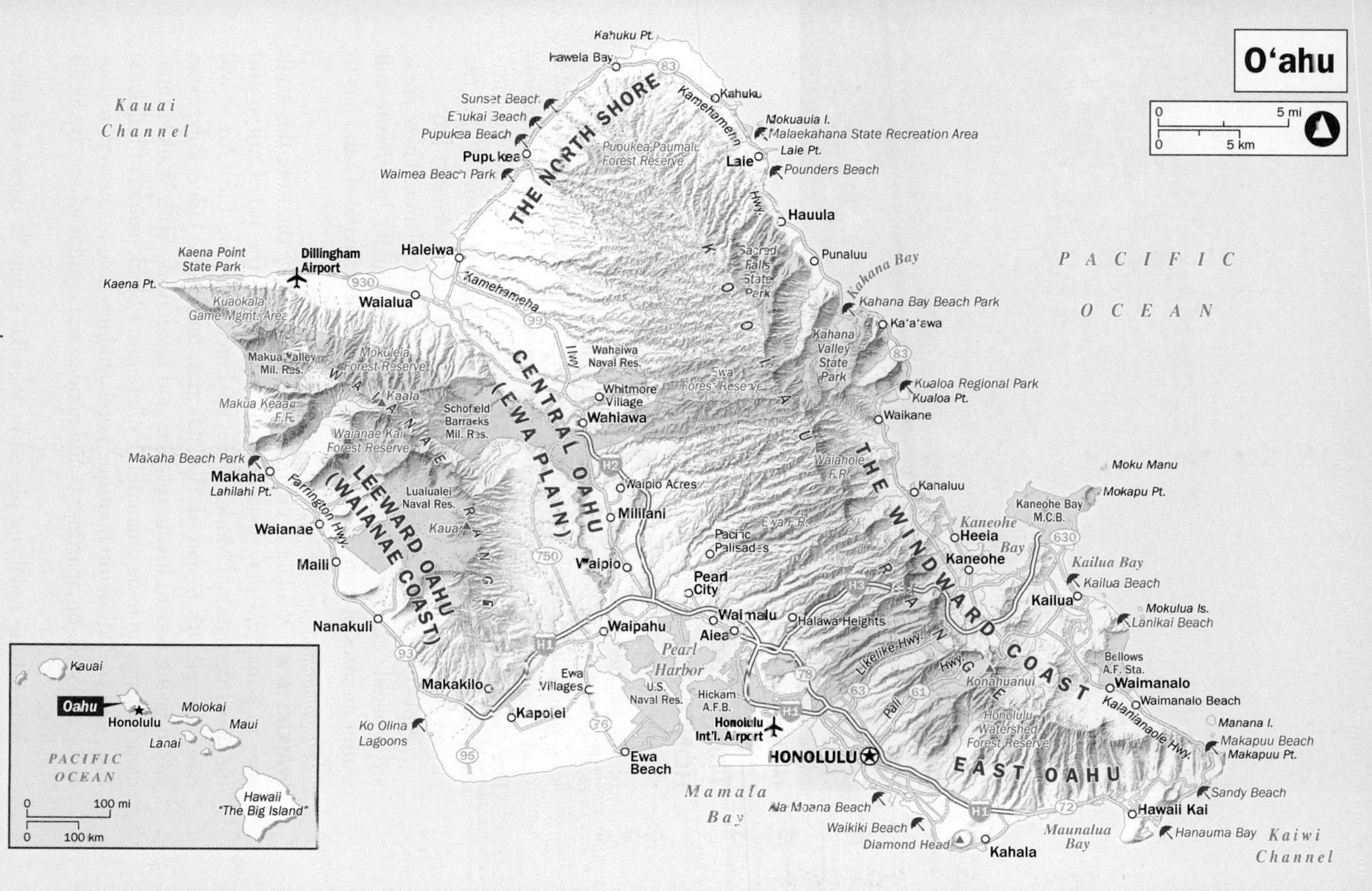
O'ahu
0 5 mi
0 5 km
PACIFIC OCEAN
Kauai Channel
Kaiwi Channel
Kahuku Pt.
Kawela Bay
Kahuku
Kamehameha
Sunset Beach
Ehukai Beach
Pupukea Beach
Pupukea
Waimea Beach Park
THE NORTH SHORE
Puoukea-Paumalu Forest Reserve
Mokuauia I.
Malaekahana State Recreation Area
Laie
Laie Pt.
Pounders Beach
Hwy.
Hauula
Sacred Falls State Park
Punaluu
Kahana Bay
Kahana Bay Beach Park
Ka'a'awa
Kahana Valley State Park
Kualoa Regional Park
Kualoa Pt.
Waikane
KOOLAU RANGE
Kaena Point State Park
Kaena Pt.
Dillingham Airport
Haleiwa
Waialua
Kuaokala Game Mgmt. Area
Kamehameha
Hwy
Wahaiwa Naval Res.
Ewa Forest Reserve
Makua Valley Mil. Res.
Mokuleia Forest Reserve
CENTRAL OAHU (EWA PLAIN)
Whitmore Village
Wahiawa
Kaala
Makua Keaau F.R.
Schofield Barracks Mil. Res.
Waianae Kai Forest Reserve
WAIANAE RANGE
Waiahole F.R.
THE WINDWARD COAST
Makaha Beach Park
Makaha
Lahilahi Pt.
Farrington Hwy.
LEEWARD OAHU (WAIANAE COAST)
Lualualei Naval Res.
Kauai
Waipio Acres
Mililani
Kanaluu
Moku Manu
Mokapu Pt.
Kaneohe Bay M.C.B.
Kaneohe Bay
Heeia
Kaneohe
Ewa F.R.
Pacific Palisades
Waianae
Maili
Waipio
Pearl City
Kailua Bay
Kailua Beach
Kailua
Mokulua Is.
Lanikai Beach
Nanakuli
Waimalu
Aiea
Halawa Heights
Waipahu
Likelike Hwy.
Hwy.
Konahuanui
Pali
Pearl Harbor
Bellows A.F. Sta.
Waimanalo
Waimanalo Beach
Kalanianaole Hwy.
Manana I.
Makapuu Beach
Makapuu Pt.
Makakilo
Ewa Villages
U.S. Naval Res.
Hickam A.F.B.
Kapolei
Honolulu Int'l. Airport
Ko Olina Lagoons
Honolulu Watershed Forest Reserve
Ewa Beach
HONOLULU
EAST OAHU
Sandy Beach
Mamala Bay
Ala Moana Beach
Waikiki Beach
Diamond Head
Kahala
Maunalua Bay
Hawaii Kai
Hanauma Bay
Kauai
Oahu
Honolulu
Molokai
Maui
Lanai
PACIFIC OCEAN
Hawaii "The Big Island"
0 100 mi
0 100 km

View from Diamond Head.

The Island in Brief

HONOLULU

Hawai'i's largest city looks like any other big metropolitan center with tall buildings. In fact, some cynics refer to it as "Los Angeles West." But within Honolulu's boundaries, you'll find rainforests, deep canyons, valleys, waterfalls, a nearly mile-high mountain range, coral reefs, and gold-sand beaches. The city proper—where most of Honolulu's residents live—is approximately 12 miles wide and 26 miles long, running east-west roughly between **Diamond Head** and **Pearl Harbor.** Within the city are seven hills laced by seven streams that run to Māmala Bay.

A plethora of neighborhoods surrounds the central area. These areas are generally quieter and more residential than Waikīkī, but they're still within minutes of beaches, shopping, and all the activities O'ahu has to offer.

WAIKĪKĪ ★★ Waikīkī is changing almost daily. By the time this book goes to print, two new, high-end developments—the Ritz Carlton and the new International Marketplace, anchored by a Saks Fifth Ave.—will have opened. It's a sign of Waikīkī's transformation: faded Polynesian kitsch giving way to luxury retailers and residences. Still, Waikīkī tenaciously hangs on to its character: Explore just 1 block *mauka* of Kalākaua Ave., and you'll find hip boutique hotels, hidden hole-in-the-wall restaurants, and walk-up apartments and nondescript condos where the locals still live.

When King Kalākaua played in Waikīkī, it was "a hamlet of plain cottages . . . its excitements caused by the activity of insect tribes and the occasional fall of a coconut." The Merrie Monarch, who gave his name to Waikīkī's main street, would love the scene today. Some 5 million tourists visit O'ahu every year, and 9 out of 10 of them stay in Waikīkī. This urban beach is where all the action is; it's backed by 175 high-rise hotels with more than 33,000 guest rooms and hundreds of bars and restaurants, all in a 1½-square-mile beach zone. Waikīkī means honeymooners and sun seekers, bikinis and bare buns, an around-the-clock beach party every day of the year. Staying in Waikīkī puts you in the heart of it all, but be aware that this on-the-go place has traffic noise 24 hours a day—and it's almost always crowded.

ALA MOANA ★★ A great beach as well as Hawai'i's largest shopping mall, Ala Moana is the retail and transportation heart of Honolulu, a place where you can both shop and suntan in one afternoon. All bus routes lead to the open-air **Ala Moana Center,** across the street from **Ala Moana Beach Park ★★**. The shopping center is one of Hawai'i's most visited destinations for its collection of luxury brands (such as Louis Vuitton and Chanel) and Hawai'i-based stores (from Tori Richard to Town & Country Surf). For our purposes, the neighborhood called "Ala Moana" extends along Ala Moana Boulevard from Waikīkī in the direction of Diamond Head to downtown Honolulu in the Ewa direction (west) and includes the **Ward Village,** as well as **Restaurant Row.**

DOWNTOWN ★★ Here, you'll find historic Honolulu, including 'Iolani Palace, the official residence of Hawai'i's kings and queens; its business center housed in high rises; and the Capitol District, all jammed in about 1 square mile. On the waterfront stands the iconic 1926 **Aloha Tower.**

On the edge of downtown is the **Chinatown Historic District,** the oldest Chinatown in America and still one of Honolulu's liveliest neighborhoods, a nonstop pageant of people, sights, sounds, smells, and tastes—not all Chinese. Southeast Asians, including many Vietnamese, share the old storefronts, as do Honolulu's oldest bar (the divey **Smith's**

Finding Your Way Around, O'ahu-Style

Mainlanders sometimes find the directions given by locals a bit confusing. Seldom will you hear the terms *east, west, north,* and *south;* instead, islanders refer to directions as either ***makai*** (ma-*kae*), meaning toward the sea, or ***mauka*** (*mow*-kah), toward the mountains. In Honolulu, people use **Diamond Head** as a direction meaning to the east (in the direction of the world-famous crater called Diamond Head), and **'Ewa** as a direction meaning to the west (toward the town called 'Ewa, on the other side of Pearl Harbor).

So if you ask a local for directions, this is what you're likely to hear: "Drive 2 blocks *makai* (toward the sea), and then turn Diamond Head (east) at the stoplight. Go 1 block, and turn *mauka* (toward the mountains). It's on the 'Ewa (western) side of the street."

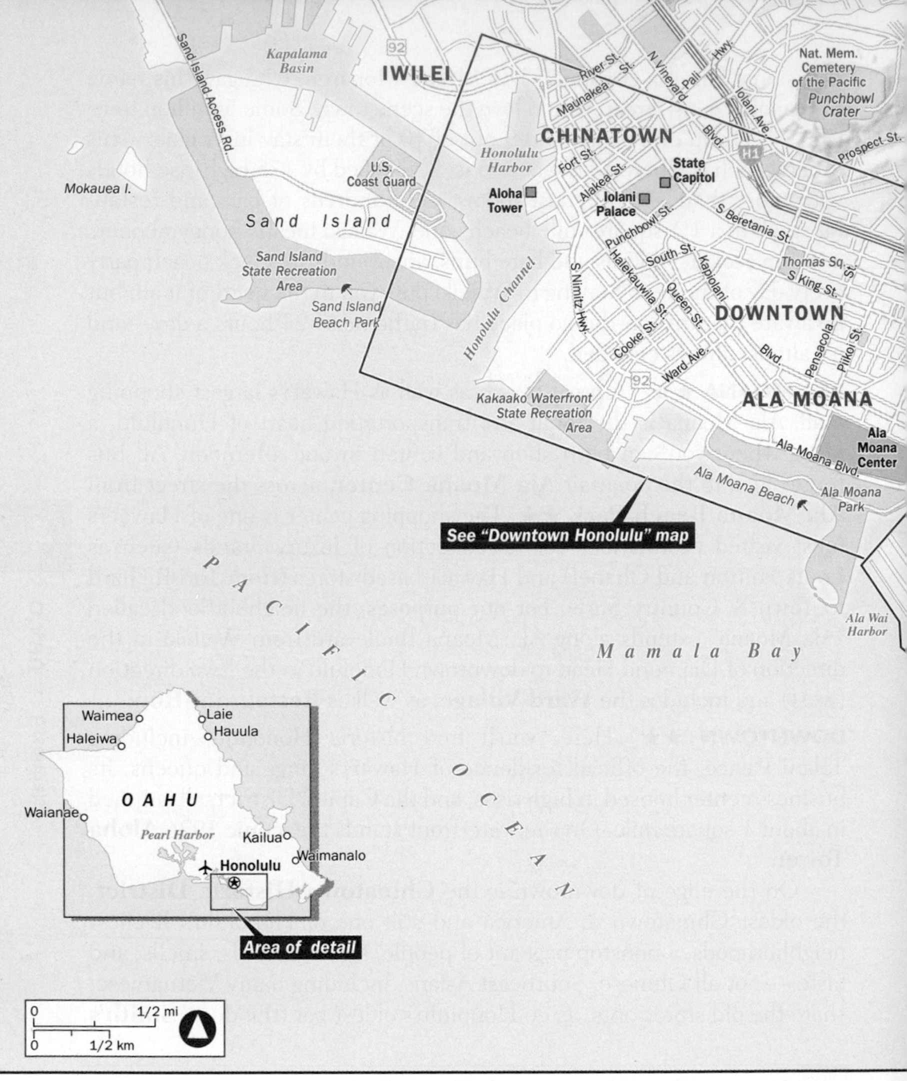

Union Bar) and some of the city's hippest clubs and chic-est boutiques. Go in the morning, when everyone shops for fresh goods such as mangoes (when in season), live fish (sometimes of the same varieties you saw while snorkeling), fresh tofu, and hogs' heads.

MĀNOA VALLEY ★ First inhabited by white settlers, Mānoa Valley, above Waikīkī, still has vintage *kama'āina* (native-born) homes, one of Hawai'i's premier botanical gardens (the **Lyon Arboretum ★**), the ever-gushing **Mānoa Falls,** and the 320-acre **University of Hawai'i** campus, where 50,000 students hit the books when they're not on the beach.

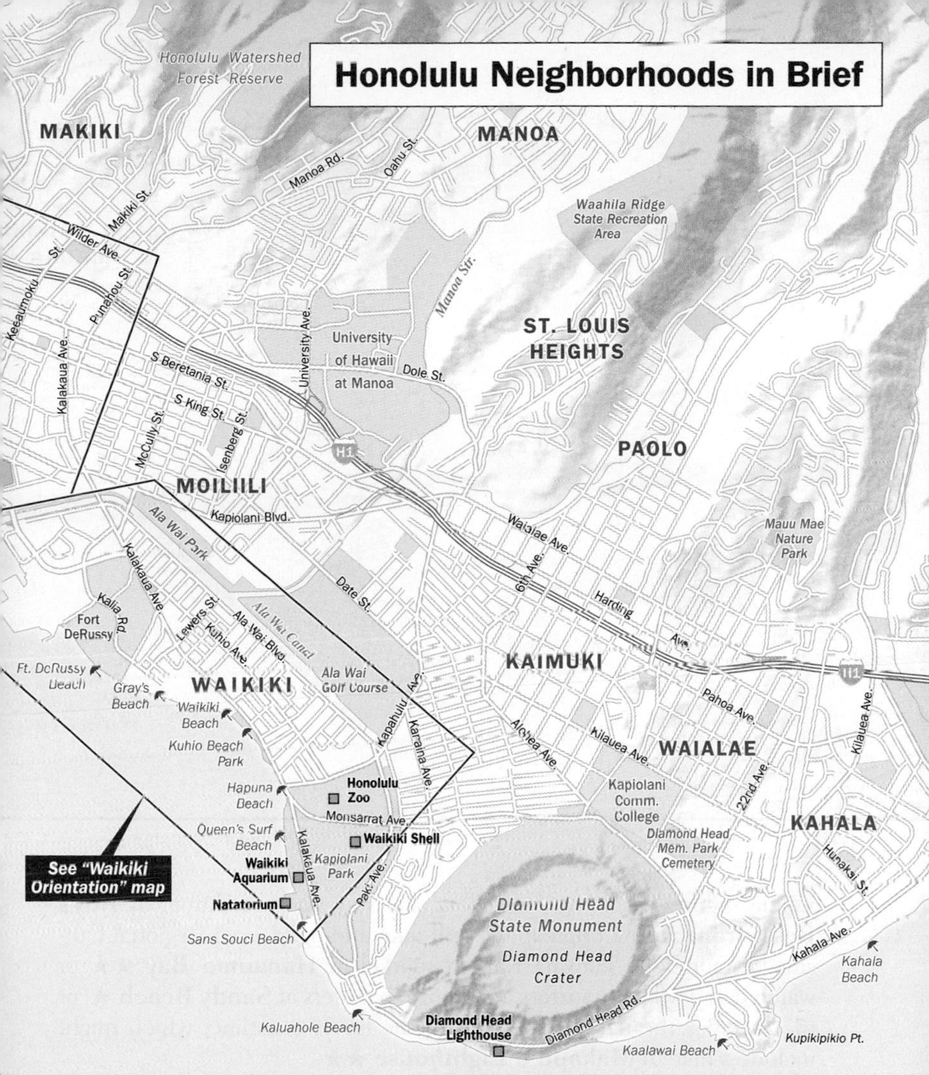

TO THE EAST: KĀHALA Except for the estates of millionaires and the luxurious **Kāhala Hotel & Resort ★★★**, there's little out this way that's of interest to visitors.

EAST O'AHU

Beyond Kāhala lies East Honolulu and suburban bedroom communities such as 'Āina Haina, Niu Valley, and Hawai'i Kai, among others, all linked by the Kalaniana'ole Highway and loaded with homes, condos, fast-food joints, and strip malls. It looks like Southern California on a good day. You'll drive through here if you take the longer, scenic route to

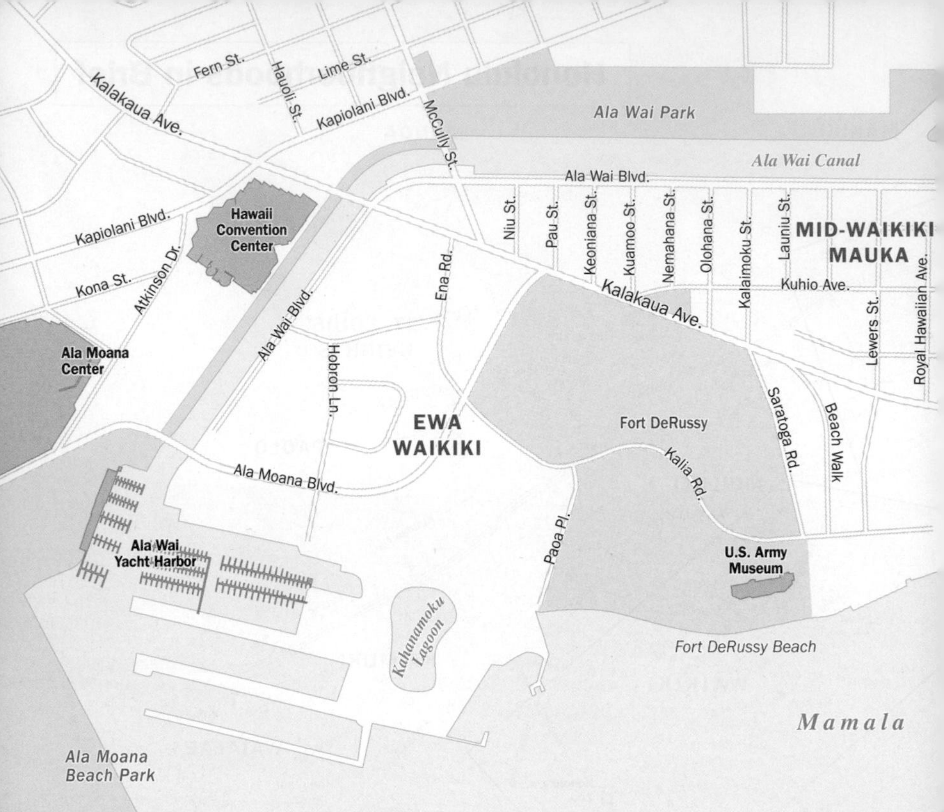

Kailua. Some reasons to stop along the way: to have dinner at **Roy's Restaurant ★**, the original and still-outstanding Hawai'i Regional Cuisine restaurant in Hawai'i Kai; to snorkel at **Hanauma Bay ★★** or watch daredevil body surfers and boogie boarders at **Sandy Beach ★**; or to just enjoy the natural splendor of the lovely coastline, which might include a hike to **Makapu'u Lighthouse ★★**.

THE WINDWARD COAST

The windward side is the opposite side of the island from Waikīkī. On this coast, trade winds blow cooling breezes over gorgeous beaches; rain squalls spawn lush, tropical vegetation; and miles of subdivisions dot the landscape. Bed-and-breakfasts, ranging from oceanfront estates to tiny cottages on quiet residential streets, are everywhere. Vacations here are spent enjoying ocean activities and exploring the surrounding areas. Waikīkī is a 20-minute drive away.

KAILUA ★★★ The biggest little beach town in Hawai'i, Kailua sits at the foot of the sheer green Ko'olau mountain range, on a great bay with two of Hawai'i's best beaches. In the past few years, the town has seen some redevelopment, with a new Target, Whole Foods, condos, and

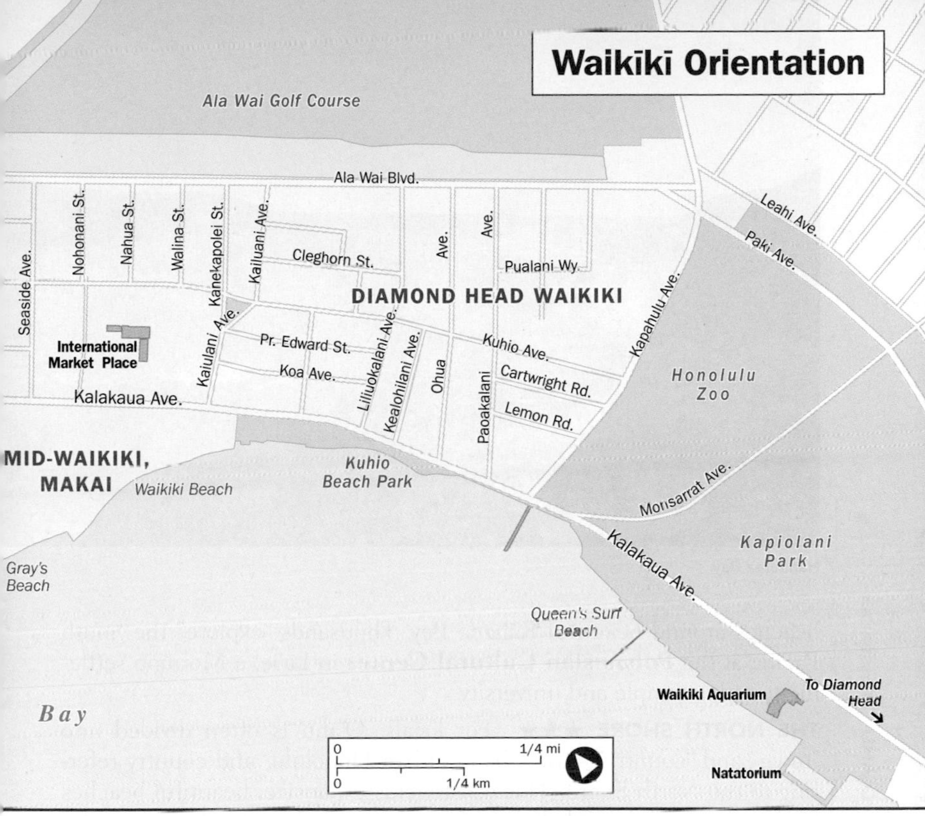

newer, bigger digs for old favorite shops and restaurants. But it's still a funky low-rise cluster of timeworn shops and homes. Kailua has become the B&B capital of Hawai'i; it's an affordable alternative to Waikīkī, with rooms and vacation rentals starting at $70 a day. With the prevailing trade winds whipping up a cooling breeze, Kailua attracts windsurfers from around the world. On calmer days, kayaking or stand-up paddling to the Mokulua Islands off the coast is a favorite adventure.

KĀNE'OHE BAY ★ Helter-skelter suburbia sprawls around the edges of Kāne'ohe, one of the most scenic bays in the Pacific. After you clear the trafficky maze of town, O'ahu returns to its more natural state. This great bay beckons you to get out on the water; you can depart from He'eia Boat Harbor on snorkel or fishing charters. From here, you'll have a panoramic view of the Ko'olau Range.

KUALOA/LĀ'IE ★ The upper-northeast shore is one of O'ahu's most sacred places, an early Hawaiian landing spot where kings dipped their sails, cliffs hold ancient burial sites, and ghosts still march in the night. Sheer cliffs stab the reef-fringed seacoast, while old fish ponds are tucked along the two-lane coast road that winds past empty gold-sand

Hanauma Bay.

beaches around beautiful Kahana Bay. Thousands "explore" the South Pacific at the **Polynesian Cultural Center** in Lā'ie, a Mormon settlement with a temple and university.

THE NORTH SHORE ★★★ For locals, O'ahu is often divided into "town" and "country"—town being urban Honolulu, and country referring to the North Shore. This coast yields expansive, beautiful beaches for swimming and snorkeling in the summer and world-class waves for surfing in the winter. Laid-back **Hale'iwa ★★** is the social hub of the North Shore, with its casual restaurants, surf shops, and clothing boutiques. Vacation rentals are the most common accommodations, but there's also the first-class **Turtle Bay Resort ★★**. Be forewarned: It's a long trip—nearly an hour's drive—to Honolulu and Waikīkī, and even longer during the surf season, when tourists and wave-seekers can jam up the roads.

CENTRAL O'AHU: THE 'EWA PLAIN

Flanked by the Ko'olau and Wai'anae mountain ranges, the hot, sunbaked 'Ewa Plain runs up and down the center of O'ahu. Once covered with sandalwood forests (hacked down for the China trade) and later the sugarcane and pineapple backbone of Hawai'i, 'Ewa today sports a new crop: suburban houses stretching to the sea. But let your eye wander west to the Wai'anae Range and Mount Ka'ala, at 4,020 feet the highest summit on O'ahu; up there in the misty rainforest, native birds thrive in the hummocky bog. In 1914, the U.S. Army pitched a tent camp on the plain; author James Jones would later call **Schofield Barracks** "the most beautiful army post in the world." Hollywood filmed Jones's *From Here to Eternity* here.

LEEWARD O'AHU: THE WAI'ANAE COAST

The west coast of O'ahu is a hot and dry place of dramatic beauty: white-sand beaches bordering the deep-blue ocean, steep verdant green cliffs, and miles of Mother Nature's wildness. Tourist services are concentrated in Ko Olina Resort, which has a Disney hotel and a brand-new Four Seasons, pricey resort restaurants, golf course, marina, and wedding chapel, should you want to get hitched. This side of O'ahu less visited—though that could change as Ko Olina lures visitors from Waikīkī—except by surfers bound for **Mākaha Beach ★★** and those coming to see needle-nose **Ka'ena Point ★** (the island's westernmost outpost), which has a coastal wilderness park.

GETTING AROUND

BY CAR O'ahu residents own more than 686,000 registered vehicles, but they have only 1,500 miles of mostly two-lane roads to use. That's 450 cars for every mile, a fact that becomes abundantly clear during morning and evening rush hours. You can (mostly) avoid the gridlock by driving between 9am and 2pm or after 7pm.

All of the major car-rental firms have agencies on O'ahu at the airport and in Waikīkī. For listings, see chapter 10. For tips on insurance and driving rules in Hawai'i, see "Getting Around Hawai'i" (p. 604).

BY BUS One of the best deals anywhere, **TheBus** will take you around the whole island for $2.50 ($1.25 for children age 6–17)—if you have time. To get to the North Shore and back takes 4 hours, twice as long as a car. But for shorter distances, TheBus is great, and it goes almost everywhere almost all the time. If you're planning on sticking to the Waikīkī–Ala Moana–Downtown region, go with TheBus, which will save you a lot of car hassle and expense. The most popular route is **no. 8,** which arrives every 10 minutes or so to shuttle people between Waikīkī and Ala Moana Center (the ride takes 15–20 min.). The **no. 19** (Airport/Hickam), **no. 20** (Airport/Hālawa Gate), and **no. 40** (Waipahu/Ala Moana) also cover the same stretch. Waikīkī service begins daily at 5am and runs until midnight; most buses run about every 15 minutes during the day and every 30 minutes in the evening.

The Circle Island–North Shore route is **no. 52** (Wahiawā/Circle Island); the Circle Island–South Shore route is **no. 55** (Kāne'ohe/Circle Island). Both routes leave Ala Moana Center every 30 minutes and take about 4½ hours to circle the island. Be aware that at Turtle Bay Resort, just outside Kahuku, the 52 becomes the 55 and returns to Honolulu via the coast, and the 55 becomes the 52 and returns to Honolulu on the inland route. (Translation: You'll have to get off and switch buses to complete your island tour.) There are express buses available to some areas (for example, **no. 54** to Pearl City, **no. 85** to Kailua and to Kāne'ohe).

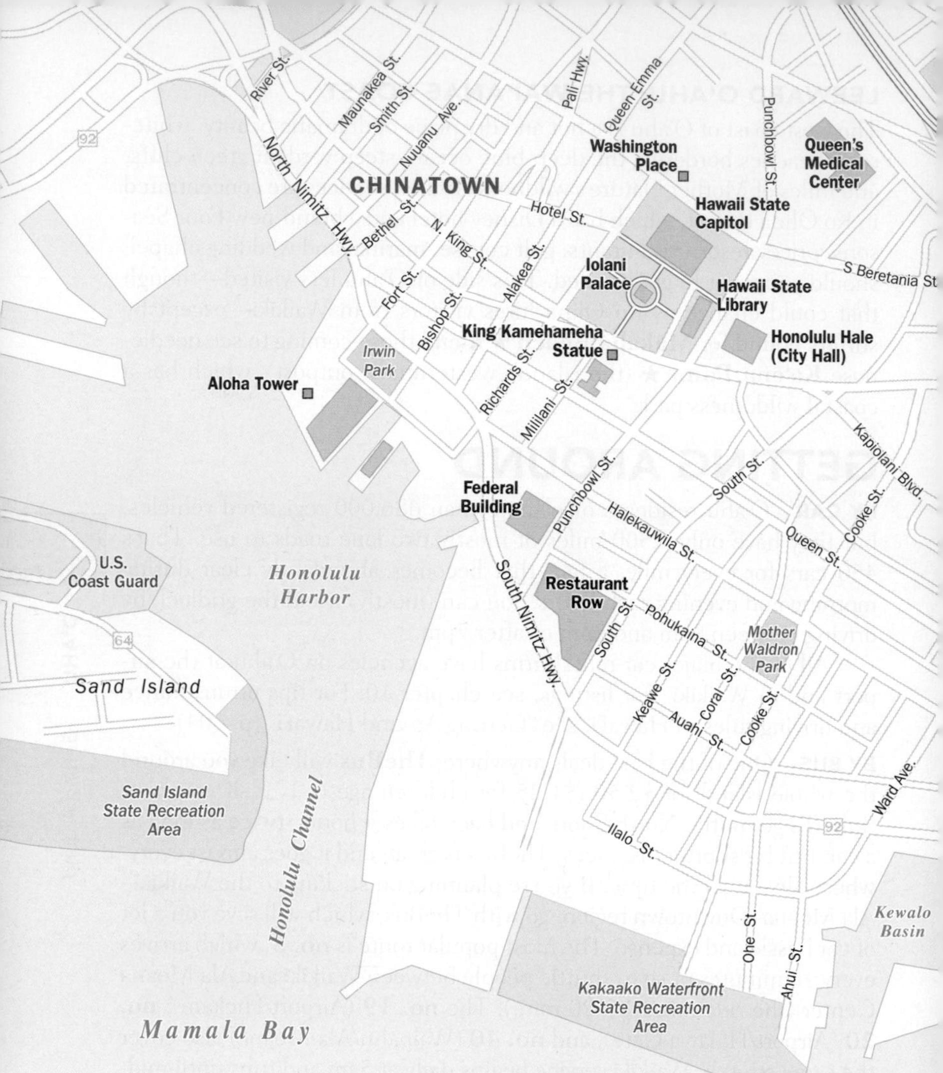

For more information on routes and schedules, call **TheBus** (✆ **808/848-5555,** or 808/296-1818 for recorded information) or check out **www.thebus.org**, which provides timetables and maps for all routes, plus directions to many local attractions and a list of upcoming events. Taking TheBus is often easier than parking your car.

BY TAXI O'ahu's major **cab companies** offer 24-hour, islandwide, radio-dispatched service, with multilingual drivers and air-conditioned cars, limos, and vans, including vehicles equipped with wheelchair lifts (there's a $9 charge for wheelchairs). Fares are standard for all taxi firms. From the airport, expect to pay about $35 to $40 to Waikīkī, about $25

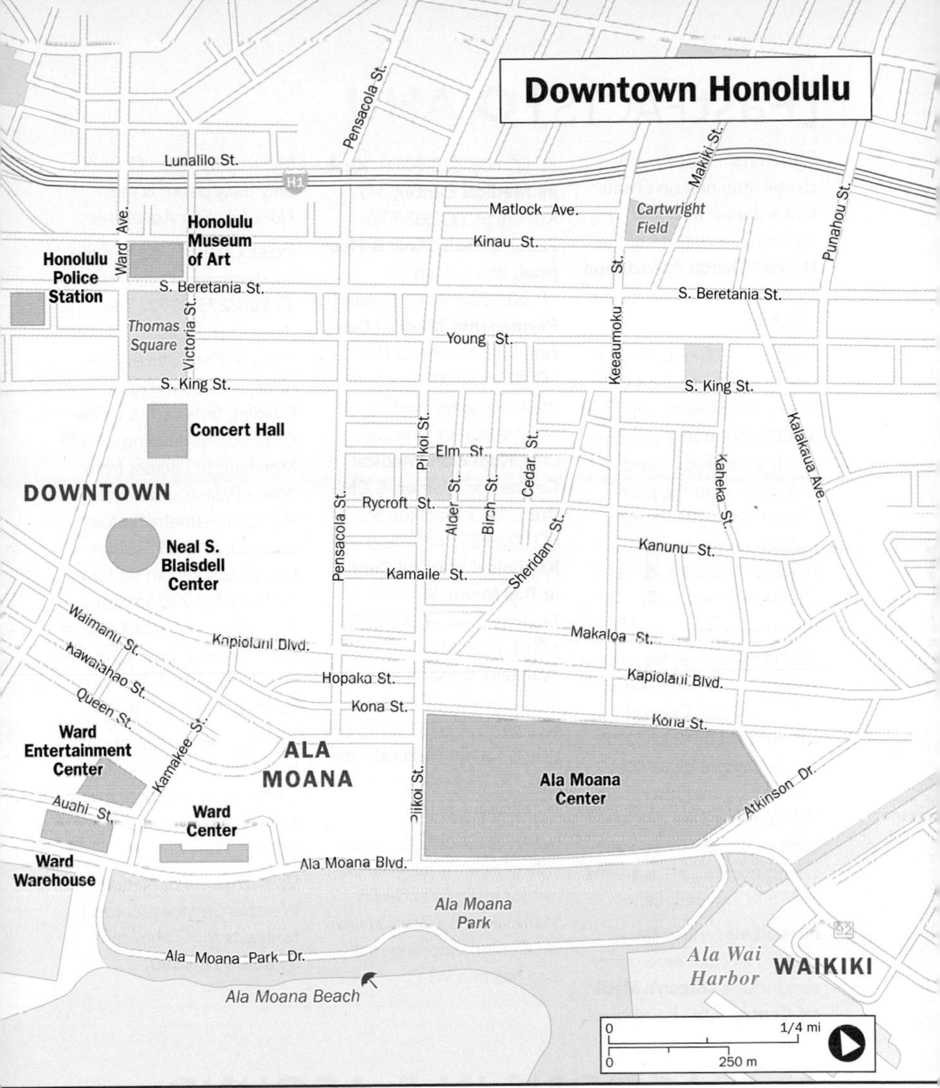

to $35 to downtown, $60 and up to Kailua, about $60-plus to Hawai'i Kai, and about $90 to $125 to the North Shore (plus tip). Plus there may be a $4.75 fee per piece of luggage.

Uber, the taxi-hailing app, has arrived in Honolulu. Use it on your phone to summon and pay for a taxi or livery (standard taxi meter rates, plus a $1 surcharge; gratuity automatically added). If you prefer to go the old-fashioned route, try **The Cab** (**© 808/422-2222**) or **EcoCab** (**© 808/979-1010**), an all-hybrid taxi fleet. **Robert's Taxi and Shuttle** (**© 808/261-8555**) serves windward O'ahu, while **Hawai'i Kai Hui/Koko Head Taxi** (**© 808/396-6633**) serves east Honolulu/southeast O'ahu.

[FastFACTS] O'AHU

Dentists If you need dental attention on O'ahu, find a dentist near you through the website of the **Hawai'i Dental Association** (www.hawaiidentalassociation.net).

Doctors Straub Clinic & Hospital's **Doctors on Call** (www.straubhealth.org; ✆ **808/971-6000**) can dispatch a van if you need help getting to the main clinic or to any of its additional clinics at the Hilton Hawaiian Village and the Sheraton Princess.

Emergencies Call ✆ **911** for police, fire, or ambulance. If you need to call the **Poison Control Center** (✆ **800/222-1222**), you will automatically be directed to the Poison Control Center for the area code of the phone you are calling from; all are available 24/7 and very helpful.

Hospitals Hospitals offering 24-hour emergency care include **Queen's Medical Center,** 1301 Punchbowl St. (✆ 808/538-9011); **Kuakini Medical Center,** 347 Kuakini St. (✆ 808/536-2236); **Straub Clinic & Hospital,** 888 S. King St. (✆ 808/522-4000); **Kaiser Permanente Medical Center,** 3288 Moanalua Rd. (✆ 808/432-0000), where the emergency room is open to Kaiser members only; **Kapi'olani Medical Center for Women & Children,** 1319 Punahou St. (✆ 808/983-8633); and **Kapi'olani Medical Center at Pali Momi,** 98-1079 Moanalua Rd. (✆ 808/486-6000). Central O'ahu has **Wahiawā General Hospital,** 128 Lehua St. (✆ 808/621-8411). On the windward side is **Castle Medical Center,** 640 Ulukahiki St., Kailua (✆ 808/263-5500).

Internet Access Outside of your hotel, your best bet for Internet access is Starbucks. The Royal Hawaiian Center shopping mall also has free Wi-Fi.

Newspapers O'ahu's only daily paper is the *Honolulu Star Advertiser.*

Post Office To find the location nearest you, call ✆ **800/275-8777.** The downtown location is in the old U.S. Post Office, Customs, and Court House Building (referred to as the Old Federal Building) at 335 Merchant St., across from 'Iolani Palace and next to the Kamehameha Statue (bus: 20, E, or 19). Other branch offices can be found in Waikīkī at 330 Saratoga Ave. (Diamond Head side of Fort DeRussy; bus: 19 or 20) and in the Ala Moana Center (bus: 8, 19, or 20).

Safety Be aware of car break-ins in touristed areas and beach parks; make sure to keep valuables out of sight.

Weather For National Weather Service recorded forecasts for O'ahu, call ✆ **808/973-4380.**

ATTRACTIONS IN & AROUND HONOLULU & WAIKĪKĪ

Historic Honolulu

The Waikīkī you see today bears no resemblance to the Waikīkī of yesteryear, a place of vast taro fields extending from the ocean to deep into Mānoa Valley, dotted with numerous fish ponds and gardens tended by thousands of people. This picture of old Waikīkī can be recaptured by following the emerging **Waikīkī Historic Trail** ★ (www.waikikihistorictrail.org), a meandering 2-mile walk with 20 bronze surfboard markers (standing 6 ft., 5 in. tall—you can't miss 'em), complete with descriptions and archival photos of the historic sites. The markers note everything from Waikīkī's ancient fishponds to the history of the Ala Wai Canal. The trail begins at Kūhiō Beach and ends at the King Kalākaua statue at the intersection of Kūhiō and Kalākaua avenues.

Bishop Museum ★★★ MUSEUM This is a museum for adults and kids alike. For the adults: the original **Hawaiian Hall,** built in 1889 to house the collection of Hawaiian artifacts and royal family heirlooms of Princess Bernice Pauahi Bishop, the last descendant of King Kamehameha I. Today, the exhibits, spread out over three floors, give the most complete sense of how ancient native Hawaiians lived. On display are carvings representing Hawaiian gods and the personal effects of Hawaiian royalty, including a feathered cape worn by Kamehameha himself. In the Hawaiian Hall Atrium, traditions come to life with the daily **hula show** (2pm). In 2013, renovations to **Pacific Hall** (previously known as Polynesian Hall) doubled the collection to include artifacts from all the Pacific Islands, including a restored Fijian fishing canoe.

For the kids, there's the 50-foot sperm whale skeleton and the **Richard T. Mamiya Science Adventure Center,** featuring interactive exhibits on how volcanoes, wind, and waves work. Don't miss the planetarium show **Wayfinders: Waves, Winds, and Stars** (Wed–Mon 1:30pm), which alternates between scenes shot on the voyaging canoe *Hōkūle'a* and interactive segments that teach the basics on navigating using the stars. It's educational and awe-inspiring to realize that ancient voyagers navigated using just the night sky, the wind, and wave patterns. It's also how the current crew of the *Hōkūle'a,* which set sail in 2014, is finding its way around the world. At the end of the presentation, you'll get an update on the crew's worldwide voyage.

The Bishop Museum.

Hungry? Stop by the new cafe by Highway Inn, a favorite local restaurant that serves 'ono (delicious) Hawaiian plate lunches.

1525 Bernice St., just off Kalihi St./Likelike Hwy. www.bishopmuseum.org. ✆ **808/847-3511.** Admission $22.95 adults, $19.95 seniors, $14.95 children 4–12. Daily 9am–5pm. Parking is $5. Bus: 2.

Hawaiian Mission Houses Historic Site and Archives ★ HISTORIC SITE Centered on the first mission houses built in the 1800s, what was formerly known

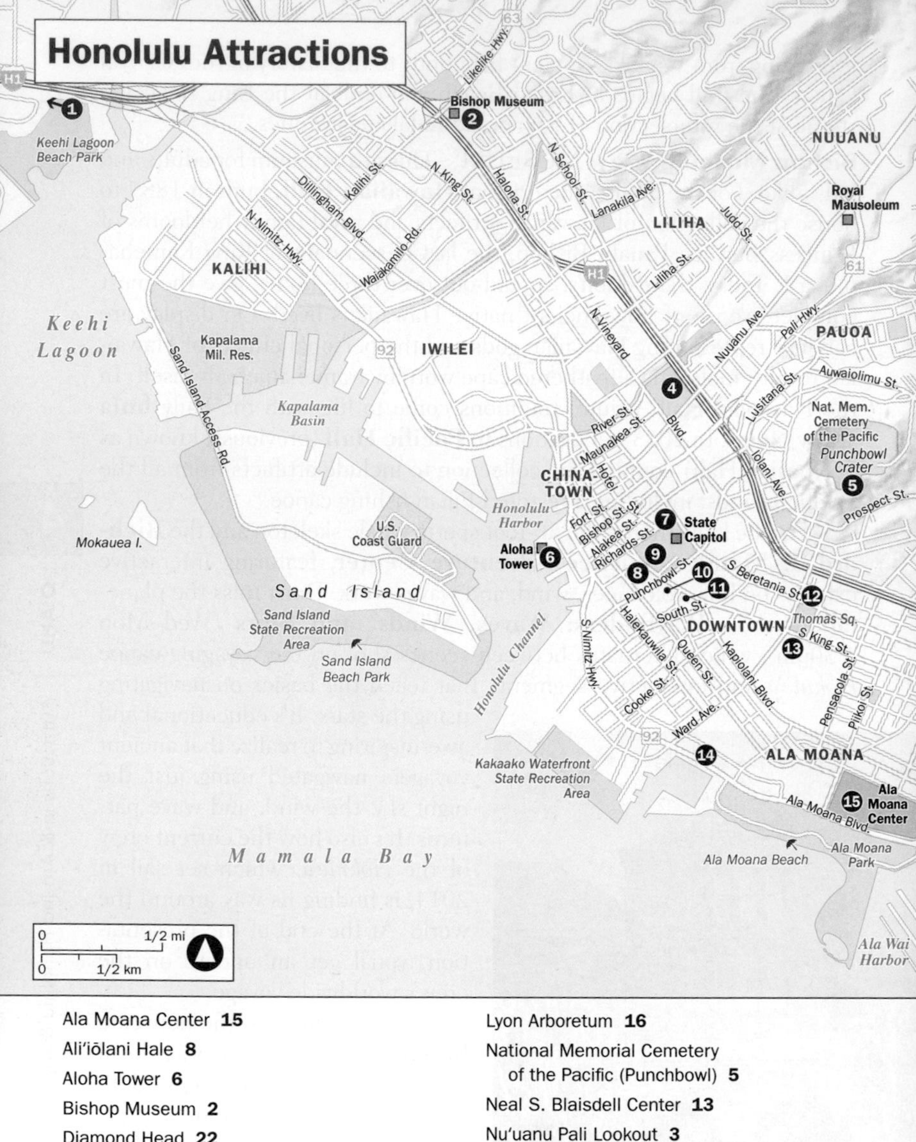

Ala Moana Center **15**
Ali'iōlani Hale **8**
Aloha Tower **6**
Bishop Museum **2**
Diamond Head **22**
Foster Botanical Garden **4**
Hawaiian Mission Houses Historic Site **11**
Hawai'i State Art Museum **7**
Honolulu Museum of Art **12**
Honolulu Zoo **19**
'Iolani Palace **9**
Kapi'olani Park **21**
Kawaiaha'o Church **10**
Lyon Arboretum **16**
National Memorial Cemetery of the Pacific (Punchbowl) **5**
Neal S. Blaisdell Center **13**
Nu'uanu Pali Lookout **3**
Pacific Aviation Museum **1**
Pu'u 'Ualaka'a State Park **18**
Queen Emma Summer Palace **3**
Spalding House **17**
USS *Arizona* Memorial at Pearl Harbor **1**
USS *Bowfin* Submarine Museum & Park **1**
USS *Missouri* Memorial **1**
Waikīkī Aquarium **20**
Ward Village **14**

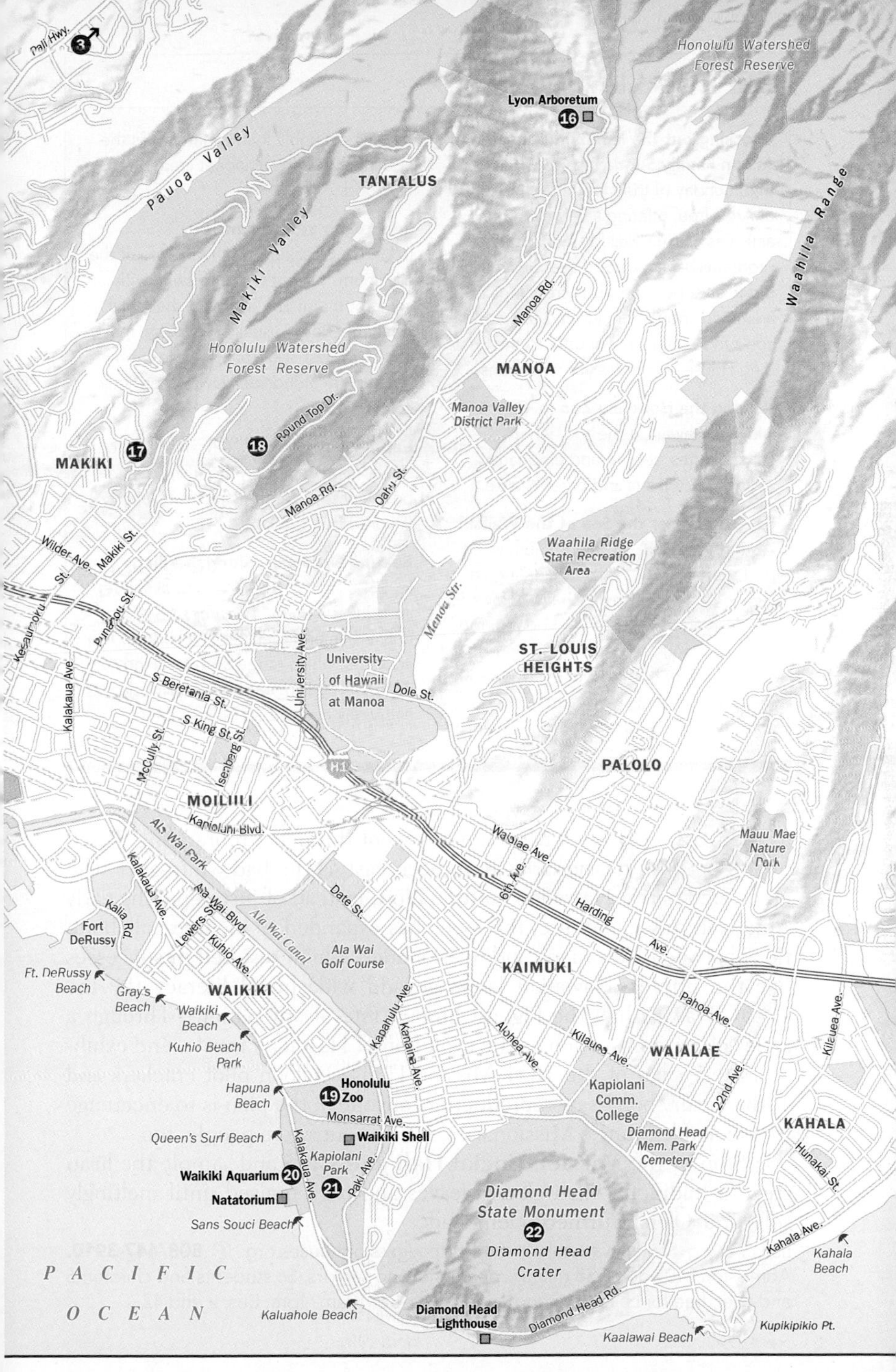

Pali Hwy.
3
Honolulu Watershed Forest Reserve
Lyon Arboretum
16
Pauoa Valley
TANTALUS
Waahila Range
Makiki Valley
Manoa Rd.
Honolulu Watershed Forest Reserve
MANOA
Manoa Valley District Park
Round Top Dr.
17
18
MAKIKI
Manoa Rd.
Oahu St.
Wilder Ave.
Makiki St.
Waahila Ridge State Recreation Area
Punahou St.
Manoa Str.
University Ave.
University of Hawaii at Manoa
ST. LOUIS HEIGHTS
Kalakaua Ave
S Beretania St.
Dole St.
S King St.
McCully St.
Isenberg St.
H1
PALOLO
MOILIILI
Kapiolani Blvd.
Ala Wai Park
Waialae Ave.
Mauu Mae Nature Park
Kalakaua Ave.
Ala Wai Blvd.
Date St.
6th Ave.
Harding Ave.
Kalia Rd.
Fort DeRussy
Lewers St.
Ala Wai Canal
Kuhio Ave.
Ala Wai Golf Course
KAIMUKI
Ft. DeRussy Beach
Gray's Beach
WAIKIKI
Waikiki Beach
Kapahulu Ave.
Pahoa Ave.
Kilauea Ave.
Kuhio Beach Park
Kanaina Ave.
Alohea Ave.
Kilauea Ave.
WAIALAE
Hapuna Beach
Honolulu Zoo
19
Kapiolani Comm. College
22nd Ave.
Monsarrat Ave.
KAHALA
Queen's Surf Beach
Waikiki Shell
Diamond Head Mem. Park Cemetery
Kalakaua Ave.
Kapiolani Park
Hunakai St.
Waikiki Aquarium
20
21
Paki Ave.
Diamond Head State Monument
Natatorium
Sans Souci Beach
22
Kahala Ave.
Diamond Head Crater
Kahala Beach
PACIFIC
OCEAN
Kaluahole Beach
Diamond Head Lighthouse
Diamond Head Rd.
Kupikipikio Pt.
Kaalawai Beach

ESPECIALLY FOR kids

Checking out the Honolulu Museum of Art on Family Sunday (p. 75) Every third Sunday of the month, the Museum of Art is free, offering a variety of art activities and movies for the kids. Past programs have included sessions making pirate sock puppets and screenings of animated shorts from around the world. You can also take the shuttle to the Spalding House, where the fun continues.

Visiting the Honolulu Zoo (p. 82) Visit Africa in Hawai'i at the zoo, where the lions, giraffes, zebras, and elephants delight youngsters and parents alike.

Peeking Under the Sea at the Waikīkī Aquarium (p. 83) The aquarium is pretty small, but it has a fascinating collection of alien-like jellyfish and allows for up-close encounters of the endangered Hawaiian monk seal and an octopus that changes color before your eyes. Check the aquarium website for family-friendly activities, including a Behind the Scenes tour, where you'll learn what makes the aquarium run, from habitat creation to fish food.

Snorkeling at Hanauma Bay (p. 111) Checked out the sea life at the aquarium? Now it's time to swim with some of them! The inside of sheltered Hanauma Bay is usually very calm, making it the best spot for first-time snorkelers to swim alongside Hawai'i's brightly colored fish.

Eating Shave Ice (p. 142) No visit to Hawai'i is complete without shave ice—powdery soft ice drenched in tropically flavored fruit syrups.

Beating Drums in a Tongan Village (p. 96) The Polynesian Cultural Center introduces kids to the games played by Polynesian and Melanesian children. The activities, which range from cracking coconuts to Tongan shuffleboard, go on every day from 12:30 to 5:30pm.

as the Mission Houses Museum just went through a rebranding. Possibly it's because missionaries have been cast as the bad white guys who eradicated native Hawaiian culture. Now, instead of just depicting early American missionary life, the focus has expanded to include collaborations between Hawaiians and missionaries, which resulted in successes like the printed Hawaiian language and widespread literacy (by the 1860s, Hawai'i had the highest literacy rate of any nation). Through a series of programs, such as the evolution of Hawaiian music, and exhibits in the cellar of the 1821 Mission House (saloon pilot crackers and 19th-century bone-saw reproduction, anyone?), the plan is to encourage "emotional learning." Missionaries, it turns out, were people, too.

Stop by the **Mission Social Hall and Café** and sample the lū'au stew (a traditional dish of taro leaves and pork braised until meltingly soft) and 'Ōlena (turmeric) lemonade.

553 S. King St. (at Kawaiaha'o St.). http://missionhouses.org. ✆ **808/447-3910.** Admission $10 adults, $8 military personnel and seniors, $6 students and children 6 and over, free for children 5 and under. Tues–Sat 10am–4pm. Bus: 2 and 42.

Honolulu Museum of Art ★ MUSEUM In 2011, the Honolulu Academy of Art merged with the Contemporary Museum and was renamed the (more apropos) Honolulu Museum of Art. It also finished a reinstallation of the European and American art galleries, bringing to light many pieces from the archives. The museum's Asian collection includes a significant number of items from Japan, China, and Korea.

The Honolulu Museum of Art is also where tours of **Shangri La ★★★** start. Shuttles from the museum take visitors to tobacco heiress Doris Duke's private palace on a 5-acre sanctuary in Black Point. It's absolutely stunning, packed with Islamic art and intricate tilework from Iran, Turkey, and Syria; textiles from Egypt and India; and custom-painted ceilings by Moroccan artisans. Outside's not so bad either, with ocean views all the way to Diamond Head. Make sure to book far in advance—the tours fill up quickly, a testament to this unique wonder. Tours take 2½ hours.

Admittedly, I love the **Spalding House** (formerly the Contemporary Museum) more for its views and surrounding gardens than for its art collection. It's in Tantalus, high above the city, and yet only a 10-minute drive from downtown. One of my favorite activities is the Lauhala and Lunch, where you picnic on the expansive lawn overlooking Honolulu. Call ahead to reserve a picnic basket from the Spalding House Café, which comes complete with tatami mats ($35 lunch for two).

900 S. Beretania St. www.honolulumuseum.org. ✆ **808/532-8700;** 808/532-3853 for Shangri La reservations; 808/237-5225 for the Spalding House Café. $10 adults; $5 students, seniors, and military personnel; free for children 12 and under. Shangri La tours $25 ($20 Hawai'i residents), children under 8 not admitted, advance reservations a must. Tues–Sat 10am–4:30pm; Sun 1–5pm.

'Iolani Palace ★★ HISTORIC BUILDING If you want to really "understand" Hawai'i, this 45-minute tour is well worth the time. The 'Iolani Palace was built by King David Kalākaua, who spared no expense. The 4-year project, completed in 1882, cost $360,000—and nearly bankrupted the Hawaiian kingdom. This four-story Italian Renaissance palace was the first electrified building in Honolulu (it had electricity before the White House and Buckingham Palace). Royals lived here for 11 years, until Queen Lili'uokalani was deposed and the Hawaiian monarchy fell forever in a palace coup led by U.S. Marines on January 17, 1893, at the demand of sugar planters and missionary descendants.

Cherished by latter-day royalists, the 10-room palace stands as an architectural statement of the monarchy period. 'Iolani attracts 60,000 visitors a year in groups of 15; everyone must don booties to scoot across the royal floors. Visitors take either a comprehensive **guided tour ★**, which offers a docent-guided tour of the interior, or a self-led **audio tour.** Finish by exploring the Basement Gallery on your own, where

'Iolani Palace.

you'll find crown jewels, ancient feathered cloaks, the royal china, and more.

364 S. King St. (at Richards St.). www.iolanipalace.org. ✆ **808/538-1471.** Guided tour $22 adults, $6 children 5–12; not available Mon; reservations required. Book online at website or visit the ticket office in the 'Iolani Barracks on the Palace Grounds. Audio tour $15 adults, $6 children 5–12. Gallery tour $7 adults, $3 children 5–12. Mon–Sat 9:30am–4pm; closed Sun. Children 4 and under allowed only in the Basement Gallery (in the company of an adult). Extremely limited parking on palace grounds; try metered parking on the street. Bus: 2.

Kawaiaha'o Church ★ CHURCH In 1842, Kawaiahaʻo Church stood complete at last. Designed by Rev. Hiram Bingham (grandfather of explorer and politician Hiram Bingham III) and supervised by Kamehameha III, who ordered his people to help build it, the project took 5 years to complete. Workers quarried 14,000 coral blocks weighing 1,000 pounds each from the offshore reefs and cut timber in the forests for the beams. This proud stone church, complete with bell tower and colonial colonnade, was the first permanent Western house of worship in the islands. It became the church of the Hawaiian royalty and remains in use today. Some fine portraits of Hawaiian royalty hang inside. English- and Hawaiian-language services are conducted on Sundays at 9am.

957 Punchbowl St. (at King St.). ✆ **808/522-1333.** Free admission (donations appreciated). Mon–Fri 8am–4:30pm; Sun services 9am. Bus: 2.

Queen Emma Summer Palace ★ PALACE Hānaiakamalama, the name of the country estate of Kamehameha IV and Queen Emma, was once in the secluded uplands of Nuʻuanu Valley. These days it's adjacent to a six-lane highway full of speeding cars. This simple, seven-room New England–style house, built in 1848 and restored by the Daughters of Hawai'i, is worth about an hour of your time to see the interesting blend of Victorian furniture and hallmarks of Hawaiian royalty, including feather cloaks and *kahili,* the feathered standards that mark the presence of *ali'i* (royalty). Other royal treasures include a canoe-shaped cradle for Queen Emma's baby, Prince Albert, who died at the age of 4. (Kaua'i's ritzy Princeville Resort is named for the little prince.)

2913 Pali Hwy. (at Old Pali Rd.). http://daughtersofhawaii.org. ✆ **808/595-3167.** Admission $10 adults, $1 children 11 and under. Daily 9am–4pm. Bus: E or 57.

Wartime Honolulu

USS Arizona Memorial at Pearl Harbor ★★★ HISTORIC SITE On December 7, 1941, the USS *Arizona,* while moored here in Pearl Harbor, was bombed in a Japanese air raid. The 608-foot battleship sank in 9 minutes without firing a shot, taking 1,177 sailors and Marines to their deaths—and catapulting the United States into World War II.

Nobody who visits the memorial will ever forget it. The deck of the ship lies 6 feet below the surface of the sea. Oil still oozes slowly up from the Arizona's engine room and stains the harbor's calm, blue water; some say the ship still weeps for its lost crew. The memorial is a stark-white,

USS *Arizona* Memorial.

Pearl Harbor Visitor Center: Getting Tickets

The **USS *Arizona* Memorial, USS *Bowfin* and Submarine Museum, USS *Missouri* Memorial,** and **Pacific Aviation Museum** are all accessed via the Pearl Harbor Visitor Center. Park here and purchase tickets for all the exhibits. (Entry to the USS *Arizona* Memorial is free, but you still must get a ticket. Better yet, for the USS *Arizona*, reserve your spot at **www.recreation.gov** to avoid a long wait.) Shuttle buses will deliver you to the sites within Pearl Harbor.

184-foot rectangular bridge that spans the sunken hull of the ship; it was designed by Alfred Preis, a German architect interned on Sand Island during the war. It contains the ship's bell, recovered from the wreckage, and a shrine room with the names of the dead carved in stone.

Today, free U.S. Navy launches take visitors to the *Arizona*. You can make an **advance reservation** to visit the memorial at the website **www.recreation.gov** for an additional $1.50 per-ticket convenience fee. This is highly recommended; if you try to get walk-up tickets directly at the visitor center, you may have to wait a few hours before the tour. While you're waiting for the free shuttle to take you out to the ship, get the **audio tour ★★★**, which will make the trip even more meaningful. The tour (on an MP3 player) is about 2½ hours long, costs $7.50, and is worth every nickel. It's like having your own personal park ranger as your guide. The tape is narrated by the late Ernest Borgnine and features stories told by actual Pearl Harbor survivors—both American and Japanese. Plus, while you're waiting for the launch, the tour will take you step by step through the museum's personal mementos, photographs, and historic documents. You can pause the tour for the moving 20-minute film that precedes your trip to the ship. The tour continues on the launch, describing the shore line and letting you know what's in store at the memorial itself. At the memorial, the tour gives you a mental picture of that fateful day, and the narration continues on your boat ride back. Allow a total of at least 4 hours for your visit.

Note that boat rides to the *Arizona* are sometimes suspended because of high winds. Check the World War II **Valor in the Pacific** Facebook page (www.facebook.com/valorNPS) for updated information on boat ride suspensions. Due to increased security measures, visitors cannot carry purses, handbags, fanny packs, backpacks, camera bags (though you can carry your camera, cellphone, or video camera with you), diaper bags, or other items that offer concealment on the boat. However, there is a storage facility where you can stash carry-on-size items (no bigger than 30×30×18 in.) for a fee. ***A reminder to parents:*** Baby strollers, baby carriages, and baby backpacks are not allowed inside the theater, on the boat, or on the USS *Arizona* Memorial. All babies must be carried. ***One last note:*** Most unfortunately, the USS *Arizona* Memorial is a high-theft area—so leave your valuables at the hotel.

Pearl Harbor. www.nps.gov/usar. ✆ **808/422-3300.** Free admission. $7.50 for the audio guide. **Highly recommended:** Make an advance reservation to visit the memorial at www.recreation.gov. Children 11 and under should be accompanied by an adult. Wheelchairs gladly accommodated. Daily 7am–5pm (programs run 8am–3pm). Drive west on H-1 past the airport; take the USS *Arizona* Memorial exit and follow the green-and-white signs; there's ample free parking. Bus: 40 or 42; or *Arizona* Memorial Shuttle Bus VIP (✆ **866/836-0317**), which picks up at Waikīkī hotels 7am–noon ($10 per person round-trip).

USS Bowfin Submarine Museum & Park ★ HISTORIC SITE Ever wonder what life on a submarine is like? Then go inside the USS *Bowfin,* aka the Pearl Harbor Avenger, to experience the claustrophobic quarters where soldiers lived and launched torpedoes. The *Bowfin* Museum details wartime submarine history and gives a sense of the impressive technical challenges that must be overcome for submarines to even exist. The Waterfront Memorial honors submariners lost during World War II.

11 Arizona Memorial Dr. (next to the USS *Arizona* Memorial Visitor Center). www.bowfin.org. ✆ **808/423-1341.** Admission $12 adults, $8 active-duty military personnel and seniors, $5 children 4–12 (children 3 and under not permitted for safety reasons). Daily 7am–5pm (last admission at 4:30pm). See USS *Arizona* Memorial, above, for driving, bus, and shuttle directions.

USS Missouri Memorial ★ HISTORIC SITE In the deck of this 58,000-ton battleship (the last one the navy launched), World War II came to an end with the signing of the Japanese surrender on September 2, 1945. The *Missouri* was part of the force that carried out bombing raids over Tokyo and provided firepower in the battles of Iwo Jima and Okinawa. In 1955, the navy decommissioned the ship and placed it in mothballs at the Puget Sound Naval Shipyard in Washington State. But the *Missouri* was modernized and called back into action in 1986, eventually being deployed in the Persian Gulf War, before retiring once again in 1992. Here it sat until another battle ensued, this time over who would get the right to keep this living legend. Hawai'i won that battle and brought the ship to Pearl Harbor in 1998. The 887-foot ship is now open to visitors as a museum memorial.

You're free to explore on your own or take a guided tour. Highlights of this massive (more than 200-ft. tall) battleship include the forecastle (or "fo'c's'le," in navy talk), where the 30,000-pound anchors are dropped on 1,080 feet of anchor chain; the 16-inch guns (each 65 ft. long and weighing 116 tons), which can accurately fire a 2,700-pound shell some 23 miles in 50 seconds; and the spot where the Instrument of Surrender was signed as Douglas MacArthur, Chester Nimitz, and "Bull" Halsey looked on.

Battleship Row, Pearl Harbor. www.ussmissouri.com. ✆ **877/MIGHTY-MO.** Admission $27 adults, $13 children 4–12. Mighty Mo Tour (35 min.); Heart of the Missouri Tour (90 min.) $27 extra. Daily 8am–5pm; guided tours 8:15am–4:15pm. Check in at the USS *Bowfin* Submarine Museum, next to the USS *Arizona* Memorial Visitor Center. See USS *Arizona* Memorial, above, for driving, bus, and shuttle directions.

National Memorial Cemetery of the Pacific ★★ CEMETERY The National Memorial Cemetery of the Pacific (aka Punchbowl) is an ash-and-lava tuff cone that exploded about 150,000 years ago—like Diamond Head, only smaller. Early Hawaiians called it Pūowaina, or "hill of sacrifice." The old crater is a burial ground for 35,000 victims of three American wars in Asia and the Pacific: World War II, Korea, and Vietnam. Among the graves, you'll find many unmarked ones with the date December 7, 1941, carved in stone. Some names will be unknown forever; others are famous, like that of war correspondent Ernie Pyle, killed by a Japanese sniper in April 1945 on Okinawa; still others buried here are remembered only by family and surviving buddies. The white stone tablets known as the Courts of the Missing bear the names of 28,788 Americans missing in action in World War II. Survivors come here often to reflect on the meaning of war and to remember those, like themselves, who stood in harm's way to win peace a half-century ago. Some fight back tears, remembering lost buddies, lost missions, and the sacrifices of those who died.

Punchbowl Crater, 2177 Pūowaina Dr. (at the end of the road). Free admission. Daily 8am–5:30pm (Mar–Sept to 6:30pm). Bus: 2 or 42, with a long walk.

Pacific Aviation Museum ★ MUSEUM The Pacific Aviation Museum is the flashiest (and newest) of the Pearl Harbor exhibits, with its propaganda-esque written histories and signs. There are two hangars: Hangar 37 includes planes involved in the 1942 attack, but the best is Hangar 79, the doors still riddled with bullet holes from the Pearl Harbor strafing. It houses military aircraft, old and new; you can even climb into the cockpit of some of them. On the far end is the Restoration Shop, where you can watch vintage aircraft actively being restored. For an additional $10, sit in a Combat Flight Simulator, like an immersive video game in which you fly a plane and shoot down the enemy.

Hanger 39, 319 Lexington Blvd., Ford Island (next to the red and white control tower). www.pacificaviationmuseum.org. ✆ **808/441-1000.** Admission $25 adults, $15 children 4–12; guided behind-the-scenes tour $35 adults, $25 children 4–12. Daily 9am–5pm. See USS *Arizona* Memorial, above, for driving, bus, and shuttle directions.

Just Beyond Pearl Harbor

Hawaiian Railway ★ TRAIN It's like a Disneyland ride . . . through Honolulu's suburbia. It's also a quirky way to see the less-traveled leeward side of O'ahu. Between 1890 and 1947, the chief mode of transportation for O'ahu's sugar mills was the O'ahu Railway and Land Co.'s narrow-gauge trains. The line carried not only equipment, raw sugar, and supplies, but also passengers from one side of the island to the other. About 6 miles of the train tracks have been restored, starting in 'Ewa and ending along the coast at Kahe Point. Don't expect ocean views all the way—you're passing through the heart of suburban Honolulu (yup, that's a Costco and a power plant) before you reach the ocean. Still, the 1½-hour narrated ride is pretty amusing. Even better, book the Sunday 3pm ride, and the train stops at Ko Olina resort for ice cream.

91-1001 Renton Rd., Ewa. www.hawaiianrailway.com. ✆ **808/681-5461.** Admission $12 adults, $8 seniors and children 2–12. Parlour Car 64 $25. Departures Sun at 1 and 3pm and weekdays by appointment. Take H-1 west to Exit 5A; take Hwy. 76 south for 2½ miles to Tesoro Gas; turn right on Renton Rd. and drive 1½ miles to end of paved section. The station is on the left. Bus: E or 42, with a 1½-mile walk.

Hawai'i's Plantation Village ★ HISTORIC SITE The hour-long tour of this restored 50-acre village offers a glimpse back in time to when sugar planters shaped the land, economy, and culture of Hawai'i. From 1852, when the first contract laborers arrived here from China, to 1947, when the plantation era ended, more than 400,000 men, women, and children from China, Japan, Portugal, Puerto Rico, Korea, and the Philippines came to work the sugarcane fields. The "talk story" tour brings the old village alive with 30 faithfully restored camp houses, Chinese and Japanese temples, the Plantation Store, and even a sumo-wrestling ring.

94-695 Waipahu St. (at Waipahu Depot Rd.), Waipahu. www.hawaiiplantationvillage.org. ✆ **808/677-0110.** Admission (including escorted tour) $13 adults, $10 seniors, $7 military personnel, $5 children 4–11. Mon–Sat 10am–2pm. Take H-1 west to Waikele-Waipahu exit (Exit 7); get in the left lane of the exit and turn left on Paiwa St.; at the 5th light, turn right onto Waipahu St.; after the 2nd light, turn left. Bus: 40 or 42.

Foster Botanical Garden.

Gardens, Aquariums & Zoos

Foster Botanical Garden ★ GARDEN You could spend days in this unique historic garden, a leafy oasis amid the high-rises of downtown Honolulu. Combine a tour of the garden with a trip to Chinatown (just across the street)

Waikīkī Aquarium.

to maximize your time and double your pleasure. The giant trees that tower over the garden's main terrace were planted in the 1850s by William Hillebrand, a German physician and botanist, on royal land leased from Queen Emma. Today this 14-acre public garden, on the north side of Chinatown, is a living museum of plants, some rare and endangered, collected from the tropical regions of the world. Of special interest are 26 "Exceptional Trees" protected by state law, a large palm collection, a primitive cycad garden, and a hybrid orchid collection.

50 N. Vineyard Blvd. (at Nu'uanu Ave.). ✆ **808/522-7066.** Admission $5 adults, $1 children 6–12. Daily 9am–4pm; guided tours Mon–Sat at 1pm (reservations recommended). Bus: 19 or E.

Honolulu Zoo ★ ZOO Nobody comes to Hawai'i to see an Indian elephant or African lions and zebras, right? Wrong. This 43-acre municipal zoo in Waikīkī attracts visitors in droves. If you've got kids, allot at least half a day. The highlight is the African Savanna, a 10-acre exhibit with more than 40 African critters, including antelope and giraffes. The zoo also has a rare Hawaiian nēnē goose, one of the few indigenous animals left in Hawai'i.

151 Kapahulu Ave. (between Paki and Kalākaua aves.), at entrance to Kapi'olani Park. www.honoluluzoo.org. ✆ **808/971-7171.** Admission $14 adults, $6 children 3–12. Daily 9am–4:30pm. Zoo parking lot (entrance on Kapahulu Ave.) $1 per hr. Bus: 8 and 42.

Lyon Arboretum ★ GARDEN The Lyon Arboretum dates from 1918, when the Hawaiian Sugar Planters Association wanted to demonstrate the value of watershed for reforestation. In 1953, it became part of the University of Hawai'i, where they continued to expand the extensive collection of tropical plants. Six-story-tall breadfruit trees, yellow orchids no bigger than a nickel, ferns with fuzzy buds as big as a human head—these are just a few of the botanical wonders you'll find at the 194-acre arboretum. A whole different world opens up to you along the self-guided, 20-minute hike through the arboretum to Inspiration Point. You'll pass more than 5,000 exotic tropical plants full of singing birds in this cultivated rainforest at the head of Mānoa Valley.

3860 Mānoa Rd. (near the top of the road). www.hawaii.edu/lyonarboretum. ✆ **808/988-0456.** Suggested donation $5. Mon–Fri 8am–4pm; Sat 9am–3pm. Bus: 5.

Waikīkī Aquarium ★★★ AQUARIUM Half of Hawai'i's beauty is its underwater world. Behold the chambered nautilus, nature's submarine and inspiration for Jules Verne's *20,000 Leagues Under the Sea.* You can see this tropical, spiral-shelled cephalopod mollusk—the only living one born in captivity—any day of the week here. Its natural habitat is the deep waters of Micronesia, but former aquarium director Bruce Carlson not only succeeded in trapping the pearly shelled creature in 1,500 feet of water (by dangling chunks of raw tuna), but also managed to breed this ancient relative of the octopus. There are plenty of other fish to see in this small but first-class aquarium, located on a live coral reef. The reef habitat features sharks, eels, a touch tank, and habitats for the endangered Hawaiian monk seal and green sea turtle. The rotating jellyfish exhibit is otherworldly—it's like watching alien life.

2777 Kalākaua Ave. (across from Kapi'olani Park). www.waikikiaquarium.org. ✆ **808/923-9741.** Admission $12 adults, $8 active military, $5 seniors and children 4–12. Daily 9am–4:30pm. Bus: 2 and Waikīkī Trolley's Green Line.

Other Natural Wonders & Spectacular Views

In addition to the attractions listed below, check out the hike to **Diamond Head Crater ★★★** (p. 114); almost everybody can handle it, and the 360-degree views from the top are fabulous.

Nu'uanu Pali Lookout ★ NATURAL ATTRACTION Gale-force winds sometimes howl through the mountain pass at this 1,186-foot-high perch guarded by 3,000 foot peaks, so hold on to your hat—and small children. But if you walk up from the parking lot to the precipice, you'll be rewarded with a view that'll blow you away. At the edge, the dizzying panorama of O'ahu's windward side is breathtaking: Clouds low enough to pinch scoot by on trade winds; pinnacles of the pali (cliffs), green with ferns, often disappear in the mist. From on high, the tropical palette of green and blue runs down to the sea. Combine this 10-minute stop with a trip over the pali to the windward side.

Near the summit of Pali Hwy. (Hwy. 61); take the Nu'uanu Pali Lookout turnoff.

Pu'u 'Ualaka'a State Park ★★★ STATE PARK/NATURAL ATTRACTION The best **sunset view** of Honolulu is from a

1,048-foot-high hill named for sweet potatoes. Actually, the poetic Hawaiian name means "rolling sweet potato hill," for the way early planters used gravity to harvest their crop. The panorama is sweeping and majestic. On a clear day—which is often—you can see from Diamond Head to the Wai'anae Range, almost the length of O'ahu. At night, several scenic overlooks provide romantic spots high above the city lights. At the end of Round Hill Dr. Daily 7am–6:45pm (to 7:45pm in summer). From Waikīkī, take Ala Wai Blvd. to McCully St., turn right, and drive *mauka* (inland) beyond the H-1 on-ramps to Wilder St.; turn left and go to Makiki St.; turn right, and continue onward and upward about 3 miles.

WALKING TOUR: HISTORIC HONOLULU

GETTING THERE: **From Waikīkī, take Ala Moana Boulevard in the Ewa direction. Ala Moana Boulevard ends at Nimitz Highway. Turn right on the next street on your right (Alakea St.). Park in the garage across from St. Andrew's Church after you cross Beretania Street. Bus: 2, 13, 19, or 20.**

START & FINISH: **St. Andrew's Church, Beretania and Alakea streets.**

TIME: **2 to 3 hours, depending on how long you linger in museums.**

BEST TIMES: **Monday through Saturday, daytime, when 'Iolani Palace is open.**

The 1800s were a turbulent time in Hawai'i. By the end of the 1790s, Kamehameha the Great had united all the islands. Foreigners then began arriving by ship—first explorers, then merchants, and then, in 1820, missionaries. The rulers of Hawai'i were hard-pressed to keep up. By 1840, it was clear that the capital had shifted from Lahaina, where the Kingdom of Hawai'i was actually centered, to Honolulu, where the majority of commerce and trade was taking place. In 1848, the Great Mahele (division) enabled commoners and, eventually, foreigners to own crown land, and in two generations, more than 80% of all private lands had shifted to foreign ownership. With the introduction of sugar as a crop, the foreigners prospered, and in time they put more and more pressures on the government.

By 1872, the monarchy had run through the Kamehameha line and, in 1873, David Kalākaua was elected to the throne. Known as the "Merrie Monarch," Kalākaua redefined the monarchy by going on a world tour, building 'Iolani Palace, having a European-style coronation, and throwing extravagant parties. By the end of the 1800s, however, the foreign sugar growers and merchants had become extremely powerful in Hawai'i. With the assistance of the U.S. Marines, they orchestrated the overthrow of Queen Lili'uokalani, Hawai'i's last reigning monarch, in 1893. The United States declared Hawai'i a territory in 1898.

You can witness the remnants of these turbulent years in just a few short blocks.

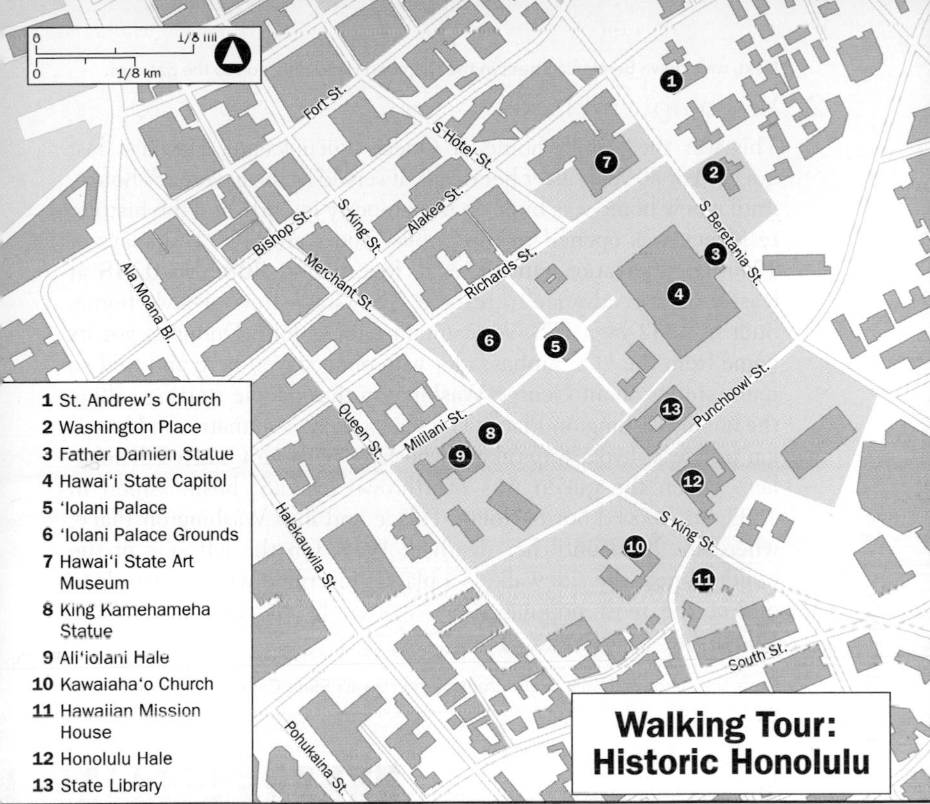

Cross the street from the garage and venture back to 1858 when you enter:

1 St. Andrew's Church

The Hawaiian monarchs were greatly influenced by the royals in Europe. When King Kamehameha IV saw the grandeur of the Church of England, he decided to build his own cathedral. He and Queen Emma founded the Anglican Church of Hawai'i in 1858. The king didn't live to see the church completed, however; he died on St. Andrew's Day, 4 years before King Kamehameha V oversaw the laying of the cornerstone in 1867. The church was named St. Andrew's in honor of King Kamehameha IV's death. This French-Gothic structure was shipped in pieces from England. Even if you aren't fond of visiting churches, you have to see the floor-to-eaves, hand-blown stained-glass window that faces the setting sun. In the glass is a mural of Rev. Thomas Staley (the first bishop in Hawai'i), King Kamehameha IV, and Queen Emma. Services are conducted in English and Hawaiian. On Sundays at 8am the Hawaiian Choir sings Hawaiian hymns, and at 10:30am the Cathedral Choir, in existence for 150 years, performs.

Next, walk down Beretania Street in the Diamond Head direction to the gates of:

2 Washington Place

This was the former home of Queen Lili'uokalani, Hawai'i's last queen. For 80 years after her death, it served as the governor's house, until a new home was built on the property in 2002 and the historic residence was opened to the public. Tours are held Thursdays at 10am by reservation only. They're free; call ✆ **808/586-0248** at least 2 days in advance to reserve. The Greek Revival–style home, built in 1842 by a U.S. sea captain named John Dominis, got its name from the U.S. ambassador who once stayed here and told so many stories about George Washington that people starting calling the home Washington Place. The sea captain's son married a Hawaiian princess, Lydia Kapa'akea, who later became Queen Lili'uokalani. When the queen was overthrown by U.S. businessmen in 1893, she moved out of 'Iolani Palace and into Washington Place, where she lived until her death in 1917. On the left side of the building, near the sidewalk, is a plaque inscribed with the words to one of the most popular songs written by Queen Lili'uokalani, "Aloha 'Oe" ("Farewell to Thee").

Cross the street and walk to the front of the Hawai'i State Capitol, where you'll find the:

3 Father Damien Statue

The people of Hawai'i have never forgotten the sacrifice this Belgian priest made to help the sufferers of leprosy when he volunteered to work with them in exile on the Kalaupapa Peninsula on the island of Moloka'i. After 16 years of service, Father Damien himself died of leprosy, at the age of 49. The statue is frequently draped in leis in recognition of Father Damien's humanitarian work.

Father Damien statue, in front of the Hawaii State Capitol.

Behind the Father Damien Statue is the:

4 Hawai'i State Capitol

Here's where Hawai'i's state legislators work from mid-January to the end of April every year. The building's unusual design has palm tree–shaped pillars, two cone-shaped chambers (representing volcanoes) for the legislative bodies, and, in the inner courtyard, a 600,000-tile mosaic of the sea (Aquarius) created by a local artist. A reflecting pool (representing the sea) surrounds the entire structure. You are welcome to go into the rotunda and see the woven hangings and murals at the entrance; pick up a self-guided-tour brochure at the governor's office on the fourth floor. The public is also welcome to observe the state government in action during legislative sessions (www.capitol.hawaii.gov).

Walk down Richards Street toward the ocean and stop at:

5 'Iolani Palace ★★

Hawai'i is the only state in the U.S. to have not one but two royal palaces: one in Kona, where the royals went during the summer, and 'Iolani Palace (*'Iolani* means "royal hawk"). Don't miss the opportunity to see this grande dame of historic buildings. Guided tours are $22 adults, $6 children 5 to 12; self-guided audio tours are $15 adults, $6 children 5 to 12; and basement gallery tours are $7 adults, $3 children 5 to 12. It's open Monday to Saturday 9:30am to 4pm and closed Sunday; call ✆ **808/522-0832** or book online (www.iolanipalace.org) to reserve in advance, as spots are limited.

In ancient times, a *heiau* (temple) stood in this area. When it became clear to King Kamehameha III that the capital should be transferred from Lahaina to Honolulu, he moved to a modest building here in 1845. The construction of the palace was begun in 1879 by King David Kalākaua; it was finished 3 years later at a cost of $350,000. The king spared no expense: You can still see the glass and iron work imported from San Francisco, and the palace had all the modern conveniences for its time. Electric lights were installed 4 years before the White House had them, and every bedroom had its own full bathroom with hot and cold running water, copper-lined tub, flush toilet, and bidet. The king had a telephone line from the palace to his boathouse on the water a year after Alexander Graham Bell introduced it to the world.

It was also in this palace that Queen Lili'uokalani was overthrown and placed under house arrest for 9 months. Later, the territorial and then the state government used the palace until it outgrew it. When the legislature left in 1968, the palace was in shambles. It has since undergone a $7-million overhaul to restore it to its former glory.

After you visit the palace, spend some time on the:

6 'Iolani Palace Grounds

You can wander around the grounds at no charge. The ticket window to the palace and the gift shop are in the former barracks of the Royal Household Guards. The domed pavilion on the grounds was originally built as a Coronation Stand by King Kalākaua (9 years after he took the throne, he decided to have a formal European-style coronation ceremony where he crowned himself and his queen, Kap'Iolani). Later he used it as a **Royal Bandstand** for concerts (King Kalākaua, along with Henri Berger, the first Royal Hawai'ian Bandmaster, wrote "Hawai'i Pono'ī," the state anthem). Today, the Royal Hawaiian Band, founded in 1836 by King Kamehameha III, plays at the Royal Bandstand every Friday from noon to 1pm.

From the palace grounds, turn in the 'Ewa direction, cross Richards Street, and walk to the corner of Richards and Hotel streets to the:

7 Hawai'i State Art Museum

Opened in 2002, the Hawai'i State Art Museum is housed in the original Royal Hawaiian hotel, built in 1872 during the reign of King Kamehameha V. Most of the art displayed in the 300-piece collection was created by local artists. The pieces were purchased by the state, thanks to a 1967 law that says that 1% of the cost of state buildings will be used to acquire works of art. Nearly 5 decades later, the state has amassed almost 6,000 pieces.

Walk *makai* down Richards Street and turn left (toward Diamond Head) on South King Street to the:

8 King Kamehameha Statue

At the juncture of King, Merchant, and Mililani streets stands a replica of the man who united the Hawaiian Islands. The striking black-and-gold bronze statue is magnificent. Try to see the statue on June 11 (King Kamehameha Day), when it is covered with leis in honor of Hawai'i's favorite son.

The statue of Kamehameha I was cast by Thomas Gould in 1880 in Paris. However, it was lost at sea somewhere near the Falkland Islands. Subsequently, the insurance money was used to pay for a second statue, but in the meantime, the original statue was recovered. The original was eventually sent to the town of Kapa'au

King Kamehameha Statue.

on the Big Island, the birthplace of Kamehameha, and the second statue was placed in Honolulu in 1883, as part of King David Kalākaua's coronation ceremony.

Right behind the King Kamehameha Statue is:

9 Ali'iōlani Hale

The name translates to "House of Heavenly Kings." This distinctive building, with a clock tower, now houses the Supreme Court of Hawai'i and the Judiciary History Center. King Kamehameha V originally wanted to build a palace here and commissioned the Australian architect Thomas Rowe in 1872. However, it ended up as the first major government building for the Hawaiian monarchy. Kamehameha V didn't live to see it completed, and King David Kalākaua dedicated the building in 1874. Ironically, less than 20 years later, on January 17, 1893, Stanford Dole, backed by other prominent sugar planters, stood on the steps to this building and proclaimed the overthrow of the Hawaiian monarchy and the establishment of a provisional government. Self-guided tours are available Monday through Friday from 7:45am to 4:30pm; admission is free.

Walk toward Diamond Head on King Street; at the corner of King and Punchbowl, stop in at the:

10 Kawaiaha'o Church ★

When the missionaries came to Hawai'i, the first thing they did was build churches. Four thatched-grass churches (one measured 54×22 ft. and could seat 300 people on lauhala mats; the last thatched church held 4,500 people) had been built on this site through 1837, before Rev. Hiram Bingham began building what he considered a "real" church: a New England–style congregational structure with Gothic influences. Between 1837 and 1842, the construction of the church required some 14,000 giant coral slabs (some weighing more than 1,000 pounds). Hawaiian divers ravaged the reefs, digging out huge chunks of coral and causing irreparable environmental damage.

Kawaiaha'o is Hawai'i's oldest church and has been the site of numerous historic events, such as a speech made by King Kamehameha III in 1843, an excerpt from which became Hawai'i's state motto (*"Ua mau ke ea o ka 'āina i ka pono,"* which translates as "The life of the land is preserved in righteousness").

The church is open Monday through Saturday 8am to 4pm; you'll find it to be very cool in temperature. Don't sit in the back pews marked with kahili feathers and velvet cushions; they are still reserved for the descendants of royalty. Sunday service (in English and Hawaiian) is at 9am.

Cross the street, and you'll see the:

11 Hawaiian Mission Houses

On the corner of King and Kawaiaha'o streets stand the original buildings of the Sandwich Islands Mission Headquarters: the **Frame House** (built in 1821), the **Chamberlain House** (1831), and the **Printing Office** (1841). The complex is open Tuesday through Saturday from 10am to 4pm; admission is $10 adults, $8 seniors and military personnel, and $6 students and children 6 and older. The tours are often led by descendants of the original missionaries to Hawai'i. For information, go to http://missionhouses.org.

Believe it or not, the missionaries brought their own prefab house along with them when they came around Cape Horn from Boston in 1819. The Frame House was designed for New England winters and had small windows (it must have been stiflingly hot inside). Finished in 1821 (the interior frame was left behind and didn't arrive until Christmas 1820), it is Hawai'i's oldest wooden structure. The Chamberlain House, built in 1831, was used by the missionaries as a storehouse.

The missionaries believed that the best way to spread the Lord's message to the Hawaiians was to learn their language, and then to print literature for them to read. So it was the missionaries who gave the Hawaiians a written language. The Printing House on the grounds was where the lead-type Ramage press (brought from New England, of course) was used to print the Hawaiian Bible.

Cross King Street and walk in the 'Ewa direction to the corner of Punchbowl and King to:

12 Honolulu Hale

The **Honolulu City Hall,** built in 1927, was designed by Honolulu's most famous architect, C. W. Dickey. His Spanish Mission–style building has an open-air courtyard, which is used for art exhibits and concerts. It's open Monday through Friday.

Cross Punchbowl Street and walk *mauka* to the:

13 State Library

Anything you want to know about Hawai'i and the Pacific can be found here, at the main branch of the state's library system. Located in a restored historic building, it has an open garden courtyard in the middle, great for stopping for a rest on your walk.

Head down Beretania in the 'Ewa direction to Alakea back to the parking garage.

BEYOND HONOLULU: EXPLORING THE ISLAND BY CAR

Urban Honolulu, with its history, cuisine, and shopping, can captivate travelers for days. But the rest of the island draws them out in its promise of wild coastlines and unique adventures.

O'ahu's Southeast Coast

From the high-rises of Waikīkī, venture down Kalākaua Avenue through tree-lined **Kapi'olani Park** to take a look at a different side of O'ahu, the arid South Shore. The landscape here is more moonscape, with prickly cacti onshore and, in winter, spouting whales cavorting in the water.

To get to this coast, follow Kalākaua Avenue past the multitiered Dillingham Fountain and around the bend in the road, which now becomes Poni Moi Road. Make a right on Diamond Head Road and begin the climb up the side of the old crater. At the top are several lookout points, so if the official Diamond Head Lookout is jammed with cars, try one of the other lookouts just down the road. The view of the rolling waves and surfers is spectacular; take the time to pull over.

Diamond Head Road rolls downhill into the ritzy community of **Kāhala.** At the fork in the road at the triangular Fort Ruger Park, veer to your right and continue on the palm tree–lined Kāhala Avenue. Make a left on Hunakai Street, and then take a right on Kīlauea Avenue and look for the sign, "H-1 west–Waimānalo." Turn right at the sign, although you won't get on the H-1 freeway; instead, get on the Kalaniana'ole Highway, a four-lane highway interrupted every few blocks by a stoplight. This is the suburban bedroom community to Honolulu, marked by malls on the left and beach parks on the right.

One of these parks is **Hanauma Bay ★★** (p. 104); you'll see the turnoff on the right when you're about half an hour from Waikīkī. This marine preserve is one of the island's best places to snorkel; you'll find the friendliest fish on the island here. ***A reminder:*** The beach park is closed on Tuesday.

Around mile marker 11, the jagged lava coast itself spouts sea foam at the **Halona Blowhole.** Look out to sea from Halona over Sandy Beach and across the 26-mile gulf to neighboring Moloka'i and the faint triangular shadow of Lāna'i on the far horizon. **Sandy Beach ★** (p. 105) is one of O'ahu's most dangerous beaches. Body boarders just love it.

The coast looks raw and empty along this stretch, but the road weaves past old Hawaiian fish ponds and the famous formation known as **Pele's Chair,** just off Kalaniana'ole Highway (Hwy. 72) above Queen's Beach. From a distance, the lava-rock outcropping looks like a mighty throne; it's believed to be the fire goddess's last resting place on O'ahu before she flew off to continue her work on other islands.

Ahead lies 647-foot-high **Makapu'u Point,** with a lighthouse that once signaled safe passage for steamship passengers arriving from San Francisco. The automated light now brightens O'ahu's south coast for passing tankers, fishing boats, and sailors. You can take a short hike up the **Makapu'u Lighthouse Trail ★★** (p. 116) for a spectacular vista.

Turn the corner at Makapu'u and you're on O'ahu's windward side, where cooling trade winds propel windsurfers across turquoise bays; the waves at **Makapu'u Beach Park ★** (p. 105) are perfect for bodysurfing.

Ahead, the coastal vista is a profusion of fluted green mountains and strange peaks, edged by golden beaches and the blue, blue Pacific. The 3,000-foot-high, sheer, green Ko'olau mountains plunge almost straight down, presenting an irresistible jumping-off spot for paragliders. Most likely, you'll spot their colorful chutes in the sky, looking like balloons released into the wind.

Winding up the coast, Kalaniana'ole Highway (Hwy. 72) leads through rural **Waimānalo,** a country beach town of nurseries and stables. Nearly 4 miles long, **Waimānalo Beach ★★** (p. 107) is O'ahu's longest beach and popular with local families on weekends. Take a swim here or head on to **Kailua Beach ★★★** (p. 106), one of Hawai'i's best.

The Windward Coast

From the **Nu'unau Pali Lookout ★**, near the summit of the Pali Highway (Hwy. 61), you get the first hint of the other side of O'ahu, a region so green and lovely that it could be an island sibling of Tahiti. With its many beaches and bays, the scenic 30-mile Windward Coast parallels the corduroy-ridged, nearly perpendicular cliffs of the Ko'olau Range, which separates the windward side of the island from Honolulu and the rest of O'ahu. As you descend on the serpentine Pali Highway beneath often-gushing waterfalls, you'll see the nearly 1,000-foot spike of **Olomana,** a bold pinnacle that beckons intrepid hikers, and, beyond, the town of **Waimānalo,** where many of Native Hawaiian descent live. Stop by **Keneke's** at 41-857 Kalaniana'ole Hwy. (© **808/259-9800**), a roadside local spot, for shave ice before continuing on your way.

From the Pali Highway, to the right is Kailua, Hawai'i's biggest beach town, with more than 50,000 residents and 2 special beaches, **Kailua Beach ★★★** (p. 106) and **Lanikai Beach ★★★** (p. 106). You can easily spend an entire day in Kailua, which I absolutely recommend, whether to laze on the sand or stand-up paddle to the Mokuloa Islands. But Kailua isn't all beach: A bevy of chic boutiques recently opened, such as **Oliver Men's Shop** and the **Aloha Beach Club,** and you can grab a shave ice at **The Local Hawai'i** (p. 162). Kailua-proud boutiques are scattered throughout town, like the **Kailua General Store,** 171 Hāmā kua Dr. (© **808/261-5681**), a cute, throwback shop with locally made souvenirs, foodstuffs, soap, and more.

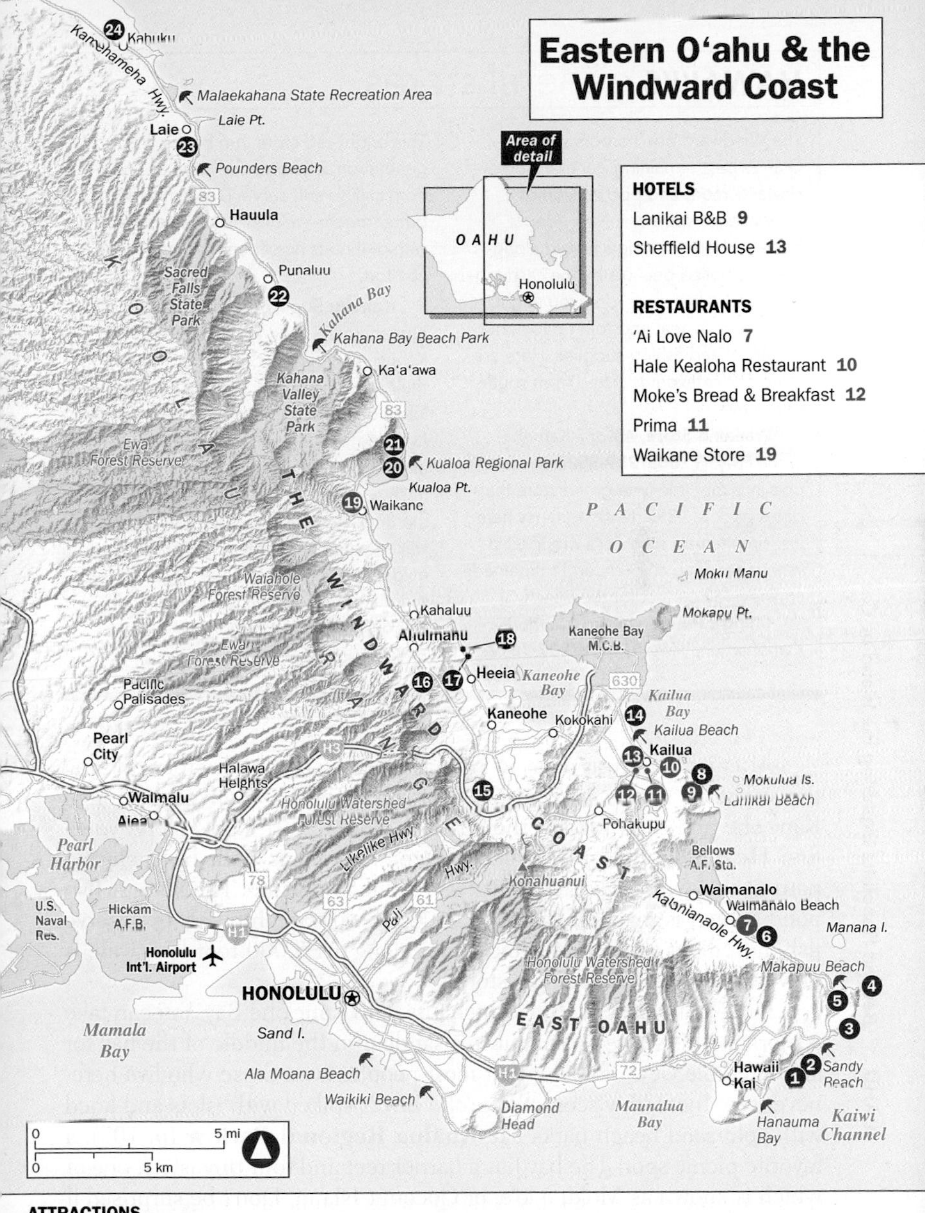

ATTRACTIONS

Ching's Punalu'u Store 22
Halona Blowhole 1
He'eia Pier 18
He'eia State Park/He'eia Fish Pond 17
Ho'omaluhia Botanical Gardens 15
Kahuku Superette 24
Kailua Beach 14
Kualoa Ranch 21
Kualoa Regional Park 20
Lanikai Beach 8
Makapu'u Beach Park 5
Makapu'u Point 4
Nu'uanu Pali Lookout 15
Pele's Chair 3
Polynesian Cultural Center 23
Sandy Beach 2
Valley of the Temples 16
Waimānalo Beach 6

HAWAI'I'S general stores

The Windward side harbors some of O'ahu's best remaining general stores—Hawai'i's mom-and-pop version of a convenience store or a New York bodega. Here, nostalgia is sold alongside the boiled peanuts by the cash register. Under the same roof, you might find smoked meat and toilet paper, butter mochi and fishing supplies. Here are three of our favorites (listed from south to north):

Waikane Store, 48-377 Kamehameha Hwy. (✆ **808/239-8522**): Locals pop into this little lime-green store that dates back to 1898. Nothing fancy here, just simple maki sushi rolls wrapped in wax paper, fried chicken, and homemade cookies—all perfect for the beach.

Ching's Punalu'u Store, 53-360 Kamehameha Hwy. (✆ **808/237-7017**): This bright-red store, run by the third generation, offers all the local favorites—from chili to soft serve. Don't miss the butter mochi—a local sweet treat made with glutinous rice flour. It's pure, chewy comfort.

Kahuku Superette ★★★, 56-505 Kamehameha Hwy. (✆ **808/293-9878**): Kahuku's shrimp trucks may entice with their potent, garlicky smells, but absolutely don't miss the poke (seasoned raw fish) from Kahuku Superette. If you're not afraid of kimchi, get the special poke: fresh ahi tuna with a housemade, fermented, gingery paste that's sure to waken your taste buds. Want something milder? Try the shoyu poke. This nondescript store is a must-stop for many of Honolulu's notable chefs.

After whiling away a day in Kailua, allocate another day for exploring the rest of the Windward coast. Take Highway 830N, which goes through Kāne'ohe and then follows the coast to He'eia State Park. Here, you'll find **He'eia Fish Pond,** which ancient Hawaiians built by enclosing natural bays with rocks to trap fish on the incoming tide. The 88-acre fish pond, which is made of lava rock and had four watchtowers to observe fish movement and several sluice gates along the 5,000-foot-long wall, is now in the process of being restored.

Drive onto **He'eia Pier,** which juts onto Kāne'ohe Bay. You can take a snorkel cruise here or sail out to a sandbar in the middle of the bay for an incredible view of O'ahu that most people, even those who live here, never see. Incredibly scenic Kāne'ohe Bay is spiked with islets and lined with gold-sand beach parks like **Kualoa Regional Park ★** (p. 107), a favorite picnic spot. The bay has a barrier reef and four tiny islets, one of which is known as Moku o lo'e, or Coconut Island. Don't be surprised if it looks familiar—it appeared in *Gilligan's Island.*

Everyone calls the other distinctively shaped island **Chinaman's Hat,** but it's really named **Mokoli'i.** It's a sacred *pu'u honua,* or place of refuge, like the restored Pu'u Honua Honaunau on the Big Island of Hawai'i. Excavations have unearthed evidence that this area was the home of ancient *ali'i* (royalty). Early Hawaiians believed that Mokoli'i

(Fin of the Lizard) is all that remains of a *mo'o,* or lizard, slain by Pele's sister, Hi'iaka, and hurled into the sea. At low tide you can swim out to the island, but keep watch on the changing tide, which can sweep you out to sea. You can also kayak to the island; park your car and launch your kayak from Kualoa Regional Park. It's about a half-hour hike to the top, which awards you views of the Ko'olau mountains and Kāne'ohe Bay.

Little poly-voweled beach towns like **Kahalu'u, Ka'a'awa, Punalu'u,** and **Hau'ula** pop up along the coast, offering passersby shell shops and art galleries to explore. Roadside fruit and flower stands vend ice-cold coconuts to drink (vendors lop off the top and provide the straws) and tree-ripened mangoes, papayas, and apple bananas (short bananas with an apple aftertaste).

Sugar, once the sole industry of this region, is gone. But **Kahuku,** the former sugar-plantation town, has found new life as a small aquaculture community with shrimp farms. Definitely stop for a poke bowl at **Kahuku Superette** (p. 94).

From here, continue along Kamehameha Highway (Hwy. 83) to the North Shore.

Attractions Along the Windward Coast

The attractions below are arranged geographically as you drive up the coast from south to north.

Ho'omaluhia Botanical Garden ★ GARDEN This 400-acre botanical garden at the foot of the steepled Ko'olau Range is the perfect place for a picnic. Its name means "a peaceful refuge," and that's exactly what the Army Corps of Engineers created when they installed a flood-control project here, which resulted in a 32-acre freshwater lake and garden. Just unfold a beach mat, lie back, and watch the clouds race across the rippled cliffs of the majestic Ko'olau Mountains. This is one of the few public places on O'ahu that provides a close-up view of the steepled cliffs. The park has hiking trails and a lovely, quiet campground (p. 137). If you like hiking and nature, plan to spend at least a half-day here. ***Note:*** Be prepared for rain, mud, and mosquitoes.

45-680 Luluku Rd., Kāne'ohe. ✆ **808/233-7323.** Free admission. Daily 9am–4pm. Guided nature hikes Sat 10am and Sun 1pm. Take H-1 to the Pali Hwy. (Hwy. 61); turn left on Kamehameha Hwy. (Hwy. 83); at the 4th light, turn left onto Luluku Rd. Bus: 55 or 56 will stop on Kamehameha Hwy.; it's a 2-mile walk to the visitor center.

Kualoa Ranch and Activity Club ★★ ACTIVITY PARK Kualoa Ranch does raise cattle, but people don't come here to see the cows. They come for adventure packages covering numerous activities on its 4,000 acres. Options include horseback riding and ATV rides that take you through the locations where movies like *Jurassic Park* and *Godzilla* were filmed. Get your adrenaline going on the new zipline course, which allows you to fly through the treetops at the ranch.

49-560 Kamehameha Hwy., Ka'a'awa. www.kualoa.com. ✆ **800/231-7321** or 808/237-7321. Reservations required. Various packages available; single activities $23–$95. Daily 8am–3:30pm. Take H-1 to the Likelike Hwy. (Hwy. 63), turn left at Kahekili Hwy. (Hwy. 83), and continue to Ka'a'awa. Bus: 55.

Polynesian Cultural Center ★ THEME PARK This is the Disneyland version of Polynesia, operated by the Mormon Church. Which means that some will see it as a tourist trap, while others, especially families, will enjoy the show. (My thoughts: I would never bring friends here when they visit, but I still remember my parents taking me when I was young and how delighted I was by the spectacle.) Here you can see the lifestyles, songs, dance, costumes, and architecture of seven Pacific islands or archipelagos—Fiji, New Zealand, Marquesas, Samoa, Tahiti, Tonga, and Hawai'i—in the re-created villages scattered throughout the 42-acre lagoon park.

You "travel" through the theme park on foot or in a canoe on a man-made freshwater lagoon. Native students from Polynesia who attend Hawai'i's Brigham Young University are the "inhabitants" of each village. They engage the audience with spear-throwing competitions, coconut tree–climbing presentations, and invitations to pound Tongan drums.

Every night except Sunday, there's ***Ha: Breath of Life,*** a coming-of-age story told through the different Polynesian dances, some full of grace, some fierce, and all thrilling. It's one of O'ahu's better shows.

Just beyond the center is the **Hawai'i Temple of the Church of Jesus Christ of Latter-day Saints,** built of volcanic rock and concrete in the form of a Greek cross; it includes reflecting pools, formal gardens, and royal palms. Completed in 1919, it was the first Mormon temple built outside the continental United States. An optional tour of the Temple Visitors Center, as well as neighboring Brigham Young University Hawai'i, is included in the package admission price.

55-370 Kamehameha Hwy., Lā'ie. www.polynesia.com. ✆ **800/367-7060,** 808/293-3333, or 808/923-2911. Various packages available for $50–$229 adults, $36–$179 children 3–11. Mon–Sat noon–9pm. Take H-1 to Pali Hwy. (Hwy. 61) and turn left on Kamehameha Hwy. (Hwy. 83). Parking $8. Bus: 55. Polynesian Cultural Center coach $22 roundtrip; call numbers above to book.

Polynesian Cultural Center.

Valley of the Temples ★ HISTORIC SITE This famous cemetery in a cleft of the pali is stalked by wild peacocks and about 700 curious people a day, who pay to see the 9-foot meditation Buddha, acres of ponds full of more than 10,000 Japanese koi carp, and a replica of Japan's 900-year-old Byodo-In Temple of Equality. The original, made of wood, stands in Uji, on the outskirts of Kyoto; the Hawai'i version, made of concrete, was erected in 1968 to commemorate the 100th anniversary of the arrival of the first Japanese immigrants to Hawai'i. It's not the same as seeing the original, but it's worth a detour.

47-200 Kahekili Hwy. (across the street from Temple Valley Shopping Center), Kāne'ohe. www.byodo-in.com. ✆ **808/239-8811.** Admission $3 adults, $2 seniors, $1 children 11 and under. Daily 9am–5pm. Take the H-1 to the Likelike Hwy. (Hwy. 63); after the Wilson Tunnel, get in the right lane and take the Kahekili Hwy. (Hwy. 63); at the 6th traffic light is the entrance to the cemetery (on the left). Bus: 65.

Central O'ahu & the North Shore

If you can afford the splurge, rent a convertible—the perfect car for O'ahu to enjoy the sun and soaring views—and head for the North Shore and Hawai'i's surf city: **Hale'iwa** ★★, a former sugar-plantation town and a designated historic site. Although in recent years, Hale'iwa has been spruced up—even the half-century old, formerly dusty Matsumoto's Shave Ice has new digs now—it still maintains a surfer/hippie vibe around the edges. For more, see "Surf City: Hale'iwa," below.

Getting there is half the fun. You have two choices: The first is to meander north along the lush Windward Coast, through country hamlets with roadside stands selling mangoes, bright tropical pareu, fresh corn, and pond-raised prawns. Attractions along that route are discussed in the previous section.

The second choice is to cruise up the H-2 through O'ahu's broad and fertile central valley, past Pearl Harbor and the Schofield Barracks of *From Here to Eternity* fame, and on through the red-earthed heart of the island, where pineapple and sugarcane fields stretch from the Ko'olau to the Wai'anae mountains, until the sea reappears on the horizon.

Once you're on H-1, stay to the right side; the freeway tends to divide abruptly. Keep following the signs for the H-1 (it separates off to Hwy. 78 at the airport and reunites later on; either way will get you there), and then the H-1/H-2. Leave the H-1 where the two highways divide; take the H-2 up the middle of the island, heading north toward the town of Wahiawā. That's what the sign will say—not North Shore or Hale'iwa, but Wahiawā.

The H-2 runs out and becomes a two-lane country road about 18 miles outside downtown Honolulu, near Schofield Barracks. The highway becomes Kamehameha Highway (Hwy. 99 and later Hwy. 83) at Wahiawā. Just past Wahiawā, about a half-hour out of Honolulu, the **Dole Pineapple Plantation,** 64-1550 Kamehameha Hwy. (www.dole-plantation.com; ✆ **808/621-8408;** daily 9:30am–5pm; bus: 52),

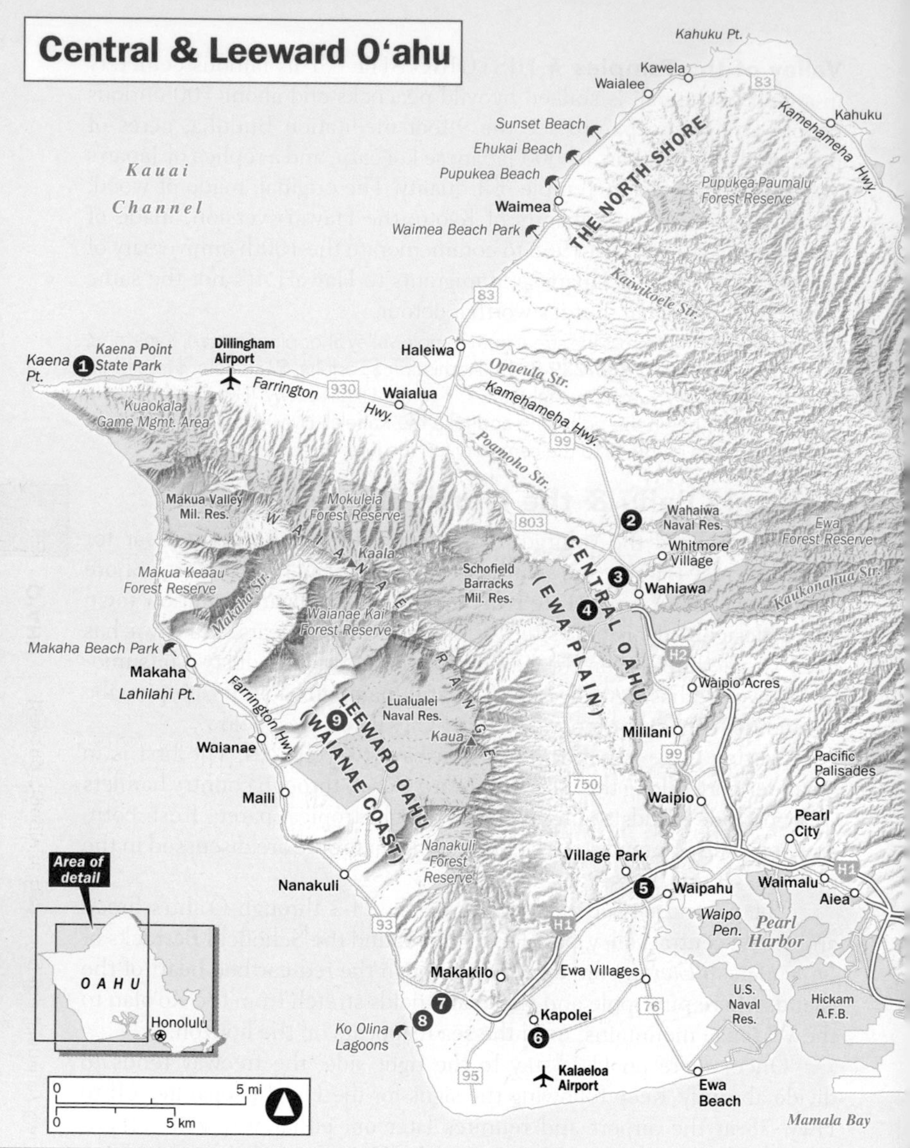

ATTRACTIONS

Dole Pineapple Plantation **2**
Hawai'i's Plantation Village **5**
Hawaiian Railway **6**
Ka'ena Point State Park **1**
Kukaniloko Birthing Stones **3**
U.S. Army Schofield Barracks **4**

HOTELS

Aulani, a Disney Resort & Spa, Ko Olina Hawai'i **7**

RESTAURANTS

Kahumana Café **9**
Monkeypod Kitchen **8**

Surfboards in Hale'iwa.

offers a rest stop, with pineapples, pineapple history, pineapple trinkets, and pineapple juice. This agricultural exhibit/retail area features a maze that kids will love to wander through; it's open daily from 9:30am to 5pm ($6 adults, $4 children 4–12).

"Kam" Highway, as everyone calls it, will be your road for most of the rest of the trip to Hale'iwa, on the North Shore.

CENTRAL O'AHU ATTRACTIONS

On the central plains of O'ahu, tract homes and malls with factory-outlet stores are now spreading across abandoned sugarcane fields. Hawaiian chiefs once sent commoners into thick sandalwood forests to cut down trees, which were then sold to China traders for small fortunes.

Kukaniloko Birthing Stones ★ HISTORIC SITE This is the most sacred site in central O'ahu. Two rows of 18 lava rocks once flanked a central birthing stone, where women of ancient Hawai'i gave birth to potential *ali'i* (royalty). The rocks, according to Hawaiian belief, held the power to ease the labor pains of childbirth. Birth rituals involved 48 chiefs who pounded drums to announce the arrival of newborns likely to become chiefs. Used by O'ahu's *ali'i* for generations of births, the *pōhaku* (rocks), many in bowl-like shapes, now lie strewn in a grove of trees that stands in a pineapple field here. Some think the site may also have served ancient astronomers—like a Hawaiian Stonehenge. Petroglyphs of human forms and circles appear on some stones.

Off Kamehameha Hwy., btw. Wahiawā and Hale'iwa, on Plantation Rd., opposite the road to Whitmore Village.

SURF CITY: Hale'iwa

Only 28 miles from Waikīkī is Hale'iwa ★★, the funky former sugar-plantation town that's now the world capital of big-wave surfing. Hale'iwa really comes alive in winter, when the waves rise; then, it seems, every surfer in the world is here to see and be seen.

Officially designated a historic cultural and scenic district, this beach town was founded by sugar baron Benjamin Dillingham, who built a 30-mile railroad to link his Honolulu and North Shore plantations in 1899. He opened a Victorian hotel overlooking Kaiaka Bay and named it Hale'iwa, or "house of the 'iwa," the tropical seabird often seen here. The hotel and railroad are gone, but the town of Hale'iwa, which was rediscovered in the late 1960s by hippies, manages to hold onto some of its rustic charm. Of course, like other places on O'ahu, that is changing; some of the older wooden storefronts are being redeveloped and local chains such as T&C Surf are moving in. Arts and crafts, boutiques, and burger joints line both sides of the town. There's also a busy fishing harbor full of charter boats and captains who hunt the Kaua'i Channel daily for tuna, mahimahi, and marlin. With a great harbor and sunset view, **Hale'iwa Joe's,** 66-011 Kamehameha Hwy. (http://haleiwajoes.com; ✆ **808/637-8005**), serves fresh local seafood and fun tropical drinks.

Once in Hale'iwa, the hot and thirsty traveler should report directly to **Matsumoto Shave Ice ★★**, 66-087 Kamehameha Hwy. (✆ **808/637-4827**). For 65 years, the Matsumoto family has served a popular rendition of the Hawai'i-style snow cone flavored with tropical tastes.

Just down the road are the fabled shrines of surfing—**Waimea Beach, Banzai Pipeline, Sunset Beach**—where some of the world's largest waves, reaching 20 feet and higher, rise up between November and January. November to December is the holding period for **Vans Triple Crown of Surfing** (http://vanstriplecrownofsurfing.com), one of the world's premier surf competition series, when professional surfers from around the world descend on the 7-mile miracle of waves. Hang around Hale'iwa and the North Shore and you're bound to run into a few of the pros and perhaps even get invited to the surf houses for a party. Battle the traffic to come up on competition days (it seems like everyone ditches work and heads north on these days): It's one of O'ahu's best shows. For details on North Shore beaches, see p. 108.

NORTH SHORE ATTRACTIONS

Pu'u o Mahuka Heiau ★ HISTORIC SITE Go around sundown to feel the *mana* (sacred spirit) of this Hawaiian place. The largest sacrificial temple on O'ahu, it's associated with the great Kaopulupulu, who sought peace between O'ahu and Kaua'i. This prescient *kahuna* predicted that the island would be overrun by strangers from a distant land. In 1794, three of Capt. George Vancouver's men of the *Daedalus* were sacrificed here. In 1819, the year before New England missionaries landed in Hawai'i, King Kamehameha II ordered all idols here to be destroyed.

A national historic landmark, this 18th-century *heiau*, known as the "hill of escape," sits on a 300-foot bluff overlooking Waimea Bay and 25

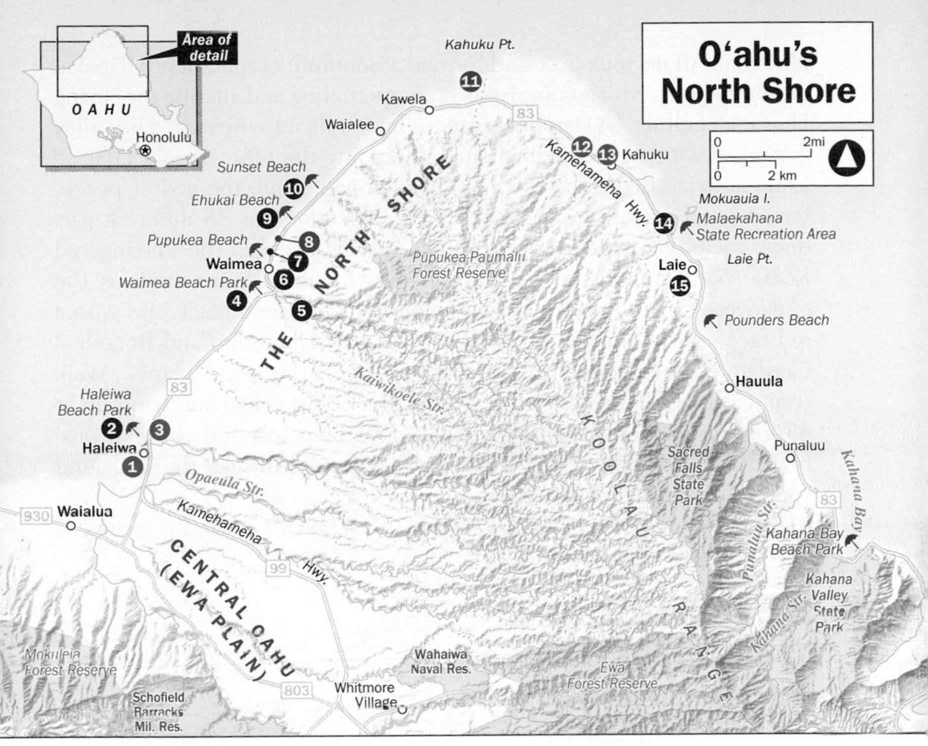

ATTRACTIONS

Banzai Pipeline ('Ehukai Beach Park) **9**
Hale'iwa Beach Park **2**
Mālaekahana Bay State Recreation Area **14**
Polynesian Cultural Center **15**
Pu'u o Mahuka Heiau **6**
Shark's Cove, Pūpūkea Beach Park **7**
Sunset Beach **10**
Waimea Beach Park **4**
Waimea Valley **5**

HOTELS

Ke Iki Beach Bungalows **8**
Turtle Bay Resort **11**

RESTAURANTS

Beet Box Café **1**
Hale'iwa Joe's **3**
Kahuku Farms **12**
Matsumoto Shave Ice **1**
Opal Thai **1**
Shrimp trucks **13**

miles of O'ahu's wave-lashed north coast—all the way to Ka'ena Point, where the Wai'anae Range ends in a spirit leap to the other world. The *heiau* appears as a huge rectangle of rocks twice as big as a football field, with an altar often covered by the flower and fruit offerings left by native Hawaiians.

1 mile past Waimea Bay. Take Pūpūkea Rd. *mauka* (inland) off Kamehameha Hwy. at Foodland, and drive 1 mile up a switchback road. Bus: 52, then walk up Pūpūkea Rd.

Waimea Valley ★ NATURAL ATTRACTION For nearly 3 decades, this 1,875-acre park has lured visitors with activities from cliff diving and hula performances to kayaking and ATV tours. In 2008, the Office of

Hawaiian Affairs took over and formed a nonprofit corporation, Hi'ipaka, to run the park, with an emphasis on perpetuating and sharing the "living Hawaiian culture." A visit here offers a lush walk into the past. The valley is packed with archaeological sites, including the 600-year-old Hale O Lono, a heiau dedicated to the Hawaiian god Lono, the god of peace, fertility, and agriculture. The botanical collection has 35 different gardens, including super-rare Hawaiian species such as the endangered *Kokia cookei* hibiscus. The valley is also home to fauna such as the endangered 'alae 'ula, or Hawaiian moorhen; look for a black bird with a red face cruising in the ponds. The 150-acre Arboretum and Botanical Garden contains more than 5,000 species of tropical plants. Walk through the gardens (take the paved paths or dirt trails) and wind up at 45-foot-high Waimea Falls—bring your bathing suit and you can dive into the cold, murky water. The public is invited to hike the trails and spend a day in this quiet oasis.

59-864 Kamehameha Hwy. © **808/638-7766.** Admission $16 adults, $12 seniors, $8 children 4–12. Daily 9am–5pm. Bus: 52.

BEACHES

The Waikīkī Coast

ALA MOANA BEACH PARK ★★

Gold-sand Ala Moana (meaning "path to the sea," in Hawaiian) stretches for more than a mile along Honolulu's coast between downtown and Waikīkī. This 76-acre midtown beach park, with spreading lawns shaded by banyans and palms, is one of the island's most popular playgrounds. It has a man-made beach, created in the 1930s by filling a coral reef with Wai'anae Coast sand, as well as its own lagoon, yacht harbor, tennis courts, music pavilion, bathhouses, picnic tables, and enough wide-open green spaces to accommodate 4 million visitors a year. The water is calm almost year-round, protected by black-lava rocks set offshore. There's a large parking lot as well as metered street parking.

WAIKĪKĪ BEACH ★★

No beach anywhere is so widely known or so universally sought after as this narrow, 1½-mile-long crescent of imported sand (from Moloka'i) at the foot of a string of high-rise hotels. Waikīkī attracts nearly 5 million visitors a year from every corner of the planet. First-timers are amazed to discover how small Waikīkī Beach really is, but there's always a place for them under the tropical sun here.

Waikīkī is actually a string of beaches that extends between **Sans Souci State Recreational Area,** near Diamond Head to the east, and **Duke Kahanamoku Beach,** in front of the Hilton Hawaiian Village to the west.

Beaches & Outdoor Activities on O'ahu

BEACHES
Ala Moana Beach Park **1**
Banzai Pipeline **26**
Hanauma Bay **6**
Kailua Beach **15**
Kualoa Regional Park **20**
Lanikai Beach **13**
Mākaha Beach Park **30**
Makapu'u Beach Park **11**
Sandy Beach **9**
Sunset Beach **25**
Waikīkī Beach **2**
Waimānalo Beach **12**
Waimea Beach Park **27**
Yokohama Bay **29**

CABINS & CAMPGROUNDS
Ho'omaluhia Botanical Garden **19**
Kahana Bay Beach Park **21**
Mālaekahana Bay State Recreation Area **22**

GOLF COURSES
Ala Wai Municipal Golf Course **3**
Hawai'i Kai Golf Course **8**
Kahuku Golf Course **23**
Ko Olina Golf Club **31**
Olomana Golf Links **14**
Pearl Country Club **18**
Turtle Bay Resort **24**
West Loch Municipal Golf Course **32**

HIKES
Diamond Head Crater **4**
Ka'ena Point **28**
Koko Crater Railway Trail **7**
Kuli'cu'ou Ridge Trail **5**
Makapu'u Lighthouse Trail **10**
Mānoa Falls Trail **16**
Pali (Maunawili) Trail **17**

Waikīkī Beach.

Waikīkī is fabulous for swimming, board surfing, bodysurfing, outrigger canoeing, diving, sailing, snorkeling, and pole fishing. Every imaginable type of watersports equipment is available for rent here. Facilities include showers, lifeguards, restrooms, grills, picnic tables, and pavilions at the **Queen's Surf** end of the beach (at Kapi'olani Park, btw. the zoo and the aquarium). The best place to park is at Kapi'olani Park, near Sans Souci.

East O'ahu

HANAUMA BAY ★★

O'ahu's most popular snorkeling spot is this volcanic crater with a broken sea wall; its small, curved, 2,000-foot gold-sand beach is packed elbow-to-elbow with people year-round. The bay's shallow shoreline water and abundant marine life are the main attractions, but this good-looking beach is also popular for sunbathing and people-watching. Serious divers shoot "the slot" (a passage through the reef) to get to Witch's Brew, a turbulent cove, and then brave strong currents in 70-foot depths at the bay mouth to see coral gardens, turtles, and even sharks. (***Divers:*** Beware of the Moloka'i Express, a strong current.) You can snorkel in the safe, shallow (10-ft.) inner bay, which, along with the beach, is almost always crowded. Because Hanauma Bay is a conservation district, you cannot touch or remove any marine life here. Feeding the fish is also prohibited.

Facilities include parking, restrooms, a pavilion, a grass volleyball court, lifeguards, barbecues, picnic tables, and food concessions.

Alcohol is prohibited in the park; there is no smoking past the visitor center. Expect to pay $1 per vehicle to park plus an entrance fee of $7.50 per person (free for children 12 and under and Hawai'i residents).

If you're driving, take Kalaniana'ole Highway to Koko Head Regional Park. Avoid the crowds by going early, about 7am, on a weekday morning; once the parking lot's full, you're out of luck. Alternatively, take TheBus to escape the parking problem: The Hanauma Bay Shuttle runs from Waikīkī to Hanauma Bay every half-hour from 8:45am to 1pm; you can catch it at the Ala Moana Hotel, the Ilikai Hotel, or other city bus stops. It returns every hour from noon to 4pm. For information, call © **808/396-4229.** Hanauma Bay is closed every Tuesday so that the fish can have a day off, but it's open all other days from 6am to 7pm in the summer and 6am to 6pm in the winter.

SANDY BEACH ★

Sandy Beach is one of the best bodysurfing beaches on O'ahu; it's also one of the most dangerous. It's better to just stand and watch the daredevils literally risk their necks at this 1,200-foot-long gold-sand beach, which is pounded by wild waves and haunted by a dangerous shore break and strong backwash. Weak swimmers and children should definitely stay out of the water here. Lifeguards post flags to alert beachgoers to the day's surf: Green means safe, yellow means caution, and red indicates very dangerous water conditions.

Facilities include restrooms and parking. Go weekdays to avoid the crowds or weekends to catch the bodysurfers in action. From Waikīkī, drive east on the H-1, which becomes Kalaniana'ole Highway; proceed past Hawai'i Kai, up the hill to Hanauma Bay, past the Halona Blowhole, and along the coast. The next big gold beach on the right is Sandy Beach. TheBus no. 22 will also bring you here.

MAKAPU'U BEACH PARK ★

Makapu'u Beach is a beautiful 1,000-foot-long gold-sand beach cupped in the stark black Ko'olau cliffs on O'ahu's easternmost point. Even if you never venture into the water, it's worth a visit just to enjoy the great natural beauty of this classic Hawaiian beach. (You've probably already seen it in countless TV shows, from *Hawaii Five-O* to *Magnum, P.I.*) In summer, the ocean here is as gentle as a Jacuzzi, and swimming and diving are perfect; come winter, however, and Makapu'u is a hit with expert bodysurfers, who come for the big, pounding waves that are too dangerous for most regular swimmers.

Facilities include restrooms, lifeguards, barbecue grills, picnic tables, and parking. To get here, follow Kalaniana'ole Highway toward Waimānalo, or take TheBus no. 22 or 23.

The Windward Coast

LANIKAI BEACH ★★★

One of Hawai'i's best spots for swimming, gold-sand Lanikai's crystal-clear lagoon is like a giant saltwater swimming pool that you're lucky enough to be able to share with the resident tropical fish and sea turtles. Almost too gorgeous to be real, this is one of Hawai'i's postcard-perfect beaches: It's a mile long and thin in places, but the sand's as soft as talcum powder. Kayakers often paddle out to the two tiny offshore Mokulua islands, which are seabird sanctuaries. Unfortunately, the secret's out about Lanikai, and the small beach is starting to feel more crowded every year; get here early to try to grab a space on the sand. Another reason to come in the morning: The Ko'olau Range tends to block the afternoon sun. Or for a rare, magical moment, come to watch the full moon rise over the water.

There are no facilities here, just off-street parking. From Waikīkī, take the H-1 to the Pali Highway (Hwy. 61) through the Nu'unau Pali Tunnel to Kailua, where the Pali Highway becomes Kailua Road as it proceeds through town. At Kalāheo Avenue, turn right and follow the coast about 2 miles to Kailua Beach Park; just past it, turn left at the T intersection and drive uphill on A'alapapa Drive, a one-way street that loops back as Mokulua Drive. Park on Mokulua Drive and walk down any of the eight public-access lanes to the shore. Or take TheBus no. 57A or 57 (Kailua), and then transfer to the no. 70 bus.

KAILUA BEACH ★★★

Windward O'ahu's premier beach is a wide, 2-mile-long golden strand with dunes, palm trees, panoramic views, and offshore islets that are home to seabirds. The swimming is excellent, and the azure waters are usually decorated with bright sails; this is O'ahu's premier windsurfing beach as well. It's a favorite spot to sail catamarans, bodysurf the gentle waves, or paddle a kayak. Water conditions are quite safe, especially at the mouth of Ka'elepulu Stream, where toddlers play in the freshwater shallows at the middle of the beach park. The water is usually about 78°F (26°C), the views are spectacular, and the setting, at the foot of the sheer green Ko'olau Range, is idyllic. It's gotten so crowded over the years that the city council banned all commercial activity on the beach, which has led to a decrease in kayak traffic jams both on the beach and in the water. These days you can usually find a less-occupied stretch of sand the farther you are from the beach park.

Facilities at the beach park include picnic tables, barbecues, restrooms, a volleyball court, a public boat ramp, and free parking. To get here, take Pali Highway (Hwy. 61) to Kailua, drive through town, turn right on Kalaheo Avenue, and go a mile until you see the beach on your left. Or take TheBus no. 57A or 57 into Kailua.

Kailua Beach.

WAIMĀNALO BEACH ★★

At almost 6 miles long, this is O'ahu's longest beach and a favorite among locals. Depending on the swell, the water can be a little rougher than at Kailua, making it fun for bodysurfing and boogie boarding. The wide, sandy beach is backed by ironwood trees, which provide shade if you tire of the sun. On weekdays, it will feel like you have the whole place to yourself; on weekends, locals bring out the grills, tents, and fishing poles. ***Note:*** Make sure your valuables are hidden in your car; break-ins have occurred in the parking lot.

Facilities include restrooms, picnic tables, outdoor showers, and parking. Waimānalo Beach has a different few points of entry to—my pick would be the Waimānalo Bay Recreation Area. To get there, follow Kalaniana'ole Highway toward Waimānalo and turn right at the Waimā nalo Bay sign, or take TheBus no. 57.

KUALOA REGIONAL PARK ★

This 150-acre coco-palm-fringed peninsula is located on Kāne'ohe Bay's north shore at the foot of the spiky Ko'olau Ridge. The park has a broad, grassy lawn and a long, narrow, white-sand beach ideal for swimming, walking, beachcombing, kite-flying, or just enjoying the natural beauty of this once-sacred Hawaiian shore, listed on the National Register of Historic Places. The waters are shallow and safe for swimming year-round. Offshore is Mokoli'i, the picturesque islet otherwise known as Chinaman's Hat. You can swim or wade out to the island (during low tide only) or kayak. A small sandy beach can be found on the backside, and it takes less than half an hour to reach the top of this tiny island.

Facilities at both sites include restrooms, outdoor showers, picnic tables, and drinking fountains. To get to the park, take the Likelike Highway (Hwy. 63); after the Wilson Tunnel, get in the right lane and turn off on Kahakili Highway (Hwy. 83). Or take TheBus no. 55.

The North Shore

WAIMEA BEACH PARK ★★★

This deep, sandy bowl has gentle summer waves that are excellent for swimming, snorkeling, and bodysurfing. To one side of the bay is a huge rock that local kids like to climb and dive from. In this placid scene, the only clues of what's to come in winter are those evacuation whistles on poles beside the road. But what a difference a season makes: Winter waves pound the narrow bay, sometimes rising to 50 feet high. When the surf's really up, very strong currents and shore breaks sweep the bay—and it seems like everyone on O'ahu drives out to Waimea to get a look at the monster waves and those who ride them. Weekends are great for watching the surfers; to avoid the crowds, go on weekdays.

Facilities include lifeguards, restrooms, showers, parking, and nearby restaurants and shops in Hale'iwa town. The beach is located on Kamehameha Highway (Hwy. 83); from Waikīkī, take TheBus no. 52.

Leeward O'ahu: The Wai'anae Coast

MĀKAHA BEACH PARK ★★★

When the surf's up here, it's spectacular: Monstrous waves pound the beach. Nearly a mile long, this half-moon, gold-sand beach is tucked between 231-foot Lahilahi Point, which locals call Black Rock, and Kepuhi Point, a toe of the Wai'anae mountain range. Summer is the best time to hit this beach—the waves are small, the sand abundant, and the water safe for swimming. Children hug the shore on the north side of the beach, near the lifeguard stand, while divers seek an offshore channel full of big fish.

Facilities include restrooms, lifeguards, and parking. To get here, take the H-1 freeway to the end of the line, where it becomes Farrington Highway (Hwy. 93), and follow it to the beach; or take TheBus no. C.

YOKOHAMA BAY ★★★

Where Farrington Highway (Hwy. 93) ends, the wilderness of **Ka'ena Point State Park** begins. It's a remote 853-acre coastline park of empty beaches, sand dunes, cliffs, and deep-blue water. This is the last sandy stretch of shore on the northwest coast of O'ahu. Sometimes it's known as Keawa'ula Beach, but everybody here calls it Yokohama, after the Japanese immigrants who came from that port city to work the cane fields and fished along this shoreline. When the surf's calm—mainly in summer—this is a good area for snorkeling, diving, swimming, shore fishing, and picnicking. There are no lifeguards or facilities, except at the park entrance, where there's a restroom and lifeguard stand. There's no bus service either.

WATERSPORTS

Boating

One of the best things about Hawai'i? The ocean. There are a million ways to enjoy it, but to get far from the shore and see the incredible beauty of the sea, hop on a boat.

Captain Bob's Picnic Sail ★ See the majestic Windward Coast the way it should be seen—from a boat. Captain Bob will take you on a 4-hour lazy-day sail of Kāne'ohe Bay aboard his 42-foot catamaran, which skims across the almost always calm water above the shallow coral reef, lands at the disappearing sandbar Ahu o Laka, and takes you past two small islands to snorkel spots full of tropical fish and sometimes turtles. The color of the water alone is worth the price. This is an all-day affair: A shuttle will pick you up at your Waikīkī hotel between 9 and 9:30am and bring you back at about 4pm.

Kāne'ohe Bay. www.captainbobspicnicsail.com. ✆ **808/942-5077.** All-day cruise $99 adults, $85 children 3–12. Rates include all-you-can-eat barbecue lunch and transportation from Waikīkī hotels. No cruises on Sun and holidays. Bus: 55.

Holokai Catamaran ★★ One of the most fun and effortless ways to get in the water is a sail off of Waikīkī. Many catamarans launch from Waikīkī, but this is our favorite of the "booze cruises." It's the least crowded and rowdy, and the drink selection is the best, with multiple Maui Brewing Co. brews and a decent island cocktail. The **Sunset Sail** is the most popular and festive, with an open bar, while the **Tradewind Sail,** which pushes off in the afternoon, is more mellow. The most romantic? The **Fireworks Sail,** which seemingly takes you right under the weekly Friday-night fireworks show.

Gray's Beach in front of the Halekulani. www.waikikibeachsailing.com. ✆ **808/922-2210.** All cruises 1½ hr. Tradewind Sail $35 adults, $25 children. Fireworks Sail $50 adults and children. Sunset Sail $55 adults; $45 children. Bus: 19 or 20.

Wild Side Tours ★★ Picture this: You're floating in the calm waters off the Wai'anae coast, where your 42-foot sailing catamaran has just dropped you off. Below, in the reef, are turtles, and suddenly in the distance, you see spinner dolphins. This happens almost every day on the 4-hour tours operated by the Cullins family, who have swum in these waters for decades. In winter, you may spot humpback whales on the morning cruise, which includes lunch, snorkel gear, instruction, and a flotation device. The other thing that sets this company apart is its small group sizes, limited to six on the **Best of the West** tour, and 10 on the **Deluxe Wildlife Charter.** The tours last from 8am to noon; check in at 7:30am.

Wai'anae Boat Harbor, 85-471 Farrington Hwy., Wai'anae. www.sailhawaii.com. ✆ **808/306-7273.** Best of the West $195 for age 12 and up (not recommended for younger children). Deluxe Wildlife Charter $175 adults; $145 children. Bus: C.

Snorkeling the Hawaiian waters.

Body Boarding (Boogie Boarding) & Bodysurfing

Good places to learn to body board are in the small waves of **Waikīkī Beach ★★★**, **Kailua Beach ★★★**, **Waimānalo Beach ★★** (reviewed under "Beaches," earlier in this chapter), and **Bellows Field Beach Park,** off Kalaniana'ole Highway (Hwy. 72) in Waimānalo, which is open to the public on weekends (from noon Fri to midnight Sun and holidays). To get here, turn toward the ocean on Hughs Road, and then right on Tinker Road, which takes you to the park.

See the introduction to this section for a list of rental shops where you can get a boogie board.

Ocean Kayaking/Stand-Up Paddling

For a wonderful adventure, rent a kayak or a stand-up paddleboard (SUP), arrive at Lanikai Beach just as the sun is appearing, and paddle across the emerald lagoon to the pyramid-shaped islands called Mokulua, or the Mokes, as locals call them—it's an experience you won't forget. On the windward side, check out **Kailua Sailboards & Kayaks,** 130 Kailua Rd., a block from Kailua Beach Park (www.kailuasailboards.com; ✆ **808/262-2555**), where single kayaks rent for $59 for a half-day and double kayaks rent for $69 for a half-day. SUP boards rent for $59 for a half-day. Note that paddling to the Mokulua Islands is not allowed on Sundays.

If you're staying on the North Shore, go to **Surf-N-Sea,** 62-595 Kamehameha Hwy., Hale'iwa (www.surfnsea.com; ✆ **800/899-7873**), where kayak rentals start at $10 per hour and go to $60 for a full day. During the summer months, you can start in Hale'iwa and kayak to Waimea Bay. SUP rentals start at $20 per hour and go to $60 for a full day. You can paddle in the bay behind the shop or in Anahula Stream, passing under the iconic Rainbow Bridge.

Scuba Diving

O'ahu is a wonderful place to scuba dive, especially for those interested in wreck diving. One of the more famous wrecks in Hawai'i is the ***Mahi,*** a 185-foot former minesweeper easily accessible just south of Wai'anae. Abundant marine life makes this a great place to shoot photos—schools of lemon butterfly fish and taape (blue-lined snapper) are so comfortable with divers and photographers that they practically pose. Eagle rays, green sea turtles, manta rays, and white-tipped sharks occasionally cruise by as well, and eels peer out from the wreck.

For non-wreck diving, one of the best dive spots in summer is **Kahuna Canyon.** In Hawaiian, *kahuna* means priest, wise man, or sorcerer; this massive amphitheater, located near Mokuleia, is a perfect example of something a sorcerer might conjure up. Walls rising from the ocean floor create the illusion of an underwater Grand Canyon. Inside the amphitheater, crabs, octopuses, slippers, and spiny lobsters abound (be aware that taking them in summer is illegal), and giant trevally, parrotfish, and unicorn fish congregate as well. Outside the amphitheater, you're likely to see an occasional shark in the distance.

Because O'ahu's greatest dives are offshore, your best bet is to book a two-tank dive from a dive boat. Hawai'i's oldest outfitter, **Aaron's Dive Shop,** 307 Hahani St., Kailua (www.aaronsdiveshop.com; © **808/262-2333**), offers dives for both first-time and certified divers. The two-tank boat dives start at $130 per person, and transportation from the Kailua shop is provided. (The boat leaves from the Hawai'i Kai Harbor.)

Snorkeling

Some of the best snorkeling in O'ahu is at **Hanauma Bay ★★**. It's crowded—sometimes it seems there are more people than fish—but Hanauma has clear, warm, protected waters and an abundance of friendly reef fish, including Moorish idols, scores of butterfly fish, damselfish, and wrasses. Hanauma Bay has two reefs, an inner and an outer—the first for novices, the other for experts. The inner reef is calm and shallow (less than 10 ft.); in some places, you can just wade and put your face in the water. Go early: It's packed by 10am. And it's closed on Tuesdays. For details, see "Beaches," earlier in this chapter.

On the North Shore, head to **Shark's Cove ★★**, just off Kamehameha Highway, between Hale'iwa and Pupukea. In the summer, this big, lava-edged pool is one of O'ahu's best snorkel spots. Waves splash over the natural lava grotto and cascade like waterfalls into the pool full of

EXPERIENCING jaws: SWIM WITH THE SHARKS

Ocean Ramsey and her crew at **One Ocean Diving ★★★** (www.oneoceandiving.com) are on a first-name basis with some of the sharks they swim with. That's right, *swim with,* cage free. And you can, too, with little more than a snorkel, mask, and fins on your feet (this is a snorkeling trip, not scuba diving). As you ride the boat out, about 3 miles offshore from Hale'iwa, where sharks are known to congregate, the crew educates you about shark behavior. For one, they're really not that interested in humans. Two, most of the sharks you'll see are sandbar and Galapagos sharks, which are not considered dangerous. And three, if you should see a potentially more threatening shark, such as a tiger shark, they teach you how to conjure your alpha shark: Stay at the top of ocean, and don't turn your back on them. Your guides are always alert and nearby; only three people are allowed in the water at a time. Once I got used to the sight of the sharks around me, I began to admire their beauty and grace. One Ocean Diving hopes to change misconceptions about sharks and bring awareness to their plight as their numbers dwindle. A dive with them is as educational as it is exciting. Rates are $150 a person, and a snorkel mask and fins are provided; must be 4 feet or taller to enter the water.

tropical fish. To the right of the cove are deep-sea caves and underwater tunnels to explore.

If you want to rent snorkel equipment, check out **Snorkel Bob's** on the way to Hanauma Bay at 700 Kapahulu Ave. (at Date St.), Honolulu (www.snorkelbob.com; ✆ **808/735-7944**).

Sport Fishing

Kewalo Basin, located between the Honolulu International Airport and Waikīkī, is the main location for charter fishing boats on O'ahu. From Waikīkī, take Kalākaua Avenue Ewa (west) beyond Ala Moana Center; Kewalo Basin is on the left, across from Ward Centers. Look for charter boats all in a row in their slips; when the fish are biting, the captains display the catch of the day in the afternoon. You can also take TheBus no. 19 or 20 (Airport).

The best sport-fishing booking desk in the state is **Sportfish Hawaii ★** (www.sportfishhawaii.com; ✆ **877/388-1376** or 808/396-2607), which books boats on all the islands. These fishing vessels have been inspected and must meet rigorous criteria to guarantee that you will have a great time. Prices range from $875 to $1,399 for a full-day exclusive charter (you, plus five friends, get the entire boat to yourself), from $650 for a half-day exclusive, or from $220 for a full-day shared charter (you share the boat with five other people).

Surfing

In summer, when the water's warm and there's a soft breeze in the air, the south swell comes up. It's surf season in Waikīkī, the best place on O'ahu to learn how to surf. For lessons, go early to **Aloha Beach Services,** next to the Moana Surfrider, 2365 Kalākaua Ave., Waikīkī (✆ **808/922-3111**). The beach boys offer group lessons for $50 an hour in the water; board rentals are $20 per hour (everything is cash only). You must know how to swim.

Hans Hedemann, a champion surfer for some 34 years, has opened the **Hans Hedemann Surf School** (www.hhsurf.com; ✆ **808/924-7778**) in Waikīkī at the Park Shore Waikīkī and Turtle Bay Resort. Hedemann himself gives private lessons—at $400 for a three-hour session. (He has taught celebrities such as Cameron Diaz and Adam Sandler.) If the expenditure is beyond your budget, go for a $75 2-hour group lesson (maximum four people).

Surfboards are also available for rent on the North Shore at **Surf-N-Sea,** 62-595 Kamehameha Hwy., Hale'iwa (www.surfnsea.com; ✆ **800/899-7873**), for $5 to $7 an hour. Lessons go for $85 for 2 to 3 hours. For the best surf shops, where you can soak in the culture as well as pick up gear, see "O'ahu Shopping" (p. 158).

More experienced surfers should drop in on any surf shop around O'ahu, or call the **Surf News Network Surfline** (✆ **808/596-SURF**) to get the latest surf conditions. The breaks at the base of Diamond Head are popular among intermediate to expert surfers.

If you're in Hawai'i in winter and want to see the serious surfers catch the really big waves, bring your binoculars and grab a front-row seat on the beach at **Waimea Bay, Sunset Beach,** or **Pipeline.**

NATURE HIKES

People are often surprised to discover that the great outdoors is often minutes from downtown Honolulu. The island's major hiking trails traverse razor-thin ridgebacks, deep waterfall valleys, and more. The best source of hiking information on O'ahu is the state's **Nā Ala Hele (Trails to Go On) Program** (www.hawaiitrails.org; ✆ **808/973-9782**). The website has everything you need: detailed maps and descriptions of 40 trails in the Nā Ala Hele program, a hiking safety brochure, updates on the trails, hyperlinks to weather information, health warnings, info on native plants, how to volunteer for trail upkeep, and more.

The **Hawaiian Trail & Mountain Club** (www.htmclub.org) offers regular hikes on O'ahu. Bring a couple of bucks for the donation, your own lunch, and drinking water, and meet up with the club members at the scheduled location to join them on a hike. In addition, the club meets for Saturday and Sunday hikes at the 'Iolani Palace at King Street between Richard and Punchbowl streets in downtown Honolulu. Generally, club members meet at 8am; look for a group of people dressed in hiking clothes and boots at the left rear of the palace.

Honolulu-Area Hikes

DIAMOND HEAD CRATER ★★★

This is a moderate but steep walk to the summit of Hawai'i's most famous landmark. Kids love to look out from the top of the 760-foot volcanic cone, where they have 360-degree views of O'ahu up the leeward coast from Waikīkī. The 1.5-mile round-trip takes about 1½ hours, and the entry fee is $5 per car load; if you walk in, it's $1 per person.

Diamond Head was created by a volcanic explosion about half a million years ago. The Hawaiians called the crater Lē'ahi (meaning "the brow of the 'ahi," or tuna, referring to the shape of the crater). Diamond Head was considered a sacred spot; King Kamehameha offered human sacrifices at a *heiau* (temple) on the western slope. It wasn't until the 19th century that Mount Lē'ahi got its current name: A group of sailors found what they thought were diamonds in the crater; it turned out they were just worthless calcite crystals, but the name stuck.

Before you begin your journey to the top of the crater, put on some decent shoes (rubber-soled tennies are fine) and don't forget water (very important), a hat to protect you from the sun, and a camera. You might want to put all your gear in a pack to leave your hands free for the climb.

Go early, preferably just after the 6am opening, before the midday sun starts beating down. The hike to the summit starts at Monsarrat and 18th avenues on the crater's inland (or *mauka*) side. To get here, take TheBus no. 58 from the Ala Moana Center or drive to the intersection of Diamond Head Road and 18th Avenue. Follow the road through the tunnel (which is closed 6pm–6am) and park in the lot. From the trail head in the parking lot, you'll proceed along a paved walkway (with handrails) as you climb up the slope. You'll pass old World War I and World War II pillboxes, gun emplacements, and tunnels built as part of the Pacific

Hiking O'ahu.

defense network. Several steps take you up to the top observation post on Point Lē'ahi. The views are incredible.

MĀNOA FALLS TRAIL ★★

This easy .75-mile (one-way) hike is terrific for families; it takes less than an hour to reach idyllic Mānoa Falls. The trail head, marked by a footbridge, is at the end of Mānoa Road, past Lyon Arboretum. The staff at the arboretum prefers that hikers not park in their lot, so the best place to park is in the residential area below Paradise Park; you can also get to the arboretum via TheBus no. 5. The often-muddy trail follows Waihi Stream and meanders through the forest reserve past guavas, mountain apples, and wild ginger. The forest is moist and humid and inhabited by giant bloodthirsty mosquitoes, so bring repellent. If it has rained recently, stay on the trail and step carefully because it can be very slippery (and it's a long way down if you slide off the side).

East O'ahu Hikes

KOKO CRATER RAILWAY TRAIL ★★

If you're looking for quiet, you'll want to find another trail. This is less a hike than a strenuous workout, and it's popular among fitness buffs who climb it daily, people trying to stick to New Year's resolutions to be more active, and triathletes in training. But first-timers and tourists also tackle the 1,048 stairs along the railway track—once part of a World War II–era tram system—for the panoramic views from the Windward Coast to Waikīkī. It's a tough hike, but you'll have lots of friendly company along the way, and the view from the top is worth it. As they say, no pain, no gain. It's unshaded the whole way, so try to go early in the morning or in the late afternoon to catch the sunset, and bring plenty of water.

To get to the trail head from Waikīkī, take Kalaniana'ole Highway (Hwy. 72) to Hawai'i Kai, turn left at Lunalilo Home Road, and then follow Anapalau Street to the trail head parking lot; you can also take TheBus no. 22 or 23.

KULI'OU'OU RIDGE TRAIL ★★

One of Honolulu's best ridge trails, this moderate 2.5-mile hike (each way) starts in the middle of a residential neighborhood, then ascends through ironwood and pine trees, and drops you in the middle of a native Hawaiian forest. Here, 'ōhi'a lehua, with its distinctive red pom-pom–like flowers grow. Hawaiian legend has it that 'ōhi'a and Lehua were lovers. Pele fell in love with ōhi'a, but when he rejected her advances, she turned him into a tree. The gods took pity on the heartbroken Lehua and turned her into a flower on the tree. According to the story, if you pick a flower from the 'ōhi'a lehua, it will rain, representing the separated lovers' tears. So avoid picking the flowers, if only to assure clear views at the top of the summit—on a good day, you can see all the way to Waimānalo.

To get there from Waikīkī, take Kalaniana'ole Highway (Hwy. 72) and turn left on Kuli'ou'ou Road. Turn right on Kala'au Place and look for street parking. You'll find the trail head at the end of the road. No bus service is available.

MAKAPU'U LIGHTHOUSE TRAIL ★★

You've seen this famous old lighthouse on episodes of *Magnum, P.I.* and *Hawaii Five-O*. No longer staffed by the Coast Guard (it's fully automated now), the lighthouse sits at the end of a precipitous cliff trail on an airy perch over the Windward Coast, Manana (Rabbit) Island, and the azure Pacific. It's about a 45-minute, 1-mile hike from Kalaniana'ole Highway (Hwy. 72), along a paved road that begins across from Hawai'i Kai Executive Golf Course and winds around the 646-foot-high sea bluff to the lighthouse lookout.

The view of the ocean all the way to Moloka'i and Lāna'i is often so clear that, from November to March, if you're lucky, you'll see migrating humpback whales.

To get to the trail head from Waikīkī, take Kalaniana'ole Highway (Hwy. 72) past Hanauma Bay and Sandy Beach to Makapu'u Head, the southeastern tip of the island; you can also take TheBus no. 22 or 23.

Blowhole alert: When the south swell is running, usually in summer, a couple of blowholes on the south side of Makapu'u Head put the famous Hālona Blowhole to shame.

Windward Coast Hikes

PALI (MAUNAWILI) TRAIL ★

For a million-dollar view of the Windward Coast, take this 11-mile (one-way) foothill trail. The trail head is about 6 miles from downtown Honolulu, on the windward side of the Nu'unau Pali Tunnel, at the scenic lookout just beyond the hairpin turn of the Pali Highway (Hwy. 61). Just as you begin the turn, look for the scenic overlook sign, slow down, and pull off the highway into the parking lot (sorry, no bus service available).

The mostly flat, well-marked, easy-to-moderate trail goes through the forest on the lower slopes of the 3,000-foot Ko'olau mountain range and ends up in the backyard of the coastal Hawaiian village of Waimā nalo. Go halfway to get the view and then return to your car, or have someone meet you in 'Nalo.

To Land's End: A Leeward O'ahu Hike

KA'ENA POINT ★

At the very western tip of O'ahu lie the dry, barren lands of **Ka'ena Point State Park,** 853 acres of jagged sea cliffs, deep gulches, sand dunes, endangered plant life, and a remote, wild, wind- and surf-battered coastline. *Ka'ena* means "red hot" or "glowing" in Hawaiian; the name refers to the brilliant sunsets visible from the point.

Ka'ena is steeped in numerous legends. A popular one concerns the demigod Maui: Maui had a famous hook that he used to raise islands from the sea. He decided that he wanted to bring the islands of O'ahu and Kaua'i closer together, so one day he threw his hook across the Kaua'i Channel and snagged Kaua'i (which is actually visible from Ka'ena Point on clear days). Using all his might, Maui was able to pull loose a huge boulder, which fell into the waters very close to the present lighthouse at Ka'ena. The rock is still called Pōhaku o Kaua'i (the Rock from Kaua'i). Like Black Rock in Kā'anapali on Maui, Ka'ena is thought of as the point on O'ahu from which souls depart.

To hike out to this departing place, take the clearly marked trail from the parking lot of Ka'ena Point State Park. The moderate 5-mile round-trip hike to the point will take a couple of hours. The trail along the cliff passes tide pools abundant in marine life and rugged protrusions of lava reaching out to the turbulent sea; seabirds circle overhead. Do *not* go off the trail; you might step on buried birds' eggs. There are no sandy beaches, and the water is nearly always turbulent here. In winter, when a big north swell is running, the waves at Ka'ena are the biggest in the state, averaging heights of 30 to 40 feet. Even when the water appears calm, offshore currents are powerful, so don't plan on taking a swim. Go early in the morning to see the schools of porpoises that frequent the area just offshore.

To get to the trail head from Honolulu or Waikīkī, take the H-1 west to its end; continue on Hwy. 93 past Mākaha and follow Hwy. 930 to the end of the road. There is no bus service.

OTHER OUTDOOR ACTIVITIES

Biking

O'ahu is not particularly bike-friendly, where drivers still need to learn to share the road. But that may be changing by the time you read this, with the installation of new bike lanes and the launch of a city bikeshare program. This system will include 2,000 bikes scattered over 200 docking stations throughout metro Honolulu. Modeled after other systems in cities such as Paris and New York, it should make short trips, such as from your hotel to the beach, or Waikīkī to Chinatown, a breeze.

For a bike-and-hike adventure, contact **Bike Hawai'i** (www.bikehawaii.com; ✆ **877/682-7433** or 808/734-4214), which has a variety of group tours, such as mountain biking in Kualoa. This guided mountain-bike tour follows dirt roads and a single track meandering through the 1,000-acre Ka'a'awa Valley on O'ahu's northeast shore, with stops at a reconstructed Hawaiian *hale* (house) and *kalo lo'i* (taro terrace) for some cultural narrative, plus an old military bunker that has been converted into a movie museum for films shot here (*Jurassic Park, Godzilla, Mighty Joe Young, Windtalkers,* and more). The 6-mile trip, which takes 2 to 3 hours of riding, includes van transportation from your hotel, a bike, helmet, snacks, picnic lunch, water bottle, and guide; it's $120 for adults and $77 for children 13 and under.

Golf

O'ahu has nearly 3 dozen golf courses, ranging from bare-bones municipal courses to exclusive country-club courses with membership fees running to six figures a year. Below are the best of a great bunch.

As you get to know O'ahu's courses, you'll see that the windward courses play much differently than the leeward courses. On the windward side, the prevailing winds blow from the ocean to shore, and the grain direction of the greens tends to run the same way—from the ocean to the mountains. Leeward golf courses have the opposite tendency: The winds usually blow from the mountains to the ocean, with the grain direction of the greens corresponding.

Tips on beating the crowds and saving money: O'ahu's golf courses tend to be

Tee-Time Discounts

For last-minute and discount tee times, call **Stand-by Golf** (www.hawaiistandbygolf.com; ✆ **888/645-BOOK** [2665]), which offers discounted tee times for same-day or next-day golfing. Call between 7am and 10pm for a guaranteed tee time with up to a 30% discount on greens fees.

crowded, so I suggest that you go midweek, if you can. Also, most island courses have twilight rates that offer substantial discounts if you're willing to tee off in the afternoon; these are included in the listings below, where applicable.

Transportation note: TheBus does not allow golf-club bags onboard, so if you want to use TheBus to get to a course, you're going to have to rent clubs there.

WAIKĪKĪ

Ala Wai Municipal Golf Course Some 500 rounds a day are played on this 18-hole municipal course within walking distance of Waikīkī's hotels. It's something of a challenge to get a tee time at this busy par-70, 6,020-yard course, and the computerized tee reservations system for all of O'ahu's municipal courses will allow you to book only 3 days in advance, but keep trying. Ala Wai has a flat layout bordered by the Ala Wai Canal on one side and the Mānoa-Pālolo Stream on the other. It's less windy than most O'ahu courses, but pay attention to the 372-yard, par-4 1st hole, which demands a straight and long shot to the very tiny green. If you miss, you can make it up on the 478-yard, par-5 10th hole—the green is reachable in two, so with a two-putt, a birdie is within reach.
404 Kapahulu Ave., Waikīkī. www.co.honolulu.hi.us/des/golf/alawai.htm. ✆ **808/733-7387** for golf course, or 808/296-2000 for tee-time reservations. Greens fees $55; twilight rates $28; cart $20. From Waikīkī, turn left on Kapahulu Ave.; the course is on the *mauka* side of Ala Wai Canal. Bus: 19, 20, or 13.

EAST O'AHU

Hawai'i Kai Golf Course This is actually two golf courses in one. The par-72, 6,222-yard **Championship Course** is moderately challenging, with scenic vistas. The course is forgiving to high-handicap golfers, although it does have a few surprises. The par-55 **Executive Course** is fun for beginners and those just getting back in the game after a few years. The course has lots of hills and valleys, with no water hazards and only a few sand traps. Lockers are available.
8902 Kalaniana'ole Hwy., Honolulu. www.hawaiikaigolf.com. ✆ **808/395-2358.** Greens fees: Championship Course $115, twilight rates $70; Executive Course $39 Mon–Fri, $44 Sat–Sun. Take H-1 east past Hawai'i Kai; it's immediately past Sandy Beach on the left. Bus: 22 and 23.

THE WINDWARD COAST

Olomana Golf Links Low-handicap golfers may not find this gorgeous course difficult, but the striking views of the craggy Ko'olau mountain ridge alone are worth the fees. The par-72, 6,326-yard course is popular with locals and visitors alike. The course starts off a bit hilly on the front 9 but flattens out by the back 9, where some tricky water hazards occur. The 1st hole, a 384-yard par-4 that tees downhill and approaches uphill, is definitely a warm-up. The next hole is a 160-yard par-3 that starts from an elevated tee to an elevated green over a severely banked V-shaped gully. Shoot long here—it's longer than you think, and short shots tend to roll all the way back down the fairway to the base of the gully. This course is very, very green; the rain gods bless it regularly with brief passing showers. You can spot the regular players here—they all carry umbrellas, wait patiently for the squalls to pass, and then resume play. Reservations are a must. Facilities include a driving range, practice greens, club rental, a pro shop, and a restaurant.

41-1801 Kalaniana'ole Hwy., Waimānalo. ✆ **808/259-7926.** Greens fees $95; twilight fees $80. Frequent player discounts. Take H-1 to the Pali Hwy. (Hwy. 61); turn right on Kalaniana'ole Hwy.; after 5 miles, it will be on the left. Bus: 23/57.

THE NORTH SHORE

Kahuku Golf Course This 9-hole budget golf course is a bit funky. It has no club rentals, no clubhouse, and no facilities other than a few pull carts that disappear with the first handful of golfers. But a round at this scenic oceanside course amid the tranquility of the North Shore is quite an experience nonetheless. Duffers will love the ease of this recreational course, and weight watchers will be happy to walk the gently sloping greens. Don't forget to bring your camera for the views (especially at holes 3, 4, 7, and 8, which are right on the ocean). No reservations are taken; tee times are first come, first served, and with plenty of retirees happy to sit and wait, the competition is fierce for early tee times. Bring your own clubs and call ahead to check the weather.

56-501 Kamehameha Hwy., Kahuku. ✆ **808/293-5842.** Greens fees $33. Take H-1 west to H-2; follow H-2 through Wahiawā to Kamehameha Hwy. (Hwy. 99, then Hwy. 83); follow it to Kahuku.

Turtle Bay Resort ★ This North Shore resort is home to two of Hawai'i's top golf courses. The 18-hole **Arnold Palmer Course** (formerly the Links at Kuilima) was designed by Arnold Palmer and Ed Seay. Now that the casuarina (ironwood) trees have matured, it's not as windy as it used to be, but this is still a challenging course. The front 9, with rolling terrain, only a few trees, and lots of wind, play like a British Isles course. The back 9 have narrower tree-lined fairways and water. The course circles Punaho'olapa Marsh, a protected wetland for endangered Hawaiian waterfowl.

Another option is the par-71, 6,200-yard **George Fazio Course**—the only Fazio course in Hawai'i. Larry Keil, pro at Turtle Bay, says that people like it because it's a more forgiving course, without all the water hazards and bunkers of the Palmer course. The 6th hole has two greens, so you can play the hole as a par-3 or par-4. The toughest hole has to be the par-3, 176-yard 2nd hole, where you tee off across a lake with a mean crosswind. The most scenic hole is the 7th, where the ocean is on your left; in winter, you might get lucky and see some whales.

Facilities include a pro shop, a driving range, putting and chipping greens, and a snack bar. Weekdays are best for tee times.

Pearl Country Club.

57-049 Kamehameha Hwy., Kahuku. www.turtlebayresort.com. ✆ **808/293-8574.** Greens fees: Palmer Course $185 before noon, $140 noon–2pm, $105 2–4pm, $85 after 4pm; Fazio Course $115 before noon, $95 noon–2pm, $75 after 2pm (after 3pm you can walk the Fazio course for $25!). Take H-1 west past Pearl City; when the freeway splits, take H-2 and follow the signs to Hale'iwa; at Hale'iwa, take Hwy. 83 to Turtle Bay Resort. Bus: 52 or 55.

CENTRAL O'AHU

Pearl Country Club Looking for a challenge? You'll find one at this popular public course, located just above Pearl City in 'Aiea. Sure, the 6,230-yard, par-72 looks harmless enough, and the views of Pearl Harbor and the USS *Arizona* Memorial are gorgeous, but around the 5th hole, you'll start to see what you're in for. That par-5, a blind 472-yard hole, doglegs seriously to the left (with a small margin of error between the tee and the steep out-of-bounds hillside on the entire left side of the fairway). A water hazard and a forest await your next two shots. Suddenly, this nice public course becomes not so nice. O'ahu residents can't get enough of it, so don't even try to get a tee time on weekends. Stick to weekdays—Mondays are usually the best bet. Facilities include a driving range, practice greens, club rental, a pro shop, and a restaurant.

98-535 Kaonohi St., 'Aiea. www.pearlcc.com. ✆ **808/487-3802.** Greens fees $140; after 3:30pm $50. Book at least a week in advance. Take H-1 past Pearl Harbor to Hwy. 78 (Moanalua Fwy.), exit 13A; stay in the left lane where Hwy. 78 becomes Hwy. 99 (Kamehameha Hwy.); turn right on Kaonohi St.; entrance is on the right. Bus: 53 and 54 (stops at Pearlridge Shopping Center at Kaonohi and Moanalua sts.; you'll have to walk about ½-mile uphill from here).

LEEWARD O'AHU

Ko Olina Golf Club ★★★ The Ted Robinson–designed course has rolling fairways and elevated tee and water features. *Golf Digest* once named it one of "America's Top 75 Resort Courses." The signature hole—the 12th, a par-3—has an elevated tee that sits on a rock garden with a cascading waterfall. At the 18th hole, you'll see and hear water all around you—seven pools begin on the right side of the fairway and slope down to a lake. A waterfall is on your left off the elevated green. You'll have no choice but to play the left and approach the green over the water. Book in advance; this course is crowded all the time. Facilities include a driving range, locker rooms, a Jacuzzi, steam rooms, and a restaurant and bar. Lessons are available.

92-1220 Aliinui Dr., Kapolei. www.koolinagolf.com. ✆ **808/676-5300.** Greens fees $199 ($179 for Ihilani Resort guests); twilight rates (after 1pm) $139. Ask about transportation from Waikīkī hotels. Collared shirts requested for men and women. Take H-1 west until it becomes Hwy. 93 (Farrington Hwy.); turn off at the Ko Olina exit; take the exit road (Aliinui Dr.) into Ko Olina Resort; turn left into the clubhouse. No bus service.

West Loch Municipal Golf Course This par-72, 6,615-yard course located just 30 minutes from Waikīkī, in Ewa Beach, offers golfers a challenge at bargain rates. The difficulties on this unusual municipal course, designed by Robin Nelson and Rodney Wright, are water (lots of hazards), constant trade winds, and narrow fairways. To help you out, the course features a "water" driving range (with a lake) to practice your drives. In addition to the driving range, West Loch has practice greens, a pro shop, and a restaurant.

91-1126 Okupe St., Ewa Beach. ✆ **808/675-6076.** Greens fees $55; 9 holes after 1pm $28; cart $20. Book 3 days in advance. Take H-1 west to the Hwy. 76 exit; stay in the left lane and turn left at West Loch Estates, just opposite St. Francis Medical Center. To park, take 2 immediate right turns. Bus: E.

Horseback Riding

You can gallop on the beach at the **Turtle Bay Resort ★★**, 57-091 Kamehameha Hwy., Kahuku (www.turtlebayresort.com; ✆ **808/293-6024;** bus: 52 or 55), where 45-minute rides along sandy beaches with spectacular ocean views and through a forest of ironwood trees cost $80 for age 7 and up (riders must be at least 4 ft., 4 in. tall). Romantic sunset rides are $110 per person. Private rides for up to four people are $130 per person.

ORGANIZED TOURS

Guided Sightseeing Tours

If your time is limited, you might want to consider a guided tour. These tours are informative, can give you a good overview of Honolulu or O'ahu in a limited amount of time, and are surprisingly entertaining.

E Noa Tours, 1141 Waimanu St., Suite 105, Honolulu (www.enoa.com; ✆ **800/824-8804** or 808/591-2561), offers a range of narrated tours, from island loops to explorations of Pearl Harbor, on air-conditioned, 27-passenger minibuses. The Majestic Circle Island Tour ($99 for adults, $80 for children 3–11) stops at Diamond Head Crater, Hanauma Bay, Byodo-In Temple, Sunset Beach, Waimea Valley (admission included), and various beach sites along the way. Other tours go to the Pearl Harbor/USS *Arizona* Memorial and the Polynesian Cultural Center.

Waikīkī Trolley Tours.

Waikīkī Trolley Tours ★, 1141 Waimanu St., Suite 105, Honolulu (www.waikikitrolley.com; © **800/824-8804** or 808/593-2822), offers four tours of sightseeing, entertainment, dining, and shopping. These are a great way to get the lay of the land. You can get on and off the trolley as needed (trolleys come along every 2–20 min.). An all-day pass (8:30am–11:35pm) is $38 for adults, $28 for children 3 to 11; a 4-day pass is $59 for adults, $41 for children. For the same price, you can experience the 2-hour narrated Panoramic Coast Line tour (Blue Line) of the southeast side of O'ahu, an easy way to see the stunning views.

Specialty Tours

Below is a sampling of specialty tours found on O'ahu.

CHOCOLATE FACTORY TOUR

Hawai'i is the only state in the U.S. to grow cacao commercially, and at bean-to-bar maker **Mānoa Chocolate ★★**, 315 Uluniu St., Suite 203 (www.manoachocolate.com; © **808/262-6789**), you can find out more about Hawai'i's burgeoning chocolate scene and see what it takes to turn cacao beans into smooth chocolate bars. You'll taste the beans through every step of the process and be able to compare Hawai'i-grown chocolate with chocolate from around the world. A rare treat.

FARM TOUR

Take a tractor-pulled wagon ride through the tropical fruit groves of **Kahuku Farms ★★**, 56-800 Kamehameha Hwy. (www.kahukufarms.com; © **808/628-0639**). For the smoothie tour, you'll learn about the

bird's-eye VIEW: AIR TOURS

To understand why O'ahu was the island of kings, you need to see it from the air. **Island Seaplane Service ★★★** (www.islandseaplane.com; ✆ **808/836-6273**) operates flights departing from a floating dock in the protected waters of Ke'ehi Lagoon in either a six-passenger de Havilland Beaver or a four-passenger Cessna 206. There's nothing quite like feeling the slap of the waves as the plane skims across the water and then effortlessly lifts into the air.

The half-hour tour ($179) gives you aerial views of Waikīkī Beach, Diamond Head Crater, Kāhala's luxury estates, and the sparkling waters of Hanauma and Kāne'ohe bays; the 1-hour tour ($299) continues on to Chinaman's Hat, the Polynesian Cultural Center, and the rolling surf of the North Shore. The flight returns across the island over Hawai'i's historic wartime sites: **Schofield Barracks** and the Pearl Harbor memorials.

apple banana (short and tart), *liliko'i* (passionfruit), and pineapple, and then taste them all in a smoothie made on the spot at the café. Oh, and definitely don't miss the grilled banana bread topped with made-on-the-farm ice cream and *haupia* (coconut) and caramel sauce.

GHOST TOURS

For a really different look at Honolulu and the island, **O'ahu Ghost Tours ★** (www.oahughosttours.com; ✆ **877/597-7325**) offers a look at the supernatural side of this ancient place. Originally started by Glen Grant, who dedicated his life to exploring stories and sightings of the paranormal, the company has continued his investigations of ghosts, unusual sightings, and the unexplainable. The offerings include **Honolulu City Haunts,** a 2-hour walking tour of places where it's rumored that supernatural events are still happening today ($39 adults, $29 children 11 and under); **Sacred Spirits,** a 5-hour walking tour of the most sacred native Hawaiian spots on O'ahu ($59 adults, $49 children); and the **Orbs of O'ahu** driving tour, which circles the island, stopping at some of the "most haunted" locations ($59 adults, $49 children).

WHERE TO STAY ON O'AHU

Before you go online to book a place to stay, consider when you'll be visiting. The high season, when hotels are full and rates are at their peak, is mid-December to March. The secondary high season, when rates are high but rooms are somewhat easier to come by, is June to September. The low seasons—when you can expect fewer tourists and better deals—are April to June and September to mid-December. (For more on Hawai'i's travel seasons, see "When to Go" on p. 47.) No matter when you travel, you can often get a good rate at many of Waikīkī's hotels by booking a package.

For a description of each neighborhood, see "The Island in Brief" (p. 60). It can help you decide where you'd like to base yourself.

Remember that hotel and room taxes of 13.962% will be added to your bill (O'ahu has a .546% additional tax that the other islands do not have). And don't forget about parking charges—at up to $30 a day in Waikīkī, they can add up quickly.

Note that more and more hotels charge a mandatory daily "resort fee" or "amenity fee," usually somewhere between $25 and $30, which can increase the room rates by 20%. Hotels say these charges cover amenities, some of which you may not need (such as movie rentals, a welcome drink, a color photograph of you on the property—drinking that welcome drink, perhaps?) and some which are awfully handy (such as Internet access and parking). We have listed resort charges next to the room rates in the reviews below.

VACATION RENTALS O'ahu has few true bed-and-breakfast inns. Instead, if you're looking for a non-hotel experience, your best bet is a vacation rental. You can rent direct from owners via **VRBO.com** (Vacation Rentals by Owner) and **airbnb.com**. On these sites, you'll find a range of offerings, from $80-a-night studios to unique, off the beaten path lodgings, like a Portlock cottage near Hanauma Bay on the water (listed on vrbo.com) or a North Shore treehouse (listed on airbnb.com). Make sure to read the reviews before booking so you have a general idea of what you're getting into. Note that for VRBO, unless you purchase VRBO's Vacation Protection Services, most places won't provide a refund if a rental is not what you expected. Airbnb.com gives renters more peace of mind; it withholds payment until check-in so renters can make sure the listing is as advertised. But I've booked places on both sites, basing my picks on reviews, and I've found the hosts friendly and listings accurate.

Waikīkī

EWA WAIKĪKĪ

All the hotels listed below are located between the ocean and Kalākaua Avenue, and between Ala Wai Terrace in the Ewa (western) direction and Olohana Street and Fort DeRussy Park in the Diamond Head (eastern) direction.

Expensive

Hawai'i Prince Hotel Waikīkī ★ These two towers look like they're from *The Jetsons,* especially with the glass-walled elevators zipping up and down the exterior. The rooms are kind of characterless, in shades of beige and gray, but you'll probably spend most of your time looking outward anyway; every room, even on the lower floors, boasts a yacht harbor view. This hotel is on the quiet side of Waikīkī. There's no beach in front, but it's about a 10-minute walk to Ala Moana Beach Park, a more local

Waikīkī Hotels
Ala Wai Park
Ala Wai Golf Course
Ala Wai Canal
Kapiolani Blvd.
McCully St.
Kalakaua Ave.
Ala Wai Blvd.
Hawaii Convention Center
Atkinson Dr.
Ala Moana Center
Hobron Ln.
Ena Rd.
Pau St.
Keoniana St.
Kuamoo St.
Nemahana St.
Olohana St.
Kalaimoku St.
Launiu St.
Kaiolu St.
Lewers St.
Royal Hawaiian Ave.
Seaside Ave.
Nohonani St.
Duke's Ln.
Nahua St.
Walina St.
Kanekapolei St.
Kaiulani Ave.
Cleghorn St.
Pr. Edward St.
Koa Ave.
Liliuokalani Ave.
Kealohilani Ave.
Ohua Ave.
Paoakalani Ave.
Pualani Wy.
Kuhio Ave.
Cartwright Rd.
Lemon Rd.
Kapahulu Ave.
Honolulu Zoo
Monsarrat Ave.
Kapiolani Park
International Market Place
Fort DeRussy
Saratoga Rd.
Beach Walk
Kalia Rd.
Ala Moana Blvd.
Paoa Pl.
U.S. Army Museum
Ala Wai Yacht Harbor
Kahanamoku Lagoon
Fort DeRussy Beach
Gray's Beach
Waikiki Beach
Kuhio Beach Park
Queen's Surf Beach
Ala Moana Beach Park
Mamala Bay
0 1/4 mi
0 1/4 km
1 2 3 4 5 6 7 8 9 10 11 12 13 14 15 16 17 18
Aqua Lotus 17
Aqua Skyline Hotel at Island Colony 6
Aqua Waikīkī Pearl 7
The Breakers 8
Coconut Waikīkī Hotel 5
Halekūlani 10
Hawai'i Prince Hotel Waikīkī 1
Hilton Hawaiian Village 3
Hotel Renew 15
Luana Waikīkī 4
Moana Surfrider 14
The Modern Honolulu 2
New Otani Kaimana Beach Hotel 18
Outrigger Reef on the Beach 9
Park Shore Waikīkī 16
Royal Hawaiian 13
Sheraton Waikīkī 12
Waikīkī Parc 11

and less-busy beach than Waikīkī. The hotel also has two of Honolulu's favorite buffets: the **Prince Court** and **Hakone.** I prefer the latter for its all-you-can-eat sashimi and made-to-order sushi.

100 Holomoana St. (just across Ala Wai Canal Bridge, on the ocean side of Ala Moana Blvd.), Honolulu. www.princeresortshawaii.com/hawaii-prince-hotel-waikiki. ✆ **888/977-4623** or 808/956-1111. 548 units. $215–$399 double; from $409 suite. Extra person $60. Children 17 and under stay free in parent's room using existing bedding. Valet parking $33, self-parking $25. Bus: 19 or 20. **Amenities:** 2 restaurants; outdoor bar; babysitting; concierge; 27-hole golf club a 40-min. drive away in 'Ewa Beach (reached by hotel shuttle); fitness room; outdoor pool; room service; small day spa; Internet ($15 per day).

Hilton Hawaiian Village Beach Resort & Spa ★★ This sprawling resort is like a microcosm of Waikīkī—on good days it feels like a lively little beach town with hidden nooks and crannies to discover and great bars in which to make new friends, and on bad days it's just an endless traffic jam, with lines into the parking garage, at the front desk, and in the restaurants. Need an oasis in the middle of it all? Choose the Ali'i Tower; it has its own lobby lounge, reception, and concierge, and even its own pool and bar; it's like a hotel within a hotel.

But there's something for everyone at the Hilton Hawaiian—I've seen families settling in for a screening of *The Lorax* on the lawn, winter breakers leaving the Tapa Tower (the largest tower) to hit the bars, and well-heeled (literally) tourists returning to the Ali'i Tower with their shopping bags. Room views can range from a straight-on view of the tower in front to oceanfront, so close to the water you can hear waves lapping. Cheaper rooms are in the Kalia, Tapa, and Diamond Head towers (which are farther from the beach), and the more expensive ones in the Rainbow and Ali'i, which are closest to the water. I found rooms in all the towers to be spacious, clean, and comfy, so ultimately it comes down to how close you want to be to the beach.

2005 Kālia Rd. (at Ala Moana Blvd.), Honolulu. www.hiltonhawaiianvillage.com. ✆ **800/HILTONS** or 808/949-4321. 2,860 units. $279–$479 double; from $499 suite. $30 resort charge per day includes Internet access and movie rentals. Extra person (over 2 adults) $50. Children 17 and under stay free in parent's room. Valet parking $36, self-parking $29. Bus: 19 or 20. **Amenities:** 9 restaurants; 4 bars; year-round children's program; concierge; fitness center; 6 outdoor pools; room service; Wi-Fi (included in resort fee).

The Modern Honolulu ★ Waikīkī's trendiest hotel is hip and modern and not your typical Hawaiian hotel, which means you won't find rattan furniture nor slack key music over the speakers. Instead, you get sleek, all-white, and blond-wood-accented rooms and electronic funk a la Ibiza played in the common areas. Come here to see and be seen, at the clubby lobby bar behind the bookcase or alongside two oceanview pools—each with its own bar and expansive daybeds. Choose this hotel, too, if you're looking to get away from the kids—the top pool is adults only. There's no beach access here, but the pool has its own beachy sand—a blend culled from all the islands—to pretend like there is.

1775 Ala Moana Blvd. (at Hobron Lane), Honolulu. www.themodernhonolulu.com. ✆ **855/970-4161** or 808/943-5800. 353 units. $280–$469 double; from $499 suite. Valet parking only (no self-parking) $28. Bus: 19 or 20. **Amenities:** Restaurant; nightclub; 4 lounges; concierge; fitness center; pool; 24-hr. room service; spa; Wi-Fi (free).

Outrigger Reef on the Beach ★★ You may arrive by car, but the Outrigger reminds you—with the 100-year-old koa wood canoe suspended in the longhouse entryway—that long ago, the Polynesians came to Hawai'i by boat, navigating their way only by the stars. The Hawai'i-based Outrigger chain has a handful of hotels on O'ahu, and this one is its most striking, with lovely Hawaiian cultural touches. You'll find the outrigger theme throughout the hotel, such as in the collection of Polynesian canoe art by Herb Kāne, who some call the "father of the Hawaiian Renaissance." (Most notably, he built the double-hulled voyaging canoe the *Hōkūle'a* in 1975, which revived ancient celestial navigation methods. In 2014, the *Hōkūle'a* was set to sail around the world—without a compass, GPS, or any other modern-day navigational equipment.) But don't worry, at Outrigger Reef, you can have your historical culture and modern amenities too, such as free Wi-Fi, a large pool, and three restaurants, including the ever-popular beachside **ShoreBird,** serving $4.50 Mai Tais until 6pm and grill-your-own steaks. Decked out in tasteful Hawaiian decor, rooms are spacious.

Note that **Outrigger Waikīkī on the Beach** (www.outriggerwaikikihotel.com) has a similar feel and price point to Outrigger Reef on the Beach, but its location in the center of Waikīkī and its resident bar—Duke's Waikīkī, the area's most happening bar—means it's a little more bustling and noisy.

2169 Kālia Rd. (at Saratoga Rd.), Honolulu. www.outriggerreef.com. ✆ **866/733-6420** or 808/923-3111. 639 units. $249–$475 hotel room double. Resort fee $30 includes Wi-Fi and rides on the Waikīkī Trolley. Extra person (over 2 adults) $75 per person per night. Children 17 and under stay free in parent's room. Valet parking only (no self-parking) $30. Bus: 19 or 20. **Amenities:** 3 restaurants; 2 bars; babysitting; fitness center; spa; outdoor pools.

MID-WAIKĪKĪ, *MAKAI*

All the hotels listed below are between Kalākaua Avenue and the ocean, and between Fort DeRussy in the Ewa (western) direction and Kaiulani Street in the Diamond Head (eastern) direction.

Expensive

Halekulani ★★★ This is one of Waikīkī's most luxurious hotels; its name means "house befitting heaven." The history of the Halekulani tracks that of Waikīkī itself: At its inception at the turn of the century, it was just a beachfront house and a few bungalows, and Waikīkī was an

AFFORDABLE parking IN WAIKĪKĪ

It *is* possible to find affordable parking in Waikīkī if you know where to look. I've divided up the parking into free or metered parking and carry-a-big-wallet parking.

FREE OR METERED PARKING:

- All side streets in Waikīkī.
- Ala Wai Boulevard along the Ala Wai Canal.
- Kalākaua Avenue along Kapi'olani Park.
- Waikīkī Zoo.

BEST OF THE NOT-SO-AFFORDABLE PARKING:

- Across from Hale Koa Hotel, 2055 Kalia Rd. (parking lot is across from the hotel; $4 for the first hour, $3 per subsequent hour, $36 maximum)
- Royal Hawaiian Shopping Center, 2201 Kalākaua Ave. (First hour free with validation, $2 per hour for the next 2 hours)
- Waikīkī Beach Marriott, 2552 Kalākaua Ave. (entrance on 'Ōhua Ave.; free if you eat here, $8 per hour if you don't)
- Waikīkī Parking Garage, 333 Seaside Ave. ($4 per hour)
- Waikīkī Shopping Plaza, 2270 Kalākaua Ave. ($5 per hour, $5 flat-rate weekends 6:30am–6pm and evenings 6pm–midnight)

undeveloped stretch of sand and drained marshland. By the 1980s, Waikīkī was a different place, and so was the Halekulani, which was relaunched by its new Japanese owners as an oasis of mostly oceanfront hotel rooms, marble foyers, and beautifully landscaped courtyards—and so it remains. It's all very understated—it actually doesn't look like much from the outside. But what it lacks in splashy grandeur, a la Royal Hawaiian, it makes up with a quiet elegance.

The large rooms are done in what the Halekulani calls its signature "seven shades of white." Generously sized tile-and-marble bathrooms and louver shutter doors separating the lanais contribute to the spare yet luxe feel. Of all the hotels in Waikīkī, this one feels the most peaceful, abetted by lovely, personable service. It's a true escape.

2199 Kālia Rd. (at the ocean end of Lewers St.), Honolulu. www.halekulani.com. ✆ **800/367-2343** or 808/923-2311. 453 units. $520–$690 double; from $1,075 suite. Extra person $125. 1 child 17 and under stays free in parent's room using existing bedding; additional rollaway bed $40. Maximum 3 people per room. Parking $35. Bus: 19 or 20. **Amenities:** 3 restaurants; 3 bars; 24-hr. concierge; fitness center; gorgeous outdoor pool; room service; spa; complimentary tickets to the Honolulu Museum of Art, Bishop Museum, and Doris Duke's Shangri La estate; Wi-Fi (free).

Moana Surfrider, a Westin Resort ★★ This is Waikīkī's oldest hotel, built in 1901. Even after more than 100 years, multiple renovations, and the construction of two towers in the '50s and '60s, the hotel has managed to retain its original and still grand Beaux-Arts main building. It's so picturesque you're likely to encounter many a Japanese wedding couple posing for a shot along the staircase and in the lobby. I prefer the rooms in the Banyan Wing for their nostalgic character, but these tend to be small in size. Larger rooms with lānais are in the Tower Wing, and although they are as well appointed as any you'll find at other Westin properties, with granite bathrooms and signature Heavenly beds, they don't feel very Hawai'i. Of course, to change that, get a room with a view of Diamond Head, or just step out under the giant banyan tree in the courtyard and enjoy the nightly live Hawaiian music and a Mai Tai. 2365 Kalākaua Ave. (ocean side of the street, across from Ka'iulani St.), Honolulu. www.moana-surfrider.com. ✆ **800/325-3535** or 808/922-3111. 793 units. $340–$610 double; from $970 suite. $31 resort charge per day (covers self-parking, Internet, and local calls). Extra person $120. Children 17 and under stay free in parent's room using existing bedding. Valet parking $8 additional. Bus: 19 or 20. **Amenities:** 3 restaurants; bar; babysitting; children's program; concierge; nearby fitness room (about a 2-min. walk down the beach at the Sheraton Waikīkī); outdoor pool; room service; Wi-Fi (included in resort fee).

Royal Hawaiian ★★★ The "Pink Palace of the Pacific" is as pink as the Halekulani is white. Everytime I step into the Royal Hawaiian, it still takes my breath away. I love its vibrant exoticism—the Spanish-Moorish architecture manifested in graceful stucco arches, the patterned floor tiles, the ornate lamps. Who knew that pink could look so good against Hawai'i's blue skies and seas? The historic rooms are my favorite, with the pink and gold-embossed wallpaper and dark-wood furniture. Rooms in the Mailani Tower wing are larger, the colors more muted (although, don't worry, there are still pink accents) and the bathrooms there have fancy Toto toilets. Here, even your *'okole* (rear end) is pampered. 2259 Kalākaua Ave. (at Royal Hawaiian Ave., on the ocean side of the Royal Hawaiian Shopping Center), Honolulu. www.royal-hawaiian.com. ✆ **800/325-3535** or 808/923-7311. 528 units. $395–$535 double; from $490 suite. $35 resort charge per day (includes Wi-Fi). Extra person $155. Bus: 19 or 20. **Amenities:** 2 restaurants; landmark bar; babysitting; bike rentals; year-round children's program (available next door at the Sheraton Waikīkī); concierge; preferential tee times at various golf courses; nearby fitness room (next door at the Sheraton Waikīkī); outdoor pool; room service; spa; Wi-Fi (included in resort fee).

Sheraton Waikīkī ★ At 30 stories tall, the Sheraton towers over its neighbors. With almost 2,000 rooms and a location right in the middle of the busiest section of Waikīkī, this is not the place to book if you're looking for a peaceful getaway. What you do get: views of the ocean (available in most rooms), the Helumoa Playground pool for kids, and a gorgeous infinity pool for adults. Expect crowds, though. Drinks at **Rumfire** are fun, with great views to match; the **Kai Market** dinner buffet offers a smorgasbord of local flavors. Dining is expensive (as is expected at most of the Waikīkī hotels); for cheap, grab-and-go meals, I like to go to **Lawson Station,** something of a Japanese version of 7-Eleven but with much better food, such as bento boxes, oden, and yummy desserts made by local companies.

2255 Kalākaua Ave. (at Royal Hawaiian Ave., on the ocean side of the Royal Hawaiian Shopping Center and west of the Royal Hawaiian), Honolulu. www.sheraton.com. ✆ **800/325-3535** or 808/922-4422. 1,852 units. $295–$495 double; from $705 suite. $30 resort charge per day for self-parking, Internet, and local and long-distance calls. Extra person $120. Children 17 and under stay free in parent's room. Valet parking $33. Bus: 19 or 20. **Amenities:** 5 restaurants; 2 bars; nightclub; babysitting; bike rentals; children's program (operated by an independent vendor, Poppins Keiki Hawai'i); concierge; fitness center; 2 large outdoor pools; room service; Wi-Fi (included in resort fee).

Moderate

Waikīkī Parc ★ This is the Halekulani's younger, hipper sister. It's right across the street and run by the same management company. The lobby entrance glows blue to the beat of electronica, and you can rent the flashy Lotus sports cars parked near the valet. The rooms aren't as posh as the rest of the hotel, though—the floors are tile and rooms feel more utilitarian than stylish. But the location—right across the street from the beach—is great. Spring for an ocean view; otherwise, you might be overlooking the parking lot.

2233 Helumoa Rd. (at Lewers St.), Honolulu. www.waikikiparc.com. ✆ **800/422-0450** or 808/921-7272. 297 units. $221–$425 double. Extra person $75. Children 17 and under stay free in parent's room. Bus: 19 or 20. **Amenities:** 2 restaurants; babysitting; concierge; fitness center; 8th-floor pool deck; room service; complimentary admission to the Bishop Museum and Honolulu Museum of Art; Wi-Fi (free).

Inexpensive

The Breakers ★ In the 1950s and '60s, thanks to statehood and the jet age, Waikīkī's low-rise skyline gave way to larger and taller hotels. A lot of the more modest hotels are long gone . . . except for the Breakers. The two-story building, built in 1954, has managed to hold on to its family feel and prime real estate (just a few minutes' walk to the beach and the center of Waikīkī). It's like a Hawai'i-style motel, built around a pool, with charming touches such as double-pitched roofs, shoji doors to the lānai, and tropical landscaping. All of the rooms come with a kitchenette, though the appliances look like they're from the '70s. Sure, the decor is dated (some say vintage), but it's clean.

250 Beach Walk (btw. Kalākaua Ave. and Kalia Rd.), Honolulu. www.breakers-hawaii.com. ✆ **800/426-0494** or 808/923-3181. 64 units, all with shower only. $150–$170 double (extra person $20 per day); $220 garden suite double. Limited free parking (just 6 stalls); additional parking across the street $16 per day. Bus: 19 or 20. **Amenities:** Restaurant; grill; outdoor pool; Wi-Fi (free, in lobby).

MID-WAIKĪKĪ, *MAUKA*

These mid-Waikīkī hotels, on the mountain side of Kalākaua Avenue, are a little farther away from the beach than those listed above. All are between Kalākaua Avenue and Ala Wai Canal, and between Kālaimoku Street in the 'Ewa (western) direction and Ka'iulani Street in the Diamond Head (eastern) direction.

AFFORDABLE Waikīkī: AQUA HOTELS

Inexpensive accommodations are few and far between on O'ahu, and especially in Waikīkī . . . at least places that you'd actually *want* to stay in. But a good bet is the Aqua chain. Its inexpensive-to-moderately-priced properties (from $119 a night) are managed by a Hawai'i-based company. Hotels do range in quality (with furnishings from dated tropical to bright and modern), but they are generally clean, well maintained, and regularly updated. Another plus? Free Wi-Fi! Book directly from the website (www.aquaresorts.com) for the best rates and special deals.

Some of the standout O'ahu hotels in the Aqua portfolio include the **Aqua Waikīkī Pearl,** 415 Nahua St. (✆ **808/954-7425**), right in the middle of Waikīkī and about a 10-minute walk to the beach. It has spacious room options, and I was able to find a 450-square-foot room for $125 online. Staying at the 44-floor **Aqua Skyline at Island Colony,** 445 Seaside Ave. (✆ **808/954-7411**), feels very urban, with a fresh new green-and-slate color scheme and views of Waikīkī's skyline. The rooms have kitchenettes, and a pool and grill area on the sixth floor means you can save even more money making meals instead of going out. Not bad for a place with rates starting at $150. Rooms in the **Luana Waikīkī,** 2045 Kalākaua Ave. (✆ **808/955-6000**), which Aqua recently acquired from Outrigger, start at $179. It offers a pool and suites with a kitchen. Best of the mid-range Aqua hotels is the **Park Shore Waikīkī,** 2586 Kalākaua Ave. (✆ **808/954-7426**), which was renovated in 2013 and offers views of Diamond Head and the ocean, starting at just $200 a night.

One of Aqua's most expensive—and nicest—hotels is the **Aqua Lotus Honolulu,** 2885 Kalākaua Ave. (✆ **808/954-7420**), on the east end of Waikīkī, facing Kapi'olani Park. It's a former W Hotel property, newly updated with dark hardwood floors, platform beds, granite-tiled bathrooms, and—in the corner units—a lānai and window that frame Diamond Head beautifully. You can sleep with the windows open here; this is the quiet side of Waikīkī. Rates start at $230.

Inexpensive

Coconut Waikīkī Hotel ★ This is a cheery, chic boutique hotel with lime-green accents, reggae-inflected "Jawaiian" music in the lobby, a super-friendly staff, and a chalkboard featuring a Hawaiian "Word of the Day" and "Local Food of the Day." Rooms are spacious and immaculate and come with a wet bar and a microwave. The small pool is kind of wedged between the hotel and a fence—better to grab the free beach-towel rental and head to the ocean sands. Its sister hotel, **Shoreline Hotel Waikīkī** (shorelinehotelwaikiki.com), is a few blocks away, with similar amenities and a midcentury modern vibe. Check out **Heavenly,** inside the Shoreline, with its surfer-chic decor and delicious brunch fare, including the French toast and loco moco.

450 Lewers St. (at Ala Wai Blvd.), Honolulu. coconutwaikikihotel.com. ✆ **808/923-8828.** 81 units. $169–$219 double; from $249 suite. Valet parking only (no self-parking) $26. Bus: 19 or 20. **Amenities:** Tiny outdoor pool w/sun deck; Wi-Fi (free).

DIAMOND HEAD WAIKĪKĪ

You'll find all these hotels between Ala Wai Boulevard and the ocean, and between Ka'iulani Street and world-famous Diamond Head itself.

Moderate

Hotel Renew ★★ This is a stylish boutique hotel just a block from the beach. Like its lobby bar, rooms at Hotel Renew are pretty small but well edited and well designed. You get a minimalist, Japanese aesthetic, mood lighting, and plush beds with a down featherbed and down comforter. The crowd that stays here are 20- and 30-somethings who don't need hibiscus and tropical prints to tell them they're vacationing in Hawai'i.

129 Paoakalani Ave. (at Lemon Rd.), Honolulu. www.hotelrenew.com. ✆ **888/485-7639** or 808/687-7700. 72 units. $190–$350 double. Amenity fee $25 per day. Valet parking $25. Bus: 19 or 20. **Amenities:** Lounge; concierge; Wi-Fi (included in amenity fee).

New Otani Kaimana Beach Hotel ★ On the other side of the park is this hotel, where the tables are Formica and the color palette grandma pastels, at least for the cheaper rooms. But also here, right in front of the New Otani, is my favorite Waikīkī beach. About a 15-minute walk from central Waikīkī, it tends to be less crowded and the water cleaner than at other spots. In the mornings and right before sunset, you'll see regulars doing laps to the windsock and back. The quieter location, plus the right-on-the-beach **Hau Tree Lānai** restaurant, makes this hotel's lower-end rooms just right for the price. If you want a more updated decor and space, you can opt for the higher-end rooms, some of which were recently renovated.

2863 Kalakaua Ave. (ocean side of the street just before Diamond Head and just past the Waikīkī Aquarium, across from Kapi'olani Park), Waikīkī. www.kaimana.com. ✆ **800/356-8264** or 808/923-1555. 124 units. $175–$350 double; from $176 studio; from $255 1-bedroom; from $400 suite. Extra person $50. Children 12 and under stay free in parent's room using existing bedding. Check website for special packages. Valet parking $23. Bus: 2 or 14. **Amenities:** 2 restaurants; beachfront bar; babysitting; concierge; room service; Wi-Fi (free).

HONOLULU BEYOND WAIKĪKĪ

Mānoa Valley

Mānoa Valley Inn ★ I'm including this bed-and-breakfast because there's really nothing like it, but it takes a unique traveler to love it. It's like staying at your eccentric great-aunt's house, if she lived in a 100-year-old Victorian and furnished it with ornate antiques, four-poster beds, lace curtains, rose wallpaper, and floral bedspreads, which have all faded over the years. The yard, accessed via an overgrown trellis, is lush and tropical, and dense vegetation surrounds a small saltwater pool. The house itself is quite grand, with three stories and a view over the city all the way to Diamond Head. Some of the rooms on the top floor have an attic-like feel with sloping ceilings and quirky, hidden corners. One of my favorites is the T. C. Davis Room (the rooms are named for prominent businessmen in Honolulu's history) for its lovely southern-facing window and smaller side windows that let in Honolulu's cooling trade winds. (Only two of the rooms have air-conditioning; the rest have fans.) A new owner took over a few years ago; the caretaker and assorted family members, two dogs, and one cat live on-site. Be aware that this house is in a residential neighborhood near the University of Hawai'i; you'll need a car to get around and see the sights.

2001 Vancouver Dr. (at University Ave.), Honolulu. www.manoavalleyinn.com. ✆ **808/947-6019.** 7 units, each with a private bathroom. $155–$195 doubles and triples. Rates include a hot breakfast. Free parking. Bus: 4 or 6. Children 12 and older preferred. **Amenities:** A/C (in some units); small saltwater pool; Wi-Fi (free).

To the East: Kāhala

Kahala Hotel & Resort ★★★ Hotel magnate Conrad Hilton opened the Kahala in 1964 as a secluded and exclusive retreat away from Waikīkī. Fifty years and a different owner later, it still retains that feeling of peacefulness and exclusivity. Its rooms convey a unique island luxury, aka "Kahala chic." In your private quarters, you'll get a plush bed and enormous bathroom with a soaking tub and separate shower. On the property, you have access to a small beach with a private feel (in Hawai'i, all beaches are public, but few people come here). There's a pool, too, but what makes the Kahala unique is the Dolphin Quest, which allows you to get up close and personal with the dolphins in the lagoon. The restaurants on the property offer experiences such as a beachfront brunch buffet, afternoon tea on the veranda, and an upscale Pacific Rim dinner, all of which make the Kahala a worthy escape from the bustle of Waikīkī.

5000 Kāhala Ave. (next to the Wai'alae Country Club), Honolulu. www.kahalaresort.com. ✆ **800/367-2525** or 808/739-8888. 343 units. From $495 double; from $1,340 suite. Extra person $100. Children 17 and under stay free in parent's room. Check Specials & Packages online discounts. Parking $32. **Amenities:** 5 restaurants; 4 bars; babysitting; year-round children's program (for a fee); concierge; nearby golf course; fitness center; large outdoor pool; room service; watersports equipment rentals, Wi-Fi (free).

THE WINDWARD COAST

Note: Windward Coast accommodations are located on the "Eastern O'ahu & the Windward Coast" map (p. 93).

Kailua

Lanikai Bed & Breakfast ★ This is one of the few options for staying in the exclusive Lanikai neighborhood, which still keeps its laidback, beachy vibe—you'll see people heading to the beach on bikes or with kayaks or stand-up paddleboards in tow. You'll feel a part of the neighborhood, staying in this old-style, homey, and comfortable Lanikai house just across the street from the beach. It has two units: the 1,000-square-foot, two-bedroom Tree House and the smaller Garden Studio, decorated in Hawaiiana print and recently updated with rattan furniture. Rick Maxey is the second-generation owner: "I grew up in this house," he says. He and his family live on the first floor, below the Tree House. Each unit has its own private entrance and kitchenette, and the Garden Studio has its own patio. Each is furnished with cooking utensils and beach equipment—all you need to make it home.

1277 Mokulua Dr. (btw. Onekea and Aala drives in Lanikai), Kailua. www.lanikaibeachrentals.com. ✆ **808/261-7895.** 2 units. $225 studio double; $250 apt double or $325 for 3 or 4. Cleaning fee $100-$158. Rates include breakfast items in fridge left at the beginning of your stay. 5-night minimum. Free parking. Bus: 56. **Amenities:** Wi-Fi (free).

Sheffield House ★ Kailua is a small beach town, with restaurants, shops, and a business center anchored by Whole Foods. Staying at Sheffield House puts you right in the middle of everything—it's just a few minutes' walk to the beach but also a short stroll to Whole Foods, the Sunday farmer's market, and "town" for groceries and entertainment. (Convenience does have its drawbacks, though—the house is on one of Kailua's busy streets, which means traffic sounds.) There are two vacation rentals here—a one-bedroom and a studio, each with its own private entry and kitchenette.

131 Ku'ulei Rd. (at Kalaheo Dr.), Kailua. www.hawaiisheffieldhouse.com. ✆ **808/262-0721.** 2 units. $144–$164 double guest room; $164–$184 1-bedroom. Extra person $20. Cleaning fee $65–$75. Rates include 1st day's continental breakfast. Free parking. Bus: 56. **Amenities:** Wi-Fi (free).

THE NORTH SHORE

The North Shore has few tourist accommodations—some say that's its charm. VRBO.com and airbnb.com (mentioned earlier in "Vacation Rentals") offer a good range of places to stay, such as a Hale'iwa studio on the first floor of a two-story home for $85 a night, a North Shore loft with three beds from $159, and a three-bedroom house steps away from Sunset Beach for $410 a night. Cleaning fees vary.

Note: North Shore accommodations are located on the "O'ahu's North Shore" map (p. 101).

Very Expensive

Turtle Bay Resort ★★★ The North Shore's only resort completed property-wide renovations in 2014, updating everything in a beachy, laid-back, but luxurious style befitting the less-developed, unhurried North Shore. The lobby and gym have been opened up with ocean views, the spa has doubled in size, the restaurants' menus have been revamped to highlight locally grown ingredients, and the refreshed rooms have a calming, neutral palette and walk-in stone showers. What hasn't changed: Every room still has an ocean view. Turtle Bay has also embraced its role as a surf-scene hub, especially in the wintertime, when the surfing season is in full swing. All the pros come to **Lei Lei's Bar and Grill** for a drink, and **Surfer, The Bar**—a collaboration between the resort and *Surfer* magazine—offers Surf Talk Story nights, bringing in pro surfers and watermen to share their tales. All in all, Turtle Bay's renovations have really made the resort feel a part of the North Shore landscape. Of all the resorts outside of Waikīkī (including Kahala and Aulani), this would be my pick, for the vibe, the value, and the surroundings.

57-091 Kamehameha Hwy. (Hwy. 83), Kahuku. www.turtlebayresort.com. ✆ **800/203-3650** or 808/293-6000. 477 units. $319–$389 double; from $599 cottage; from $499 suite; from $1,169 villa. Daily $38 resort fee for self-parking, Internet access, and more. Extra person $50. Children 17 and under stay free in parent's room. **Amenities:** 5 restaurants; 2 bars; concierge; 36 holes of golf; stable w/horseback riding; 2 outdoor heated pools (with 80-ft. water slide); room service; spa w/fitness center; 4 tennis courts; watersports equipment rentals; Wi-Fi (included in resort fee).

Inexpensive

Ke Iki Beach Bungalows ★ These bungalows are right on a beautiful, wide, and uncrowded beach, between Sharks Cove (great for snorkeling in the summer) and Pipeline (for the best pro-surfer wave-watching come winter). Ranging from basic studios to two bedrooms, each unit comes with bamboo furniture and a full kitchen, plus its own grill. Stock up on groceries at the nearby Foodland (part of the largest locally owned supermarket chain in Hawai'i). Be aware that units have no air-conditioning, but ceiling fans and North Shore breezes are usually enough to keep the air cool. Settle into one of the hammocks strung up between the palm trees overlooking the beach—this is island living.

59-579 Ke Iki Rd. (off Kamehameha Hwy.), Hale'iwa. www.keikibeach.com. ✆ **866/638-8229** or 808/638-8229. 11 units. $135 double gardenview studio or 1-bedroom; $185–$215 double beachfront 1-bedroom; $155–$185 double gardenview 2-bedroom; $210–$230 double beachfront 2-bedroom. Extra person stays free. Cleaning fee $55–$100 per week or per visit (if less than a week). Free parking. Bus: 52. **Amenities:** Complimentary bikes; CD player; kitchen; TV; complimentary watersports equipment; Wi-Fi (free).

LEEWARD O'AHU: THE WAI'ANAE COAST

Ko Olina will soon be hotel hub of the Leeward coast, and a luxury one at that. The Aulani opened in 2011, the Four Seasons in late 2016, and two more hotels are slated for the area by 2018. The new resorts are in sharp contrast to the rest of the coast, which is O'ahu's poorest.

Aulani, a Disney Resort & Spa, Ko Olina, Hawai'i ★★★ Aulani offers plenty of fun from Mickey Mouse and friends to entertain the kids, such as a character breakfast with photo ops, but it's also a celebration of Hawaiian culture. Disney's "imagineers" worked with locals to get many of the details just right, from murals and woodcarvings throughout the property that tell the story of Hawai'i, to the **'Ōlelo Room,** one of the resort bars, where you can learn the Hawaiian language from bartenders who are fluent in Hawaiian (everyone learns a new language better when they're drinking, right?). A 900-foot-long lazy river threads the resort, which—along with children's programs like storytelling nights under the stars, Hawaiian crafts classes, and Disney movies on the lawn—makes the Aulani, perhaps unsurprisingly, one of the best lodging choices for families. Even I, by now a cynical adult, am always delighted when I set foot on this property.

92-1185 Ali'inui Dr., Kapolei. http://resorts.disney.go.com/aulani-hawaii-resort. © **714/520-7001** (reservations) or 808/674-6200 (hotel). 359 units in hotel, $449–$670 hotel room, from $1,340 suite. Parking $35. No bus service. Take H-1 west toward Pearl City/Ewa Beach; stay on H-1 until it becomes Hwy. 93 (Farrington Hwy.); look for the exit sign for Ko Olina Resort; turn left on Ali'inui Dr. **Amenities:** 3 restaurants; 3 bars; babysitting; championship 18-hole Ko Olina Golf Course designed by Ted Robinson; numerous outdoor pools and water features; room service; spa; watersports equipment rentals; Wi-Fi (free).

Camping & Wilderness Cabins

If you plan to camp, you must bring your own gear or buy it here—no one on O'ahu rents gear. If you are bringing your own equipment, remember that you can't transport fuel (even in a canister) on the plane.

The best places to camp on O'ahu are listed below. TheBus's Circle Island route can get you to or near all these sites, but remember: On TheBus, you're allowed only one bag, which has to fit under the seat. If you have more gear, you're going to have to drive or take a cab.

THE WINDWARD COAST

Ho'omaluhia Botanical Garden ★

This little-known windward campground outside Kāne'ohe is a real treasure. It's hard to believe that it's just half an hour from downtown Honolulu. The name Ho'omaluhia, or "peace and tranquility," accurately describes this 400-acre botanical garden at the foot of the jagged Ko'olau Range. In this lush setting, gardens are devoted to plants specific to tropical America, native Hawai'i, Polynesia, India, Sri Lanka, and Africa. A 32-acre lake sits in the middle of the scenic park (no swimming or boating allowed), and there are numerous hiking trails. The visitor center offers free guided walks Saturday at 10am and Sunday at 1pm (call © **808/233-7323** to register).

Facilities for this tent-camp area include restrooms, cold showers, dishwashing stations, picnic tables, and water. Shopping and gas are available in Kāne'ohe, 2 miles away. Stays are limited to 3 nights, from 9am Friday to 4pm Monday only. Reserve a campsite up to 2 weeks in advance at **camping.honolulu.gov**. Permits are $32, valid for the entire weekend (Fri–Sun). To get here from Waikīkī, take H-1 to the Pali Highway (Hwy. 61); turn left on Kamehameha Highway (Hwy. 83); and at the fourth light, turn left on Luluku Road. TheBus nos. 55 and 65 stop nearby on Kamehameha Highway; from here, you'll have to walk 2 miles to the visitor center.

Kahana Bay Beach Park ★

Lying under Tahiti-like cliffs, with a beautiful gold-sand crescent beach framed by pine-needle casuarina trees, Kahana Bay Beach Park is a place of serene beauty. You can swim, bodysurf, fish, hike, and picnic or just sit and listen to the trade winds whistle through the beach pines (and sometimes, cars—the campsite is along Kamehameha Highway).

Facilities include restrooms, outdoor showers, picnic tables, and drinking water. ***Note:*** The restrooms are located at the north end of the beach, far away from the camping area.

Permits can be obtained at **camping.ehawaii.gov** for $18 a night. Camping is only allowed from Friday through Wednesday.

Kahana Bay Beach Park is set in the 52-222 block of Kamehameha Highway (Hwy. 83) in Kahana. From Waikīkī, take the H-1 west to the Likelike Highway (Hwy. 63). Continue north on the Likelike, through the Wilson Tunnel, turning left on Hwy. 83; Kahana Bay is 13 miles down the road on the right. You can also get here via TheBus no. 55.

THE NORTH SHORE

Mālaekahana Bay State Recreation Area ★★

This is one of the most beautiful beach-camping areas in the state, with a mile-long, gold-sand beach on O'ahu's North Shore. During low tide, you can wade/swim out to Goat Island, a sanctuary for seabirds and turtles. There are two areas for tent camping. Facilities include picnic tables, restrooms, showers, sinks, and drinking water. For your safety, the park gate is closed between 6:45pm and 7am; vehicles cannot enter or exit during those hours. Groceries and gas are available in Lā'ie and Kahuku, each less than a mile away.

Permits are $18 a night and available at **camping.ehawaii.gov**. Camping is limited to Friday through Wednesday.

The recreation area is located on Kamehameha Highway (Hwy. 83) between Lā'ie and Kahuku. Take the H-2 to Hwy. 99 to Hwy. 83 (both roads are called Kamehameha Hwy.); continue on Hwy. 83 just past Kahuku. You can also get here via TheBus no. 55.

WHERE TO EAT ON O'AHU

Hawai'i offers food experiences that exist nowhere else in the world, from dishes based on foods eaten by ancient Native Hawaiians to plate lunches in which you can see the history of Hawai'i, from postwar-era hole-in-the-walls (where the only thing that's changed is the prices) to fancy dining rooms that spawned the birth of Hawai'i Regional Cuisine. Asian food dominates, thanks to the state's demographics (as of 2012, Hawai'i was the country's only majority-Asian state, comprising 56.9% of the total population). On O'ahu, the most promising places to eat are often found in the most unexpected places. For the adventurous, eating here is like a treasure hunt.

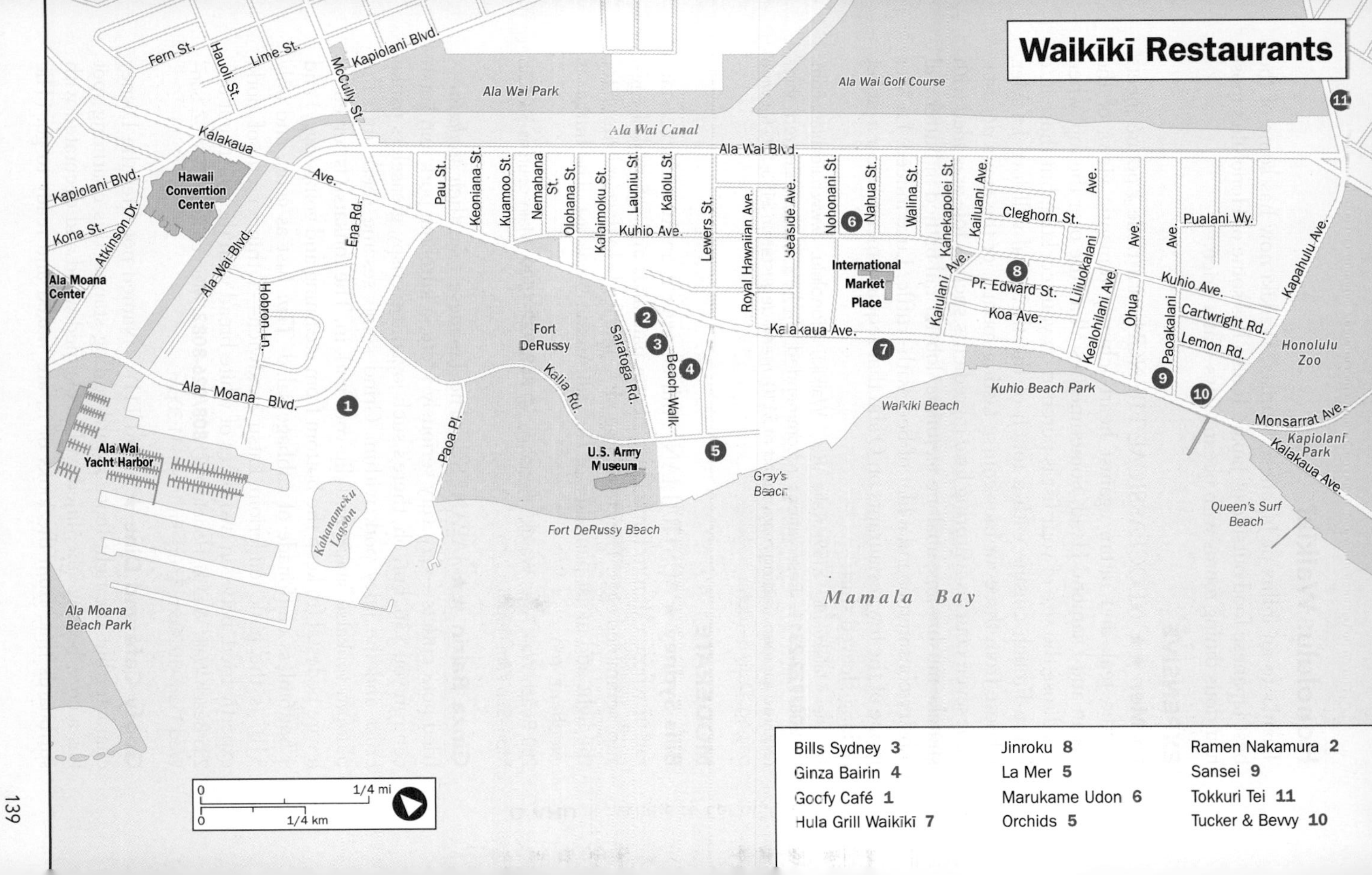

Waikīkī Restaurants
Bills Sydney 3
Ginza Bairin 4
Goofy Café 1
Hula Grill Waikīkī 7
Jinroku 8
La Mer 5
Marukame Udon 6
Orchids 5
Ramen Nakamura 2
Sansei 9
Tokkuri Tei 11
Tucker & Bevvy 10
Ala Wai Golf Course
Ala Wai Park
Ala Wai Canal
Ala Wai Blvd.
Fern St.
Hauoli St.
Lime St.
McCully St.
Kapiolani Blvd.
Kalakaua Ave.
Hawaii Convention Center
Kona St.
Atkinson Dr.
Ala Moana Center
Ala Wai Blvd.
Hobron Ln.
Ena Rd.
Pau St.
Keoniana St.
Kuamoo St.
Nemahana St.
Olohana St.
Kalaimoku St.
Launiu St.
Kalolu St.
Kuhio Ave.
Lewers St.
Royal Hawaiian Ave.
Seaside Ave.
Nohonani St.
Nahua St.
Walina St.
Kanekapolei St.
Kailuani Ave.
Cleghorn St.
Pualani Wy.
Kapahulu Ave.
International Market Place
Kaiulani Ave.
Pr. Edward St.
Koa Ave.
Liliuokalani Ave.
Kealohilani Ave.
Ohua Ave.
Paoakalani Ave.
Cartwright Rd.
Lemon Rd.
Honolulu Zoo
Fort DeRussy
Saratoga Rd.
Beach Walk
Kalia Rd.
Ala Moana Blvd.
Paoa Pl.
U.S. Army Museum
Ala Wai Yacht Harbor
Kahanamoku Lagoon
Gray's Beach
Fort DeRussy Beach
Waikiki Beach
Kuhio Beach Park
Monsarrat Ave.
Kapiolani Park
Queen's Surf Beach
Mamala Bay
Ala Moana Beach Park
0
1/4 mi
0
1/4 km

Honolulu: Waikīkī

Thanks to an influx of Japanese tourists, Waikīkī now has some of the best Japanese food outside of Japan. It also has some of Honolulu's most luxurious dining rooms with ocean views—at a price.

EXPENSIVE

La Mer ★★ NEOCLASSICAL FRENCH La Belle Époque meets Pacific teak and rattan against heart-achingly romantic views of the ocean and Diamond Head. Sometimes it's all a little over the top, when a red rose the size of your fist is perched on your cocktail, but those into haute French cuisine with a touch of the theatrical will love La Mer. Choose from three- or four-course tasting menus, or the *menu dégustation,* seven courses featuring luxe ingredients such as foie gras tiled with shiitake mushrooms, abalone *meunière,* lobster tail bathed in butter and lobster consommé, and a filet of beef with truffle. Luxe indeed. La Mer is one of the few restaurants on O'ahu that requires men to wear a jacket or long-sleeved shirt.

At the Halekulani, 2199 Kalia Rd., Waikīkī, Honolulu. www.halekulani.com. ✆ **808/923-2311.** Reservations recommended. Jackets or long-sleeved shirts required for men. Tasting menus start at $110, *menu dégustation* $195, $95 for wine pairing. Daily 6–10pm.

MODERATE

Bills Sydney ★ AUSTRALIAN Bill Granger is an Australian restaurateur whose claim to fame is his ricotta pancakes and scrambled eggs. Yup, scrambled eggs. They're that good. Come for breakfast or brunch for the light and moist pancakes or the full Aussie breakfast. The burger is excellent, too.

280 Beach Walk Ave., Waikīkī, Honolulu. ✆ **808/922-1500.** Main courses $8–$28. Mon–Sun 7am–10pm.

Ginza Bairin ★★ JAPANESE The Japanese take their *tonkatsu*—fried pork cutlets—very, very seriously. Here, a kurobota pork loin katsu can run you $36, but, oh, there's such joy in the crispy, greaseless panko crust and the juicy pork within. Grind some sesame seeds into the plummy tonkatsu sauce, and dip your pork in. The tonkatsu is served on a wire pedestal (to keep the bottom from steaming and going soggy) and a bottomless chiffonade of cabbage salad. ***Tip:*** Just as good, and only $10, is the pork tenderloin katsu sandwich—a thinner cut of pork, expertly fried, between two slices of white bread with the crusts cut off.

255 Beach Walk, Waikīkī, Honolulu. ✆ **808/926-8082.** Main courses $12–$32. Sun–Wed 11am–10:30pm; Thurs–Fri 11am–11:30pm.

Goofy Café and Dine ★ HEALTHY Named not after the Disney character but the right-foot-forward surfing stance, this charming spot has a cozy, beachy vibe, lined with reclaimed wood and decorated with surfboards that, from the looks of it, are waxed and ready to go. (The

dining out **AT THE HALEKULANI**

Sure, dining in Waikīkī's high-end hotels is often an overpriced affair, but sometimes the occasion warrants everything that comes with it—including oceanside views and upscale service. My pick for special events is the **Halekulani ★★★** (p. 128). Here are my favorite ways to soak up the Halekulani's rarefied restaurant experiences:

- The **Sunday brunch buffet** at **Orchids** is a must—it's the best in Hawai'i, with everything from a roast-suckling-pig carving station to a sashimi and poke bar. Leave room for the ice cream sundae bar, the Halekulani's signature fluffy coconut cake, and lots of dainty desserts. (***Note:*** Reserve a spot weeks in advance.) Love afternoon tea? Orchids also serves my favorite **afternoon tea** service on the island, with an array of sandwiches and sweets, as well as an excellent selection of premium teas.
- Come sunset, head to **House Without a Key** for a Mai Tai and the lovely hula of former Miss Hawai'is, including the legendary Kanoe Miller.
- If the occasion calls for something more romantic and intimate, I go to **L'Aperitif,** the bar inside La Mer, where drinks are inspired by 19th-century French cocktail culture and each glass is accompanied by a delightful amuse bouche.

popular locals' surfing spot, Bowls, is nearby.) It's a surfer's cafe as envisioned by a Japanese company that also runs Aloha Table in Waikīkī. Goofy has a breakfast, lunch, and dinner menu, but breakfast (served all day) is the best part: Look for eggs Benedict, French toast drizzled with creamy Big Island honey, green smoothies poured over chia seeds, and huge acai bowls mounded over with fresh fruit. Come later, for dinner or to sit at the bar, and you can get a shochu sour, shaken with Hawaiian Shochu Co.'s unique, Hale'iwa-made sweet-potato spirit.
1831 Ala Moana Blvd., Suite 201., Waikīkī, Honolulu. © **808/943-0077.** Breakfast $10–$14. Daily 7am–11pm.

Hula Grill Waikīkī ★ AMERICAN The night before, you might be slamming back tiki drinks and making new friends at the ever-popular and rowdy Duke's down below. For the morning after, head to Hula Grill (owned by the same restaurant group as Duke's), where the ocean views, pineapple-coconut pancakes, and sweet potato-chorizo hash will smooth out any hangover. Not so adventurous in the morning? There's standard waffle-and-omelet breakfast fare, too. Breakfast and brunch are the most reasonably priced meals; dinner gets into the $30 range and isn't worth it.
At the Outrigger Waikīkī on the Beach, 2335 Kalākaua Ave., Waikīkī, Honolulu. www.hulagrillwaikiki.com. © **808/923-HULA** [4852]. Reservations recommended for dinner. Breakfast $7–$14; main courses $21–$35. Daily 6:30–11pm, 4–6pm (happy hour with light menu).

going local: UNIQUELY HAWAIIAN EATS

Talk to locals who move away from Hawai'i, and these are the foods they miss. Everyone's got their own go-to place and go-to dishes—people here could spend hours arguing over the best. Here are some of my favorites:

Poke Ruby-red cubes of fresh 'ahi (tuna), tossed with limu (seaweed), kukui nut, and Hawaiian chili pepper: Ahi poke (pronounced "*po*-keh") doesn't get better than the Hawai'ian-style version at **Ono Seafood ★★** (p. 145).

Saimin An only-in-Hawai'i mashup of Chinese-style noodles in a Japanese dashi broth. Join the regulars at the communal table at **Palace Saimin,** 1256 N. King St. (✆ **808/841-9983**), where the interior is as simple as this bowl of noodles. Palace Saimin has been around since 1946, and it looks like it. (I mean that in the nicest way possible.)

Loco moco Two sunny-side up eggs over a hamburger patty and rice, all doused in brown gravy. I love it at **Liliha Bakery ★★** (p. 150).

Spam *musubi* Ah yes, Spam. Hawai'i eats more Spam per capita than any other state. A dubious distinction to some, but don't knock it before you try it. Spam *musubi* (think of it as a giant sushi topped with Spam) is so ubiquitous you can find it at 7-Elevens and convenience stores (where it's pretty good). But for an even finer product, **Mana Bu,** 1618 S. King St. (✆ **808/358-0287**), is the tops. Get there early; the musubi, made fresh daily, are often sold out by 9am.

Hawaiian plate *Laulau* (pork wrapped in taro leaves), kālua pig (shredded, roasted pork), poi (milled taro), and *haupia* (like coconut Jell-O): It's Hawaiian lū'au food, based on what native Hawaiians used to eat. Find it at **Helena's Hawaiian Food ★★** (p. 149), **Highway Inn ★★** (p. 147), and **Ono Hawaiian Food,** 726 Kapahulu Ave. (✆ **808/737-2275**). (Sorry, I couldn't pick a favorite for this one!)

Malasadas Hole-less doughnuts, rolled in sugar, by way of Portugal. **Leonard's Bakery,** 933 Kapahulu Ave. (✆ **808/737-5571**), opened in 1946 by the descendants of Portuguese contract laborers brought to work in Hawai'i's sugarcane fields. I love Leonard's malasadas dusted with *li hing mui* powder (made from sweet-tart plums).

Shave ice Nothing cools better on a hot day than powdery-soft ice drenched in tropical fruit syrups. I go to **Waiola Shave Ice,** 3113 Mokihana St. (✆ **808/735-8886**), for the nostalgia factor, but since you'll probably need more than one shave ice while you're in town, also hit up **Ailana Shave Ice,** 1430 Kona St. (✆ **808/955-8881**), which offers a variety of homemade syrups from real fruit (a rarity).

Jinroku ★★ JAPANESE The specialty here is *okonomiyaki,* a cross between an omelet and a savory pancake, topped with fluttering bonito flakes. Try the mochi shiso one, with chewy rice cakes and an herb that's like a mint and basil hybrid, or pork kimchi okonomiyaki. They can take almost 20 minutes to cook on the teppan grill, but it's oh-so-worth-it. The open-air setting—one side opens onto bustling Kūhiō Street—is like Osaka meets Waikīkī.

2427 Kūhiō Ave., Waikīkī, Honolulu. www.jinrokupacific.com. ✆ **808/926-8955.** Appetizers $6–$14; main courses $20–$72. Daily 11:30am–2:30pm, 5:30–10:30pm.

Sansei Seafood Restaurant & Sushi Bar ★ SUSHI/PACIFIC RIM Sushi purists and sticklers for rice/fish ratios need not come. But those looking for creativity in their sushi should make their way to restaurateur D. K. Kodama's most popular spot. The best rolls here don't even have rice, like the moi sashimi wrapped around sweet Maui onions in a pool of ponzu, or the panko-crusted ahi in a soy mustard sauce. Don't miss the crab truffle ramen. ***Tip:*** Sushi is half off from 10pm to 1am Friday and Saturday, although you might have to put up with some very loud karaoke. Just hope your fellow diners are good singers.

At the Waikīkī Beach Marriott Resort, 2552 Kalākaua Ave., 3rd floor, Waikīkī, Honolulu. www.sanseihawaii.com. ✆ **808/931-6286.** Reservations recommended. Sushi $3–$18; main courses $16–$35. Sat–Wed 5:30–10pm; Thurs–Fri 5:30pm–1am.

INEXPENSIVE

Marukame Udon ★★ JAPANESE/UDON There's always a line out the door at this cafeteria-style noodle joint, but it moves quickly. Pass the time by watching the cooks roll out and cut the dough for udon right in front of you. Bowls of udon, hot or cold, with toppings such as a soft poached egg or Japanese curry, are all under $7.

2310 Kūhiō Ave., Waikīkī, Honolulu. ✆ **808/931-6000.** Noodles $4–$7. Daily 11am–10pm.

Ramen Nakamura ★ JAPANESE/RAMEN Squeeze into this narrow ramen bar, grab a seat at the U-shaped counter, and get ready to slurp some noodles. It's famous for its oxtail ramen (think of oxtail like ribs—meaty chunks eaten off the bone—but from the tail), served with a side of fresh grated ginger and soy sauce for dipping. The spicy ramen is also a winner.

2141 Kalākaua Ave., Waikīkī, Honolulu. ✆ **808/922-7960.** Noodles $10–$22. Daily 11am–11:30pm.

Tucker & Bevvy ★ HEALTHY Aussie slang for "food and drink" (owner Cecily Ho Sargent was born in Honolulu, but spent 17 years in Australia), this white clapboard cafe with blackboard menus offers food for an instant picnic: grab-and-go sandwiches and salads, like a smoked ahi wrap, sesame chicken salad with beets and almonds, and quinoa tabbouleh. You can get hot sandwiches, too, such as a pastrami Reuben or turkey Brie. Come in the morning, and you'll find surfers rehydrating at the fresh juice and smoothie bar, post–dawn patrol.

At the Park Shore Hotel, 2586 Kalākaua Ave., Waikīkī, Honolulu. www.tuckerandbevvy.com. ✆ **808/922-0099.** Most items under $10. Daily 7am–7pm.

Honolulu Beyond Waikīkī

KAPAHULU

Moderate

Side Street Inn on Da Strip ★ LOCAL This newer and bigger version of Side Street Inn opened in 2010. You can still go to the original

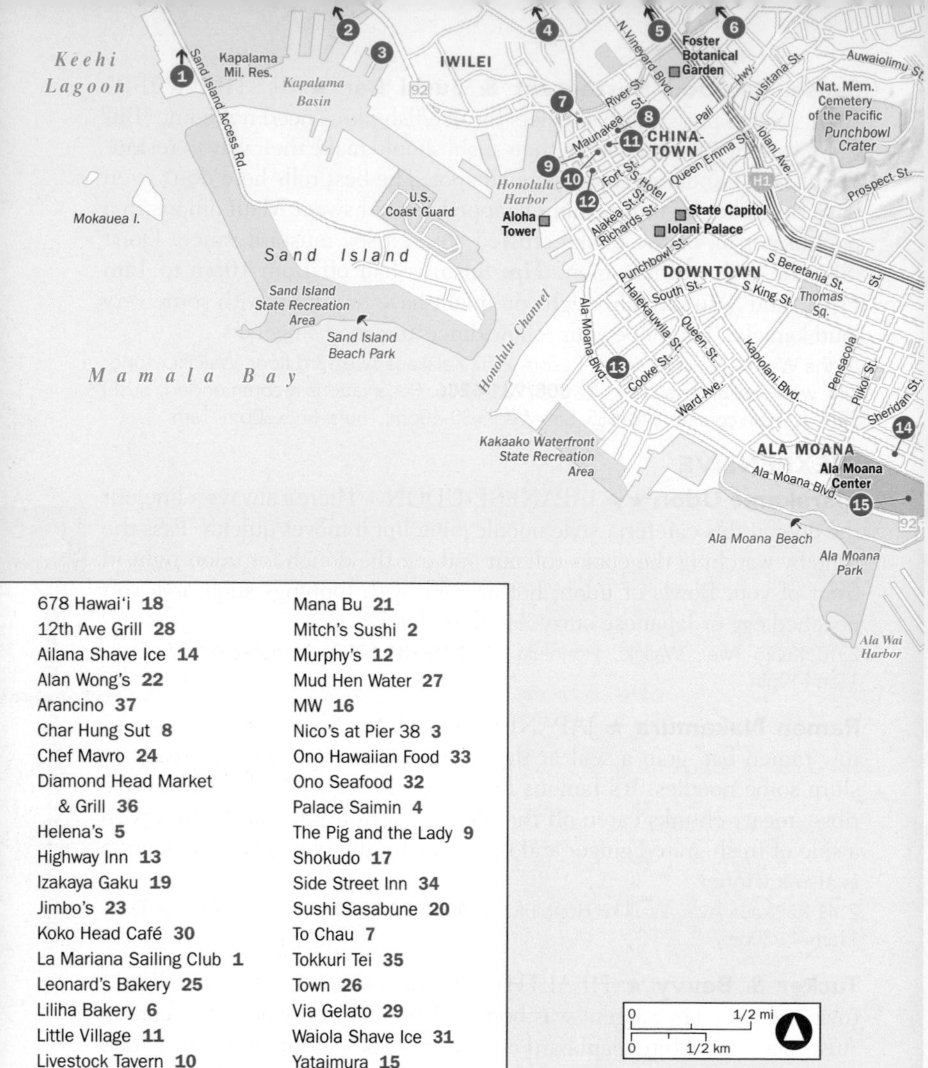

one near Ala Moana for the divey, locals-only atmosphere. But I've found that the food is better prepared at this new location, even though it's pretty much the same menu of fried pork chops and kimchi fried rice with bacon, Portuguese sausage, and *char siu*. The portion sizes are still as big as ever.

614 Kapahulu Ave., Honolulu. ✆ **808/739-3939.** Starters $8–$14; main courses $13–$23. Mon–Fri 3–11:30pm; Sat–Sun 1–11:30pm.

Tokkuri Tei ★ LOCAL/JAPANESE/SUSHI This is a local-style *izakaya,* a Japanese pub with snacks made for sharing. The menu is long and quirky—before diving in to make sense of it all, start with the squid

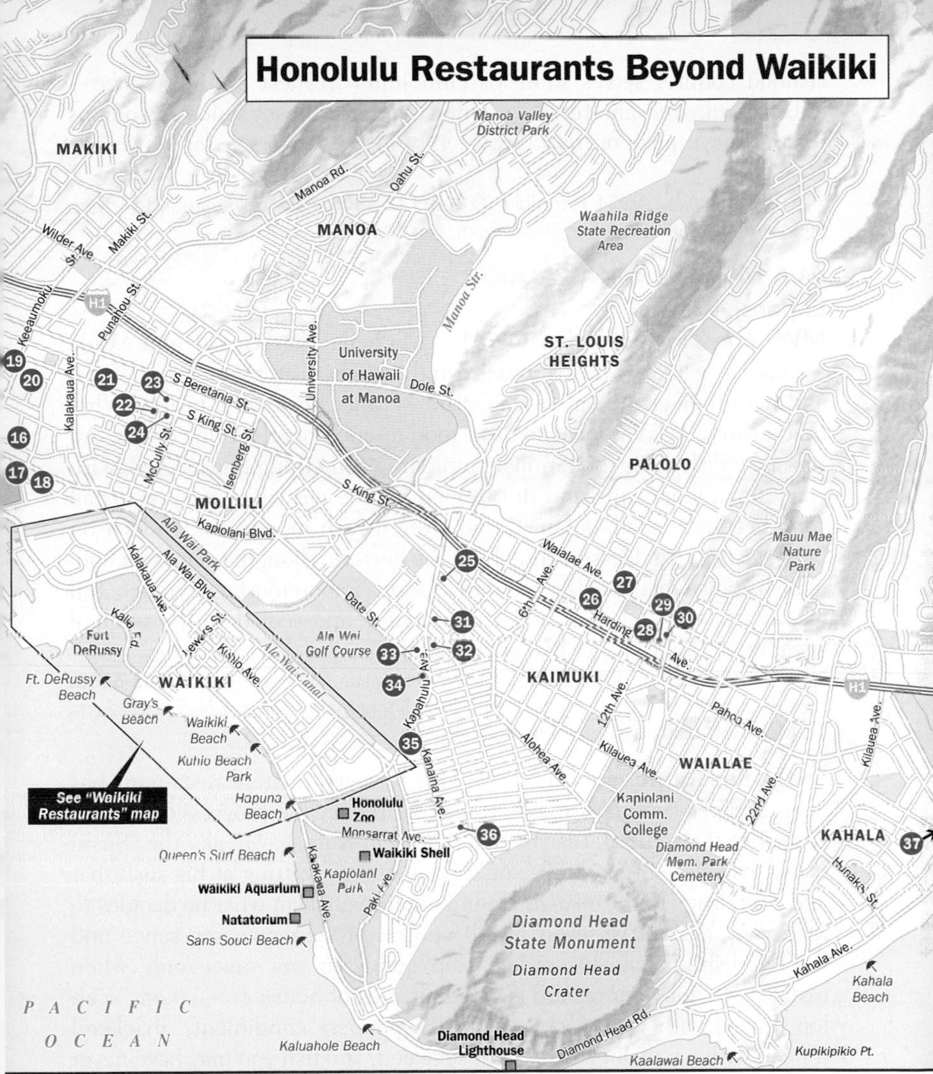

pancake and *Nori-chos,* strips of nori tempura-battered and fried, topped with nacho cheese, tobiko, and teriyaki sauce. For purists, there are simple nigiri sushi.

449 Kapahulu Ave., Honolulu. ✆ **808/732-6480.** Sushi $5–$50. Mon–Sat 10:30am–2pm and 5:30pm–midnight; Sun 5:30–10pm.

Inexpensive

Ono Seafood ★★ LOCAL Not to be confused with Ono Hawaiian Food (though that restaurant, immediately recognizable with its long line of tourists and locals, is also worth going to for its monster-size *laulau* and other more reasonably sized portions of Hawaiian food). This little seafood counter serves some of Honolulu's freshest and best poke—cubes of ruby-red 'ahi (tuna) seasoned to order with soy sauce and onions for the shoyu poke or *limu* (seaweed) and Hawaiian salt for Hawaiian-style poke.

747 Kapahulu Ave., Apt. 4, Honolulu. ✆ **808/732-4806.** Poke bowls around $8. Mon and Wed–Sat 8am–6pm; Sun 10am–3pm.

ALA MOANA & KAKA'AKO

Expensive

MW ★★ HAWAI'I REGIONAL Michelle Karr-Ueoka and Wade Ueoka, the wife-and-husband team in the kitchen, are Alan Wong alums, and here they give their own take on Hawai'i Regional Cuisine. What that means at MW is local comfort food re-envisioned for fine dining. An 'ahi poke dish turns the familiar staple into something unexpected, with spicy tuna, ikura, 'ahi, and uni topped with crispy rice crackers. Oxtail soup becomes oxtail, deboned and stuffed with more meat, and set on beef-stew risotto. Desserts outshine the entrees, though, such as a chocolate banana cream pie layered into a jar or a lemon meringue brûlée, full of custard, chewy jellies, and lemon sorbet and sealed with a torched sugar crust. You've never had anything like it.

1538 Kapi'olani Blvd., #107, Honolulu. www.mwrestaurant.com. ✆ **808/955-6505.** Reservations recommended. Lunch $14–$26; dinner main courses $24–$36; desserts $9. Mon–Sat 10:30am–10pm; Sun 10:30am–9pm.

Sushi Sasabune ★★ SUSHI This formerly austere restaurant has been updated with faux maple trees that reflect the progression of seasons. But if you think that means that Seiji Kumagawa, aka the "Sushi Nazi," has also softened up, you'd be mistaken. Sitting at his sushi bar and submitting to the *omakase* menu means you'll eat what he decides to feed you, and you've given up all control of your own soy sauce and wasabi dish. Follow his orders (dip gently in soy sauce only when instructed), and your reward is gorgeous orbs of house-cured *ikura,* scallop dusted with *yuzu kosho* (a citrusy, peppery condiment), mackerel topped with a translucent sheet of seaweed, and fish you may have never heard of. The rice is just as important—watch how Kumagawa molds it, just so, and then feel it break apart softly in your mouth, melding with the fish. This is sushi art. ***Tip:*** Want to experience the sushi without the stress? Sit at the tables, and you're free to order sushi a la carte.

1417 S. King St., Honolulu. ✆ **808/947-3800.** Reservations recommended. Sushi $5–$50; *omakase* $80–$100 per person. Tues–Fri noon–2pm and Tues–Sat 5:30–10pm.

Moderate

678 Hawai'i ★★ KOREAN This is Honolulu's hippest Korean barbecue restaurant, where different cuts of high-quality pork and beef sizzle on the tabletop grill in front of you. It was started by the Korean celebrity Kang Ho Dong (that's his likeness in the glowing cutout in front), who has also opened other locations in Korea, Los Angeles, and Atlanta. The atmosphere draws young and old alike, with everyone reaching over for bits of meat to dip into the moat of corn cheese and egg custard warmed by the grill. Servers are quick and cheerful—call them by pressing a button on the table—and happy to replenish the *banchan,* or little side dishes, until you can't eat anymore. If only all eating experiences were this fun!

1726 Kapi'olani Blvd., Honolulu. ✆ **808/941-6678.** Reservations recommended. Combination meal for 2–3 people $44–$55. Sun–Thurs 11am–1am; Fri–Sat 11am–2am.

Highway Inn ★ HAWAIIAN/LOCAL The original Highway Inn in Waipahu opened in 1947, serving Hawaiian food such as *laulau* (pork wrapped in taro leaves and steamed), kālua pig (smoky, roasted pork), and poi (mashed taro). Also on the menu: classic American fare such as beef stew and hamburgers, recipes that founder Seiichi Toguchi picked up in internment-camp mess halls during World War II. For decades, Highway Inn remained a snapshot of food in post-war Hawai'i. Then, in 2012, it opened a new location in Honolulu and introduced some new twists, such as a Smokin' Moco—smoked meat over rice and topped with two eggs—and a hō'i'o salad, made with locally gathered fiddlehead ferns. The old favorites still remain, though, in the new, plantation-era-style restaurant.

680 Ala Moana Blvd., Honolulu. www.myhighwayinn.com. ✆ **808/954-4955.** Plates $10–$14. Mon–Thurs 8:30am–8:30pm; Fri–Sat 8:30am–9pm; Sun 9am–2:30pm.

Inexpensive

Shokudo ★ JAPANESE What you cannot miss here: the honey toast—as in, you literally won't miss it as servers bring it to the tables around you. Get your own—it's a tower of toast, practically half a loaf of Japanese bread, griddled in butter, cubed, drizzled with honey, and topped with ice cream. It sounds simple, but it's ridiculously enjoyable. As for the rest of the menu, Shokudo is sort of a cross between Denny's and Morimoto—a fun, trendy, stylish, eclectic eatery offering Japanese comfort food and decent (but not the best) sushi. Try the fresh tofu and mochi cheese gratin, too.

At the Ala Moana Pacific Center, 1585 Kapi'olani Blvd., Honolulu. www.shokudojapanese.com. ✆ **808/941-3701.** Main courses $7–$25; sushi $6.50–$15. Sun–Thurs 11:30am–1am; Fri–Sat 11:30am–2am.

Yataimura at Shirokiya ★★ JAPANESE Yes, it's a food court in a department store, but if you love Japanese food, you have to go. Shirokiya emulates Japan's busy street food scene by devoting its entire top floor to food. It can be overwhelming with the sights and sounds and smells—almost 2 dozen stalls and vendors are packed in here. Here's where to go: **Takoyaki Yama-chan** for *takoyaki,* little doughy pancake balls crisp on the outside and filled with chopped octopus; **Menya Ifu Do** for *tonkotsu* (pork bone) ramen; and affordable chirashi bowls at **Maguro Zanmai.** At the Ala Moana Center, 1450 Ala Moana Blvd., Honolulu. www.shirokiya.com. Plates $5–$15. Daily 10am–9pm.

DOWNTOWN/CHINATOWN

Char Hung Sut ★ LOCAL CHINESE For locals, this 60-year-old Chinatown institution is synonymous with *manapua,* Hawai'i's version of Chinese *char siu bao.* At Char Hung Sut, they're big, fluffy steamed buns stuffed with slightly sweet, shredded pork. Go early and watch them being made right in front of you. It's takeout only here—the shop is more factory than restaurant. Also try the pork hash (also known as *siu mai* on the Mainland)—juicy ground pork steamed in wonton-style wrappers. 64 N. Pauahi St., Honolulu. ✆ **808/538-3335.** Under $10. Cash only. Mon and Wed–Sat 5:30am–2pm; Sun 5:30am–1pm.

Little Village Noodle House ★ CHINESE For almost every year it's been open, Little Village has been awarded Best Chinese Restaurant by readers of local publications. It's Chinese food geared toward local tastes, but that doesn't mean it's not tasty. Added plus: a clean, charming interior decorated with Christmas lights and bamboo, a nice change from the sometimes harsh spaces of Chinatown's other restaurants. I like the Shanghai mochi stir fry, honey walnut shrimp, dried green beans, and beef chow fun.
1113 Smith St., Honolulu. www.littlevillagehawaii.com. ✆ **808/545-3008.** Most items under $17. Sun–Thurs 10:30am–10pm; Fri–Sat 10:30am–midnight.

Livestock Tavern ★★ AMERICAN For the past two decades, restaurateurs and artists have been trying to revitalize Chinatown, which in the second half of the 20th century became more well known as a red-light district than a place to eat and hang out. Restaurateurs Jesse Cruz and Dusty Grable have helped make Chinatown a destination with their three places—**Lucky Belly,** which serves modern Asian comfort food; **Tchin Tchin!,** a bar and lounge; and **Livestock Tavern.** All are great, but Livestock Tavern is my favorite. This is modern American food at its finest, with an excellent cocktail menu to boot. The menu changes seasonally (yes, even Hawai'i has seasons, however subtle), with heartier dishes like a mushroom bread pudding in the winter and lighter ones such as the grilled catch of the day in the summer. The hamburger is a staple on the menu and it's one of Honolulu's best.
49 N. Hotel St., Honolulu. www.livestocktavern.com. ✆ **808/537-2577.** Main courses $16–$32. Mon–Sat 11am–2pm and 5–10pm.

Murphy's Bar and Grill ★ IRISH Maybe you didn't come to Honolulu to hang out in an Irish bar. But if you did, Murphy's is the place to be. At lunch, it's packed with downtown businessmen tucking into Blarney Burgers (a hamburger with Guinness cheese) or open-face turkey sandwiches. After work, this is one of Honolulu's favorite *pau hana* (after-work) spots with great wings, local beers on draft (get anything from Maui Brewing Co.), and some of the friendliest bartenders in town. You would expect nothing less from an Irish bar.

2 Merchant St., Honolulu. http://murphyshawaii.com. ✆ **808/531-0422.** Main courses $12–$23. Lunch daily 11:30am–2:30pm; dinner Sun–Wed 5:30–9pm; Thurs–Sat 5:30–10pm.

The Pig and the Lady ★★★ MODERN VIETNAMESE It's one of Chinatown's liveliest dining rooms, with brick walls, long communal tables hewed from single slabs of mango wood, benches reupholstered with burlap rice bags, and a rotating display of fun, bright prints by local, young artists. The Pig and the Lady introduces you to a world of Vietnamese noodle soups beyond pho—such as one with oxtail, another with crab and tomato. But chef Andrew Le also applies creative twists to Southeast Asian food for unique eats like a pho French dip banh mi—an absolute must with its melting slices of braised brisket, smeared with a bright Thai basil chimichurri and served with a side of pho broth for dipping. Everything is en pointe here, from the cocktails to the dessert.

83 N. King St., Honolulu. http://thepigandthelady.com. ✆ **808/383-2152.** Reservations recommended. Main courses $11–$30. Mon–Fri 10:30am–2pm; Sat 10:30am–3pm; Tue–Sat 5:30–10pm.

To Chau ★★ VIETNAMESE PHO Is there anything on the menu other than pho? I couldn't even tell you. I just walk in, order a medium number 9, meat outside, and iced coffee with milk. What arrives: strong, black coffee percolating into a mug and a cup of ice and condensed milk. When the coffee is finished brewing, dump it into the cup and stir. By that time, you'll have a plate mounded with bean sprouts, Thai basil, sawtooth coriander, jalapeños, and lemon wedges. Soon after, the bowl of pho arrives, with flank, tendon, and tripe, as well as slices of rare steak on the side to dip into the hot broth-like fondue. You can also get your pho with all the meat in and just steak if you want; there are 14 different possible combinations. That's the only hard choice in this Chinatown Vietnamese restaurant. Getting the pho and Vietnamese coffee shouldn't be one.

1007 River St., Honolulu. ✆ **808/533-4549.** Reservations not accepted. All items under $10. Cash only. Mon–Fri 8:30am–2:30pm.

KALIHI/LILIHA/SAND ISLAND

Helena's Hawaiian Food ★★ HAWAIIAN Definitely seek out this humble little restaurant, winner of the James Beard Regional Classics award in 2000. When first-generation-Chinese Helen Chock started Helena's in 1946 (she added an "a" at the end to make it sound more "Hawaiian"), she served Chinese and Hawaiian food. Eventually, she pared down the menu to the most popular items—Hawaiian food such as *laulau*, kalua pig, and poi. Sixty years later, her grandson runs the

tasty TOURS

See Honolulu—one restaurant at a time. Former Honolulu newspaper food critic Matthew Gray has put together **Hawai'i Food Tours** to give you a taste of Hawai'i. He offers two tours, all with transportation from your Waikīkī hotel in an air-conditioned van and all with running commentary on Hawai'i's history, culture, and architecture. The **Hole-in-the-Wall Tour,** a lunch tour from 9am to 2pm ($139 per person), includes stops at Honolulu institutions, a noodle factory, and a behind-the-scenes look at Chinatown. You'll sample some only-in-Hawai'i treats. For details and booking, go to www.hawaiifoodtours.com or call ✆ **808/926-FOOD.**

place, and it's as popular as ever. What makes Helena's stand out among other Hawaiian food restaurants? The *pipikaula:* marinated, bone-in short ribs hung above the stove to dry and fried right before they land on your table.

1240 N. School St., Honolulu. www.helenashawaiianfood.com. ✆ **808/845-8044.** Full meals $9–$20. Cash only.

La Mariana Sailing Club ★ AMERICAN Only one authentic vintage tiki bar remains in Honolulu, and it's in the industrial wasteland near the airport (which makes it awfully convenient to have your last drink here before getting on the plane). But once you enter, you'll feel as if you've stepped back into 1955, the year La Mariana opened. It's pure kitsch, with glass floats and puffer fish lamps hanging from the ceiling. Come for a Mai Tai or a Zombie and watch the sunset over the docked sailboats. Stay for the live piano entertainment nightly, when regulars croon their favorite Hawaiian and American songs. You're here more for the ambience and entertainment than for the forgettable food.

50 Sand Island Rd., Honolulu. www.lamarianasailingclub.com. ✆ **808/848-2800.** Reservations recommended, especially Sat–Sun. Main courses $8–$16 lunch, $15–$29 dinner. Daily 11am–9pm. Turn *makai* (toward the ocean) on Sand Island Rd. from Nimitz Hwy.; immediately after the first light on Sand Island, take a right and drive toward the ocean; it's not far from the airport.

Liliha Bakery ★ AMERICAN/LOCAL It's a bakery, well known for its Coco Puffs (similar to cream puffs), but it's also one of O'ahu's favorite old-school diners, beloved by young and old alike. Sit at the Formica counter and watch the ladies expertly man the flattop and grill, turning out light and fluffy pancakes, crispy and seriously buttery waffles, loaded country-style omelets, and satisfying hamburgers and hamburger steaks. There's a newer location on Nimitz, but I prefer the ambience of the original.

515 N. Kuakini St., Honolulu. www.lilihabakeryhawaii.com. ✆ **808/531-1651.** Most items under $10. Open 24 hr. from Tues at 6am to Sun at 8pm.

Mitch's Sushi ★★ SUSHI The family that owns Mitch's Sushi also owns a seafood import business, which is why Mitch's has some of the freshest fish around. It's one of Honolulu's most expensive sushi bars, as well as its most casual, a place where slippers (local lingo for flip-flops) and T-shirts are the norm, along with a cooler of beer (Mitch's is BYOB). Here you'll find New Zealand salmon, as luxurious as fatty tuna belly, and Mitch's famous lobster sashimi, which you inspect as it's brought to your table, alive and kicking, and then sample in the form of sashimi and lobster miso soup.

524 Ohohia St., Honolulu. http://mitchssushi.com. ✆ **808/837-7774.** Reservations recommended. Sushi $4–$30. Daily 11:30am–8:30pm.

Nico's at Pier 38 ★ FRESH FISH Nico's has expanded from a hole in the wall to a gleaming, open-air restaurant almost four times its original size. The food isn't quite as good as it used to be, but it's still one of the best places around to get fresh fish plates for under $20. I also love its setting along the industrial waterfront, where Hawai'i's commercial fishing fleet resides—this isn't a fake fisherman's wharf but the real deal. Popular dishes here are the furikake pan-seared 'ahi and the catch-of-the-day special—perhaps opah sauced with tomato beurre blanc or swordfish topped with crab bisque (the chef, Nico Chaize, is French born). As part of the expansion, there's also a fish market next door where you can take out fresh poke and smoked swordfish to eat on the tables outside. Renting a place with a kitchen? Pick up fresh fish filets to take home and cook.

Pier 38, 1129 N. Nimitz Hwy., Honolulu. www.nicospier38.com. ✆ **808/540-1377.** Takeout orders accepted by phone. Lunch $8–$13; dinner $14–$26. Mon–Sat 6:30am–9pm; Sun 10am–9pm.

MĀNOA VALLEY/MŌ'ILI'ILI/MAKIKI

Expensive

Alan Wong's Restaurant ★★★ HAWAI'I REGIONAL Alan Wong was one of the founders of Hawai'i Regional Cuisine, which championed Hawai'i farmers and local flavors back in the '90s when most restaurants were of the Continental variety and flying in frozen seafood and meat. Wong brought uniquely local flavors to the fine-dining table, in dishes such as a ginger-crusted onaga, soy-braised short ribs, and *li hing mui* tomato salad. To this day, Alan Wong's remains one of Honolulu's best restaurants. Its menu retains many of the classics—for newer dishes, try the chef's tasting menu, which features the kitchen's latest, creative dishes, such as a pan-seared *opakapaka* on kimchi risotto or Maui Cattle Co. rib steak with a beef and foie gras "burger."

1857 S. King St., 3rd floor, Honolulu. www.alanwongs.com. ✆ **808/949-2526.** Reservations highly recommended. Main courses $28–$55; tasting menu $85 ($125 with wine). Daily 5–10pm.

Chef Mavro Restaurant ★★★ HAWAI'I REGIONAL James Beard Award–winner George Mavrothalassitis melds his French background with pristine Hawaiian ingredients for one of Hawai'i's top fine-dining experiences. The menu changes quarterly to reflect the seasons. A recent menu featured onaga baked in a Hawaiian salt crust, lamb loin with a vadouvan curry, and liliko'i malasadas. Four- and six-course menus are offered. Wine is only available as pairings for each course, which elevates the experience to divine.

1969 S. King St., Honolulu. www.chefmavro.com. ✆ **808/944-4714.** Reservations recommended. Prix-fixe menu $105–$148 ($162–$211 with wine pairings). Tues–Sun 6–9pm.

Izakaya Gaku ★★★ JAPANESE There is life beyond maguro and hamachi nigiri, and the best place to experience it is at Izakaya Gaku. The Izakaya restaurants embrace small plates as the best way to eat and drink with friends; although Honolulu offers many of them, Izakaya Gaku is the best. Here you can get uncommon seasonal sushi and seafood, such as wild yellowtail and grilled ray. One of the best dishes here is a hamachi tartare, with hamachi scraped off the bones and topped with tobiko and raw quail egg, served with sheets of crisp nori. But you're not likely to be disappointed with any dish.

1329 S. King St., Honolulu. ✆ **808/589-1329.** Reservations highly recommended. Sashimi $12–$40; small plates $4–$13. Mon–Sat 5–11pm.

Inexpensive

Jimbo's Restaurant ★ JAPANESE Jimbo's offers fresh noodles made by hand—or should we say foot? To give the udon noodles their characteristic chew, Jimbo's cooks stomp on the noodle dough (wrapped, of course) before rolling it out. Enjoy it cold with a dipping sauce or hot in a shoyu and dashi-based broth. For sumo-sized appetites, get the *nabeyaki* udon, brought to the table in a heavy pot and filled with udon, vegetable and shrimp tempura, chicken, and an egg.

1936 S. King St., Honolulu. ✆ **808/947-2211.** Main courses $10–$14. Daily 11am–2:30pm and 5–9:45pm (Fri–Sat until 10:30pm).

KAIMUKĪ

Moderate

Mud Hen Water ★ MODERN HAWAIIAN This is the sister restaurant to Town (see below). Whereas Town is Italian in its flavors, Mud Hen Water draws inspiration from all of the cultures influencing Hawai'i. What that translates into: *lup cheong* (a Chinese sausage) madeleines with miso-whipped lardo and *i'a lawalu,* fish wrapped in a banana leaf and grilled over an open fire. You won't find dishes like this anywhere else. Plates are small and made for sharing.

3452 Wai'alae Ave. (at 9th St.), Honolulu. www.mudhenwater.com. ✆ **808/737-6000.** Reservations highly recommended for dinner. Small plates $8–$28. Tues–Sat 5:30–10pm (Fri–Sat until midnight).

Town ★★ CONTEMPORARY ITALIAN Town's motto is "Local first, organic whenever possible, with Aloha always." Chef/owner Ed Kenney lovingly showcases local ingredients: in a pork sugo on the lightest gnocchi you may ever have, or as the seasonal produce tossed with hand-cut pasta. Kenney definitely has a way with pork: If you see it on the menu—as charcuterie, porchetta, or roasted shoulder—get it. I also love the mussels in a fennel and Cinzano broth. Order it with a side of fries, and use them to soak up all the goodness. Also worth checking out: **Kaimukī Superette** across the street, Chef Kenney's casual breakfast and lunch spot specializing in sandwiches.

3435 Wai'alae Ave. (at 9th St.), Honolulu. www.townkaimuki.com. ✆ **808/735-5900.** Reservations highly recommended for dinner. Main courses $9–$16 lunch, $16–$26 dinner. Mon–Sat 7am–2:30pm and 5:30–9:30pm (Fri–Sat until 10pm).

12th Ave Grill ★★ CONTEMPORARY AMERICAN Outside of Waikīkī and the Ke'eaumoku region, Honolulu lacks dense, walkable neighborhoods—it's more like L.A. than San Francisco. One of the few urban neighborhoods is Kaimukī, with a cluster of some of Honolulu's best restaurants. This is one of them, with a menu leaning towards comfort food, like baked mac 'n' cheese, and locally raised meat, such as pork chops with potato pancakes and ribeye on fresh pappardelle. Another reason why I love this place? It's the rare restaurant that serves good food *and* good cocktails. ***Tip:*** Sit in the bar area during opening or closing hours, when the bar serves a special menu of terrifically satisfying hamburgers and meatloaf sandwiches, and nothing costs more than $10.

1120 12th Ave., Honolulu. http://12thavegrill.com. ✆ **808/732-9469.** Reservations recommended. Small plates $7–$13; large plates $23–$36. Daily 5:30–11pm.

Inexpensive

Koko Head Café ★ BREAKFAST/BRUNCH This "island style brunch house" offers inspired takes on breakfast favorites. There's the cornflake French toast, extra crunchy on the outside and custardy on the inside, crowned with frosted flake gelato, and the Don Buri Chen, a rice bowl for carnivores, with miso-smoked pork, five-spice pork belly and eggs.

1145c 12th Ave., Honolulu. www.kokoheadcafe.com. ✆ **808/732-8920.** Main courses $9–$16. Daily 7am–2:30pm.

Via Gelato ★ DESSERT When you've had your fill of shave ice, come here for gelato churned daily in island-inspired flavors such as guava, lychee, strawberry, and *ume* (salted plum). It's a tough decision, though, choosing between those and other favorites such as green tea Oreo and black sesame. The flavors change daily. Be sure to get here early on weekend nights before they run out.

1142 12th Ave., Honolulu. www.viagelatohawaii.com. ✆ **808/732-2800.** Scoops starting at $3. Tues–Sun 11am–10pm (Fri–Sat until 11pm).

TO THE EAST: DIAMOND HEAD AND KĀHALA

Arancino at The Kahala ★★ MODERN ITALIAN This, Arancino's third location (the other two are in Waikīkī), opened a few years ago. Befitting its new digs, it isn't a casual trattoria; it's meant to be a fine-dining destination with a dress code (pants and shoes required for the men). Standouts on the menu include a *bagna cauda,* with the vegetables planted in a pot of cremini mushroom "dirt"; grilled calamari, shrimp, and seafood over housemade squid-ink chitarra; and a decadent uni spaghetti. For a town surprisingly short on alfresco dining, Arancino at the Kahala is a breath of fresh air (even if it is facing the Kahala Resort's valet).

At the Kahala Hotel Resort, 5000 Kāhala Ave., Honolulu. www.kahalaresort.com. ✆ **808/380-4400.** Reservations recommended. Collared shirts and long pants preferred for men. Main courses $18–$32 lunch; $18–$80 dinner. Daily 11:30am–2:30pm and 5–9:30pm.

Diamond Head Market & Grill ★ AMERICAN/LOCAL Here you'll find some of our favorite plate lunches, near the base of Diamond Head. For breakfast, the pancakes with mac nuts or pineapple are a winner, or start the morning with a savory plate like the kimchi fried rice. Lunch and dinner offer tasty ʻahi steaks and kalbi (Korean-marinated short ribs). Don't miss dessert: The lemon crunch cake is the perfect capper to a Diamond Head hike.

3158 Monsarrat Ave., Honolulu. www.diamondheadmarket.com. ✆ **808/732-0077.** Plates $6–$17. Daily 6:30am–9pm.

East O'ahu

Roy's Restaurant ★ HAWAIʻI REGIONAL This is the original Roy's, the one that launched more than 30 Roy's restaurants around the world (six of them in Hawaiʻi). One of Hawaiʻi Regional Cuisine's most famous founders, Roy Yamaguchi started fusing local flavors and ingredients with European techniques 20 years ago. The original menu items are still here, such as blackened island ʻahi with spicy soy mustard and Roy's famous melting-hot chocolate soufflé. Sit on the lānai to watch the sunset over Maunalua Bay.

6600 Kalaniana'ole Hwy., Hawai'i Kai. www.roysrestaurant.com. ✆ **808/396-7697.** Reservations recommended. Main courses $20–$40; 3-course prix-fixe $42. Mon–Thurs 5:30–9pm; Fri 5:30–9:30pm; Sat 5–9:30pm; Sun 5–9pm.

The Windward Coast

Note: The following restaurants are located on the "Eastern Oʻahu & the Windward Coast" map (p. 93).

'Ai Love Nalo ★ LOCAL/VEGAN This roadside gem offers a plant-based take on local favorites, such as the *laulau,* here a package of *kalo* (taro, a staple in the Hawaiian diet), *ʻulu* (breadfruit), Okinawan sweet potato, and carrot, all bundled in a *lūʻau* leaf (taro leaf) and slow-cooked in coconut milk. Everything is lovely and full of flavor. Try the poi parfait or the soft serve, both topped with fresh, seasonal fruit and toasted cacao coconut flakes.

41-1025 Kalaniana'ole Hwy., Waimānalo. www.ailovenalo.com. Everything under $11. Wed–Mon 9am–5pm.

Hale Kealoha Restaurant ★ LOCAL Eating here feels like hanging out at a friend's backyard lū'au, complete with foldout picnic tables and chairs and Christmas lights. On Saturday nights, there's even live Hawaiian music. Order the Pa Pā'ina plate for the full experience, a Hawaiian plate lunch with all the fixin's—kālua pig, chicken long rice, squid lū'au, lomi salmon, poke, rice, poi, haupia, 'uala (sweet potato), and mamaki tea.

120 Hekili St., Kailua. www.halekealoharestaurant.com. ✆ **808/262-1100.** Plates $10–$28. Wed–Thurs 10am–8pm, Fri–Sat 10am–10pm.

Moke's Bread and Breakfast ★ BREAKFAST/BRUNCH Of all the pancake joints in Kailua, Moke's is my pick—their *liliko'i* pancakes are unparalleled. A light passionfruit cream sauce cascades over tender, fluffy pancakes, a perfect blend of tart and sweet, simple and decadent. Other staples, such as the loco moco and omelets, are also spot-on.

27 Ho'olai St., Kailua. www.mokeskailua.com. ✆ **808/261-5565.** Entrees $8–$14. Wed–Mon 6:30am–2pm.

Prima ★ ITALIAN O'ahu's best Neopolitan-style pizzas come out of the wood-burning oven at Prima. What that translates into: a thin crust that gives way to puffy edges, spare toppings, fresh-pulled mozzarella, and a bright, San Marzano tomato sauce. Sample a classic margherita

The Shrimp Trucks

Shrimp farming took hold in Kahuku in the '90s and, before long, the first shrimp truck set up, serving fresh shrimp from a lunch wagon window. Now you can smell the garlic cooking before you see all the trucks and shrimp shacks—at least five, by last count. **Giovanni's Original White Shrimp Truck,** 56-505 Kamehameha Hwy. (✆ **808/293-1839**), is the most popular—so popular that a makeshift food court with picnic tables, shade, and a handful of other businesses has sprung up around the beat-up old white truck scrawled with tourists' signatures. Even though the shrimp are now imported and previously frozen, Giovanni's knows how to cook them perfectly. Scampi style is my favorite—shell-on shrimp coated in lots of butter and garlic. Twelve bucks gets you a dozen, plus two scoops of rice. Head north from Giovanni's about a mile, and you'll hit **Romy's,** 56-781 Kamehameha Hwy. (✆ **808/232-2202**), a shrimp shack instead of a truck. Here the shrimp actually come from the farm behind it. Romy's is my favorite for the sauce—tons of sautéed and fried garlic over a half-pound of head-on shrimp, plus a container of spicy soy sauce for dipping. The shrimp, however, are inconsistent—sometimes firm and sweet, sometimes mealy.

pizza or my favorite, the Five P, with pickled piquillo pepper, pepperoncini, and pepperoni.

108 Hekili St. #107, Kailua. www.primahawaii.com. ✆ **808/888-8933.** Pizzas $16–$22. Mon–Sun 10am–9:30pm.

The North Shore

Note: The following are on the "O'ahu's North Shore" map (p. 101).

INEXPENSIVE

Beet Box Café ★★ VEGETARIAN For me, a perfect day on the North Shore involves waves and a stop at Beet Box. It recently moved into a bigger space with warm wood paneling (upcycled, of course), and it's now open for dinner, too (try the cauliflower steak). For lunch, veggies are transformed into tasty, satisfying sandwiches with portobello and feta or avocado and local greens. The breakfast burritos and smoothies are popular, too.

66-437 Kamehameha Hwy., Hale'iwa. www.thebeetboxcafe.com. ✆ **808/637-3000.** Breakfast and lunch $8–$12; dinner $14–$17. Mon–Sun 7am–4pm; Wed–Sat 6–9:30pm.

Kahuku Farms ★ SANDWICHES & SNACKS Not a fan of shrimp? Then stop by Kahuku Farms' Farm Café, where you can get a simple grilled veggie panini made with veggies all grown right here on the farm, and a smoothie with papaya and banana, also grown here. If I'm driving up this way, I always try to stop for the grilled banana bread topped with caramel and *haupia* (coconut) sauce and a scoop of ice cream. Yup, so decadent and so good.

56-800 Kamehameha Hwy., Kahuku. www.kahukufarms.com. ✆ **808/293-8159.** Items $8–$10. Wed–Mon 11am–4pm.

Opal Thai ★ THAI Once a popular food truck, now a no-frills, sit-down restaurant in Hale'iwa Town Center, Opal Thai serves the best Thai food on the island. My favorites: crab stir-fried noodles, duck curry, and fried tofu with garlic sauce and fried basil leaves. If it's hard for you to choose, leave the ordering up to owner Opel Sirichandhra, giving your spice preference and favorite Thai dishes as a guide.

66-197 Kamehameha Hwy., Hale'iwa. ✆ **808/381-8091.** Dishes $11–$20. Tues–Sat 11am–3pm and 5–10pm.

Leeward O'ahu: The Wai'anae Coast

Kahumana Café ★ FARM The fare here is simple but fresh and tasty; the setting is right on an organic farm. Enjoy a veggie-tofu stir-fry or veggie wrap while overlooking the herbs and vegetables grown right there. There aren't a lot of eating options on the west side, which makes Kahumana Café even more welcome.

86-660 Lualualei Homestead Rd., Wai'anae. www.kahumana.org. ✆ **808/696-2655.** Main courses $10–$15. Tues–Sat 11:30am–2:30pm and 6–7:30pm. Head up

LŪ'AU!

The sun is setting, the tiki torches are lit, the pig is taken from the *imu* (an oven in the earth), the *pū* (conch) sounds—it's lū'au time! Few experiences say "Hawai'i" to visitors as the lū'au. In ancient times, the lū'au was called 'aha 'āina ('aha means means gathering and 'āina, land); these were celebrations with family and friends to mark important occasions, such as a victory at war or a baby surviving its first year. Lū'au are still a part of life in Hawai'i; in particular, the legacy of the baby's first lū'au lives on.

For visitors, lū'au are a way to experience a feast of food and entertainment, Hawaiian style. The lū'au at the **Royal Hawaiian,** 2259 Kalākaua Ave. (www.royal-hawaiian.com; ✆ **888/808-4668**), is the priciest of all the options, but it's the only beachfront one in Waikīkī and offers the best food, an open bar, and quality entertainment. It takes place every Monday from 5:30 to 9pm, costing $179 for adults, $101 for children 5 to 12.

About an hour outside of Waikīkī on the Leeward coast, **Paradise Cove Lū'au,** 92-1089 Ali'i Nui Dr., Kapolei (www.paradisecovehawaii.com; ✆ **808/842-5911**), is a popular option. It has a lovely setting, perfect for sunset photos, and the evening starts with arts and crafts and activities for the kids. As for the buffet, you'll find better food at the Hawaiian restaurants listed on p. 156. Waikīkī bus pickup and return is included in the package prices: Paradise Cove's lū'au is nightly at 6pm and costs $85 to $156 for adults, $75 to $137 for teens 13 to 18, $65 to $123 for children 4 to 12, and free for children 3 and under.

Farrington Hwy. and turn right on Mā'ili'ili Rd. Go straight for 2 miles, past Pūhāwai Rd. Continue until you reach the Kahumana gate. The cafe is the blue building at the end of the driveway.

Monkeypod Kitchen ★ AMERICAN This is the best dining option at Ko Olina Station, a strip mall of casual eateries servicing Ko Olina Resort. Monkeypod Kitchen is one of the latest ventures from Peter Merriman, who pioneered farm-to-table fine dining on the Big Island in the '80s. This is his larger and more casual restaurant (with another location on Maui). The vibe in this two-story space is welcoming and friendly, with live music on the lānai and a long bar with 36 (!) beers on tap. Expect fresh salads and entrees like fish and chips and burgers. I always go for the saimin, which is nothing like the traditional version you'll find elsewhere; here it comes with kālua pork and fresh vegetables. To drink: the bracingly zingy housemade ginger beer. ***Tip:*** Want a more intimate bar experience? Head upstairs, where the bartenders spend a little more time making your cocktails, which include fresh takes on the Mai Tai (topped with a honey *liliko'i* foam) and the Makawao Ave., made with rye and that terrific ginger beer.

At Ko Olina Station, 92-1048 Olani St., Suite 4-107, Kapolei. www.monkeypod kitchen.com. ✆ **808/380-4086.** Reservations recommended. Main courses $12–$35. Daily 11am–11pm.

O'AHU SHOPPING

The trend in Honolulu shopping of late has been toward luxury brands, catering to Japanese (and increasingly, Chinese) tourists and leading to the demise, at the end of 2013, of the International Marketplace. Truthfully, the open-air Waikīkī marketplace had become a maze of kitschy junk, but it had a 56-year run, long enough for many people to feel sentimental about it. In its place is the new, high-end **International Marketplace mall** anchored by Saks Fifth Avenue.

You can also find plenty of luxury goods at the new **Ala Moana Center** wing. But just as the luxury market is growing, so is Honolulu's boutique culture and the vitality of the local crafts scene, as artisans endeavor to capture what makes Hawai'i so unique. You'll find the best boutique shopping in Chinatown and Hale'iwa, but you'll find gems even at the malls.

Classic Hawaiian aloha shirt.

Shopping in & Around Honolulu & Waikīkī

CLOTHING

The **aloha shirt** is alive and well, thanks to a revival of vintage aloha wear and the modern take, which features more subdued prints and slimmer silhouettes.

Vintage 1930s to 1950s Hawaiian wear is still beautiful, found in collectibles shops, such as the packed-to-the-rafters **Bailey's Antiques and Aloha Shirts,** 517 Kapahulu Ave.

(© **808/734-7628**). Of the contemporary aloha-wear designers, one of the best O'ahu-based ones is **Tori Richard,** who creates tasteful tropical prints in the form of linen and silk shirts for the men and flowy dresses for women. **Reyn Spooner,** Ala Moana Center (www.reynspooner.com; with three other O'ahu locations), is another source of attractive aloha shirts in traditional and contemporary styles; the new Modern Collection appeals to younger tastes, combining more fitted sleeves and a 1960s preppy look with some of Reyn Spooner's classic prints. Also check out **Kahala Sportswear,** Ala Moana Center (www.kahala.com), which has been designing aloha shirts since 1936 and remains an island favorite.

The hippest guys and gals go to **Roberta Oaks,** 19 N. Pauahi St. (www.robertaoaks.com; © **808/428-1214**), in Chinatown, where a slew of trendy boutiques has opened in recent years. Roberta Oaks ditches the too-big aloha shirt for a more stylish, fitted look, but keeps the vintage designs. Plus, she even has super-cute, tailored aloha shirts for the ladies.

EDIBLES

Nisshodo Candy Store ★ Mochi (Japanese rice cake) is so essential to locals' lives that even the drugstores sell it. But for the freshest and widest variety, go straight to the source: Nisshodo, an almost century-old business. Choose among pink-and-white *chichi dango* (or milk mochi), mochi filled with smooth azuki bean, *monaka* (delicate rice wafers sandwiching sweetened lima-bean paste), and much more. 1095 Dillingham Blvd. © **808/847-1244.**

Padovani's Chocolates ★ Brothers Philippe and Pierre Padovani are two of Hawai'i's best chefs, involved with the Hawai'i Regional Cuisine movement. In recent years, they've been devoting their attention to chocolate truffles. Their edible gems come in delightful flavors such as a calamansi (a small Filipino lime) and pirie mango ganache, flavored with fragrant, local mangoes picked at the height of the season. Other favorites incorporate ginger, Mānoa honey, and *liliko'i* (Hawaiian passionfruit). You might pick up some of these to bring home, but I'm guessing they'll never make it. 650 Iwilei Rd., #280. © **808/536-4567.**

Whole Foods ★ Whole Foods does a great job of sourcing local, both in produce and in specialty items such as honey, jams, hot sauces, coffee, and chocolate. It's also got one of the best selections of locally made soaps, great for gifts to take home. 4211 Wai'alae Ave at Kahala Mall. © **808/738-0820.**

FLOWERS & LEIS

The best place to shop for leis is in Chinatown, where lei vendors line Beretania and Maunakea streets and the fragrances of their wares mix with the earthy scents of incense and ethnic foods. My top picks are **Lita's Leis,** 59 N. Beretania St. (© **808/521-9065**), which has fresh

Farmer's MARKETS

Farmer's markets have proliferated on O'ahu—there's now one for every neighborhood for every day of the week. Unfortunately, the number of farmers has not kept up. In fact, some of the markets have vendors that sell repackaged Mainland produce. The best farmer's markets are those run by the **Hawai'i Farm Bureau Federation** (**HFBF;** www.hfbf.org/markets) and **FarmLovers** (www.farmloversmarkets.com), which mandate locally grown meats, fruits, and veggies. Check their websites for detailed information. Here are my favorites:

- **Kapi'olani Community College:** The original and still the biggest and best. Unfortunately, you'll have to deal with crowds—busloads of tourists get dropped off here. But you'll find items unavailable at any other market—endless varieties of bananas and mangoes, tropical fruit you've never seen before, persimmons, and local duck eggs. Pick up cut, chilled pineapple or jackfruit to snack on, yogurt from O'ahu's one remaining dairy, perhaps some grilled abalone from Kona, and corn from Kahuku. And with a healthy dose of prepared-food vendors serving everything from fresh tomato pizzas to raw and vegan snacks, you won't go hungry (4355 Diamond Head Rd.; © **808/848-2074;** Sat 7:30–11am; TheBus: 23 or 24).
- **Honolulu Farmer's Market:** This HFBF market is less crowded and has more locals stopping by to pick up groceries after work, plus some of the same vendors as the Kapi'olani Community College market (777 Ward Ave.; © **808/848-2074;** Wed 4–7pm; TheBus: 13).

puakenikeni, gardenias that last, and a supply of fresh and reasonable leis; **Lin's Lei Shop,** 1017-A Maunakea St. (© **808/537-4112**), with creatively fashioned, unusual leis; and **Cindy's Lei Shoppe,** 1034 Maunakea St. (© **808/536-6538**), with terrific sources for unusual leis such as feather dendrobiums and firecracker combinations, as well as everyday favorites like ginger, tuberose, orchid, and *pikake.*

HAWAIIANA & GIFT ITEMS

Visit the **Museum Shop** at the Honolulu Museum of Art, 900 S. Beretania St. (© **808/532-8703**), for crafts, jewelry, and prints, including Georgia O'Keefe's illustrations from her time in Hawai'i. You'll find gifts to bring home, such as lauhala clutches, macadamia nut oil soaps, and color-saturated screenprints. I'm a fan of the local artists' limited-edition T-shirts and collection of beautiful ceramics.

Native Books/Na Mea Hawai'i ★ Recently joined by the Hula Supply Center, the space is now a one-stop shop and resource for all things local and Hawaiian. You'll find hula stones and *ipu* (gourds); Ni'ihau shell lei; prints, crafts, and jewelry from local artists; local jams and coffee; and shelves of Hawaiian history and culture books. Regular classes in lauhala weaving, Hawaiian featherwork, 'ukulele, the

Hawaiian language, and more are also held here. Call for the schedule. At the Ward Warehouse, 1050 Ala Moana Blvd. ✆ **808/596-8885.**

Nohea Gallery ★ During its 25 years in business, Nohea Gallery has carried the work of more than 2,100 artists, almost all local. Here you'll find original *gyotaku,* or prints using real fish such as ono and 'opelu by Naoki Hayashi, and woodwork, including beautiful bowls made of mango wood and koa. I love that you can buy everything from trinkets such as koa wood magnets to ki*ele's beachy, delicate jewelry using sea glass and shells to a Russell Lowrey original (painting) of Pounder's Beach for $7,500. At the Ward Warehouse, 1050 Ala Moana Blvd. www.noheagallery.com. ✆ **808/596-0074.**

Tin Can Mailman ★ What, not looking for a 1950s oil hula lamp? Check out this shop anyway. It's packed with vintage Hawaiiana to emulate old-school general stores. The emphasis is on ephemera, such as pinups, postcards, old sheet music and advertisements, and the elusive Betty Boop hula girl bobblehead. 1026 Nu'unau Ave. ✆ **808/524-3009.**

SHOPPING CENTERS

Ala Moana Center ★★ Hawai'i's largest mall includes luxury brands and mainstream chains. But it also offers a selection of local stores. Make sure to browse **Manaola,** a locally designed line of luxury Hawaiian wear that draws inspiration from Hawaiian culture. You'll also find **Tori Richard** and **Reyn Spooner** (see "Clothing," above, for both); for surf-and-skate wear, check out **Hawaiian Island Creations** or **T&C Surf Designs.** Local boutique **Cinnamon Girl** is a perennial favorite for ultra-feminine dresses and mother-and-daughter matching outfits. For presents to bring home, stop in **Blue Hawai'i Lifestyle,** which offers locally made food gifts such as chocolate and honey, as well as Hawai'i-made soaps and beauty products. Pick up beautifully packaged, chocolate-dipped macnut shortbread at **Big Island Candies** and only-in-Hawai'i treats such as *manju* (resembling a filled cookie) and ume-shiso chocolates. Hungry? Head to the food court at **Shirokiya ★★** (p. 147) or treat yourself to a slice of cake and a plantation iced-tea jelly at the Japanese/French patisserie **Palme D'Or.** The center is open Monday to

Flower leis.

Saturday 9:30am to 9pm, and Sunday 10am to 7pm. 1450 Ala Moana Blvd. www.alamoanacenter.com. ✆ **808/955-9517.** Bus: 8, 19, or 20. Various shuttle services also stop here. For Waikīkī Trolley information, see "Getting Around" (p. 67). Farmers Market Sat 9am–1pm, Level 2 across from Sears.

Ward Village Shops ★ Gems here include **Native Books/Na Mea Hawai'i** and the **Nohea Gallery** (see "Hawaiiana & Gift Items," above, for both). Find more unique gifts at **Red Pineapple,** such as Sumadra clutches printed with silhouettes of the Mokulua Islands off Kailua, and Saffron James' scents, which capture the exoticism of Hawai'i's flowers. Don't miss the Everything Is Jake! retro-styled travel posters of O'ahu's Hale'iwa town and other iconic Hawai'i landscapes. **Kaypee Soh,** a local designer, opened his eponymous store here recently, showcasing colorful, tropical designs on housewares, from pillows to rugs, bowls to plates. Ward Village Shops is open Monday through Saturday 10am to 9pm, Sunday 10am to 6pm. ***Note:*** This area is currently being redeveloped, and the intent is to find new spaces for many of the current tenants while bringing in new stores for the mixed-use condo and retail development, dubbed Ward Village. To find the most up-to-date store directory, visit the Ward Village website. 1200 Ala Moana Blvd. www.wardvillageshops.com. ✆ **808/591-8411.**

Shopping in Kailua

Befitting O'ahu's favorite beach town, many of the boutiques in Kailua offer plenty of swimsuits, breezy styles for men and women, and T-shirts from homegrown brands.

Aloha Beach Club ★ One of Kailua's newer boutiques, Aloha Beach Club also designs and makes its own aloha shirts and board shorts in Hawai'i. The style is updated retro. You'll also find tasteful Aloha Beach Club logo wear. Make sure to grab a shave ice in the shop-within-a-shop, **The Local Hawai'i,** made with locally grown fruit (a rarity in the artificially flavored shave ice world). 131 Hekili St., Suite 108, Kailua. www.alohabeachclub.com.

Oliver ★ This tiny, quirky shop for stylish men sells aloha shirts from local brand Salvage Public, pocket knives for the urban explorer, and soaps to clean up with when you're done exploring. Browse the shop's collection of vinyl records for some great vintage surf-band finds. Next door, **Olive** is for women, offering beach blankets, über-stylish swimsuits (to match Oliver's über-stylish man), and beachy, well-made dresses. 49 Kihapai St., Kailua. www.oliverhawaii.com. ✆ **808/261-6587.**

Madre Chocolate ★ Honolulu's first bean-to-bar maker pays homage to chocolate's origins—no surprise, considering owner Nat Bletter's career as an ethnobotanist. The Triple Cacao bar blends cacao in all its forms: cacao pulp from Brazil, and nibs and chocolate from Mexico, reflecting the origin of the cacao trees in South America and chocolate's

Shopping in **CHINATOWN**

In the 1840s, Honolulu's Chinatown began to take shape as many Chinese brought in to work on the sugar plantations opted not to renew their contracts and instead moved to Chinatown to open businesses. Fronting Honolulu harbor, Chinatown catered to whalers and sailors. It reached its zenith in the 1920s, with restaurants and markets flourishing by day, and prostitutes and opium dens doing brisk business at night. As its reputation as a red-light district began to eclipse everything else, the neighborhood slowly declined. That is, until recent decades. Fresh boutiques and restaurants are filling in previously abandoned storefronts—which retain much of their original architectural details from the 1900s—as Chinatown once again attracts the entrepreneurial.

At the original location of **Fighting Eel,** 1133 Bethel St. (www.fightingeel.com; ✆ **808/738-9300**), you'll find bright, easy-to-wear dresses and shirts with island prints that are in every local fashionista's closet—perfect for Honolulu weather, but chic enough to wear back home. **Owens and Co.,** 1152 Nu'uanu Ave. (www.owensandcompany.com; ✆ **808/531-4300**), offers a colorful selection of housewares and accessories, including candles, stationery, jewelry, and totes, many of which are locally made or island inspired. Go treasure hunting at **Tin Can Mailman** (p. 161) and the funky **Hound & Quail,** 920 Maunakea St. (www.houndandquail.com; ✆ **808/779-8436**), where a collection of antiques and curiosities, from a taxidermied ostrich to old medical texts, make for a fascinating perusal. Find nostalgia in a 1950s tiki print dress or red silk kimono at **Barrio Vintage,** 1161 Nu'uanu Ave. (www.barriovintage.com; ✆ **808/674-7156**), one of the island's best shops for vintage clothing. At **Ginger13,** 22 S. Pauahi St. (www.ginger13.com; ✆ **808/531-5311**), local jewelry designer Cindy Yokoyama offers a refreshing change from the delicate jewelry found all over Hawai'i by creating asymmetrical styles with chunky stones such as agate and opal.

invention in Central America. Other chocolate-bar flavors include *liliko'i* (passionfruit) and coconut milk with candied ginger. 20A Kainehe St., Kailua. www.madrechocolate.com. ✆ **808/262-6789.**

Shopping on the North Shore

The newly developed **Hale'iwa Store Lots,** 66-087 Kamehameha Hwy. (www.haleiwastorelots.com), replaces some of the old, dusty buildings (some would say charming) in Hale'iwa with an open-air, plantation-style shopping center. Here's the famous **Matsumoto Shave Ice,** in new, bigger digs but with the same powdery-soft ice drenched in island flavors. You'll also find the **Clark Little Gallery,** showcasing the photographer's shorebreak photos, which capture the fluidity, beauty, and power of a wave just as it's about to hit the shoreline. Don't miss **Greenroom Hawai'i** (which also has a location in the Sheraton Waikīkī), featuring local artists' work, including Heather Brown's bold and bright surf art and Kris Goto's quirky drawings combining manga sensibilities with Hawai'i surf culture. **Guava Shop** is Hale'iwa's quintessential clothing boutique.

Its beachy, bohemian styles capture the aesthetic of a North Shore surfer girl.

Farther south into Hale'iwa is **Coffee Gallery,** 66-250 Kamehameha Hwy., Suite C106 (www.roastmaster.com; ✆ **808/637-5571**), the best cafe in town, with a great selection of locally grown coffee beans to take home. **Tini Manini,** 66-250 Kamehameha Hwy., Suite C101 (www.tinimanini.com; ✆ **808/637-8464**), is an adorable children's shop with everything from bathing suits to baby blankets for your little one. North Shore residents are relentlessly active, keeping in shape through running, surfing, stand-up paddling, and yoga. **Mahiku,** 66-165 Kamehameha Hwy. (www.mahiku.com; ✆ **808/888-6857**), keeps them stylish, with fun and bright activewear that can go straight from the yoga mat into the ocean.

Over in Waialua, a collection of surfboard shapers and small businesses have turned the **Waialua Sugar Mill,** which stopped producing sugar in 1996, into a low-key retail and industrial space. Stop by the **North Shore Soap Factory,** 67-106 Kealohanui St. (www.northshoresoapfactory.com; ✆ **808/637-8400**), to watch its all-natural and fragrant soaps being made. You can even stamp your bar of soap with a shaka or the silhouette of the sugar mill. It also has a line of bath and body care, including scrubs, lotions, and moisturizing kukui-nut oil.

O'AHU NIGHTLIFE

Nightlife in Hawai'i begins at sunset, when all eyes turn westward to see how the day will end. Sunset viewers always seem to bond in the mutual enjoyment of a natural spectacle.

Enjoy hula dancing and a torch-lighting ceremony on Tuesday, Thursday, Saturday, and Sunday from 6:30 to 7:30pm (6–7pm Nov–Jan), as the sun casts its golden glow on the beach at the **Kūhiō Beach Hula Mound,** close to Duke Kahanamoku's statue (Ulunui and Kalākaua sts.). This is a thoroughly delightful free offering of hula and music by some of the Hawai'i's finest performers. Start off early with a picnic basket and walk along the oceanside path fronting Queen's Beach near the Waikīkī Aquarium. (You can park along Kapi'olani Park or near the zoo.) There are few more pleasing spots in Waikīkī than the benches at water's edge at this Diamond Head end of Kalākaua Avenue. It's a short walk to where the seawall and daring boogie boarders attract hordes of spectators. To check the schedule, go to www.waikikiimprovement.com/waikiki-calendar-of-events/kuhio-beach-hula-show and click Events.

The Bar Scene

ON THE BEACH Waikīkī's beachfront bars offer many possibilities, from the **Mai Tai Bar** (✆ **808/923-7311**) at the Royal Hawaiian (p. 130) a few feet from the sand, to the **Beach Bar** (✆ **808/921-4600**)

A trio plays to a sunset crowd at House Without a Key.

under the banyan tree at the Moana Surfrider (p. 129), to the unfailingly enchanting **House Without a Key** (© **808/923-2311**) at the Halekulani (p. 128) where the breathtaking **Kanoelehua Miller** dances hula to the riffs of Hawaiian steel-pedal guitar under a century-old *kiawe* tree with the sunset and ocean glowing behind her—a romantic, evocative, nostalgic scene. (It doesn't hurt, either, that the Halekulani happens to make the best Mai Tais in the world.) The Halekulani has the after-dinner hours covered, too, with light jazz by local artists in the Lewers Lounge from 9pm to 2am nightly (see "Live Blues, R&B, Jazz & Pop," below).

Another great bar for watching the sun sink into the Pacific is **Duke's Waikīkī** (www.dukeswaikiki.com; © **808/922-2268**) in the Outrigger Waikīkī Beach Resort. The outside Barefoot Bar is perfect for sipping a tropical drink, watching the waves and sunset, and listening to music. It can get crowded, so get here early. Hawai'i sunset music is usually from 4 to 6pm daily, and there's live entertainment nightly from 9:30pm to midnight.

DOWNTOWN/CHINATOWN **First Fridays,** which originally started as an art gallery walk on the first Friday of the month, has now evolved into a club and bar crawl that can sometimes turn Chinatown into a frat party on the streets. Go on a non–First Friday weekend for a mellower scene. The activity is concentrated on Hotel Street, on the block between Smith and Nu'unau. That's where you'll find **Tchin Tchin!** (p. 148) and **Manifest,** 32 N. Hotel St., one of the best craft cocktail bars in town, with a great selection of whiskey and gin. The bartenders here are happy to

get down with **ARTAFTERDARK**

On the last Friday of every month (except Nov–Dec), the place to be after the sun goes down is **ARTafterDARK,** a *pau hana* (after-work) mixer in the **Honolulu Academy of Arts,** 900 S. Beretania St. (www.artafterdark.org; © **808/532-8700**), that brings residents and visitors together around a theme combining art with food, music, and dancing. In addition to the exhibits in the gallery, ARTafterDARK features visual and live performances. Previous themes have ranged from "Plant Rice"—with rice and sake tastings, rice dishes, Asian beers, live Asian fusion music, and a tour of the "Art of Rice" exhibit—to "'80s Night," "Turkish Delights," "Cool Nights, Hot Jazz and Blues," and "Havana Heat." The entrance fee is $10. The party gets going around 6 and lasts till 9pm. The crowd ranges from 20s to 50s, and the dress is everything from jeans and T-shirts to cocktail-party attire.

whip up complex whiskey drinks or simple, classic cocktails. After 10pm, DJs and live music make the laidback bar more clubby. Across the street is **Bar 35,** 35 N. Hotel St. (© **808/537-3535**), whose claim to fame is its 110 beers available, plus wine, cocktails, and even pizza. You must be 21 to enter (strictly enforced).

Hanks Cafe, around the corner on Nu'unau Avenue between Hotel and King streets (http://hankscafehawaii.com; © **808/526-1410**), is a tiny, kitschy, friendly pub with live music nightly, open-mic nights, and special events that attract great talent and a supportive crowd. On some nights, the music spills out into the streets and it's so packed you have to press your nose against the window to see what you're missing. Upstairs at the **Dragon Upstairs,** there's more live music Tuesday through Sunday nights (http://thedragonupstairs.com; © **808/526-1411**). At the *makai* end of Nu'unau, toward the pier, **Murphy's Bar and Grill ★** (p. 148) is a popular downtown ale house and media haunt.

Hawaiian Music

O'ahu has several key spots for Hawaiian music. **House Without a Key** (see "The Bar Scene," above) is one of my favorite places to listen to Hawaiian music, both for the quality and the ambience.

Kana ka pila means to make music, so it makes sense then that the **Kana Ka Pila Grille** (© **808/924-4994**) at the Outrigger Reef on the Beach has one of the city's best Hawaiian-music lineups, including slack key guitarists Cyril Pahinui (son of famed guitarist Gabby Pahinui).

The **Brothers Cazimero** remain one of Hawai'i's most gifted duos (Robert on bass, Roland on 12-string guitar). In early December, the Brothers Caz do a Christmas show at the **Hawai'i Theatre** (www.hawaiitheatre.com) that is not to be missed. Locals dress up in their leis and best aloha shirts, and you can feel the holidays in the air.

Every year, hālau (hula schools) and Hawaiian musicians from around the state gather for **Ola Ka Hā,** to honor 'Iolani Palace through song and dance. It's a free event; find this year's date at www.olakaha.com.

Live Blues, R&B, Jazz & Pop

Blue Note Hawai'i, inside the Outrigger Waikīkī, 2335 Kalākaua Ave. (www.bluenotehawaii.com; © **808/777-4890**), from the owner of the Blue Note jazz club in New York City, is the state's newest venue for jazz, blues, and favorite local entertainers. Past performers have included Dee Dee Bridgewater and 'ukulele virtuoso Jake Shimabukuro.

Tops in taste and ambience is the perennially alluring **Lewers Lounge** in the Halekulani, 2199 Kalia Rd. (www.halekulani.com; © **808/923-2311**). Comfy intimate seating around the pillars makes this a great spot for contemporary jazz nightly from 8:30pm to midnight.

Outside Waikīkī, the **Veranda,** at the Kahala Hotel & Resort, 5000 Kāhala Ave. (www.kahalaresort.com; © **808/739-8888**), is a popular spot for the over-40 crowd, with nightly jazz music and a dance floor.

Check www.honolulujazzscene.com for daily listings.

Showroom Acts & Revues

Te Moana Nui, at the Sheraton Princess Kai'ulani, is a theatrical journey of fire dancing, special effects, illusions, hula, and dances from Hawai'i and the South Pacific. Shows are Sunday, Wednesday, and Friday (dinner show starts at $105 adults, $79 children 5–12; cocktail show $60 adults).

Also worth experiencing, even if you don't spend the day at the Polynesian Cultural Center, is ***Hā: Breath of Life*** (p. 96).

The Performing Arts

"Aloha shirt to Armani" is how I describe the night scene in Honolulu—mostly casual, but with ample opportunity to part with your flip-flops and dress up.

Audiences have grooved to the beat of the Hawai'i International Jazz Festival, the American Repertory Dance Company, barbershop quartets, and John Ka'imikaua's *halau*—all at the **Hawai'i Theatre,** 1130 Bethel St., downtown (www.hawaiitheatre.com; © **808/528-0506**). The theater is basking in its renaissance as a leading multipurpose center for the performing arts. The neoclassical Beaux-Arts landmark features a dome from 1922, 1,400 plush seats, a hydraulically elevated organ, breathtaking murals, and gilt galore.

In 2011, a new symphony orchestra was reborn from the disbanded century-old Honolulu Symphony Orchestra: **Hawai'i Symphony** (http://hawaiisymphonyorchestra.org; © **808/593-2468**). Meanwhile, the **Hawai'i Opera Theatre** (www.hawaiiopera.org; ✆ **808/596-7372** or 800/836-7372), celebrating more than 50 seasons, still draws fans to the **Neal S. Blaisdell Center** (www.blaisdellcenter.com; ✆ **808/591-2211**), as does **Ballet Hawai'i** (www.ballethawaii.org). Contemporary performances by **Iona** (www.iona360.com), a strikingly creative group whose dance evolved out of Butoh (a contemporary dance form that originated in Japan), are worth tracking down if you love the avant-garde.

HAWAI'I, THE BIG ISLAND

by Jeanne Cooper

5

Larger than all the other Hawaiian Islands combined, the Big Island truly deserves its nickname. Its 4,028 square miles—a figure that's growing, thanks to an active volcano—contain 10 of the world's 13 climate zones. In less than a day, a visitor can easily traverse tropical rainforest, lava desert, verdant pastures, misty uplands, and chilly tundra, the last near the summit of Mauna Kea, almost 14,000 feet above sea level. The shoreline also boasts diversity, from golden beaches to enchanting coves with black, salt-and-pepper, even olivine sand. Above all, the island home of Kamehameha the Great and Pele, the volcano goddess, is big in *mana:* power and spirituality.

ESSENTIALS

Arriving

The Big Island has two major airports for interisland and trans-Pacific jet traffic: Kona and Hilo.

Most people arrive at **Kona International Airport** (**KOA;** http://hawaii.gov/koa) in Keāhole, the island's westernmost point, and can be forgiven for wondering if there's really a runway among all the crinkly black lava and golden fountain grass. Leaving the airport, the ritzy Kohala Coast is to the left (north) and the town of Kailua-Kona—often just called "Kona," as is the airport—is to the right (south).

U.S. carriers offering nonstop service to Kona, in alphabetical order, are **Alaska Airlines** (www.alaskaair.com; ✆ **800/252-7522**), with flights from the Pacific Northwest hubs of Seattle, Portland, and Anchorage, and from San Diego, San Jose, and Oakland, California; **American Airlines** (www.aa.com; ✆ **800/433-7300**), departing from Los Angeles and Phoenix; **Delta Air Lines** (www.delta.com; ✆ **800/221-1212**), flying from Los Angeles and Seattle; **Hawaiian Airlines** (www.hawaiianairlines.com; ✆ **800/367-5320**), offering summer service from Oakland and Los Angeles; **United Airlines** (www.united.com; ✆ **800/241-6522**), with year-round flights from Los Angeles, San Francisco, and Denver, and seasonal service from Chicago.

Air Canada (www.aircanada.com; ✆ **888/247-2267**) and **WestJet** (www.westjet.com; ✆ **888/937-8358**) also offer nonstop service to Kona, with frequency changing seasonally, from Vancouver.

PREVIOUS PAGE: **Hawai'i Volcanoes National Park.**

Coast of Kailua-Kona.

Only United offers nonstop service from the mainland to **Hilo International Airport** (**ITO;** http://hawaii.gov/ito), via Los Angeles.

For connecting flights or island-hopping, Hawaiian (see above) is the only carrier offering interisland jet service, available from Honolulu and Kahului, Maui, to both Kona and Hilo airports; its **Ohana by Hawaiian** subsidiary also flies from Kona and Hilo to Kahului on 48-passenger, twin-engine turboprops. **Mokulele Airlines** (www.mokuleleairlines.com; **© 866/260-4040**) flies nine-passenger, single-engine turboprops to Kona from Moloka'i (Ho'olehua) and Maui's Kahului and Kapalua airports. It also flies to the Big Island's upcountry town of Waimea from Kahului. ***Note:*** Mokulele discreetly weighs passengers and their carry-ons before boarding to determine seating; those totaling 350 pounds or more are not permitted to fly.

Visitor Information

The **Big Island Visitors Bureau** (www.gohawaii.com/big-island; **© 800/648-2441**) has two offices: one in the Shops at Mauna Lani, 68-1330 Mauna Lani Dr., Suite 109B, in the Mauna Lani Resort (**© 808/885-1655**); the other at 101 Aupuni St., Suite 238, Hilo (**© 808/961-5797**).

This Week (www.thisweekhawaii.com/big-island) and ***101 Things to Do on Hawai'i the Big Island*** (www.101thingstodo.com/big-island) are free publications that offer lots of useful information amid the advertisements, as well as discount coupons for a variety of island adventures. Copies are easy to find all around the island.

Konaweb.com has an extensive event calendar and handy links to sites and services around the island, not just the Kona side. Those fascinated by the island's active volcanoes should check out the detailed daily lava reports, maps, photos, videos, and webcams on the U.S. Geological Survey's **Hawaiian Volcano Observatory** website (http://hvo.wr.usgs.gov), which also tracks the island's frequent but usually minor earthquake activity.

The national historic park at Hōnaunau.

The Island in Brief

Note: The spelling of Hawaiian words in the names of businesses below reflects their particular preference.

THE KONA COAST

Kona means "leeward side" in Hawaiian—and that means hot, dry weather virtually every day of the year on the 70-mile stretch of black lava shoreline encompassing the North and South Kona districts.

NORTH KONA With the exception of the sumptuous but serenely low-key **Four Seasons Resort Hualalai ★★★** north of the airport, most of what everyone just calls "Kona" is an affordable vacation spot. An ample selection of midpriced condo units, timeshares, and several recently upgraded hotels lie between the bustling commercial district of **Kailua-Kona ★★★**, a one-time fishing village and royal compound now renowned as the start and finish of the Ironman World Championship, and Keauhou, an equally historic area about 6 miles south that boasts upscale condominiums, a shopping center, and golf-course homes.

The rightly named Ali'i ("Royalty") Drive begins in Kailua-Kona near King Kamehameha's royal compound at **Kamakahonu Bay,** which includes the off-limits temple complex of **Ahu'ena Heiau,** and continues past **Hulihe'e Palace ★★★**, an elegant retreat for later royals that sits across from the oldest church in the islands. Heading south, the road passes by the snorkelers' haven of **Kahalu'u Beach ★★**, as well as sacred and royal sites on the former Keauhou Beach Resort, before the intersection with King Kamehameha III Road, which leads to that monarch's birthplace by Keauhou Bay. Several kayak excursions and snorkel boats leave from Keauhou, but Kailua Pier sees the most traffic—from cruise-ship tenders to fishing and dive boats, dinner cruises, and other sightseeing excursions.

Beaches between Kailua-Kona and Keauhou tend to be pocket coves, but heading north toward South Kohala (which begins near the entrance to the Waikoloa Beach Resort), beautiful, uncrowded sands lie out of sight from the highway, often reached by unpaved roads across vast lava fields. Among the steep coffee fields in North Kona's cooler upcountry, you'll find the rustic, artsy village of **Hōlualoa.**

SOUTH KONA The rural, serrated coastline here is indented with numerous bays, from **Kealakekua,** a marine life and cultural preserve that's the island's best diving spot, down to **Hōnaunau,** where a national historical park recalls the days of old Hawai'i. This is a great place to stay, in modest plantation-era inns or bed-and-breakfasts, if you want to get away from the crowds but still be within driving distance of beaches and the sights of Kailua. The higher, cooler elevation of the main road means you'll pass many coffee, macadamia nut, and tropical fruit farms, some with tours or roadside stands.

THE KOHALA COAST

Also on the island's "Kona side," sunny and dry Kohala is divided into two distinctively different districts, although the resorts are more glamorous and the rural area that much less developed.

SOUTH KOHALA Pleasure domes rise like palaces no Hawaiian king ever imagined along the sandy beaches carved into the craggy shores here, from the more moderately priced **Waikoloa Beach Resort** at 'Anaeho'omalu Bay to the posher **Mauna Lani** and **Mauna Kea** resorts to the north. Mauna Kea is where Laurance Rockefeller opened the area's first resort in 1965, a virtual mirage of opulence and tropical greenery rising from bleak, black lava fields, framed by the white sands of Kauna'oa Beach and views of the eponymous mountain. But you don't have to be a billionaire to enjoy South Kohala's fabulous beaches and historic sites (such as petroglyph fields), all open to the public, with parking and other facilities (including restaurants and shopping) provided by the resorts.

Several of the region's attractions are also located off the resorts, including the white sands of **'Ōhai'ula Beach** at **Spencer Park ★★**; the massive **Pu'ukoholā Heiau ★★★**, a lava rock temple commissioned by King Kamehameha the Great; and the excellent restaurants and handful of stores in **Kawaihae,** the commercial harbor just after the turnoff for upcountry Waimea. ***Note:*** Despite its name, the golf course community of **Waikoloa Village** is not in the Waikoloa Beach Resort but instead lies 5½ miles uphill from the coastal highway.

Keck Observatory.

WAIMEA (KAMUELA) & MAUNA KEA Officially part of South Kohala, the old upcountry cow town of Waimea on the northern road between the coasts is a world unto itself, with rolling green pastures, wide-open spaces dotted by *pu'u* (cindercone hills), and real cowpokes who work mammoth **Parker Ranch,** the state's largest working ranch. The postal service gave it the name Kamuela, after ranch founder Samuel (Kamuela) Parker, to distinguish it from another cowboy town, Waimea, Kaua'i. It's split between a "dry side" (closer to the Kohala Coast) and a "wet side" (closer to the Hāmākua Coast), but both sides can be cooler than sea level. It's also headquarters for the **Keck Observatory,** whose twin telescopes atop the nearly 14,000-foot **Mauna Kea ★★★**, some 35 miles away, are the largest and most powerful in the world. Waimea is home to shopping centers and affordable B&Bs, while the recently expanded **Merriman's ★★★** remains a popular foodie outpost at Opelo Plaza.

NORTH KOHALA Locals may remember when sugar was king here, but for visitors, little-developed North Kohala is most famous for another king, Kamehameha the Great. His birthplace is a short walk from one of the Hawaiian Islands' largest and most important temples, **Mo'okini Heiau ★**, which dates to A.D. 480; you'll want a four-wheel-drive (4WD) for the rugged road there. Much easier to find: the yellow-cloaked bronze statue of the warrior-king in front of the community center in **Kapa'au,** a small plantation-era town. The road ends at the breathtaking **Pololū Valley Overlook ★★★**.

Once the center of the Big Island's sugarcane industry, **Hawi** remains a regional hub, with a 3-block-long strip of sun-faded, false-fronted buildings holding a few shops and restaurants of interest to visitors. Eight miles south, **Lapakahi State Historical Park ★★** merits a stop to explore how less-exalted Hawaiians than Kamehameha lived in a simple village by the sea. Beaches are less appealing here, with the northernmost coves subject to strong winds blowing across the ʻAlenuihāhā Channel from Maui, 26 miles away and visible on clear days.

THE HĀMĀKUA COAST

This emerald coast, a 52-mile stretch from Honokaʻa to Hilo on the island's windward northeast side, was once planted with sugarcane; it now blooms with flowers, macadamia nuts, papayas, vanilla, and mushrooms. Resort-free and virtually without beaches, the Hāmākua Coast includes the districts of Hāmākua and North Hilo, with two unmissable destinations. Picture-perfect **Waipiʻo Valley ★★★** has impossibly steep sides, taro patches, a green riot of wild plants, and a winding stream leading to a broad, black-sand beach, while **ʻAkaka Falls State Park ★★★** offers views of two lovely waterfalls amid lush foliage. Also worth checking out: **Laupāhoehoe Point ★**, with its mournful memorial to young victims of a 1946 tsunami; and the quirky assortment of shops in the plantation town of **Honokaʻa.**

HILO

The largest metropolis in Hawaiʻi after Honolulu is a quaint, misty, flower-filled city of Victorian houses overlooking a half-moon bay, with a restored historic downtown and a clear view of Mauna Kea, often snow-capped in winter. Hilo catches everyone's eye until it rains—and it rains a lot in Hilo, with 128 inches of rain annually. It's ideal for growing ferns, orchids, and anthuriums, but not for catching constant rays.

Yet there's a lot to see and do in Hilo and the surrounding South Hilo district, both indoors and out—including visiting the bayfront Japanese-style **Liliʻuokalani Gardens ★★**, the **Pacific Tsunami Museum ★**, the **Mokupāpapa Discovery Center ★★**, and **Rainbow Falls (Waiānueanue) ★**—so grab your umbrella. The rain is warm (the temperature seldom dips below 70°F/21°C), and there's usually a rainbow afterward.

The town also holds the island's best bargains for budget travelers, with plenty of hotel rooms—most of the year, that is. Hilo's magic moment comes in spring, the week after Easter, when hula *hālau* (schools) arrive for the annual **Merrie Monarch Hula Festival** hula competition (www.merriemonarch.com). Plan ahead if you want to go: Tickets are sold out by the first week in January, and hotels within 30 miles are usually booked solid. Hilo is also the gateway to **Hawaiʻi Volcanoes National Park ★★★**, where hula troupes perform chants and dances before the Merrie Monarch festival; the park is 30 miles away, or about an hour's drive up-slope.

Hula dancer at the Merrie Monarch Hula Festival in Hilo.

PUNA DISTRICT

PĀHOA, KAPOHO & KALAPANA Between Hilo and Hawai'i Volcanoes National Park lies the "Wild Wild East," an emerging visitor destination with geothermal wonders such as the ghostly hollowed trunks of **Lava Tree State Monument ★★**, the volcanically heated waters of **Ahalanui Park ★★** and the **Kapoho warm ponds,** and the acres of lava from a 1986 flow that rolled through the Hawaiian hamlet of **Kalapana** and covered a popular black-sand beach. The ocean has since carved out a new, more rugged cove, while Kalapana's Wednesday-night farmer's market and live music on Friday nights attract a large local crowd all may join. On June 27, 2014, a new lava flow from Kīlauea's East Rift Zone began oozing toward the part-Hawaiian, part-hippie plantation town of **Pāhoa,** the region's funky gateway. The flow consumed miles of forest before stopping in early 2015 within 550 yards of Hwy. 130, the only road in and out of lower Puna; the flow remained stalled at press time, although active "breakouts" were still occurring upslope.

HAWAI'I VOLCANOES NATIONAL PARK ★★★ This is America's most exciting national park, where a live volcano called Kīlauea has been continuously erupting since 1983. Depending on where the flow is, you may not be able to witness molten lava—or have to walk across miles of rough lava rock to do so—but there's always something else impressive to see. A plume of ash, which at night reflects the glow of the lava lake below it, has been rising from Kīlauea's Halema'uma'u Crater since 2008, while steam vents have been belching sulphurous odors since long before

Mark Twain visited in 1866. Ideally, you should plan to spend 3 days at the park exploring its many trails, watching the volcano, visiting the rainforest, and just enjoying this spectacular place. But even if you have only a day, it's worth the trip. Bring your sweats or jacket (honest!); it's cool up there.

VOLCANO VILLAGE If you're not camping or staying at historic, 33-room **Volcano House ★★** inside the park, you'll want to overnight in this quiet hamlet, just outside the national park entrance. Several cozy inns and B&Bs, some with fireplaces, reside under tree ferns in this cool mountain hideaway. The tiny highland community (elevation 4,000 ft.), first settled by Japanese immigrants, is now inhabited by artists, soul-searchers, and others who like the crisp high-country air.

KA'Ū DISTRICT

Written variously as *Ka'ū* or *Kā'ū,* and pronounced *"kah-oo,"* this windswept, often barren district between Puna and South Kona is one visitors are most likely to just drive through on their way to and from the national park. Nevertheless, it contains several noteworthy sites.

KA LAE (SOUTH POINT) This is the Plymouth Rock of Hawai'i. The first Polynesians are thought to have arrived in seagoing canoes, probably from the Marquesas Islands, around A.D. 500 at this rocky promontory 500 feet above the sea. To the west is the old fishing village of Wai'ahukini, populated from A.D. 750 until the 1860s; ancient canoe moorings, shelter caves, and *heiau* (temples) poke through windblown pili grass today. The east coast curves inland to reveal **Papakōlea (Green Sand) Beach ★★**, a world-famous anomaly that's best accessed on foot. Along the point, the southernmost spot in the 50 states, trees grow sideways due to the relentless gusts that also power wind turbines. It's a slow, nearly 12-mile drive from the highway to the tip of Ka Lae, so many visitors simply stop at the marked overlook on Highway 11, west of South Point Road.

NĀ'ĀLEHU, WAI'ŌHINU & PĀHALA Nearly every business in Nā'ālehu and Wai'ōhinu, the two wide spots on the main road near South Point, claims to be the southernmost this or that. But except for delicious *malasadas* (doughnut holes) or another pick-me-up from the **Punalu'u Bake Shop ★** or **Hana Hou Restaurant ★**, there's no reason to linger before heading to **Punalu'u Beach ★★★**, between Nā'ālehu and Pāhala. Protected green sea turtles bask on the fine black-sand beach when they're not bobbing in the clear waters, chilly from fresh springs bubbling from the ocean floor. Pāhala is the center of the burgeoning Ka'ū coffee-growing scene ("industry" might be overstated), so caffeine fans should also allot at least 45 minutes for a visit to the **Ka'ū Coffee Mill ★**.

Ka Lae.

GETTING AROUND

The Hawaiian directions of *makai* (toward the ocean) and *mauka* (toward the mountains) come in handy when looking for unfamiliar sites, especially since numbered address signs may be invisible or nonexistent. They're used with addresses below as needed.

BY TAXI Taxis are readily available at both Kona and Hilo airports, although renting a car (see below) is a more likely option. On the Kona side, call **Kona Taxicab** (www.konataxicab.com; ✆ **808/324-4444**), which can also be hailed via smartphone using its "Hail-a-Cab" function and booked in advance for airport pickups (see website for details); drivers will check on your flight's arrival. In Hilo or Puna, call **Kwiki Taxi** (www.kwikitaxi.wordpress.com; ✆ **808/498-0308**). Set by the county, rates start at $3, plus $3.20 each additional mile—about $25 to $30 from the Kona airport to Kailua-Kona and $50 to $60 to the Waikoloa Beach Resort.

BY CAR You'll want a rental car on the Big Island; not having one will really limit you. All major car-rental agencies have airport pickups in Kona and Hilo; some even offer cars at Kohala and Kona resorts. For tips on insurance and driving rules, see "Getting Around Hawai'i" (p. 604).

The Big Island has more than 480 miles of paved road. The highway that circles the island is called the **Hawai'i Belt Road.** From North Kona to South Kohala and Waimea, you have two driving choices: the scenic "upper" road, **Māmalahoa Highway** (Hwy. 190), or the speedier "lower" road, **Queen Ka'ahumanu Highway** (Hwy. 19). South of

Kailua-Kona, the Hawai'i Belt Road continues on Māmalahoa Highway (Hwy. 11) all the way to downtown Hilo, where it becomes Highway 19 again and follows the Hāmākua Coast before heading up to Waimea.

North Kohala also has upper and lower highways. In Kawaihae, you can follow **Kawaihae Road** (Hwy. 19) uphill to the left turn onto the often-misty **Kohala Mountain Road** (Hwy. 250), which eventually drops down into Hawi. The **Akoni Pule Highway** (Hwy. 270) hugs the coast from Kawaihae to pavement's end at the Pololū Valley Lookout.

Note: **Saddle Road** (Hwy. 200) snakes between Mauna Kea and Mauna Loa en route from Hilo to Māmalahoa Highway (Hwy. 190). Despite recent improvements to its once-rough pavement and narrow shoulders, it's still frequented by large military vehicles and plagued by bad weather; as a result, most rental-car agencies forbid you from driving on it. However, I've found the 29 miles from Hilo to the Mauna Kea Access Road to be very easy to navigate in good conditions.

BY BUS & SHUTTLE **SpeediShuttle** (www.speedishuttle.com; ✆ **808/329-5433**) and **Roberts Hawaii** (www.robertshawaii.com; ✆ **866/570-2536** or 808/954-8640) offer door-to-door airport transfers to hotels and other lodgings. Sample shared-ride rates from the Kona airport are $28 per person to Kailua-Kona, and $60 per person to the Mauna Lani Resort; Roberts' agents meet you outside security and provide porter service in baggage claim, but be aware there may be up to five stops before your destination.

The islandwide bus system, the **Hele-On Bus** (www.heleonbus.org; ✆ **808/961-8744**), offers a great flat rate for riders: $2 general; $1 for students, seniors, and people with disabilities; and free for children under 5. Most routes have limited value for visitors, other than the Hilo–Hawai'i Volcanoes National Park bus or the Intra-Kona line between Kailua-Kona's big-box stores (Wal-Mart, Costco) and the Keauhou Shopping Center; the latter also stops at the Old Kona Airport Beach.

Travelers staying in Kailua-Kona and the Keauhou Resort can hop on the open-air, 44-seat **Keauhou Resort Trolley** operated by Roberts Hawaii (✆ **808/329-1688**), running from 9am to 9:15pm daily along Ali'i Drive. It makes six stops a day at 31 locations from the Sheraton Kona Resort and Keauhou Shopping Center to Kahalu'u Beach, Kailua Pier, and the shops of downtown Kailua-Kona. The fare is $2, free for those with vouchers from their hotel (such as the Sheraton) or stores in the Keauhou or Kona Commons shopping centers, which give them to customers who spend $25 or more.

The **Waikoloa Beach Resort shopping trolley** runs from 10am to 10pm daily from Hilton Waikoloa Village and the Waikoloa Beach Marriott to the Kings' Shops and Queens' MarketPlace; it costs $2 adults, $1 ages 5 to 12 (younger free). Guests at Kings' Land by Hilton Grand Vacations can catch a free van shuttle to Hilton Waikoloa Village and pick up the trolley from there.

BY BIKE Due to elevation changes, narrow shoulders (with the notable exception of the Queen Ka'ahumanu Hwy. between Kailua-Kona and Kawaihae), and high traffic speeds, point-to-point bike travel without a tour guide isn't recommended. However, several areas are ideal for recreational cycling and sightseeing. See "Biking" under "Other Outdoor Activities" for rental shops and routes.

BY MOTORCYCLE & SCOOTER The sunny Kohala and Kona coasts are ideal for tooling around on a motorcycle, while those sticking to one resort or Kailua-Kona can easily get around by scooter. **Big Island Motorcycle Co.,** in Kings' Shops in the Waikoloa Beach Resort, 69-250 Waikoloa Beach Rd. (www.thrillseekershawaii.com; ✆ **808/886-2011**), rents a variety of motorbikes to those 21 and older with a valid motorcycle license (from $100 a day, including gear, insurance, and unlimited miles). Moped rentals, available to those 18 and up with a standard driver's license, are $20 an hour, $45 half-day, and $60 full day ($75 for 24 hr.). In Kailua-Kona, **Big Island Harley-Davidson,** 75-5633 Palani Rd. (www.bigislandharley.com; ✆ **888/904-3155** or 808/217-8560), rents a variety of Harleys starting at $99 daily ($639 weekly), with gear and unlimited mileage, to qualified drivers, while **Big Island Mopeds** (www.konamopedrentals.com; ✆ **808/443-6625**) will deliver mopeds to your door for $40 day ($200 weekly; note prices rise to $100 daily/$500 weekly during Ironman week in mid-Oct).

[Fast FACTS] THE BIG ISLAND

ATMs/Banks ATMs are located everywhere on the Big Island, at banks, supermarkets, Long's Drugs, and at some shopping malls. The major banks on the Big Island are First Hawaiian, Bank of Hawaii, American Savings, and Central Pacific, all with branches in both Kona and Hilo.

Business Hours Most businesses on the island are open from 8 or 9am to 5 or 6pm.

Dentists In Kohala, contact **Dr. Craig C. Kimura** at Kamuela Office Center, 65-1230 Māmalahoa Hwy., Waimea (✆ **808/885-5947**). In Kailua-Kona, call **Dr. Christopher Bays** at **Kona Coast Dental Care,** 75-5591 Palani Rd., in the Frame 10 Center above the bowling alley (www.konacoastdental.com; ✆ **808/329-8067**). In Hilo, **Kuhio Dental Group,** in Prince Kuhio Plaza, 111 E. Puainako St. (✆ **808/959-3433**), is open daily from 8am to 5pm, with dental surgeon **Jonathan Mah** on staff.

Doctors For minor emergencies or drop-in appointments on weekdays, visit **Urgent Care of Kona,** 77-311 Sunset Dr., off Highway 11, Kailua-Kona (www.urgentcareofkona.com; ✆ **808/327-4357**). In Hilo, **Urgent Care** (✆ **855/580-5923**) has offices open 8:30am–9pm weekdays and 9:30am–4pm weekends at 45 Mohouli St., Hilo, and 16-612 Old Volcano Rd., Kea'au.

Emergencies For ambulance, fire, or rescue services, dial ✆ **911.**

Hospitals Hospitals offering 24-hour, urgent-care facilities include the **Kona Community Hospital,** 79-1019 Haukapila St., off Highway 11, Kealakekua (www.kch.hhsc.org; ✆ **808/322-9311**); **Hilo**

Medical Center, 1190 Waiānuenue Ave., Hilo (www.hilomedicalcenter.org; ✆ **808/932-3000**); and **North Hawaii Community Hospital,** 67-1125 Māmalahoa Hwy., Waimea (www.nhch.com; ✆ **808/885-4444**).

Internet Access Pretty much every lodging on the island has Wi-Fi; resorts typically include it in their exorbitant resort fees, but some offer it for a daily charge. **Starbucks** (six free-standing locations), **McDonald's** (nine locations), and numerous local coffee shops also offer free Wi-Fi.

Pharmacies The only 24-hour pharmacy is in Hilo at **Long's Drugs,** 555 Kīlauea Ave., one of 12 around the island (www.cvs.com; ✆ **808/935-9075**). The rest open as early as 7am and close as late as 9pm Monday through Saturday; some are closed Sunday. Kona and Hilo's national chain stores such as **Kmart, Target, Wal-Mart,** and **Costco** (Kailua-Kona only) also have pharmacies with varying hours.

Police Dial ✆ **911** in case of emergency; otherwise, call the **Hawai'i Police Department** at ✆ **808/935-3311** islandwide.

Post Office The **U.S. Postal Service** (www.usps.com; ✆ **800/275-8777**) has more than 2 dozen branches around the island, including in Kailua-Kona at 74-5577 Palani Rd., in Waimea at 67-1197 Māmalahoa Hwy., and in Hilo at 1299 Kekūanaō'a St. All are open weekdays; some are also open Saturday morning.

Volcanic Activity Check the website of **Hawai'i Volcanoes National Park**, www.nps.gov/havo/planyourvisit/index.htm, to see what's going on with the volcano and to check for road closures. For daily **air-quality reports,** based on sulfur dioxide and particulates from eruptions measured at eight sites around the island, visit http://hiso2index.info.

EXPLORING THE BIG ISLAND

Attractions & Points of Interest

Although parks are open year-round, some of the other attractions below may be closed on major holidays such as Christmas, New Year's, or Thanksgiving Day. Admission is often reduced for Hawai'i residents (*kama'āina*) with state ID.

NORTH KONA

Hulihe'e Palace ★★★ HISTORIC SITE John Adams Kuakini, royal governor of the island, built this stately, two-story New England–style mansion overlooking Kailua Bay in 1838. It later became a summer home for King Kalākaua and Queen Kapi'olani and, like Queen Emma's Summer Palace and 'Iolani Palace on O'ahu, is now lovingly maintained by the Daughters of Hawai'i as a showcase for royal furnishings and Native Hawaiian artifacts, from hat boxes to koa furniture and a 22-foot spear. You can take a self-guided tour of its six spacious rooms, but guided tours, offered throughout the day, are worth the extra $2 to learn more of the monarchs' history and cultural context; guided tours are also the only ones permitted on the oceanfront lanai. A sign directs you to remove shoes before entering; free booties are provided upon request.

The palace lawn hosts 12 free events a year honoring a different member of Hawaiian royalty, with performances by local hula *hālau*

Hulihe'e Palace.

(schools) and musicians. Called **Afternoon at the Palace,** they're generally held at 4pm on the third Sunday of the month (except June and Dec, when the performances are held in conjunction with King Kamehameha Day and Christmas). Check the Daughters of Hawai'i website for dates.

75-5718 Alii Dr., Kailua-Kona. http://daughtersofhawaii.org. ✆ **808/329-1877.** Admission $8 adults, $6 seniors, $1 children 17 and under. $2 more per adult for guided tours. Mon–Sat 9am–4pm (arrive by 3pm for guided tour).

Kaloko-Honokōhau National Historical Park ★★ HISTORIC SITE/NATURAL ATTRACTION With no erupting volcano, impressive tikis, or massive temples, this 1,160-acre oceanfront site just north of Honokōhau Harbor tends to get overlooked by visitors in favor of its showier siblings in the national park system. That's a shame for several reasons, among them that it's a microcosm of ancient Hawai'i, from fish ponds (one with an 800-ft.-long rock wall), house platforms, petroglyphs, and trails through barren lava to marshlands with native waterfowl, reefs teeming with fish, and a tranquil beach where green sea turtles bask in the shadow of Pu'uoina Heiau. Plus, it's rarely crowded, and admission is free. Stop by the small visitor center to pick up a brochure and ask about ocean conditions (if you're planning to snorkel), and then backtrack to Honokōhau Harbor, a half-mile south, to park closer to the beach.

Ocean side of Hwy. 19, 3 miles south of Kona airport. www.nps.gov/kaho. ✆ **808/326-9057.** Visitor center and parking lot ½-mile north of Honokōhau Harbor daily 8:30am–4pm. Kaloko Rd. gate daily 8am–5pm. No time restrictions on parking at Honokōhau Harbor; from Hwy.19, take Kealakehe Pkwy. west into harbor, then take 1st right, and follow to parking lot near Kona Sailing Club, a short walk to beach.

Moku'aikaua Church ★ RELIGIOUS/HISTORIC SITE In 1820, just a few months after King Kamehameha II and Queen Regent Ka'ahumanu had broken the *kapu* system (taboos) at Ahu'ena Heiau, the first missionaries to land in Hawai'i arrived on the brig *Thaddeus* and received the royals' permission to preach. Within a few years a thatched-roof structure had risen on this site, on land donated by Gov. Kuakini, owner

Ahalanui Park (Hot Pond) **24**

Ahu'ena Heiau (King Kamehameha's Compound) **15**

'Akaka Falls **12**

Cape Kumukahi Lighthouse **21**

Hamakua Macadamia Nut Factory **5**

Hawaii Tropical Botanical Garden **13**

Hawai'i Volcanoes National Park **26**

Hulihe'e Palace **15**

Kaloko-Honokōhau National Historical Park **14**

Kealakekua Bay State Historical Park **18**

King Kamehameha Statue **3**

Kings' Trail Petroglyphs **10**

Kohala Historical Sites State Monument **1**

Lapakahi State Historical Park **2**

Laupāhoehoe Point **8**

Lava Tree State Monument **22**

Mauna Kea Summit **11**

Mauna Loa Macadamia Nut Factory **17**

Moku'aikaua Church **15**

Painted Church (St. Benedict's) **19**

Pana'ewa Rainforest Zoo and Garden **16**

Pololū Valley Overlook **4**

Puakō Petroglyph Archaeological Preserve **9**

Pu'uhonua O Hōnaunau National Historical Park **20**

Pu'ukoholā Heiau National Historic Site **6**

South Point (Ka Lae) **27**

Star of the Sea (Painted Church) **25**

Wai'ōpae Tidepools **23**

Waipi'o Valley Overlook **7**

Moku'aikaua Church.

of Hulihe'e Palace across the road. But after several fires, Rev. Asa Thurston had this massive, New England–style structure erected, using lava rocks from a nearby *heiau* (temple) held together by coral mortar, with gleaming koa for the lofty interior; the 112-foot steeple is still the tallest structure in Kailua-Kona. Visitors are welcome to view the sanctuary, open daily, and a rear room with a small collection of artifacts, including a model of the *Thaddeus,* a rope star chart used by Pacific Islanders, and a poignant plaque commemorating Henry 'Ōpūkaha'ia. As a teenager, the Big Island native (known then as "Obookiah") boarded a ship to New England in 1807, converted to Christianity, and helped plan the first mission to the islands, but he died of a fever in 1818, the year before the *Thaddeus* sailed. (In 1993 his remains were reinterred at Kahikolu Congregational Church, 16 miles south of Moku'aikaua.) Moku'aikaua hosts a free history talk most Sundays at 12:15pm, following the 11am service.
75-5713 Ali'i Dr., Kailua-Kona, across from Hulihe'e Palace. www.mokuaikaua.org. ✆ **808/329-0655.** Daily 7:30am–5:30pm.

Ocean Rider Seahorse Farm ★★ AQUACULTURE On the coastline just behind the Natural Energy Lab (NELHA) lies this 3-acre, conservation-oriented "aqua-farm," which breeds and displays more than half of the world's 36 species of seahorses. The farm began breeding seahorses in 1998 as a way of ending demand for wild-collected seahorses and, once successful, expanded its interests to include similarly threatened sea dragons and reef fish. Although the $40 online ticket cost of the biologist-led, 1-hour tour (the only way to see the farm) may seem excessive, proceeds benefit the farm's research and conservation. In any case, people still find their way here in droves, excited to see pregnant male

CRAZY FOR KONA coffee

More than 600 farms grow coffee in the Kona Coffee Belt on the slopes of Hualālai, from Kailua-Kona and Hōlualoa in North Kona to Captain Cook and Hōnaunau in South Kona. The prettiest time to visit is between January and May, when the rainy season brings white blossoms known as "Kona snow." Harvesting is by hand—one reason Kona coffee is so costly—from late August through early winter. At least 40 farms offer regular **tours with tastings,** and many more provide samples. You can make impromptu stops along Māmalahoa Highway (Hwy. 11 and Hwy. 180) or find more obscure farms and those requiring reservations via the **Kona Coffee Farmers Association** (www.konacoffeefarmers.org). Some highlights, heading north to south:

- **Mountain Thunder Coffee Plantation,** 73-1944 Hao St. (off Kaloko Dr.), Kailua-Kona (www.mountainthunder.com; ✆ **808/325-2136**): In the hills known as Kaloko Mauka above the airport, Trent Bateman mills award-winning coffee from his own 21-acre organic farm Mountain Thunder, as well as from other Kona growers. Mountain Thunder also grows organic coffee, pineapple, *mamaki* (used for herbal tea), cacao, sugarcane, and green tea at another location: Kainaliu, on Highway 11, just south of mile marker 113. Both farms offer free tours on the hour from 10am to 4pm daily; farmstands open at 9am.
- **Kona Blue Sky Coffee Company,** 76-973 Hualālai Rd., Hōlualoa (www.konablueskycoffee.com; ✆ **877/322-1700** or 808/322-1700): The Christian Twigg-Smith family and staff grows and sells its coffee on a 400-acre estate, with free, 15-min. guided walking tours and tastings weekdays from 9am to 4pm (first tour at 10am, then hourly through 3pm).
- **Holualoa Kona Coffee Company,** 77-6261 Māmalahoa Hwy. (Hwy. 180), Holulaloa (www.konalea.com; ✆ **800/334-0348** or 808/322-9937): Owned by Desmond and Lisen Twigg-Smith, this organic farm and mill sells its own and others' premium Kona coffee. Tour the orchards (mowed and fertilized by a flock of about 50 geese) and witness all phases of processing, weekdays from 8am to 4pm.
- **Kona Joe Coffee,** 79-7346 Māmalahoa Hwy. (Hwy. 11 between mile markers 113 and 114), Kainaliu; www.konajoe.com; ✆ **808/322-2100**): The home of the world's first trellised coffee farm offers a free, self-guided tour with 8-minute video, as well as guided tours by request ($15 adults, free for kids 12 and under), daily from 8am to 5pm. Guided tours of the 20-acre estate include a mug, coffee, and chocolate, with reservations recommended for groups of six or more.
- **Greenwell Farms,** 81-6581 Māmalahoa Hwy. (*makai* side of Hwy. 11, south of mile marker 112), Kealakekua (www.greenwellfarms.com; ✆ **808/323-2295**): If any farm can claim to be the granddaddy of Kona coffee, this would be it. Englishman Henry Nicholas Greenwell began growing coffee in the region in 1850. Now operated by his great-grandson and agricultural innovator Tom Greenwell, the farm offers free tours daily from 8:30am to 4pm. On Thursday, join volunteers farm to bake Portuguese sweet bread in a stone oven at the **Greenwell Store Museum** ★ just south of the from 10am to 1pm; bread sales ($8) start at 12:30pm and sell out quickly.

seahorses and their babies, and to have one of the delicate creatures wrap its tail around their fingers.

73-4388 'Ilikai Place (behind the Natural Energy Lab), Kailua-Kona. From Hwy. 19 (at mile marker 94), follow OTEC Rd. past Wawalaloli Beach Park to 1st left; farm is on the right. www.seahorse.com. ✆ **808/329-6840.** Online tickets: $40 adults, $30 children 7–12, $28 children 3–6, free 2 and under; $2 more per ticket purchased at the door. Tours Mon–Fri noon and 2pm; also 10am Thanksgiving week (late Nov), Dec 19–Apr 30, and June 1–Labor Day (early Sept). Reservations recommended. Gift shop Mon–Fri 9:30am–3:30pm.

SOUTH KONA

Kealakekua Bay State Historical Park ★★ NATURAL ATTRACTION The island's largest natural sheltered bay, a marine life conservation district, is not only one of the best places to snorkel on the Big Island, but it's also an area of deep cultural and historical significance. On the southern side, now called Nāpo'opo'o *(nah-poh-oh-poh-oh)*, stands the large stacked-rock platform of **Hikiau Heiau,** a temple once used for human sacrifice and still considered sacred today. A rocky beach park here includes picnic tables, barbecues, and restrooms. On the north side, a steep but relatively broad 2-mile trail leads down to the historic Ka'awaloa area, where *ali'i* (royalty) once lived; when they died, their bodies were taken to **Puhina O Lono Heiau** on the slope above them, prepared for burial, and hidden in caves on the 600-foot-cliff above the central bay. An obelisk known as the **Captain Cook Monument** stands on Ka'awaloa Flat, near where the British explorer was slain in 1779, after misunderstandings between Hawaiians and Cook's crew led to armed conflict. The Hawaiians then showed respect by taking Cook's body to Puhina O Lono before returning some of the remains to his crew. Please do not walk on the reef or any cultural sites; to protect the area, only hikers and clients of three guided kayak tour companies have access to Ka'awaloa Flat (see "Kayaking" on p. 231).

From Hwy. 11 in Captain Cook heading south, take right fork onto Nāpo'opo'o Rd. (Hwy. 160). Ka'awaloa trail head is about 500 ft. on right. By car, continue on Nāpo'opo'o Rd. 4¼-mile to left on Pu'uhonua Rd.; go ⅕-mile to right on Manini Beach Rd. www.hawaiistateparks.org. Daily during daylight hours.

SWEET ON chocolate

Tucked between coffee orchards in the uplands of Keauhou, the **Original Hawaiian Chocolate Factory** (www.ohcf.us; ✆ **888/447-2626,** 808/322-2626) began growing cacao in 1993. It was the first in the islands to produce 100% Hawaiian chocolate. The 1-hour walking tour ($15 adults, free kids 11 and under) includes the orchard, small factory, and chocolate sampling, plus the option to buy the expensive but delectable chocolate bars and pieces shaped like plumeria flowers. Tours take place at 9am Wednesday and 9 and 11am Friday by reservation only; book well in advance. The factory store is open Tuesday through Friday 10am to 3pm.

The Painted Church.

The Painted Church (St. Benedict's) ★★ RELIGIOUS SITE Beginning in 1899, Father John Berchman Velghe (a member of the same order as Father Damien of Moloka'i) painted biblical scenes and images of saints inside quaint St. Benedict's Catholic Church, built in 1842 and restored in 2002. As with stained-glass windows of yore, his pictures, created with simple house paint, were a way of sharing stories with illiterate parishioners. It's a wonderfully trippy experience to look up at arching palm fronds and shiny stars on the ceiling. Health issues forced the priest to return to Belgium in 1904 before finishing all the pictures. The oceanview church is typically open during daylight hours, but keep in mind it's an active parish, with Mass celebrated most days. 84-5140 Painted Church Rd., Captain Cook. www.thepaintedchurch.org. ✆ **808/328-2227.** From Kailua-Kona, take Hwy. 11 south 20 miles to a right on Rte. 160. Go 1 mile to the 1st turnoff on the right, opposite from a King Kamehameha sign. Follow the narrow, winding road about ¼-mile to church sign and turn right. Free admission.

Pu'uhonua O Hōnaunau National Historical Park ★★★ HISTORIC SITE With its fierce, haunting idols *(ki'i),* this sacred site on the black-lava Kona Coast certainly looks forbidding. To ancient Hawaiians, it served as a 16th-century place of refuge *(pu'uhonua),* providing sanctuary for defeated warriors and *kapu* (taboo) violators. A great rock wall—1,000 feet long, 10 feet high, and 17 feet thick—defines the refuge where Hawaiians found safety. On the wall's north end is **Hale O Keawe Heiau,** which holds the bones of 23 Hawaiian chiefs. Other archaeological finds include a royal compound, burial sites, old trails,

Some of the *ki'i* at Pu'uhonua O Hōnaunau National Historical Park.

and a portion of an ancient village. On a self-guided tour of the 420-acre site—much of which has been restored to its pre-contact state—you can learn about reconstructed thatched huts, canoes, and idols, and feel the *mana* (power) of old Hawai'i, but do try to include one of the free daily ranger talks (10:30am and 2:30pm in a covered amphitheater). ***Note:*** The park has no concessions other than bottled water at the bookstore, but there are picnic tables on the sandy stretch of the south side.

Hwy. 160, Hōnaunau. From Kailua-Kona, take Hwy. 11 south 20 miles to a right on Hwy. 160. Head 3½ miles and turn left at park sign. www.nps.gov/puho. ✆ **808/328-2288.** Admission $5 per vehicle; $3 per person on foot, bicycle, or motorcycle; good for 7 days. Visitor center daily 8:30am–4:30pm; park daily 7am–sunset.

SOUTH KOHALA

Hamakua Macadamia Nut Factory ★ FACTORY TOUR The self-guided tour of shelling, roasting, and other processing that results in flavored macadamia nuts and confections is not that compelling if production has stopped for the day, so go before 3pm or plan to watch a video to get caught up. But who are we kidding—it's really all about the free tastings here, generous samples of big, fresh nuts in island flavors such as chili "peppah," Spam, and Kona coffee glazed. Outside the hilltop factory warehouse are picnic tables with an ocean view.

61-3251 Maluokalani St., Kawaihae. www.hawnnut.com. ✆ **888/643-6688** or 808/882-1690. Free admission. Daily 9am–5:30pm. From Kawaihae Harbor, take Hwy. 270 north ¾-mile, turn right on Maluokalani St., and drive ⅕-mile uphill; factory is on right.

Kohala Petrogylph Fields ★★★ ROCK CARVINGS The Hawaiian petroglyphs are a great enigma of the Pacific—no one knows who made them or why. They appear at 135 different sites on six inhabited islands, but most are found on the Big Island, including images of dancers and paddlers, fishermen and chiefs, and tools of daily life such as fish hooks and canoes. The most common representations are family groups, while some petroglyphs depict post–European contact objects such as ships, anchors, horses, and guns. Simple circles with dots were used to mark the *puka,* or holes, where parents would place their child's umbilical cord *(piko).*

The largest concentration of these stone symbols in the Pacific lies in the 233-acre **Puakō Petroglyph Archaeological Preserve** next to the Fairmont Orchid, Hawaii, at the Mauna Lani Resort. Some 3,000 designs have been identified. The 1.5-mile **Malama Trail** through a kiawe field to the large, reddish lava field starts north of the hotel, *makai* side. Take Highway 19 to the resort turnoff and drive toward the coast on North Kaniku Drive, which ends at the Holoholokai Beach parking lot; the trail head on your right is marked by a sign and interpretive kiosk. Go in the early morning or late afternoon when it's cooler; bring water, wear shoes with sturdy soles (to avoid kiawe thorns), and stay on the trail.

Local expert Kaleiʻula Kaneau leads a **free 1-hour tour** of the petroglyphs near the Kings' Shops in the Waikoloa Beach Resort Thursdays at 9:30am; meet lakeside by Island Fish & Chips. You can also follow the signs to the trail through the petroglyph field on your own, but be aware that the trail is exposed, uneven, and rough; wear closed-toe shoes, a hat, and sunscreen.

Note: The petroglyphs are thousands of years old and easily destroyed. Do not walk on them or take rubbings (the Puakō preserve has a replica petroglyph you may use instead). The best way to capture a petroglyph is with a photo in the late afternoon when the shadows are long.

Pu'ukoholā Heiau National Historic Site ★★★ HISTORIC SITE This seacoast temple, called "the hill of the whale," is the single most imposing and dramatic structure of the early Hawaiians, built by Kamehameha I from 1790 to 1791. The *heiau* stands 224 feet long by 100 feet wide, with three narrow terraces on the seaside and an amphitheater to view canoes. Kamehameha built this temple to Kū, the war god, after a prophet told him he would conquer and unite the islands if he did so. He also slayed his cousin on the site, and 4 years later fulfilled his kingly goal. The site includes an interactive visitor center; a smaller *heiau*-turned-fort; the homestead of John Young (a trusted advisor of Kamehameha); and, offshore, the submerged ruins of what is believed to be **Hale O Kapuni,** a shrine dedicated to the shark gods or guardian spirits called *ʻaumākua.* (You can't see the temple, but shark fins are often spotted slicing through the waters.) Paved trails lead around the complex, with restricted access to the heiau.

62-3601 Kawaihae Rd. (Hwy. 270, *makai* side, south of Kawaihae Harbor). www.nps.gov/puhe. © **808/882-7218.** Daily 8am–4:45pm. Free admission.

NORTH KOHALA

It takes some effort to reach the **Kohala Historical Sites State Monument ★**, but for those with four-wheel-drive (4WD) vehicles or the ability to hike 3 miles round-trip, visiting the windswept, culturally important site on the on the island's northern tip may be worth it. The 1,500-year-old **Moʻokini Heiau,** once used by kings to pray and offer human sacrifices, is among the oldest, largest (the size of a football field), and most significant shrines in Hawaiʻi. It's off a coastal dirt road, 1½ miles southwest of ʻUpolu Airport (http://dlnr.hawaii.gov/dsp/parks/hawaii; Thurs–Tues 9am–8pm; free admission).

King Kamehameha Statue ★★ MONUMENT Here stands King Kamehameha the Great, right arm outstretched, left arm holding a spear, as if guarding the seniors who have turned a century-old, New England–style courthouse into an airy civic center. There's one just like it in Honolulu, across the street from ʻIolani Palace, and another in the U.S. Capitol, but this is the original: an 8-foot, 6-inch bronze by Thomas R. Gould, a Boston sculptor. Cast in Europe in 1880, it was lost at sea on its way to Hawaiʻi. After a sea captain recovered the statue, it was placed here, near Kamehameha's Kohala birthplace, in 1912. Kamehameha is believed to have been born in 1758 under Halley's Comet and became ruler of Hawaiʻi in 1810. He died in Kailua-Kona in 1819, but his burial site remains a mystery.

In front of North Kohala Civic Center, *mauka* side of Hwy. 270, Kapaʻau, just north of Kapaʻau Rd.

Lapakahi State Historical Park ★★ HISTORIC SITE This 14th-century fishing village on a hot, dry, dusty stretch of coast offers a glimpse into the lifestyle of the ancients. Lapakahi is the best-preserved fishing village in Hawaiʻi. Take the self-guided, 1-mile loop trail past stone platforms, fish shrines, rock shelters, salt pans, and restored *hale* (houses) to a coral-sand beach and the deep-blue sea of Koaie Cove, a marine life conservation district. Wear good walking shoes and a hat, go early in the morning or late in the afternoon to beat the heat, and bring your own water. Facilities include porta-potties and picnic tables.

Makai side of Hwy. 270, Mahukona, 12.4 miles north of Kawaihae. http://dlnr.hawaii.gov/dsp/parks/hawaii. ✆ **808/327-4958.** Free admission. Daily 8am–4pm.

Pololū Valley Lookout ★★★ NATURAL ATTRACTION At this end-of-the-road scenic lookout, you can gaze at the vertical dark-green cliffs of the Hāmākua Coast and two islets offshore or peer back into the often-misty uplands. The view may look familiar once you get here—it often appears on travel posters. Linger if you can; adventurous travelers can take a switchback trail (a good 45-min. hike) to a secluded black-sand beach at the mouth of a wild valley once planted in taro; bring water and bug spray, and avoid the surf, subject to strong currents.

At the northern end of Hwy. 270, 5½ miles east of Kapaʻau.

Polulū Valley Lookout.

WAIMEA & MAUNA KEA

Mauna Kea ★★★ NATURAL ATTRACTION The 13,796-foot summit of Mauna Kea, the world's tallest mountain if measured from its base on the ocean floor, is one of the best places on earth for astronomical observations, thanks to pollution-free skies, pitch-black nights, and a tropical location. Here are the world's largest telescopes—and at press time, some environmentalists and Native Hawaiians who still worship here were fighting construction of an even larger one—but the stargazing is fantastic even with the naked eye. ***Note:*** Some spell it Maunakea, a contraction of *Mauna a Wakea,* or "the mountain of Wākea" (the sky father and ancestor of all Hawaiians), in lieu of Mauna Kea, or "white mountain."

SAFETY TIPS Check the weather and Mauna Kea road conditions before you head out (http://mkwc.ifa.hawaii.edu/current/road-conditions; ✆ **808/935-6268**). Dress warmly; it's chilly and windy by day, and after dark, temperatures drop into the 30s (from 3°C to -1°C). Don't go within 24 hours of scuba diving to avoid the bends, and bring a flashlight with a red filter for night visits. Pregnant women, children under 16, and those with heart or lung conditions should skip this trip. ***Note:*** Many rental-car agencies still ban driving on Saddle Road—the only access to Summit Road, which requires a four-wheel-drive (4WD) vehicle—so a private tour, while pricey, is probably the safest and easiest bet (see "Seeing Stars While Others Drive," below).

VISITOR CENTER Named for the Big Island astronaut aboard the ill-fated *Challenger,* the **Ellison Onizuka visitor center** (www.ifa.hawaii.edu/info/vis; ✆ **808/961-2180**) is 6¼ miles up Summit Road and at

Observatories near the summit of Mauna Kea.

9,200 feet elevation. It's open daily 9am to 10pm, with interactive exhibits, 24-hour restrooms, and a bookstore with food, drink, gloves, and other gear for sale. Stay here at least 30 minutes to acclimate before ascending to the summit. From 6 to 10pm nightly, a guide leads a free **stargazing** program that starts with a screening of *First Light,* a documentary about the cultural and astronomical significance of Mauna Kea.

AT THE SUMMIT It's another steep 6 miles, most of them unpaved, to the summit from the visitor center, which at press time unfortunately had suspended indefinitely its free weekend summit caravan tours. If you're driving, make sure your four-wheel-drive (4WD) vehicle has plenty of gas and is in good condition before continuing on. Up here, 11 nations have set up 13 peerless infrared telescopes to look into deep space, making this the world's largest astronomical observatory. The **W. M. Keck Observatory** has a visitor gallery (open weekdays 10am–4pm) with informational panels and a viewing area of the eight-story-high telescope and dome. For cultural reasons, visitors are discouraged from hiking the narrow footpath across the road to the actual, unmarked summit where ancient astronomers and priests came to study the skies and where cultural practitioners still worship today. No matter: From the summit parking lot you have an unparalleled view of other peaks, such as Mauna Loa and Haleakalā, and the bright Pacific.

Another sacred site is **Lake Waiau,** which, at 13,020 feet above sea level, is one of the highest in the world. Although it shrinks drastically in time of drought, it has never dried up. It's named for one of the sisters of Poli'ahu, the snow goddess said to make her home atop Mauna Kea. To see it, you must take a brief hike: On the final approach to the summit, on the blacktop road, go about 600 feet to the major switchback and make a hard right turn. Park on the shoulder of the road and look for the obvious .5-mile trail, following the base of the large cinder cone on your left to the small, greenish lake. ***Note:*** Please respect cultural traditions by not drinking or entering the water, and leave all rocks undisturbed.

THE HĀMĀKUA COAST

Don't forget the bug spray when exploring this warm, moist region, beloved by mosquitoes, and be ready for passing showers—you're in rainbow territory here. Note that some sights below are in the North Hilo district, which shares the rural character of the Hāmākua District, its northern neighbor.

'Akaka Falls State Park ★★★ NATURAL ATTRACTION See one of the most scenic waterfalls in Hawai'i via a relatively easy .4-mile paved loop through a rainforest, past bamboo and flowering ginger, and down to an observation point. You'll have a perfect view of 442-foot 'Akaka Falls, plunging down a horseshoe-shaped green cliff, and nearby Kahuna Falls, a mere 100-footer. Keep your eyes peeled for rainbows; your ears are likely to pick up the two-note chirp of coqui frogs (see below). Facilities include restrooms and drinking water.

End of 'Akaka Falls Rd. (Hwy. 220), Honomu. http://dlnr.hawaii.gov/dsp/parks/hawaii. From Hilo, drive north 8 miles on Hwy. 19 to left at 'Akaka Falls Rd. Follow 3½ miles to parking lot. $5 per car, $1 per person on foot or bicycle.

Lake Waiau, inside the cinder cone just below the summit of Mauna Kea.

'Akaka Falls.

Botanical World Adventures ★ WATERFALL/GARDEN Just north of Hilo is one of the largest botanical gardens in Hawai'i, with some 5,000 species. Although it no longer offers a vista of spectacular, triple-stacked Umauma Falls (see below), it still lays claim to a huge children's maze (second in size only to Dole Plantation's on O'ahu), a tropical fruit arboretum, ethnobotanical and wellness gardens, and flower-lined walks. Waterfall lovers will be heartened to note that the owners have also created a road and trail leading to viewing areas above and below the previously hidden 100-foot **Kamae'e Falls** ($6 if you want to go there only), as well as a trail leading past a series of shorter, bubbling cascades in **Hanapueo Stream.** If that's just too peaceful for you, opt for one of the **Segway tours,** ranging from 30 minutes to 3 hours ($57–$187) or a **zipline tour** ($167), which should be reserved in advance; tour rates include garden admission.

31-240 Old Māmalahoa Hwy., Hakalau. www.worldbotanicalgardens.com. ✆ **888/947-4753** or 808/963-5427. Admission $15 adults, $7 teens 13–17, $3 children 5–12, free for children 4 and under. Guided 2-hr. garden/waterfall tours $57 adults, $33 children 5–12, free for children 4 and under; 24-hr. advance reservation required. Daily 9am–5:30pm. From Hilo, take Hwy. 19 north past mile marker 16, turn left on Leopolino Rd., and then right on Old Māmalahoa Hwy.; entrance is 1⁄10-mile on right.

Hawaii Tropical Botanical Garden ★★ GARDEN More than 2,000 species of tropical plants thrive in this little-known Eden by the sea. The 40-acre valley garden, nestled between the crashing surf and a thundering waterfall, includes torch gingers (which tower on 12-ft.

seeing stars **WHILE OTHERS DRIVE**

Two excellent companies offer Mauna Kea tour packages that provide cold-weather gear, dinner, hot drinks, guided stargazing, and, best of all, someone else to worry about maneuvering the narrow, unpaved road to the summit. All tours are offered weather permitting, but most nights are clear—that's why the observatories are here, after all—with pickups from several locations. Read the fine print on health and age restrictions before booking, and don't forget to tip your guide ($5–$10 per person).

- **Hawaii Forest & Trail** (www.hawaii-forest.com; ✆ **800/464-1993** or 808/331-8505), the island's premier environmentally- and culturally-oriented outfitter, operates a daily **Mauna Kea Summit & Stars Adventure,** including a late-afternoon picnic dinner, sunset at the summit, and stargazing at the visitor center, for $209. The company uses two customized off-road buses (14 passengers max each) for the 7- to 8-hour tour. A daytime option from Hilo, **Maunakea Voyage** ($169), swaps dinner and stargazing for lunch and a private tour of the 'Imiloa Astronomy Center, with a peek inside a summit observatory; it's limited to 12 passengers. Like all of Hawaii Forest & Trail's tours, these are exceptional, with well-informed guides.
- **Monty "Pat" Wright** was the first to run a Mauna Kea stargazing tour when he launched **Mauna Kea Summit Adventures** (www.maunakea.com; ✆ **888/322-2366** or 808/322-2366) in 1983. Guests now ride in a large-windowed, four-wheel-drive (4WD) van instead of a Land Cruiser and don parkas instead of old sweaters; otherwise, it's much the same, with dinner at the visitor center before a spectacular sunset. The 7½- to 8-hour tour costs $204 (check for discounts online).

stalks), a banyan canyon, an orchid garden, a banana grove, a bromeliad hill, an anthurium corner, and a golden bamboo grove, which rattles like a jungle drum in the trade winds. Some endangered Hawaiian specimens, such as the rare *Gardenia remyi,* flourish in this habitat. The

Co-key, Co-key: What Is That Noise?

That loud, chirping noise you hear after dark, especially on the eastern side of the Big Island, is the cry of the male coqui frog looking for a mate. A native of Puerto Rico, where the frogs are kept in check by snakes, the coqui frog came to Hawai'i in some plant material, found no natural enemies, and spread quickly across the Big Island, concentrated on the Hilo side. (A few have made it to O'ahu, Maui, and Kaua'i, where they've been swiftly captured by state agriculture teams devoted to eradicating the invasive species.) A few frogs will sound like singing birds; a chorus of thousands can be deafening—and on the Big Island, they can reach densities of up to 10,000 an acre. Coqui frogs don't like the cool weather of Waimea and Volcano as much, but anywhere else that's lush and rural is likely to have large populations. Pack earplugs if you're a light sleeper.

self-guided tour takes about 90 minutes, but you're welcome to linger. Pick up a loaner umbrella in the visitor center, where you register, so that passing showers don't curtail your visit. ***Note:*** You enter the garden via a 500-foot-long boardwalk that descends along a verdant ravine. Free golf-cart assistance is provided for wheelchair users to reach the wheelchair-accessible path below; for those without wheelchairs but with limited physical ability, the cost to ride the cart there and back is $5.

27-717 Old Māmalahoa Hwy. (4-Mile Scenic Route), Pāpa'ikou. www.htbg.com. ✆ **808/964-5233.** Admission $15 adults, $5 children 6–16, free for children 5 and under. Daily 9am–5pm (admissions end promptly at 4pm). From Hilo, take Hwy. 19 north 7 miles to right turn on Scenic Route; visitor center is 2 miles on the left.

Laupāhoehoe Point ★ HISTORIC SITE/NATURAL ATTRACTION This idyllic place holds a grim reminder of nature's fury. On April 1, 1946, a tsunami swept across the schoolhouse that once stood on this peninsula of leaf-shaped lava *(laupāhoehoe)* and claimed the lives of 24 students, teachers, and residents. Their names are engraved on a stone memorial in this pretty little beach park, and a display holds newspaper stories on the tragedy. The land here ends in black sea stacks that resemble tombstones; when high surf crashes on them, it's positively spooky (and dangerous if you stand too close). The unprotected shoreline is not a place to swim, but the views are spectacular. Facilities include restrooms, picnic tables, and drinking water.

Laupāhoehoe. From Hilo, take Hwy. 19 north 25 miles to Laupāhoehoe Point exit, *makai* side; the exit is 31 miles south of Waimea.

Umauma Falls ★★ WATERFALL/GARDEN Formerly accessed through the Botanical World Adventures (see above), the triple-tiered, cascading pools of Umauma Falls are now the exclusive province of visitors to the neighboring Umauma Experience, which offers an array of ziplining, hiking, swimming, and kayaking excursions on its lush 90 acres. The less adventurous can also just pay $10 to drive the paved road to the waterfall lookout, and then take a self-guided garden hike with several more overlooks; it's worth it. Pick up a map at the visitor center, which also sells snacks and drinks. You can enjoy your repast at the river walk's observation area, under guava trees (feel free to sample their fruit when ripe), or on the visitor center's back lanai, which overlooks the river and the last line on the zip course (see "Ziplining" on p. 250). If you book a tour package that includes a swim in a waterfall pool, you'll also get to see one of the only petroglyphs on the island's east side.

31-313 Old Mamalahoa Hwy., Hakalau. http://umaumaexperience.com. ✆ **808/930-9477.** Admission $10 adults, free for children 11 and under; includes waterfall viewing, garden, and river walk. Daily 8am–5pm. Various times: Zipline tours $189–$239; hike/swim/picnic $125; kayak/swim/picnic $49. From Hilo, take Hwy. 19 north past mile marker 16, turn left on Leopolino Rd., then right on Old Māmalahoa Hwy., and follow ½-mile to entrance.

Waipi'o Valley ★★★ NATURAL ATTRACTION/HISTORIC SITE This breathtakingly beautiful valley has long been a source of fascination, inspiring song and story. From the black-sand bay at its

Waipi'o Valley.

A TASTE OF the Hāmākua coast

When the Hamakua Sugar Company—the Big Island's last sugar plantation—closed in 1996, it left a huge void in the local economy, transforming already shrinking villages into near ghost towns. But some residents turned to specialty crops that are now sought after by chefs throughout the islands. Hidden in the tall eucalyptus trees outside the old plantation community of Pa'auilo, the **Hawaiian Vanilla Company ★★** (www.hawaiianvanilla.com; ✆ **808/776-1771**) is the first U.S. farm to grow vanilla. The farm hosts one of the truly sensuous experiences on the Big Island—the **Hawaiian Vanilla Luncheon**—plus shorter tastings and a weekly afternoon tea. Before you even enter the huge Vanilla Gallery, you will be embraced by the heavenly scent of vanilla. The four-course luncheon ($39 for age 12 and up; $19 for kids 4–11) takes place weekdays from 12:30 to 2:30pm; the 45-minute **Farm Tour** ($25 for age 4 and up; free for kids 3 and under), including dessert and tastings, happens on weekdays at 1pm; and the **Upcountry Tea** ($29), featuring vanilla-flavored savories and desserts, takes place on 3pm Saturday. Reservations required.

mouth, Waipi'o ("curving water") sweeps 6 miles between sheer, cathedral-like walls some 2,000 feet high. The tallest waterfall in Hawai'i, Hi'ilawe, tumbles 1,300 feet from its rear cliffs. Called "the valley of kings" for the royal burial caves dotting forbiddingly steep walls, this was Kamehameha's boyhood residence; up to 10,000 Hawaiians are thought to have lived here before Westerners arrived. Chinese immigrants later joined them and a modest town arose, but it was destroyed in 1946 by the same tsunami that devastated Hilo and Laupāhoehoe, though luckily without fatalities. The town was never rebuilt; only about 50 people live here today, most with no electricity or phones, although others come down on weekends to tend taro patches, camp, and fish.

To get to Waipi'o Valley, take Highway 19 from Waimea or Hilo to Highway 240 in Honoka'a, and follow the highway almost 10 miles to Kukuihaele Road and the **Waipi'o Valley Lookout ★★★**, a grassy park and picnic area on the edge of Waipi'o Valley's sheer cliffs, with splendid views of the wild oasis below.

To explore the valley itself, a guided tour is best, for reasons of safety and access. The steep road has a grade of nearly 40% in places and is narrow and potholed; by law, you must use a four-wheel-drive (4WD) vehicle, and even then rental-car agencies ban their vehicles from it, to avoid pricey tow jobs. Hiking down the 900-foot-road is hard on the knees going down and the lungs coming up, and requires dodging cars in both directions. Most of the valley floor is privately owned, with trespassing actively discouraged. Note that unmarked burial sites lie just behind the black-sand beach, which is not good for swimming or snorkeling and has no facilities.

Instead, book a ride on the **Waipio Valley Shuttle ★★** (www.waipiovalleyshuttle.com; ✆ **808/775-7121**) for a 90- to 120-minute guided tour that begins with an exciting (and bumpy) drive down in an open-door van. Once on the valley floor, you'll be rewarded with breathtaking views of Hiilawe, plus a narrated tour of the taro patches *(lo'i)* and ruins from the 1946 tsunami. The tour is offered Monday through Saturday at 9am, 11am, 1pm, and 3pm; tickets are $59 for adults and $32 for kids 10 and under (minimum two adult fares); reservations recommended. Check-in is less than a mile from the lookout at **Waipio Valley Artworks** (www.waipiovalleyartworks.com; ✆ **808/775-0958**), on Kukuihaele Road. Waipio Valley Artworks is also the pickup point for Na'alapa Stables' **Waipi'o Valley Horseback Adventure ★★** (www.naalapastables.com; ✆ **808/755-0419**), a 2½-hour guided ride ($94) for ages 8 and up; see "Horseback Riding" (p. 248) for details.

All ages may take the mule-drawn surrey ride offered by **Waipio Valley Wagon Tours ★** (www.waipiovalleywagontours.com; ✆ **808/775-9518**), a narrated, 90-minute excursion that starts with a van ride down to the valley stables. Tours are offered Monday through Saturday at 10:30am, 12:30pm, and 2:30pm; cost is $60 adults, $55 seniors 65 and older, and $30 children 3 to 12. Reservations are a must; weight distribution is a factor on the rides. Check-in is at **Neptune's Gardens Gallery** on Kukuihaele Road (www.neptunesgarden.net; ✆ **808/775-1343**).

HILO

Pick up the map to a self-guided walking tour of Hilo, which focuses on 21 historic sites dating from the 1870s to the present, at the information kiosk of the **Downtown Hilo Improvement Association** (www.downtownhilo.com; ✆ **808/935-8850**) in the Mo'oheau Bus Depot, 329 Kamehameha Ave.—the first stop on the tour.

Hilo Bay ★★★ NATURAL ATTRACTION Old banyan trees shade **Banyan Drive ★**, the lane that curves along the waterfront from Kamehameha Avenue (Hwy. 19) to the Hilo Bay hotels. Most of the trees were planted in the mid-1930s by visitors like Cecil B. DeMille (here in 1933 filming *Four Frightened People*), Babe Ruth (his tree is in front of the Hilo Hawaiian Hotel), King George V, Amelia Earhart, and celebs whose fleeting fame didn't last as long as the trees themselves.

It's worth a stop along Banyan Drive—especially if the coast is clear and the summit of Mauna Kea is free of clouds—to make the short walk across the concrete-arch bridge in front of the Hilo Naniloa Hotel to **Moku Ola (Coconut Island) ★**, if only to gain a panoramic sense of Hilo Bay and its surroundings.

Continuing on Banyan Drive, just south of Coconut Island, are **Lili'uokalani Gardens ★★**, the largest formal Japanese garden this side of Tokyo. This 30-acre park, named for the last monarch of Hawai'i,

Queen Lili'uokalani, and dedicated in 1917 to the islands' first Japanese immigrants, is as pretty as a postcard (if occasionally a little unkempt), with stone lanterns, koi ponds, pagodas, rock gardens, bonsai, and a moon-gate bridge. Admission is free; it's open 24 hours.

Kaumana Caves Park ★★ NATURAL ATTRACTION Pick up an inexpensive flashlight or headlight ($5–$15) at Walmart in Hilo or Kona before visiting this wilder, longer sibling to the more famous Nāhuku (Thurston) lava tube (p. 209) in Hawai'i Volcanoes National Park. As the sign warns, there are "no lights, no walkway" in this eerily fascinating set of caves formed by an 1881 lava flow that threatened downtown Hilo. Princess Ruth is credited with saving the town by praying to Pele to halt the lava. You can thank the county for maintaining the steep concrete stairs leading into the lava tube's fern-lined "skylight," where the larger right entrance offers a short loop trail and the left entrance leads to a more challenging (that is, watch your head) out-and-back path. Your flashlight will help you spot the lava that cooled fast enough to keep its red cover, and help you avoid stumbling over protruding roots. Wear long sleeves, since it can be cool and dripping, and sturdy shoes, to avoid slipping on the often-slick cave floor.

Kaumana Dr. (Hwy. 200), west of 'ākala Road (4-mile marker), Hilo. Driving from Hilo, park is on right and parking lot is on left across the road. Free admission.

Lyman Museum & Mission House ★★ MUSEUM/HISTORIC SITE Yankee missionaries Rev. David and Sarah Lyman had been married for just 24 days before they set sail for Hawai'i in 1832, arriving 6 months later in a beautiful but utterly foreign land. Seven years later, they built this two-story home for their growing family (eventually seven children) in a blend of Hawaiian and New England design, with plastered walls, koa floors, and lanais on both floors. Long a museum of 19th-century missionary life, the **Mission House** was completely restored in 2010, and Rev. Lyman's office in an 1845 annex was opened to the public for the first time. You can only visit the house as part of a guided tour, offered twice daily except Sunday.

The larger, modern **Lyman Museum** next door gives a broader perspective of Hawaiian history and culture. Walk through a lava tube and make your way through multiple climate zones in the **Earth Heritage Gallery**'s "Habitats of Hawai'i" exhibit, with recorded bird sounds and full-scale replicas of sea life; mineral and shell enthusiasts can pore over an extensive collection. The **Island Heritage Gallery** examines the life of early Hawaiians, with artifacts such as stone poi pounders, wooden bowls, and *kapa,* the delicate bark cloth.

276 Haili St. (at Kapi'olani St.). www.lymanmuseum.org. ✆ **808/935-5021.** Admission $10 adults, $8 seniors 60 and over, $5 college students, $3 children 6–17; $21 per family. Mon–Sat 10am–4:30pm; guided house tours at 11am and 2pm (call to reserve).

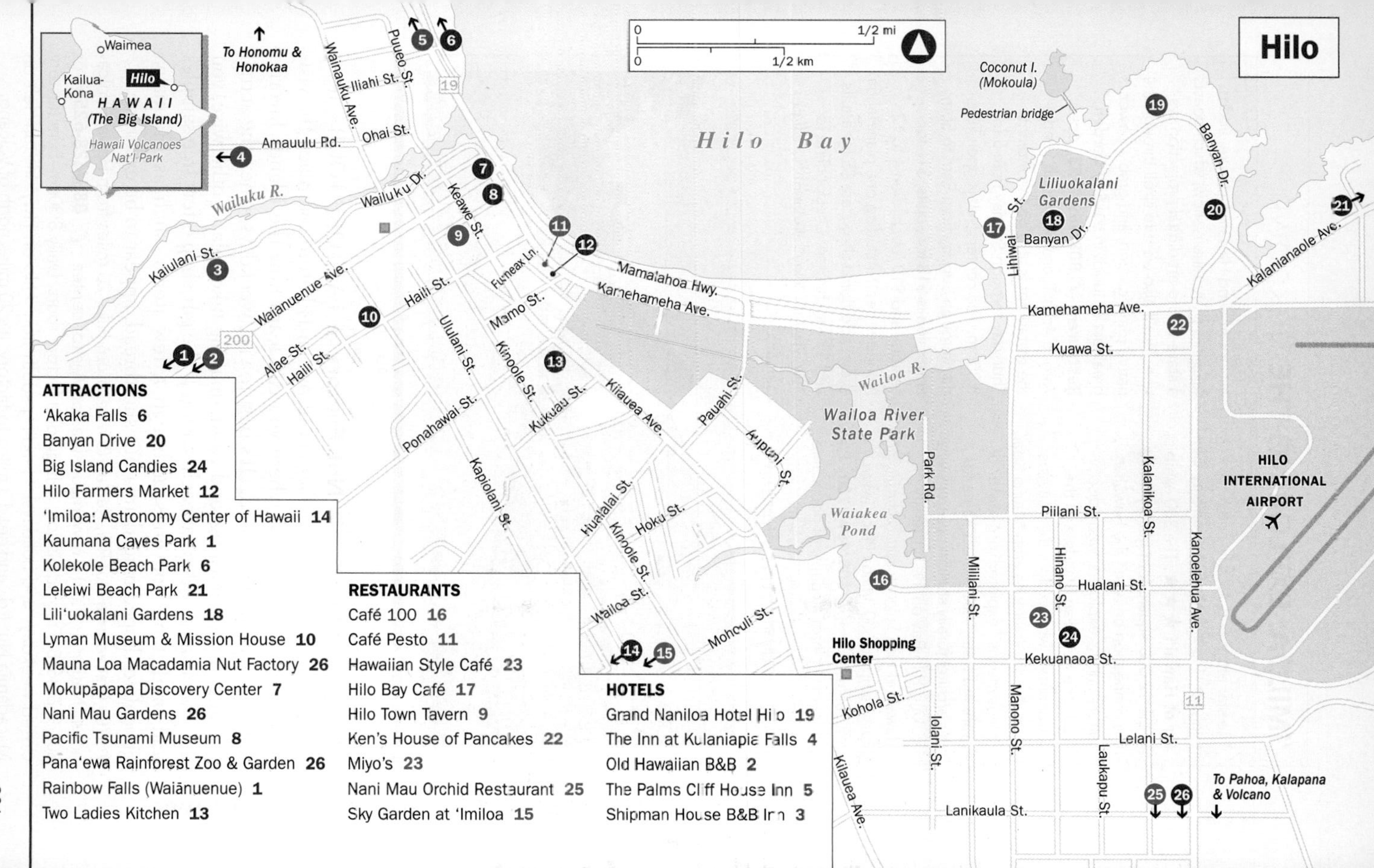

Hilo
To Honomu & Honokaa
Waimea
Kailua-Kona
Hilo
HAWAII
(The Big Island)
Hawaii Volcanoes Nat'l Park
0
1/2 mi
1/2 km
Hilo Bay
Coconut I. (Mokoula)
Pedestrian bridge
Liliuokalani Gardens
Banyan Dr.
Kalanianaole Ave.
Lihiwai St.
Kamehameha Ave.
Mamalahoa Hwy.
Kuawa St.
Wailoa R.
Wailoa River State Park
Waiakea Pond
HILO INTERNATIONAL AIRPORT
Park Rd.
Piilani St.
Kalanikoa St.
Kanoelehua Ave.
Mililani St.
Hinano St.
Hualani St.
Kekuanaoa St.
Hilo Shopping Center
Kohola St.
Iolani St.
Manono St.
Lelani St.
Laukapu St.
Lanikaula St.
Kilauea Ave.
To Pahoa, Kalapana & Volcano
Wainauku Ave.
Puueo St.
Iliahi St.
Ohai St.
Amauulu Rd.
Wailuku R.
Wailuku Dr.
Keawe St.
Kaiulani St.
Waianuenue Ave.
Haili St.
Alae St.
Funeax Ln.
Mamo St.
Ululani St.
Kinoole St.
Ponahawai St.
Kapiolani St.
Kukuau St.
Pauahi St.
Hualalai St.
Hoku St.
Wailoa St.
Mohouli St.
19
200
11
ATTRACTIONS
'Akaka Falls 6
Banyan Drive 20
Big Island Candies 24
Hilo Farmers Market 12
'Imiloa: Astronomy Center of Hawaii 14
Kaumana Caves Park 1
Kolekole Beach Park 6
Leleiwi Beach Park 21
Lili'uokalani Gardens 18
Lyman Museum & Mission House 10
Mauna Loa Macadamia Nut Factory 26
Mokupāpapa Discovery Center 7
Nani Mau Gardens 26
Pacific Tsunami Museum 8
Pana'ewa Rainforest Zoo & Garden 26
Rainbow Falls (Waiānuenue) 1
Two Ladies Kitchen 13
RESTAURANTS
Café 100 16
Café Pesto 11
Hawaiian Style Café 23
Hilo Bay Café 17
Hilo Town Tavern 9
Ken's House of Pancakes 22
Miyo's 23
Nani Mau Orchid Restaurant 25
Sky Garden at 'Imiloa 15
HOTELS
Grand Naniloa Hotel Hilo 19
The Inn at Kulaniapia Falls 4
Old Hawaiian B&B 2
The Palms Cliff House Inn 5
Shipman House B&B Inn 3

'IMILOA: EXPLORING THE unknown

The star attraction, literally and figuratively, of Hilo is **'Imiloa: Astronomy Center of Hawai'i ★★★**. The 300 exhibits in the 12,000-square-foot gallery make the connection between the Hawaiian culture and its explorers, who "discovered" the Hawaiian Islands, and the astronomers who explore the heavens from the observatories atop Mauna Kea. *'Imiloa* means "explorer" or "seeker of profound truth," the perfect name for this architecturally stunning center overlooking Hilo Bay on the University of Hawai'i at Hilo Science and Technology Park campus, 600 'Imiloa Place (www.imiloahawaii.org; ✆ **808/969-9700**). Plan to spend at least a couple of hours here to allow time to browse the excellent, family-friendly interactive exhibits on astronomy and Hawaiian culture, and to take in a planetarium show, which boasts a state-of-the-art digital projection system. You'll also want to stroll through the native plant garden, and grab a power breakfast or lunch in the **Sky Garden Restaurant** (✆ **808/969-9753**), open 7am to 4pm Tuesday through Sunday; the restaurant is also open for dinner Thursday through Sunday from 5 to 8:30pm. The center itself is open Tuesday through Sunday from 9am to 5pm; admission is $18 for adults, $16 for seniors, and $10 for children 4 to 12 (younger free), including one planetarium show; additional shows are $5 for adults and $3 for children. Check online for "Word of the Day" discount ($2 off per person).

Maunaloa Macadamia Nut Factory ★ FACTORY TOUR It's a 3-mile drive through macadamia nut orchards before you reach the visitor center of this factory, where you can learn how the islands' favorite nut is grown and processed. (It's best to visit weekdays, when the actual husking, drying, roasting, and candy-making takes place; otherwise, you can watch short videos at each station.) The gift shop offers free samples and predictable souvenirs, although a few items, such as Maunaloa chocolate-dipped macadamia nut shortbread, appear to be exclusive.

16-701 Macadamia Nut Rd., Kea'au (5 miles from Hilo, 20 miles from Hawai'i Volcanoes National Park). www.maunaloa.com/visitor-center. ✆ **888/628-6256** or 808/966-8618. Free admission; self-guided factory tours. Daily 8:30am–5pm (factory closed weekdays and holidays). Heading south from Hilo on Hwy. 11, turn left on Macadamia Nut Rd., and head 3 miles to factory; it's 20 miles north of Volcano.

Mokupāpapa Discovery Center ★★ MUSEUM You may never get to the vast coral-reef system that is the Northwest Hawaiian Islands—the protected chain of islets and atolls spanning 1,200 nautical miles is remote (stretching from Nīhoa, 155 miles northwest of Kaua'i, to Kure Atoll, 56 miles west of Midway), and visitation is severely limited. But enough people have been intrigued by the wonders of the Papahā naumokuākea Marine National Monument that in spring 2014 its educational center moved into much larger quarters in a handsomely renovated, century-old building on the Hilo waterfront. The new center has 20,000 square feet to reveal the beauties and mysteries of the region's ecosystem and its relationship with Hawaiian culture—a prime reason why the region was named a World Heritage Site in 2010. Exhibits include a 3,500-gallon saltwater aquarium with brilliant coral and reef fish; the sounds of Hawaiian chants and seabirds; interactive displays on each of the islets; a life-size Hawaiian monk seal exhibit; and a giant mural by Hilo artist Layne Luna, who also created the life-size models of giant fish, sharks, and the manta ray. Both the content and the cost of admission—free—are great for families.

76 Kamehameha Ave. (on the corner of Waiānuenue Ave.). www.papahanaumokuakea.gov/education/center.html. ✆ **808/933-8180.** Free admission. Tues–Sat 9am–4pm.

Nani Mau Gardens ★ GARDEN In 1972 Makato Nitahara turned a 20-acre papaya patch just outside Hilo into a tropical garden. Today Nani Mau ("forever beautiful") holds more than 2,000 varieties of plants, from fragile hibiscus, whose blooms last only a day, to durable red anthuriums imported from South America. It also has rare palms, a fruit orchard, Japanese gardens (with a bell tower built without nails), an orchid walkway, and a ginger garden. The gardens went through a rough patch a few years ago, even closing the doors before Los Angeles tour operator Helen Koo purchased the site in 2012. With the help of four full-time gardeners working around the clock, she reopened the gardens in 2013, along with a **garden restaurant** that offers a surprisingly delicious buffet lunch ($17, including garden admission) daily 10:30am to 2pm.

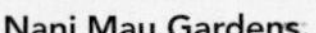

Nani Mau Gardens.

421 Makalika St. www.nanimaugardens.com. ✆ **808/959-3500.** Admission $10 adults, $5 seniors and children 4–10; with lunch, $17 adults, $15 seniors and children 4–10. Daily 10am–3pm. From Hilo Airport, take Hwy. 11 south 2 miles to second left turn at Makalika St., and continue ¾-mile.

Pacific Tsunami Museum ★ MUSEUM Poignant exhibits on Japan's 2011 tsunami (which caused significant property damage on the Big Island) and the 2004 Indian Ocean tragedy have broadened the international perspective in this compact museum in a former bank, where displays explain the science of the deadly phenomenon. Still, the stories and artifacts related to Hilo's two most recent catastrophic tsunamis are impressive, including a parking meter nearly bent in two by the force of the 1960 killer waves, and accounts from survivors of the 1946 tsunami that washed away the school at Laupāhoehoe. Many of the volunteers have hair-raising stories of their own to share—but you'll feel better after reading about the warning systems now in place.
130 Kamehameha Ave. (at the corner of Kalākaua Ave.). www.tsunami.org. ✆ **808/935-0926.** Admission $8 adults, $7 seniors, $4 children 6–17, free for children 5 and under. Tues–Sat 10am–4pm.

Pana'ewa Rainforest Zoo & Gardens ★ ZOO/GARDEN This 12-acre zoo, in the heart of the Pana'ewa Forest Reserve south of Hilo, is the only outdoor rainforest zoo in the U.S. Some 80 species of animals from rainforests around the globe call Panaewa home, as do a couple of "Kona nightingales"—donkeys that escaped decades ago from coffee farms. (Though highway signs still warn of them, virtually all were relocated to California in 2011 during a prolonged drought.) The Pana'ewa residents enjoy fairly natural, sometimes overgrown settings. Look for cute pygmy goats, capuchin monkeys, and giant anteaters, among other critters. This free attraction includes a covered playground.
800 Stainback Hwy., Kea'au (off Hwy. 11, 5 miles south of its intersection with Hwy. 19 in downtown Hilo). www.hilozoo.com. ✆ **808/959-7224.** Free admission. Daily 9am–4pm. Petting zoo Sat 1:30–2:30pm.

Rainbow Falls (Waiānueanue) ★ WATERFALL Go in the morning, around 9 or 10am, just as the sun comes over the mango trees, to see Rainbow Falls, or Waiānuenue, at its best. Part of **Wailuku River State Park,** the 80-foot falls (which can be slender in times of drought) spill into a big round natural pool surrounded by wild ginger. If you're lucky, you'll catch the rainbow created in the falls' mist. According to legend, Hina, the mother of demigod Māui, once lived in the cave behind the falls. Swimming in the pool is not allowed, but you can follow a trail left through the trees to the top of the falls (watch your step).
Off Rainbow Dr., just past the intersection of Waiānuenue Ave. (Hwy. 200) and Pu'uhina St. http://dlnr.hawaii.gov/dsp/parks/hawaii. Free admission.

PUNA

Most visitors understandably want to head straight to **Hawai'i Volcanoes National Park ★★★** (p. 207) when exploring this region, where Pele still consumes the land and creates still more. But the celebrated national park is far from the only place where you can experience Puna's geothermal wonders, or see the destruction the volcano has wrought. At press time, residents in Pāhoa were still warily monitoring a slow-moving lava flow that began June 27, 2014, and halted just 550 yards before reaching Hwy. 130, the sole paved access to the rest of the island. (Officials have prepared unpaved roads as resident-only alternates.)

For now, the easiest way to explore the **Pāhoa-Kapoho-Kalapana** triangle is still by taking Highway 130 west from Pāhoa about 9 miles to Kalapana. Along the way, you'll pass **steam vents** on the *makai* side of the two-lane highway in the Keauohana Forest Reserve, near mile marker 15. (Though some have been used as natural saunas, do not enter the caves on your own.) **Star of the Sea Painted Church ★** will also be on your left, shortly before Highway 130 meets Highway 137. The wooden church was moved here in advance of the 1990 lava flow that destroyed area homes, buried the black-sand beach at Kaimū, and severed the highway link to Chain of Craters Road in the national park. The church is open daily 9am to 4pm; visitor donations help pay for upkeep.

In Kalapana, you'll want to see the **new black-sand beach,** reached by walking carefully along a short red cinder trail, past fascinating fissures and dramatically craggy rocks. A crafts stand near the start often has sprouting coconuts for you to wedge into the ground, available for a few dollars' donation; no digging is required—like the 'ōhi'a lehua that have started to reappear here, coconut palms are used to tough conditions. So are the people of Puna, who gather in great numbers at the open-air **Uncle Robert's 'Awa Club** for the Wednesday-night market and Hawaiian music on Fridays. During the day, it's open for snacks and drinks, sold "by donation" for permit purposes (be aware they'll let you know *exactly* how much to donate).

From Kalapana/Kaimū, you'll pick up Highway 137 (the Kapoho-Kalapana Rd.), and follow it east to Kapoho along 15 miles of nearly pristine coastline, past parks, forests, rugged beaches, and tide pools, some geothermally heated. The highway is nicknamed the **Red Road,** for the terra-cotta-hued cinders once used to pave it, although it's now mostly covered by black asphalt.

The adventurous (or exhibitionists) may want to make the tricky hike down to unmarked **Kehena Black Sand Beach ★,** off Highway 137 about 3½ miles east of Kalapana. Here the law against public nudity is widely ignored, although the view of the ocean is usually more entrancing. (Clothed or not, avoid going into the water—currents are dangerous.) It's easier to take a brief detour to see the waves pounding the base of ironwood-shaded cliffs in the **MacKenzie State Recreation Area ★,**

9 miles northeast of Kalapana. Another 3 miles east leads to the scenic "hot pond" at **Ahalanui Park ★★** (see below); both MacKenzie and Ahalanui have picnic and restroom facilities.

From Ahalanui, Highway 137 veers inland; drive 1¾ miles to a right turn on Kapoho Kai Road and follow it for a mile to the small parking area for the **Wai'ōpae Tidepools ★★**, a state marine-life conservation district (http://dlnr.hawaii.gov/dar). Snorkelers will go crazy here; with proper footwear, you can also walk along the edges of numerous tide pools, many very shallow and teeming with coral and juvenile fish, while the breakers crash in the distance. (***Note:*** The private road and parking lot are maintained by the community, with a volunteer usually on hand to collect a $3 fee.)

Back on Highway 137, head 1 mile north to Kapoho Beach Road. On your left is the **Green Lake Fruit Stand,** named for the unusual, freshwater **Green Lake,** inside nearby **Kapoho Crater ★**. The lake is actually a crater within the 360-foot-tall Kapoho Crater, formed 200 to 400 years ago. If she's not at the stand, call caretaker Smiley Burrows (**© 808/965-5500**) to arrange a scenic hike or drive up the crater for $5. (You can also swim in the lake, one of only two on the island, but no one knows its depths, and algae sometimes obscure the water.)

Just east of the Green Lake Fruit Stand, Highway 137 intersects Highway 132 (Kapoho Rd.). A right turn leads on an upaved road to the island's easternmost point and **Cape Kumukahi Lighthouse ★**, which miraculously survived the 1960 lava flow that destroyed the original village of Kapoho. Who cares if its modern steel frame isn't all that quaint? The fact that it's standing at all is impressive—the molten lava parted in two and flowed around it—while its bright-white trusses make a great contrast in photos against the black lava, dotted with a few green trees and framed by a cerulean sea.

A left turn onto paved Highway 132 takes you back 9 miles to the funky, somewhat ramshackle village of Pāhoa, passing eerie **Lava Tree State Monument ★★** (see below) and the towering monkeypod and invasive albizia trees of **Nanawale Forest Reserve** as you go.

Ahalanui Park (Hot Pond) ★★ PARK Warmed by one of the area's many volcanically heated springs, this balmy, shallow pool lined with lava rocks and shady trees is protected from the surging ocean by a concrete wall, although very high surf can crash over it and cool the pond. It's not a snorkeling site per se, but silver fish use inlets to dart around the pool's usually clear waters, while a few eels hide in the rocks (if you don't bother them, they won't bother you). Shaded by tall palms, it's a pretty setting even if you don't plan to go into the water (which you shouldn't if you have any open cuts, due to possible bacteria, although the county does perform regular tests). Facilities include a lifeguard station, picnic tables, shower, and porta-potties—wear your bathing suit under your clothes so you don't have to change in one.

Makai side of Hwy. 137, between mile markers 10 and 11, Pāhoa (9 miles southeast of town). Free admission. Daily 7am–7pm (closed until 1pm 2nd Wed each month for maintenance).

Lava Tree State Monument ★★ NATURAL ATTRACTION In 1790, a fast-moving lava flow raced through a grove of ʻōhiʻa lehua trees here, cooling quickly and creating lava rock molds of their trunks. Today the ghostly sentinels punctuate a well-shaded, paved .7-mile loop trail through the rich foliage of the 17-acre park. Facilities include restrooms and a few spots for picnicking (or ducking out of the rain during one of the area's frequent showers). Some areas with deep fissures are fenced off, but keep to the trail regardless for safe footing.
Makai side of Hwy. 132 (Pāhoa–Pohoiki Rd.), 2¾ miles southeast of Pāhoa. http://dlnr.hawaii.gov/dsp/parks/hawaii. Free admission. Daily during daylight hours.

HAWAIʻI VOLCANOES NATIONAL PARK ★★★

Before tourism became the islands' middle name, their singular attraction for visitors wasn't the beach, but the volcano. From the world over, curious spectators gathered on the rim of Kīlauea's Halemaʻumaʻu crater to see one of the greatest wonders of the globe. A century after it was named a national park in 1916, **Hawaiʻi Volcanoes National Park** (www.nps.gov/havo; ✆ **808/985-6000**) remains the state's premier natural attraction, home to an active volcano and one of only two World Heritage Sites in the islands.

There's never a guarantee you'll see flowing lava from the ground—helicopter flights are another matter—but it's undeniably spectacular even without liquid rocks (check the website for updates before you go). Sadly, after driving to the park, about 100 miles from Kailua-Kona and 29 miles from Hilo, many visitors pause only briefly by the highlights along **Crater Rim Drive ★★★** before heading back to their hotels. To allow the majesty and *mana* (spiritual energy) of this special place to sink in, you should really take at least 3 days—and certainly 1 night—to explore the park, including its miles of trails.

Fortunately, the admission fee ($15 per vehicle, $8 per bicyclist or hiker) is good for 7 days. Be prepared for rain and bring a jacket, especially in winter, when it can be downright chilly at night, in the 40s or 50s (single digits to midteens Celsius). ***Note:*** For details on hiking and camping in the park, see "Hiking" (p. 244) and "Camping" (p. 267).

Crater Rim Drive Tour

Stop by the **Kīlauea Visitor Center** (daily 9am–5pm) to get the latest updates on lava flows and the day's free ranger-led tours and watch an informative 25-minute film, shown on the hour from 9am to 4pm. Just beyond the center lies vast **Kīlauea Caldera ★★★**, a circular depression nearly 2 miles by 3 miles and 540 feet deep. It's easy to imagine

VOG & OTHER volcanic VOCABULARY

Hawaiian volcanoes have their own unique vocabulary. The lava that resembles ropy swirls of brownie batter is called ***pāhoehoe*** *(pah-hoy-hoy)*; it results from a fast-moving flow that ripples as it moves. The chunky, craggy lava that looks like someone put asphalt in a blender is called ***'a'ā*** *(ah-ah)*; it's caused by lava that moves slowly, breaking apart as it cools, and then overruns itself. **Vog** is smog made of volcanic gases and smoke, which can sting your eyes and can cause respiratory illness. Since Halema'uma'u began spewing its dramatic plume of smoke in 2008, vog has been more frequent, particularly on the Kona and Kohala coasts, thanks to wind patterns. The state **Department of Health** (www.hiso2index.info) lists current air-quality advisories for the Big Island, based on sulfur dioxide levels.

Mark Twain marveling over the sights here in 1866, when a wide, molten lava lake bubbled within view in the caldera's **Halema'uma'u Crater ★★★**, itself 3,000 feet across and 300 feet deep.

Though different today, the caldera's panorama is still compelling. Since 2008, a plume of ash, often visible from miles away, has billowed from Halema'uma'u, the legendary home of Pele. The sulfurous smoke has forced the ongoing closure of nearly half of Crater Rim Drive, now just a 6-mile crescent. The fumes normally drift northwest, where they often create vog (see "Vog & Other Volcanic Vocabulary" on p. 208), to the dismay of Kona residents. (Scientists monitor the park's air quality closely, just in case the plume changes direction, with rangers ready to evacuate the park quickly if needed.) In the evening the pillar of smoke turns a rosy red, reflecting the lava lake that rises and falls deep below and even overflowed onto the crater floor in 2015. You can also admire Halema'uma'u's fiery glow over a drink or dinner in **Volcano House ★★** (p. 266), the only inn in the park.

Less than a mile from the visitor center, several **steam vents ★★★** line the rim of the caldera, puffing out moist warm air. Across the road, a boardwalk leads through the stinky, smoking **sulphur banks ★★★**, called Ha'akulamanu in Hawaiian, and home to ōhi'a lehua trees and unfazed native birds. (As with all trails here, stay on the path to avoid possible serious injury, or worse.)

Shortly before Crater Rim Drive closes to traffic (due to the current eruption), the **observation deck ★★★** at **Thomas A. Jaggar Museum ★★** offers a prime spot for viewing the crater and its plume, especially at night. By day you can also see the vast, barren Ka'ū Desert and the massive sloping flank of Mauna Loa. The museum itself is open daily 10am to 8pm, and admission is free; watch videos from the days when the volcano was really spewing, learn about the cultural significance of Pele, and track earthquakes (a precursor of eruptions) on a seismograph.

Heading southeast from the visitor center, Crater Rim Drive passes by the smaller but still impressive **Kīlauea Iki Crater ★★**, which in 1959 was a roiling lava lake spewing lava 1,900 feet into the air. From here, you can walk or drive to **Thurston Lava Tube ★★★**, a 500-year-old lava cave in a pit of giant tree ferns. Also called Nāhuku, it's partly illuminated, but take a flashlight and wear sturdy shoes so you can explore the unlit area for another half-mile or so.

Continuing on Crater Rim Drive leads to the **Pu'u Pua'i Overlook ★** of Kīlauea Iki, where you find the upper trail head of the aptly named half-mile **Devastation Trail ★★**, an easy walk through a cinder field that ends where Crater Rim Drive meets **Chain of Craters Road ★★★**.

Pedestrians and cyclists only can continue on Crater Rim Drive for the next .8 mile of road, closed to vehicular traffic since the 2008 eruption. The little-traveled pavement leads to **Keanakāko'i Crater ★★**, scene of several eruptions in the 19th and 20th centuries. It provides yet another dazzling perspective on the Kīlauea Caldera; turn your gaze north for an impressive view of Mauna Loa and Mauna Kea, the world's two highest mountains when measured from the sea floor.

Hawai'i Volcanoes National Park.

Chain of Craters Road ★★★

It's natural to drive slowly down the 19-mile **Chain of Craters Road,** which descends 3,700 feet to the sea and ends in a thick black mass of rock from a 2003 lava flow. You feel like you're driving on the moon, if the lunar horizon were a brilliant blue sea. Pack food and water for the journey, since there are officially no concessions after you pass the Volcano House; the nearest fuel lies outside the park, in Volcano Village.

> **Please Brake for Nēnē**
>
> Nēnē, the endangered native Hawaiian goose and state bird, are making a comeback in Hawai'i Volcanoes National Park and other high-altitude areas in the islands, where they feast on the cranberry-like *'ōhelo* berries that grow at upper elevations. Unfortunately, these uplands are often misty, and the birds' feathers blend easily with the pavement, making it hard for inattentive drivers to see them. Drive carefully, and to discourage nēnē from approaching cars, don't feed them.

Two miles down, before the road really starts twisting, the one-lane, 8½-mile **Hilina Pali Road ★★** veers off to the west, crossing windy scrublands and old lava flows. The payoff is at the end, where you stand nearly 2,300 feet above the coast along the rugged 12-mile *pali* (cliff). Some of the most challenging trails in the park, across the Ka'ū Desert and down to the coast, start here.

Back on Chain of Craters Road, 10 miles below the Crater Rim Drive junction, the picnic shelter at **Kealakomo ★** provides another sweeping coastal vista. At mile marker 16.5, you'll see the parking lot for **Pu'u Loa ★★★**, an enormous field of some 23,000 petroglyphs—the largest in the islands. A three-quarter-mile, gently rolling lava trail leads to a boardwalk where you can view the stone carvings, 85% of which are *puka,* or holes (aka cupules); Hawaiians often placed their infants' umbilical cords in them. At the end of Chain of Craters Road, a lookout area allows a glimpse of 90-foot **Holei Sea Arch ★★**, one of several striking formations carved in the oceanside cliffs. Stop by the ranger station before treading carefully across the 21st-century lava, "some of the youngest land on Earth," as the park calls it. In the distance you may spot fumes from the Pu'u 'Ō'ō vent, or a red glow at night (bear in mind it's a slow drive back up in the dark.)

KA'Ū

At the end of 11 miles of bad road that peters out at Kaulana Bay, in the lee of a jagged, black-lava point, is *Ka Lae* ("The Point")—the tail end of the United States, often called South Point. From the tip, the nearest continental landfall is Antarctica, 7,500 miles away. It's a rugged 2-mile hike down a cliff from Ka Lae to the anomaly known as **Papakōlea (Green Sand) Beach ★★**, described on p. 224. Beware the big waves that lash the shore there.

Chain of Craters Road.

Kahuku Unit, Hawai'i Volcanoes National Park ★★ NATURAL ATTRACTION Few visitors (or even residents) are familiar with this 116,000-acre portion of the national park, some 24 miles from the Kīlauea Visitor Center and accessible only since 2009. But if your timing is right—it's only open weekends, and closed holidays—you can hike, bike, or drive on a 12-mile loop to see a forested pit crater, cinder cone, and tree molds from an 1866 lava flow, plus ranch-era relics. Rangers also frequently lead free hikes; check the online schedule. ***Note:*** There are restrooms but no water; bring your own food and drinks. Four-wheel-drive (4WD) is advised for the upper road, and drivers should yield to uphill traffic.

Mauka side of Hwy. 11, btw mile markers 70 and 71, Pāhala. www.nps.gov/havo/planyourvisit/kahuku-hikes.htm. ✆ **808/985-6000.** Free admission. Sat–Sun 9am–3pm.

Ka'ū Coffee Mill ★ FACTORY TOUR In the former sugarcane fields on the slopes of Mauna Loa, a number of small farmers are growing coffee beans whose quality equals—some say surpasses—Kona's. More and more tasting competitions seem to agree; in any case, this farm and mill in tiny Pāhala provides an excellent excuse to break up the long drive to the main entrance of Hawai'i Volcanoes National Park, 23 miles northeast. Free 45-minute guided tours are offered three times daily; enjoy tastings of coffee and macadamia nuts throughout the day in the pleasant visitor center. In May, the 10-day **Ka'ū Coffee Festival** (www.kaucoffeefestival.com) includes hikes, music, hula, and farm tours.

THE BRUTE FORCE OF THE volcano

Volcanologists refer to Hawaiian volcanic eruptions as "quiet" eruptions because gases escape slowly instead of building up and exploding violently all at once. The Big Island's eruptions produce slow-moving, oozing lava that generally provide excellent, safe viewing when they're not in remote areas. Even so, **Kīlauea** has still caused its share of destruction. Since the current eruption began on January 3, 1983, lava has covered more than 50 square miles of lowland and rainforest, ruining 215 homes and businesses, wiping out the pretty, black-sand beach of Kaimū, and burying other landmarks. Kīlauea has also added more than 500 acres of new land on its southeastern shore. (Such land occasionally collapses under its own weight into the ocean, which is why Hawai'i Volcanoes National Park discourages hiking there.) The most prominent vent of the eruption has been Pu'u 'Ō'ō, a 760-foot-high cinder-and-spatter cone 10 miles east of Kīlauea's summit, in an off-limits natural reserve. Scientists are also keeping an eye on the active volcanoes of **Mauna Loa,** which has been swelling since its last eruption in 1984, and **Hualālai,** which hovers above Kailua-Kona and last erupted in 1801.

96-2694 Wood Valley Rd., Pāhala. http://kaucoffeemill.com. © **808/928-0550.** Free admission. Daily 8:30am–4:30pm. Guided tours 10am, noon, and 2pm, weather permitting. From Kailua-Kona, take Hwy. 11 71 miles to a left on Kamani St., take 3rd right at Pīkake St., which becomes Wood Valley Rd., and follow uphill 2½ miles to farm on left.

Kula Kai Caverns ★★ NATURAL ATTRACTION Before you trudge up to Pele's volcanic eruption, take a look at its underground handiwork. Ric Elhard and Rose Herrera have explored and mapped out the labyrinth of lava tubes and caves, carved out over the past 1,000 years or so, that crisscross their property near South Point. Their "expeditions" range from the Lighted Trail tour, an easy, half-hour walk suitable for families, to longer (up to 2 hr.), more adventurous caving trips, where you crawl through tunnels and wind through labyrinthine passages (some restricted to kids 8 and older). Wear sturdy shoes.
92-8864 Lauhala Dr., Ocean View (46 miles south of Kailua-Kona). www.kulakaicaverns.com. © **808/929-9725.** Lighted Trail tour $20 adults, $10 children 6–12, free for children 5 and under; longer tours $60–$95 adults ($60–$65 children 8–12). By reservation only; gate security code provided at booking.

Organized Tours

Farms, gardens, and historic houses that may be open only to guided tours are listed under "Attractions & Points of Interest," above. For boat, kayak, bicycle, and similar tours, see listings under "Outdoor Activities."

HELICOPTER TOURS ★★

Don't believe the brochures with pictures of fountains of lava and "liquid hot magma," as Dr. Evil would say. Although there are no guarantees you'll see red-hot lava (and for safety reasons, you're not going to fly all that close to it), a helicopter ride offers a unique perspective on the island's thousands of acres of hardened black lava, Kīlauea's enormous fuming caldera, and the remote, still-erupting Pu'u 'Ō'ō vent—the likeliest place to spot flowing lava, with scattered "breakouts" on the 2014 flow that threatened Pāhoa. If you're pressed for time, a helicopter ride beats driving to the volcano and back from Kohala and Kona resorts.

Blue Hawaiian Helicopters ★★ (www.bluehawaiian.com; ✆ **800/786-2583** or 808/886-1768), a professionally run, locally based company with comfortable, top-of-the-line copters and pilots who are extremely knowledgeable about everything from volcanology to Hawai'i lore, flies three different tours out of Waikoloa, at Highway 19 and Waikoloa Road. The 2-hour **Big Island Spectacular** ★★ stars the volcano, tropical valleys, the Hāmākua Coast waterfalls, and the Kohala Mountains, and costs $464 to $579 ($408–$510 online with a 5-day advance booking). If time is money for you, and you've got all that money, it's an impressive trip, particularly if you ride in the roomier and quieter Eco-Star (the higher price in ranges quoted here). If you just want to admire waterfalls, green mountains, and the deep valleys, including Waipi'o, of North Kohala and the Hāmākua Coast, the 50-minute **Kohala Coast Adventure** ★ is a less exorbitant but reliably picturesque outing, costing $249 to $302 ($219–$266 online).

If you've "done" the volcano and have an adventurous spirit, consider Blue Hawaiian's 2-hour **Big Island–Maui tour** ★★, which includes the Kohala Mountains/Hāmākua waterfalls leg and also crosses the 'Alenuihāhā Channel to Maui, where you view massive Haleakalā (a long-dormant volcano) and dozens of waterfalls in the verdant Hānā rainforest. It costs $515 to $579 ($453–$510 online, with advance booking). Blue Hawaiian also operates out of the Hilo airport (✆ **808/961-5600**), flying the 50-minute **Circle of Fire Plus Waterfalls** ★★ tour, which is significantly cheaper—$229 to $282 ($202–$248 online)—because it's closer to the volcano and waterfalls. On the other hand, if you're willing to drive to Hilo, you really should continue on to the national park. ***Tip:*** Ask about a AAA discount when booking flights.

The similarly professional **Sunshine Helicopters** ★★ (www.sunshinehelicopters.com; ✆ **866/501-7738** or 808/270-3999) offers a **Volcano Deluxe Tour** ★, a 105-minute ride out of the Hāpuna heliport, which includes Kohala Mountains/Hāmākua waterfalls. It's even pricier: $560 for open seating, $635 reserved seating next to the pilot on the six-passenger Whisper Star choppers ($520–$595 online). Less of a splurge—and less dependent on the ooh factor of oozing lava—is Sunshine's 30- to 40-minute **Kohala/Hāmākua Coast Tour** ★★, which hovers above waterfall-lined sea cliffs and the Pololū, Waimanu, and Waipi'o valleys, for $199 ($169 online).

Note: On all rides, your weight may determine where you sit in the helicopter. You should wear dark shades to prevent glare, and dress in light layers; both cool rain and strong sun can occur.

VAN & BUS TOURS

Intrigued by the island lifestyle? Take a delectable peek inside private residences and gardens on one of the culinary home tours of **Home Tours Hawai'i** ★★★ (www.hometourshawaii.com; ✆ **808/325-5772**). Groups of 6 to 20 (maximum) travel in air-conditioned vans from Kona to unique properties, dining on either an island brunch on the 5-hour tour ($189) or a decadent, multicourse chocolate tasting on a 3-hour tour ($89) that visits Kokoleka Lani ("Heavenly Chocolate") Farm, home to the Kona Natural Soap Factory and affable host **Greg Colden.**

Many of the outdoor-oriented, but not especially physically taxing, excursions of **Hawaii Forest & Trail** ★★★ (www.hawaii-forest.com; ✆ **800/464-1993** or 808/331-8505) include a significant time in comfy vans heading to and from remote areas, with well-briefed guides providing narration along the way. Thus, they're ideal for seeing a large chunk of the island without having to drive yourself. The island's premier outfitter, this eco-friendly company also has exclusive access to many sites, including the waterfalls on its **Kohala Waterfalls Adventure** ($179 adults, $129 children 12 and under) and **Swim Kohala Falls** tours ($89 adults, $79 children). Most of its dozen tours depart daily from several locations on the Kona side ($89–$249 adults, $79–$179 children). Tours from Hilo—exploring volcano country, Mauna Kea, or Hilo's waterfalls ($129–$169 adults, $99–$139 children)—are perfect for cruise passengers or anyone else on the Hilo side. ***Note:*** Mauna Kea tours are restricted to ages 16 and older, due to the high elevation.

From Kailua-Kona, it's easy to book other all-day volcano and "circle" tours, which include the black-sand **Punalu'u Beach** ★★★ (p. 224), the national park, Hilo, and Waimea. I recommend the environmentally conscious, community-oriented **KapohoKine Adventures** ★★ (www.kapohokine.com; ✆ **808/964-1000**), which offers a variety of tours from Kona and Hilo ($119–$229 adults, $99–$219 children 12 and under). Its 11-hour **Waipio Valley Explorer** tour, offered Monday and Wednesday through Saturday ($229 adults, $219 children, including lunch), departs from Waikoloa, with stops at Rainbow Falls, Hilo Farmer's Market, Hawaii Tropical Botanical Garden, and 'Akaka Falls before switching to a four-wheel-drive (4WD) van for the descent into Waipi'o Valley.

Note: Tipping the tour guide/driver $10 to $20 per person, depending on length and cost of the tour, is customary.

PLANTING A koa legacy tree

One of the most inspiring and memorable experiences I've ever had in Hawai'i has been with **Hawaiian Legacy Tours** ★★★ (www.hawaiianlegacytours.com; ✆ **877/707-8733**), which allows visitors to help restore the native koa forest high above the Hāmākua Coast. More koa means more native birds and less runoff, which can harm the reefs far below. Over its lifetime, the tree can also offset the carbon impact of a week's vacation on this beautiful island. The freshly baked scones that await in the welcome center are pretty awesome, too.

After you check in at the welcome center, a handsomely restored ranch house in the tiny village of 'Umikoa (at 3,200 ft. elevation), guides in ATVs, or a Pinzgauer six-wheeler for larger groups, drive you even higher up the misty slopes of Mauna Kea, to the former personal forest of King Kamehameha the Great. Amid the new groves growing on the mountainside, where the *mana* (spiritual power) and beauty of your surroundings are spine-tingling, you'll be shown how to plant a seedling. You can dedicate it to a loved one on a special commemorative certificate, and you'll also receive its GPS coordinates, allowing you to monitor its growth via Google Earth.

The 2-hour **Planters Tour,** including one tree for planting, costs $110 for adults, $55 for kids 5 to 18, while the 3½-hour **Grand Tour,** which spends more time in the nurseries and on the 'Umikoa Trail, costs $180 for adults, $90 for kids 5 to 18. (Children's rates exclude a tree for planting, but additional trees may be purchased for $60 each.) Private tours and shuttles (from the Kona and Hilo airports, Four Seasons Resort Hualalai, and Hilo cruise terminal) are available for additional fees. ***Note:*** If you can't take a tour, you can pay to have a koa ($60) or an even rarer sandalwood tree ($100) planted for you; see www.legacytrees.org for details.

BEACHES

Too young geologically to have many great beaches, the Big Island instead has more colorful ones: brand-new black-sand beaches, salt-and-pepper beaches, and even a green-sand beach. If you know where to look, you'll also find some gorgeous pockets of golden sand off the main roads here and there, plus a few longer stretches, often hidden from view by either acres of lava or high-end resorts. Thankfully, by law all beaches are public, so even the toniest hotel must provide access (including free parking) to its sandy shores. ***Note:*** Never leave valuables in your trunk, particularly in remote areas, and always respect the privacy of residents with homes on the beach. For details on shoreline access around the island, see the maps and descriptions at www.hawaiicounty.gov/pl-shoreline-access-big-island. For more information on state beach parks and reserves, visit **http://dlnr.hawaii.gov/dsp/parks/hawaii**.

Note: You'll find relevant sites on the "Big Island" map on p. 183.

North Kona

KAHALU'U BEACH ★★

The most popular beach on the Kona Coast has reef-protected lagoons and county park facilities that attract more than 400,000 people a year, making it less attractive than in years past. Coconut trees line a narrow salt-and-pepper-sand shore that gently slopes to turquoise pools, home to schools of brilliantly colored tropical fish. In summer, it's an ideal spot for children and beginning snorkelers; the water is so shallow you can just stand up if you feel uncomfortable—but please, not on the living coral, which can take years to recover. In winter, there's a rip current when the high surf rolls in; look for any lifeguard warnings. Kahalu'u isn't the biggest beach on the island, but it's one of the best equipped, with off-road parking, beach-gear rentals, a covered pavilion, restrooms, barbecue pits, and a food concession. It gets crowded, so come early to stake out a spot. If you have to park on Ali'i Drive, be sure to poke your head into tiny, blue-roofed **St. Peter's by the Sea,** a Catholic chapel next to an old lava rock *heiau* where surfers once prayed for waves.

KEKAHA KAI STATE PARK ★★

Brilliant white sand offsets even more brilliant turquoise water at this beach park with several sandy bays and coves well hidden from the highway and two official entrances. About 4½ miles north of the airport off Highway19 (across from West Hawai'i Veterans Cemetery) is the turnoff for Manini'ōwali Beach, better known as **Kua Bay.** A thankfully paved road crosses acres of craggy lava, leading to the parking lot and a short, paved walkway to an even shorter, sandy scramble down a few rocks to the beach. It has restrooms and showers, but absolutely no shade or drinking water. Locals flock here to sunbathe, swim, bodyboard, and bodysurf, especially on weekends, so go during the week, and in mornings, when it's cooler. If you have a four-wheel-drive (4WD) vehicle, you can take the marked turnoff 2½ miles north of the airport off Highway 19 and drive 1½ bumpy miles over a rough lava road to the parking area for sandy **Mahai'ula Beach,** reached by another short trail. Sloping more steeply than Kua Bay, this sandy beach has stronger currents too, although if you're fit you can still swim or snorkel in calm conditions. You can also just laze under the shade—you're likely to see a snoozing green sea turtle or two. The park is open 8am to 7pm daily.

KĪHOLO STATE PARK RESERVE ★★★

To give yourself a preview of why to come here, pull over at the marked Scenic Overlook on Highway 19 north of Kekaha Kai State Park, between mile markers 82 and 83. You'll see a shimmering pale blue lagoon, created by the remains of an ancient fish pond, and the bright cerulean **Kīholo Bay,** jewels in a crown of black lava. Now take the unmarked lava-gravel road (much smoother than Kekaha Kai's road to Mahai'ula Beach) just

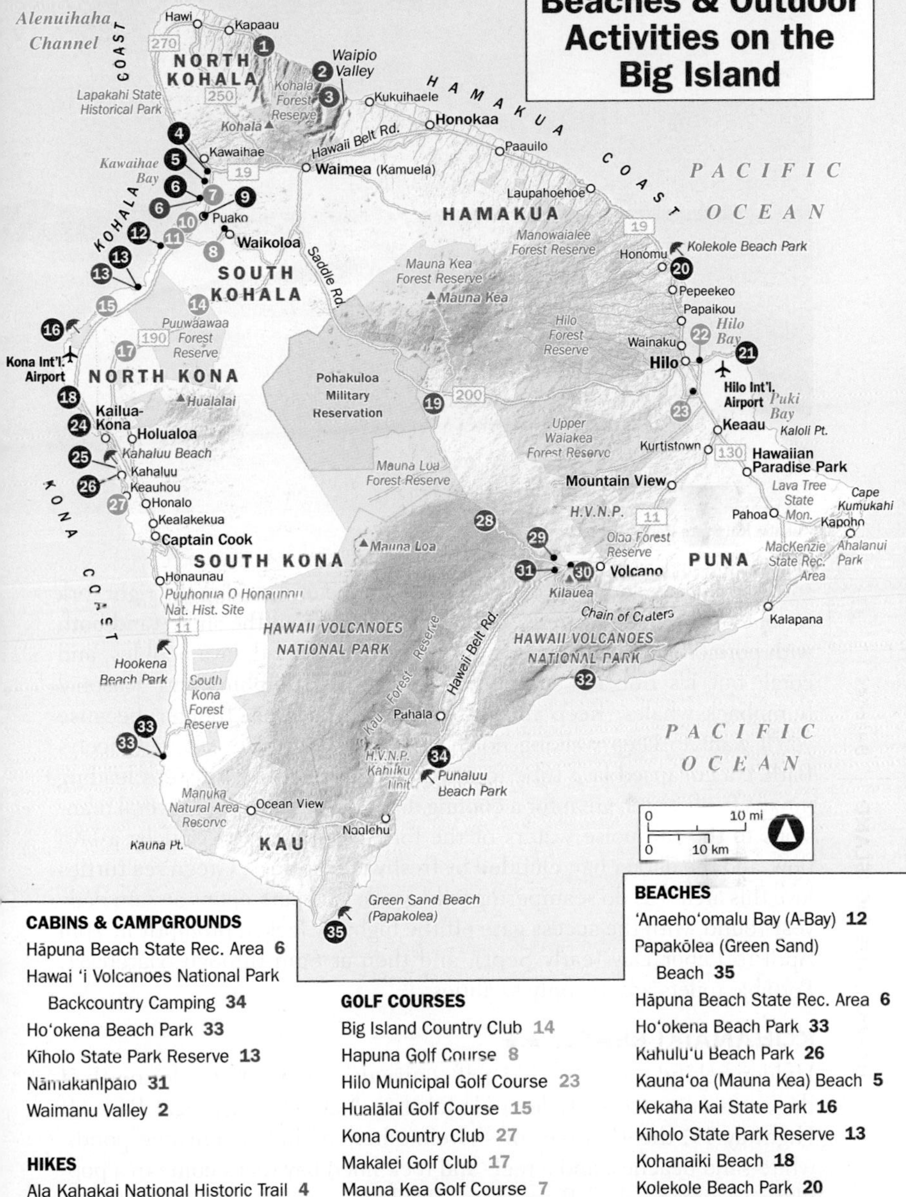

CABINS & CAMPGROUNDS

Hāpuna Beach State Rec. Area 6
Hawai 'i Volcanoes National Park Backcountry Camping 34
Ho'okena Beach Park 33
Kīholo State Park Reserve 13
Nāmakanipaio 31
Waimanu Valley 2

HIKES

Ala Kahakai National Historic Trail 4
Kīlauea Caldera Trails 30
Kīpukapuaulu (Bird Park) Trail 29
Mauna Loa Trail 28
Muliwai Trail 3
Pu'u Huluhulu Trail 19
Pololū Valley Trail 1

GOLF COURSES

Big Island Country Club 14
Hapuna Golf Course 8
Hilo Municipal Golf Course 23
Hualālai Golf Course 15
Kona Country Club 27
Makalei Golf Club 17
Mauna Kea Golf Course 7
Mauna Lani Francis I'i Brown Championship Courses 10
Naniloa Golf Course 22
Waikoloa Beach Resort Courses 11
Waikoloa Village Golf Course 8

BEACHES

'Anaeho'omalu Bay (A-Bay) 12
Papakōlea (Green Sand) Beach 35
Hāpuna Beach State Rec. Area 6
Ho'okena Beach Park 33
Kahulu'u Beach Park 26
Kauna'oa (Mauna Kea) Beach 5
Kekaha Kai State Park 16
Kīholo State Park Reserve 13
Kohanaiki Beach 18
Kolekole Beach Park 20
La'aloa (White Sands) Beach 25
Leleiwi Beach Park 21
Old Kona Airport Park 24
Punalu'u Beach Park 34
'Ōhai'ula Beach at Spencer Park 4
Waialea Bay (Beach 69) 9

Kekaha Kai State Park.

south of the overlook and drive carefully to the end, taking the right fork for one of two parking areas, both a short walk from the shore (and both with portable toilets). The "beach" here is black sand, lava pebbles, and coral, but it's fine for sunbathing or spotting dolphins and seasonal humpback whales. Keep your sturdy-soled shoes on, though, because you'll want to keep walking north to **Keanalele** (also called "Queen's Bath"), a collapsed lava tube found amid kiawe trees with steps leading into its fresh water, great for a cooling dip. Continue on past several mansions to the turquoise waters of the former fishpond, cut off by a lava flow, and the darker bay, clouded by freshwater springs. Green sea turtles love this area—as do scampering wild goats. The park opens at 7am daily year-round, with the access gate off the highway locked promptly at 7pm April to Labor Day (early Sept), and then at 6pm through March 31. Portable toilets are the only facilities.

KOHANAIKI BEACH ★★

Hidden behind the Kohanaiki golf course development, 2 miles north of the main entrance to Kaloko-Honokōhau National Historical Park off Highway 19, the 1½ miles of shoreline here include anchialine ponds, white-sand beaches, and a reef- and rock-lined bay that's home to a popular surf break called Pine Trees. Paddlers, snorkelers, and fishermen also flock to the rugged coastline, which became a county park in 2013—giving it improved access and parking, restrooms, showers, water fountain, campsites, and a *hālau* (covered pavilion) for cultural practices;

there's also a well-marked petroglyph. Since you can't turn left from northbound Hwy. 19, directions are easiest from the airport: Head 2.2 miles south on Hwy. 19 to the Kohanaiki entrance on the right (past mile marker 95); turn right at the first fork and follow nearly 1 mile to the first parking lot for beach access; facilities and more parking are farther south along the one-lane paved road, but you can also explore the shore to the left. It's open daily from 5:30am to 9pm (no camping Tues–Wed).

LA'ALOA BEACH (WHITE SANDS/MAGIC SANDS BEACH) ★★

Don't blink as you cruise Ali'i Drive, or you'll miss La'aloa, often called White Sands, Magic Sands, or Disappearing Beach. That's because the sand at this small pocket beach, about 4½ miles south of Kailua-Kona's historic center, does occasionally vanish, especially at high tide or during storms. On calm summer days, you can swim here, next to bodyboarders and bodysurfers taking advantage of the gentle shorebreak; you can also snorkel in a little rocky cove just to the south. In winter, though, a dangerous rip develops and waves swell, attracting expert surfers and spectators; stay out of the water then, but enjoy the gawking. The palm-tree lined county beach park includes restrooms, showers, a lifeguard station, and a small parking lot off Ali'i Drive.

Kohanaiki Beach.

OLD KONA AIRPORT PARK ★

Yes, this used to be the airport for the Kona side of the island—hence the copious parking on the former runway at the end of Kuakini Highway about a half-mile north of Palani Road in Kailua-Kona. Now it's a park jointly managed by the county and state, which in 1992 designated its waters a marine life conservation district. It's easy to get distracted by all the other free amenities: two Olympic-size pools in the **Kona Community Aquatic Center** (**© 808/327-3500**), a gym, tennis courts, ball fields. Yet there's a mile of sandy beach here, fronting tide pools perfect for families with small children, and Pāwai Bay, whose reefs draw turtles and rays, and thus snorkelers and divers. The beach area also has covered picnic tables and grills, restrooms, and showers.

South Kona

HO'OKENA BEACH PARK ★

A community group known as **Friends of Ho'okena** (www.hookena.org) took responsibility for upkeep and concessions at this secluded, taupe-colored sandy beach (technically a county park) in 2007. Visitors can rent kayaks and snorkel gear on site to explore Kauhakō Bay's populous reefs (avoid during high surf), or beach and camping gear to enjoy the view—sometimes including wild spinner dolphins—from the shore. Reservations for gear and campgrounds can be made online; the welcome concession stand at this remote spot even accepts credit cards. Facilities include showers, restrooms, water fountains, picnic tables, pavilions, and parking. From Kailua-Kona, take Highway 11 22 miles south to the Ho'okena Beach Road exit (just past Ho'okena Elementary School), between mile markers 101 and 102. Follow it downhill 2 miles to the end, and turn left on the one-lane road to the parking area.

The Kohala Coast

'ANAEHO'OMALU BAY ★★★

The Big Island makes up for its dearth of beaches with a few spectacular ones, like 'Anaeho'omalu, or A-Bay, as many call it. This popular gold-sand beach, fringed by a grove of palms and backed by royal fishponds still full of mullet, is one of the most beautiful in Hawai'i. It fronts the Waikoloa Beach Marriott Resort & Spa and is enjoyed by guests and locals alike (it's busier in summer, but doesn't ever get truly crowded). The beach slopes gently from shallow to deep water; swimming, snorkeling, diving, kayaking, and windsurfing are all excellent here. At the northern edge of the bay, snorkelers and divers can watch endangered green sea turtles line up and wait their turn to have small fish clean them. Equipment rental and snorkeling, scuba, and windsurfing instruction are available at the north end of the beach. Facilities include restrooms, showers, picnic tables, and plenty of parking; look for access signs off Waikoloa Beach Road, about 1 mile west of Highway 19. No lifeguards.

HĀPUNA BEACH ★★★

Just off Queen Ka'ahumanu Highway, below the Hāpuna Beach Prince Hotel, lies this crescent of gold sand—a half-mile long and up to 200 feet wide. In summer, when the beach is widest, the ocean calmest, and the crowds biggest, this is a terrific place for swimming, bodysurfing, and snorkeling. But beware of Hāpuna in winter or stormy weather, when its thundering waves and strong rip currents should only be plied by local experts. Facilities at Hāpuna Beach, part of the **Hāpuna Beach State Recreation Area,** include A-frame cabins (for camping by permit), picnic tables, restrooms, showers, water fountains, a lifeguard station, and parking. You can also pick up the coastal **Ala Kahakai National Historic Trail** (p. 244) here to Spencer or Holoholokai parks to the north and south, respectively.

KAUNA'OA BEACH (MAUNA KEA BEACH) ★★★

Nearly everyone refers to this gold-sand beach at the foot of Mauna Kea Beach Hotel by its hotel nickname, but its real name is Hawaiian for "native dodder," a lacy, yellow-orange vine that once thrived on the shore. A coconut grove sweeps around this golden crescent, where the water is calm and protected by two black-lava points. The sandy bottom slopes

'Ōhai'ula Beach at Spencer Park.

gently into the bay, which often fills with tropical fish, sea turtles, and manta rays, especially at night, when lights shine down from a viewing promontory. Swimming is excellent year-round, except in rare winter storms. Snorkelers prefer the rocky points, where fish thrive in the surge. Facilities include restrooms, showers, and public-access parking (go early). No lifeguards.

SPENCER PARK ('ŌHAI'ULA BEACH) ★★

Virtually in the shadow of the massive Pu'ukoholā Heiau (p. 189) to the north, this is a great place to stop when heading to or from the scenic and historic sites in North Kohala. The gently sloping, white-yellow sand beach is **'Ōhai'ula,** though most just call it "Spencer," since it's part of **Samuel M. Spencer County Park.** Protected by both a long reef and Kawaihae Harbor, the beach has relatively safe swimming year-round. Parking is plentiful, but it may fill up on weekends and holidays. From the intersection of highways 19 and 270, take Highway 270 a half-mile north to a left turn at the sign for the park and Pu'ukoholā Heiau, and follow this to either of two parking areas at the end of the road. Facilities include picnic tables, restrooms, showers, grassy lawns, and shade trees; lifeguards are on duty weekends and holidays. Campsites at either end of the beach often serve the area's homeless population. (It's safe during daylight hours, but I'd avoid walking through the tents section.)

WAIALEA BAY (BEACH 69) ★★

Once a hidden oasis, this light-golden sandy beach in Puakō, between the Waikoloa Beach and Mauna Lani resorts, earned its nickname from the number on a former telephone pole off Old Puakō Road, which signaled one of the public-access points. Still tucked behind private homes, it's now a proper beach park, with a paved parking lot, a trail to the beach, restrooms, and water fountains—but no lifeguards. The bay is generally calm in summer, good for swimming and snorkeling; waves can get big in winter, when surfers and bodyboarders tend to show up. From Kailua-Kona, take Highway 19 north to a left on Puakō Road, and then a right on Old Puakō Road; the access road to the parking area is on your left, near telephone pole No. 71 (the nickname has not caught up with the times).

Hilo

LELEIWI BEACH PARK ★★

This string of palm-fringed, black-lava tide pools fed by freshwater springs and rippled by gentle waves is a photographer's delight—and the perfect place to take a plunge. In winter, big waves can splash these ponds, but the shallow pools are generally free of currents and ideal for families with children, especially in the protected inlets at the center of the park. Leleiwi often attracts endangered sea turtles, making this one

Leleiwi Beach.

of the island's most popular snorkeling spots. Open 7am to 7pm, the beach park is 4 miles east of town on Kalaniana'ole Avenue. Facilities include a lifeguard station (staffed weekends, holidays, and summer), picnic tables, pavilions, and parking. A second section of the park, known **as Richardson's Ocean Park,** includes showers, restrooms, daily lifeguards, and the marine life exhibits of Richardson Ocean Center. ***Tip:*** If the area is crowded, check out the tide pools and/or small sandy coves in the five other beach parks along Kalaniana'ole Avenue between Banyan Drive and Leleiwi, especially the protected white-sand lagoon of **Carlsmith Beach Park ★,** just a 2-minute drive west. It has lifeguard service in summer and on weekends and holidays, as does the rocky but kid-friendly **Onekahaha Beach Park ★,** at the end of Onekahakaha Road off Kalaniana'ole Avenue, just under a mile west from Carlsmith.

KOLEKOLE BEACH PARK ★

Not a place to enter the rough water, this streamside park is nonetheless an unusually picturesque spot for a picnic. The lush greenery around you contrasts with the black rock beach, aquamarine sea, and white sea foam where waves meet Kolekole Stream, several miles below **'Akaka Falls ★★★** (p. 193) in Honomū. You may see local kids jumping from a rope swing into the stream, which also has a small waterfall. Facilities include picnic pavilions, grills, restrooms, and parking. It's open 6am to 11pm. From Hilo, take Highway 19 north 11 miles to a left turn on Old Māmalahoa Highway, and take the first (sharp) right, which descends a quarter-mile down to the park. No lifeguard.

Puna District

Most of the shoreline in this volcanically active area is craggy, with rough waters and dangerous currents, although the oceanfront thermal pond at **Ahalanui ★★** (p. 206) and the **Wai'ōpae Tidepools ★★** (p. 206) are certainly worth seeking out. The still-forming black-sand beach near **Kalapana,** born in the 1990 lava flow that buried Kaimū Beach, is best viewed from the cliff above it; rogue waves may suddenly break much higher down on the beach. ***Note:*** Although nudism is common at secluded, unmarked **Kehena Beach** (p. 205), it is illegal.

Ka'ū District

PAPAKŌLEA (GREEN SAND) BEACH ★★

The island's famous green-sand beach is located at the base of Pu'u o Mahana, an old cinder cone spilling into the sea. It's difficult to reach; the open bay is often rough; there are no facilities, fresh water, or shade; and howling winds scour the point. Nevertheless, each year the unusual olive-brown sands—made of crushed olivine, a semiprecious green mineral found in eruptive rocks and meteorites—attract thousands of oglers. From Highway 11, between mile markers 69 and 70, take South Point Road about 8 miles south to a left fork for the Papakōlea parking lot; be aware much of it is one lane. Driving from there to the top of the cinder cone is no longer permitted by the Department of Hawaiian Homelands, although enterprising locals now offer a round-trip shuttle for $10 to $20 (cash only); you can also do the windy, challenging hike along the remaining 2½ miles across unshaded dirt roads and lava rock (wear closed-toe shoes, sunglasses, and a hat, and bring lots of water). In either case, you'll still need to clamber carefully down the steep eroded cinder cone to the sand. If the surf's up, check out the beach from the cliff's edge; if the water's calm, you can go closer, but keep an eye on the ocean at all times (there are strong rip currents here).

PUNALU'U BEACH ★★★

Green sea turtles love to bask on this remote, black-sand beach, beautifully framed by palm trees and easily photographed from the bluff above. The deep-blue waters can be choppy; swim only in very calm conditions, as there's no lifeguard present. You're welcome to admire the turtles, but at a respectful distance; the law against touching or harassing them is enforced here (if not by authorities, then by locals who also like to congregate in the park). Park facilities include camping, restrooms, showers, picnic tables, pavilions, water fountains, a concession stand, and parking. There are two access roads from Highway 11, at 7¾ and 8 miles northeast of Na'alehu. The first, Nīnole Loop Road, leads past the somewhat overgrown-looking Sea Mountain golf course to a turnoff for a paved parking lot by the bluff. The second access from Highway 11, Punalu'u Road, has a turnoff for a smaller, unpaved parking area.

Papakōlea (Green Sand) Beach.

WATERSPORTS

Boat, Raft & Submarine Tours

The relatively calm waters of the Kona and Kohala coasts are home to inquisitive reef fish, frolicking spinner dolphins, tranquil green sea turtles, spiraling manta rays, and spouting whales and their calves in season (Dec–Mar). A wide variety of vessels offer sightseeing and snorkel/dive tours (gear provided). Cocktail and dinner cruises take advantage of the region's predictably eye-popping sunsets. On the wild Puna side of the island, boat rides pass green clefts and coastal waterfalls. For fishing charters, see p. 236.

KONA COAST

Atlantis Submarines ★ If you have what it takes (namely, no claustrophobia), head 100 feet below the sea in a 65-foot **submarine,** with a large porthole for each of the 48 passengers. During the 45 minutes underwater, the sub glides slowly through an 18,000-year-old, 25-acre coral reef in **Kailua Bay,** teeming with fish (including, unfortunately, invasive goatfish and ta'ape) and two shipwrecks encrusted in coral. You'll take a 5-minute boat shuttle from Kailua Pier, across from the ticket office, to the air-conditioned submarine. ***Note:*** Children are allowed, but all passengers must be at least 3 feet tall.

75-5669 Ali'i Dr. (across the street from Kailua Pier), Kailua-Kona. ✆ **800/548-6262.** www.atlantisadventures.com/kona. Trips leave four times a day 10am–2:30pm (check-in 30 min. earlier). $115 age 13 and older, $48 under 13; book online for $10 off or $115 special for one adult with one child.

Body Glove Cruises ★★ Body Glove's *Kanoa II,* a 65-foot, solar-powered catamaran carrying up to 100 passengers, runs an environmentally-friendly, 4½-hour **snorkel/dive** morning cruise, along with shorter lunch and dinner excursions for those who just want to enjoy the views, as well as seasonal whale-watching trips; all depart from Kailua Pier. In the morning, you'll be greeted with fresh Kona coffee, fruit, and breakfast pastries before heading north to **Pāwai Bay,** a marine preserve where you can snorkel, scuba dive, swim, or just hang out on the deck. Before chowing down on the deli lunch buffet, take the plunge off the boat's 20-foot water slide or 15-foot-high diving board. The only thing you need to bring is a towel; all gear is provided, along with "reef safe" sunscreen. Dinner and lunch cruises feature a historian who points out significant sites on the 12 miles from Kailua Pier to **Kealakekua Bay,** where passengers feast on a buffet spread and enjoy live Hawaiian music by notable entertainer LT Smooth. All cruises are free for children 5 and under, and the boat is wheelchair accessible, including restrooms.
Kailua Pier, Kailua-Kona. www.bodyglovehawaii.com. ✆ **800/551-8911** or 808/326-7122. Snorkel cruises (daily 8am) $132 adults, $88 children 6–17; see website for additional scuba charges. Dinner cruise (Thurs–Tues 4pm) $128 adults, $88 children 6–17. Lunch cruise (Wed 1pm) $98 adults, $78 children 6–17. Whale-watching cruises (Dec–Apr only; daily 1pm) $98 adults, $78 children 6–17.

Snorkeling the Big Island seas.

Captain Dan McSweeney's Whale Watch Learning Adventures ★★★ The islands' most impressive visitors—45-foot humpback whales—return to warm Hawaiian waters, including those on the Big Island's **Kona side,** each winter. Capt. Dan McSweeney, who founded the Wild Whale Research Foundation in 1979, has no problem finding them. During the 3-hour **whale-watching tours,** typically offered January through March, he drops a hydrophone (an underwater microphone) into the water so you can listen to their songs, and sometimes uses an underwater video camera to show you what's going on. Cruises are aboard the *Lady Ann,* which has restrooms and a choice of sunny or shaded decks; cold drinks and snacks are provided. Trips depart from Honokōhau Harbor, where parking is free and typically easy.

Honokōhau Harbor, 74-380 Kealakehe Pkwy. (off Hwy. 19), Kailua-Kona. www.ilovewhales.com. ✆ **888/942-5376** or 808/322-0028. Departures 7 and 11am Mon–Tues and Thurs–Fri Jan–March. $110 adults, $99 children 11 and under who also weigh under 90 lb.

Captain Zodiac ★ It's a wild, 14-mile ride to **Kealakekua Bay** aboard one of Captain Zodiac's 16-passenger, 24-foot **rigid-hull inflatable rafts,** or Zodiacs. There you'll spend about an hour snorkeling in the bay, perhaps with spinner dolphins, and enjoy snacks and beverages at the site. The small size of the craft mean no restrooms, but it also means you can explore sea caves on this craggy coast. Four-hour **snorkel trips** take place twice daily, with morning and afternoon departures; the 5-hour midday tour ingeniously arrives at Kealakekua when most other boats have left, with extra time for a second snorkel site, seasonal **whale-watching,** or other experiences at the captain's discretion, plus a deli lunch. Be prepared to get wet regardless (that includes your camera). There's also a 3-hour **swim with wild dolphins**—an activity I typically don't recommend, due to the disruption it causes to the pods of dolphins who need to rest during the day and feed at night. But Captain Zodiac claims to follow federal guidelines in these encounters and briefs passengers on proper protocol for letting the marine mammals approach them, rather than vice versa.

In Gentry's Kona Marina, Honokōhau Harbor, 74-425 Kealakehe Pkwy. (off Hwy. 19), Kailua-Kona. www.captainzodiac.com. ✆ **808/329-3199.** 4-hr. snorkel cruise (Wed–Thurs and Sat–Sun 8am and 12:30pm) $110 adults, $84 children 5–12; 5-hr. snorkel cruise (Mon–Tues and Fri 9:45am), $125 adults, $94 children 5–12. Dolphin swim (Tues, Thurs, Sun 8am), $110 adults, $80 children 8–12. Whale-watching cruises (Jan–Apr only; Tues, Thurs, Sat 8:45am) $84 adults, $59 children 5–12. Online booking discounts ($15 adults, $5–$10 children) available.

Fair Wind Snorkeling & Diving Adventures ★★★ I love Fair Wind, for several reasons, starting with its home in Keauhou Bay, 8 miles south of Kailua Pier and so that much closer to **Kealakekua Bay,** where its two very different but impressively equipped boats head for **snorkel/dive tours:**

FAIR WIND II When traveling with kids, I book a cruise on the ***Fair Wind II,*** a 60-foot catamaran that includes two 15-foot water slides, a high-dive jump, playpens, and child-friendly flotation devices with viewfinders, so even toddlers can peek at Kealakekua's glorious sea life. Year-round, the *Fair Wind II* offers a 4½-hour morning snorkel cruise that includes breakfast and barbecue lunch; most of the year it also sails a 3½-hour afternoon snorkel cruise that provides snacks, which in summer becomes a deluxe 4½-hour excursion with barbecue dinner. Swimmers age 8 and up can also try **SNUBA**—kind of a beginner's version of scuba—for an optional $69, with an in-water guide.

HULA KAI When traveling with teens or adults, I prefer the *Hula Kai,* the Fair Wind's 55-foot foil-assist catamaran, open only to ages 7 and up. The boat provides a plusher experience (such as comfy seating with headrests) and, on its 5-hour morning snorkel cruise, a faster, smoother ride to two uncrowded Kona Coast snorkeling sites (usually neither is Kealakekua Bay), based on conditions. Guests have the option to try **stand-up paddleboarding, SNUBA** (see above), or the propulsive **"Sea Rocket"** ($25 per half-hour) to cover even more ground underwater. The *Hula Kai* also offers a fascinating night snorkel/dive with **manta rays,** a 1½-hour tour that doesn't have to voyage far from **Keauhou Bay** to find them. At night these gentle giants (no stingers!) are lured closer to the ocean's surface by the plankton that also rise there. Like other tour companies, Fair Wind uses dive lights to attract even more plankton; on the off chance you don't get to see a manta ray, you're welcome back another evening or an afternoon snorkel tour. Wetsuits, warm soup, and hot drinks are provided to ward off chills. One-tank scuba dives are also available on all *Hula Kai* excursions ($31 without gear; $45 with); the manta night trip also charges $45 per "ride-along" (non-snorkeling) passenger.

Note: Many of Fair Wind cruises sell out several days in advance, or as much as 2 to 3 weeks in peak season, so book ahead.

Keauhou Bay Pier, 78-7130 Kaleiopapa St., Kailua-Kona. www.fair-wind.com. ✆ **800/677-9461** or 808/322-2788. *Fair Wind II* morning snorkel cruise (daily 9am) $135 adults, $79 children 4–12, $29 children 3 and under. Afternoon snack snorkel cruise (Tues, Thurs, Sat 2pm) $79 adults, $49 children 4–12, free for children 3 and under. *Hula Kai* deluxe morning snorkel/dive cruise (Mon–Thurs and Sat 9:30am) $149 age 7 and up (younger not permitted). Manta ray snorkel/dive (daily; time varies by sunset) $119 age 7 and up (younger not permitted). Parking is on opposite side of Keauhou Bay, at end of King Kamehameha III Rd.

Kamanu Charters ★★ The *Kamanu,* a sleek, 38-foot sailing catamaran, provides a laidback **sail-and-snorkel cruise** from Honokōhau Harbor to the marine preserve of **Pāwai Bay.** The 3½-hour trip includes a tropical lunch (deli sandwiches, chips, fresh fruit, and drinks), snorkeling gear, and personalized instruction for first-time snorkelers; weather permitting, it sails at 9am and 1:30pm. It can hold up to 24 people but often has fewer, making it even more relaxed. Depending on bookings, morning cruises may instead focus on a swim with wild dolphins; the *Kamanu* also sails at sunset to snorkel with manta rays, with afternoon whale-watching offered in season. *Kamanu Elua,* a 31-foot, rigid-hull inflatable with seating, offers similar morning tours, but heads to **Kealakekua Bay**. ***Note:*** This Zodiac-style boat is not advised for children under 7, pregnant women, or those with back or neck injuries.

Honokōhau Harbor, 74-7380 Kealakehe Pkwy. (off Hwy. 19), Kailua-Kona. www.kamanu.com. ✆ **800/348-3091** or 808/329-2021. Snorkel cruises 9am daily, $95 adults, $50 children 12 and under; 1pm, $85 adults, $55 children. Dolphin swim and snorkel (9am daily) $99 all ages. Sunset manta ray snorkel (times/days vary) $95. Whale-watching Dec 15–Apr 15 (daily 1:30pm) $80 adults, $55 children 7 and older.

Sea Quest ★ With a head start from Keauhou Bay, Sea Quest's four **rigid-hull inflatable rafts** offer three varieties of **Kealakekua Bay snorkeling cruises** and one excursion to **swim with spinner dolphins,** which may also include a Kealakekua snorkel. The Zodiac-style rafts hold 18 passengers, but Sea Quest takes just 14; rafts on longer tours include shade. Both the 5-hour Expedition South Kona and 4-hour Deluxe Morning Adventure depart in the mornings and include snorkeling among the incredibly diverse marine life of **Hōnaunau Bay,** within view of the towering wood tikis and restored cultural sites at **Pu'uhonua O Hōnaunau National Historical Park** (p. 187); the Expedition includes a third site and deli lunch. The aptly named 3-hour **Captain Cook Express** heads straight to Kealakekua in the afternoon; all three tours explore Kona Coast lava tubes and sea caves that larger boats can't maneuver. On the daily dolphin swim, Sea Quest passengers are briefed by a certified dive master on how to float near wild spinner dolphins before their late-morning sleep. Afterward, it's off to Kealakekua or another Kona Coast reef for snorkeling and lunch. An **evening manta**

High & Dry: Glass-Bottomed Boats

If you're not a swimmer, no need to forgo seeing the multihued marine life for which the Kona and Kohala coasts are justly famous. Of the Big Island's several glass-bottomed boat cruises, **Kailua Bay Charters'** tour on the 36-foot *Marian,* which has comfy benches and shade, is well suited to families. The trip is just an hour long, with a naturalist on board to explain what you're seeing. Tours leave Kailua Pier at 11:30am Thursday to Tuesday and 12:30pm Wednesday (www.konaglassbottomboat.com; ✆ **808/324-1749;** $50 adults, $25 children under 12; reservations required). See the underwater sights of 'Anaeho'omalu Bay on **Ocean Sports'** 26-foot glass-bottom boat; it too has benches, shade, and a naturalist. Half-hour tours depart from the beach six times daily from 9:15am to 1:15pm (www.hawaiioceansports.com; ✆ **888/724-5924,** ext. 103, or 808/886-6666, ext. 103; $27 adults, $14 children 6 to 12, and free for children under 6).

experience takes advantage of the graceful creatures' favorite feeding spot a few minutes from the dock.

Keauhou Bay Pier, 78-7128 Kaleiopapa St., Kailua-Kona. www.seaquesthawaii.com. ✆ **808/329-7238.** Morning snorkel tour (daily 8am) $112 adults, $92 children 5–12. Afternoon snorkel tour (daily 12:30pm) $88 adults, $76 children 5–12. South Kona snorkel tour (weekdays 8am year-round; also weekends in summer and holiday periods) $128 adults, $105 children 5–12. Dolphin tours (ages 10 and older; 8am daily) $148. Night manta experience (ages 8 and older; daily 6pm) $98. $10 discount for booking online. Children under 6, pregnant women, and people with bad backs not allowed. Park in lot at end of King Kamehameha III Rd. across from pier.

KOHALA COAST

Kohala Sail & Sea ★★★ It took 2 decades of waiting before Capt. Steve Turner finally realized his dream of sailing from the small-boat harbor in Kawaihae, which finally opened in 2015. But it was a dream worth waiting for. Passengers (no more than six at a time) board his gleaming white, 34-foot Islander sloop, *Riva*, on the sunny, sparsely developed coast next to Puʻukoholā Heiau, a short drive from the Mauna Lani and Mauna Kea resorts. Turner and his knowledgeable crew share a deep respect for the ocean and local culture, easy to impart on these intimate cruises. In humpback-whale-watching season (Dec–Apr), they make four 2¼-hour trips daily ($85), including the year-round **sunset cruise** departing at 4:15pm. The 3½-hour **morning snorkel tours** ($125) take advantage of the Kohala Coast's brilliantly clear waters with dazzling sea life, especially in the reef off Puakō, and include all gear, snacks, and drinks; they're also available by charter.

Kawaihae South Harbor, Slip No. 8, 61-3527 Kawaihae Rd., Kawaihae. www.kohalasailandsea.com. ✆ **808/895-1781.** Whale-watching (7am, 9:35am, 12:50pm, 4:15pm daily Dec–Apr) and sunset cruises (daily 4:15pm May–Nov) $85. Morning snorkel trips (daily 8am May–Nov) $125 per person; minimum four; by year-round charter $750–$950 for up to six passengers.

Kohala Tours ★★ The second skipper to begin tours out of Kawaihae, Capt. Shane Turpin also takes the proper approach to wildlife encounters, albeit on a motorized boat. Instead of putting morning snorkelers into the middle of dolphin pods, which can deprive the animals of much-needed rest, "we invite them to check us out on the reef," Turpin says, adding that the dolphins usually comply. He exercises the same discretion on whale-watching cruises (Dec–Apr) and night snorkels with manta rays, using high-powered LED lights to attract the plankton they crave.

South Harbor, 61-3527 Kawaihae Rd., Kawaihae. www.kohalatours.com. ✆ **808/966-4200.** Dolphin snorkel cruise (Mon and Thurs 8am) $125 adults, $75 children 6–12. Whale-watching (daily 8am, 10am, noon, 4pm Dec–Apr) $99 adults, $50 children 6–12. Manta night snorkel (Mon, Wed, Fri, Sat 5:30pm) $109 adults, $99 children 6–12. All tours free for ages 5 and younger with adult.

HILO, THE HĀMĀKUA COAST & PUNA DISTRICT

Lava Ocean Tours ★★ The unpredictability of Pele means there may or may not be **sunset lava-viewing tours** aboard the *Lava Kai* catamaran (34 ft. long; 24-passenger capacity but limited to 12). When Kīlauea does send molten rock into the ocean, Capt. Shane Turpin's **Volcano Boat Tour** ($145 adults, $119 children 12 and under) departs from Pohoiki Harbor near Pāhoa. For reliable departures and luscious scenery, you can always count on the 3-hour **Hilo waterfall cruises** from Wailoa Harbor, with guaranteed whale sightings in season, and a 2.5-hour sunset option.

Wailoa Harbor, off Hwy. 11, Hilo. www.facebook.com/lavakai. ✆ **808/966-4200.** Volcano boat tours Sun and Wed 4:30pm; $145 adults, $119 children 12 and under.

Body Boarding (Boogie Boarding) & Bodysurfing

As with other watersports, it's important to stay out of rough surf in winter or during storms that bring big surf. In normal conditions, the best beaches for body boarding and bodysurfing on the Kona side of the island are **Hāpuna Beach** at the Mauna Kea Resort, **La'aloa Beach (White Sand/Magic Sands Beach) ★★** in Kailua-Kona, and **Kua Bay** (Maniniowali Beach) in **Kekaha Kai State Park,** north of the airport. Experienced bodysurfers may want to check out South Kona's **Ho'okena Beach Park,** if it has reopened. On the Hilo side, try **Leleiwi Beach Park.** See "Beaches" (p. 215) for details.

Hotel beach concessions and most surf shops (see "Surfing" on p. 237) rent body boards, but you can also find inexpensive rentals at **Snorkel Bob's** in the parking lot of Huggo's restaurant, 75-5831 Kahakai St. at Ali'i Drive, Kailua-Kona (www.snorkelbob.com; ✆ **808/329-0770**), and on the Kohala Coast in the Shops at Mauna Lani, 68-1330 Mauna Lani Dr., facing the road on the Mauna Lani Resort (✆ **808/885-9499**). Both stores are open 8am to 5pm daily.

Kayaking

Imagine sitting at sea level, eye to eye with a turtle, a dolphin, even a whale—it's possible in an ocean kayak. After a few minutes of instruction and a little practice in a calm area (like **Kamakahonu Cove** in front of the Courtyard King Kamehameha Kona Beach Hotel), you'll be ready to explore. Beginners can practice their skills in **Kailua Bay,** intermediate kayakers might try paddling from **Honokōhau Harbor** to **Kekaha Kai State Park,** and the more advanced can tackle the 5 miles from **Keauhou Bay** to **Kealakekua Bay** or the scenic but challenging **Hāmā kua Coast.** You can also rent kayaks, including a clear "peekaboo" version that allows you to view sea life, at **Ho'okena Beach Park** (p. 220) for $40 to $50 a day (assuming it has reopened, after the 2015–16 incidences of dengue fever caused the county to close it).

KEALAKEKUA BAY GUIDED TOURS & RENTALS Although technically you can rent kayaks for exploring Kealakekua Bay on your own (and even land near the Captain Cook Monument, if you follow the arduous process of snagging one of 10 daily state permits), it's best to go with a guided tour. Only three kayak companies are allowed to offer guided tours in Kealakekua Bay that land at the Cook monument (Ka'awaloa), all launching from Nāpo'opo'o Wharf. All tours include equipment, snorkeling gear, snacks or lunch, and drinks, and they should be booked in advance, due to the 12-guest limit per tour. Note that Nāpo'opo'o is a residential area, where parking can be difficult if you're not on a tour.

Kona Boys ★★ (www.konaboys.com; ✆ **808/328-1234**) was the first outfit to offer kayak rentals in Kona and is still widely regarded as the best. Its Kealakekua Bay tours, held daily by reservation, meet at the shop at 79-7539 Māmalahoa Hwy. (Hwy. 11), Kealakekua, at 7:15am, and finish at noon. Tours cost $169 for adults $149 for children. You can also rent gear from Kona Boys' **beach shack** at Kamakahonu Bay (✆ **808/329-2345**), the only one of its two sites to offer kayaks by the hour, not just by the day or week. Rentals include kayak, paddles, backrests, cooler, life jackets, dry bag, and a soft rack to carry kayaks on top of your car (including convertibles). Hourly rates are $19 single kayak, $29 double, with daily rates $54 and $74, respectively (weekly $174/$249).

Owned by a Native Hawaiian family, **Aloha Kayak ★★** (www.alohakayak.com; ✆ **877/322-1444** or 808/322-2868) offers two tours of different lengths to Kealakekua Bay and Ka'awaloa Flats, where the memorial to Captain Cook stands. The 3½-hour tour (add an hour for check-in/check-out) departs at 8am and noon Monday, Wednesday, Friday, and Saturday; it's $99 for adults and $55 for children 11 and under. The 5-hour tour, which allows more time at Ka'awaloa and its cultural sites, departs at 7:15am Sunday, Tuesday, and Thursday; it's $129 for adults and $70 for children (check website for $20-off coupon). Half-day rental rates are $25 for a single and $45 for a double; full-day rates are $35 for a single and $60 for a double, with triple kayaks and discounts for longer periods also available. Aloha Kayak's original shop is in Honalo, about 8½ miles south of Kailua-Kona, at 79-7248 Māmalahoa Hwy. (Hwy. 11), just south of its intersection with Highway 180. In 2015 the family opened a second site, including a shave ice stand and other beach gear rentals, on Nāpo'opo'o Road just below the Kona Pacific Farmers Cooperative mill.

The environmentally conscious **Adventures in Paradise ★★** (www.bigislandkayak.com; ✆ **888/210-5365** or 808/447-0080) has a small office at 82-6020 Māmalahoa Hwy. (Hwy. 11) in Captain Cook, but generally meets clients at Nāpo'opo'o for its 3½-hour Kealakekua tours ($90–$100 for ages 5 and up), departing at 7 and 11:30am daily. (***Tip:*** Book the early tour for the least crowded snorkeling.)

Parasailing

Get a bird's-eye view of the Big Island's pristine waters with **UFO Parasail** (www.ufoparasail.net; ✆ **800/FLY-4-UFO** or 808/325-5836), which offers parasail rides daily between 8am and 5:30pm from Kailua Pier. The cost is $85 for the standard flight of 8 minutes of air time at 800 feet, and $95 for a deluxe 10-minute ride at 1,200 feet. You can go up alone or with a friend (or two); no experience is necessary, but single riders must weigh at least 130 pounds, and groups no more than 450 pounds. The boat may carry up to eight passengers (observers pay just $38), and the total time in the boat, around an hour, varies on the rides they've booked. ***Tip:*** Save $9 by booking online per ride.

Scuba Diving

The Big Island's leeward coast offers some of the best diving and snorkeling in the world; the water is calm, warm, and clear. Want to swim with fast-moving game fish? Try **Ulua Cave,** at the north end of the Kohala Coast, from 25 to 90 feet deep; dolphins, rays, and the occasional Hawaiian monk seal swim by. And don't forget to book a night dive to see the majestic **manta rays,** regularly seen in greater numbers here than anywhere else in Hawai'i (or most of the world, for that matter). More than 2 dozen dive operators on island offer everything from scuba-certification courses to guided dives to snorkeling cruises.

Founded in 1984, **Kohala Divers** (www.kohaladivers.com; ✆ **808/882-7774**) has daily two-tank dives ($139–$149) to spectacular sites off North and South Kohala, including a 30-foot-high lava dome covered in plate and knob coral that attracts huge schools of fish, and several spots off Puakō frequented by green sea turtles. Snorkelers (gear included) and ride-alongs pay $85 to join these and other charters aboard the 42-foot dive boat, which books just 15 of its 24-passenger capacity. You can also rent scuba and snorkel gear at its shop in Kawaihae Harbor Shopping Center, 61-3665 Akoni Pule Hwy. (Hwy. 270), about a mile north of its intersection with Highway 19. It's open daily 8am to 6pm.

"This is not your mother or father's dive shop," says owner Simon Key of the **Kona Diving Company** in the Old Industrial area, 74-5467 Luhia St. (at Eho St.), Kailua-Kona (www.konadivingcompany.com; ✆ **808/331-1858**). "This is a dive shop for today's diver." What sets Kona Diving Company apart, Simon claims, is its willingness to take its 34-foot catamaran (complete with showers, TV, and restrooms) to unusual dive sites, and "not those sites just 2 minutes from the mouth of the harbor." Kona Diving also offers introductory dives ($205), two-tank morning dives ($130), and one- and two-tank manta ray night dives from Honokōhau Harbor ($120–$140). Snorkelers and ride-alongs pay $80 to $115, gear included, depending on the trip; scuba gear costs $30 a day.

One of Kona's oldest and most eco-friendly dive shops, **Jack's Diving Locker,** in the Coconut Marketplace, 75-5813 Ali'i Dr., Kailua-Kona (www.jacksdivinglocker.com; © **800/345-4807** or 808/329-7585), boasts an 8,000-square-foot dive center with solar-heated swimming pool (and underwater viewing windows), classrooms, full-service rentals, and sports-diving and technical-diving facilities. It offers the classic two-tank dive for $135 ($65 snorkelers) and a two-tank manta ray night dive for $155 ($125 snorkelers) on four roomy boats taking 10 to 18 divers (split into groups of six). Another night dive: **Pelagic Magic,** a one-tank descent into dark water that reveals iridescent jellies and evanescent zooplankton ($175), offered Tuesday and Thursday.

Snorkeling

If you come to Hawai'i and don't snorkel, you'll miss half the fun. The clear waters along the dry Kona and Kohala coasts, in particular, are home to spectacular marine life, including spinner dolphins by day and giant manta rays by night. You'll want to take an evening **boat tour** (p. 225) or **kayak tour** (p. 231) to see the latter (and please heed instructions to just watch the mantas and not touch them, which harms their skin). For dolphins and reef denizens, go in the mornings, before afternoon clouds and winds lessen visibility. At all snorkeling sites, please be very careful not to stand on, kick, or touch the live coral, which takes years to grow.

GEAR RENTALS If you're staying at a Kona or Kohala resort, the hotel concession should have basic gear for hourly rental. If you're thinking of exploring more than the beach outside your room, an inexpensive place to get basic rental equipment ($9 per week) is **Snorkel Bob's,** in the parking lot of Huggo's restaurant, 75-5831 Kahakai St. at Ali'i Drive, Kailua-Kona (www.snorkelbob.com; © **808/329-0770**), and on the Kohala Coast in the Shops at Mauna Lani, 68-1330 Mauna Lani Dr., facing the road on the Mauna Lani Resort (© **808/885-9499**). Higher-quality gear costs $35 a week for adults, $22 for children ($44/$32 for prescription masks). Both stores are open 8am to 5pm daily.

You can also rent high-quality gear from **Jack's Diving Locker,** Coconut Grove Shopping Center (next to Outback Steak House), 75-5813 Ali'i Dr., Kailua-Kona (www.jacksdivinglocker.com; © **800/345-4807** or 808/329-7585), open 8am to 8pm Monday to Saturday, until 6pm Sunday. Snorkel sets cost $9 a day. On the Kohala Coast, visit **Kohala Divers** (www.kohaladivers.com; © **808/882-7774**) in the Kawaihae Shopping Center, 61-3665 Akoni Pule Highway (Hwy. 270), in Kawaihae, a mile north of the intersection with Highway 19. It's open 8am to 6pm daily, with snorkel sets starting at $10 a day.

On the island's east side, **Nautilus Dive Center,** 382 Kamehameha Ave. at Nāwahi Lane (next to the Shell gas station) in Hilo (www.

nautilusdivehilo.com; ✆ **808/935-6939**), rents snorkel packages for $6 a day; it's open 9am to 5pm Mon–Sat.

TOP SNORKEL SITES If you've never snorkeled in your life, **Kahalu'u Beach ★★** (p. 216) is the best place to start, as long as the crowds don't throw you off. Just wade in on one of the small, sandy paths through the lava-rock tide pools and you'll see colorful fish. Even better, swim out to the center of the shallow, well-protected bay to see schools of surgeonfish, Moorish idols, butterflyfish, and even green sea turtles. The friendly and knowledgeable volunteers of the **Kahalu'u Bay Education Center (KBEC;** www.kahaluubay.org; ✆ **808/640-1166**) are on-site daily from 9:30am to 4:30pm to explain reef etiquette—essentially: "Look, but don't touch"—and answer questions about its marine life. The KBEC even rents snorkel gear ($14) from Jack's Diving Locker and boogie boards with viewing windows ($10) if you don't want to put your face underwater; proceeds benefit conservation at this popular spot visited annually by some 400,000 snorkelers, swimmers, and surfers.

Kealakekua Bay ★★★ may offer the island's best overall snorkeling (coral heads, lava tubes, calm waters, underwater caves, and more), but because it's a marine life conservation district and state historical park (p. 186), access is restricted to preserve its treasures. The best way to snorkel here is via permitted **boat tours** (p. 225), generally departing from Kailua Pier or Keauhou Bay, or **kayak tours** (p. 232) with permits to launch from Nāpo'opo'o Wharf and land near the Captain Cook Monument. You can paddle a rental kayak, canoe, or stand-up paddleboard from Nāpo'opo'o on your own if the company has acquired a special permit; otherwise, it's about a 10-mile round-trip paddle from Keauhou. Carrying your snorkel gear down and up the steep 5-mile trail from the highway is possible but not recommended. Watch out for spiny urchins as well as fragile coral when entering the water from lava rocks along the shore.

Much more easily accessible snorkeling, with a terrific display of aquatic diversity, can be found at **Hōnaunau Bay,** nicknamed "Two Step" for the easy entry off flat lava rocks into the crystalline waters just before **Pu'uhonua O Hōnaunau National Historical Park** (p. 187). Snorkeling is not permitted in the park itself, but you can pay the entrance fee to park your car there and walk to the bay if the 25 or so spaces on the bayfront road—look for the coastal access sign off Highway 160—are taken.

North of the Kohala resort, the well-protected waters of **'Ōhai'ula Beach** at **Spencer Park** (p. 222) are a great site for families to snorkel, with convenient facilities (restrooms, showers, picnic tables), not to mention a lifeguard on weekends and holidays, and a reputation for attracting green sea turtles (let them come to you, but don't touch or approach them.) It can get windy, so mornings are your best bet here.

Sport Fishing: The Hunt for Granders ★★

Big-game fish, including gigantic blue marlin and other Pacific billfish, tuna, sailfish, swordfish, ono (wahoo), and giant trevallies *(ulua),* roam the waters of the Kona Coast, known as the marlin capital of the world. When anglers catch marlin weighing 1,000 pounds or more, they call them "granders"; there's even a "wall of fame" in Kailua-Kona's Waterfront Row shopping mall honoring those who've nailed more than 20 tons of fighting fish. Nearby photos show celebrities such as Sylvester Stallone posing with their slightly less impressive catches. The celebrities of the fishing world descend on Kailua-Kona in August for the 5-day **Hawaiian International Billfish Tournament** (www.hibtfishing.com), founded in 1959. Note that it's not all carnage out there: Teams that tag and release marlin under 300 pounds get bonus points.

Nearly 100 charter boats with professional captains and crew offer fishing charters out of **Keauhou, Kawaihae, Honokōhau,** and **Kailua Bay** harbors. If you're not an expert angler, the best way to arrange a charter is through a booking agency such as the **Charter Desk at Honokōhau Marina** (www.charterdesk.com; ✆ **888/566-2487** or 808/326-1800), which can sort through the more than 60 different types of vessels and fishing specialties to match you with the right boat. Prices range from $750 to $3,500 or so for a full-day exclusive charter (you and up to five friends have an entire boat to yourselves) or $450 to $600 for a half-day. One or two people may be able to book a "share" on boats that hold four to eight anglers, who take turns fishing—generally for smaller

Wahoo caught in Big Island waters.

catch—to increase everyone's chances of hooking something. Shares start at $95 to $150 per person for half-day trips, $250 for a full day.

Note: Most big-game charter boats carry six passengers max, and the boats supply all equipment, bait, tackle, and lures. No license is required. Many captains now tag and release marlins; other fish caught belong to the boat, not to you—that's island style. If you want to eat your catch or have your trophy mounted, arrange it with the captain before you go.

Stand-Up Paddleboarding (SUP)

Anywhere the water is calm is a fine place to learn stand-up paddleboarding (SUP), which takes much less finesse than traditional surfing but offers a fun alternative to kayaking for exploring the coast. Numerous hotel concessions offer rentals and lessons, as do traditional surf shops.

Kona Boys ★★ (www.konaboys.com; ✆ **808/328-1234**) has the best locale in Kailua-Kona to try your hand at SUP: **Kamakahonu Cove,** next to Kailua Pier and King Kamehameha's royal (and sacred) compound. The spring water in the well-protected cove is a little too cool and murky for snorkeling, but just right for getting your bearings. The 90-minute lessons costs $99 in a group setting, $149 private; once you've got the hang of it, you can also reserve one of Kona Boys' 90-minute tours ($99 group/$149 private) or just pick up a rental ($29 hourly, $74 daily). It also offers lessons and rentals at its Kealakekua location, 79-7539 Māmalahoa Hwy. (Hwy. 11), 1¼ miles south of its intersection with Highway 180. Both sites are open daily until 5pm; the Kamakahonu beach shack opens at 8am, Kealakekua at 7:30am.

Another good option in North Kona is at Keauhou Bay where **Ocean Safaris** (www.oceansafariskayaks.com; ✆ **808/326-4699**) offers 2-hour lessons and tours, each $79; rentals are $25 for 2 hours, but paddlers must stay within Keauhou Bay.

On the Kohala Coast, the smooth crescents of **'Anaeho'omalu Bay** and **Puakō Bay** are also well suited to exploring via SUP. **Ocean Sports** (www.hawaiioceansports.com) rents boards for $30 a half-hour ($50 hourly) from its kiosk on the sand in front of the Waikoloa Beach Marriott; see website for details on its other Kohala locations. **Hulakai** rents all kinds of beach gear from its outlet in the Shops at Mauna Lani (http://hulakai.com; ✆ **808/896-3141**). Open 10am–4pm daily, it offers 1-hour SUP lessons ($68) and 90-minute "adventures" ($98), plus rentals for $69 a day, $249 a week.

Surfing

Most surfing off the Big Island is for the experienced only, thanks to rocks, coral reef, and rip currents at many of the reliable breaks. As a general rule, the beaches on the North and West Shores of the island get northern swells in winter, while those on the South and East shores get southern swells in summer. You'll also need to radiate courtesy and expertise in the lineup with local surfers, understandably territorial about their challenging breaks.

In Kailua-Kona, experienced surfers should check out the two breaks in **Hōlualoa Bay** off Ali'i Drive between downtown Kailua-Kona and Keauhou: **Banyans** near the northern point and **Lyman's** near the southern point, once home to a surfers' temple. If you don't have the chops, don't go in the water; just enjoy the show. Another surfing shrine, its black-lava rock walls still visible today, stands near **Kahalu'u Beach ★★** (p. 216), where the waves are manageable most of the year and there's also a lifeguard. Less-experienced surfers can also try **Pine Trees** north of town at **Kohanaiki Beach ★★** (p. 218), where it's best to avoid the busy weekends.

Surf breaks on the east side of the island are also generally best left to skilled surfers. They include **Honoli'i Point,** north of Hilo; **Richardson's Point** at **Leleiwi Beach Park** (p. 222); **Hilo Bay Front Park;** and **Pohoiki Bay,** home to **Isaac Hale Beach Park** near Pāhoa.

PRIVATE & GROUP LESSONS You can have a grand time taking a surf lesson, especially with instructors who know where the breaks are best for beginners and who genuinely enjoy being out in the waves with you. The Native Hawaiian–owned **Hawaii Lifeguard Surf Instructors** (www.surflessonshawaii.com; © **808/324-0442**), which gives lessons at Kahalu'u Beach, has an especially good touch with kids and teens. For $110, adults and children as young as 3 can take a 90-minute private lesson (little ones under 55 pounds ride on the same board as their lifeguard/teacher). Lessons for ages 11 and up cost $75 per person for small groups (no more than three students per instructor) and $185 for a group of just two. On days when the waves are tame, HLSI offers the same lessons with stand-up paddleboards. Classes are three times a day, Monday through Saturday.

BOARD RENTALS You're never going to rent a board as good as your own, but you'll enjoy getting to know the local vibe at the appropriately named **Pacific Vibrations,** 75-5702 Likana Lane, tucked off Ali'i Drive just north of Moku'aikaua Church (© **808/329-4140**), founded in 1978 by the McMichaels, a Native Hawaiian family with deep ties to surfing and the Ironman triathlon. It's a trip just to visit the densely stocked surf shop in downtown Kailua-Kona. Surfboards rent for $10 to $20 a day, and body boards for just $5. Stand-up paddleboards go for $15 an hour. The staff is happy to help steer you to waves to match your skills.

Founded in Puakō in 1997, surfboard shaper **Hulakai** (http://hulakai.com) also rents surfboards for $20 a day ($80 a week) from two locations: the Shops at Mauna Lani (© **808/896-3141**) on the Mauna Lani Resort and in downtown Hilo (© **808/993-4852**) at 284 Kamehameha Ave. (at Furneaux Lane). You can also sign up for 2-hour private and semiprivate surfing lessons ($150 or $125, respectively).

OTHER OUTDOOR ACTIVITIES

Biking

Note: In addition to the rental fees mentioned below, expect to put down a deposit on a credit card or leave your credit card number on file.

KONA & KOHALA COASTS

When you're planning to spend a fair amount of time in Kailua-Kona, where parking can be at a premium, consider renting a bicycle for easy riding and sightseeing along flat, often oceanview Ali'i Drive. A cruiser can also be handy if you're staying at a Kohala Coast resort and want an easy way to shuttle around shops, beaches, and condos without having to jump in the car. Experienced cyclists may also want to trace part of the Ironman course (112 miles round-trip) along the wide-shouldered "Queen K" and Akoni Pule highways from Kailua-Kona to Hawi, or join in one of several weekly group rides of the **Hawaii Cycling Club** (www.hawaiicyclingclub.com).

For simple cruisers, head to **Hawaiian Pedals,** Kona Inn Shopping Village, 75-5744 Ali'i Dr., Kailua-Kona (www.hawaiianpedals.com; ✆ **808/329-2294**), which has 7-speed hybrid bikes for $25 a day and $91 a week; a 24-speed city bike is $30 a day, $112 a week. Pros and amateurs alike flock to its sister store, **Bike Works,** Hale Hana Centre, 74-5583 Luhia St., Kailua-Kona (www.bikeworkskona.com; ✆ **808/326-2453**) for an even bigger selection of bikes, including mountain bikes ($40 a day), road bikes ($50), and triathlon bikes ($60), with large discounts for longer bookings. Bike Works also has a shop in **Queens' MarketPlace,** Waikoloa Beach Resort (www.bikeworkshawaii.com; ✆ **808/886-5000**), with road and city bike rentals ($25–$75 daily). Both locations offer weekly group rides open to all.

Note: Reserve well in advance for rentals in the first 2 weeks of October, during the leadup to the Ironman World Championship.

HAWAI'I VOLCANOES NATIONAL PARK

The national park has miles of paved roads and trails open to cyclists, from easy, flat rides to challenging ascents, but you'll need to watch out for cars and buses on the often winding, narrow roads, and make sure you carry plenty of water and sunscreen. Download a cycling guide on the park's website (www.nps.gov/havo/planyourvisit/bike.htm) or pick one up at the Kīlauea Visitor Center. The closest bike-rental shops are in Hilo, including **Mid-Pacific Wheels,** 1133 Manono St. (www.midpacificwheelsllc.com; ✆ **808/935-6211**), which has mountain and road bikes for $25 to $45 a day, including a helmet; bike racks are $10 a day. Or leave the planning to **Volcano Bike Tours** (www.bikevolcano.com; ✆ **888/934-9199** or 808/934-9199), which offers fully supported half- and full-day guided tours ($110–$134) in the national park that include some off-road riding and, on the longer tour, a van trip to the end of Chain of Craters Road.

Golf

All greens fees below are for visitors; those with Hawai'i state ID (*kama'ā ina)* may receive substantial discounts. Rates include carts unless noted.

THE KONA COAST

The fabulous **Hualālai Golf Course ★★★** at the Four Seasons Resort Hualalai (p. 256) is open only to members and resort guests—but for committed golfers, this Jack Nicklaus–designed championship course is reason enough to book a room and pay the sky-high greens fee of $285 ($150 for kids 13–18, free for children 12 and under with paying guest).

Big Island Country Club ★★ Designed by Perry Dye, this par-72, 18-hole course offers sweeping views of towering Mauna Kea and the bright blue coastline from its perch 2,000 feet above sea level. Although it's not on the ocean, water features wind around nine of the holes, including the spectacular par-3 No. 17. Waterfalls, tall palms, and other lush greenery add to the tropical feel; look for native birds such as the nēnē (Hawaiian goose), hawks, stilts, and black-crowned night herons. The wide fairways and gently rolling terrain make it appropriate for players of every level. Facilities include club rentals, driving range, pro shop, lounge, and snack bar.

71-1420 Māmalahoa Hwy. (Hwy. 190), Kailua-Kona. www.bigislandcountryclub.com. ✆ **808/325-5044.** Greens fees $95 before noon; $66–$79 after noon.

Kona Country Club ★★ Although the 18-hole Mountain Course has permanently closed, the popular Keauhou club has reopened its Ocean Course, originally designed by William Bell, in 2015 with expanded greens, new cart paths and bunkers, and a new irrigation system. The views of pounding waves on lava rock—also visible from the well-stocked pro shop—remain impressive. Other facilities include club rentals, driving range, pro shop, locker rooms, and putting and chipping greens.

78–7000 Ali'i Dr., Kailua-Kona. www.konagolf.com. ✆ **808/322-3431.** Greens fees $150–$180; juniors ages 8 to 17, $90; 9 holes after 2pm, $90.

Makalei Golf Club ★ This par-72, 18-hole upcountry course—some 1,800 to 2,850 feet in elevation—goes up and down through native forests, cinder cones, and lava tubes over its championship length of 7,091 yards. The signature hole is the par-3 No. 15, offering a distant view of Maui and the best chance for a hole-in-one. A local favorite, Makalei is visited by wild peacocks, pheasants, and turkeys. Facilities include a golf shop, driving range, putting greens, club rentals (drop-off and pickup available), and the **Peacock Grille** restaurant, offering a full bar and a menu of burgers, salads, and snacks from 11am to 2:30pm.

72-3890 Hawai'i Belt Rd. (Māmalahoa Hwy./Hwy. 190), Kailua-Kona. www.makalei.com. ✆ **808/325-6625.** Greens fees $119 before noon; $99 after noon. From the intersection of Palani Rd. and Hwy. 11 in Kailua-Kona, take Palani Rd. (which becomes Hwy. 190) east 7¼ miles, and look for green gates and small white sign on right.

THE KOHALA COAST

Hapuna Golf Course ★★★ Since its opening in 1992, this 18-hole championship course has been named the most environmentally-sensitive course by *Golf* magazine, as well as "Course of the Future" by the U.S. Golf Association. Designed by Arnold Palmer and Ed Seay, the links-style course extends nearly 6,900 yards from the shoreline to 700 feet above sea level, with views of the pastoral Kohala Mountains and the Kohala coastline; look for Maui across the channel from the signature 12th hole. The elevation changes on the course keep it challenging (and windy the higher you go). There are a few elevated tee boxes and only 40 bunkers. Facilities include putting and chipping greens, driving range, practice bunker, lockers, showers, a pro shop, rental clubs, fitness center, and spa.

At the Hapuna Beach Prince Hotel, Mauna Kea Resort, off Hwy. 19 (near mile marker 69). www.princeresortshawaii.com. ✆ **808/880-3000.** Greens fees $160–$175 ($140–$150 hotel guests) before 1pm; $85–$95 after 1pm. Second round same day $50 $55. Ages under 18 $55.

Mauna Kea Golf Course ★★★ This breathtakingly beautiful, par-72, 7,114-yard championship course designed by Robert Trent Jones, Jr., and later updated by son Rees Jones, is consistently rated one of the top golf courses in the United States. The signature 3rd hole is 175 yards long; the Pacific Ocean and shoreline cliffs stand between the tee and the green, giving every golfer, from beginner to pro, a real challenge. Another par-3 that confounds duffers is the 11th hole, which drops 100 feet from tee to green and plays down to the ocean, into the steady trade winds. When the trades are blowing, 181 yards might as well be 1,000 yards. Book ahead; the course is very popular, especially for early weekend tee times. Facilities include a pro shop and clubhouse with restaurant, named **Number 3** for the hole Jones, Sr., once called "the most beautiful in the world."

At the Mauna Kea Beach Hotel, Mauna Kea Resort, off Hwy. 19 (near mile marker 68). www.princeresortshawaii.com. ✆ **808/882-5400.** Greens fees $275 ($235 hotel guests) before 11am; $185–$195 11am–1:30pm; $165 after 1:30pm. Back 9 holes or second round same day, $125. Ages under 18, $95.

Mauna Lani Francis H. I'i Brown Championship Courses ★★★ Carefully wrapped around ancient trails, fish ponds, and petroglyphs, the two 18-hole courses here have won *Golf* magazine's Gold Medal Award every year since the honor's inception in 1988. The **South Course,** a 7,029-yard, par-72, has two unforgettable ocean holes: the over-the-water 15th hole and the downhill, 221-yard, par-3 7th, which is

Manua Kea Golf Course.

bordered by the sea, a salt-and-pepper sand dune, and lush kiawe trees. The **North Course** may not have the drama of the oceanfront holes, but because it was built on older lava flows, the more extensive indigenous vegetation gives the course a Scottish feel. The hole that's cursed the most is the 140-yard, par-3 17th: It's beautiful but plays right into the surrounding lava field. Facilities include two driving ranges, a golf shop (with teaching pros), a restaurant, and putting greens. Mauna Lani also has the island's only *keiki* (children's) course, a 9-hole walking course for juniors, beginners, and families (golfers under 14 must be with an adult). At the Mauna Lani Resort, Mauna Lani Dr., off Hwy. 19 (20 miles north of Kona Airport). www.maunalani.com. ✆ **808/885-6655.** Greens fees: $225 ($160–$170 for hotel guests) before 10am; $185 ($150–$160 guests) 10am–noon; $145 ($125 guests) after noon. Keiki course: $25 children, including clubs; $35 adults ($15 clubs).

Waikoloa Beach Resort Courses ★★ Two 18-hole courses beckon here. The pristine 18-hole, par-70 Beach Course certainly reflects the motto of designer Robert Trent Jones, Jr.: "Hard par, easy bogey." Most golfers remember the par-5, 505-yard 12th hole, a sharp dogleg left with bunkers in the corner and an elevated tee surrounded by lava. The Kings' Course, designed by Tom Weiskopf and Jay Morrish, is about 500 yards longer. Its links-style tract has a double green at the 3rd and 6th holes, and carefully placed bunkers see a lot of play, courtesy of the ever-present trade winds. Facilities include a golf shop, 15-acre practice range (with complimentary clubs and unlimited balls for just $15), and chef Allen Hess' excellent **Mai Grille** restaurant, serving gourmet comfort food (see p. 273); call for a free shuttle within the resort.

At the Waikoloa Beach Resort, 600 Waikoloa Beach Dr., Waikoloa. www.waikoloabeachgolf.com. ✆ **808/886-7888.** Greens fees: $145–$180 ($145 for resort guests) before 11:30am; $125 ($120 guests) 11:30am–1pm; $115 ($110 guests) 1–2pm; $95 after 2pm. 9 holes after 8:30am, $69. Children 6 to 17, $60. Second round same day, $55.

Waikoloa Village Golf Course ★ This semiprivate 18-hole course, with a par-72 for each of the three sets of tees, is hidden in the town of Waikoloa, next to the Paniolo Greens timeshare resort. Overshadowed by the glamorous resort courses of the Kohala Coast, it's nevertheless a beautiful course with terrific views and some great golfing. The wind can play havoc with your game here (like most Hawai'i golf courses). Robert Trent Jones, Jr., in designing this challenging course, inserted his trademark sand traps, slick greens, and great fairways. The par 5, 490-yard 18th hole is a thriller: It doglegs to the left, and the last 75 yards up to the green are water, water, water. Enjoy the fabulous views of Mauna Kea and Mauna Loa, and—on a very clear day—Maui's Haleakalā in the distance.

In Waikoloa Village, 68-1793 Melia St., Waikoloa. www.waikoloavillagegolf.com. ✆ **808/883-9621.** Greens fees $98 ($72 Paniolo Greens guests) before 2pm; $60 after 2pm. Children 7 to 17 $45 before 2pm; $40 after 2pm. From the airport, turn left on Hwy. 19; head 18 miles to stoplight at Waikoloa Rd. Turn right, drive uphill 6½ miles to left on Paniolo Ave. Take 1st right onto Lua Kula St. and follow ½-mile to Melia St.

HILO

Hilo Municipal Golf Course ★ This 146-acre course, renovated in 2016, is great for the casual golfer: It's flat, scenic, and often fun. Just don't go after a heavy rain (especially in winter); the fairways can get really soggy and play can slow way down. The rain does keep the 18-hole course green and beautiful, though. Wonderful trees (monkeypods, coconuts, eucalyptus, banyans) dot the grounds, and the views—of Mauna Kea on one side and Hilo Bay on the other—are breathtaking. There are four sets of tees, with a par-71 from all; the back tees give you 6,325 yards of play. It's the only municipal course on the island, so getting a tee time can be a challenge; weekdays are the best bet. Facilities include a driving range, pro shop, club rentals, restaurant, and snack bar.

340 Ha'iha'i St. (btw. Kino'ole and 'Iwalani sts.), Hilo. www.hawaiicounty.gov/pr-golf. ✆ **808/959-7711.** Greens fees $34 Mon–Fri, $45 Sat–Sun and holidays; carts $16.

Naniloa Golf Course ★ At first glance, this semiprivate 9-hole course just off Hilo Bay looks pretty flat and short, but once you get beyond the 1st hole—a wide, straightforward 330-yard par-4—things get challenging. The tree-lined fairways require straight drives, and the huge lake on the 2nd and 5th holes is sure to haunt you. This course is very popular with locals and visitors alike. Facilities include a driving range, putting green, pro shop, and club rentals.

120 Banyan Dr. (at the intersection of hwys. 11 and 19), Hilo. ✆ **808/935-3000.** Greens fees: 9 holes, $10 adults ($9 seniors 62 and over, $5 children under 17); 18 holes, $15 adults ($12 seniors 62 and over, $9 children under 17). Cart $10 ($15 for 18 holes).

Hiking

Trails on the Big Island wind through fields of coastal lava rock, deserts, rainforests, and mountain tundra, sometimes covered with snow. It's important to wear sturdy shoes, sunscreen, and a hat, and take plenty of water; for longer hikes, particularly in remote areas, it may also be essential to bring food, a flashlight, and a trail map—not one that requires a cellphone signal to access (coverage may be nonexistent). Hunting may be permitted in rural, upcountry, or remote areas, so stay on the trails and wear bright clothing.

The island has 16 trails in the state's **Nā Ala Hele Trail & Access System** (www.hawaiitrails.org; ✆ **808/974-4382**), highlights of which are included below; see the website for more information. For an even greater number of trails on a variety of public lands, see the detailed descriptions on **www.bigislandhikes.com**.

KONA & KOHALA COASTS

The **Ala Kahakai National Historic Trail** (www.nps.gov/alka; ✆ **808/326-6012,** ext. 101) is the designation for an ancient, 175-mile series of paths through coastal lava rock, from ʻUpolu Point in North Kohala along the island's west coast to Ka Lae (South Point) and east to Puna's Wahaʻula Heiau, an extensive temple complex. Some were created as long-distance trails, others for fishing and gathering, while a few were reserved for royal or chiefly use. There's unofficial access through the four national park sites—Puʻukoholā Heiau, Kaloko-Honokōhau, Puʻuhonua O Hōnaunau, and Hawaiʻi Volcanoes (see "Attractions & Points of Interest" on p. 181)—but it's easy, free, and fun to walk a portion of the 15.4-mile stretch between Kawaihae and ʻAnaehoʻomalu Bay, part of the state's **Nā Ala Hele** trails system (www.hawaiitrails.org; ✆ **808/974-4382**). Signs mark only the 8-mile portion of Ala Kahakai between the northern terminus of **ʻŌhaiʻula Beach** at **Spencer Park** (p. 222) through Puakō to **Holoholokai Beach Park,** near the petroglyph field on the Mauna Lani Resort, but it's fairly simple to follow farther south by hugging the shoreline, past resort hotels and multimillion-dollar homes, anchialine ponds, and jagged lava formations.

For those not satisfied with the view from the **Pololū Valley Lookout** (p. 190), the steep, 1-mile **Pololū Valley Trail** will lead you just behind the black-sand beach (beware of high surf and riptides). In addition to a 420-foot elevation change, the trail's challenges can include slippery mud and tricky footing over ancient cobblestones. As with all windward areas, be prepared for pesky mosquitos and/or cool mist.

If you're willing to venture on Saddle Road (Hwy. 200), which some rental-car companies still forbid, the **Pu'u Huluhulu Trail** is an easy, .6-mile hike that gradually loops around both crests of this forested cinder cone, with panoramic views of Mauna Kea and Mauna Loa between the trees. There's a parking lot in front of the hunter check-in station at the junction of the Mauna Loa observatory access road and Saddle Road.

THE HĀMĀKUA COAST

The 25% grade on the 1-mile "hike" down the road to **Waipi'o Valley** (p. 197) is a killer on the knees, and no picnic coming back up, but that's just the start of the epic, 18-mile round-trip adventure involving the **Muliwai Trail,** a very strenuous hike to primeval, waterfall-laced **Waimanu Valley.** This trail is the island's closest rival to Kaua'i's **Kalalau Trail** (p. 513), and so is only worth attempting by very physically fit and well-prepared hikers. Once in Waipi'o Valley, you must follow the beach to Wailoa Stream, ford it, and cross the dunes to the west side of the valley. There the zigzag Muliwai Trail officially begins, carving its way some 1,300 feet up the cliff; the reward at the third switchback is a wonderful view of Hi'ilawe Falls. Ahead lie 5 miles of 12 smaller, tree-covered gulches to cross before your first view of pristine Waimanu Valley, which has nine campsites (see "Camping" on p. 267) and two outhouses, but no drinking water. The trail is eroded in places and slippery when wet—which is often, due to the 100-plus inches of rain, which can also flood streams. This explains why the vast majority of those who see Waimanu Valley do so via helicopter (p. 212).

HAWAI'I VOLCANOES NATIONAL PARK

This magnificent national treasure and Hawaiian cultural icon (p. 207) has more than 150 miles of trails, including many day hikes, most of which are well maintained and well marked; a few are paved or have boardwalks, permitting strollers and wheelchairs. ***Warning:*** If you have heart or respiratory problems or if you're pregnant, don't attempt any hike in the park; the fumes will bother you. Also: Stacked rocks known as *ahu* mark trails crossing lava; please do not disturb or create your own.

Plan ahead by downloading maps and brochures on the park website (www.nps.gov/havo), which also lists areas closed due to current eruptions. Always check conditions with the rangers at the Kīlauea Visitor Center, where you can pick up detailed trail guides. ***Note:*** All overnight backcountry hiking and camping require a free permit, available only the day of or the day before your hike, from the park's **Backcountry Office** (**© 808/985-6178**).

In addition to sights described on the **Crater Rim Drive** tour (p. 207) and **Chain of Craters Road** tour (p. 210), here are some of the more accessible highlights for hikers, all demonstrating the power of Pele:

KĪLAUEA IKI TRAIL The 4-mile loop trail begins 2 miles from the visitor center on Crater Rim Road, descends through a forest of ferns into still-fuming Kīlauea Iki Crater, and then crosses the crater floor past the vent where a 1959 lava blast shot a fountain of fire 1,900 feet into the air for 36 days. Allow 2 hours for this fair-to-moderate hike, and look for white-tailed tropicbirds and Hawaiian hawks above you.

DEVASTATION TRAIL ★★ Up on the rim of Kīlauea Iki Crater, you can see what an erupting volcano did to a once-flourishing ohia forest. The scorched earth with its ghostly tree skeletons stands in sharp contrast to the rest of the lush forest. Everyone can take this 1-mile round-trip hike on a paved path across the eerie bed of black cinders. The trail head is on Crater Rim Road at Pu'u Puai Overlook.

KĪPUKA PUA'ULU (BIRD PARK) TRAIL This easy 1.2-mile round-trip hike lets you see native Hawaiian flora and fauna in a little oasis of living nature in a field of lava, known as a *kīpuka*. For some reason, the once red-hot lava skirted this mini-forest and let it survive. Go early in the morning or in the evening (or, even better, just after a rain) to see native birds like the *'apapane* (a small, bright-red bird with black wings and tail) and the *'i'iwi* (larger and orange-vermilion colored, with a curved salmon-hued bill). Native trees along the trail include giant ohia, koa, soapberry, kolea, and mamane.

Devastation Trail hiking path.

GUIDED hikes

A guided day or night hike is a safe but stimulating way for city slickers to explore natural Hawai'i. Book one of these excursions before you arrive; trips fill up quickly.

Hawaiian Walkways ★ (www.hawaiianwalkways.com; ✆ **800/457-7759** or 808/775-0372), now owned by veteran tour guide Richard Hawkins, offers hikes in Waipi'o and Pololū valleys, at Hawai'i Volcanoes National Park, and in the Kona Cloud Forest Sanctuary ($129–$190 adults, $99–$130 ages 7 to 11). Lunch, bottled water, snacks, and rain gear (if needed) are provided; custom hikes and off-road jeep tours (see www.lavajeep.com) are also available.

Naturalist and educator Rob Pacheco of **Hawaii Forest & Trail** ★★★ (www.hawaii-forest.com; ✆ **800/464-1993** or 808/331-8505) offers fully outfitted day trips to some of the island's most remote, pristine areas, including lands to which his company has exclusive access. His well-trained guides narrate the entire trip, offering extensive ecological, geological, and cultural commentary (and more than a little humor). Tours are limited to 12 to 14 people and are highly personalized to meet the group's interests and abilities. Options include my personal favorite, the 8-hour **Kohala Waterfalls Adventure** ★★★ ($179 for adults, $129 for children 12 and under), which you can pair with ziplining (p. 250); exceptionally well-run, all-day **birding tours,** for ages 8 and older ($192); all-day trips to **Hawai'i Volcanoes National Park** ★★★, some 300 miles round-trip ($192 for adults, $159 for children) and some shorter ones (6–7 hr.); and stargazing atop **Mauna Kea** ★★★ ($209; for ages 16 and up only). A daytime Mauna Kea tour ★★★ departs from Hilo ($169).

PU'U HULUHULU This moderate 3-mile round-trip to the summit of a cinder cone (which shares its name with the one on Saddle Rd., described above) crosses lava flows from 1973 and 1974, lava tree molds, and *kīpuka.* At the top is a panoramic vista of Mauna Loa, Mauna Kea, the coastline, and the often steaming vent of Pu'u 'Ō'ō. The trail head is in the Mauna Ulu parking area on Chain of Craters Road, 8 miles from the visitor center. (Sulfur fumes can be stronger here than on other trails.)

For avid trekkers, several long, steep, unshaded hikes lead to the beaches and rocky bays on the park's remote shoreline; they're all considered overnight backcountry hikes and thus require a permit. Only hiking diehards should consider attempting the **Mauna Loa Trail,** perhaps the most challenging hike in all of Hawai'i. Many hikers have had to be rescued over the years due to high-altitude sickness or exposure after becoming lost in snowy or foggy conditions. From the trail head at the end of scenic but narrow Mauna Loa Road, about an hour's drive from the visitor center, it's a 7.5-mile trek to the Pu'u 'Ula'ula ("Red Hill") cabin at 10,035 feet, and then 12 more miles up to the primitive Mauna Loa summit cabin at 13,250 feet, where the climate is subarctic and overnight temperatures are below freezing year-round. In addition to backcountry permits (see above), this 4-day round-trip requires special gear, great physical condition, and careful planning.

Horseback Riding

Although vast Parker Ranch, the historic center of Hawaiian ranching, no longer offers horseback tours, several other ranches in upcountry Waimea provide opportunities for riding with sweeping views of land and sea. Picturesque Waipi'o Valley is also another focus of equestrian excursions. ***Note:*** Most stables require riders to be at least 8 years old and weigh no more than 230 pounds; confirm before booking.

The 11,000-acre Ponoholo Ranch, whose herd of cattle (varying between 6,000 and 8,000) is second only to Parker Ranch's, is the scenic home base for **Paniolo Adventures** (www.panioloadventures.com; ✆ **808/889-5354**). Most of its five rides are open-range style and include brief stretches of trotting and cantering, although the gorgeous scenery outweighs the equine excitement—all but the 4-hour Wrangler Ride ($175) are suitable for beginners. The tamest option is the 1-hour City Slicker ride ($69), but the 1½-hour Sunset Ride ($89) appears to be the most popular. Boots, light jackets, Australian dusters, chaps, helmets, hats, drinks, and even sunscreen are provided. Look for Paniolo Adventures' red barn on Kohala Mountain Road (Hwy. 250), just north of mile marker 13.

Na'alapa Stables (www.naalapastables.com; ✆ **808/889-0022**) operates rides at Kahua Ranch, which also has an entrance on Kohala Mountain Road, north of mile marker 11. Riding open-range style, you'll pass ancient Hawaiian ruins, through lush pastures with grazing sheep and cows, and along mountaintops with panoramic coastal views. The horses and various riding areas are suited to everyone from first-timers to experienced equestrians. There are several trips a day: a 2½-hour tour at 9am and 1pm for $94, and a 1½-hour tour at 10am and 1:30pm for $73; check-in is a half-hour earlier.

Horseback riders in the Waipi'o Valley.

Na'alapa has another stable in Waipi'o Valley (✆ **808/775-0419**), which offers the more rugged **Waipi'o Valley Horseback**

Adventure ★★, a 2½-hour ride that starts with a four-wheel-drive (4WD) van ride down to this little-inhabited but widely revered valley (p. 197). The horses are sure-footed in the rocky streams and muddy trails, while the guides, who are well versed in Hawaiian history, provide running commentary. The cost is $94 for adults, with tours at 9:30am and 12:30pm Monday to Saturday. Don't forget your camera or bug spray; check in a half-hour earlier at **Waipio Valley Artworks,** 48-5415 Kukuihaele Rd., off Highway 240, about 8 miles northwest of Honoka'a.

Waipio Valley Artworks (see above) is also the check-in point for **Waipio Ridge Stables** (www.waipioridgestables.com; **© 877/757-1414**), which leads riders on a 2½-hour **Valley Rim Ride** ($90), including views of the beach below and Hi'ilawe waterfall at the rear of the deep valley. The 5-hour **Hidden Waterfalls Ride** ($175) includes the sights along the rim ride and then follows the stream that feeds Hi'ilawe through the rainforest to a picnic and swim in a bracingly cool waterfall pool, but it's rather long if you're not into riding. ***Note:*** Fog sometimes obscures views of Waipi'o Valley from the rim.

Tennis

Although some resorts only allow guests to use their tennis facilities, the Kohala Coast has several delightful exceptions. The 11-court **Seaside Tennis Club (© 808/882-5420)** at the Mauna Kea Beach Hotel (p. 260) is frequently ranked among the world's finest for good reason: Three of the courts ($25 per person) are right on the ocean and all enjoy beautiful landscaping. The club also boasts luxurious locker rooms, a pro shop with racket and ball machine rentals, daily clinics, round robins, and lessons for ages 4 and up. Those not staying at the hotel just need to make a reservation for a court (open daily 8am–5pm) or lesson.

Just as highly ranked, the **Hawaii Tennis Center © 808/887-7532**) at the Fairmont Orchid Hawaii (p. 258) offers 10 courts (including one stadium court), with evening play available until 9pm by reservation. It has a pro shop, rents rackets and ball machines, and offers lessons. Fees are $30 per court; check in at pro shop. The **Pā Le'a Le'a Ocean Sports Tennis** program (www.hawaiioceansports.com; **© 808/886-6666,** ext. 108) at Hilton Waikoloa Village (p. 259) provides five cushioned courts and one stadium court, plus lessons, clinics, and racket and ball machine rentals. Court fees are $20 per hour ($30 per day if available).

You can also play for free at any Hawai'i County tennis court; the easiest way to find one nearest you is to visit **www.tennisinhawaii.com**. For those in Kailua-Kona, the four courts at **Old Kona Airport Park** (p. 220) offer the best experience.

Ziplining

Ziplining gives Big Island visitors an exhilarating way to view dramatic gulches, thick forests, gushing waterfalls, and other inspiring scenery—without significantly altering the landscape. Typically, the pulley-and-harness systems have redundant safety mechanisms, with lines and gear inspected daily and multiple checks of your equipment during the tour; your biggest worry may be losing your cellphone or anything not in a zipped pocket. Most outfitters also rent GoPro video cameras that attach to your helmets, so you can relive your whizzing rides at home.

Note: For safety reasons, tours have minimum ages (listed below) and/or minimum and maximum weights; read the fine print carefully before booking.

NORTH KOHALA The Australian eucalyptus and native kukui trees on **Kohala Zipline's Canopy Tour ★★** (www.kohalazipline.com; ✆ **800/464-1993** or 808/331-3620) might not provide the most colorful panoramas, but this nine-line adventure ($169 adults, $129 kids 8–12) emphasizes environmental awareness and cultural history in a compelling way—and the extra-quiet ziplines and multiple suspension bridges are a hoot, too. You'll fly from platform to platform in a sylvan setting that includes ancient taro terraces believed to have been farmed by Kamehameha before he became king. Tours depart from the zip station on Highway 270 between Hawi and Kapa'au up to 16 times daily; shuttle service is also available from South Kohala and North Kona resorts for the 8:30am and 1pm tours ($209 adults, $179 children 8–12, lunch included). For a very special splurge, take the outfitter's 8-hour **Kohala Zip & Dip ★★★**, which combines the Canopy Tour with Hawaii Forest & Trail's fascinating Kohala Waterfalls Adventure (p. 247), including a waterfall swim and picnic overlooking beautiful Pololū Valley. The Zip & Dip tours ($249 adults, $209 for ages 8–12, with lunch) depart from Queens' MarketPlace in Waikoloa Beach Resort and Hawaii Forest & Trail headquarters on Highway 19 in Kailua-Kona, 74-5035 Queen Ka'ahumanu Hwy. (north of Kealakehe Parkway).

THE HĀMĀKUA COAST I don't like the misleading name, but I can't begrudge the thrills involved on the **Akaka Falls Skyline Adventure ★★** (www.zipline.com/bigisland; ✆ **888/864-6947**), which actually zips past the nearly 250-foot-tall **Kolekole Falls,** downstream from the taller and more famous **'Akaka Falls** (p. 193) in Honomū, about 12 miles north of Hilo. The seven-line course builds in length and speed, while the well-informed guides share insights on local flora and fauna—including banana, taro, and wild pigs—and the area's history as a sugar plantation. The 2½- to 3-hour tour costs $170 (ages 10 and older), with 10% off for online bookings.

The **Umauma Falls Zipline Tour ★★★** (www.ziplinehawaii.com; ✆ **808/930-9477**) lives up to its name, where you see the captivating, three-tiered falls (p. 197) and 13 other smaller cascades as you zip along its 2-mile, 9-line course ($189 ages 4 and older) in Hakalau, about 16 miles north of Hilo. The **Zip & Dip** option ($239 ages 4 and older) includes an hour of kayaking and swimming under a waterfall, next to the Hilo side's only known petroglyph. For a quicker thrill, try the three-person giant swing ($40), which soars 150 feet over the falls.

WHERE TO STAY ON THE BIG ISLAND

For additional **bed-and-breakfasts**, visit the website of the **Hawaii Island B&B Association** (www.stayhawaii.com), which only allows licensed, inspected properties to become members; 30 are currently listed. **Vacation rentals,** which Hawai'i County does not regulate the way it does B&Bs and hotels, are currently less of a hot-button issue here than on other islands. You'll find numerous listings of condos and houses on sites such as VRBO.com and airbnb.com. To help you compare units and complexes, as well as guarantee rapid assistance should issues arise during your stay, though, consider booking vacation rentals through an island-based company, such as those listed for specific regions below.

All rooms listed below come with a private bathroom and free parking unless otherwise noted, all pools are outdoors. Rates do not include the state's 13.41% tax, while cleaning fees refer to one-time charges, not daily service.

The Kona Coast

Many of the lodgings in Kailua-Kona and Keauhou are timeshares or individually owned condos; rates, decor, and amenities in the latter may vary widely by unit. For a broad selection of well-managed condos and a smaller selection of homes (most with pools), contact **Kona Rentals** (www.konarentals.com; © **800/799-5662**) or **Kona Hawaii Vacation Rentals** (www.konahawaii.com; © **809/244-4752** or 808/329-3333). ***Note:*** Prices and minimum-stay requirements may be significantly higher during the week before and after the Ironman World Championship (usually the second Sat in Oct), as well as during holidays.

CENTRAL KAILUA-KONA

In addition to the lodgings below, consider booking a condo at the **Royal Sea Cliff ★★**, on the ocean side of Ali'i Drive about 2 miles south of the Kailua Pier. There's no beach, but it has two oceanfront pools, often the site of free entertainment, and a tennis court. **Outrigger Hotels & Resorts** (www.outrigger.com; © **800/688-7444** or 808/329-8021) manages 62 of the 148 large air-conditioned units, ranging from studios (650 sq. ft.) up to two-bedroom, two-bathroom units (1,100–1,300 sq. ft.), all with full kitchens and washer/dryers. Outrigger charges $139 to

$399, plus cleaning fees of $110 to $245, for its well-appointed accommodations, with free parking and Wi-Fi.

Moderate

Courtyard King Kamehameha Kona Beach Hotel ★★★ Thanks to a 2009 renovation—partially repeated after the 2011 Fukushima tsunami sent waves rolling through its lobby—this Courtyard Marriott–managed hotel lives up to its premium setting in front of King Kamehameha's royal compound on Kailua Bay. Rooms boast not only flatscreen TVs, updated bathrooms, and modern furnishings but also a sense of history and place. Subtle patterns in the stylish guest rooms reflect lava, native plants, and traditional tattoo designs, while colors suggest sand, coffee, and rainforest ferns. The high-ceilinged, bright-toned lobby is home to a gallery of royal portraits and Hawaiian cultural scenes by the late Herb Kawainui Kāne. More recently, the hotel restored its two tennis courts and pro shop, added a yoga studio, and expanded the offerings at **Honu's on the Beach ★★**, its popular indoor/outdoor restaurant. ***Note:*** In early October, this is Ironman central, full of buff bodies and international triathletes, all abuzz about the world championship that starts and ends just outside the hotel's front door.

75-5660 Palani Rd., Kailua-Kona. www.konabeachhotel.com. ✆ **800/367-2111** or 808/329-2911. 452 units. $159–$309 up to 4 people; from $399 one-bedroom suite. Check for online discounts and packages. Parking $16. **Amenities:** 2 restaurants; poolside bar; convenience store; fitness center; coin-operated laundry; lū'au; infinity pool; hot tub; Dollar and Hertz rental-car agencies; room service; spa; 2 lighted tennis courts and pro shop; watersports equipment rentals; Wi-Fi (free); yoga studio.

Holiday Inn Express Kailua-Kona ★ Its neutral-toned, modern "chain hotel" decor may seem out of place in Hawai'i, but this 75-room hotel, opened in late 2014, is nevertheless a very welcome addition to the area. Tucked on a one-way street between Ali'i Drive and Kuakini Highway, the three-story building offers surprisingly quiet rooms, some with a glimpse of the ocean, including suites with a sofa sleeper. All have 42-inch flatpanel TVs, ample desk space, and gleaming bathrooms; the pool, hot tub, and fitness center are compact but also immaculate. The hot breakfast buffet may lack tropical touches, but it's free. The only downside: The hotel has just 55 parking spaces ($10) in a shared lot. Luckily, the hospitable staff can advise you where to nab another spot.

77-146 Sarona Rd., Kailua-Kona. www.hiexpress.com/kailua-kona. ✆ **855/373-5450** or 808/329-2599. 75 units. $151–$169 room, $160–$219 suite, $178–$239 oceanview suite with king or two queens, plus sofa sleeper; rates include up to 4 people per room. Parking $10. **Amenities:** Free breakfast buffet; business center; fitness center; hot tub; pool; Wi-Fi (free).

Kona Magic Sands ★ With Kailua-Kona's largest (if somewhat fickle) sandy beach next door, and oceanfront lanais on every unit to soak in the sunsets and let in the sound of pounding waves, this location is ideal for couples who don't want to spend a bundle at a resort. All the

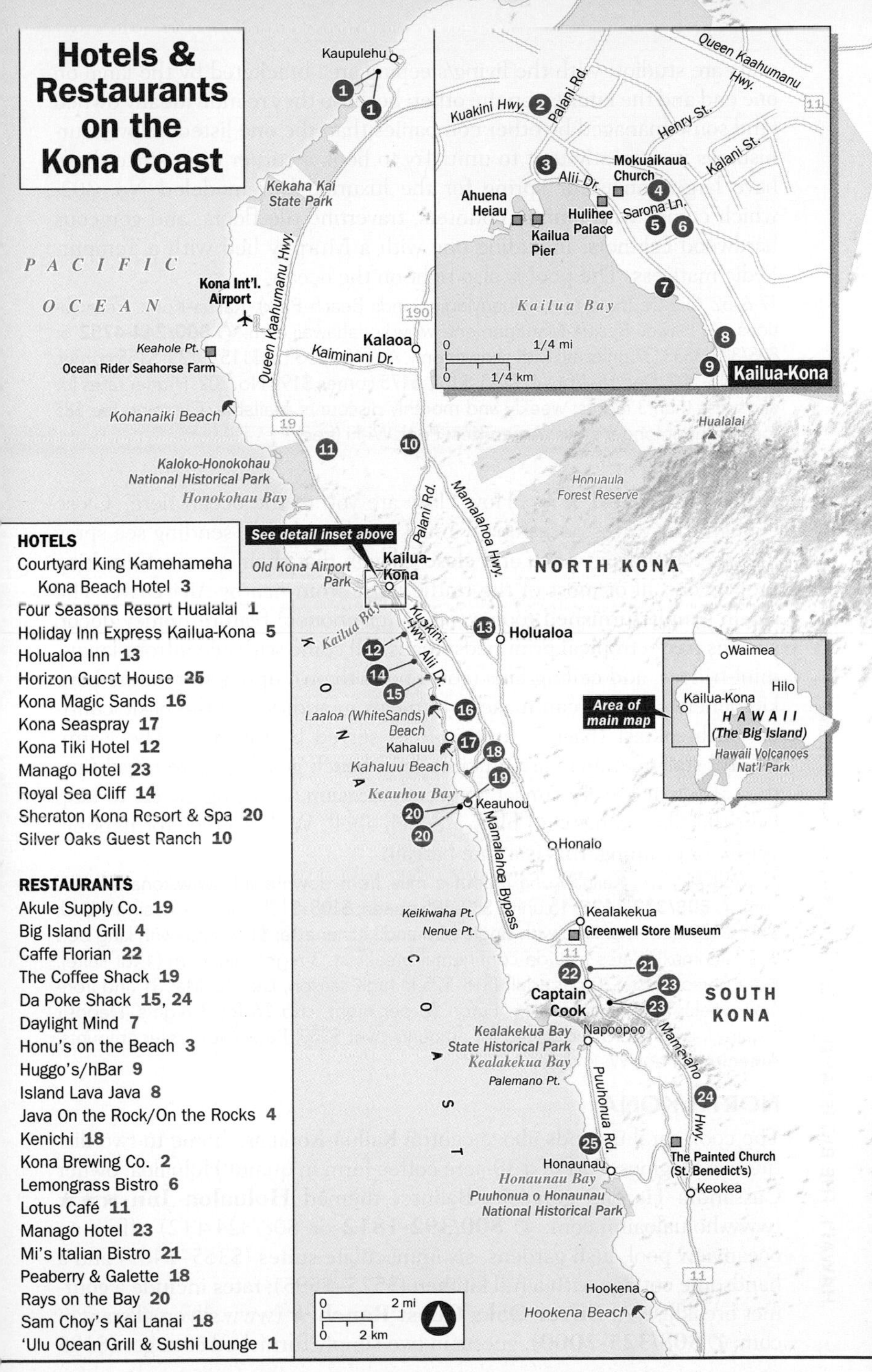
Hotels & Restaurants on the Kona Coast
HOTELS
Courtyard King Kamehameha Kona Beach Hotel 3
Four Seasons Resort Hualalai 1
Holiday Inn Express Kailua-Kona 5
Holualoa Inn 13
Horizon Guest House 25
Kona Magic Sands 16
Kona Seaspray 17
Kona Tiki Hotel 12
Manago Hotel 23
Royal Sea Cliff 14
Sheraton Kona Resort & Spa 20
Silver Oaks Guest Ranch 10
RESTAURANTS
Akule Supply Co. 19
Big Island Grill 4
Caffe Florian 22
The Coffee Shack 19
Da Poke Shack 15, 24
Daylight Mind 7
Honu's on the Beach 3
Huggo's/hBar 9
Island Lava Java 8
Java On the Rock/On the Rocks 4
Kenichi 18
Kona Brewing Co. 2
Lemongrass Bistro 6
Lotus Café 11
Manago Hotel 23
Mi's Italian Bistro 21
Peaberry & Galette 18
Rays on the Bay 20
Sam Choy's Kai Lanai 18
'Ulu Ocean Grill & Sushi Lounge 1
Kaupulehu
Kekaha Kai State Park
PACIFIC OCEAN
Kona Int'l. Airport
Queen Kaahumanu Hwy.
Keahole Pt.
Ocean Rider Seahorse Farm
Kalaoa
Kaiminani Dr.
Kohanaiki Beach
Kaloko-Honokohau National Historical Park
Honokohau Bay
Palani Rd.
Mamalahoa Hwy.
See detail inset above
Old Kona Airport Park
Kailua-Kona
Kailua Bay
Kuakini Hwy.
Alii Dr.
Holualoa
NORTH KONA
Hualalai
Honuaula Forest Reserve
Laaloa (WhiteSands) Beach
Kahaluu
Kahaluu Beach
Keauhou Bay
Keauhou
Mamalahoa Bypass
Honalo
KONA COAST
Keikiwaha Pt.
Nenue Pt.
Kealakekua
Greenwell Store Museum
Captain Cook
SOUTH KONA
Napoopoo
Kealakekua Bay State Historical Park
Kealakekua Bay
Palemano Pt.
Puuhonua Rd.
Mamalaho Hwy.
The Painted Church (St. Benedict's)
Honaunau
Honaunau Bay
Puuhonua o Honaunau National Historical Park
Keokea
Hookena
Hookena Beach
0 2 mi
0 2 km
Queen Kaahumanu Hwy.
Kuakini Hwy.
Palani Rd.
Henry St.
Kalani St.
Mokuaikaua Church
Alii Dr.
Ahuena Heiau
Hulihee Palace
Sarona Ln.
Kailua Pier
Kailua Bay
0 1/4 mi
0 1/4 km
Kailua-Kona
Waimea
Hilo
Kailua-Kona
Area of main map
HAWAII (The Big Island)
Hawaii Volcanoes Nat'l Park

units are studios, with the living/sleeping area bracketed by the lanai on one end and the kitchen on the other; because they're individually owned (and some managed by other companies than the one listed below), furnishings vary greatly unit to unit. Try to book a corner unit, since those have larger lanais, or spring for the luxuriously remodeled No. 302, which comes with granite counters, travertine tile floors, and gorgeous hardwood cabinets, including one with a Murphy bed with a Tempur-Pedic mattress. The pool is also right on the ocean.

77-6452 Ali'i Dr. (next to La'aloa/Magic Sands Beach Park), Kailua-Kona. Reservations c/o Hawaii Resort Management. www.konahawaii.com. ✆ **800/244-4752** or 808/329-3333. 37 units, all with shower only. Apr 15–Dec 15: $115, $125–$155 corner, $189 No. 302. Dec 16–Apr 14: $185, $160–$175 corner, $199 No. 302. Higher rates for stays less than 3 nights; weekly and monthly discounts available. Cleaning fee $85 for 3-night or longer stays. **Amenities:** Pool; Wi-Fi (free).

Inexpensive

Kona Tiki Hotel ★★ How close are you to the ocean here? Close enough that waves occasionally break on the seawall, sending sea spray into the oceanfront pool, and close enough that their constant crashing drowns out all or most of the traffic noise from nearby Ali'i Drive. The small, simply furnished rooms (no TV or phones) feature homey decor, such as pastel tropical print bedspreads. All come with oceanfront lanais, mini-fridges, and ceiling fans (you'll need them); upper-story units have kitchenettes so you can make light meals in addition to the basic continental breakfast (bagels, fruit, coffee) served by the pool. The warm, helpful staff members are quick to lend beach gear and give travel tips; they also make every sunset a special occasion, enlisting guests to help light the tiki torches and blow a conch shell. With no fees for parking, Wi-Fi, or cleaning, this is a true bargain.

75-5968 Ali'i Dr., Kailua-Kona (about a mile from downtown). www.konatikihotel.com. ✆ **808/329-1425.** 15 units. $89–$95 queen; $108–$115 queen with single bed; $119–$129 queen or king with single bed and kitchenette; $179 suite with king bed (2 adults max). Rates include continental breakfast. 3-night minimum (4 for suite). Extra person $15–$20 per adult ($18–$25 in high season, Dec 15–Mar 31 and Ironman week), $7 per child 6–11. Futon $6 per night, crib $6 for 3 nights. Deposit required; credit cards accepted for amounts over $350; PayPal for lesser amounts. **Amenities:** Pool; Wi-Fi (free).

NORTH KONA

The cool, rural uplands above central Kailua-Kona are home to two distinctive lodgings. Part of a 30-acre coffee farm in quaint Hōlualoa, owner Cassandra Hazen's gorgeous Balinese-themed **Holualoa Inn ★★★** (www.holualoainn.com; ✆ **800/392-1812** or 808/324-112) offers an oceanview pool, lush gardens, six immaculate suites ($365–$465) and a handsome cottage with a full kitchen ($525–$595); rates include a gourmet breakfast. At **Silver Oaks Guest Ranch ★** (www.silveroaksranch.com; ✆ **808/325-2000**), guests in two simply furnished cottages ($195

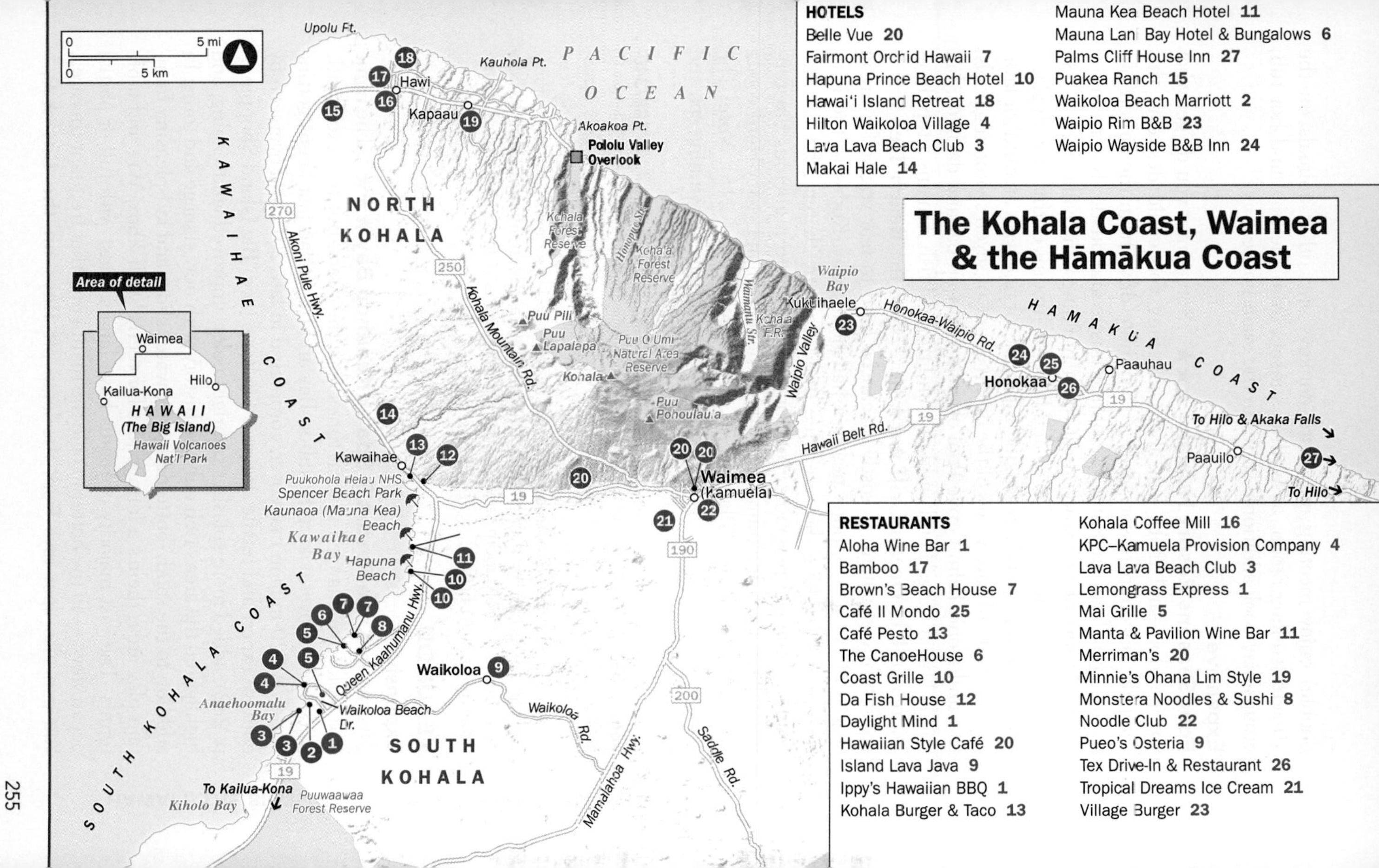

The Kohala Coast, Waimea & the Hāmākua Coast
HOTELS
Belle Vue 20
Fairmont Orchid Hawaii 7
Hapuna Prince Beach Hotel 10
Hawai'i Island Retreat 18
Hilton Waikoloa Village 4
Lava Lava Beach Club 3
Makai Hale 14
Mauna Kea Beach Hotel 11
Mauna Lani Bay Hotel & Bungalows 6
Palms Cliff House Inn 27
Puakea Ranch 15
Waikoloa Beach Marriott 2
Waipio Rim B&B 23
Waipio Wayside B&B Inn 24
RESTAURANTS
Aloha Wine Bar 1
Bamboo 17
Brown's Beach House 7
Café Il Mondo 25
Café Pesto 13
The CanoeHouse 6
Coast Grille 10
Da Fish House 12
Daylight Mind 1
Hawaiian Style Café 20
Island Lava Java 9
Ippy's Hawaiian BBQ 1
Kohala Burger & Taco 13
Kohala Coffee Mill 16
KPC–Kamuela Provision Company 4
Lava Lava Beach Club 3
Lemongrass Express 1
Mai Grille 5
Manta & Pavilion Wine Bar 11
Merriman's 20
Minnie's Ohana Lim Style 19
Monstera Noodles & Sushi 8
Noodle Club 22
Pueo's Osteria 9
Tex Drive-In & Restaurant 26
Tropical Dreams Ice Cream 21
Village Burger 23
0 5 mi
0 5 km
PACIFIC OCEAN
Upolu Pt.
Kauhola Pt.
Akoakoa Pt.
Pololu Valley Overlook
Hawi
Kapaau
NORTH KOHALA
KAWAIHAE COAST
Akoni Pule Hwy.
Kohala Mountain Rd.
Kohala Forest Reserve
Honopue Str.
Kohala Forest Reserve
Puu Pili
Puu Lapalapa
Puu O Umi Natural Area Reserve
Kohala
Puu Pohoulaula
Waimanu Str.
Kohala F.R.
Waipio Valley
Waipio Bay
Kukuihaele
Honokaa-Waipio Rd.
HAMAKUA COAST
Honokaa
Paauhau
Paauilo
Hawaii Belt Rd.
To Hilo & Akaka Falls
To Hilo
Waimea (Kamuela)
Kawaihae
Puukohola Heiau NHS
Spencer Beach Park
Kaunaoa (Mauna Kea) Beach
Kawaihae Bay
Hapuna Beach
Queen Kaahumanu Hwy.
Waikoloa
Waikoloa Rd.
Waikoloa Beach Dr.
Anaehoomalu Bay
SOUTH KOHALA
SOUTH KOHALA COAST
Mamalahoa Hwy.
Saddle Rd.
To Kailua-Kona
Kiholo Bay
Puuwaawaa Forest Reserve
270
250
19
190
200
Area of detail
Waimea
Hilo
Kailua-Kona
HAWAII (The Big Island)
Hawaii Volcanoes Nat'l Park

double) enjoy meeting miniature donkeys and other animals on the 10-acre working ranch, as well as sunsets from the pool and hot tub; groups may book additional suites in the main house.

Expensive

Four Seasons Resort Hualalai ★★★ Sometimes you do get what you pay for—and that's just about anything you could desire at this serenely welcoming resort, only a 15-minute drive from the airport but worlds away from anything resembling hustle and bustle. Rooms in the small clusters of two-story guest-room buildings and villa start at 635 square feet, with private lanais and large bathrooms outfitted with glass-walled showers and deep soaking tubs; ask for one with an outdoor lava-rock shower. All have views of the ocean or one of seven swimming pools; the adults-only Palm Grove Pool offers a swim-up bar and daybeds, but snorkeling in Kings' Pond amid rays and tropical fish remains a top draw. Dinner at **'Ulu Ocean Grill ★★★** (p. 270) or the **Beach Tree ★★** is consistently excellent, if costly; it can be hard to tear yourself away in search of cheaper options nearly a half-hour away. Kudos to the Four Seasons for bucking the resort-fee trend, for not charging for its children's or cultural programs, and for committing to numerous environmental measures, including support for the Hawaiian Legacy Hardwoods' koa reforestation (see "Planting a Koa Legacy Tree," p. 215). ***Note:*** The 18-hole Jack Nicklaus signature golf course and award-winning spa and fitness center are open only to hotel guests and members.

72-100 Ka'ūpūlehu Dr., Kailua-Kona. www.fourseasons.com/hualalai. ✆ **888/340-5662** or 808/325-8000. 243 units. $745–$1,495 double; from $1,645 suite. Children 18 and under stay free in parent's room (maximum occupancy in guest rooms is 3 people; couples with more than 1 child must get a suite or 2 rooms). Self-parking free; valet parking $20 per day. **Amenities:** 5 restaurants and lounges; 2 bars; babysitting; complimentary children's program; concierge; cultural center; fitness center; 18-hole golf course, 7 pools; room service; spa; 8 tennis courts (4 lit for night play); watersports rentals; Wi-Fi (free).

KEAUHOU

Expensive

Sheraton Kona Resort & Spa at Keauhou Bay ★★★ The name and look have changed several times over the years, but this excellently priced resort overlooking Keauhou Bay and the ocean just keeps getting better. A $20-million makeover, completed in late 2012 and overseen by cultural expert and textile designer Sig Zane (see "Big Island Shopping," p. 282), added more splashes of bright color, improved landscaping, and highlighted the area's rich cultural history with new signage and tours. In addition to the sandy-bottomed pool, water slide, and kid-pleasing fountain play area, there's a lounge just for teens, with Xbox, Wii, and table tennis. The vast majority of rooms have lanais, most with full or partial ocean views—all the better to ogle the manta rays that frequent this area. You can also spot rays from the lanai off **Rays on the Bay ★★**, a vivacious restaurant/lounge with fire pits and tasty cocktails. ***Note:*** Check online for one of the frequent deals with prices at the "moderate" level, even with the $31 daily resort fee. Upgrade to the Club Level for access to the breakfast buffet and evening pupus and cocktails at the oceanview Kaiulu Club Lounge, opened in 2016.

78-128 'Ehukai St., Kailua-Kona. www.sheratonkona.com. ✆ **888/488-3535** or 808/930-4900. 509 units. $170–$432 double; from $399 two-room suite with king and sofa bed. Online packages available. Daily resort fee $31, includes self-parking (valet $7 additional per day), bottled water, local calls, Kona Trolley, yoga, cultural tours, Wi-Fi, and more. Extra person or rollaway $65. Children 18 and under stay free in adult's room using existing bedding. **Amenities:** 3 restaurants; cafe; 2 bars; babysitting; rental bikes; concierge; fitness center; weekly lū'au (p. 288); multilevel pool w/ water slide; room service; spa; 2 tennis courts, basketball court, and sand volleyball court; whirlpool; Wi-Fi (included in resort fee).

Moderate

Kona Seaspray ★ Pay close attention to the details when booking a unit here, across Ali'i Drive from bustling Kahalu'u Beach, because the eight, spacious two-bedroom/two-bathroom units in the three-story main building have varying bedding configurations, views, and decor. All offer ocean views (best from the top two floors), full kitchens, and washer/dryers, but some have been remodeled with granite counters in the kitchen and slate tiles on the lanai. Two one-bedroom units in the adjacent, two-story Seaspray building share laundry facilities. A pretty blue-tiled wall provides privacy for the ground-floor pool, with lounges and a hammock next to a covered grill and dining area.

78-6671 Ali'i Dr., Kailua-Kona. www.konaseaspray.com. ✆ **808/322-2403.** 10 units. Main building: $175–$205 1-bedroom for 2 (sleeps up to 4); $190–$215 2-bedroom for 4 (sleeps up to 6). Seaspray building: $175–$205 double (sleeps up to 4). 5% discount for weekly rentals, 10% discount May and Sept. Extra person $20. Cleaning fee $85 1-bedroom, $110 2-bedroom, plus $20 per 5th or more person. 3-night minimum. **Amenities:** Barbecue; pool; whirlpool spa; Wi-Fi (free).

SOUTH KONA

This rural region of steeply sloping hills, often dotted with coffee and macadamia nut farms, is home to many unassuming B&Bs that may appeal to budget travelers who don't mind being far from the beach.

At the higher end, in every sense, **Horizon Guest House ★★** (www.horizonguesthouse.com; ✆ **808/938-7822**) offers four suites ($250–$350) with private entrances and lanais on a 40-acre property, including a spacious pool and whirlpool spa, at 1,100 feet of elevation in Hōnaunau, 21 miles south of Kailua-Kona. Rates include a gourmet breakfast by host Clem Classen; children 13 and under are not allowed.

Inexpensive

Manago Hotel ★ You can't beat the bargain rates at this plantation-era hotel, opened in 1917 and now run by the third generation of the friendly Manago family. Although clean, the 22 original rooms with shared bathrooms ($38 double) should be considered just above camping; they're ultra-spartan and subject to highway noise; children younger than 18 are not allowed. The 42 newer rooms in the three-story wing at the rear also have rather bare walls, but they come with private bathrooms and views of the coast that improve with each floor. Book the third-floor corner Japanese room for a *ryokan* experience, sleeping on a futon and soaking in the *ofuro* (hot tub). ***Note:*** There's no elevator. Walls are thin, and sound can carry through jalousie windows used to let cooling breezes in, but neighbors tend to be considerate. The lounge next to the **Manago Hotel Restaurant ★★** (p. 273) has a TV.

82-6151 Māmalahoa Hwy., Captain Cook (Hwy. 11, *makai* side, between mile markers 109 and 110, 12 miles south of Kailua-Kona). www.managohotel.com. ✆ **808/323-2642.** 64 units. $41 double with shared bathroom; $67–$72 double with private bathroom; $86 double Japanese room with private bathroom. Extra person $3. 4-person maximum. **Amenities:** Restaurant; bar; Wi-Fi (free).

The Kohala Coast

SOUTH KOHALA

There's no way around it: The three resort areas here are very costly, but the beaches, weather, amenities, and services at their hotels are among the best in the state. Although you'll miss out on fabulous pools and other hotel perks, you can shave costs (and save money on dining) by booking a vacation rental. **South Kohala Management** boasts the most listings (100-plus) of condos and homes in the Mauna Lani, Mauna Kea, and Waikoloa Beach resorts (www.southkohala.com; ✆ **800/822-4252**). **Outrigger Hotels & Resorts** also manages well-maintained condos and townhomes in five complexes in the Mauna Lani and Waikoloa Beach resorts (www.outrigger.com; ✆ **866/956-4262**).

Right on the sand at ʻAnaehoʻomalu Bay, the lively **Lava Lava Beach Club** restaurant and bar (www.lavalavabeachclub.com/bigisland; ✆ **808/769-5282**) also offers four luxurious **beach cottages ★★** ($500–$675), with kitchenettes and king beds; just keep in mind the nearby bar is open until 10pm nightly, with live music until 9pm.

Expensive

Fairmont Orchid Hawaii ★★★ The two guest wings at this polished but inviting sanctuary are set off the main lobby like two arms ready to embrace the well-manicured grounds and rugged shoreline; you may feel like hugging it, too, when you have to leave. Tucked among burbling waterfalls and lush greenery are 10 thatched-roof huts in the **Spa Without Walls,** which has another five oceanfront cabanas. Beyond the 10,000-square-foot swimming pool lies a cove of soft sand, where the Hui Holokai Beach Ambassadors make guests feel at home in the water and on shore, teaching all kinds of Hawaiiana and sharing their knowledge about the area's cultural treasures, such as the nearby Puakō Petroglyph Archaeological Preserve (p. 189). The elegant, generously proportioned rooms (starting at 510 sq. ft.) with lanais were completely renovated in 2013—the largest redo since the hotel opened in 1990—adding subtle island accents such as rattan and carved wood to marble bathrooms and other luxurious fittings. Golf, tennis, and dining are also exceptional here, as befits the prices.

At the Mauna Lani Resort, 1 N. Kanikū Dr., Waimea. www.fairmont.com/orchid-hawaii. ✆ **800/845-9905** or 808/885-2000. 540 units. $263–$899 double; $529–$879 Gold Floor double; from $699 suite. Check for online packages. Extra person $75. Children 17 and under stay free in parent's room. Daily resort fee $30, includes self-parking and Wi-Fi. Valet parking $22. **Amenities:** 6 restaurants; 3 bars; babysitting; bike rentals; year-round children's program; concierge; concierge-level rooms; 2 championship golf courses; fitness center; lū'au (p. 258); pool; room service; spa; theater; 10 tennis courts (7 lit for night play); watersports rentals; Wi-Fi (included in resort fee).

Hapuna Beach Prince Hotel ★★★ Now that an evening shuttle links this larger, more low-key hotel to its sister property, the Mauna Kea Beach Hotel, this hidden gem may not be a secret for long. It's never really been hidden, hovering as it does above the wide sands of **Hāpuna Beach ★★★**. Cognoscenti relish the fact that rooms start at 600 square feet (the largest standard rooms on the Kohala Coast), all with balconies and an ocean view. Substantial upgrades in 2013 also brought touches of Hawaiiana in subdued colors and improved the deck around the long, large pool, great for lap swimming; a complete room overhaul is said to be in the works. The sprawling, terraced grounds host an 18-hole championship golf course (p. 241) and several open-air restaurants, among them the wonderful **Coast Grille ★★★** (p. 274) and a small cafe with affordable (for this area) takeout fare. The 8,000-square-feet Hapuna Villa, a four-bedroom residence with butler service and pool, is a truly hidden gem, albeit one that starts at a princely $7,000 a night. ***Tip:*** Rates dip sharply in the off season.

At the Mauna Kea Resort, 62-100 Kauna'oa Dr., Waimea. www.princeresortshawaii.com. ✆ **800/882-6060** or 808/880-1111. 351 units. $275–$475 double; from $699 suite. Extra person $60. Children 17 and under stay free in parent's room using existing bedding. Daily resort fee $30, includes self-parking and Wi-Fi. Valet parking $20. **Amenities:** 3 restaurants; 2 bars; babysitting; cafe/gift shop; seasonal children's program; concierge; 18-hole championship golf course (p. 241); fitness center; pool; room service; spa; access to Mauna Kea Beach Hotel tennis center; watersports rentals; Wi-Fi (included in resort fee).

Hilton Waikoloa Village ★★ It's up to you how to navigate this 62-acre oceanfront Disneyesque golf resort, laced with fantasy pools, lagoons, and a profusion of tropical plants in between three low-rise towers. If you're in a hurry, take the Swiss-made air-conditioned tram; for a more leisurely ride, handsome mahogany boats ply canals filled with tropical fish. Or just walk a half-mile or so through galleries of Asian and Pacific art on your way to the ample-sized rooms designed for families. Among the best are the 161 rooms and eight suites in the Lagoon Tower's

Makai section—all ocean view, with upgraded bathrooms (including dual vanities), roomier closets, and high-end bedding, with a sophisticated palette evoking lava and sand. The 395 renovated Hale ʻIke rooms in the Palace Tower, which offer digital check-in, debuted in late 2015. Kids will want to head straight to the 175-foot water slide and 1-acre pool, and will pester you to pony up for the DolphinQuest encounter with Pacific bottlenose dolphins. The actual beach is skimpy, hence an enormous swimming and watersports lagoon that's home to green sea turtles and other marine life. You won't want for places to eat here either, although much more affordable options await at the two nearby shopping centers and Allen Hess's Mai Grille.

69-425 Waikoloa Beach Dr., Waikoloa. www.hiltonwaikoloavillage.com. ✆ **800/445-8667** or 808/886-1234. 1,241 units. $219–$409 double (Hale ʻIke, from $269; Makai, from $279); from $619 suite with king and sofa bed. Daily resort fee $30, includes Wi-Fi, local/toll-free calls, cultural lessons, in-room PlayStation3 with unlimited movies and games, and more. Extra person $50. Children 18 and under stay free in parent's room. Self-parking $25; valet parking $30. **Amenities:** 9 restaurants; 5 bars; babysitting; bike rentals; children's program; concierge; concierge; fitness center; 2 18-hole golf courses; lūʻau (p. 288); 3 pools (1 adults-only); room service; spa; 6 tennis courts; watersports rentals; Wi-Fi (included in resort fee).

Mauna Kea Beach Hotel ★★★ Old-money travelers have long embraced this golf-course resort, which began as a twinkle in Laurance Rockefeller's eye and in 1965 became the first hotel development on the rugged lava fields of the Kohala Coast. The 2006 earthquake provided the literal shakeup behind $150 million in renovations that reduced the number of rooms but expanded their size, creating spacious, modern bathrooms and closets. Further renovations in 2013 brightened the family-size rooms and suites in the Beachfront Wing, now with picture windows above the soaking tubs. Dining, particularly at **Manta ★★★** (p. 274) and the **Copper Bar ★★★** (p. 288), is top-notch, with glorious views from both the golf course (p. 241) and tennis center (p. 249). The pool is small by today's standards, but sandy **Kaunaʻoa Beach ★★★** (p. 221), where manta rays skim the north point, is just a few steps away. The true pearls are the gracious staff members, many of whom know several generations of guests by name. ***Note:*** The hotel is now part of Marriott's Autograph Collection, although management hasn't changed.

At the Mauna Kea Resort, 62-100 Mauna Kea Beach Dr., Waimea. www.princeresorts hawaii.com. ✆ **866/977-4589** or 808/882-7222. 252 units. $339–$1,150 double; from $1,000 suite. Extra person $75. 3-adult maximum. Valet parking $20; self-parking $15. **Amenities:** 4 restaurants; 3 bars; cafe; babysitting; seasonal children's program; concierge; 18-hole championship golf course (p. 241); fitness center; pool; hot tub; room service; 11 tennis courts; watersports rentals; Wi-Fi ($15 per day).

Mauna Lani Bay Hotel & Bungalows ★★ After a $30-million renovation that wrapped up in late 2013, the posh guest rooms gleam with understated elegance, outfitted in mahogany cabinets, stone-tiled bathrooms, and ceiling fans behind the signature plantation shutters, also refinished. All have private lanais, some with ocean views looking over the ancient fishponds and historic cottage where the popular "Twilight at Kalahuipua'a" monthly storytelling (p. 287)—one of many free cultural programs—takes place. Book carefully, though—some garden-view rooms hover just above the busy porte-cochère. Koi ponds and evening entertainment add life to the somewhat skeletal lobby. Although the opulent two-bedroom bungalows (2,700 sq. ft.) have also been updated, it's less costly to splurge on dining at the **CanoeHouse** ★ (p. 274) or on a treatment at the spa, with an outdoor lava rock sauna. The two beach areas are small but popular with green sea turtles, some that had even been raised by the hotel and released at the annual July 4th celebration.

At the Mauna Lani Resort, 68-1400 Mauna Lani Dr., Puakō. www.maunalani.com. ✆ **800/367-2323** or 808/885-6622. 341 units. $339–$939 double; from $1,089 suite; $4,000–$5,000 bungalow (sleeps up to 6). Extra person $75. Daily resort fee $25, includes valet or self-parking, Wi-Fi, local calls, beach cabana, and more. **Amenities:** 3 restaurants; lounge; babysitting; free bike rentals; concierge; children's program; 2 18-hole golf courses; multi-room fitness center with 25-meter lap pool; oceanfront pool; hot tub; room service; spa; access to 10 tennis courts at the Fairmont Orchid Hawaii; watersports rentals; Wi-Fi (free).

Waikoloa Beach Marriott Resort & Spa ★★ Of all the lodgings in the Waikoloa Beach Resort, this hotel has the best location on **'Anaeho'omalu Bay** ★★ (nicknamed "A-Bay"; p. 220), with many rooms offering views of the crescent beach and historic fishponds; others look across the parking lot and gardens toward Mauna Kea. Besides all kinds of beach watersports, kids enjoy the sandy-entrance children's pool, while adults delight in the heated infinity-edge pool, the two-level **Mandara Spa,** and the spacious, well-equipped fitness center. The light-hued rooms are also enticing, with glass-walled balconies and plush beds with down comforters in crisp white duvets. Families should book one of the spacious corner rooms, which include a king-size bed and a sofa bed; despite the resort fee ($30 daily), this hotel typically offers the best prices of the Kohala Coast resorts, with access to nearby golf courses.

69-275 Waikoloa Beach Dr., Waikoloa. www.marriotthawaii.com. ✆ **888/236-2427** or 808/886-6789. 555 units. $219–$547 double; from $720 suite. Check for online packages. Daily $30 resort fee includes self-parking (valet parking $3 more), local and mainland U.S./Canada calls, cultural activities, Wi-Fi, and more. Extra person $45. Children 17 and under stay free in parent's room. Valet parking $21. **Amenities:** Restaurant; bar; babysitting; cafe; concierge; cultural activities; fitness center; Jacuzzi; lū'au; 3 pools; rental-car desk; room service; spa; watersports rentals; Wi-Fi free in public areas, $15 a day in room ($19 for enhanced high speed).

NORTH KOHALA

This rural area, steeped in Hawaiian history and legend, has few overnight visitors, given its distance from swimmable beaches and other attractions. But it does include two luxurious accommodations that reflect its heritage in unique ways. At eco-friendly **Puakea Ranch** ★★

(www.puakearanch.com; ✆ **808/315-0805**), west of Hawi and 400 feet above the coast, three plantation-era bungalows and a former cowboy bunkhouse have been beautifully restored as vacation rentals ($289–$899; 3- to 7-night minimum, $200 cleaning fee). Sizes vary, as do amenities such as soaking tubs and swimming pools, but all have access to the organic farm produce and eggs, plus fast Wi-Fi. On the ocean bluff between Hawi and Kapa'au, hidden from the road, the "eco-boutique" **Hawai'i Island Retreat** ★★ (www.hawaiiislandretreat.com; ✆ **808/889-6336**) offers 13 posh guest rooms with large bathrooms and balconies ($425–$500 double, 2-night minimum). Clustered near the spa and saltwater infinity pool are seven yurts (large tent-like structures) with private bathrooms and shared indoor/outdoor showers ($195 double). Rates include a sumptuous, homegrown organic breakfast.

For a more economical stay, consider **Makai Hale** ★★, a bed-and-breakfast in windy, higher-elevation Kohala Ranch, with panoramic ocean and Maui views. It has one guest suite with queen bed, kitchenette, and bath ($155–$175) and the option of an additional queen bedroom with private bath ($85), both with access to the private pool and whirlpool spa (www.makaihale.com; ✆ **808/880-1012**).

The cowboy town of Waimea offers a few very basic motels (not recommended) and a few more comfortable options, all within a 15-minute drive or less of Hāpuna Beach. Close to the center of town, the two-story, two-unit **Belle Vue** ★ (www.hawaii-bellevue.com; ✆ **800/772-5044** or 808/885-7732) vacation rental has a penthouse apartment with high ceilings and views from the mountains to the distant sea, and a downstairs studio ($95–$175 double). Both sleep four and have private entrances and kitchenettes with breakfast fixings. ***Note:*** Check VRBO.com and airbnb.com for even more listings, such as the well-equipped, roomy **Banana Hale** ★★ studio ($95), with bananas growing just outside your window; it's off Hwy. 19, a few miles west of Waimea (www.airbnb.com/rooms/6392442).

The Hāmākua Coast

This emerald-green, virtually empty coast is a far drive from resort-worthy beaches and Hawai'i Volcanoes National Park and so is less frequented by overnight visitors (other than coqui frogs). Those who do choose to spend a night or more, though, will appreciate getting away from it all. Two miles north of Honoka'a off Hwy. 240, the **Waipio Wayside Inn Bed & Breakfast** ★★ (www.waipiowayside.com; ✆ **800/833-8849** or 808/775-0275) perches on a sunny ocean bluff. A restored former plantation supervisor's residence, the inn has five antiques-decorated rooms with modern bathrooms ($125–$200 double) and a handsome living/dining room, where owner Jacqueline Horne serves hot organic breakfasts promptly at 8am.

At the northern end of Hwy. 240, you'll find an amazing vista of Waipi'o Valley and privacy at **Waipio Rim B&B ★★★** (www.waipiorim.com; ✆ **808/775-1727**). There's only one unit: a second-floor, detached studio ($220) with flatscreen TV, kitchenette, and Wi-Fi for when you tire of the panorama. The hot breakfast even comes to you, at 8am; enjoy it on the oceanview deck.

Closer to Hilo, in rustic Honomū, the sprawling, Victorian-inspired **Palms Cliff House Inn ★★** (www.palmscliffhouse.com; ✆ **866/963-6076** or 808/963-6076) serves a full breakfast on its lanai overlooking. Pohakumanu Bay. Some of its eight large suites ($199–$449) come with air-conditioning and jetted tubs; all have an ocean view.

Note: You'll find these accommodations on "The Kohala Coast, Waimea & the Hāmākua Coast" map on p. 255.

Hilo

Although several hotels line scenic Banyan Drive, most fall short of visitors' expectations, with the exception of the **Grand Naniloa Hotel Hilo ★★**, described below. You'll find more character in lodgings elsewhere in and around Hilo, but be aware you may hear coqui frogs throughout the night.

Jack London and Queen Lili'uokalani are said to have stayed at the gracious Victorian mansion on Reed's Island now known as **Shipman House Bed & Breakfast Inn ★★** (www.hilo-hawaii.com; ✆ **800/627-8447** or 808/934-8025). The restored inn includes five rooms ($219–$249) with modern conveniences such as mini-fridges and fans tucked among the heirlooms, and lavish continental breakfast on the lanai. The **Old Hawaiian Bed & Breakfast ★** (www.thebigislandvacation.com; ✆ **877/961-2816** or 808/961-2816) provides easy access to Waiānuenue (Rainbow Falls) from a quaint 1930s house with three rooms ($85–$125, with full breakfast); children under 12 not permitted.

On a hilltop 22-acre compound boasting its own waterfall swimming pool, the **Inn at Kulaniapia Falls ★★** (www.waterfall.net; ✆ **808/935-6789**) offers a choice of 10 Asian- or Hawaiian-themed rooms ($189–$269, with full breakfast) or the Pagoda Cottage ($289, with kitchen stocked with breakfast supplies). Kayaks, paddleboards, yoga, and light lunches are also available.

Note: The lodgings in this section are on the "Hilo" map on p. 201.

INEXPENSIVE

Grand Naniloa Hotel Hilo—A DoubleTree by Hilton ★★ The bright spot on somewhat rundown Banyan Drive is this 12-story oceanfront hotel (formerly the Hilo Naniloa Hotel), next to the 9-hole **Naniloa Golf Course** (p. 243) with wonderful views of Hilo Bay. The refurbished rooms (312–330 sq. ft.) have new marble bathrooms and floors, 32-inch flatscreen TVs, and triple-sheet white bedding. Families should consider the oceanfront suite (660 sq. ft.; $238–$269), with two king beds, kitchenette, and living area. The pool can be a bit chilly, but it also overlooks the sparkling bay. ***Note:*** Rates and amenities below may change under the new Hilton management.

93 Banyan Dr., Hilo. http://doubletree3.hilton.com/en/hotels/hawaii/grand-naniloa-hotel-hilo-a-doubletree-by-hilton-ITOHNDT/index.html. ✆ **808/969-3333.** 407 units. $129–$189 double; from $269 suite w/2 kings. Most rates include free round of golf daily. **Amenities:** 9-hole golf course (free); pool; Wi-Fi in lobby (free).

Puna

An unusual collection of more than 350 species of palm trees—some 5,000 trees in all—shelter the four luxurious yet off-the-grid Balinese-style bamboo cottages ($255–$338) of **Kīpuka ★★** in Kapoho, all of which sleep two to six, and all have access to a saline pool (http://kipuka.co; ✆ **808/339-3027**). Yoga and nature lovers should investigate the variety of rustic lodgings ($95–$245) and classes at the bohemian, gay-friendly **Kalani Oceanside Retreat ★** on Highway 137 about halfway between Kapoho and Kalapana (www.kalani.com; ✆ **800/800-6886;** 808/965-7828). Be prepared for the evening symphony of coqui frogs.

In **Volcano Village,** the frogs don't like the misty, cool nights as much—the village is at 3,700 feet—but ask about heating when booking a rental. Joey Gutierrez of **Hawaii Volcano Vacations** (www.hawaiivolcanovacations.com; ✆ **800/709-0907** or 808/967-7178) manages a great selection of cottages, cabins, and houses ranging from $99 to $199 a night. **Mahinui Na Lani ★★★** (www.mahinui.com; ✆ **510/965-7367;** $235) is a romantic, eco-friendly hideaway; the whimsical two-level treehouse studio offers a kitchenette and cedar hot tub for two, with a ship's ladder leading to a cozy sleeping loft.

Note: You'll find Mahinui Na Lani and the following accommodations on the "Hotels & Restaurants in the Volcano Area" map.

VOLCANO VILLAGE

Expensive

Volcano Village Lodge ★★★ Built as an artists' retreat in 2004, the five romantic cottages in this leafy, 2-acre oasis offer gleaming hardwood floors and paneled walls, vaulted ceilings, fireplaces, kitchenettes, and endless walls of windows—the lush rainforest envelops the oh-so-peaceful lodge in privacy. Fixings for a full breakfast are left in your room each night. Enjoy the communal hot tub in the gardens after a day of hiking in the national park. For true sumptuousness or extra guests, book the two-room Mauna Loa cottage ($375), which includes a "meditation" loft under the eaves. ***Note:*** Families should also consider the lodge's **5th Street Ohana** (www.5thstohana.com; ✆ **808/985-9500**). On the other side of Hwy. 11, this modern vacation rental offers a two-bedroom suite ($225) plus studio ($175), both with full kitchens, which can be combined as one unit ($375).

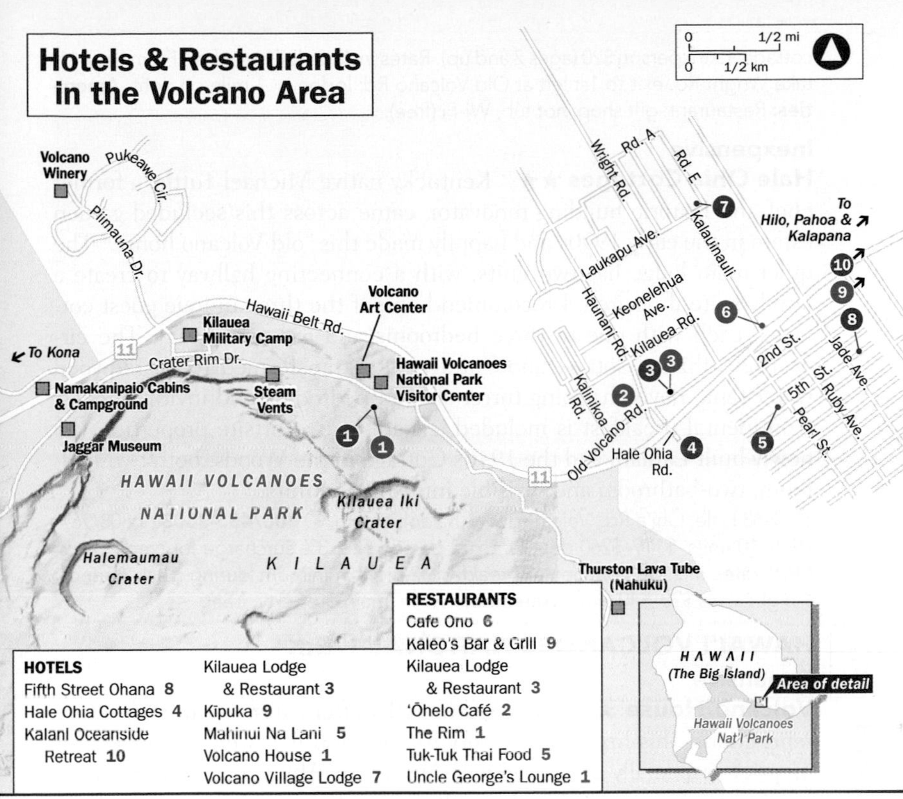

19-4183 Road E, Volcano. www.volcanovillagelodge.com. ✆ **808/985-9500.** 5 units. $280–$375 double (up to 4 guests). Rates include full breakfast. From Hwy. 11, take Wright Rd. exit, and head .8 mile north to right on Laukapu St.; it ends at Road E. Turn left; lodge is first driveway on the left. **Amenities:** Hot tub; DVD library; Wi-Fi (free).

Moderate

Kilauea Lodge ★★ This former YMCA camp, built in 1938, has served as a gracious inn since 1986. The 10-acre main campus has 12 units in two wings and two cottages; most have gas fireplaces, along with European-Hawaiian decor and thoughtful touches such as heated towel racks. Another four cottages lie within a walk or short drive of the lodge; my favorites are the two-bedroom, two-bathroom Pi'i Mauna, overlooking the Volcano Golf Course, and the two-bedroom, one-bathroom Ola'a Plantation House, an elegantly restored 1935 home with a huge kitchen, breakfast room, and living room. All rates include gourmet breakfast in the superb **Kilauea Lodge Restaurant ★★★** (p. 280). ***Note:*** The lodge and restaurant were both for sale at press time.

19-3948 Old Volcano Rd., Volcano. www.kilauealodge.com. ✆ **808/967-7366.** 12 units on main property, 4 cottages nearby. $195–$215 double room; $230–$300 cottage. Extra person $20 (ages 2 and up). Rates include full breakfast. From Hwy. 11, take Wright Rd. exit to 1st left at Old Volcano Rd; lodge is .1 mile on right. **Amenities:** Restaurant; gift shop; hot tub; Wi-Fi (free).

Inexpensive

Hale Ohia Cottages ★★ Kentucky native Michael Tuttle, a former chef and historic building renovator, came across this secluded garden estate in the early 1990s and happily made this "old Volcano home." The quiet main lodge has two units, with a connecting hallway to create a family suite if desired. I recommend one of the three unique guest cottages, each with one to three bedrooms and greater privacy. The circa-1920s Ihilani Cottage and Cottage 44, a transformed 1930s redwood water tank, have charming turret-shaped bedrooms and inviting nooks. Continental breakfast is included, except at two offsite properties: the newly built Laulani and the 1940s Cottage in the Woods, both two-bedroom, two-bathroom and divisible into smaller units.

11-3968 Hale 'Ōhi'a Rd., Volcano. www.haleohia.com. ✆ **800/455-3803** or 808/967-7986. 10 units. $119–$260 double. Extra person $20. 3% surcharge for credit cards. Most rates include continental breakfast. 2-night minimum during peak periods; 1-night stays $20–$40 extra. **Amenities:** Wi-Fi (main property; free).

HAWAI'I VOLCANOES NATIONAL PARK

Expensive

Volcano House ★ Reopened in 2013 after extensive infrastructure renovations, this historic two-story wooden inn is extremely modest for its price, especially compared with Yosemite's Ahwahnee and the grand lodges of other national parks. Still, its location on the very rim of the Kīlauea Caldera is nothing short of spectacular—to wake up to that view is very special indeed. Rooms are on the small and plain side and the vintage bathrooms downright tiny, so explore your surroundings during the day and then enjoy dinner and drinks at **The Rim ★★** (p. 281) or **Uncle George's Lounge** downstairs, before falling into the comfy beds. Now that the crater-view rooms have risen to $335 to $385, this is a real splurge. The hotel also manages 10 cabins and 16 campsites in the park; see "Camping," below.

1 Crater Rim Dr., Hawai'i Volcanoes National Park. www.hawaiivolcanohouse.com. ✆ **866/536-7972** or 808/756-9625. 33 units. $285–$385 double. Extra person $30. 1-time $15 park entrance fee. Check for online packages. **Amenities:** Restaurant; bar; bicycles; gift shops; Wi-Fi (free).

Ka'ū

As with the Hāmākua Coast, few visitors overnight in this virtually undeveloped area, halfway between Kailua-Kona and Hawai'i Volcanoes National Park, but there is one lodging that encourages guests to linger. In a tranquil setting above the road to Ka Lae (South Point), luxurious **Kalaekilohana ★★** (www.kau-hawaii.com; ✆ **808/939-8052**) has four large guest suites ($349) in a modern plantation-style home. After one night in a plush bed, with a beautifully presented breakfast on the lanai, and true Hawaiian hospitality from hosts Kenny Joyce and Kilohano Domingo, many guests kick themselves for not having booked a second night or more—and multi-night discounts start at $40 off a 2-night stay. Kenny's delicious dinners ($25–$45 per person) are a nightly option.

Camping

Camping is available at **10 county beach parks, six state parks and reserves,** a few **private campgrounds,** and **Hawai'i Volcanoes National Park.** I don't recommend the county parks, because of noise at popular sites (such as **Spencer Park,** p. 222) and security concerns at more remote ones (such as **Punalu'u Beach,** p. 224). All county campsites require advance-purchase permits, which cost $20 a night per person for nonresidents (http://hawaiicounty.ehawaii.gov; © **808/961-8311**).

State campsites also require permits that must be booked in advance (http://camping.ehawaii.gov; © **808/961-9540**). The most desirable are at **Hāpuna Beach** (p. 221), which offers six A-frame screened shelters with wooden sleeping platforms and a picnic table, plus communal restrooms and cold showers. Nonresidents pay $50 per shelter per night for permits; purchase at least a week in advance. Friday through Sunday nights, **Kīholo State Park Reserve** (p. 216) allows tent camping in a kiawe grove on a pebbly beach, with portable toilets but no water; nonresidents pay $18 per campsite per night. For hard-core backpackers, camping in the state preserve of remote **Waimanu Valley** is typically the reward for tackling the extremely arduous Muliwai Trail (p. 245). Permits for nonresident campers cost $20 per site (for up to six people); it was closed indefinitely in early 2016 due to concerns over dengue fever.

At South Kona's **Ho'okena Beach Park** (p. 220), which reopened in March 2016 after a dengue-fever scare closed it for several months, the private campground with local security is perfect for pitching a tent by the waves. Campsites cost $21 per person per night for ages 7 and older; reservations are not required, though recommended (www.hookena.org; © **808/328-7321**). You can also rent tents, camping stoves, tables, and chairs for use on site.

In **Hawai'i Volcanoes National Park** (p. 207), the only campground accessible by car is **Nāmakanipaio ★★,** which has 10 cabins and 16 campsites managed by **Volcano House** (www.hawaiivolcanohouse.com, © **866/536-7972** or 808/441-7750). The one-room cabins sleep four apiece, with bed linens and towels provided, grills, and a community restroom with hot showers; the cost is $80 a night. Tent campers have restrooms but not showers; sites cost $15 a night, on a first-come, first-served basis, with a 7-night maximum stay. Call the hotel in advance to rent a tent set up for you with a comfy foam mattress, linens, cooler, lantern, and two chairs for $55 a night. ***Note:*** Cabins and campground were undergoing renovations at press time, so prices may change once they reopen.

Backpack camping is allowed at seven remote areas in the park, some with shelters and cabins, but first you must register for a free permit at the **Backcountry Office** (www.nps.gov/havo; © **808/985-6178**), no more than 1 day in advance.

Note: No island merchants rent camping gear, but you can buy some at the **Hilo Surplus Store,** 148 Mamo St., Hilo (www.hilosurplusstore.com; © **808/935-6398**), or at a big-box store such as **Kmart,** 74-5456 Kamaka 'Eha Ave., Kailua-Kona (© **808/326-2331**).

Island RV & Safari Activities (www.islandrv.com; © **800/406-4555** or 808/960-1260) offers weekly rentals of a 22-foot, class-C motor home, which sleeps up to four, for $2,400. Included are airport transfers, linens, barbecue grill, a last night in a hotel, and help with itinerary planning; you must book county campsite permits in advance. ***Note:*** RV camping is not allowed in state or national parks in Hawai'i.

WHERE TO EAT ON THE BIG ISLAND

Thanks to its deep waters, green pastures, and fertile fields, the Big Island provides local chefs with a cornucopia of fresh ingredients. The challenge for visitors is finding restaurants to match their budgets. Don't be afraid to nosh at a roadside stand or create a meal from a farmer's market (see "Big Island Shopping," p. 282), as locals do, but indulge at least once on an oceanfront sunset dinner for the best of all the Big Island has to offer.

The Kona Coast

CENTRAL KAILUA-KONA

With few exceptions, this is a no-man's-land for memorable, sensibly priced dining; chains abound, and service is often slow. One bright spot: **Honu's on the Beach ★★** (daily 6–10:30am and 5:30–10pm), the indoor/outdoor restaurant at the Courtyard King Kamehameha Kona Beach Hotel (p. 252). Fresh sushi Sunday to Thursday nights attracts both locals and visitors; chef Roy Basilio's well-prepared farm-to-table Hawai'i Regional Cuisine is available nightly (main courses $15–$28), with a prime rib/seafood buffet ($45) Friday and Saturday nights.

In a less scenic setting, duck into **Lemongrass Bistro ★**, 75-5742 Kuakini Hwy. (*makai* side, at Hualālai Rd), for fragrant curry and noodle dishes ($13–$25). It's open daily for lunch ($10 specials) and dinner, as late as 10:30pm weekdays (www.lemongrassbistrokona.com; © **808/331-2708**). Big appetites should head to the **Big Island Grill ★**, 75-5702 Kuakini Hwy. (*makai* side, south of Henry St.), for local and American classics ($5–$17 breakfast, $8–$20 lunch, $9–$24 dinner) in a strip mall, with parking. It's open daily 7am to 9pm except Sunday (www.facebook.com/BigIslandGrill; ✆ **808/326-1153**). **Lotus Cafe ★**, near Costco 5 miles north of town at 73-5617 Maiau St., caters to gluten-free diners but will appeal to anyone seeking fresh, pan-Asian fare ($14–$20); it's open Monday through Saturday 10:30am to 9pm (www.thelotuscafe.com; ✆ **808/327-3270**).

Expensive

Daylight Mind ★★ HAWAI'I REGIONAL Bakery, coffee bar, restaurant, coffee roaster, community center—this two-story complex with vaulted wooden ceilings and a large, wraparound oceanfront lanai tries to be many things to many people, and mostly succeeds. Many of the ingredients are locally sourced, of course, including Kona, Ka'ū, and other Hawaiian coffees. The coffee bar also serves tropical kombucha (fermented tea), coffee cherry tisane, and other brews; check the bakery for fresh sourdough bread. In the restaurant, the eclectic brunch and dinner menu runs the gamut from trendily healthful (quinoa porridge with chia seed yogurt) to utterly rich (Keahole lobster BLT). ***Note:*** A second, smaller location opened in the Queens' MarketPlace in the Waikoloa Beach Resort in 2015; the food is tasty, but service seems slower here.

At rear of Waterfront Row, 75-5770 Ali'i Dr., Kailua-Kona. www.daylightmind.com. ✆ **808/339-7824.** Daily brunch 8am–3pm, bar 3–9pm, dinner 5–9pm. Also: 69-201 Waikoloa Beach Dr., Waikoloa. ✆ **808/339-7824.** Coffee bar 6am–9:30pm; restaurant 7am–9:30pm. Main courses $10–$19 brunch, $15–$36 dinner.

Huggo's ★★★ PACIFIC RIM/SEAFOOD The setting doesn't get any better in Kailua-Kona than this, a covered wooden deck overlooking tide pools and the sweep of Kailua Bay. But executive chef Alan Heap adds literal sizzle with crackling-hot dishes, such as brussels sprouts and cauliflower with kimchi puree and bacon; Kona Kai shrimp with butter, garlic, and herbs; and Hāmākua mushrooms in Asian spices. The seared sesame ahi and chips with avocado fries is also a must. Huggo's new lounge, **hBar ★★★,** has its own chic vibe and inventive small-plates menu, as well as Kona's first truly artisan cocktail menu. Next door is the more casual and moderately priced **On the Rocks ★**; it's a pulsating nightclub after sunset. ***Note:*** **Java on the Rock** occupies the same space from 6 to 11am, with brisk (bordering on brusque) counter service for Kona coffee, bagels, papaya, and a few egg dishes ($12) on paper plates.

75-5828 Kahakai Rd., Kailua-Kona. www.huggos.com. ✆ **808/329-1493.** Reservations recommended. Main courses $30–$41. Sun–Thurs 5–9pm, Fri–Sat 5–10pm. hBar: Mon–Thurs 4–10pm, Fri–Sat 4–midnight, Sun 5–10pm. Appetizers $12–$17. On the Rocks: Main courses $13–$20. Mon–Thurs 11:30am–11pm, Fri–Sat 11:30am–midnight, happy hour 3–5pm. Java on the Rock: www.javaontherock.com. ✆ **808/329-9262.** Main courses $8–$12. Daily 6–11am.

Moderate

Da Poke Shack ★★★ SEAFOOD Nestled in an out-of-sight corner of an unassuming stretch of vacation rental condos, with just a couple of picnic tables for seating, Da Poke Shack has nevertheless put itself on the culinary (and social media) map with a lineup of eight or so *poke*—diced raw seafood with different marinades and seasonings—that are so fresh you may spot fishermen delivering their latest catch. Go early for the best selection, since it often sells out; the spicy Pele's Kiss and creamy avocado versions are first-rate. Prices vary daily and are on the high side for lunch plates and bowls with quinoa, rice, or potato salad; although you can get kalua pork plates here ($10–$15), it's the seafood that's the star. A second location, convenient for those en route to Pu'uhonua O Hōnaunau, opened in Captain Cook in 2014.

At the Kona Bali Kai, 76-6246 Ali'i Dr., Kailua-Kona. www.dapokeshack.com. ✆ **808/329-7653.** Reservations not accepted. Market price, averaging $20 per pound, plates $22, bowls $14. Daily 10am–6pm. Also at 83–5308 Māmalahoa Hwy. (*mauka* side, at mile marker 106), Captain Cook. ✆ **808/328-8862.** Daily 11am–7pm.

Island Lava Java ★★ AMERICAN Residents of upcountry Waikoloa Village were thrilled when this perennial favorite opened a branch there in 2012, but there's no competing with the lively ambience and oceanview setting of the Kailua-Kona original. Founded in 1994, the former espresso bar blossomed into a full-service cafe for breakfast, lunch, and dinner, with most tables on a patio overlooking the breakers across the Ali'i Drive seawall. Pluses: The coffee is 100% Kona; breads, pastries, and desserts are made in house; and organic salads, sandwiches, and pizzas feature mostly local ingredients. Minuses: With the exception of the Big Island grass-fed beef burger ($15) or pizzas to share ($18–$24), dinner plates are expensive, and service can be leisurely; order online for takeout. Enjoy the people- and surf-watching while you wait, and bring your own beer or wine—there's no corkage fee.

75-5799 Ali'i Dr., Kailua-Kona. www.islandlavajava.com. ✆ **808/327-2161.** Main courses $7–$18 breakfast; $10–$20 lunch; $15–$30 dinner. Daily breakfast 6:30am–11:30am, lunch 11:30am–5pm, dinner 5–9:30pm. Also in the Waikoloa Highlands Shopping Center, 68-1845 Waikoloa Rd., Waikoloa. ✆ **808/769-5202.** Same hours and prices as Kailua-Kona location.

NORTH KONA

'Ulu Ocean Grill & Sushi Lounge ★★★ ISLAND FARM/SEAFOOD With executive chef Massimo Falsini, formerly of Harry's Bar in Rome, at the helm, the Four Seasons' beachfront destination restaurant remains a superb showcase for the wares of 160 local fishermen and farmers. Refined yet approachable dishes include roasted pineapple mahi in a Thai chili black bean sauce and black pepper-crusted New York steak with kiawe-smoked potatoes. Jewel-like sashimi and artful sushi rolls can be ordered in the oceanview lounge (with fire pits) or the

TAPPING INTO kona brewing co.

Father and son Cameron Healy and Spoon Khalsa opened microbrewery and pub **Kona Brewing Co.** ★★ (www.konabrewingco.com; ✆ **808/334-2739**) in an obscure warehouse in Kailua-Kona in 1998; now they also run a restaurant at the Koko Marina on O'ahu and enjoy widespread Mainland distribution of their most popular brews, including Fire Rock Pale Ale and Longboard Lager. While they're building a new Kona facility, due to open in 2018, the original brewpub, 75-5629 Kuakini Hwy., still offers affordable lunch specials (pizzas, fish tacos), a palm-fringed patio, and short free tours daily at 10:30am and 3pm. It's open daily 11am to 10pm.

open-air dining room, behind roe-like curtains of glass balls. Browse the extensive wine list on an iPad, or simply ask the expert waitstaff for advice. On Saturday, sign up for the four-course, prix-fixe Farm-to-Table dinner with wine pairings ($150), limited to 40 guests, who meet with the chef de cuisine and dine on a private lanai. ***Note:*** The breakfast menu is also locally sourced but seems more exorbitant.

At the Four Seasons Resort Hualalai, 72-100 Ka'ūpūlehu Dr., Kailua-Kona (off Hwy. 19, 6 miles north of Kona airport). ✆ **808/325-8000.** www.uluoceangrill.com. Reservations recommended. Breakfast buffet $30–$44; dinner main courses $32–$55. Daily 6:30–11am (buffet 6:30–10:30am) and 5:30–9pm (sushi until 9:30pm).

KEAUHOU

High above Ali'i Drive, Keauhou Shopping Center has several more affordable options than Sam Choy's Kai Lanai (below) and **Kenichi** ★★ (www.kenichipacific.com; ✆ **808/322-6400**), a stylish but high-priced Asian fusion/sushi dinner spot, open daily 5 to 9:30pm. The best is **Peaberry & Galette** ★ (www.peaberryandgalette.com; ✆ **808/322-6020**), a small cafe with a wide selection of savory and sweet crepes ($9–$14), plus a few sandwiches, salads, and good, 100 percent Kona coffee; it's open 7am to 5pm Monday to Saturday, 8am to 5pm Sunday.

Ultra-casual **Akule Supply Co.** ★★ (www.akulesupply.com; ✆ 808/498-4987) may not be a culinary rival to any of the above, but it can claim the best setting: Keauhou Harbor, at the end of Kaleiopapa St. Open 8am to 8pm daily, it serves local favorites like fish and eggs ($10) and Spam musubi ($4) at breakfast; sandwiches and burgers ($10–$14) at lunch and dinner; and a 10-ounce steak ($25) and market-rate fish plates at dinner only (5–8pm). At sunset, relax by the bayfront fire pit until your order's ready.

Sam Choy's Kai Lanai ★ HAWAI'I REGIONAL The miles-long coastal views from this former Wendy's are spectacular—if only the service and food consistently measured up. When they're in top form, this aerie nominally run by renowned Honolulu chef Sam Choy is hard to beat. Lunch offers the most bargains, with local dishes such as loco moco (with veggie and smoked pork options in lieu of the burger over eggs, gravy, and rice), Portuguese bean soup, and beef stew omelet. For weekend breakfasts, the Samoan-style pani popo pancakes with *haupia* (coconut) sauce and macadamia nuts and French toast with a trio of taro, guava, and plain sweet bread are decidedly decadent. Appetizers and dinner courses veer into the expensive category, but the fried poke ($12) and seafood *laulau* (fish and seafood in steamed ti leaves, $28) merit the expense. Go early to nab a happy-hour seat by the fire pits or at the bar.

In Keauhou Shopping Center, 78-6831 Ali'i Dr., Kailua-Kona. ✆ **808/333-3434.** Reservations recommended for dinner. Lunch main courses $8–$14; dinner main courses $15–$36. Sun–Thurs 11am–9pm, Fri–Sat 11am–9:30pm; daily happy hour 3–5pm. Breakfast (main courses $6–$12) Sat–Sun 7–11am.

SOUTH KONA

For pastries, breakfast, lunch, elevated ocean views, and, of course, Kona coffee, consider two cafes on the *makai* side of Hwy. 11. **Kona Coffee Shack ★**, 83-5799 Māmalahoa Hwy. (between mile marker 108 and 109) in Captain Cook, serves egg dishes ($11–$15), plump sandwiches on fresh-baked bread ($12), and pizza ($14–$15); it's open daily 7:30am to 3pm (www.coffeeshack.com; ✆ **808/328-9555**). The more modern, Italian-themed **Caffe Florian ★** offers counter service for a light menu that includes panini ($10–$12); it's open 6:30am to 4pm weekdays, 7am to 2pm Saturday, and 8am to 1pm Sunday at 81-6637 Māmalahoa Hwy., Kealakekua (at Ke'e-Ke'e Rd.; www.caffefloriankona.com; ✆ **808/238-0861**). For fresh seafood to go, don't forget the southern outpost of Kailua-Kona's **Da Poke Shack ★★★** (see p. 270).

Expensive

Mi's Italian Bistro ★★★ ITALIAN Chef Morgan Starr, formerly at Four Seasons Resort Hualalai, is the "M" and wife Ingrid Chan is the "I" in Mi's, a small, dark-toned restaurant that opened in late 2007 in a drab shopping strip to rave reviews. There's no fabulous view here, only superbly executed, thoughtfully created Italian dishes using fresh ingredients from Starr's own garden, local beef, handmade pasta, and off-the-hook ahi. They've maintained their commitment to top-notch, well-priced cuisine (and wine list) while raising two children, often at their mother's side. Porcini-crusted pork tenderloin ($23) with gnocchi comes with a velvety Hāmākua mushroom sauce, while grilled rack of lamb in a Chianti demi-glaze ($35) is worth the splurge. Save some calories for dessert, such as Meyer lemon crème brûlée or white pineapple sorbet.

81-6372 Māmalahoa Hwy. (Hwy. 11, *makai* side), Kealakekua; park in lot next to Captain Cook Mini Market. www.misitalianbistro.com. ✆ **808/323-3880.** Main courses $14–$35. Daily 4:30–8:30pm.

Inexpensive

Manago Hotel Restaurant ★★ AMERICAN Like its clean but plain-spun hotel, the family-run dining room with Formica tabletops and vinyl-backed chairs has changed little over the years. Service is friendly and fairly swift, with family-style servings of rice, potato salad, and fresh vegetables accompanying the generous portions of their signature pork chops with gravy and grilled onions ($12), teriyaki chicken, and sautéed mahimahi, among other popular choices. Breakfast is a steal: papaya or juice, toast or rice, two eggs, breakfast meat, and coffee for $7.
At the Manago Hotel, 82-6151 Māmalahoa Hwy. (Hwy. 11), Captain Cook, between mile markers 109 and 110, *makai* side. www.managohotel.com/rest.html. ✆ **808/323-2642.** Reservations recommended for dinner. Breakfast $5–$6, lunch and dinner $7–$19. Tues–Sun 7–9am, 11am–2pm, and 5–7:30pm.

The Kohala Coast

Note: You'll find the following restaurants on the "Kohala Coast, Waimea & the Hāmākua Coast" map on p. 255.

SOUTH KOHALA

For convenient alternatives to pricey hotel dining, the Waikoloa Beach Resort has several hidden treasures. The Queens' MarketPlace food court includes **Lemongrass Express ★** (✆ **808/886-3400**), a compact version of Kailua-Kona's tasty **Lemongrass Bistro** (p. 268), with indoor-outdoor seating and seafood specials that rival those of resort chefs, and **Ippy's Hawaiian BBQ ★** (✆ **808/886-8600**), serving well-seasoned plate lunches with ribs, chicken, and fish, under the aegis of Food Network celebrity Philip "Ippy" Aiona. **Aloha Wine Bar ★,** on the west side of the mall's Island Gourmet Markets, has tasty burgers, pizzas, and sushi, as well as good wine specials; it's open 3 to 10pm daily (✆ **808/886-3500**).

Views of 'Anaeho'omalu Bay, especially at sunset, never fail to please at **Lava Lava Beach Club ★★**, which serves fresh American and island food from 11am to 9pm daily on the beach. At lunch, main courses run $15 to $26; at dinner, they're $19 to $37. Owned by the team behind **Huggo's** (p. 269), it's at the end of Ku'uali'i Place in the Waikoloa Beach Resort (www.lavalavabeachclub.com; ✆ **808/769-5282**).

Chef Allen Hess, formerly of CanoeHouse, features well-crafted, farm-to-table comfort food (that is, plenty of housemade bacon) at **Mai Grille ★★,** opened in late 2015. Overlooking the Kings' Golf Course, it's open for breakfast, lunch, and *pupu* from 7:30am to 6pm daily; dinner ($12–$29) is served Thursday to Saturday 6 to 9pm, with reservations a must (www.maigrille.com; ✆ **808/886-7600**).

The commercial port of Kawaihae also harbors several inexpensive, homespun eateries, including **Kohala Burger and Taco ★**, upstairs in the Kawaihae Shopping Center (www.kohalaburgerandtaco.com;

SORTING OUT THE resorts

There's no getting around sticker shock when dining at the South Kohala resort hotels, especially at breakfast and lunch. Dazzling sunsets help soften the blow at dinner, when chefs at least show more ambition. Here's a quick guide to help you distinguish among the top dinner-only hotel restaurants, all serving excellent (for the most part) yet costly variations on farm-to-table Hawai'i Regional Cuisine:

- **Mauna Lani: Brown's Beach House** ★★ at the **Fairmont Orchid Hawaii** (p. 258) offers attentive service at tables on a lawn just a stone's throw from the water; main courses are $35 to $54. At the **CanoeHouse** ★★ in the **Mauna Lani Bay Hotel** (p. 260), chef Allan Nagun personally presents each dish of his "Captain's Table" Blind Tasting Menu ($110; $160 with wine pairings), offered Thursday to Saturday by 24-hour reservation (✆ **808/881-7911;** main courses $36–$52).
- **Mauna Kea: Manta & Pavilion Wine Bar** ★★★ at the **Mauna Kea Beach Hotel** (p. 260) offers a sweeping ocean view, artful cuisine, and 48 high-end wines by the glass from the nifty Enomatic dispenser; main courses are $35 to $52. A bit more casual, **Coast Grille** ★★ at the **Hapuna Beach Prince Hotel** (p. 259) also provides an expansive view, plus good value; main courses cost $23 to $45, with moderately priced small plates, flatbreads, salads, and other dishes featuring herbs, fruits, and vegetables from the hotel garden by homegrown chef Moki Tavares.
- **Waikoloa Beach: KPC–Kamuela Provision Company** ★ at the **Hilton Waikoloa Village** (p. 259) has the oceanfront setting to rival other resorts' restaurants, although its culinary ambitions are not as high as its prices (main courses $42 to $82). Book an outdoor table for at least a half-hour before sunset.

✆ **808/880-1923**). Its burgers are made with local grass-fed beef, while buns and tortillas (used for fresh fish tacos, burritos, and quesadillas) are housemade. It opens daily at 11am; closing hours vary widely by season. The lunch wagon next to **Da Fish House** fish market (p. 286) has very fresh fish plates ($9–$12) though little seating; it's open weekdays 10:30am to 2:30pm and takes cash only.

Expensive

Monstera Noodles & Sushi ★★ JAPANESE Master sushi chef Norio Yamamoto left his namesake restaurant (still called Norio's) at the Fairmont Orchid Hawaii to open this bright, less formal dining room in the Shops at Mauna Lani. His "sizzling plates" menu includes New York strip steak in a choice of sauces, boneless fried chicken in spicy garlic-sesame sauce, and pork loin stir-fried with kimchi. But it would be a shame to skip seafood specialties like his volcano roll (a combination of spicy tuna and shrimp tempura with local avocado) or ultra-fresh, silken sashimi such as Hawaiian fatty tuna *(chu toro)*. In 2015, Yamamato and partner Wes Monty opened the downstairs **Blue Room Brasserie & Bar ★★**, a charming French/island-style bistro inspired by a room at 'Iolani Palace; it's open for lunch and dinner, notably with Belgian beers on tap, an oyster bar, excellent seafood entrees, and leafy patio seating.

Monstera: The Shops at Mauna Lani, 68-1330 Mauna Lani Dr., Waimea. www.monsterasushi.com. ✆ **808/887-2711.** Reservations recommended. Main courses $18–$30; sushi rolls $10–$22; sashimi $17–$20. Daily 5:30–9:30pm. Blue Room: http://theblueroomhi.com. ✆ **808/887-0999.** Lunch main courses $14–$39 (most under $20); dinner main courses, $18–$39. Daily 11:30am–10pm.

Moderate

Café Pesto ★★ PIZZA/PACIFIC RIM Locals may dart in and out for wood-fired pizzas to go, but there's something to be said for enjoying the capable service and cozy yet uncluttered atmosphere of the original Café Pesto, which opened in 1988, joined by a Hilo branch (p. 279) 4 years later. More local produce and proteins appear on the menu now, but otherwise the pizzas, meal-size salads, hearty pastas, and "creative island cuisine" (such as zesty wok-fired shrimp and scallops in a red coconut curry) continue to impress. The playful children's menu ($8) also brims with healthful but enticing choices, including kalua turkey over rice.

Lower level of Kawaihae Shopping Center, 61-3665 Akoni Pule Hwy. (Hwy. 270, *makai* side), Kawaihae. www.cafepesto.com. ✆ **808/882-1071.** Main courses $11–$17 lunch, $15–$37 dinner. Pizza $10–$21. Sun–Thurs 11am–9pm; Fri–Sat 11am–10pm. To park on the restaurant level, take Kawaihae Harbor spur from Hwy. 270; Cafe Pesto is on the right.

Pueo's Osteria ★★★ ITALIAN Upcountry residents and night owls rejoiced when this inviting bistro opened in Waikoloa Village Highlands Center in 2013, but its appeal goes far beyond its location (an 8-minute drive uphill of the Waikoloa Beach Resort) and late hours. Executive chef-owner James Babian, who lined up more than 150 local food purveyors for Four Seasons Hualalai during his tenure there, continues to work his connections for the freshest seafood, meat, and produce, while importing only the finest of everything else (including olive oil and well-priced wines) to create a delicious Italian menu. Bargain hunters will love the "early owl" specials ($8) and bar menu, which includes a Tuscan burger made with local beef, provolone, and bruschetta tomatoes, served with house-made fries for just $12, plus build-your-own wood-fired pizzas starting at $13. Babian has a tender touch with fresh pasta, such as potato gnocchi with Hāmākua mushrooms and prosciutto, but also adds zest to hearty dishes such as chicken Milanese and Ni'ihau lamb ossobuco. Reserve early.

In Waikoloa Village Highlands Center, 68-1845 Waikoloa Rd., Waikoloa. www.pueososteria.com. ✆ **808/339-7566.** Main courses $18–$39; pizza $17–$22; bar menu $7–$13. Reservations recommended. Dinner 5–9pm daily; bar Sun–Thurs 5pm–1am, Fri–Sat 5pm–2am (bar menu 5pm–midnight daily).

NORTH KOHALA

For a light meal or snack, stop at **Kohala Coffee Mill ★**, 55-3412 Akoni Pule Hwy. (*mauka* side, across from Bamboo, discussed below; www.facebook.com/kohala.coffeemill; © **808/889-5577**). Known best for scoops of Tropical Dreams ice cream (p. 277) and well-crafted coffee drinks, it's open weekdays 6am to 6pm, weekends 7am to 6pm. In Kapa'au, homey **Minnie's Ohana Lim Style ★**, 54-3854 Akoni Pule Hwy. (*mauka* side, at Kamehameha Rd.), serves heaping portions of fresh fish, roast pork, Korean fried chicken, and local staples ($9–$15; © **808/889-5288;** Mon–Thurs 11am–8pm, Fri 11am–3pm and 6–8pm).

Moderate

Bamboo ★★ PACIFIC RIM Dining here is a trip, literally and figuratively. A half-hour away from the nearest resort, Bamboo adds an element of time travel, with vintage decor behind the screen doors of its pale-blue, plantation-era building; an art gallery and quirky gift shop provide great browsing if you have to wait for a table. The food is well worth the wait, from local lunch faves like barbecued baby-back ribs to a veggie stir-fry of soba noodles or grilled chicken with a kicky Thai-style coconut sauce. Dinner adds more fresh-catch preparations, including a grilled filet with a tangy *liliko'i* mustard sauce balanced by crispy goat cheese polenta. Friday and Saturday night often have live music.

55-3415 Akoni Pule Hwy. (Hwy. 270, just west of Hwy. 250/Hawi Rd.), Hawi. www.bamboorestaurant.info. © **808/889-5555.** Dinner reservations recommended. Main courses $10–$20 lunch, $15–$35 dinner (full- and half-size portions available at dinner). Tues–Sat 11:30am–2:30pm and 6–8pm; Sun brunch 11:30am–2:30pm.

WAIMEA

Daunted by high-priced hotel breakfast or lunch? Visit the inexpensive **Hawaiian Style Café ★,** 65-1290 Kawaihae Rd. (Hwy. 19, 1 block east of Opelo Rd.; www.hawaiianstylecafe.com; © **808/885-4925**), which serves pancakes bigger than your head (try them with warm *haupia,* a coconut pudding), kalua pork hash, Portuguese blood sausage, and other local favorites, along with burgers and sandwiches. It's cash only, and very crowded on weekends (Mon–Sat 7am–1:30pm; until noon Sun).

Expensive

Merriman's ★★★ HAWAI'I REGIONAL This is where it all began in 1988 for chef Peter Merriman, one of the founders of Hawai'i Regional Cuisine and an early adopter of the farm-to-table trend. Now head of a culinary empire with various Merriman's and Monkeypod Kitchen incarnations on four islands, the busy Merriman has entrusted chef Eric Purugganan with maintaining his high standards and inventive flair. Lunch offers terrific values, such as the grilled fresh fish ($15), while weekend brunch includes a luscious eggs Benedict with jalapeño hollandaise, and a less guilt-inducing kale and beet salad with chèvre and shaved Waimea sweet onion. At dinner, you can order Merriman's famed wok-charred ahi, grass-fed steak, or molten chocolate purse with vanilla bean ice cream—but you'll also want to consider Purugganan's fresh-catch dish, often inspired by his herb garden, or his family-style, four-course tasting menu for four or more diners ($75 per person).

In Opelo Plaza, 65-1227 Opelo Rd., off Hwy. 19, Waimea. www.merrimanshawaii.com. ✆ **808/885-6822.** Reservations recommended. Main courses $13–$18 lunch, $28–$58 dinner (half-portions $23–$44). Mon–Fri 11:30am–1:30pm; daily 5:30–9pm; Sat–Sun brunch 10am–1pm.

Tropical Dreams: Ice Cream Reveries

Founded in North Kohala in 1983, ultra-rich **Tropical Dreams ★★★** ice cream is sold all over the island now, but you'll find the most flavors at the retail store next to its Waimea factory, 66-1250 Lālāmilo Farm Rd. (off Hwy. 19; www.tropicaldreamsicecream.com; ✆ **888/888-8031**). Try the Tahitian vanilla, lychee, or poha, or sorbets like dragonfruit, passion-guava, or white pineapple ($3.50 for an 8 oz. cup—the smallest size). It's open weekdays 8am to 4:30pm.

Moderate

Village Burger ★★ BURGERS Tucked into a cowboy-themed shopping center with a drafty food court (bring a jacket or sit by the fireplace), this burger stand run by former Four Seasons Lanai chef Edwin Goto has a compact menu: plump burgers made with local grass-fed beef, grilled ahi, taro, or Hāmākua mushrooms; thick, sumptuous shakes made from Tropical Dreams ice cream (see above); and hand-cut, twice-cooked fries. Other than that, there's just a grilled ahi Niçoise salad featuring island greens—but it's also delicious. A few doors down is Goto's **Noodle Club ★★,** opened in 2015. A casual sit-down restaurant, it features artfully presented interpretations of local and Asian specialties such as saimin, pork belly bao buns, pho, and ramen; the yuzu pudding cake is a melt-away marvel. ***Note:*** Look for hours to expand as service expands.

Village Burger: In the Parker Ranch Center, 67-1185 Māmalahoa Hwy., Waimea. www.villageburgerwaimea.com. ✆ **808/885-7319.** Burgers $8–$12. Mon–Sat 10:30am–8pm; Sun 10:30am–6pm. Noodle Club: Same address. www.facebook.com/noodleclubwaimea. ✆ **808/885-8825.** Main courses $9–$13. Tues–Thurs 10:30am–3pm; Fri–Sat 2:30pm–8pm; Sun 10:30am–5pm.

The Hāmākua Coast

This lovely but little-populated area holds few dinner options, and those tend to close early, so plan ahead. ***Note:*** You'll find these restaurants on "The Kohala Coast, Waimea & the Hāmākua Coast" map on p. 255.

Café Il Mondo ★ PIZZA/ESPRESSO BAR To order a medium or large version of the pleasantly crusty, stone-oven-baked pizzas, you'll have to get it to go. But if you can find a space in this very cozy bistro, pick your own pie ($12–$15), or consider one of the calzones ($11) with the cafe's signature pesto sauce, made with macadamia nuts in lieu of pine nuts. The best values may be the Mama Mia dinners ($13): roast chicken with twice-baked potatoes or beef lasagna with focaccia, both with a garden salad. ***Note:*** Bring your own beer and wine (**Mālama Market** is just around the corner); the pizzeria charges $2 to $5 for corkage, depending on how many are imbibing.

45-3626 Māmane St. (Hwy. 240, at Lehua St.), Honoka'a. © **808/775-7711.** Main courses $7–$15 lunch, $11–$15 dinner. No credit cards. Mon–Sat 11am–8pm.

Tex Drive-In & Restaurant ★★ AMERICAN/LOCAL The two stars here are only for the *malasadas,* Portuguese sweetbread doughnut holes fried to order, dusted in sugar, and available (for 65¢ more) with a filling, such as Bavarian cream, tropical jellies—guava, mango, pineapple—and chocolate. Founded in 1969, Tex sells malasadas that are square, larger, and a little chewier than the traditional version, and they sometimes run out of certain fillings, but the plain are quite satisfying. Tex also serves burgers, hot dogs, sandwiches, and Hawaiian plate lunches that are modestly priced but adequate at best.

45-690 Pakalana St., off Hwy. 19, Honoka'a. www.texdriveinhawaii.com. © **808/775-0598.** Malasadas $1.10 each, fillings 65¢. Main courses $5–$7 breakfast, $4–$11 lunch and dinner. Daily 6am–8pm.

Hilo

The second largest city in Hawai'i hosts a raft of unpretentious eateries serving plate lunches and Japanese cuisine, reflecting the plantation heritage and largest ethnic group of East Hawai'i. A prime example of the former is **Ken's House of Pancakes** ★, 1730 Kamehameha Ave., at the corner of Hwys. 19 and 11 (www.kenshouseofpancakes.com; © **808/935-8711**), which serves heaping helpings of local dishes and American fare 24/7. The **Hawaiian Style Café** ★, 681 Manono St. (www.hawaiianstylecafe.com; © **808/969-9265**), is an outpost of the

A TASTE of volcano wines

Volcano Winery (www.volcanowinery.com; © **808/967-7772**) has been a unique pit stop for visitors since 1993, when it began selling traditional grape wines, honey wines, and grape wines blended with tropical fruits in a location near Hawai'i Volcanoes National Park. Del and Marie Bothof have owned the winery since 1999, planting Pinot Noir and Cayuga White grapes in 2000 and expanding into tea in 2006. Wine tastings, for ages 21 and up, are $7 to $10; there's also a picnic area under cork and koa trees. The tasting room and store, 35 Pi'i Mauna Dr. in Volcano (just off Hwy. 11 near the 30-mile marker), are open 10am to 5:30pm daily.

Waimea breakfast/lunch favorite (p. 276) but with dinner hours Tuesday through Saturday as well.

The ambience is even more basic (plastic trays and paper plates) at the venerable **Café 100** ★ (www.cafe100.com; ✆ **808/935-8683**), 969 Kīlauea Ave., but the price is right, with hefty plate lunches ($8–$10), burgers $3.95 and up, and more than 30 varieties of loco moco—meat, eggs, rice, and gravy—starting around $4; opt for brown rice to lessen the guilt. It's open daily at 6:15am, closing at 8:30pm Monday to Thursday, 9pm Friday, and 7:30pm Saturday.

Miyo's ★, 564 Hinano St. (www.miyosrestaurant.com; ✆ **808/935-8825**), prides itself on "home-style" Japanese cooking, with locally sourced ingredients and a few welcome surprises, such as pumpkin flan and a fluffy cheesecake. It's open daily except Sunday, 11am to 2pm for lunch (main courses $12–$16) and 5:30 to 8:30pm for dinner ($14–$18).

Note: You'll find the following restaurants and those listed above on the "Hilo" map on p. 201.

Café Pesto ★★ PIZZA/PACIFIC RIM The menu of wood-fired pizzas, pastas, risottos, fresh local seafood, and artfully prepared "creative island cuisine" such as mango-glazed chicken is much the same as at the original Kawaihae location (p. 275), and that's a good thing. Even better: The airy dining room in a restored 1912 building, with black-and-white tile floors and huge glass windows overlooking the vintage wooden buildings and palm trees of downtown Hilo. Service is attentive and swift, especially by island standards, but don't shy away from the two counters with high-backed chairs if tables are full.

At the S. Hata Bldg., 308 Kamehameha Ave., Hilo. www.cafepesto.com. ✆ **808/969-6640.** Pizzas $10–$21; main courses $11–$17 lunch, $19–$30 dinner. Sun–Thurs 11am–9pm; Fri–Sat 11am–10pm.

Hilo Bay Café ★★ PACIFIC RIM Hidden in a strip mall for years, this ambitious restaurant moved in late 2013 to an elevated perch overlooking Hilo Bay, next to Suisan Fish Market and the lovely Liliʻuokalani Gardens. Fittingly, sushi and seafood dishes are the most reliable pleasers, including horseradish panko-crusted ono and grilled asparagus salad with pan-roasted salmon, but fresh produce from the Hilo Farmer's Market also inspires several dishes. Vegetarians will appreciate thoughtful options such as the Hāmākua mushroom curry pot pie (one can add chicken or shrimp). The drink list is similarly creative, including locally sourced kombucha and craft beer. During daylight, ask for a seat on the covered lanai deck or at a table with a bay view.

123 Lihiwai St., just north of Banyan Dr., Hilo. www.hilobaycafe.com. ✆ **808/935-4939.** Reservations recommended for dinner. Main courses $13–$17 lunch, $13–$35 dinner. Mon–Sat lunch 11am–2:30pm, limited menu 2:30–5pm, dinner 5–9pm.

Puna District

Options are limited and frankly often disappointing here, so plan mealtimes carefully and stock up on picnic supplies in Kailua-Kona or Hilo. ***Note:*** You'll find the following restaurants on the "Hotels & Restaurants in the Volcano Area" map (p. 265).

VOLCANO VILLAGE

In addition to the listings below, look for the **Tuk-Tuk Thai Food ★★** truck in front of the Volcano Inn, 19-3820 Old Volcano Rd. (www.tuk-tukthaifood.com; ✆ **808/747-3041**), from 11am to 6pm Tuesday to Saturday. You can even call ahead for its hearty curries and noodle dishes ($8–$10), about half the price of the Thai restaurant down the road.

Opened in late 2015, **'Ōhelo Café ★★**, 19-4005 Haunani Rd., may have a casual ambience but aims high with wood-fired pizzas ($12–$14), fresh catch ($25), pastas, and salads. It mostly succeeds; hence long lines of drop-ins—best to call for reservations. It's open daily 11:30am to 2:30pm and 5:30 to 9pm (www.ohelocafe.com; ✆ **808/339-7865**).

Expensive

Kilauea Lodge Restaurant ★★ CONTINENTAL Like his inn (for sale at press time), owner-chef Albert Jeyte's woodsy restaurant radiates *Gemütlichkeit,* that ineffable German sense of warmth and cheer, symbolized by the "International Fireplace of Friendship" studded with stones from around the world. Although starters can be ho-hum, the European-style main courses showcase unique meats such as rabbit, antelope, buffalo, and duck, along with local grass-fed beef and lamb, plus the fresh catch (recommended). The wine list is well priced, although *liliko'i* margaritas are refreshing after a long day exploring the nearby national park. Dinner prices are steep (due in part to the lack of competition), but lunch offers good values, including Kuahiwi Ranch grass-fed beef, buffalo and antelope burgers, and a curried chicken bowl. Breakfast is another winner, especially the French toast made with Punalu'u Bake Shop's guava, taro, and white Portuguese sweetbread.

19-3948 Old Volcano Rd., Volcano. www.kilauealodge.com. ✆ **808/967-7366.** Reservations recommended. Main courses $9–$14 breakfast, $11–$14 lunch, $23–$38 dinner. Daily breakfast 7:30–10am, lunch 10am–2pm, and dinner 5–9pm; Sun brunch 10am–2pm.

Moderate

Café Ono ★ VEGETARIAN When burgers and plate lunches start to pall, this cafe and tearoom hidden in Ira Ono's quirky art studio/gallery provides a delectably light alternative. The all-vegetarian menu is concise: a soup or two, chili, lasagna, quiche (highly recommended), and sandwiches, most accompanied by a garden salad. Don't pass up the peanut butter and pumpkin soup if available, and ask if you can give Ernest the goat a bite to eat before you explore the lush gardens outside.

In Volcano Garden Arts, 19-3834 Old Volcano Rd., Volcano. www.cafeono.net. ✆ **808/985-8979.** Main courses $10–$15. Lunch Tues–Sun 11am–3pm, coffee/dessert menu 10am to 4pm.

HAWAI'I VOLCANOES NATIONAL PARK

The Rim ★★ ISLAND FARM/SEAFOOD By no means is this your typical national park concession, as some hot dog–seeking visitors are discouraged to find. Since the restored Volcano House hotel reopened in 2013, The Rim and the adjacent **Uncle George's Lounge ★★** have tried to match their three-star views of Kīlauea Caldera with a menu that's both artful and hyper-local. The bountiful breakfast buffet includes made-to-order eggs and waffles, tropical fruit smoothies, turkey hash, and housemade granola. Bento lunch boxes ($19) offer a choice of kalua pork, teriyaki chicken, an organic veggie/tofu stir fry, or macadamia-nut mahimahi, plus four tasty sides, Hilo poi, and *haupia* pudding. Pizza, burgers, and salads are also available. Reserve well in advance for a window table at dinner, when lights are periodically dimmed to showcase the glow from Halema'uma'u Crater. Culinary highlights include *'opakapaka* (pink snapper) wrapped in white pineapple, pan-seared Kona *kampachi*, and Hilo coffee-rubbed rack of lamb. The lounge serves excellent *pupu* ($12–$17) such as chicken satay and avocado dip. ***Note:*** Diners must pay park admission ($15 a vehicle, good for 7 days).

In Volcano House, 1 Crater Rim Dr., Volcano. www.hawaiivolcanohouse.com. ✆ **808/756-9625.** Reservations recommended. Breakfast buffet $18 adults, $9 children; lunch main courses $12–$19; dinner main courses $19–$39. Daily breakfast buffet 7–10am, lunch 11am–2pm, dinner 5–9pm. Lounge daily 11am–10pm.

PĀHOA

Kaleo's Bar & Grill ★★ ECLECTIC/LOCAL The best restaurant for miles around has a wide-ranging menu, ideal for multiple visits, and a welcoming, homey atmosphere. Local staples such as chicken katsu and spicy Korean kalbi ribs won't disappoint, but look for dishes with slight twists, such as tempura ahi roll with spicy *liliko'i* sauce or the blackened-ahi BLT with avocado and mango mayo. Save room for the *liliko'i* cheesecake or banana spring rolls with vanilla ice cream.

15-2969 Pāhoa Village Rd., Pāhoa. www.kaleoshawaii.com. ✆ **808/965-5600.** Main courses $8–$18 lunch, $14–$32 dinner. Daily 11am–9pm.

Ka'ū District

When you're driving between Kailua-Kona and Hawai'i Volcanoes National Park, it's good to know about two places on Highway 11 in Nā'ālehu for a quick pick-me-up. The **Punalu'u Bake Shop ★** (www.bakeshophawaii.com; ✆ **866/366-3501** or 808/929-7343) is the busier tourist attraction, famed for its varieties of Portuguese sweetbread (including taro, mango, and guava), now seen in stores across the islands; clean restrooms, a deli counter, and gift shop are also part of the appeal. It's open 9am to 5pm daily. Across the highway off a small lane lies **Hana Hou Restaurant** ★ (www.hanahourestaurant.com; ✆ **808/929-9717**), which boasts a bakery counter with equally tempting sweets (try the macnut pie or *liliko'i* bar) and a small, retro dining room serving simple but fresh and filling plate lunches ($13–$16), burgers, sandwiches, and quesadillas; look for the large sign saying Eat. It's open Sunday through Thursday 8am to 7pm, 8am to 8pm Friday and Saturday.

BIG ISLAND SHOPPING

This island is fertile ground, not just for coffee, tea, chocolate, macadamia nuts, honey and other tasty souvenirs, but also for artists inspired by the volcanic cycle of destruction and creation, the boundless energy of the ocean, and the timeless beauty of native crafts. For those cooking meals or packing a picnic, see the "Edibles" listings.

Note: Stores are open daily unless otherwise stated.

The Kona Coast

KAILUA-KONA

For bargain shopping with an island flair, bypass the T-shirt and trinket shops and head 2 miles south from Kailua Pier to **Ali'i Gardens Marketplace,** 75-6129 Ali'i Dr., a friendly, low-key combination farmer's market, flea market, and crafts fair, with plenty of parking and tent-covered stalls. You'll find fun items handmade in Hawai'i as well as China's factories. On Tuesday, Wednesday, and Saturday, visit the **Kona Natural Soap Company** stand (www.konanaturalsoapcompany.com) and let Greg Colden explain the all-natural ingredients he uses, many grown at his farm in Keauhou.

In Kailua-Kona's historic district, the funky, family-run **Pacific Vibrations** (✆ **808/329-4140**) has colorful surfwear; it's at 75-5702 Likana Lane, an alley off Ali'i Drive just north of Moku'aikaua Church. Across the street, the nonprofit **Hulihe'e Palace Gift Shop** stocks arts and crafts by local artists, including gorgeous feather lei, silk scarves, art cards, aprons, and woven lauhala hats (www.daughtersofhawaii.org; ✆ **808/329-6558;** closed Sun).

Keauhou Shopping Center, above Ali'i Drive at King Kamehameha III Road (www.keauhouvillageshops.com), has more restaurants and services than shops, but check out **Kona Stories** (www.konastories.com; ✆ **808/324-0350**) for thousands of books, especially Hawaiiana and children's titles. Also in the mall, **Jams World** (www.jamsworld.com; ✆ **808/322-9361**) has kicky, comfortable resort wear for men and women, from a Hawai'i company founded in 1964. Local hula *hālau* perform hour-long shows Fridays at 6pm on the Heritage Court Stage.

HŌLUALOA

Charmingly rustic Hōlualoa, 1,400 feet and 10 minutes above Kailua-Kona at the top of Hualālai Road, is the perfect spot for visiting coffee farms (p. 185) and tasteful galleries, with a half-dozen or more within a short distance of each other on Māmalahoa Highway (Hwy. 180). Among them, **Studio 7 Fine Arts** (www.studio7hawaii.com; ✆ **808/324-1335**), a virtual Zen garden with pottery, wall hangings, and paper collages by Setsuko Morinoue, as well as paintings and prints by husband Hiroki. ***Note:*** Most galleries are closed Sunday and Monday; see **www.holualoahawaii.com** for more listings.

Revel in the Hawaiian art of weaving leaves *(lau)* from the pandanus tree *(hala)* at **Kimura's Lauhala Shop,** farther south on the *makai* side of Māmalahoa Hwy., at 77-996 Hualālai Rd. Founded in 1914, the store brims with locally woven mats, hats, handbags, and slippers, plus Kona coffee, koa wood bowls, and feather hatbands. It's closed Sunday.

SOUTH KONA

Many stores along Highway 11, the main road, are roadside fruit and/or coffee stands, well worth pulling over for, if only to "talk story" and pick up a snack. Fabric aficionados must stop at **Kimura Store,** a quaint general store and textile emporium with more than 10,000 bolts of aloha prints and other colorful cloth, at 79-7408 Māmalahoa Hwy. (*makai* side), Kainaliu (✆ **808/322-3771;** closed Sun).

The Kohala Coast

SOUTH KOHALA

Three open-air shopping malls claim the bulk of stores here, with a few island-only boutiques amid state and national chains. The real plus is the malls' free entertainment (check their websites for current calendars) and prices somewhat lower than those of shops in resort hotels.

The Waikoloa Beach Resort has two malls, both off its main drag, Waikoloa Beach Road. **Kings' Shops** (www.kingsshops.com) has a *keiki* (children's) hula performance at 6pm most Fridays and live music at 7pm Mon–Thurs. Along with luxury stores such as **Tiffany** and **Coach,** you'll find affordable swimwear at **Making Waves** (✆ **808/886-1814**) and batik-print fashions at **Noa Noa** (✆ **808/886-5449**). Shops at **Queens' MarketPlace** (http://queensmarketplace.net) include the **Hawaiian Quilt Collection** (✆ **808/886-0494**), which also offers purses, placemats, and pottery with the distinctive quilt patterns of the islands, and **Starscape Gallery** (✆ **808/430-5864**), featuring stunning night and astral photography. Free shows include hula and Polynesian dance Monday, Wednesday, and Friday at 6pm.

In the **Shops at Mauna Lani** (www.shopsatmaunalani.com), on the main road of the Mauna Lani Resort, **Hawaiian Island Creations** (www.hicsurf.com; ✆ **808/881-1400**) stands out for its diverse lineup of local, state, and national surfwear brands. Look for hula and Polynesian fire dancing at the shops on Monday and Thursday at 7pm.

In **Kawaihae,** an unassuming shopping strip on Highway 270, just north of Highway 19, hosts **Harbor Gallery** (www.harborgallery.biz; ✆ **808/882-1510**). Browse the works of more than 150 Big Island artists, specializing in koa and other wood furniture, bowls, and sculpture; Sew Da Kine cork purses are an easy-to-pack item. Stock up on savory souvenirs at **Hamakua Macadamia Nut Factory** (p. 188).

NORTH KOHALA

When making the trek to the Pololū Valley Lookout, you'll pass a few stores of note along Hwy. 270. **As Hawi Turns,** 2 miles west of the Kohala Mountain Road (Hwy. 250), features eclectic women's clothing, locally made jewelry, home decor, and a consignment area cheekily called **As Hawi Returns** (✆ **808/889-5203**). Across from the King Kamehameha Statue in Kapa'au, **Ackerman Gallery** features Big Island arts and crafts (including paintings by owner Gary Ackerman), colorful clothing, and gifts (www.ackermanhawaii.com; ✆ **808/889-5138**).

WAIMEA

The barn-red buildings of **Parker Square,** on the south side of Highway 19 east of Opelo Road, hold several pleasant surprises. The **Gallery of Great Things** (www.galleryofgreatthingshawaii.com; ✆ **808/885-7706**) has high-quality Hawaiian artwork, including quilts and Ni'ihau shell leis, as well as pieces from throughout the Pacific. Sticking closer to home, literally, **Bentley's Home & Garden Collection** (www.bentleyshomecollection.com; ✆ **808/885-5565**) is chock-full of Western and country-inspired clothes, accessories, and cottage decor.

East Hawai'i

HĀMĀKUA COAST

Park on Māmane Street (Hwy. 240) in "downtown" **Honoka'a** and peruse the mom-and-pop shops, such as the **Green Chair** (✆ **808/747-4046;** closed Wed and Sun), which includes collectibles and thrift clothing among brightly hued home furnishings and small gifts. If you'd like something newer, head to **Big Island Grown,** selling edibles such as coffee, tea, and honey, plus locally made gifts and clothing (✆ **808/775-9777;** closed Sun), or **Taro Patch Gifts** (www.taropatchgifts.com; ✆ **808/775-7228**), which adds books and international goodies to the mix. **Waipio Valley Artworks** (www.waipiovalleyartworks.com; ✆ **808/775-0958**), on Kukuihaele Road near the overlook, has many handsome wood items, plus a café.

HILO

The second-largest city in Hawai'i has both mom-and-pop shops and big-box stores. The **Hilo Farmer's Market** is the prime attraction (see "A

Hilo Farmer's Market.

Feast for the Senses," below), but you should also hit the following for *omiyage,* or edible souvenirs: **Big Island Candies,** 585 Hinano St. (www.bigislandcandies.com; ✆ **808/935-5510**), and **Two Ladies Kitchen,** 274 Kīlauea Ave. (✆ **808/961-4766**). Big Island Candies is a busy tourist attraction that cranks out addictive macadamia-nut shortbread cookies. A cash-only hole-in-the-wall, Two Ladies Kitchen makes delicious *mochi,* a pounded-rice treat (try the one with a giant strawberry inside, if available), and *manju,* a kind of mini-turnover.

Visit **Sig Zane Designs,** 122 Kamehameha Ave. (www.sigzane.com; ✆ **808/935-7077,** closed Sun), for apparel and home items with Zane's fabric designs, inspired by native Hawaiian plants and culture, including wife Nālani Kanaka'ole's hula lineage. **Basically Books,** 160 Kamehameha Ave. (www.basicallybooks.com; ✆ **808/961-0144**), has a wide assortment of maps and books emphasizing Hawai'i and the Pacific.

PUNA DISTRICT

One of the prettiest places to visit in **Volcano Village** is **Volcano Garden Arts,** 19-3834 Old Volcano Rd. (www.volcanogardenarts.com; ✆ **808/985-8979;** closed Mon), offering beautiful gardens with sculptures and open studios; delicious **Café Ono** (p. 280); and an airy gallery of artworks (some by owner Ira Ono), jewelry, and home decor by local artists. Look for Hawaiian quilts and fabrics, as well as island-made butters and jellies, at **Kilauea Kreations,** 19-3972 Old Volcano Rd. (www.kilaueakreations.com; ✆ **808/967-8090**).

In Hawai'i Volcanoes National Park, the two **gift shops** at Volcano House (p. 266) have surprisingly tasteful gifts, many made on the Big Island, as well as attractive jackets for chilly nights. The original 1877

Volcano House, a short walk from the Kīlauea Visitor Center, is home to the nonprofit **Volcano Art Center** (www.volcanoartcenter.org; ✆ **808/967-7565**), which sells locally made artworks, including the intricate, iconic prints of Dietrich Varez, who worked at the modern Volcano House in his youth.

A Feast for the Senses: Hilo Farmer's Market

You can't beat the **Hilo Farmer's Market** (www.hilofarmersmarket.com), considered by many the best in the state, from its dazzling display of tropical fruits and flowers (especially orchids) to savory prepared foods such as pad Thai and bento boxes, plus locally made crafts and baked goods, all in stalls pleasantly crammed around the corner of Kamehameha Avenue and Mamo Street. The full version with 200-plus farmers and artisans takes place 6am to 4pm Wednesday and Saturday; go early for the best selection. (About 30 vendors set up at 7am to 4pm the rest of the week, but it's not quite the same experience.)

Edibles

Since most visitors stay on the island's west side, the Hilo Farmer's Market isn't really an option to stock their larders. The **Keauhou Farmer's Market** (www.keauhoufarmersmarket.com), held from 8am to noon Saturday at the **Keauhou Shopping Center** (near Ace Hardware), can supply locally grown produce, fresh eggs, baked goods, coffee, and flowers. Pick up the rest of what you need at the center's **KTA Super Stores** (www.ktasuperstores.com; ✆ **808/323-2311**), a Big Island grocery chain founded in 1916 at which you can find island-made specialties (poke, mochi) as well as national brands. Another **KTA** is in the Kona Coast Shopping Center, 74-5588 Palani Rd. (✆ **808/329-1677**), open daily until 11pm. Wine aficionados will be amazed at the large and well-priced selection in **Kona Wine Market,** now near Home Depot at 73-5613 Olowalu St. (www.konawinemarket.com; ✆ **808/329-9400**). For **Costco** members, its local warehouse is at 73-4800 Maiau St., near Highway 19 and Hina Lani Street (✆ **808/331-4800**).

On the Kohala Coast, the best prices are in **Waimea,** home to a **KTA** in Waimea Center, Highway 19 at Pulalani Road (✆ **808/885-8866**). Buy smoked meat and fish, hot *malasadas* (doughnut holes), baked goods, and ethnic foods along with a cornucopia of produce at the **Waimea Homestead Farmer's Market,** Saturday 7am to noon at the Waimea Middle School playground, behind the post office, at 67-1229 Māmalahoa Hwy. (www.waimeafarmersmarket.com). The best deals for fresh fish are at **Da Fish House,** 61-3665 Akoni Pule Hwy. (Hwy. 270) in Kawaihae (✆ **808/882-1052;** closed Sun). Among resort options, **Foodland Farms** in the Shops at Mauna Lani (www.foodland.com; ✆ **808/887-6101**), has top-quality local produce and seafood, while the Kings' Shops hosts a decent **farmer's market** Wednesday 8:30am to

3pm. **Island Gourmet Markets** (www.islandgourmethawaii.com; ✆ **808/886-3577**), centerpiece of the Queens' MarketPlace, has an almost overwhelming array of delicacies, including 200-plus kinds of cheese.

BIG ISLAND NIGHTLIFE

With few exceptions, the Big Island tucks in early, all the better to rise at daybreak, when the weather is cool and the roads (and waves) are open. But live Hawaiian music is everywhere, and it's easy to catch free, engaging hula shows, too, at several open-air resort malls (see "Big Island Shopping," p. 282).

Kailua-Kona

When the sun goes down, the scene heats up around Ali'i Drive. Among the hot spots: **On the Rocks,** next to Huggo's restaurant (see p. 269) at 75-5824 Kahakai Rd., has Hawaiian music and hula nightly, going until midnight Friday to Saturday and 10pm Sunday (www.huggosontherocks.com; ✆ **808/329-1493**). Inside Huggo's, the stylish, oceanview **hBar** (www.huggos.com/hbar) offers the area's best artisanal cocktails; it's open till midnight Friday to Saturday. Across the way in the Coconut Grove Market Place, **Laverne's Sports Bar** (www.laverneskona.com; ✆ **808/331-2633**) draws a 20-something crowd with happy-hour specials, theme nights, and late-night DJs on weekends; it's open until 2am nightly. Next door, an eclectic mix of local musicians perform at **Bongo Ben's,** 75-5819 Ali'i Dr. (www.bongobens.com; ✆ **808/329-9203**), open until 10pm nightly.

Farther afield, **Rays on the Bay,** at the **Sheraton Kona Resort & Spa** (p. 256), lures locals and visitors to Keauhou with fire pits, a great happy hour, nightly live music, and free valet parking. The motto of the lively, gay-friendly **MyBar,** 74-5606 Luhia St., a block *makai* of Hwy. 19 (www.mybarkona.com; ✆ **808/331-8789**), is "We accept everyone as long as you want to have fun." It's darts, drag nights, and $6 cocktails.

Sharing Stories & Aloha Under the Stars

Twilight at Kalahuipua'a, a monthly Hawaiian-style celebration, takes place on the lawn in front of the oceanside Eva Parker Woods Cottage on the Mauna Lani Resort (www.maunalani.com/about/big-island-hawaii-events; ✆ **808/881-7911**). On the Saturday closest to the full moon, revered entertainers and local *kūpuna* (elders) gather to "talk story," play music, and dance hula. The 3-hour show starts at 5:30pm, but the audience starts arriving an hour earlier, with picnic fare and beach mats. Bring yours, and plan to share food as well as the fun. Parking is free, too.

lū'aus' new taste **OF OLD HAWAI'I**

Let's face it: You may never have a truly great meal at a lū'au, due to the numbers served, but on the Big Island you can have a very good one, with a highly enjoyable—and educational—show to boot. Buffets now offer more intriguing, tasty items such as pohole ferns and Moloka'i sweet potatoes, while shows feature more local history, from the first voyagers to *paniolo* days, plus a spectacular fire knife dance and Polynesian revue. I recommend one of these oceanfront affairs:

- **Hāleo** (www.haleoluau.com) at the **Sheraton Kona Resort & Spa** (p. 256) is simply the best in Kailua-Kona (Mon 4:30pm; $95 adults, $45 children 6–12).
- **Gathering of the Kings** (www.gatheringofthekings.com) at the **Fairmont Orchid Hawaii** (p. 258), has the best selection of island-style food, including the taro leaf stew that gave lū'au its name (Sat 4:30pm; $109 adults, $75 children 5–12).
- **Legends of Hawai'i** (www.hiltonwaikoloavillage.com/resort-experiences) at **Hilton Waikoloa Village** (p. 258) is the most family-friendly, with pillow seating upfront for kids (Tues, Fri, and Sun 5:30pm; $125 adults, $68 children 5–12; free for children 4 and under). Add VIP options for $29 more per person.

The Kohala Coast

All the resort hotels have at least one lounge with nightly live music, usually Hawaiian, often with hula. Members of the renowned **Lim Family** perform at varying times and venues in the **Mauna Lani Bay Hotel & Bungalows** (p. 260), while award-winning singer **Darlene Ahuna** typically sings from 7 to 10pm Tues–Thurs by the pool at the **Hapuna Beach Prince Hotel** (p. 259). **Lava Lava Beach Club** (p. 258) has created a lively scene at the Waikoloa Beach Resort with nightly music and hula right on the sand. The gleaming **Copper Bar** at the **Mauna Kea Beach Hotel** (p. 260) also serves nightly music and hula with creative cocktails and choice small plates.

Just beyond the resorts, the **Blue Dragon,** 61-3616 Kawaihae Rd., Kawaihae (www.bluedragonrestaurant.com; ✆ **808/882-7771**), is a great open-air music spot. Here you can enjoy music—jazz, rock, Hawaiian swing—often with dancing, Thursday through Sunday.

For a uniquely Big Island alternative to a lū'au, try **An Evening at Kahua Ranch** (www.kahuaranch.com; ✆ **808/882-7954**), a barbecue with an open bar, line dancing, rope tricks, a campfire singalong, and stargazing, on a working North Kohala ranch. The 3-hour event costs $134 for adults and $67 for kids 6 to 11 (free for kids under 6) with hotel shuttle; drive yourself and it's $109 and $55, respectively. Festivities typically start at 6pm Wednesday in summer, 5:30pm in winter.

Hilo & the Hāmākua Coast

Opened in 1925, the neoclassical **Palace Theater,** 38 Haili St., Hilo (www.hilopalace.com; ✆ **808/934-7010**), screens first-run independent movies and hosts concerts, festivals, hula, and theater to pay for its ongoing restoration. **Hilo Town Tavern,** 168 Keawe St. (✆ **808/935-2171**), is a Cajun restaurant and dive bar open until 2am daily, with a pool room and live music from hip-hop to Hawaiian. **Honoka'a First Friday,** a mini-festival on the first Friday of each month, features stores open late, sidewalk vendors, and live music from 5 until 9pm.

Puna District

Although the revered founder of **Uncle Robert's Awa Club** (✆ **808/443-6913**), Robert Keli'iho'omalu, passed away in 2015, the bustling Wednesday-night marketplace (5–10pm) continues at his family compound at road's end in Kalapana, with live music from 6 to 9pm. Sample the mildly intoxicating *'awa* (the Hawaiian word for kava) at the tiki bar, or come back Friday at 6pm for more live music. In Pāhoa, **Kaleo's Bar & Grill** ★★ (p. 281) offers nightly live music, including jazz and slack key.

6

MAUI

by Shannon Wianecki

For many, Maui inhabits the sweet spot. Hawaii's second-largest island is a tangle of lovely contradictions, with a Gucci heel on one foot and a *puka*-shell anklet on the other. Culturally, it's a mix of farmers, *paniolo* (Hawaiian cowboys), aspiring chefs, artists, New Age healers, and big-wave riders. The landscape runs the gamut from sun-kissed golden beaches and fragrant rainforests to the frigid, wind-swept summit of Haleakalā. Sure, more traffic lights sprout up around the island every year and spurts of development have turned cherished landmarks into mere memories. But even as Maui transforms, its allure remains.

ESSENTIALS

Arriving

BY PLANE If you think of the island of Maui as the shape of a person's head and shoulders, you'll probably arrive near its neck, at **Kahului Airport** (OGG). Many airlines offer direct flights to Maui from the mainland U.S., including **Hawaiian Airlines** (www.hawaiianair.com; ✆ **800/367-5320**), **Alaska Airlines** (www.alaskaair.com; ✆ **800/252/7522**), **United Airlines** (www.united.com; ✆ **800/241-6522**), **Delta Air Lines** (www.delta.com; ✆ **800/221-1212**), **American Airlines** (www.aa.com; ✆ **800/882-8880**), and the newest arrival, **Virgin America** (www.virginamerica.com; ✆ **877/359-8474**). The only international flights to Maui originate in Canada, via **Air Canada** (www.aircanada.com; ✆ **888/247-2262**) and **West Jet** (www.westjet.com; ✆ **888/937-8538**), which both fly from Vancouver.

Other major carriers stop in Honolulu, where you'll catch an inter-island flight to Maui on **Hawaiian Airlines** or **Island Air** (www.islandair.com; ✆ **800/652-6541**). The latter airline, acquired by Larry Ellison after the billionaire purchased 98% of the island of Lāna'i, has a reputation for canceled and delayed flights. Our fingers are crossed that it improves. A small commuter service, **Mokulele Airlines** (www.mokuleleairlines.com; ✆ **866/260-7070**), recently expanded its routes to include flights from Honolulu to Kahului Airport and to Maui's two other airstrips.

FACING PAGE: **Windsurfing in Pā'ia.**

If you're staying in Lahaina or Ka'anapali, you might consider flying in or out of **Kapalua–West Maui Airport** (JHM). From this tiny, one-pony airfield, it's only a 10- to 15-minute drive to most hotels in West Maui, as opposed to an hour or more from Kahului. Same story with **Hāna Airport** (HNM): Flying directly here will save you a 3-hour drive.

Mokulele also flies between Maui, Moloka'i, the Big Island, and by charter to Lāna'i. Check-in is a breeze: no security lines (unless leaving from Honolulu). You'll be weighed, ushered onto the tarmac, and welcomed aboard a nine-seat Cessna. The plane flies low, and the views between the islands are outstanding.

LANDING AT KAHULUI If you're renting a car, proceed to the car-rental desks just beyond baggage claim. All of the major rental companies have branches at Kahului. Each rental agency has a shuttle that will deliver you to the car lot a half-mile away. For tips on insurance and driving rules in Hawai'i, see "Getting Around Hawai'i" in chapter 10.

If you're not renting a car, the cheapest way to exit the airport is the **Maui Bus** (www.mauicounty.gov/bus; ✆ **808/871-4838**). For $2, it will deposit you at any one of the island's major towns. Simply cross the street at baggage claim and wait under the awning. Unfortunately, bus stops are far and few between, so you'll end up lugging your suitcase a long way to your destination. A much more convenient option is **Roberts Hawai'i Express Shuttle** (www.robertshawaii.com/mauiexpress; ✆ **866/293-1782** or 808/954-8630), which offers curb-to-curb service in a shared van or small bus. Booking is a breeze on their new website. Plan to pay $18 (one-way) to Kīhei, $24 to Wailea, $34 to Ka'anapali, and $44 to Kapalua. Prices drop if you book round-trip. **SpeediShuttle** (www.speedishuttle.com; ✆ **877/242-5777**) also services Kahului Airport. Rates are $41 (one-way) to Wailea, $58 to Ka'anapali, and $80 to Kapalua. You need to book in 24 hours in advance. Bonus: You can request a fresh flower-lei greeting for an added fee.

Taxis usually cost 30% more than the shuttles—except when you're traveling with a large party, in which case they're a deal. **West Maui Taxi** (www.westmauitaxi.com; ✆ **888/661-4545**), for example, will drive up to six people from Kahului Airport to Ka'anapali for $80.

Visitor Information

The website of the **Hawai'i Tourism Authority** (www.gohawaii.com/maui) is chock-full of helpful facts and tips. Visit the state-run **Visitor Information Center** at the Kahului Airport baggage claim for brochures and the latest issue of *This Week Maui,* which features great regional maps.

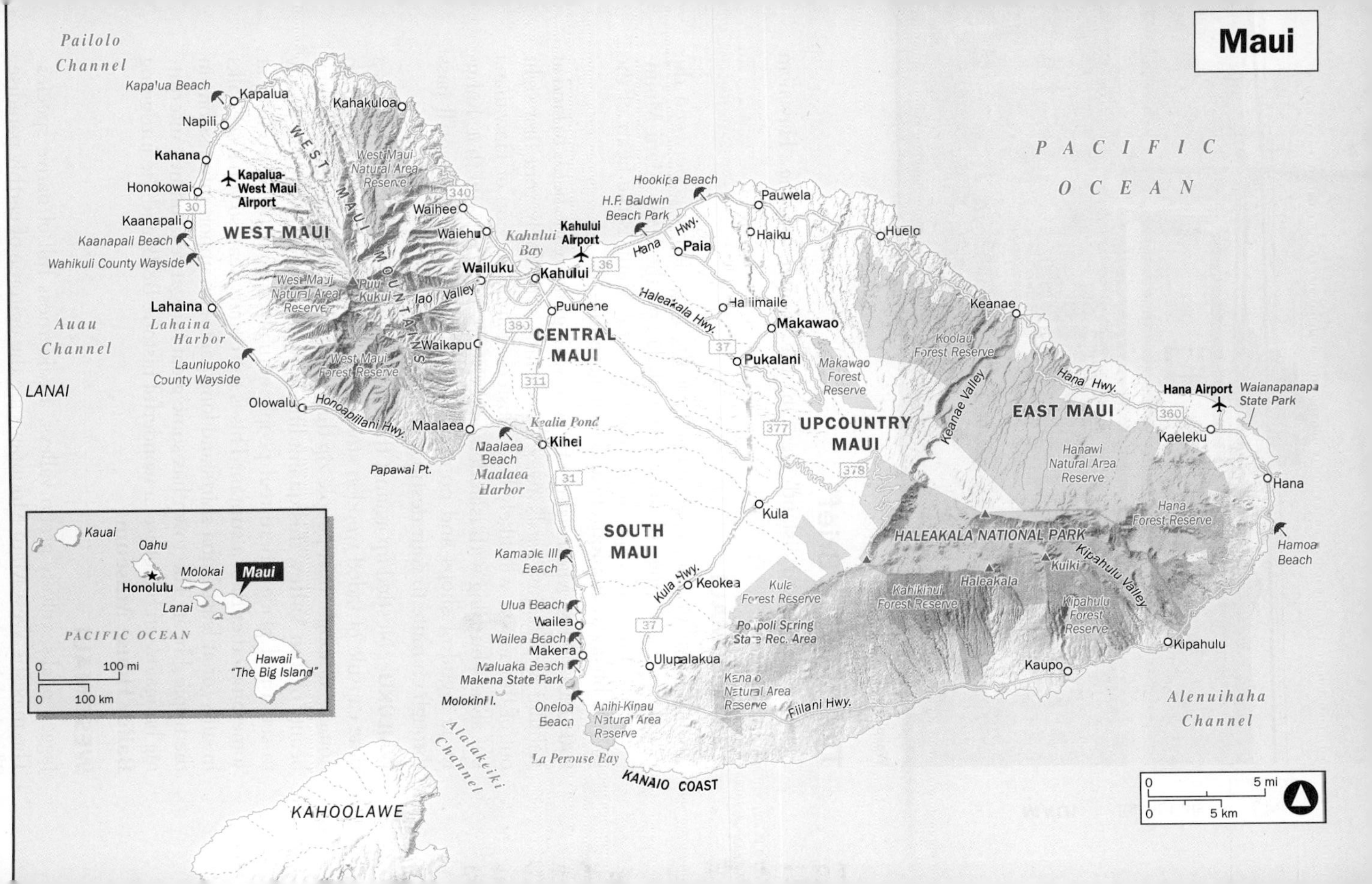

Maui

PACIFIC OCEAN
Pailolo Channel
Auau Channel
Alalakeiki Channel
Alenuihaha Channel
LANAI
KAHOOLAWE
WEST MAUI
CENTRAL MAUI
SOUTH MAUI
UPCOUNTRY MAUI
EAST MAUI
HALEAKALA NATIONAL PARK
KANAIO COAST
WEST MAUI MOUNTAINS
Kapalua Beach
Kapalua
Napili
Kahana
Kapalua-West Maui Airport
Honokowai
Kaanapali
Kaanapali Beach
Wahikuli County Wayside
Lahaina
Lahaina Harbor
Launiupoko County Wayside
Olowalu
Honoapiilani Hwy.
Papawai Pt.
Maalaea
Maalaea Beach
Maalaea Harbor
Kahakuloa
West Maui Natural Area Reserve
West Maui Forest Reserve
Puu Kukui
Iao Valley
Waikapu
Waihee
Waiehu
Wailuku
Kahului
Kahului Bay
Kahului Airport
Puunene
Kealia Pond
Kihei
Kamaole III Beach
Ulua Beach
Wailea
Wailea Beach
Makena
Maluaka Beach
Makena State Park
Molokini I.
Oneloa Beach
La Perouse Bay
Ahihi-Kinau Natural Area Reserve
H.F. Baldwin Beach Park
Hookipa Beach
Paia
Hana Hwy.
Haleakala Hwy.
Haliimaile
Pukalani
Makawao
Makawao Forest Reserve
Haiku
Pauwela
Huelo
Koolau Forest Reserve
Keanae
Keanae Valley
Kula
Kula Hwy.
Keokea
Kula Forest Reserve
Polipoli Spring State Rec. Area
Kanaio Natural Area Reserve
Ulupalakua
Piilani Hwy.
Kahikinui Forest Reserve
Haleakala
Kaupo
Kipahulu Forest Reserve
Kuiki
Kipahulu Valley
Kipahulu
Hanawi Natural Area Reserve
Hana Forest Reserve
Kaeleku
Hana Airport
Waianapanapa State Park
Hana
Hamoa Beach
30
36
37
311
377
378
380
31
340
360
0
5 mi
5 km
Kauai
Oahu
Honolulu
Molokai
Lanai
Maui
Hawaii "The Big Island"
PACIFIC OCEAN
100 mi
100 km

Wailuku.

The Island in Brief

This medium-sized island lies in the center of the Hawaiian archipelago.

CENTRAL MAUI

Maui, the Valley Isle, is so named for the large isthmus between the island's two towering volcanoes: Haleakalā and the West Maui Mountains. The flat landscape in between, Central Maui, is the heart of the island's business community and local government.

KAHULUI Most Maui visitors fly over waving sugarcane fields to land at Kahului Airport, just yards away from rolling surf. Sadly, your first sight out of the airport will likely be a Costco—hardly an icon of Hawaiiana but always bustling with islanders and visitors alike. Beyond that, Kahului is a grid of shops and no-nonsense neighborhoods that you'll pass through en route to your destination.

WAILUKU Nestled up against the West Maui Mountains, Wailuku is a time capsule of faded wooden storefronts, old churches, and plantation homes. Although most people zip through on their way to see the natural beauty of **'Īao Valley,** this quaint little town is worth a brief visit, if only to see a real place where real people actually appear to be working at something other than a suntan. This is the county seat, so you'll see folks in suits (or at least aloha shirts and long pants) on important missions in the tropical heat. The town has some great budget restaurants, interesting bungalow architecture, a wonderful historic B&B, and the intriguing **Bailey House Museum.**

WEST MAUI

Jagged peaks, velvety green valleys, a wilderness full of native species: The majestic West Maui Mountains are the epitome of earthly paradise. The beaches below are crowded with condos and resorts, but still achingly beautiful. This stretch of coastline from Kapalua to the historic port of Lahaina, is the island's busiest resort area (with South Maui close behind). Expect slow-moving traffic on the two main thoroughfares: Honoapi'ilani Highway and Front Street.

Vacationers on this coast can choose from several beachside neighborhoods, each with its own identity and microclimate. The West Side tends to be hot, humid, and sunny year-round. As you travel north, the weather grows cooler and mistier. Starting at the southern end of West Maui and moving northward, the coastal communities look like this:

LAHAINA In days past, Lahaina was the seat of Hawaiian royalty. Legend has it that a powerful *mo'o* (lizard goddess) dwelt in a moat surrounding a palace here. Later this hot and sunny seaport was where raucous whalers swaggered ashore in search of women and grog. Modern Lahaina is a tame version of its former self. Today Front Street teems with restaurants, T-shirt shops, and galleries. Action revolves around the town's giant, century-old banyan tree and busy recreational harbor. Lahaina is rife with tourist traps, but you can still find plenty of authentic history here. It's also a great place to stay; accommodations include a few old hotels (such as the 1901 Pioneer Inn on the harbor), quaint bed-and-breakfasts, and a handful of oceanfront condos.

KA'ANAPALI Farther north along the West Maui coast is Hawai'i's first master-planned destination resort. Along nearly 3 miles of sun-kissed golden beach, pricey midrise hotels are linked by a landscaped parkway and a beachfront walking path. Golf greens wrap around the slope between beachfront and hillside properties. Convenience is a factor here: **Whalers Village** shopping mall and numerous restaurants are easy to reach on foot or by resort shuttle. Shuttles serve the small West Maui airport just to the north and also go to Lahaina (see above), 3 miles to the south, for shopping, dining, entertainment, and boat tours. Ka'anapali is popular with groups and families—and especially teenagers, who like all the action.

HONOKŌWAI, KAHANA In the building binge of the 1970s, condominiums sprouted along this gorgeous coastline like mushrooms after a rain. Today these older oceanside units offer excellent bargains for astute travelers. The great location—along sandy beaches, within minutes of both the Kapalua and Ka'anapali resort areas, and close enough to the goings-on in Lahaina town—makes this area a haven for the budget-minded.

In **Honokōwai** and **Māhinahina,** you'll find mostly older, cheaper units. There's not much shopping here (mostly convenience stores), but you'll have easy access to the shops and restaurants of Ka'anapali. **Kahana** is a little more upscale than Honokōwai and Māhinahina, and most of its condos are big high-rise types, newer than those immediately to the south.

NĀPILI A quiet, tucked-away gem, with temperatures at least 5 degrees cooler than in Lahaina, this tiny neighborhood feels like a world unto itself. Wrapped around deliciously calm Nāpili Bay, Nāpili offers convenient activity desks and decent eateries and is close to the gourmet restaurants of Kapalua. Lodging is generally more expensive here—although I've found a few hidden jewels at affordable prices.

KAPALUA Beyond the activity of Ka'anapali and Kahana, the road starts to climb and the vista opens up to include unfettered views of Moloka'i across the channel. A country lane lined with Cook pines brings you to Kapalua. It's the exclusive domain of the luxurious Ritz-Carlton resort and expensive condos and villas, set above two sandy beaches. Just north are two jeweled bays: marine-life preserves and world-class surf spot in winter. Although rain is frequent here, it doesn't dampen the enjoyment of this wilder stretch of coast.

Anyone is welcome to visit Kapalua, guest of the resort or not. The Ritz-Carlton provides free public parking and beach access. The resort has swank restaurants, spas, golf courses, and hiking trails—all open to the general public.

SOUTH MAUI

The hot, sunny South Maui coastline is popular with families and sun worshippers. Rain rarely falls here, and temperatures hover around 85°F (29°C) year-round. Cows once grazed and cacti grew wild on this former scrubland from Mā'alaea to Mākena, now home to four distinct areas—**Mā'alaea, Kīhei, Wailea,** and **Mākena.** Mā'alaea is off on its own, at the mouth of an active small boat harbor, Kīhei is the working-class, feeder community for well-heeled Wailea, and Mākena is a luxurious wilderness at the road's end.

MĀ'ALAEA If West Maui is the island's head, Mā'alaea is just under the chin. This windy, oceanfront village centers on a small-boat harbor (with a general store and a handful of restaurants) and the **Maui Ocean Center,** an aquarium/ocean complex. Visitors should be aware that tradewinds are near constant here, so a stroll on the beach often comes with a free sandblasting.

KĪHEI Kīhei is less a proper town than a nearly continuous series of condos and mini-malls lining South Kīhei Road. This is Maui's best vacation bargain. Budget travelers swarm like sun-seeking geckos over the eight sandy beaches along this scalloped, 7-mile stretch of coast. Kīhei is neither charming nor quaint; what it lacks in aesthetics, though, it more than makes up for in sunshine, affordability, and convenience. If you want the beach in the morning, shopping in the afternoon, and Hawai'i Regional Cuisine in the evening—all at bargain prices—head to Kīhei.

WAILEA Just 4 decades ago, the road south of Kīhei was a barely paved path through a tangle of *kiawe* trees. Now Wailea is a manicured oasis of multimillion-dollar resorts along 2 miles of palm-fringed gold coast.

Wailea has warm, clear water full of tropical fish; year-round sunshine and clear blue skies; and hedonistic pleasure palaces on 1,500 acres of black-lava shore indented by five beautiful beaches, each one prettier than the next.

This is the playground of the stretch-limo set. The planned resort community has a shopping village, a plethora of award-winning restaurants, several prized golf courses, and a tennis complex. A growing number of large homes sprawl over the upper hillside, some offering excellent B&Bs at reasonable prices. The resorts along this fantasy coast are spectacular. Next door to the Four Seasons Resort Maui at Wailea, the most elegant, is the Grand Wailea, built by Tokyo developer Takeshi Sekiguchi, who dropped $500 million in 1991 to create the most opulent Hawaiian resort to date. Stop in and take a look—sculptures by Botero and Léger populate its open-air art gallery and gardens. Stones imported from Mount Fuji line the resort's Japanese garden.

MĀKENA Suddenly, the road enters raw wilderness. After Wailea's overdone density, the thorny landscape is a welcome relief. Although beautiful, this is an end-of-the-road kind of place: It's a long drive from Mākena to anywhere on Maui. If you're looking for an activity-filled vacation, stay elsewhere, or you'll spend most of your vacation in the car. But if you want a quiet, relaxing respite, where the biggest trip of the day is from your bed to the beach, Mākena is the place.

Pu'u Ōlai stands like Maui's Diamond Head near the southern tip of the island. The red cinder cone shelters tropical fish and **Mākena State Beach Park,** a vast stretch of golden sand spanked by feisty swells. Beyond Mākena, you'll discover Haleakalā's most recent lava flow; the bay famously visited by French explorer La Pérouse; and a sunbaked lava-rock trail known as the King's Highway, which threads around Maui's southernmost shore through the ruins of bygone fishing villages.

La Pérouse Bay, Mākena.

UPCOUNTRY MAUI

After a few days at the beach, you'll probably notice the 10,023-foot mountain towering over Maui. The leeward slopes of Haleakalā (House of the Sun) are home to cowboys, farmers, and other rural folks who wave as you drive by. They're all up here enjoying the

Haleakalā.

crisp air, emerald pastures, eucalyptus, and flower farms of this tropical Olympus.

The neighborhoods here are called "upcountry" because they're halfway up the mountain. You can see a thousand tropical sunsets reflected in the windows of houses old and new, strung along a road that runs like a loose hound from Makawao to Kula, leading up to the summit and **Haleakalā National Park.** If you head south on Kula Highway, beyond the tiny outpost of Kēōkea, the road turns feral, undulating out towards the **Tedeschi Vineyards,** where cattle, elk, and MauiWine grapes flourish on 'Ulupalakua Ranch. A stay upcountry is usually affordable and a nice contrast to the sizzling beaches and busy resorts below.

MAKAWAO This small, two-street town has plenty of charm. It wasn't long ago that Hawaiian *paniolo* (cowboys) tied up their horses to the hitching posts outside the storefronts here; working ranchers still stroll through to pick up coffee and packages from the post office. The eclectic shops, galleries, and restaurants have a little something for everyone—from blocked Stetsons to wind chimes. Nearby, the **Hui No'eau Visual Arts Center,** Hawai'i's premier arts collective, is definitely worth a detour. Makawao's only accommodations are reasonably priced bed-and-breakfasts, perfect for those who love great views and don't mind slightly chilly nights.

KULA A feeling of pastoral remoteness prevails in this upcountry community of old flower farms, humble cottages, and new suburban ranch houses with million-dollar views that take in the ocean, the isthmus, the West Maui Mountains, and, at night, the lights that run along the gold coast like a string of pearls from Mā'alaea to Pu'u Ōlai. Everything flourishes at a cool 3,000 feet (bring a jacket), just below the cloud line, along a winding road on the way up to Haleakalā National Park. Everyone here grows something—Maui onions, lavender, orchids, and proteas—and B&Bs cater to guests seeking cool tropical nights, panoramic views, and a rural upland escape. Here you'll find the true peace and quiet that only rural farming country can offer—yet you're still just 40 minutes away from the beach and a little more than an hour's drive from Lahaina.

ON THE ROAD TO HĀNA On Maui's North Shore, **Pā'ia** was once a busy sugar plantation town with a railroad, two movie theaters, and a double-decker mercantile. As the sugar industry began to wane, the tuned-in, dropped-out hippies of the 1970s moved in, followed shortly by a cosmopolitan collection of windsurfers. When the international wave riders discovered **Ho'okipa Beach Park** just outside of town, their minds were blown; it's one of the best places on the planet to catch air. Today high-tech windsurf shops, trendy restaurants, bikini boutiques, and modern art galleries inhabit Pā'ia's rainbow-colored vintage buildings. The Dalai Lama himself blessed the beautiful Tibetan stupa in the center of town. **Mama's Fish House** is located east of Pā'ia in the tiny community of **Kū'au.**

Ten minutes farther east is **Ha'ikū.** Once a pineapple plantation village, complete with two canneries (both now shopping complexes), Ha'ikū offers vacation rentals and B&Bs in a pastoral setting. It's the perfect base for those who want to get off the beaten path and experience the quieter side of Maui.

HĀNA Set between an emerald rainforest and the blue Pacific is a Hawaiian village blissfully lacking in golf courses, shopping malls, and fast-food joints. Hāna is more of a sensory overload than a destination; here you'll discover the simple joys of rain-misted flowers, the sweet taste of backyard bananas and papayas, and the easy calm and unabashed aloha spirit of old Hawai'i. What saved "Heavenly" Hāna from the inevitable march of progress? The 52-mile **Hāna Highway,** which winds around 600 curves and crosses more than 50 one-lane bridges on its way from Kahului. You can go to Hāna for the day—it's 3 hours (and a half-century) from Kīhei and Lahaina—but 3 days are better.

GETTING AROUND

BY CAR The simplest way to see Maui is by rental car; public transit is still in its infancy here. All of the major car-rental firms—including Alamo, Avis, Budget, Dollar, Enterprise, Hertz, National, and Thrifty—have agencies on Maui. If you're on a budget or traveling with sports gear, you can rent an older vehicle by the week from **Kimo's Rent-a-Car** (www.kimosrentacar.com; ✆ **808/280-6327,** ext. 5). For tips on insurance and driving rules in Hawai'i, see "Getting Around Hawai'i" (p. 604).

Maui has only a handful of major roads, and you can expect a traffic jam or two heading into Kīhei, Lahaina, or Pā'ia. In general, the roads hug the coastlines; one zigzags up to Haleakalā's summit. When asking locals for directions, don't bother using highway numbers; residents know the routes by name only.

Traffic advisory: Be alert on the Honoapi'ilani Highway (Hwy. 30) en route to Lahaina. Drivers ogling whales in the channel between Maui and La¯na'i often slam on the brakes and cause major tie-ups and accidents. This is the main road connecting the west side to the rest of the island; if an accident, rockslide, flooding, or other road hazard occurs, traffic can back up for 1 to 8 hours (no joke). So before you set off, check with Maui County for road closure advisories (www.co.maui.hi.us; ✆ **808/986-1200**). The most up-to-date info can be found on its Twitter feed (@CountyofMaui) or that of a local news agency (@MauiNow).

BY MOTORCYCLE Feel the wind on your face and smell the salt air as you tour the island on a Harley, available for rent from **Cycle City Maui,** 150 Dairy Rd., Kahului, and 602 Front St., Lahaina (www.cyclecitymaui.com; ✆ **808/831-2698**). Rentals start at $99 a day.

BY TAXI Because Maui's various destinations are so spread out, taxi service can be quite expensive and should be limited to travel within a neighborhood. **West Maui Taxi** (www.westmauitaxi.com; ✆ **888/661-4545**) offers 24-hour service island-wide. Call **Kīhei Wailea Taxi** (✆ **808/879-3000**) if you need a ride in South Maui. The metered rate is $3 per mile.

BY BUS The **Maui Bus** (www.mauicounty.gov/bus; ✆ **808/871-4838**) is a public/private partnership that provides affordable but sadly inconsistent public transit to various communities across the island. Expect hour waits between rides. Air-conditioned buses service 13 routes, including several that stop at the airport. All routes operate daily, including holidays. Suitcases (one per passenger) and bikes are allowed; surfboards are not. Fares are $2.

[Fast FACTS] MAUI

Dentists Emergency dental care is available at **Hawai'i Family Dental,** 1847 S. Kīhei Rd., Kīhei (✆ **808/874-8401**), or at **Aloha Lahaina Dentists,** 134 Luakini St. (in the Maui Medical Group Bldg.), Lahaina (✆ **808/661-4005**).

Doctors **Urgent Care West Maui,** located in the Fairway Shops, 2580 Keka'a Dr., Suite 111, Ka'anapali (www.westmauidoctors.com; ✆ **808/667-9721**), is open 365 days a year; no appointment necessary. In Kīhei, call **Urgent Care Maui,** 1325 S. Kīhei Rd., Suite 103 (at Lipoa St., across from Times Market), Kīhei (✆ **808/879-7781**), open Monday to Saturday 7am to 9pm and Sunday 8am to 2pm.

Emergencies Call ✆ **911** for police, fire, and

ambulance service. District stations are located in Lahaina (✆ **808/661-4441**) and in Hāna (✆ **808/248-8311**).

Hospitals In Central Maui, **Maui Memorial Hospital** is at 221 Mahalani, Wailuku (✆ **808/244-9056**). East Maui's **Hāna Community Health Center** is open weekdays at 4590 Hāna Hwy. (www.hanahealth.org; ✆ **808/248-7515**). In upcountry Maui, **Kula Hospital** is at 100 Kēōkea Pl. (off of Kula Highway), Kula (✆ **808/878-1221**).

Internet Access Many places offer free Wi-Fi. **Whole Foods** (www.wholefoodsmarket.com/stores/maui) has Wi-Fi at the Maui Mall in Kahului, and **Starbucks** (www.starbucks.com/store-locator) provides Internet service in its stores in Kahului, Pukalani, Lahaina, and Kīhei.

Post Office To find the nearest post office, call ✆ **800/ASK-USPS.** In Lahaina, branches are located at the Lahaina Civic Center, 1760 Honoapi'ilani Hwy., and at the Lahaina Shopping Center, 132 Papalaua St. In Kahului, there's a branch at 138 S. Pu'unēnē Ave., and in Kīhei, there's one at 1254 S. Kīhei Rd.

Weather For the current weather, the Haleakalā National Park weather, or the marine and surf conditions, call the **National Weather Service's Maui forecast** (✆ **866/944-5025**) or visit www.prh.noaa.gov/hnl and click on the island of Maui.

EXPLORING MAUI

Attractions & Points of Interest

Tip: If you're a history buff, buy a "Passport to the Past" for $10 and gain admission to four of Maui's museums: the Baldwin Home and Wo Hing Museum in Lahaina, the Bailey House in Wailuku, and the A&B Sugar Museum in Pu'unēnē.

CENTRAL MAUI

Kahului

Under the airport flight path, next to Maui's busiest intersection and across from Costco and Kmart in Kahului's business park, is a most unlikely place: the **Kanahā Wildlife Sanctuary,** Haleakalā Highway Extension and Hāna Highway (✆ **808/984-8100**). Look for the parking area off the Haleakalā Highway Extension (just past Krispy Kreme), and you'll find a 50-foot trail that meanders along the shore to a shade shelter and lookout. A sign proclaims that this is the permanent home of the endangered black-neck Hawaiian stilt, whose population is now down to about 1,000. Naturalists say this is also a good place to see endangered Hawaiian *kōloa* ducks, stilts, coots, and other migrating shorebirds. For a quieter, more natural-looking wildlife preserve, head to the **Keālia Pond National Wildlife Preserve** in Kīhei (p. 307).

Maui Nui Botanical Garden ★ GARDEN This garden is a living treasure box of native Hawaiian coastal species and plants brought here by Polynesian voyagers in their seafaring canoes. Stroll beneath the shade of the *hala* and breadfruit trees. Learn how the first Hawaiians made everything from medicine to musical instruments out of the plants they found growing in these islands. Ask to see the *hāpai* (pregnant) banana tree—a variety with fruits that grow inside the trunk! Take a self-guided audio tour or come between Tuesday and Thursday at 10am, when docents lead tours ($10 per person). If the garden happens to be hosting a lei-making or *kapa*-dyeing workshop while you're on the island, don't miss it.

150 Kanaloa Ave., Kahului. www.mnbg.org. © **808/249-2798.** Admission $5 adults, free for seniors and children 12 and under. Free admission on Sat.

Wailuku

Wailuku, the historic gateway to 'Īao Valley, is worth a visit for a little shopping and a stop at the small but fascinating Bailey House.

Bailey House Museum ★ HISTORIC SITE Since 1957, the Maui Historical Society has welcomed visitors to the charming former home of Edward Bailey, a missionary, teacher, and accomplished artist. The 1833 building—a hybrid of Hawaiian stonework and Yankee-style architecture—is a treasure trove of Hawaiiana. Inside you'll find pre-contact artifacts: precious feather lei, *kapa* (barkcloth) samples, a wooden spear so large it defies believability, and a collection of gem-like Hawaiian tree-snail shells. Bailey's exquisite landscapes decorate the rock walls, capturing on canvas a Maui that exists only in memory.

2375-A Main St., Wailuku. www.mauimuseum.org. © **808/244-3326.** Admission $7 adults, $5 seniors/military, $2 children 7–12. Mon–Sat 10am–4pm.

Maui Tropical Plantation GARDEN About 3 miles south of Wailuku lies the tiny village of Waikapū, which has an attraction that's worth exploring. There's plenty to do here: shop for locally made souvenirs, learn how to husk a coconut, gawk at the longhorn cattle, and zoom on a zipline over the plantation's lush landscape. Relive Maui's past by taking a 40-minute narrated tram ride around fields of pineapple, sugarcane, and papaya trees at a working plantation. Tram tours start at 10am and leave about every 45 minutes. The grounds are fantastically landscaped with tropical plants and sculptures made from repurposed sugarcane-harvesting equipment. The **Mill House** restaurant offers exceptional, inventive cuisine for lunch and dinner from 11am to 9pm.

1670 Honoapi'ilani Hwy. www.mauitropicalplantation.com. © **808/270-0333.** Free admission. Tram tours $16 adults, $6 children 3–12. Daily 9am–5pm.

'Īao Valley ★

A couple of miles north of Wailuku, where the little plantation houses stop and the road climbs ever higher, Maui's true nature begins to reveal itself. The transition from suburban sprawl to raw nature is so abrupt that most people who drive up into the valley don't realize they're suddenly in a rainforest. This is 'Īao Valley, a beautiful 6¼-acre state park whose verdant nature, waterfalls, swimming holes, and hiking trails have been enjoyed by millions of people from around the world for more than a century. The head of the valley is a broad circular amphitheater where four major streams converge into 'Īao Stream. At the back of the amphitheater is rain-drenched Puu' Kukui, the West Maui Mountains' highest point.

To get here from Wailuku, take Main Street to 'Īao Valley Road to the entrance to the state park. Two paved walkways loop into the massive green amphitheater, across the bridge of 'Īao Valley Stream, and along the stream itself. This paved .35-mile loop is Maui's easiest hike—you can take your grandmother on this one. The leisurely walk will allow you to enjoy lovely views of 'Īao Needle and the lush vegetation.

'Iao Needle.

The feature known as **'Īao Needle** is an erosional remnant consisting of basalt dikes. This phallic rock juts an impressive 2,250 feet above sea level. Youngsters play in **'Īao Stream,** a peaceful brook that belies its bloody history. In 1790, King Kamehameha the Great and his men engaged in the battle of 'Īao Valley to gain control of Maui. When the battle ended, so many bodies blocked 'Īao Stream that the battle site was named Kepaniwai, or "Damming of the Waters." An architectural heritage park of Hawaiian, Japanese, Chinese, Filipino, Korean, Portuguese, and New England–style houses stands in harmony by 'Īao Stream at **Kepaniwai Heritage Garden.** This is a good picnic spot, with plenty of tables and benches. You can see ferns, banana trees, and other native and exotic plants in the **'Īao Valley Botanic Garden** along the stream.

WHEN TO GO The park is open daily 7am to 7pm; the entrance fee is $5 per car. Go early in the morning or late in the afternoon when the sun's rays slant into the valley and create a mystical mood. You can bring a picnic and spend the day, but be prepared at any time for one of the frequent tropical cloudbursts that soak the valley and swell both waterfalls and streams.

The Scenic Route to West Maui: The Kahekili Highway

The main route to West Maui is the Honoapi'ilani Highway, which sidles around the southern coastline along the *pali* (cliffs) to Lahaina. But those who relish adventures should consider exploring the backside of the West Maui Mountains.

From Wailuku, head north on the **Kahekili Highway** (Hwy. 340)—though "highway" is a bit of a misnomer for this paved and sometimes precarious road. It's named after a fierce Maui king who built houses out of the skulls of his enemies. The narrow and sometimes white-knuckle road weaves for 20 miles along an ancient Hawaiian coastal footpath to Honokōhau Bay, at the island's northernmost tip, past blowholes, sea stacks, seabird rookeries, and the imposing 636-foot Kahakuloa headland. On the *mauka* (mountain) side, you'll pass high cliffs, deep valleys dotted with plantation houses, cattle grazing on green plateaus, old wooden churches, taro fields, and houses hung with fishing nets. It's slow going (you often have to inch past oncoming traffic on what feels like a one-lane track) but a spectacular drive. In Kahakuloa, between mile markers 12 and 13, stop in at the wooden roadside stand known as **Julia's Best Banana Bread** for world-famous warm, sweet loaves and coconut candy. Check for road closures before heading out, especially if it's been raining heavily.

At Honokōhau, pick up Hwy. 30 and continue on to the West Maui resorts; the first one you'll reach is Kapalua (see below).

WEST MAUI

For a map of attractions in Lahaina and Ka'anapali, see p. 353.

Baldwin Home Museum ★ HISTORIC SITE Step into this coral-and-rock house on Lahaina's Front Street and travel back in time. Built in 1835, it belonged to Rev. Dwight Baldwin, a missionary, naturalist, and self-trained physician who saved many Native Hawaiians from devastating influenza and smallpox epidemics. Baldwin's rudimentary medical tools (on display here) bear witness to the steep odds he faced. He was rewarded with 2,600 acres in Kapalua, where he grew pineapple—then an experimental crop. His children later became some of Hawai'i's most powerful landholders and business owners. Tour the Baldwin family home and pick up a walking-tour map to Lahaina's most historic sites on your way out. On Friday night, docents dressed in period attire offer candlelit tours and serve free refreshments on the lānai.

120 Dickenson St. (at Front St.). www.lahainarestoration.org. ✆ **808/661-3262.** Admission $7 adults, $5 seniors/military, free for children 12 and under (admission also grants entry to Wo Hing Museum). Sat–Thurs 10am–4pm, Fri 10am–8:30pm.

Banyan Tree NATURAL ATTRACTION Of all the Indian banyan trees in Hawai'i, this is the greatest—so big you can't fit it in your camera's viewfinder. It was 8 feet tall when planted in 1873. Today the arboreal octopus rises more than 50 feet high, has 12 major trunks, and shades artists and crafters selling their wares in Courthouse Square.

Wo Hing Museum & Cookhouse ★ HISTORIC SITE Sandwiched between souvenir shops and restaurants on Front Street, this ornate building once served as a fraternal and social meeting hall for Lahaina's Chinese immigrants. Today it houses fascinating Asian artifacts, artwork, and a lovely shrine in the altar room upstairs. Beside the

The banyan tree in Courthouse Square.

temple is a rustic cookhouse where you can watch some of Thomas Edison's first movies, filmed here in Hawai'i. The footage of *paniolo* (cowboys) wrangling steer onto ships offshore and Honolulu circa 1898 is mesmerizing. Wo Hing hosts Lunar New Year festivals and other celebrations that are catnip for kids.

858 Front St. www.lahainarestoration.org. ✆ **808/661-3262.** Admission $7 adults, $5 seniors/military, free for children 12 and under (admission also grants entry to Baldwin House Museum; see above). Daily 10am–4pm.

Ka'anapali

Whalers Village Museum ★ MUSEUM ***Note: This museum was closed for renovation at press time.*** As you enter Ka'anapali's posh shopping center, you're greeted by the almost life-size metal sculpture of a mother whale and two nursing calves. A few steps in is the impressive, bleached-white skeleton of a 40-foot sperm whale. On the mall's second floor, a small interactive museum illuminates the "Golden Era of Whaling" from 1825 to 1860. Follow the self-guided audio tour, check out the harpoons and scrimshaw collection, and experience the cramped quarters of a whaleboat's forecastle. The videos of whale-hunting carnage may be a bit much for youngsters, but the free talks by marine biologists every Monday, Wednesday, and Friday at 11am are terrific. ***Tip:*** You can get 3 hours' free parking validated here.

In Whalers Village Shopping Mall, 2435 Ka'anapali Pkwy. www.whalersmuseum.com. ✆ **808/661-5992.** Admission $3 adults, $2 seniors/students/military, $1 children 6–18, free for children under 6. Daily 10am–4pm.

SOUTH MAUI

Mā'alaea

Maui Ocean Center ★★★ AQUARIUM This 5-acre facility houses the largest aquarium in the state and features one of Hawai'i's largest predators: the tiger shark. As you walk past the 3 dozen or so tanks and countless exhibits, you'll slowly descend from the tide pools to the pelagic zone—without ever getting wet. Start at the outdoor surge pool, where you'll see shallow-water spiny urchins and cauliflower coral; and then move on to the turtle pool and eagle-ray pools before heading indoors for the star of the show: a 100-foot-long, 600,000-gallon main tank featuring tiger, gray, and white-tip sharks, as well as feisty ulua, colorful surgeonfish, and numerous others. The walkway tunnels right through the tank, so you're surrounded on three sides by marine creatures. Check out the hammerhead exhibit, where juvenile scalloped hammerhead sharks are on display, and the Shark Dive Maui Program, where scuba divers plunge into the tank with sharks, stingrays, and tropical fish. You, too, can sign up to dive with sharks, and fish-loving kids can book a sleepover in the aquarium, staying up into the wee hours to watch glowing jellyfish and other nocturnal animals.

At the Mā'alaea Harbor Village, 192 Mā'alaea Rd. (the triangle btw. Honoapi'ilani Hwy. and Mā'alaea Rd.). www.mauioceancenter.com. ✆ **808/270-7000.** Admission $28 adults, $25 seniors, $20 children 3–12 (book online for a week pass upgrade). Daily 9am–5pm (until 6pm July–Aug).

Maui Ocean Center.

Kīhei

West of the junction of Pi'ilani Highway (Hwy. 31) and Mokulele Highway (Hwy. 350) is **Kealia Pond National Wildlife Preserve** (www.fws.gov/kealiapond; © **808/875-1582**), a 700-acre U.S. Fish & Wildlife wetland preserve where endangered Hawaiian stilts, coots, and ducks splash about. These ponds work both as bird preserves and as sedimentation basins that keep coral reefs from silting from runoff. You can take a self-guided tour along a boardwalk dotted with interpretive signs and shade shelters, through sand dunes, and around ponds to Mā'alaea Harbor. The boardwalk starts at the outlet of Kealia Pond on the ocean side of North Kīhei Road (near mile marker 2 on Pi'ilani Hwy.). Among the Hawaiian water birds seen here are the black-crowned high heron, Hawaiian coot, Hawaiian duck, and Hawaiian stilt. From July to December, the hawksbill turtle comes ashore here to lay its eggs.

Wailea

The best way to explore this golden resort coast is to head for Wailea's 1.5-mile **coastal nature trail ★**, stretching between the Fairmont Kea Lani Maui and the *kiawe* thicket just beyond the Marriott Wailea Beach Resort. The serpentine path meanders past an abundance of native plants (on the *makai,* or ocean side), old Hawaiian habitats, and a billion dollars' worth of luxury hotels. You can pick up the trail at any of the resorts or from clearly marked shoreline access points along the coast. As the path crosses several bold black-lava points, it affords new vistas of islands and ocean; benches allow you to pause and contemplate the view across 'Alalākeiki Channel, where you may spy whales in season. It's nice in the cool hours of the morning (though often clogged with joggers) and at sunset, when you can watch the burning sun sink into the Pacific.

Mākena

A few miles south of Wailea, the manicured coast returns to wilderness; now you're in Mākena. At one time cattle were driven down the slope from upland ranches, lashed to rafts, and sent into the water to swim to boats that waited to take them to market. Now **Mākena Landing ★** is a great spot to launch kayaks and dive trips.

From the landing, go south on Mākena Road; on the right is **Keawalai Congregational Church** (© **808/879-5557**), built in 1855, with walls 3 feet thick. Surrounded by *ti* leaves, which by Hawaiian custom provide protection, and built of lava rock with coral used as mortar, this church sits on its own cove with a gold-sand beach. It always attracts a Sunday crowd for its 7:30am and 10am Hawaiian-language services.

Farther south on the coast is **La Pérouse Monument,** a pyramid of lava rocks that marks the spot where French explorer Adm. Comte de la Pérouse set foot on Maui in 1789. He described the "burning climate" of the leeward coast, observed several fishing villages near Kīhei, and sailed on into oblivion, never to be seen again. To get here, drive south to 'Āhihi Bay, where the road turns to gravel. Just beyond this is **'Āhihi-Kīna'u Natural Preserve,** 1,238 acres of rare anchialine ponds and sunbaked lava fields from the last eruption of Haleakalā between 200 and 500 years ago. The state closed the preserve to all traffic—both land and sea—hoping to give the fragile ecosystem a chance to rebound. Continue another 2 miles past 'Āhihi-Kīna'u to La Pérouse Bay; the monument sits amid a clearing in black lava at the end of the dirt road. If you've got plenty of water, sunblock, and sturdy shoes, you can embark on foot on the **King's Trail,** a rugged path built by ancient Hawaiian royals.

UPCOUNTRY MAUI

Makawao

Makawao is Hawaiian cowboy country—yup, the islands have a long-standing tradition of ranchers and rodeo masters, and this cool, misty upcountry town is its Maui epicenter. Modern-day *paniolo* come here to fuel up on cream puffs and stick donuts from **Komoda Store & Bakery,** 3674 Baldwin Ave. (✆ **808/572-7261**), a 100-year-old family grocery that seems frozen in time. Neighboring shops offer Tibetan jewelry, shabby-chic housewares, and marvelous paintings by local artists. A handful of decent restaurants crowd the intersection of Baldwin and Makawao avenues; take your pick of sushi, Maui cattle ribeye, or pasta.

Five minutes down Baldwin Avenue, the **Hui No'eau Visual Arts Center,** 2841 Baldwin Ave. (www.huinoeau.com; ✆ **808/572-6560**), occupies a two-story, Mediterranean-style stucco home designed in 1917 by C. W. Dickey, one of Hawai'i's most prominent architects. The sprawling 9-acre estate, known as **Kaluanui,** hosts visiting artists for lectures and classes in basketry, jewelry making, ceramics, painting, and other media, all at reasonable prices. Call for details. The gallery's rotating exhibits include work by established and emerging artists, and the gift shop features many one-of-a-kind works, including ceramic seconds at a steal. Hours are Monday through Saturday 10am to 4pm.

Kula

While in the upcountry Kula region, visit one of the area's many farms (see "Maui Farms: Stop & Smell the Lavender," p. 323).

Kula Botanical Garden ★ GARDEN You can take a self-guided, informative, leisurely stroll through this collection of more than 700 native and exotic plants—including three unique assemblages of orchids, proteas, and bromeliads—at this 5-acre garden. It offers a good overview of Hawai'i's exotic flora in one small, cool place.

638 Kekaulike Ave, Kula. www.kulabotanicalgarden.com. ✆ **808/878-1715.** Admission $10 adults, $3 children 6–12. Daily 8am–4pm.

MauiWine (Tedeschi Vineyards) ★ VINEYARD/WINERY On the southern shoulder of Haleakalā is **'Ulupalakua Ranch,** a 20,000-acre spread once owned by the legendary sea captain James Makee, celebrated in the Hawaiian song and dance "Hula O Makee." Wounded in a Honolulu waterfront brawl in 1843, Makee moved to Maui and bought 'Ulupalakua. He renamed it Rose Ranch, planted sugar as a cash crop, and grew rich. Still in operation, the ranch is now home to Maui's only winery, established in 1974 by Napa vintner Emil Tedeschi, who began growing California and European grapes here and produces serious still and sparkling wines, plus a silly wine made of pineapple juice. The rustic grounds are the perfect place for a picnic. Settle in under the sprawling camphor tree, pop the cork on a blanc de blanc, and toast your good fortune in being here.

Off Hwy. 37 (Kula Hwy.). https://mauiwine.com. ✆ **808/878-6058.** Free tastings daily 10am–5:30pm. Free tours at 10:30am, 1:30pm, and 2:30pm.

House of the Sun: Haleakalā National Park ★★★

The summit of Haleakalā, the House of the Sun, is a spectacular natural phenomenon. More than 1.3 million people a year ascend the 10,023-foot-high mountain to peer into the world's largest dormant volcano. Haleakalā has not rumbled for at least 100 years, but it's still officially considered active. The lunar-like volcanic landscape is a national park, home to numerous rare and endangered plants, birds, and insects. Hardy adventurers hike and camp inside the crater's wilderness (see

Leleiwi Overlook.

"Hiking," p. 344, and "Camping," p. 386). Those bound for the interior should bring survival gear, for the terrain is raw and rugged—not unlike the moon. Note that the Haleakalā Crater is one of the world's quietest places—so silent that it exceeds the technical capacity of microphones.

Haleakalā National Park extends from the volcano's summit down its southeast flank to Maui's eastern coast, beyond Hāna. There are actually two separate districts within the park: **Haleakalā Summit** and **Kīpahulu** (see "Tropical Haleakalā: 'Ohe'o Gulch at Kīpahulu," p. 320). No roads link the summit and the coast; you have to approach them separately, and you need at least a day to see each place.

WHEN TO GO Many drive up to the summit in predawn darkness to watch the sunrise over Haleakalā, though I recommend sunset instead. It's equally beautiful—and warmer! Plus, you're more likely to explore the rest of the park when you're not sleep-deprived and hungry for breakfast. Weather is extreme at the summit, ranging from blazing sun to sudden snow flurries. If you go at sunrise, bring every warm thing you can swaddle yourself with. Full-moon nights are especially ethereal. But remember, glorious views aren't guaranteed; the summit may be misty or overcast at any time of day. Before you go, get current weather conditions from the park (✆ **808/572-4400**) or the **National Weather Service** (✆ **866/944-5025,** option 4).

THE DRIVE TO THE SUMMIT

Just driving up the mountain is an experience. **Haleakalā Crater Road (Hwy. 378)** is one of the fastest-ascending roads in the world. Its 33 switchbacks travel through numerous climate zones, passing in and out of clouds to finally deliver a view that extends for more than 100 miles. The trip takes 1½ to 2 hours from Kahului. No matter where you start out, follow Highway 37 (Haleakalā Hwy.) to Pukalani, where you'll pick up Highway 377 (also called Haleakalā Hwy.), which you take to Highway 378. Fill up your gas tank before you go—Pukalani is the last stop for fuel. Along the way, expect fog, rain, and wind. Be on the lookout for downhill bicyclists, stray cattle, and naïve **nēnē,** the native Hawaiian geese.

Remember, you're entering a high-altitude wilderness area; some people get dizzy from lack of oxygen. Bring water, a jacket, and, if you go up for sunrise, every scrap of warmth you can find. There are no concessions in the park—not even a coffee urn in sight. If you plan to hike, bring extra water and snacks.

At the **park entrance,** you'll pay a fee of $25 per car or $20 per motorcycle. It's good for 3 days and includes access to the Kīpahulu district on the east side of the island. (***Tip:*** If you plan on visiting more than once, or also visiting Hawai'i Volcanoes National Park on the Big Isle, purchase a tri-park pass for $5. It allows unlimited access for one year to Haleakalā, Hawai'i Volcanoes, and Pu'uhonua o Hōnaunau National

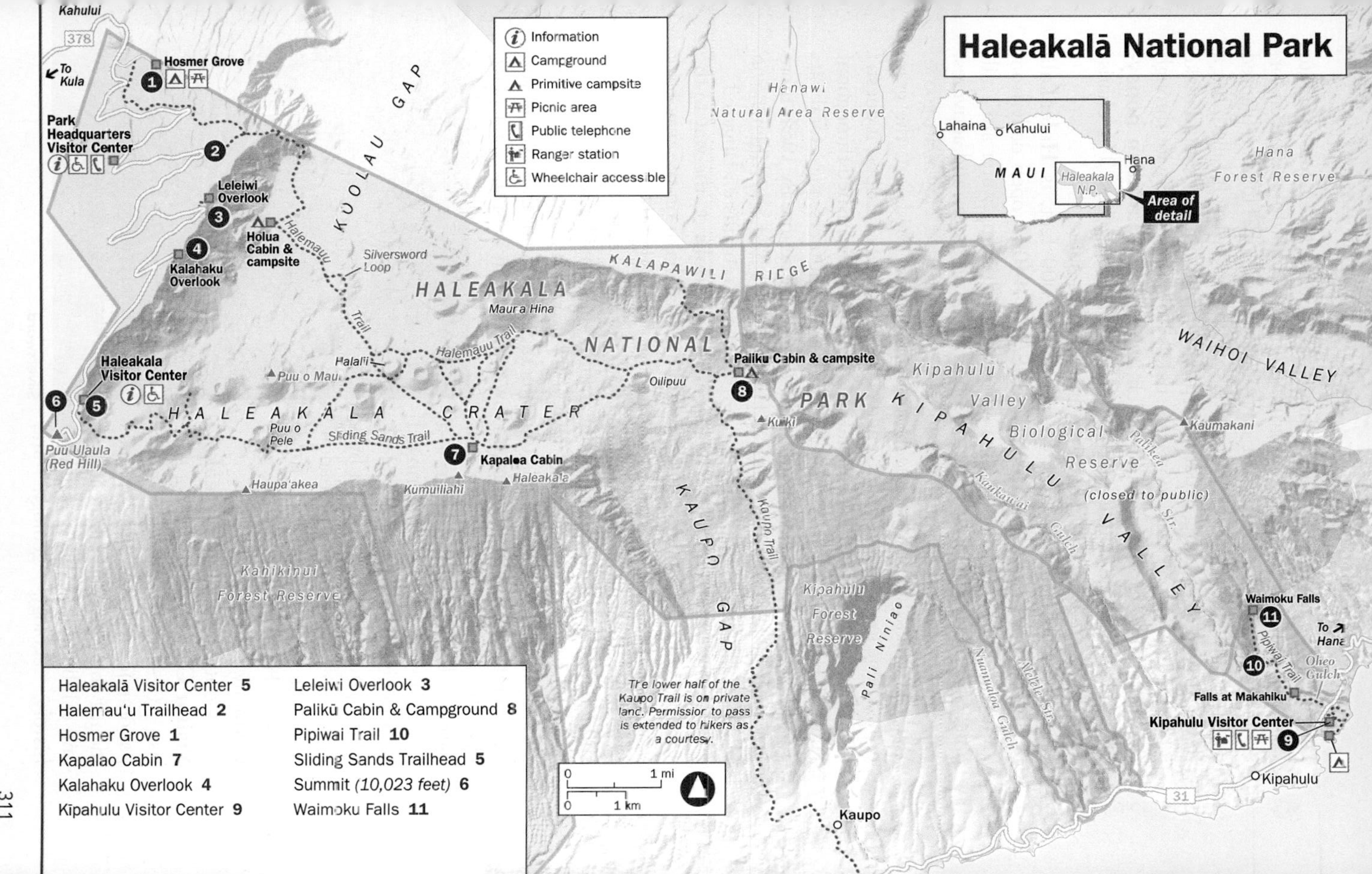

Haleakalā National Park
Information
Campground
Primitive campsite
Picnic area
Public telephone
Ranger station
Wheelchair accessible
Lahaina
Kahului
Hana
MAUI
Haleakala N.P.
Area of detail
Kahului
378
To Kula
Hosmer Grove
Park Headquarters Visitor Center
KOOLAU GAP
Leleiwi Overlook
Holua Cabin & campsite
Kalahaku Overlook
Halemauu Trail
Silversword Loop
HALEAKALA NATIONAL PARK
Maui Hina
Halemauu Trail
Halali'i
Puu o Maui
Haleakala Visitor Center
HALEAKALA CRATER
Puu o Pele
Sliding Sands Trail
Puu Ulaula (Red Hill)
Kapalaoa Cabin
Haupa'akea
Kumuiliahi
Haleakala
Kahikinui Forest Reserve
Hanawi Natural Area Reserve
KALAPAWILI RIDGE
Oilipuu
Paliku Cabin & campsite
Kuiki
KAUPO GAP
Kaupo Trail
Kipahulu Valley Biological Reserve (closed to public)
KIPAHULU VALLEY
Kaumakani
Palikea Str.
Kaukaiwai Gulch
Hana Forest Reserve
WAIHOI VALLEY
Kipahulu Forest Reserve
Pali Ninao
Nuanualoa Gulch
Alelele Str.
The lower half of the Kaupo Trail is on private land. Permission to pass is extended to hikers as a courtesy.
0 1 mi
0 1 km
Kaupo
Waimoku Falls
Pipiwai Trail
Oheo Gulch
To Hana
Falls at Makahiku
Kipahulu Visitor Center
Kipahulu
31
Haleakalā Visitor Center 5
Halemau'u Trailhead 2
Hosmer Grove 1
Kapalao Cabin 7
Kalahaku Overlook 4
Kīpahulu Visitor Center 9
Leleiwi Overlook 3
Palikū Cabin & Campground 8
Pipiwai Trail 10
Sliding Sands Trailhead 5
Summit (10,023 feet) 6
Waimoku Falls 11

Park in Kona.) Immediately after the park entrance, take a left turn into **Hosmer's Grove.** A small campground abuts a beautiful evergreen forest. During Hawai'i's territorial days, forester Ralph Hosmer planted experimental groves, hoping to launch a timber industry. It failed, but a few of his sweet-smelling cedars and pines remain. Birders should make a beeline here. A half-mile loop trail snakes from the parking lot through the evergreens to a picturesque gulch, where rare **Hawaiian honeycreepers** flit above native ***'ōhi'a*** and **sandalwood trees.** The charismatic birds are best spotted in the early morning hours.

One mile from the park entrance, at 7,000 feet, is **Haleakalā National Park Headquarters** (**© 808/572-4400**), open daily from 7am to 3:45pm. Restrooms, a pay phone, and drinking water are available. Stop here to pick up information on park programs and activities, get camping permits, and, occasionally, see a native Hawaiian goose. With its black face, buff cheeks, and partially webbed feet, the gray-brown nēnē looks like a small Canada goose with zebra stripes; it doesn't migrate and prefers lava beds to lakes. Nēnē once flourished throughout Hawai'i, but habitat destruction and predators (hunters, pigs, feral cats and dogs, and mongooses) nearly caused their extinction. By 1951, there were only 30 left. Now protected as Hawai'i's state bird, the wild nēnē on Haleakalā number fewer than 400—the species remains endangered.

Beyond headquarters are **two scenic overlooks** on the way to the summit; stop at Leleiwi on the way up and Kalahaku on the way back down, if only to get out, stretch, and get accustomed to the heights. Take a deep breath, look around, and pop your ears. If you feel dizzy, or get a sudden headache, consider turning around and going back down.

The **Leleiwi Overlook** is just beyond mile marker 17. From the parking area, a short trail leads to a spectacular view of the colorful volcanic crater. When the clouds are low and the sun is in the right place (usually around sunset), you may witness the "Brocken Spectre"—a reflection of your shadow, ringed by a rainbow, in the clouds below. This optical illusion—caused by a rare combination of sun, shadow, and fog—occurs in only three places: Haleakalā, Scotland, and Germany.

Silversword.

Continue on to the **Haleakalā Visitor Center,** open daily at sunrise (5:45am–3pm). It offers panoramic views, with photos identifying the various features, and exhibits that explain the area's history, ecology, geology, and volcanology. Park staff members are often on hand to answer questions. Restrooms and water are available. The actual summit is a little farther on, at **Pu'u Ula'ula Overlook** (also known as Red Hill), the volcano's highest point, where you'll see Haleakalā Observatories' cluster of buildings—known unofficially as **Science City.** The Pu'u Ula'ula Overlook, with its glass-enclosed windbreak, is a prime viewing spot, crowded with shivering folks at sunrise. It's also the best place to see a rare **silversword.** This botanical wonder is the punk of the plant world—like a spacey artichoke with attitude. Silverswords grow only in Hawai'i, take from 4 to 30 years to bloom, and then, usually between May and October, send up a 1- to 6-foot stalk covered in multitudes of reddish, sunflower-like blooms. Don't walk too close to silversword plants, as footfalls can damage their roots.

On your way back down, stop at the **Kalahaku Overlook.** On a clear day you can see all the way across Alenuihaha Channel to the often snowcapped summit of Mauna Kea on the Big Island. ***Tip:*** Put your car in low gear when driving down the Haleakalā Crater Road, so you don't destroy your brakes by riding them the whole way down.

East Maui & Heavenly Hāna

Hāna is about as close as you can get to paradise on Earth. In and around Hāna, you'll find a lush tropical rainforest dotted with cascading waterfalls, trees spilling ripe fruits onto the grass, and the sparkling blue Pacific, skirted by red- and black-sand beaches.

THE ROAD TO HĀNA ★★★

Top down, sunscreen on, Hawaiian music playing on a breezy morning it's time to head out along the Hāna Highway (Hwy. 36), a wiggle of a road that runs along Maui's northeastern shore. The drive takes at least 3 hours from Lahaina or Kīhei, but don't shortchange yourself—take all day. Going to Hāna is about the journey, not the destination.

There are wilder, steeper, and more dangerous roads, but in all of Hawai'i, no road is more celebrated than this one. It winds 50 miles past taro patches, magnificent seascapes, waterfall pools, botanical gardens, and verdant rainforests, and ends at one of Hawai'i's most beautiful tropical places.

The outside world discovered the little village of Hāna in 1926, when pickax-wielding convicts carved a narrow road out of the cliff's edge. Often subject to landslides and washouts, the mud-and-gravel track was paved in 1962, when tourist traffic began to increase; it now sees around 1,000 cars and dozens of vans a day. That translates into half a million people a year, which is way too many. Go at the wrong time, and you'll be stuck in a bumper-to-bumper rental-car parade—peak traffic hours are midmorning and midafternoon year-round, especially on weekends.

The road to Hāna.

In the rush to "do" Hāna in a day, most visitors spin around town in 10 minutes and wonder what all the fuss is about. It takes time to soak up the serene magic of Hāna, play in the waterfalls, sniff the rain-misted gingers, hike through clattering bamboo forests, and merge with the tension-dissolving scenery. Stay overnight if you can, and meander back in a day or two. If you really must do the Hāna Highway in a day, go just before sunrise and return after sunset.

Tips: Practice aloha. Yield at one-lane bridges, wave at oncoming motorists, let the big guys in 4×4s have the right of way—you're not in a hurry, after all! If the guy behind you blinks his lights, let him pass. Unless you're rounding a blind curve, don't honk your horn—in Hawai'i, it's considered rude. ***Safety note:*** Be aware of the weather when hiking in streams. Flash floods happen frequently in this area. *Do not attempt to cross rising stream waters.* In the words of the Emergency Weather Forecast System: "Turn around. Don't drown."

THE JOURNEY BEGINS IN PĀ'IA Before you start out, fill up on fuel. Pā'ia is the last place for gas until you get to Hāna, some 50-plus bridges and 600-plus hairpin turns down the road. (It's fun to make a game out of counting the bridges.)

Pā'ia ★★ was once a thriving sugar-mill town. The skeletal mill is still here, but in the 1950s the bulk of the population (10,000 in its heyday) shifted to Kahului. Like so many former plantation towns, Pā'ia nearly foundered, but its beachfront charm lured hippies, followed by adrenaline-seeking windsurfers and, most recently, young families. The town has proven its adaptability. Now chic eateries and trendy shops occupy the old ma-and-pa establishments. Plan to get here early, around

7am, when **Charley's ★**, 142 Hāna Hwy. (✆ **808/579-8085**), opens. Enjoy a big, hearty breakfast for a reasonable price or continue a few minutes down the road to the little town of **Kū'au.** A rainbow fence made of surfboards announces **Kū'au Store** (✆ **808/579-8844**), a great stop for smoothies and snacks.

WINDSURFING MECCA Just before mile marker 9 is **Ho'okipa Beach Park ★★★**, where top-ranked windsurfers come to test themselves against thunderous surf and forceful wind. On nearly every windy day after noon (the board surfers have the waves in the morning), you can watch dozens of windsurfers twirling and dancing in the wind like colored butterflies. To watch them, do not stop on the highway, but go past the park and turn left at the entrance on the far side of the beach. Park on the high grassy bluff or drive down to the sandy beach and park alongside the pavilion. **Green sea turtles** haul out to rest on the east end of the beach. Go spy on them, but stay a respectful distance (15 ft.) away. Facilities include restrooms, a shower, picnic tables, and a barbecue area.

INTO THE COUNTRY Past Ho'okipa Beach, the road winds down into **Māliko Gulch.** Big-wave surfers use the boat ramp here to launch jet skis and head out to **Jaws,** one of the world's biggest surf breaks a few

Windsurfers at Ho'okipa Beach Park.

coves over. Back on the Hāna Highway, for the next few miles you'll pass through the rural area of **Ha'ikū,** where banana patches and guava trees litter their sweet fruit onto the street.

At mile marker 16, the curves begin, one right after another. Slow down and enjoy the view of fern-covered hills and plunging valleys punctuated by mango and *kukui* trees. After mile marker 16, the road is still called the Hāna Highway, but the number changes from Highway 36 to Highway 360, and the mile markers go back to 0.

TWIN FALLS Not far beyond mile marker two, you'll see a large fruit stand on the *mauka* (mountain) side of the road—most likely surrounded by lots of cars. This is **Twin Falls** (www.twinfallsmaui.net; © **808/463-1275**), a privately owned piece of paradise with more waterfalls than anyone can count. A gravel road leads to the first waterfall pool. Continue up the mountain path to find many more. Swimming is safe as long as it's not raining and you don't have open wounds. (Bacterial infections aren't uncommon.) Be respectful of the residents and pack out your trash.

From here on out, there's a waterfall (and one-lane bridge) around nearly every turn in the road, so drive slowly and be prepared to stop and yield to oncoming cars.

WILD CURVES About a half-mile after mile marker 6, there's a sharp U-curve in the road, going uphill. The road is super narrow here, with a brick wall on one side and virtually no maneuvering room. Sound your horn at the start of the U-curve to let approaching cars know you're coming. Take the curve slowly.

Just before mile marker 7, a forest of waving **bamboo** takes over the right-hand side of the road. To the left, you'll see a stand of **rainbow eucalyptus trees,** recognizable by their multicolored trunks. Drivers are often tempted to pull over here, but there isn't any shoulder. Continue on; you'll find many more beautiful trees to gawk at down the road.

AN EASY FAMILY HIKE At mile marker 9, a small state wayside area has restrooms, picnic tables, and a barbecue area. The sign says KO'OLAU FOREST RESERVE, but the real attraction here is the **Waikamoi Nature Trail,** an easy .75-mile loop. The start of the trail is just behind the Quiet: Trees at Work sign. The well-marked trail meanders through eucalyptus, ferns, and hala trees.

CAN'T-MISS PHOTO OPS Just past mile marker 12 is the **Kaumahina State Wayside Park ★**. This is a good pit stop and a great vista point. You can see all the way down the rugged coastline to the jutting Keanae Peninsula.

Another mile and a couple of bends in the road, and you'll enter the Honomanu Valley, with its beautiful bay. To get to the **Honomanū Bay,** look for the turnoff on your left, just after mile marker 14, as you begin your ascent up the other side of the valley. The rutted dirt-and-cinder

A church built in 1860 in Ke'anae.

road takes you down to the rocky black sand beach. There are no facilities here. Because of the strong rip currents offshore, swimming is best in the stream inland from the ocean. You'll consider the detour worthwhile as you stand on the beach, well away from the ocean, and turn to look back on the steep cliffs covered with vegetation.

KE'ANAE PENINSULA & ARBORETUM At mile marker 17, the vintage Hawaiian village of **Ke'anae** ★★ stands out against the Pacific like a place time forgot. Here, on an old lava flow graced by an 1860 stone church and swaying palms, is one of the last coastal enclaves of native Hawaiians. They still grow taro in patches and pound it into poi, the staple of the old Hawaiian diet, and they still pluck *opihi* (limpets) from tide pools along the jagged coast and cast thrownets for fish. Pick up a loaf of still-warm banana bread from **Aunty Sandy's** (10 Ke'anae Rd.; **✆ 808/344-1885**).

At nearby **Ke'anae Arboretum,** Hawai'i's botanical world is divided into three parts: native forest, introduced forest, and traditional Hawaiian plants, food, and medicine. You can swim in the pools of Piinaau Stream or press on along a mile-long trail into Ke'anae Valley, where a lovely tropical rainforest waits at the end. Had enough foliage for one day? This is the prime spot to turn around.

PUA'A KA'A STATE WAYSIDE Tourists and locals alike often overlook this convenient, rejuvenating stop, a half-mile past mile marker 22. Park by the restrooms; then cross the street to explore a jade green waterfall pool. Break out your picnic lunch here at the shaded tables. Practice saying the park's name, pronounced pooh-*ahh*-ahh kahh-*ahh,* which means "rolling pig." If you're daring, climb beyond the first waterfall to find another.

For the world's best dessert (only a slight exaggeration), continue on to **Nāhiku,** near mile marker 27.5 (yes, half-mile markers come into play in this wild territory). You'll see the rainbow-splashed sign for **Coconut Glen's ★★** (www.coconutglens.com; ✆ **808/248-4876**). Pull over and indulge in some truly splendid ice cream—dairy-free and made with coconut milk! Scoops of chocolate chili, *lilikoi,* and honey macadamia nut ice cream are served in coconut bowls, with coconut chips as spoons. This whimsical stand oozes with aloha. From here, you're only 20 minutes away from Hāna.

KAHANU GARDENS & PI'ILANIHALE HEIAU ★★★ To see one of Hawai'i's most impressive archeological sites, take a detour off of Hāna Highway down 'Ula'ino Road. The National Tropical Botanical Garden maintains the world's largest breadfruit collection here—including novel varieties collected from every tropical corner of the globe. Ancient Hawaiian history comes alive when you walk through the manicured canoe garden and first glimpse the monumental 3-acre Pi'ilanihale *heaiu* (temple). Built 800 years ago from stacked rocks hand-carried from miles away, it is a testament to the great chiefdoms of the past. Gaze in wonder at the 50-foot retaining wall and thatched canoe *hale* (house). Imagine steering a war canoe onto the wave-swept shore. Take time to soak in the site's *mana* (spiritual power). Admission is $10; 2-hour guided tours are $25 (650 'Ula'ino Rd., Hāna; www.ntbg.org; ✆ **808/248-8912**).

WAI'ĀNAPANAPA STATE PARK ★★★ On the outskirts of Hāna, the shiny black-sand beach appears like a vivid dream, with bright-green jungle foliage on three sides and cobalt-blue water lapping at its shore. The 120-acre state park on an ancient lava flow includes sea cliffs, lava tubes, arches, and the beach—plus a dozen rustic cabins. See p. 388 for a review of the cabins. Also see "Beaches" and "Camping," below.

HĀNA ★★★

Green, tropical Hāna, which some call heavenly, is a destination all its own, a small coastal village in a rainforest inhabited by 2,500 people, many part-Hawaiian. Beautiful Hāna enjoys more than 90 inches of rain a year—more than enough to keep the scenery lush. Banyans, bamboo, breadfruit trees—everything seems larger than life, especially the flowers, like wild ginger and plumeria. Several roadside stands offer exotic blooms for $5 a bunch. As the signs say, just Put Money in Box. It's the Hāna honor system. The best farm stand of the bunch is **Hāna Farms ★★**, 2910 Hāna Hwy. (✆ **808/248-7371;** see p. 417 for details).

The last unspoiled Hawaiian town on Maui is, oddly enough, the home of Maui's first resort, which opened in 1946. Paul Fagan, then owner of the San Francisco Seals baseball team, bought an old inn and

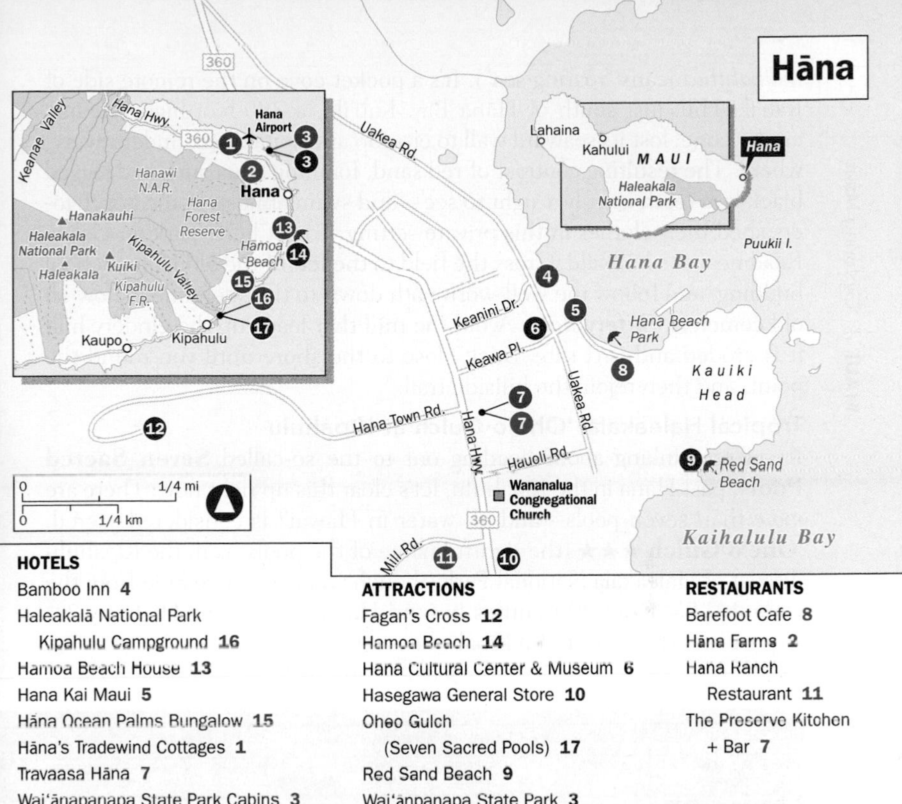

turned it into Hāna's first and only resort, now called **Travaasa Hāna.** Others have tried to open hotels and golf courses, but the Hāna community always politely refuses. Several great B&Bs are scattered around town, though; see p. 383 for reviews.

A wood-frame 1871 building that served as the old Hāna District Police Station now holds the **Hāna Cultural Center & Museum,** 4974 Uakea Rd. (www.hanaculturalcenter.org; © **808/248-8622**). The center tells the history of the area, with some excellent artifacts, memorabilia, and photographs. Also stop in at **Hasegawa General Store,** a Maui institution. Buy a T-shirt or bumper sticker and check out the machete display above the office window.

On the green hills above Hāna stands a 30-foot-high white cross made of lava rock. Citizens erected the cross in memory of Paul Fagan, who helped keep the town alive. The 3-mile hike up to **Fagan's Cross** provides a gorgeous view of the Hāna coast, especially at sunset, when Fagan himself liked to climb this hill (see p. 348 for details).

Most day-trippers to Hāna miss the most unusual natural attraction of all: **Red Sand Beach ★★**, officially named Kaihalulu Beach (*kaihalulu* means "roaring sea"). It's a pocket cove on the remote side of Kau'iki Hill, just south of Hāna Bay. Kau'iki, a 390-foot-high volcanic cinder cone, lost its seaward wall to erosion and spilled red cinders everywhere. The resulting contrast of red sand, foaming aqua surf, and jagged black lava teeth is truly a sight to see—and swim amidst. Some beachgoers shed their clothes in this private setting. To get here, park on Uakea Road near the ballfield. Cross the field to the left of the old Hāna School building, and follow the well-worn path down to the shoreline, below an old cemetery. ***Safety note:*** Avoid the trail that leads up the cindery hill; it is eroded and isn't safe. Stick close to the shore until you round the point, and then rejoin the hillside trail.

Tropical Haleakalā: 'Ohe'o Gulch at Kīpahulu

If you're thinking about heading out to the so-called **Seven Sacred Pools,** past Hāna in the Kīpahulu, let's clear this up right now: There are *more* than seven pools—and *all* water in Hawai'i is considered sacred. **'Ohe'o Gulch ★★★** (the rightful name of the pools) is in the Kīpahulu district of Haleakalā National Park (though you can't drive here from the summit). It's about 30 minutes beyond Hāna town, along Highway 31. Expect rain showers on the Kīpahulu coast.

Red Sand (Kaihalulu) Beach.

The **Kīpahulu Ranger Station** (© **808/248-7375**) is staffed from 8:30am to 5pm daily. Here you'll find park-safety information, exhibits, and books. Rangers offer a variety of walks and hikes year-round; check at the station for current activities. The fee to enter is $20 per car or $15 per motorcycle. The Highway 31 bridge passes over some of the pools near the ocean; the others, plus magnificent 400-foot **Waimoku Falls,** are uphill, via an often muddy but always rewarding hour-long hike. Restrooms are available, but there's no drinking water. Tent camping is permitted in the park; see "Camping" (p. 386) for details.

From the ranger station, it's just a short hike above the famous 'Ohe'o Gulch to two spectacular **waterfalls.** Check with park rangers before hiking up to or swimming in the pools, and always keep an eye on the water in the streams. The sky can be sunny near the coast, but flood-waters travel 6 miles down from the Kīpahulu Valley, and the water level can rise 4 feet in less than 10 minutes. It's not a good idea to swim in the pools in winter.

Makahiku Falls is easily reached from the central parking area; the trailhead begins near the ranger station. **Pipiwai Trail** leads up to the road and beyond for .5 miles to the overlook. If you hike another 1.5 miles up the trail across two bridges and through a magical bamboo forest, you reach **Waimoku Falls.** It's a hard uphill hike, but worth every step.

Beyond 'Ohe'o Gulch

A mile past 'Ohe'o Gulch on the ocean side of the road is **Lindbergh's Grave.** First to fly across the Atlantic Ocean, Charles A. Lindbergh found peace in the Pacific; he settled in Hāna, where he died of cancer in 1974. The famous aviator is buried under river stones in a seaside graveyard behind the 1857 **Palapala Ho'omau Congregational Church.**

Adventurers can continue on around Haleakalā, back towards civilization in Kula. Be warned that the route, Old Pi'ilani Highway (Hwy. 31), is full of potholes and unpaved in parts. But it threads through ruggedly beautiful territory. Most rental-car companies warn you against traveling down this road, but it's really not so bad—just make sure a rockslide hasn't closed it before you go. If it's open, stop in for ice cream at **Kaupō General Store,** 34793 Pi'ilani Hwy. (© **808/248-8054**). This remote outpost has a wonderful antique camera collection and many tempting souvenirs.

Organized Tours

Atlantis Submarine ★ TOUR Descend more than 100 feet below the ocean's surface in air-conditioned comfort aboard this 48-passenger submarine. You'll see colorful fish, corals, and other marine creatures populating the waters off of Lahaina. Occasionally, eagle rays, white tip sharks, or a rare monk seal will swim past the submerged ship's windows. Whales have even been known to cruise alongside—filling the cabin with their otherworldly song. One guaranteed highlight is the sunken *Carthaginian,* a 19th-century replica supply boat that was scuttled to become an artificial reef.

At Pioneer Inn Hotel, 658 Wharf St., Lahaina. www.atlantisadventures.com/maui. ✆ **808/667-2224.** 1-hr. and 45-min. tours offered daily from 9am to 2pm. Admission $115 adults, $48 children 12 and under (book online for specials).

Blue Hawaiian Helicopters ★★ TOUR Some of Maui's most spectacular scenery—3,000-foot-tall waterfalls thundering away in the chiseled heart of the West Maui Mountains, say, or Pi'ilanihale, an impressive 3-acre *heaiu* (temple) hidden away in Hāna—can only be seen from the air. Blue Hawaiian can escort you there on one of their two types of helicopters: A-star or Eco-Star. Both are good, but the latter is worth the extra cash for its bucket seats (raised in the rear) and wraparound windows. Tours range from 30-minute flyovers to 2-hour excursions exploring Maui and Moloka'i or the Big Island. Be aware that if you visit another island, a good portion of the tour will be over ocean—not much to see. The 65-minute Complete Island Tour is the best value, especially if it's been raining and the waterfalls are gushing. After exploring West Maui, your pilot will flirt at the edges of Haleakalā National Park so you can peer into the crater's paint-box colors, and then zip over Oprah's organic farm in Kula. ***Tip:*** Book on the website for substantial savings.

1 Kahului Airport Rd., Kahului. www.bluehawaiian.com. ✆ **800/745-2583** or 808/871-8844. Flight times range 45–90 min. and cost $153–$510. Parking & flight video extra.

Temptation Tours ★ TOUR If you'd rather leave the driving to someone else, this tour company will chauffeur you to Maui's top sites in a comfy deluxe van—much more luxurious than the large, crowded buses used by other agencies. Book a pre-dawn trip to the summit of Haleakalā to witness the sunrise (followed by tasting tours at Surfing Goat Dairy and Ocean Organic Vodka; see below) or a picnic out in Hāna. You'll pass numerous waterfalls and stop often, but don't expect to swim or get muddy hiking. The Hāna Sky-Trek is actually a pretty great value; the half-day adventure starts with a drive along the lush East Maui coast to Hāna, where you board a helicopter for a scenic flight back home over hidden waterfalls and Haleakalā National Park. The eight-person vans are safe and roomy, tour guides are generally knowledgeable, and the chicken wraps, seared ono, and brownies for lunch are tasty.

www.temptationtours.com. ✆ **808/878-1715.** All-day tours $225–$344. Free hotel pickup.

MAUI FARMS: stop & smell the lavender

Idyllic farms abound in upcountry Maui. Many open their doors to visitors and have terrific Maui-made products for purchase.

ALI'I KULA LAVENDER Stop and smell the lavender when you visit these gorgeous grounds, set high up on the leeward slope of Haleakalā, scented by multiple varieties of lavender, tropical flowers, and fruit trees. On the 30-minute walking tour (5 tours daily; $10 with advance reservation), you can sniff lavender cuttings and leave with a fragrant bouquet. The store is chock-full of great culinary products (lavender seasonings, honey, jelly, and teas) and bath and body goodies (the salve is a lifesaver). General admission is $3; lunches and treasure hunts for the kids can be arranged with 24-hour notice. 1100 Waipoli Rd., Kula (www.aliikulalavender.com; ✆ **808/878-3004**).

MAUI COUNTRY FARM TOURS Marilyn Jansen Lopes and her husband, Rick, are sweet, knowledgeable guides who visit the farms listed here as well as others. They offer an overview of agriculture on the Valley Isle and regale guests with plenty of anecdotes and extra treats along the way. They share their love of Maui along with the historic background of the island's sugar mills, coffee plantations, family farms, and vineyards. Tours in eight-seat, air-conditioned buses start at $160 and include lunch. Their new **Halfway to Hana** tour features tropical fruit tasting and waterfall dips when weather allows (www.mauicountryfarmtours.com; ✆ **808/283-9131**).

OCEAN ORGANIC VODKA Never heard of a vodka farm? Neither had I until this business opened just below Surfing Goat Dairy on Ōma'opio Road. Sustainably harvested organic sugarcane is blended with deep ocean mineral water to make fine-quality liquor. See how it's done at this solar-powered distillery halfway up the leeward slope of Haleakalā. (The views alone are worth the price of admission.) Fun and informative tours are $10 a person (12 years and up). Lunch can be added for $25 with 24-hour advance notice. Those 21 and over get to sample various spirits (and vodka-filled truffles!) and take home a souvenir shot glass. 4051 Ōma'opio Rd., Kula (www.oceanvodka.com; ✆ **808/877-0009;** daily 9:30am–5pm).

SURFING GOAT DAIRY When heading upcountry, take a detour on wild ōma'opio Road to meet the frisky kids at this sweet, off-the-beaten-path destination for those who love goats and/or cheese. When you spot the surfboard nailed to the tree, you'll know you're close. Daily farm tours are $12 adults and $8 for kids. Book in advance if you want to help with evening chores—milking mama goats (Mon–Sat 3:15pm; $17 adults, $14 children). Cheese aficionados will appreciate the **Grand Dairy Tours**: 2 hours of cheesemaking and sampling the farm's award-winning chèvre, quarks, and truffles. 3651 Ōma'opio Rd., Kula (www.surfinggoatdairy.com; ✆ **808/878-2870;** Mon–Sat 9am–5pm, Sun 9am–2pm).

BEACHES

West Maui

KA'ANAPALI BEACH ★★

Four-mile-long Ka'anapali is one of Maui's most famous beaches, with sugary golden sand as far as the eye can see. A paved walkway links hotels, open-air restaurants, and the Whalers Village shopping center. Ka'anapali is so long and broad, and most hotels have adjacent swimming pools, so the beach is crowded only in pockets; there's plenty of room to find seclusion. Summertime swimming is excellent. The best snorkeling is around Black Rock, in front of the Sheraton, where the water is clear, calm, and populated with clouds of tropical fish. Facilities include outdoor showers; you can also use the restrooms at the hotel pools. Various watersports outfitters and beach vendors line up in front of the hotels. Turn off Honoapi'ilani Highway into the Ka'anapali Resort. Parking can be a problem—the free lots that have been reserved for public access are small and hard to find. Look for the blue shoreline access signs at the Hyatt's southernmost lot, between Whalers Village and the Westin, and just before the Sheraton. Otherwise, park (for top dollar) at the mall or any resort.

KAPALUA BEACH ★★

This beach cove is the stuff of dreams: a golden crescent bordered by two palm-studded points. The sandy bottom slopes gently to deep water at the bay mouth; the water's so clear that you can see it turn to green and then deep blue. Protected from strong winds and currents by the lava-rock promontories, Kapalua's calm waters are ideal for swimmers of all abilities. The bay is big enough to paddle a kayak around in without getting into the more challenging channel that separates Maui from Moloka'i. Fish hang out by the rocks, making it decent for snorkeling. The sandy strip isn't so wide that you burn your feet getting in or out of the water, and it's edged by a shady path and cool lawns. Access the beach via a small tunnel beside Merriman's restaurant. Parking is limited to about 30 spaces in a small lot off Lower Honoapi'ilani Road by Nāpili Kai Beach Resort, so arrive early. Facilities include showers, restrooms, lifeguards, a rental shack, and plenty of shade.

South Maui

Wailea's beaches may seem off limits, hidden from plain view as they are by an intimidating wall of luxury resorts, but all are public. Look for the shoreline access signs along Wailea Alanui Drive, the resort's main boulevard.

KAMA'OLE III BEACH PARK ★

Three beach parks—Kama'ole I, II, and III—stand like golden jewels in the front yard of suburban Kīhei. This trio is popular with local residents

Beaches & Outdoor Activities on Maui

CABINS & CAMPGROUNDS

Camp Olowalu **3**
Hōlua Cabin & Campground **12**
Hosmer Grove Campground **11**
Kapalaoa Cabin **14**
Kīpahulu Campground **16**
Palikū Cabin & Campground **15**
Polipoli Spring State Recreation Area Campground **9**
Wai'ānapanapa State Park **19**

GOLF COURSES

Ka'anapali Golf Resort 2
Kapalua Resort 1
Mau Nuii Golf Club 4
Pukalani Country Club 6
Wailea Golf Club 5

HIKES

Fagan's Cross **17**
Halemau'u Trail **13**
Hana-Waianapanapa Coast Trail **18**
Hosmer Grove Nature Trail **11**
Polipoli Loop **8**
Skyline Trail **7**
Slicing Sands Trail **10**

Ka'anapali Beach.

and visitors alike because each is easily accessible and all three have shady lawns. On weekends, they're jam-packed with picnickers, swimmers, and snorkelers. The most popular is Kama'ole III, or "Kam-3." It's the biggest of the three beaches, with wide pockets of gold sand, a huge grassy lawn, and a children's playground. Swimming is safe here, but scattered lava rocks are toe-stubbers at the water line. Both the North and South Shores are rocky fingers with a surge big enough to attract fish and snorkelers; the winter waves appeal to bodysurfers. Kam-3 is also a wonderful place to watch the sunset. Facilities include restrooms, showers, picnic tables, barbecue grills, and lifeguards. There's plenty of parking on South Kīhei Road across from the Maui Parkshore condos.

KEAWAKAPU BEACH PARK ★★

You can't see this mile-long beauty from the road, so keep an eye out for the blue shoreline-access signs as you head towards Wailea on South Kīhei Road. The long expanse of soft, white-gold sand has more than enough room for the scores of people who come here to stroll and swim. Clear, aquamarine waves tumble to shore just the right size for gentle riding, with or without a board. During winter, mama whales come in close to give birth and teach their calves the finer points of whale acrobatics. Dip your head underwater to eavesdrop on the humpbacks' songs. At any time of year, gorge yourself on phenomenal sunsets here. The beach has three separate entrances: The first is an unpaved lot just past the Mana Kai Maui hotel, the second is a shady paved lot at the corner of South Kīhei Road and Kilohana Drive (cross the street to the beach), and the third is a large lot at the terminus of South Kīhei Road. Facilities include restrooms (at the third entrance only), showers, and parking.

ULUA BEACH ★★

Ulua is a golden stretch of sand that's popular with sunbathers, snorkelers, and scuba divers alike. Some of Wailea's best snorkeling is found on the adjoining reef. The ocean bottom is shallow and gently slopes down to deeper waters, making swimming generally safe. In high season (Christmas–Mar and June–Aug), it's carpeted with beach towels and packed with sunbathers like sardines in cocoa butter. Facilities include showers and restrooms. Beach equipment is available for rent at the nearby Wailea Ocean Activity Center. Look for the blue shoreline access sign on Wailea Alanui Drive near the Wailea Beach Marriott Resort & Spa.

WAILEA BEACH ★

Brigades of resort umbrellas and beach chairs make it challenging to appreciate this beach's pristine beauty. It's the front yard of the Four Seasons and the Grand Wailea, and hotel staff makes plenty use of the deep sand. Still, the view out to sea is magnificent, framed by neighboring Kaho'olawe, Lāna'i, and the tiny crescent of Molokini. From shore, you

Turtle off Ulua Beach.

can see Pacific humpback whales in season (Dec–Mar) and unreal sunsets nightly. Facilities include restrooms, outdoor showers, and limited free parking at the blue shoreline access sign, just south of the Grand Wailea on Wailea Alanui Drive.

MALUAKA BEACH ★★★

For a less crowded beach experience, head south. Development falls off dramatically as you travel towards Mākena and its wild, dry countryside of thorny *kiawe* trees. Just beyond the Mākena Beach & Golf Resort is Maluaka Beach, notable for its serene beauty and its views of Molokini Crater, the offshore islet, and Kaho'olawe, the so-called "target" island (it was used as a bombing target from 1945 until the early 1990s). This sandy, sun-kissed crescent is bound on one end by a grassy knoll and has little shade, so bring your own umbrella. Swimming is idyllic here, where the water is calm and sea turtles paddle by. Facilities include restrooms, showers, picnic tables, and parking. Along Mākena Alanui, just past Mākena Beach & Golf Resort, turn right on Mākena Rd., and head down to the shore.

MĀKENA STATE BEACH PARK (BIG BEACH) ★★★

One of the most popular beaches on Maui, Mākena is so vast it never feels crowded. Locals call it "Big Beach"—it's more than 100 feet wide and stretches out 3,300 feet from Pu'u 'Olai, the 360-foot cinder cone on

Mākena Beach.

Ho'okipa Beach Park.

its north end to its southern rocky point. The golden sand is luxuriant, deep, and soft, but the shorebreak is steep and powerful. Many a visitor has broken an arm in the surf here. If you're an inexperienced swimmer, better to watch the pros shred waves on skimboards. Facilities are limited to portable toilets, but there's plenty of parking and lifeguards at the first two entrances. Dolphins often frequent these waters, and nearly every afternoon a heavy cloud rolls in, providing welcome relief from the sun.

If you clamber up the Pu'u 'Olai, you'll find **Little Beach** on the other side, a small crescent of sand where assorted nudists work on their all-over tans in defiance of the law. The shoreline doesn't drop off quite so steeply here, and bodysurfing is terrific—no pun intended.

Upcountry & East Maui

HO'OKIPA BEACH PARK ★★★

Ho'okipa means "hospitality," and the wild North Shore beach of the same name is certainly hospitable to wave riders. Two miles past Pā'ia on the Hāna Highway, it's among the world's top spots for windsurfing and kiting—thanks to tradewinds that kick up whitecaps offshore. Ho'okipa offers no less than five surf breaks, and daring watermen and -women paddle out to carve waves up to 25 feet tall. Voyeurs are welcome as well; the cliff-top parking lot claims a bird's-eye view. On flat days, snorkelers explore the reef's treasure trove of marine life: Gentle garden eels wave below the surface, and turtles hunt for jellyfish or haul out on the sand to nap. More than once, a rare Hawaiian monk seal has popped ashore during a surf contest. Facilities include restrooms, showers, pavilions, picnic tables, barbecue grills, and parking.

WAI'ĀNAPANAPA STATE PARK ★★★

Jet-black sand, a cave pool, sea arches, blowholes, and historic *hala* groves: This dramatic 120-acre beach park offers many jewels. Listen to the lava boulders wash up in the foamy surf. Swim with caution; the sea here is churned by strong waves and rip currents. Watch the seabirds circle the offshore islet. Follow moss-covered stone steps through the tunnel of *hau* branches and dare yourself to plunge into the chilly freshwater cave. These are experiences that will make a deep impression on your psyche. Wai'ānapanapa offers wonderful shoreline hikes and picnicking spots. You can follow the coastal trail for a long distance in both directions from the parking lot. Facilities include picnic tables, barbecue grills, restrooms, showers, tent sites, and 12 cabins (p. 388).

HAMOA BEACH ★★

James Michener called Hamoa "a beach so perfectly formed that I wonder at its comparative obscurity." This half-moon-shaped, gray-sand beach (a mix of coral and lava) in a truly tropical setting is a favorite of sunbathers seeking rest and refuge. The Travaasa Hāna resort maintains the beach and acts as though it's private, which it isn't—so just march down the lava-rock steps and grab a spot on the sand. The wide beach is three football fields long and sits below 30-foot black-lava sea cliffs. Surf on this unprotected beach breaks offshore and rolls in, making it a popular surfing and bodysurfing area. Hamoa is often swept by powerful rip currents, so take care. The calm left side is best for snorkeling in summer. The hotel has numerous facilities for guests, plus outdoor showers and restrooms for nonguests. Parking is limited. Look for the Hamoa Beach turnoff from Hāna Highway.

WATERSPORTS

The watersports options on Maui are mind-boggling—from lazy snorkeling to high-energy kitesurfing and everything in between. Colorful, fish-filled reefs are easily accessible, often from a sandy beach.

You'll find rental gear and ocean toys all over the island. Most seaside hotels and resorts are stocked with watersports equipment (complimentary or rentals), from snorkels to kayaks to Hobies. **Snorkel Bob's** (www.snorkelbob.com) rents snorkel gear, boogie boards, wetsuits, and more at numerous locations: At Nāpili Bay, 5425 C Lower Honoapi'ilani Hwy., Lahaina (✆ **808/669-9603**); 1217 Front St. (behind Cannery Mall), Lahaina (✆ **808/661-4421**); 3350 Lower Honoapi'ilani Hwy. #201 (Near Times Supermarket), Honokowai (✆ **808/667-9999**); in Azeka's II Shopping Center, 1279 S. Kīhei Rd., Kīhei (✆ **808/875-6188**); 2411 S. Kīhei Rd., Kīhei (✆ **808/879-7449**); and 100 Wailea Ike Dr., Wailea (✆ **808/874-0011**). All locations are open daily from

8am to 5pm. If you're island-hopping, you can rent from a Snorkel Bob's location on one island and return to a branch on another.

Boss Frog's Dive, Surf, and Bike Shops (www.bossfrog.com) has eight locations for snorkel, boogie board, longboard, and stand-up paddleboard rentals and other gear, including these locations: 150 Lahainaluna Rd. in Lahaina (✆ **808/661-3333**); 3636 Lower Honoapi'ilani Rd. in Ka'anapali (✆ **808/665-1200**); Nāpili Plaza, 5095 Nāpilihau St. in Nāpili (✆ **808/669-4949**); and 1215 S. Kīhei Rd. (✆ **808/891-0077**), 1770 S. Kīhei Rd. (✆ **808/874-5225**), and Dolphin Plaza, 2395 S. Kīhei Rd. (✆ **808/875-4477**) in Kīhei. Their 2-for-1 $20 weekly snorkel rentals are the best deal.

Boating

You'll need a boat to visit the crescent-shaped islet **Molokini,** one of the best snorkel and scuba spots in Hawai'i. Trips to the island of **Lāna'i** (see chapter 8) are also popular for a day of snorkeling. Remember to bring a towel, a swimsuit, sunscreen, and a hat on a snorkel cruise; everything else is usually included. If you'd like to go a little deeper than snorkeling allows, consider trying **SNUBA,** a shallow-water diving system in which you are connected by a 20-foot air hose to an air tank that floats on a raft at the water's surface. Most of these snorkel boats offer it for an additional cost; it's usually around $60 for a half-hour or so. No certification is required for SNUBA. For fishing charters, see "Sport Fishing," below.

Maui Classic Charters ★ TOUR Maui Classic Charters offers morning and afternoon **snorkel cruises to Molokini** on *Four Winds II,* a 55-foot glass-bottom catamaran. Rates for the morning sail are $105 for adults and $75 for children 3 to 12, and include a continental breakfast and a barbecue lunch. The afternoon sail is a steal at $49; though the captain usually only visits Coral Gardens, which is accessible from shore. All *Four Winds* trips include complimentary beer, wine, and soda; snorkeling gear and instruction; and sport fishing along the way. Those looking for speed should book a trip on the state-of-the-art catamaran *Maui Magic.* A 5-hour snorkel journey to both Molokini and Mākena costs $120 for adults and $90 for children 5 to 12, including a continental breakfast; a barbecue lunch; beer, wine, and soda; snorkel gear; and instruction.

Mā'alaea Harbor, slip 55 and slip 80. www.mauicharters.com. ✆ **800/736-5740** or 808/879-8188. Prices vary depending on cruise; check website for discounts.

Pacific Whale Foundation ★★ TOUR This not-for-profit foundation supports its whale research, public education, and conservation programs by offering **whale-watch cruises, wild dolphin encounters,** and **snorkel tours,** some to Molokini and Lāna'i. Numerous daily trips

are offered out of both Lahaina and Mā'alaea harbors. Two special tours include the **Island Rhythms Sunset Cruise** with Marty Dread (a local entertainer who woos whales with his rollicking tunes) and **full moon cruises** with Harriet Witt, a wonderful astronomer and storyteller.
300 Mā'alaea Rd., Suite 211, Wailuku. (Also: Lahaina Ocean Store, 612 Front St., Lahaina.) www.pacificwhale.org. ✆ **800/942-5311** or 808/249-8811. Trips from $29 adults, $20 children 7–12, free for 1 child 6 and under per adult; snorkeling cruises from $80 adults, $35 children. Book online for a 10% discount.

Scotch Mist Sailing Charters TOUR This 50-foot Santa Cruz sailboat offers intimate, exhilarating 4-hour **snorkel-sail cruises,** limited to 25 passengers max. You'll visit the glittering outer reefs at Olowalu. The cost is $109 for ages 13 and up, $55 for children 5 to 12. Rates include a fruit platter and beverages, gear, and instruction. Other options include afternoon sails, whale-watches ($60 ages 13 and up; $30 children 5–12), and evening champagne sunset cruises ($70 ages 13 and up; $35 children 5–12). ***Note:*** Children under 5 are not allowed unless the whole boat is chartered.
Lahaina Harbor, slip 2. www.scotchmistsailingcharters.com. ✆ **808/661-0386.** Prices vary depending on cruise.

Hawaiian reef.

Trilogy Excursions ★★★ TOUR Trilogy offers my favorite **snorkel-sail trips.** The family-run company prioritizes environmental stewardship—along with insuring you have a stellar marine adventure. Hop aboard one of Trilogy's fleet of custom-built catamarans, from 54 to 65 feet long, for a **9-mile Maui-to-Lāna'i sail** from Lahaina Harbor to Hulopo'e Marine Preserve and a fun-filled day of sailing and snorkeling. This is the only cruise that offers a personalized ground tour of the island and the only one with rights to take you to Hulopo'e Beach. The full-day trip costs $205 for adults, $153 for teens (ages 13–18), and $100 for children 3 to 12.

Trilogy also offers **snorkel-sail trips to Molokini.** This half-day trip leaves from Mā'alaea Harbor and costs $125 for adults, $89 for teens, and $60 for kids 3 to 12, including breakfast and a barbecue lunch. These are the most expensive sail-snorkel cruises on Maui, but they're worth every penny. The crews are fun and knowledgeable, and the boats are comfortable and well equipped. All trips include breakfast (Mom's homemade cinnamon buns) and a very good barbecue lunch (onboard on the half-day trip; on land on the Lana'i trip). During winter, 2-hour **whale watches** depart conveniently right from the sand on Ka'anapali Beach ($59 adults, $45 teens, $30 children).

The **Captain's Sunset Dinner Sail** is a romantic adults-only adventure. Couples enjoy a four-course feast at private, candlelit tables, complete with handcrafted cocktails and cozy blankets ($129 per person).

www.sailtrilogy.com. ✆ **888/225-MAUI** or 808/874-5649. Prices and departure points vary depending on cruise.

DAY CRUISES TO MOLOKA'I

You can travel across the seas by ferry from Maui's Lahaina Harbor to Moloka'i's Kaunakakai Wharf on the Hawaiian Ocean Project's ***Moloka'i Princess*** (www.hawaiioceanproject.com; ✆ **877/500-6284** or 808/667-6165). Twice daily the 100-foot ferry makes the 2-hour journey from Lahaina to Kaunakakai; the round-trip cost is $126 for adults and $63 for children 3 to 12. I recommend spending 2 or more days on Moloka'i, but if you can't swing that, try one of the following single-day trips. The guided **Ali'i Tour** hits Moloka'i's major sites in an air-conditioned motor coach ($260 per adult and $160 per child, including round-trip passage, breakfast, and lunch). For more independent travelers, the **Cruise-Drive** package is a good deal. Hop on the ferry and pick up your rental car and maps on arrival ($130 per adult, $59 per child, plus $145 car rental fee). Load up on ginger cookies before you go; the ferry can be a bumpy ride, especially during winter.

DAY CRUISES TO LĀNA'I

You can visit the island of Lāna'i by booking a trip with **Trilogy** (see above) or by taking the passenger ferry.

Expeditions Lahaina/Lāna'i Passenger Ferry ★ FERRY The cheapest way to reach Lāna'i is via ferry, which runs five times a day, 365 days a year. It leaves Lahaina at 6:45 and 9:15am, and 12:45, 3:15, and 5:45pm; the return ferry from Lāna'i's Mānele Bay leaves at 8 and 10:30am, and at 2, 4:30, and 6:45pm. The 9-mile channel crossing takes between 45 minutes and an hour, depending on sea conditions. Reservations are strongly recommended. During winter, the trip doubles as a free whale watch. You can walk from the harbor to Hulopo'e Beach, but if you want to explore the island further, you'll have to rent a car or book a tour. See p. 467 in the Lāna'i chapter for details.

Ferries depart from Lahaina Harbor; office: 658 Front St., Suite 127, Lahaina. www.go-lanai.com. ✆ **800/695-2624** or 808/661-3756. Round-trip fares from Maui to Lāna'i $60 adults, $40 children 2–11.

Ocean Kayaking

For beginners, **Mākena Kayak and Tours** ★ (www.makenakayak.com; ✆ **808/879-8426**) is an excellent choice. Professional guide Dino Ventura leads a 2½-hour trip from Mākena Landing and loves taking first-timers over the secluded coral reefs and into remote coves. His wonderful tour will be a highlight of your vacation. This outfitter has kept its low price of $65, which includes snorkel and kayak equipment; the 4-hour tour costs $95.

South Pacific Kayaks ★ (www.southpacifickayaks.com; ✆ **808/875-4848**) is another terrific kayak-tour company. Its experts lead ocean-kayak trips that include lessons, a guided tour, and snorkeling. Tours run from 3 to 5 hours and range in price from $74 to $225 for private trips. The company rents equipment, too, and will meet you at Mākena Landing with kayaks ready to go.

Outrigger Canoe

Outrigger canoes are much revered in Hawaiian culture, and several hotels—among them, the Fairmont Kea Lani Maui and the Andaz Maui—offer this wonderful cultural activity right off the beach. If you want to give paddling a try, expect to work as a team with five other paddlers. Your guide and steersman will show you how to haul the sleek boat into the water, properly enter and exit the boat, and paddle for maximum efficiency.

Hawaiian Paddle Sports ★★★ CANOE TOUR For an intimate adventure on the great blue, book an outrigger canoe trip with Hawaiian Paddle Sports. Learn how to paddle in sync with your family or friends, just as the ancient Polynesians did when colonizing these islands. You'll

visit some of Maui's very best snorkel spots: Mākena Landing or the outer reef at Olowalu. The owner, Tim Lara, is one of the best in the business, brimming with knowledge about the island's culture, history, and marine life. When turtles, whales, manta rays, or monk seals surface alongside your canoe, you'll feel like a *National Geographic* explorer. And you'll have the pictures to prove it. Lara is a whiz with a Go-Pro camera; after the trip he'll send you under- and abovewater shots guaranteed to dazzle your friends. If you're feeling sporty, book a **canoe surfing trip** and race down the face of breaking waves. Hawaiian Paddle Sports also offers **kayak tours,** and **surf** and **stand-up paddle instruction.**
Departs from various locations. www.hawaiianpaddlesports.com. ✆ **808/660-4228.** $149–$199 per person.

Ocean Rafting

If you're semi-adventurous and looking for a wetter, wilder experience, try ocean rafting. The inflatable rafts hold 6 to 24 passengers. Tours usually include snorkeling and coastal cruising.

One of the best (and most reasonable) outfitters is **Hawai'i Ocean Rafting** (www.hawaiioceanrafting.com; ✆ **808/661-7238**), which operates out of Lahaina Harbor. The best deal is the 5-hour morning tour ($77 adults, $68 children 5–12); it includes three snorkeling stops and time spent watching for dolphins, plus continental breakfast and midmorning snacks. Check the website for discounts.

Captain Steve's Rafting Excursions (www.captainsteves.com; ✆ **808/667-5565**) offers 7-hour snorkel trips from Māla Wharf in Lahaina to the waters around **Lāna'i** (you don't actually land on the island). **Dolphin sightings** are almost guaranteed on these action-packed excursions. Discounted online rates of $135 for adults and $95 for children 5 to 12 include breakfast, lunch, snorkel gear, and wetsuits.

Scuba Diving

Maui offers plenty of undersea attractions worth strapping on a tank for. Most divers start with **Molokini** (see "Snorkeling," below). In addition to the popular basin, experienced divers can explore the crater's dramatic **back wall ★★★**, which plunges 350 feet and is frequented by larger marine animals and schools of rare butterflyfish. Other top sites include **Māla Wharf,** the **St. Anthony** (a sunken longliner), and **Five Graves** at Mākena Landing. Don't be scared off by the latter's ominous name—it's a magical spot with sea caves and arches.

Ed Robinson's Diving Adventures ★★ DIVE COMPANY Ed Robinson, a widely published underwater photographer, offers specialized charters for small groups. Two-tank dives are $130 ($150 with all the gear). The check-in for the dive is at 165 Halekuai St. in Kīhei, and the boat departs from the Kīhei Boat Ramp.
165 Halekuai St., Kīhei. www.mauiscuba.com. ✆ **808/879-3584.**

Maui Dreams Dive Company ★★★ DIVE COMPANY Run by husband-and-wife team Rachel and Don Domingo, this is the best full-service dive operation on the island. Stop in at their South Maui shop, and you might just end up scuba certified ($420 for a 3-day course). The skilled dive masters and instructors are so fun, they make every aspect of getting geared up to go underwater enjoyable. You don't need certification for an intro shore dive at Ulua Beach ($69), but you do for a two-tank adventure to **Molokini** aboard the *Maui Diamond II* ($159). Captain Don regales his passengers with jokes, snacks, and local trivia. Rachel has a knack for finding camouflaged **frogfish** on the reef. Even experienced divers will be dazzled by the **guided scooter dives** ($99–$129). The rideable rockets allow you to zip along the ocean's floor and visit sunken **World War II wrecks,** caves, and turtle-cleaning stations. The community-minded Domingos host regular reef cleanups, **pirate- and princess-themed dives,** and underwater Easter egg hunts. 1993 S. Kīhei Rd. www.mauidreamsdiveco.com. ✆ **808/874-5332.**

Mike Severns Diving ★★★ DIVE COMPANY For personalized diving tours on a 38-foot Munson/Hammerhead boat (with a freshwater shower), call Pauline Fiene at Mike Severns Diving. She and her fellow dive masters lead trips for a maximum of 12 people, divided into two groups of six. Exploring the underwater world is educational and fun with Fiene, a biologist who has authored several spectacular marine-photography books and leads dives during **coral spawning** events. She's particularly knowledgeable about nudibranchs, two of which have been named for her, *Hallaxa paulinae* and *Hypselodoris paulinae*. Two-tank dives are $145, including equipment rental, or $139 if you bring all your own equipment. Experienced divers can rent underwater cameras and tag along behind the pro photographers. Trips depart from Kīhei Boat Ramp. www.mikesevernsdiving.com. ✆ **808/879-6596.**

Snorkeling

Snorkeling on Maui is easy—there are so many great spots where you can just wade in the water with a mask and look down and see tropical fish. If you haven't snorkeled before, or are a little rusty, practice breathing through your snorkel before you get out on the water. Mornings are best; blustery trade winds kick in around noon. Maui's best snorkeling spots include **Ulua** and **Mokapu Beaches** in Wailea; **Olowalu** along the Honoapi'ilani Highway; **Black Rock** at the north end of Ka'anapali Beach; and, just beyond Black Rock, **Kahekili Beach ★★**.

The snorkeling at **Honolua Bay ★★★** is worth the drive out to West Maui's far corner. Spectacular coral formations glitter beneath the surface. Turtles, rays, and a variety of snappers and goatfish cruise along beside you. In the crevices are eels, lobster, and an array of rainbowed fish. Dolphins sometimes come into the bay to rest.

Two **truly terrific snorkel spots** are difficult to get to but rewarding—they're home to Hawai'i's tropical marine life at its best:

Molokini ★★ NATURAL ATTRACTION A sunken crater that sits like a crescent moon fallen from the sky, almost midway between Maui and the uninhabited island of Kaho'olawe, Molokini stands like a scoop against the tide. This offshore site is very popular, thanks to astounding visibility (you can often peer down 100 ft.) and an abundance of marine life, from manta rays to clouds of yellow butterflyfish. On its concave side, Molokini serves as a natural sanctuary and preserve for tropical fish. Molokini is accessible only by boat, and snorkelers commute here daily in a fleet of dive boats. See "Boating," above, for outfitters that can take you here. Expect crowds in high season.

'Āhihi-Kina'u Natural Preserve ★★ NATURAL ATTRACTION The 2,000-acre state natural area reserve in the lee of Cape Kina'u, on Maui's rugged south coast, is home to bejeweled 'āhihi Bay. It was here that Haleakalā spilled its last red-hot lava into the sea, so the entrance to the ocean is sharp and rocky. Ease into the water to see brilliant corals and abundant fish. Fishing is strictly forbidden, and the fish know it; they're everywhere in this series of rocky coves and black-lava tide pools. To get here, drive south of Makena and watch for signs. A state naturalist is often onsite to offer advice. ***Note:*** The Hawai'i Department of Land and Natural Resources has temporarily restricted access to portions of

Snorkeling with sea turtle.

the popular and heavily used preserve. Visit www.hawaii.gov/dlnr/dofaw/nars for details.

Sport Fishing

The best way to reserve a sport-fishing charter is through the experts; the top booking desk in the state is **Sportfish Hawai'i ★** (www.sportfishhawaii.com; ✆ **877/388-1376**), which books boats on all the islands. These fishing vessels have been inspected and must meet rigorous criteria to guarantee that you'll have a great time. Prices start at $1,095 for a full-day exclusive charter (meaning you, plus five friends, get the entire boat to yourself); it's $699 for a half-day exclusive. **Bottom-fishing** trips for delicious snappers run $149 per adult; you'll share the boat with up to nine other anglers.

Surfing

If you want to learn to surf, the best beginners' spots are **Charley Young Cove** in Kīhei (the far north end of Kalama Beach Park), the break in front of **505 Front Street** in Lahaina, and several breaks along Honoapi'ilani Highway, including **Ukumehame.** The first two are the most convenient, with surf schools nearby. The breaks along Honoapi'ilani Highway tend to be longer, wider, and less crowded—perfect if you're confident enough to go solo.

During summer, gentle swells roll in long and slow along the South Shore. It's the best time to practice your stance on a longboard. During winter, the North Shore becomes the playground for adrenaline junkies who drop in on thundering waves 30 feet tall and higher. If you want to watch, head to **Ho'okipa** or **Honolua Bay,** where you can view the action from a cliff above.

Maui Surfer Girls ★★★ SURF INSTRUCTION Despite its name, MSG offers coed surf instruction for groms and Betties alike. Owner Dustin Tester is a big-wave surf pioneer; she's among the first women to charge "Jaws," one of the planet's biggest breaks, and her commitment to helping others shred waves is inspirational. (She even coached her dog Luna to hang ten alongside her.) Personalized lessons at Ukumehame Beach Park with Tester or her teammates start at $85. But MSG's best offering is the **weeklong surf camp.** If you've got a teen girl who dreams of growing gills, sign her up for 7 saltwater-soaked days full of watersports, camaraderie, healthy food, island adventures, and campfire counsel. The Olowalu Campground serves as headquarters for a transformational experience.
www.mauisurfergirls.com. ✆ **808/270-8769.**

Nancy Emerson School of Surfing ★ SURF INSTRUCTION Nancy has been surfing since 1961 and has even been a stunt performer for various movies such as *Waterworld.* She's pioneered an instructional technique called "Learn to Surf in One Lesson." It's $85 per person for a 2-hour group lesson; private 2-hour classes are $170. All instructors are lifeguard certified.

505 Front St., Suite 224B, Lahaina. www.mauisurfclinics.com. © **808/244-SURF [7873].**

Zack Howard Surf ★ SURF INSTRUCTION Zack is a lifelong waterman who will help you stand up and surf—even on your very first wave. While most surf schools take newbies out into the crowded breaks at Charley Young in Kīhei or the Lahaina Breakwall, Zack steers beginning students into the surf at Ukumehame, a gentle, consistent rolling break alongside Honoapi'ilani Highway. He also helps intermediate surfers sharpen their skills at world-famous Ho'okipa. In between swells, Zack offers tips on how to improve your stance and technique. Lessons start at $90 per person for 1½ hours.

www.zackhowardsurf.com. © **808/214-7766.**

Whale-Watching

Maui is a favorite with Hawaiian humpback whales, who get downright frisky in the surrounding waters from about November to May (though Jan and Feb are the peak months). Seeing the massive marine mammals leap out of the sea or perfect their tail slap is mesmerizing. You can hear them sing underwater, too! Just duck your head a foot below the surface and listen for creaks, groans, and otherworldly serenades.

WHALE-WATCHING FROM SHORE Just look out to sea anytime during the winter months. There's no best time of day, but it seems that when the sea is glassy and there's no wind, the whales appear. Others claim the opposite: that whales are most active when the water is pocked with whitecaps.

Good whale-watching spots on Maui include:

MCGREGOR POINT On the way to Lahaina, there's a scenic lookout at mile marker 9 (just before you get to the Lahaina Tunnel); it's a good viewpoint to scan for whales.

OLOWALU REEF Along the straight part of Honoapi'ilani Highway, between McGregor Point and Olowalu, you'll sometimes see whales leap out of the water. Their appearance can bring traffic to a screeching halt: People abandon their cars and run down to the sea to watch, causing a major traffic jam. If you stop, pull off the road so others can pass.

WAILEA BEACH MARRIOTT RESORT & SPA In the Wailea coastal walk, stop at this resort to look for whales through the telescope installed as a public service by the Hawai'i Island Humpback Whale National Marine Sanctuary.

WHALE-WATCHING BY KAYAK & RAFT ★★ I recommend viewing humpback whales from a maneuverable, high-speed raft—you'll be close to the water and that much closer to the cetaceans. **Capt. Steve's Rafting Excursions** (www.captainsteves.com; © **808/667-5565**) offers 2-hour whale-watching excursions out of Lahaina Harbor (from $55 adults, $45 children 5–12). ***Tip:*** Save $10 by booking the early-bird adventure, which leaves at 7:30am.

WHALE-WATCHING CRUISES Just about all of Hawai'i's snorkel and dive boats become whale-watching boats in season; some of them even carry professional naturalists onboard so you'll know what you're seeing and drop hydrophones in the water so you can better hear the whales' song. For options, see "Boating," earlier in this section.

Windsurfing

Maui has Hawai'i's best windsurfing beaches. In winter, windsurfers from around the world flock to the town of **Pā'ia** to ride the waves; **Ho'okipa Beach ★★★**, known all over the globe for its brisk winds and excellent waves, is the site of several world championship contests. **Kanahā Beach,** west of Kahului Airport, also has dependable winds. When the winds turn northerly, **North Kīhei** is the place to be (some days, you can even spot whales in the distance behind the windsurfers). **'Ōhūkai Park,** the first beach as you enter South Kīhei Road from the northern end, has good winds, plus parking, a long strip of grass to assemble your gear, and easy access to the water.

EQUIPMENT RENTALS & LESSONS **Hawaiian Island Surf & Sport,** 415 Dairy Rd., Kahului (www.hawaiianisland.com; © **800/231-6958** or 808/871-4981), offers rentals, repairs, and private lessons for $100 per hour. **Hawaiian Sailboarding Techniques,** 425 Koloa St., Kahului (www.hstwindsurfing.com; © **800/968-5423** or 808/871-5423), offers rentals and 2½-hour lessons from $99 and Kanahā Beach. **Maui Windsurf Company,** 22 Hāna Hwy., Kahului (www.mauiwindsurfcompany.com; © **808/877-4816**), offers complete equipment rental (board, sail, rig harness, and roof rack) from $59, plus 2½-hour group lessons from $89 and private instruction at $85 per hour.

DAILY WIND & SURF CONDITIONS For reports on wind and surf conditions, call Hi-Tech's **Wind & Surf Report** at © **808/877-3611,** ext. 2.

SURF VAN Since most windsurf gear won't fit into a typical rental car, call Al West at **Al West's Surf Vans** to rent a newish (or old) van by the week (www.mauivans.com; © **808/877-0090**).

OTHER OUTDOOR ACTIVITIES

Biking

CRUISING HALEAKALĀ

Several companies offer the opportunity to coast down Haleakalā, from near the summit to the shore, on basic cruiser bikes. It can be quite a thrilling experience—but one that should be approached with caution if you aren't a seasoned cyclist. Bike tours aren't allowed in Haleakalā National Park, so your van will take you to the summit first, and then drop you off just outside of the park. You'll descend through multiple climates and ecosystems, past eucalyptus groves and flower-filled gulches. But bear in mind: The roads are steep and curvy without designated bike lanes and little to no shoulder. During winter and the rainy season, conditions can be particularly harsh; you'll be saran-wrapped in raingear. Temperatures at the summit can drop below freezing and 40-mph winds howl, so wear warm layers whatever the season. Despite what various companies claim about their safety record, people have been injured and killed participating in this activity. If you do choose to go, pay close attention to the safety briefing.

Maui's oldest downhill company is **Maui Downhill** (www.mauidownhill.com; ✆ **808/871-2155**), which offers sunrise bike tours, including breakfast and lunch stops (not hosted), starting at $149 (discounted if booked online). Be prepared for a 3am departure! **Mountain Riders Bike Tours** (www.mountainriders.com; ✆ **800/706-7700** or 808/877-4944) offers sunrise rides for $150 and midday trips for $130 (discounted if booked online). If you want to avoid the crowds and go down the mountain at your own pace (rather than in a choo-choo train of other bikers), call **Haleakalā Bike Company** (www.bikemaui.com; ✆ **888/922-2453**). After assessing your skill, they'll outfit you with the latest gear and shuttle you up Haleakalā.

RENTALS

Maui offers dynamic terrain for serious and amateur cyclists. If you've got the chops to pedal *up* Haleakalā, the pros at **Maui Cyclery ★★★** (99 Hāna Hwy., Pā'ia; www.gocyclingmaui.com; ✆ **808/579-9009**) can outfit you and provide a support vehicle. Tour de France athletes launch their Maui training sessions from this full-service Pā'ia bike shop, which rents top-of-the-line equipment and offers a range of guided tours. Shop owner Donny Arnoult hosts 6-day cycling camps and sponsors the annual Cycle to the Sun contest; riders travel from around the globe to tackle the 10,023-foot volcano on two wheels.

If **mountain biking** is more your style, hit up Moose at **Krank Cycles ★★★** (1120 Makawao Ave., Makawao; www.krankmaui.com; ✆ **808/572-2299**) for a tricked-out bike and directions to the Makawao Forest trails.

Maui County has produced a **full-color map** of the island with various cycling routes, information on road suitability, climate, mileage, elevation changes, bike shops, and safety tips. It's available at most bike shops. You can also download it at **www.southmauibicycles.com**.

Golf

Golfers have many outstanding greens to choose from on Maui, from world championship courses to municipal parks with oceanfront views.

Greens fees are pricy, but twilight tee times can be a giant deal. Be forewarned; the tradewinds pick up in the afternoon and can seriously alter your game. **Stand-by Golf** (www.hawaiistandbygolf.com; © **888/645-2665**) rents clubs and offers savings off greens fees at Ka'anapali, Wailea Gold and Emerald, and Pukalani golf courses. **Golf Club Rentals** (www.mauiclubrentals.com; © **808/665-0800**) has custom-built clubs for men, women, and juniors (both right- and left-handed) that can be delivered island-wide; the rates are $25 a day for steel clubs, and a full graphite set is $30 a day.

WEST MAUI

Ka'anapali Golf Resort ★ Both courses at Ka'anapali will challenge golfers, from high-handicappers to near-pros. The par-72, 6,305-yard **Royal (North) Course** is a true Robert Trent Jones, Sr., design: It has an abundance of wide bunkers; several long, stretched-out tees; and the largest, most contoured greens on Maui. The tricky 18th hole (par-4, 435-yard) has a water hazard on the approach to the green. The par-72, 6,250-yard **Kai (South) Course** is an Arthur Jack Snyder design; although shorter than the North Course, it requires more accuracy on the narrow, hilly fairways. It also has a water hazard on its final hole, so don't tally up your scorecard until you sink the final putt. Facilities include a driving range and putting course. The clubhouse restaurant is run by celebrated chef Roy Yamaguchi.

Off Ka'anapali Pkwy., Ka'anapali (1st building on right). www.kaanapali-golf.com. © **808/661-3691.** Greens fees: Royal Course $255 ($169 for Ka'anapali guests), twilight rates (starting at 1pm) $129, super twilight rates (starting at 3pm) $109; Kai Course $205 ($129 for Ka'anapali guests), twilight rates (starting at 1pm) $99, super twilight rates (starting at 3pm) $79.

Kapalua Resort ★★★ The views from these two championship courses are worth the greens fees alone. The par-72, 6,761-yard **Bay Course** was designed by Arnold Palmer and Ed Seay. This course is a bit forgiving, with its wide fairways; the greens, however, are difficult to read. The oft-photographed 5th overlooks a small ocean cove; even the pros have trouble with this rocky par-3, 205-yard hole. The **Plantation Course,** site of the PGA Hyundai Tournament of Champions, is a Ben Crenshaw/Bill Coore design. The 6,547-yard, par-73 course, set on a rolling hillside, is excellent for developing your low shots and precise chipping. Facilities for both courses include locker rooms, a driving range, and excellent dining. Sharpen your skills at the attached golf academy, which offers half-day golf school, private lessons, club fittings, and special clinics for beginners. Weekends are your best bet for tee times.

Off Hwy. 30, Kapalua. www.kapaluamaui.com/golf. © **877/KAPALUA** or 808/669-8877. Greens fees: Bay Course $219 ($199 for resort guests), twilight rates (starting at 1pm) $159; Plantation Course $299 ($239 for guests), twilight rates $199. Call for special packages.

SOUTH MAUI

Maui Nui Golf Club The name has changed, but the Kīhei course is the same forgiving, beautiful playground. Unspooling across the foothills of Haleakalā, it's just high enough to afford spectacular ocean vistas from every hole. ***One caveat:*** Go in the morning. Not only is it cooler, but (more important) it's also less windy. In the afternoon, the winds bluster down Haleakalā with gusto. It's a fun course to play, with some challenging holes; the par-5 2nd hole is a virtual minefield of bunkers, and the par-5 8th hole shoots over a swale and then uphill. Premium clubs rent for $50, and slightly older irons for just $25.

470 Lipoa Pkwy., Kīhei. www.mauinuigolfclub.com. ✆ **808/874-0777.** Greens fees: $119 7:30–11am, $89 before 7:30am and after 11am. Check website for specials and off-season rates.

Wailea Golf Club ★★ You'll have three courses to choose from at Wailea. The **Blue Course,** a par-72, 6,758-yard course designed by Arthur Jack Snyder and dotted with bunkers and water hazards, is for duffers and pros alike. The wide fairways appeal to beginners, while the undulating terrain makes it a course everyone can enjoy. More challenging is the par-72, 7,078-yard championship **Gold Course,** designed by Robert Trent Jones, Jr., with narrow fairways and several tricky dogleg holes, not to mention such natural hazards as lava-rock walls. The **Emerald Course,** also designed by Robert Trent Jones, Jr., is Wailea's most scenic, with tropical landscaping and a player-friendly design. Sunday mornings are the least crowded times. Facilities include a complete golf training facility, two pro shops, locker rooms, and two restaurants: **Gannon's,** by celebrity chef Bev Gannon, and **Mulligan's,** a popular Irish pub.

Blue Course: 100 Wailea Ike Dr. www.waileagolf.com. ✆ **808/879-2530.** Emerald and Gold Courses: 100 Wailea Golf Club Dr., Wailea. www.waileagolf.com. ✆ **888/328-MAUI** or 808/875-7450. Greens fees: Blue Course $190 ($150 for resort guests), $120 after noon, $99 after 2pm; Gold Course and Emerald Course $240 ($199 for resort guests), $160 after 1pm, $109 after 3:30pm. Check website for specials and unlimited passes.

UPCOUNTRY MAUI

Pukalani Country Club This cool par-72, 6,962-yard course at 1,100 feet offers a break from the resorts' high greens fees, and it's really fun to play. The 3rd hole offers golfers two different options: a tough (especially into the wind) iron shot from the tee, across a gully (yuck!) to the green, or a shot down the side of the gully across a second green into sand traps below. (Most people choose to shoot down the side of the gully; it's actually easier than shooting across a ravine.) High handicappers will love this course, and more experienced players can make it more challenging by playing from the back tees. Facilities include club and shoe rentals, practice areas, lockers, a pro shop, and a restaurant.

360 Pukalani St., Pukalani. www.pukalanigolf.com. ✆ **808/572-1314.** Greens fees for 18 holes (including cart) $89, $63 noon–2:30pm, $53 after 2:30pm. Take the Hāna

Hwy. (Hwy. 36) to Haleakalā Hwy. (Hwy. 37) to the Pukalani exit; turn right onto Pukalani St. and go 2 blocks.

Hiking

Over a few brief decades, Maui transformed from a rural island to a fast-paced resort destination, but its natural beauty has remained largely inviolate. Many pristine places can be explored only on foot. Those interested in seeing the backcountry—complete with virgin waterfalls, remote wilderness trails, and quiet, meditative settings—should head to Haleakalā or the tropical Hāna Coast.

For details on Maui hiking trails and free maps, contact **Haleakalā National Park** (www.nps.gov/hale; © **808/572-4400**), the **Hawai'i State Department of Land and Natural Resources** (www.dlnr.hawaii.gov/dsp/hiking/maui; © **808/984-8109**) or the state's **Nā Ala Hele program** (www.hawaiitrails.org; © **808/873-3508**). Choose different tabs on the Nā Ala Hele website to access downloadable maps.

GUIDED HIKES If you'd like a knowledgeable guide to accompany you on a hike, call **Maui Hiking Safaris** ★ (www.mauihikingsafaris.com; © **888/445-3963** or 808/573-0168). Owner Randy Warner takes eight or fewer adventurers on half- and full-day hikes into valleys, rainforests, and coastal areas. Randy's been hiking around Maui for more than 30 years and is wise in the ways of Hawaiian history, native flora and fauna, and volcanology. His rates range from $69 for a half-day to $169 for a full day, and hikes include daypacks, rain parkas, snacks, water, and, on full-day hikes, sandwiches. Private half-day tours are $150 per person ($75 per additional person).

Maui's oldest hiking-guide company is **Hike Maui** ★ (www.hikemaui.com; © **866/324-6284** or 808/879-5270), headed by Ken Schmitt, who pioneered guided hikes on the Valley Isle. Hike Maui offers numerous treks island-wide, ranging from an easy 1-mile, 3-hour hike to a waterfall ($85) to a strenuous full-day hike in Haleakalā Crater ($179). On the popular East Maui waterfall trips ($124), you can swim and jump from the rocks into rainforest pools. Guides share cultural and botanical knowledge along the trail. All prices include equipment and transportation. Hotel pickup costs an extra $25 per person.

The Maui chapter of the **Sierra Club** ★★ offers the best deal by far: guided hikes for a $5 donation. Volunteer naturalists lead small groups along historic coastlines and up into forest waterfalls. Call © **808/573-4147** or go to www.mauisierraclub.org.

HALEAKALĀ NATIONAL PARK ★★★

For complete coverage of the national park, see p. 309.

Wilderness Hikes: Sliding Sands & Halemau'u Trails

Hiking into Maui's dormant volcano is an experience like no other. The terrain inside the wilderness area of the volcano, which ranges from

The desert landscape of Haleakalā National Park.

burnt-red cinder cones to ebony-black lava flows, is astonishing. There are some 27 miles of hiking trails, two camping sites, and three cabins.

Entrance to Haleakalā National Park is $25 per car. The rangers offer free guided hikes (usually Mon and Thurs), a great way to learn about the unusual flora and geological formations here. Wear sturdy shoes and be prepared for wind, rain, and intense sun. Bring water, snacks, and a hat. Additional options include full-moon hikes and star-program hikes. The hikes and briefing sessions may be canceled, so check first. Call ✆ **808/572-4400** or visit www.nps.gov/hale.

Avid hikers should plan to stay at least 1 night in the park; 2 or 3 nights will allow more time to explore the fascinating interior of the volcano (see below for details on the cabins and campgrounds in the wilderness area of the valley). If you want to venture out on your own, the best route takes in two trails: into the crater along **Sliding Sands Trail,** which begins on the rim at 9,800 feet and descends to the valley floor at 6,600 feet, and back out along **Halemau'u Trail.** Before you set out, stop at park headquarters to get trail updates.

The trailhead for Sliding Sands is well marked and the trail easy to follow over lava flows and cinders. As you descend, look around: The view is breathtaking. In the afternoon, waves of clouds flow into the Kaupō and Ko'olau gaps. Vegetation is spare to nonexistent at the top, but the closer you get to the valley floor, the more growth you'll see: bracken ferns, pili grass, shrubs, even flowers. On the floor, the trail travels across rough lava flows, passing by rare silversword plants, volcanic vents, and multicolored cinder cones.

The Halemau'u Trail goes over red and black lava and past native ohelo berries and *'ōhi'a* trees as it ascends up the valley wall.

'Ohe'o Gulch.

Occasionally, riders on horseback use this trail. The proper etiquette is to step aside and stand quietly next to the trail as the horses pass.

Some shorter and easier hiking options include the .5-mile walk down the **Hosmer Grove Nature Trail,** or just the first mile or two down **Sliding Sands Trail.** (Even this short hike is exhausting at the high altitude.) A good day hike is **Halemau'u Trail** to Hōlua Cabin and back, an 8-mile, half-day trip.

Kīpahulu

All the way out in Hāna, lush and rainy Kīpahulu is one section of Haleakalā National Park that is not accessible from the summit. From the ranger station just off of Hāna Highway, it's a short hike above the famous **'Ohe'o Gulch** (aka the Seven Sacred Pools) to two spectacular waterfalls. The first, **Makahiku Falls,** is easily reached from the central parking area; the trailhead begins near the ranger station. Pipiwai Trail leads you up to the road and beyond for .5 miles to the overlook. Continue on another 1.5 miles across two bridges and through a magical bamboo forest to **Waimoku Falls.** It's a challenging uphill trek, but mostly shaded and sweetened by the sounds of clattering bamboo canes. In times of hard rain, streams swell quickly. Never attempt to cross flooding waters.

POLIPOLI SPRINGS AREA ★

At this state recreation area, part of the 21,000-acre Kula and Kahikinui forest reserves on the slope of Haleakalā, it's hard to believe that you're in Hawai'i. First of all, it's cold, even in summer, because the elevation is

5,300 to 6,200 feet. Second, this former forest of native *koa,* 'ōhi'a, and *māmane,* which was overlogged in the 1800s, was reforested in the 1930s with introduced species: pine, Monterey cypress, ash, sugi, red alder, redwood, and several varieties of eucalyptus. The result is a cool area, with muted sunlight filtered by towering trees. In addition to trails, there's a campground here. See p. 388 for details.

Skyline Trail

This is some hike—strenuous but worth every step if you like seeing the big picture. It's 8 miles, all downhill, with a dazzling 100-mile view of the islands dotting the blue Pacific, plus the West Maui Mountains, which seem like a separate island.

The trail is just outside Haleakalā National Park at Polipoli Spring State Recreation Area; however, you access it by going through the national park to the summit. It starts just beyond the Pu'u Ula'ula summit building on the south side of Science City and follows the southwest rift zone of Haleakalā from its lunar-like cinder cones to a cool redwood grove. The trail drops 3,800 feet on a 4-hour hike to the recreation area in the 12,000-acre Kahikinui Forest Reserve. If you'd rather drive, you'll need a four-wheel-drive vehicle.

Polipoli Loop

One of the most unusual hiking experiences in the state is this easy 3.5-mile hike, which takes about 3 hours; dress warmly for it. Take the Haleakalā Highway (Hwy. 37) to Kēōkea and turn right onto Hwy. 337; after less than a half-mile, turn on Waipoli Road, which climbs swiftly. After 10 miles, Waipoli Road ends at the Polipoli Spring State Recreation Area campgrounds. The well-marked trailhead is next to the parking lot near a stand of Monterey cypress; the tree-lined trail offers the best view of the island.

Polipoli Loop is really a network of three trails: **Haleakalā Ridge, Plum Trail,** and **Redwood Trail.** After .5 miles of meandering through groves of eucalyptus, blackwood, swamp mahogany, and hybrid cypress, you'll join the Haleakalā Ridge Trail, which, about a mile in, joins with the Plum Trail (named for the plums that ripen in June and July). This trail passes through massive redwoods and by an old Conservation Corps bunkhouse before joining up with the Redwood Trail, which climbs through Mexican pine, tropical ash, Port Orford cedar, and, of course, redwood.

WAI'ĀNAPANAPA STATE PARK ★★★

Tucked in a tropical jungle on the outskirts of the little coastal town of Hāna is this state park, a black-sand beach nestled against vine-strewn cliffs.

The **Hāna-Wai'ānapanapa Coast Trail** is an easy 6-mile hike that takes you back in time. Allow 4 hours to walk along this relatively flat trail, which parallels the sea, along lava cliffs and a forest of lauhala trees. The best time to take the hike is either early morning or late afternoon, when the light on the lava and surf makes for great photos. Midday is the worst time; not only is it hot (lava intensifies the heat), but there's also no shade or potable water available.

There's no formal trailhead; join the route at any point along the Wai'ānapanapa Campground and go in either direction. Along the trail, you'll see remains of an ancient *heiau* (temple), stands of lauhala trees, caves, a blowhole, and a remarkable plant, the naupaka, which flourishes along the beach. Upon close inspection, you'll see that the naupaka have only half-blossoms; according to Hawaiian legend, a similar plant living in the mountains has the other half of the blossoms. One ancient explanation is that the two plants represent never-to-be-reunited lovers: The couple bickered so much that the gods, fed up with their incessant quarreling, banished one lover to the mountain and the other to the sea.

Hāna: The Hike to Fagan's Cross

This 3-mile hike to the cross erected in memory of Paul Fagan, the founder of Hāna Ranch and the former Hotel Hāna-Maui (now the Travaasa Hāna), offers spectacular views of the Hāna Coast, particularly at sunset. The uphill trail starts across Hāna Highway from the Hotel Hāna-Maui. Enter the pastures at your own risk; they're often occupied by glaring bulls with sharp horns and cows with new calves. Watch your step as you ascend this steep hill on a jeep trail across open pastures to the cross and breathtaking views.

Horseback Riding

Maui offers spectacular horse rides through rugged ranchlands and into tropical forests. I recommend riding with **Mendes Ranch Trail Rides ★**, 3530 Kahekili Hwy., 6¼ miles past Wailuku (www.mendesranch.com; ✆ **808/871-5222**). The 3,000-acre Mendes Ranch is a real-life working cowboy ranch with all the essential elements of an earthly paradise: rainbows, waterfalls, palm trees, coral-sand beaches, lagoons, tide pools, a rainforest, and its own volcanic peak (more than a mile high). Your guides, bona fide wranglers, will take you from the edge of the rainforest out to the sea and even teach you to lasso. They'll field questions and point out native flora, but generally just let you soak up Maui's natural splendor in golden silence. Experienced riders can run their horses. A 1½-hour morning or afternoon ride costs $110; add a barbecue lunch at the corral for an additional $30.

Another one of my favorites is **Pi'iholo Ranch Adventures ★** in Makawao (www.piiholo.com; ✆ **808/270-8750**). This working cattle ranch owned by the *kama'āina* (long-time resident) Baldwin family offers a variety of horseback adventures to suit your ability. Among them, the 2- to 3-hour private rides meander through the misty slopes of Haleakalā with stops for picnic lunches (starting at $229). You can play "Cowboy for a Day" and learn how to round up cattle ($349). For a truly special occasion, book the **Heli Ranch Experience** ($3,823 for two people): A limo delivers you to the Kahului heliport, where you board an A-Star helicopter and fly to a private ranch cabin for breakfast and a 2-hour horseback ride. The ranch also has a zipline; check "Ziplining," below, for more details.

Pony Express Tours (www.ponyexpresstours.com; © **808/667-2200** or 808/878-6698) offers 1½- and 2-hour rides at Haleakalā Ranch, located on the beautiful lower slopes of the volcano ($95–$110; book via the website for a 10% discount). Pony Express provides well-trained horses and experienced guides, and accommodates all riding levels. You must be at least 10 years old, weigh no more than 235 pounds, and wear long pants and closed-toe shoes.

Tennis

Maui has excellent public tennis courts; all are free and available from daylight to sunset (a few are even lit until 10pm for night play). For a complete list of public courts, call **Maui County Parks and Recreation** (www.co.maui.hi.us/facilities.aspx; © **808/270-7383**). The courts are available on a first-come, first-served basis; when someone's waiting, limit your play to 45 minutes. Most public courts require a wait and aren't especially convenient for visitors. Exceptions include the courts in Kīhei (in Kalama Park on South Kīhei Rd. and in Waipualani Park on West Waipualani Rd. behind the Maui Sunset condo), in Lahaina (in Malu Ulu Olele Park at Front and Shaw sts.), and in Hāna (in the Hāna Ballpark just off of Hau'oli Rd.).

Private tennis courts are available at most resorts and hotels on the island. The **Kapalua Tennis Garden and Village Tennis Center,** Kapalua Resort (www.kapalua.com/activities/tennis; © **808/662-7730**), is home to the Kapalua Open, which features the largest purse in the state, held on Labor Day weekend. Court rentals are $15 per person. Drop-in Doubles and Stroke of the Day clinics are offered most days at 8 and 9am. In Wailea, try the **Wailea Tennis Club,** 131 Wailea Ike Place (www.waileatennis.com; © **808/879-1958**), with 11 Plexipave courts. Court fees are $20 per player, with 2-day advance reservations required.

Ziplining

Pi'iholo Ranch Adventures ★ Explore this family ranch in the Makawao forest from above—flying through the eucalyptus canopy on one of six ziplines. Tour packages include access to the aerial bridge, tree platforms, ziplines (including side-by-side lines that you can ride with friends), and private waterfalls where you can take a refreshing dip.

799 Piiholo Rd., Makawao. www.piiholozipline.com. © **808/374-7050.** Tours: $99–$219.

ESPECIALLY FOR kids

Take a Submarine Ride The **Atlantis Submarine** (p. 321) takes you and the kids down into the shallow coastal waters off Lahaina in a real sub, where you'll see plenty of fish (and maybe even a shark!). They'll love it, and you'll all stay dry the entire time. Allow about 2 hours for the trip.

Sleep with the Sharks What do fish do when the lights go out? Find out during one of the family sleepovers at the **Maui Ocean Center** (p. 306). The fun starts at 7pm, when kids help feed the turtles and rays, witness sharks and jacks on the prowl in the Open Ocean exhibit, and then snuggle into their sleeping bags. ***Note:*** Each child must be accompanied by an adult. The $75 per-person fee includes snacks, breakfast, a souvenir, and aquarium admission the following day.

Tour the Stars After sunset, the stars over Ka'anapali shine big and bright: That's because the tropical sky is almost pollutant free and no big-city lights interfere with the cosmic view. Amateur astronomers can probe the Milky Way, see the rings of Saturn and Jupiter's moons, and scan the Sea of Tranquillity in a 60-minute star search on the world's first recreational computer-driven telescope. It takes place nightly at 8 and 9pm on the rooftop of the **Hyatt Regency Maui Resort** (p. 356). The cost for hotel guests is $25 for adults and $15 for children 12 and under; nonguests pay $30 for adults and $20 for children 12 and under. (There's also a 10pm tour for couples only; it's $40, and champagne and chocolate-covered strawberries are served.) Reservations are a must.

Skyline EcoAdventures ★ Go on, let out a wild holler as you soar above a rainforested gulch in Ka'anapali or down the slope of Haleakalā. Pioneers of this internationally popular activity, the Skyline owners brought the first ziplines to the U.S. and launched them from their home, here on Maui. Skyline has two courses, one on the west side and the other halfway up Haleakalā. Both are fast and fun, the guides are savvy and safety-conscious, and the scenery is breathtaking. In Ka'anapali, you can even "zip and dip": drop off your line into a mountain pool.

Beyond that, this eco-conscious company is carbon-neutral and donates thousands of dollars to local environmental agencies.

2½ miles up Haleakalā Hwy., Makawao. www.zipline.com. ✆ **808/878-8400.** Skyline EcoAdventures Ka'anapali: 2580 Kekaa Dr. #122 (meet at Fairway Shops), Lahaina (✆ **808/662-1500**). Tours: $135–$249.

WHERE TO STAY ON MAUI

Maui has accommodations to fit every kind of vacation, from deluxe oceanfront resorts to reasonably priced condos to historic bed-and-breakfasts. Be sure to reference "The Island in Brief," earlier in this chapter, to help you settle on a location.

Remember that Hawai'i's 13.416% accommodations tax will be tacked on to your final bill. Also, if you're staying at an upscale hotel or resort, expect to pay a daily "resort fee" ($20–$35 a day) in addition to your room rate. Parking is free unless otherwise noted. All hotels are nonsmoking.

Central Maui

KAHULUI

Marriot Courtyard Business travelers and vacationers looking to save on airport drive time will find a comfortable night's sleep here. Built in 2012, the hotel has soundproofed walls that adequately muffle noise from the neighboring airport. Spacious rooms are attractively furnished, featuring contemporary, island-inspired artwork. Suites come with full kitchens—super convenient considering the lobby has a 24-hour market, and several grocery stores are a 5-minute drive away. The palm-fringed pool deck is especially nice at night when it's lit by the glow of the fire pit.

532 Keolani Place, Kahului. ✆ **808/871-1800.** www.marriott.com. 138 units. $269 double; $339 suite; $399 1-bedroom; $609 2-bedroom. Parking $10. Free airport shuttle. **Amenities:** Deli-style restaurant; fitness center; Jacuzzi; coin-operated laundry; 24-hr. market; pool; Wi-Fi (free).

WAILUKU

Old Wailuku Inn at Ulupono ★★ Innkeepers Janice and Thomas Fairbanks and their daughter Shelly offer genuine Hawaiian hospitality at this lovingly restored 1928 estate hidden down a sleepy side street in old Wailuku town. The nostalgic decor pays homage to Don Blanding, Hawai'i's bygone poet laureate. Rooms in both the inn and the three-bedroom Vagabond House are lavishly decorated with native *'ōhi'a*-wood or marble floors, high ceilings, and traditional Hawaiian quilts—most with king-size beds. Each room has a private, ultraluxurious bathroom stocked with plush towels and Aveda toiletries and either a claw-foot tub, a whirlpool tub, or a deluxe multihead shower. You'll want to linger in the fragrant gardens and curl up with a book on the enclosed lānai. Your hosts pull out all the stops at breakfast, serving tropical fruits and pastries to early birds and Belgian waffles, five-cheese frittatas, and Moloka'i sweet potato pancakes after 8am. The inn is located in Wailuku's historic center, just 5 minutes' walk from the Bailey House Museum, Market Street's antique shops, and several good restaurants. 'Īao Valley is a 5-minute drive away.

2199 Kahookele St. (at High St., across from the Wailuku School), Wailuku. www.mauiinn.com. ✆ **800/305-4899** or 808/244-5897. 10 units. $165–$215 double. Check website for specials. Rates include full breakfast. 2-night minimum. **Amenities:** Jacuzzi; Wi-Fi (free).

Inexpensive

Maui Seaside As if frozen in time, this harborside hotel looks much the same as it did in the 1970s: rattan furniture, aloha print bedspreads, and faux-leather booth seating in Tante's, the attached restaurant. The vintage decor has been updated and is now trendy. Rooms in the two-story building face the pool and Kahului Harbor with its sandy beach, where canoe clubs launch their paddling practice.

100 W. Kaahumanu Ave., Kahului. ✆ **800/560-5552** or 808/877-3311. www.mauiseasidehotel.com. 180 units. $114–$209 double. Children under 12 stay free in parent's room using existing bedding. Extra person $15. Parking $5. **Amenities:** Restaurant; laundry room; pool; Wi-Fi (free).

West Maui

LAHAINA

Expensive

Outrigger 'Āina Nalu ★ This lushly landscaped condo complex sprawls over 9 acres on a relatively quiet side street—a rarity in downtown Lahaina. The good-size units are tastefully decorated with modern tropical accents; all have kitchens or kitchenettes, laundry facilities, air-conditioning (a must in Lahaina), and bathrooms with large granite showers (but no tubs). Both pools are appealing places to retreat during the midday heat—particularly the infinity pool deck with its bright red cabanas and pavilion for poolside picnics. All of the historic whaling town's excitement—restaurants, shops, galleries, marine activities, and the small sandy cove at 505 Front St.—is within a 10-minute stroll.

660 Wainee St. (btw. Dickenson and Prison sts.), Lahaina. www.outriggerainanalucondo.com. ✆ **866/733-6420** or 808/667-9766. 197 units. $129–$175 studio with kitchenette; $139–$315 1-bedroom with kitchen (sleeps up to 4); $179–$365 2-bedroom with 1 bathroom and kitchen (sleeps 6); $199–$395 2-bedroom with 2 bathrooms and kitchen (sleeps 6). 2-night minimum. Parking $17.50. **Amenities:** Concierge; grills; whirlpool; 2 pools; Wi-Fi (free).

The Plantation Inn ★★ Tucked away behind **Gerard's** (Maui's award-winning French restaurant), this romantic inn was built in 1987 but looks as if it has been here since the days of Hawaiian royalty—an artful deception. Rooms are tastefully furnished with vintage touches:

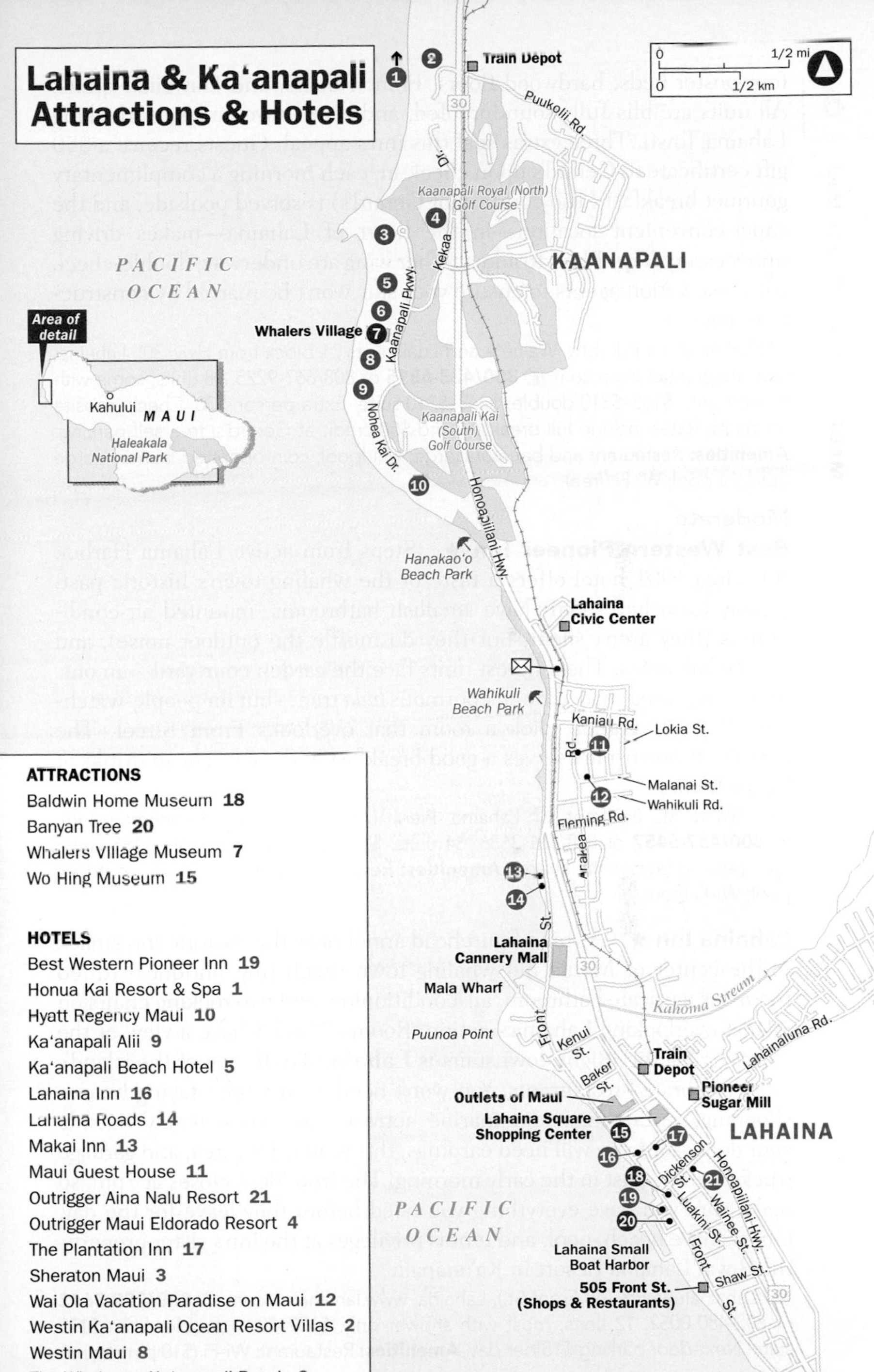
Lahaina & Ka'anapali Attractions & Hotels
0
1/2 mi
0
1/2 km
Train Depot
Puukoli Rd.
30
Kekaa Dr.
Kaanapali Royal (North) Golf Course
KAANAPALI
PACIFIC OCEAN
Area of detail
Kahului
MAUI
Haleakala National Park
Whalers Village
Kaanapali Pkwy.
Nohea Kai Dr.
Kaanapali Kai (South) Golf Course
Honoapiilani Hwy.
Hanakao'o Beach Park
Lahaina Civic Center
Wahikuli Beach Park
Kaniau Rd.
Lokia St.
Malanai St.
Wahikuli Rd.
Fleming Rd.
Ara-kea
Front St.
Lahaina Cannery Mall
Mala Wharf
Kahoma Stream
Puunoa Point
Kenui St.
Lahainaluna Rd.
Train Depot
Baker St.
Pioneer Sugar Mill
Outlets of Maui
Lahaina Square Shopping Center
LAHAINA
Dickenson St.
Honoapiilani Hwy.
Luakini St.
Wainee St.
PACIFIC OCEAN
Lahaina Small Boat Harbor
Front St.
Shaw St.
505 Front St. (Shops & Restaurants)
ATTRACTIONS
Baldwin Home Museum 18
Banyan Tree 20
Whalers Village Museum 7
Wo Hing Museum 15
HOTELS
Best Western Pioneer Inn 19
Honua Kai Resort & Spa 1
Hyatt Regency Maui 10
Ka'anapali Alii 9
Ka'anapali Beach Hotel 5
Lahaina Inn 16
Lahaina Roads 14
Makai Inn 13
Maui Guest House 11
Outrigger Aina Nalu Resort 21
Outrigger Maui Eldorado Resort 4
The Plantation Inn 17
Sheraton Maui 3
Wai Ola Vacation Paradise on Maui 12
Westin Ka'anapali Ocean Resort Villas 2
Westin Maui 8
The Whaler on Ka'anapali Beach 6

four-poster beds, hardwood floors, French doors, and Hawaiian quilts. All units are blissfully soundproofed, and some have lānais overlooking Lahaina Town. Three extras seal this inn's appeal: Guests receive a $50 gift certificate to Gerard's upon check-in, each morning a complimentary gourmet breakfast (also courtesy of Gerard's) is served poolside, and the super-convenient location—in the heart of Lahaina—makes driving unnecessary. ***Tip:*** Plans to add another wing are underway; double-check with reservation agents to ensure your stay won't be marred by construction noise.

174 Lahainaluna Rd. (btw. Waine'e and Luakini sts., 1 block from Hwy. 30), Lahaina. www.theplantationinn.com. ✆ **800/433-6815** or 808/667-9225. 18 units, some with shower only. $165–$310 double; $248–$310 suite. Extra person $30. Check website for deals. Rates include full breakfast and $50 credit at Gerard's; free self-parking. **Amenities:** Restaurant and bar; concierge; whirlpool; coin-operated laundry; large outdoor pool; Wi-Fi (free).

Moderate

Best Western Pioneer Inn ★ Steps from active Lahaina Harbor, this circa-1901 hotel offers a taste of the whaling town's historic past. Simply furnished rooms have smallish bathrooms, mounted air-conditioners (they aren't silent, but they do muffle the outdoor noise), and private balconies. The quietest units face the garden courtyard—an outdoor dining area shaded by an enormous *hala* tree—but for people-watching off your veranda, pick a room that overlooks Front Street. The restaurant downstairs serves a good breakfast and great, cheap drinks at happy hour.

658 Wharf St. (in front of Lahaina Pier), Lahaina. www.pioneerinnmaui.com. ✆ **800/457-5457** or 808/661-3636. 34 units. $162–$207 double; from $185 suite. Free parking (across the street). **Amenities:** Restaurant; bar w/live music; outdoor pool; Wi-Fi (free).

Lahaina Inn ★ A ship's figurehead announces this historic inn smack in the center of Maui's old whaling town. Each tiny, antiques-stuffed room has a private bathroom, air-conditioning, and two rocking chairs on a lānai overlooking Lahaina's action. Rooms 7 and 8 have a view of the glittering Pacific. Right downstairs is **Lahaina Grill,** one of the island's most celebrated restaurants. You won't need a car while staying here—shopping, restaurants, and marine activities are immediately outside your door—but you will need earplugs; this is an urban area, and garbage trucks rumble past in the early morning. The front desk closes at 7pm, so make sure you have everything you need before they leave for the day. Guests have beach, pool, and tennis privileges at the inn's sister property, the Royal Lahaina Resort in Ka'anapali.

127 Lahainaluna Rd. (off Front St.), Lahaina. www.lahainainn.com. ✆ **800/222-5642** or 805/480-0052. 12 units, most with shower only. $109–$221 double; from $195 suite. Next-door parking $15 per day. **Amenities:** Restaurant; Wi-Fi ($10 per day).

Lahaina Roads ★ Named for the Māla Wharf roadstead where a string of pretty boats anchor offshore, this older condominium complex offers compact, individually owned units. It's located on the northern end of Lahaina, away from crowded downtown, but just down the street from Lahaina Cannery Mall, Old Lahaina Lū'au, and several terrific restaurants. One- and two-bedroom units benefit from full kitchens, oceanfront lānais, and a seaside pool. The drawbacks: Bedrooms face the road, which can make nights noisy, and some units lack air-conditioning (it can be boiling hot in Lahaina). I've listed one property manager, but a quick Internet search will turn up others.

1403 Front St. (1 block north of Lahaina Cannery Mall), Lahaina. Book with Chase'N Rainbows: www.westmauicondos.com/resorts/lahaina-roads. ✆ **877/661-6022** or 808/359-2636. 17 units. $155–$250 1-bedroom (sleeps up to 4), $225–$405 2-bedroom (sleeps up to 6). 5-night minimum. **Amenities:** Oceanside outdoor pool; Internet/Wi-Fi (free) in some units.

Maui Guest House ★★ Tanna Swanson offers guests many extras at her charming bed-and-breakfast, tucked away in a residential Lahaina neighborhood. For starters, each private room has a full-size Jacuzzi (seriously!), noiseless air-conditioning, and gorgeous, custom stained-glass windows depicting reef fish, flowers, and other Hawaiian scenes. Guests also have access to the saltwater pool; large, fully stocked kitchen; and 30-foot sundeck for sunbathing, stargazing, and whale-watching. Tanna is a wealth of local information and an experienced scuba diver who takes good care of fellow aqua-holics. She also operates Trinity Tours, a discount activity agency. Her home is 1½ miles from Lahaina's shopping and restaurants and the same distance from Ka'anapali's beaches.

1620 Ainakea Rd. (off Fleming Rd.), north of Lahaina town. www.mauiguesthouse.com. ✆ **800/621-8942** or 808/661-8085. 5 rooms. $169 single, $189 double. Rates include continental breakfast. Take Fleming Rd. off Hwy. 30; turn left on Ainakea; it's 2 blocks down. **Amenities:** Concierge; saltwater pool; watersports equipment; Wi-Fi (free).

Inexpensive

Makai Inn ★ You can't miss this turquoise-blue, two-story apartment complex at the north end of Lahaina, right on the water. A mermaid fountain decorates the parking lot. Each of the eclectically furnished units is small (averaging 400 sq. ft.) but clean, with a full kitchen and a gas stove. Rooms have no phones or TVs, but most have ocean views with Moloka'i in the distance. This funky, U-shape "inn" surrounds a tropical garden frequented by colorful Java sparrows. The largish Paradise Found unit on the southern corner has a private lānai that overlooks the Pacific on two sides. There's no beach access here, but the Lahaina Cannery Mall and several great restaurants are a short walk away.

1415 Front St., Lahaina. www.makaiinn.net. ✆ **808/662-3200.** 18 units. $110–$190 double. Extra person $15. **Amenities:** laundry room; Wi-Fi (free).

KA'ANAPALI

Starwood's Maui properties (Sheraton Maui Resort & Spa, Westin Maui Resort & Spa, or the Westin Ka'anapali Ocean Resort Villas) provide complimentary shuttle service to Lahaina and back.

Note: You'll find Ka'anapali hotels on the "Lahaina & Ka'anapali Attractions & Hotels" map (p. 353).

Expensive

Honua Kai Resort & Spa ★★ This North Ka'anapali Beach resort is a favorite with residents and locals alike. The property sits on Kahekili Beach, immediately north of busier, flashier Ka'anapali Beach, and boasting a much better reef for snorkeling. The resort's upscale-relaxed atmosphere takes a cue from its natural surroundings. Island-inspired artwork in the lobby gives way to colorful koi ponds, artfully landscaped grounds, and meandering swimming pools. Luxury accommodations range from huge 590-square-foot studios to even bigger 2,800-square-foot three-bedroom units, with top-of-the-line appliances, private lānais, and ocean views. The resort's sociable restaurant, **Duke's Maui Beach House,** offers an "ono-licious" breakfast and live music from 3 to 5pm. Stock up on organic snacks, gelato, and local coffee at **'Āina Gourmet Market** in the lobby. **Ho'ola Spa** has the island's only therapeutic Himalayan salt room and incorporates organic, made-in-Hawai'i products in its treatments.

130 Kai Malina Pkwy., North Ka'anapali Beach. www.honuakai.com. ✆ **888/718-5789** or 808/662-2800. 628 units. $274–$607 studio double; $284–$814 1-bedroom (sleeps up to 4); $442–$1,022 2-bedroom (sleeps up to 6); $900–$3,074 3-bedroom (sleeps up to 8). Daily $29 resort fee. Free parking. **Amenities:** Restaurant; deli; bar; fitness center; nearby 36-hole golf course; 5 whirlpools; 5 pools; spa w/therapeutic salt room; nearby tennis courts; watersports equipment rentals; Wi-Fi (free).

Hyatt Regency Maui Resort & Spa ★★ You'll feel like royalty when you walk into this palatial resort with exotic parrots and South African penguins in the lobby. The southernmost property on Ka'anapali Beach, it covers some 40 acres with 9 man-made waterfalls, abundant Asian and Pacific artwork, and a waterpark pool with a swim-up grotto bar, rope bridge, and 150-foot lava-tube slide that keeps kids occupied for hours. Spread out among three towers, the resort's ample rooms have huge marble bathrooms, feather-soft platform beds, and private lānais with eye-popping views of the Pacific or the West Maui Mountains. Two Regency Club floors offer a private concierge, complimentary breakfast, sunset cocktails, and snacks—not a bad choice for families looking to save on meals. Daily activities range from sushi-making classes at **Japengo,** the resort's superb Japanese restaurant, to stargazing on the rooftop. Camp Hyatt offers pint-size guests weekly scavenger hunts, penguin-feeding opportunities, and access to a game room. The oceanfront **Marilyn Monroe Spa,** a 20,000-square-foot wellness retreat, boasts 15 treatment rooms, sauna and steam rooms, and a huge menu of celebrity-inspired body treatments.

200 Nohea Kai Dr., Lahaina. www.maui.hyatt.com. © **808/661-1234.** 806 rooms; 31 suites. $246–$534 double; $359–$609 Regency Club double; from $671 suite. Daily $31 resort fee. Extra person $75 ($125 in Regency Club rooms). Children 18 and under stay free in parent's room using existing bedding. Packages available. Valet parking $28; self-parking $18. **Amenities:** 5 restaurants; 3 bars; on-site lū'au; babysitting; children's program; concierge; club floor; 36-hole golf course; health club w/ weight room and classes; whirlpool; half-acre outdoor pool; room service; state-of-the-art spa; 6 tennis courts; watersports equipment rentals; Wi-Fi (free).

Ka'anapali Ali'i ★ This luxurious oceanfront condo complex sits on 8 landscaped acres in the center of Ka'anapali Beach. Units are individually owned and decorated—which means some are considerably fancier than others. Both one- (1,500-sq.-ft.) and two bedroom (1,900-sq.-ft.) units come with all the comforts of home: spacious living areas, gourmet kitchens, washer/dryers, lānais, and two full bathrooms. Resort-like extras include bell service, daily housekeeping, and a complimentary kids' lessons (summer only). Views from each unit vary dramatically; if watching the sun sink into the ocean is important to you, request a central unit on floor six or higher. Mountain View units shouldn't be disregarded, though. They're cooler throughout the day, and the West Maui Mountains are arrestingly beautiful—particularly on full-moon nights. It's got a swimming pool, a children's pool, barbecues and picnic areas, and tennis courts. You can even take yoga classes on the lawn.

50 Nohea Kai Dr., Lahaina. www.kaanapalialii.com. © **866/664-36410** or 808/667-1400. 264 units. $550–$695 1-bedroom for 4; $800–$1100 2-bedroom for 6. Check Internet for specials. Free parking. **Amenities:** Babysitting; concierge; fitness center; fitness and yoga classes; 36-hole golf course; kids' club (June–Aug); 2 outdoor pools; 3 lighted tennis courts; watersports equipment; Wi-Fi (free).

Sheraton Maui Resort & Spa ★★★ The Sheraton occupies the nicest spot on Ka'anapali Beach, built into the side of Pu'u Keka'a, the dramatic lava rock point at the beach's north end. The stretch of golden sand fronting the resort is widest here and the snorkeling is best around the base of the point, also known as Black Rock. At sunset, cliff divers swan-dive into the sea from the torch lit cliff. The resort's prime location, ample amenities, and great service make it an all-around ideal place to stay. Rooms feature Hawaiian-inspired decor, private lānais, and trademark Sweet Sleeper beds, which live up to their name. The *ohana* (family) suites accommodate all ages with two double beds plus a *punee* (sleeping chaise). The lagoon-like pool is refreshing but doesn't beat the sea full of real live fish and turtles just steps away. Activities ranging from outrigger canoe to hula and 'ukulele lessons will immerse you in Hawaiian culture; at night the Maui Nui Lū'au has an exciting fire-knife dance finale. The elegant **Spa at Black Rock** lacks the steam rooms and saunas of other resort spas, but treatments here—especially those catering to couples—are exquisite. Fans of **Hank's Haute Dogs** on O'ahu will find their favorite gourmet dogs here, and DJs spin tunes from 10pm to midnight on weekends at the **Black Rock Lounge.**

2605 Ka'anapali Pkwy., Lahaina. www.sheraton-maui.com. ✆ **866/716-8109** or 808/661-0031. 508 units. $296–$569 double; from $699 suite. Daily $25 resort fee. Extra person $89. Children 17 and under stay free in parent's room using existing bedding. Valet parking $30 (free first day); self-parking $20. **Amenities:** 3 restaurants; 1 poolside bar; weekly lū'au; indoor lounge; babysitting; children's program (at the Westin); lobby and poolside concierge; 36-hole golf course; fitness center; Jacuzzi; lagoon-style pool; room service; shuttle service; day spa; 3 tennis courts; watersports equipment/rentals; Wi-Fi (free).

The Westin Ka'anapali Ocean Resort Villas ★★ In contrast to the hotel-style Westin (see below), this elegant condo complex is so enormous it has two separate lobbies. The 26 acres fronting serene Kahekili Beach function as a small town with two grocery stores (stock up on marinated meats, local eggs, and Maui-grown coffee), three pools (yes, that's a life-size pirate ship in the kids' pool), three restaurants (hit **Pailolo Sports Bar** during a game), a Hawaiian cultural advisor, the luxurious **Spa Helani** (the 80-min. Polynesian ritual is unforgettable), and a high-energy gym with its own steam rooms, saunas, and lockers. Managed by Westin, the individually owned units (ranging from studios to two-bedrooms) are uniformly outfitted with trademark Heavenly beds, huge soaking tubs with jets, and upscale kitchen appliances. Despite its seemingly massive footprint, the resort has accrued numerous awards for its eco-friendly practices. One fun example: On July 4th, the resort ditches the usual fireworks display (which spreads ash on the fragile coral reefs) and opts instead to celebrate with "flower-works," dropping 60,000 orchids on the property. The lucky guest who finds the rose amid the orchids gets a free spa treatment or snorkel cruise. ***Note:*** Construction will take place next door through the fall of 2017; lower room rates are available. ***Tip:*** Ask for some leeway with the 4pm check-in and 10am checkout times.

6 Kai Ala Dr., Ka'anapali Resort. www.westinkaanapali.com. ✆ **866/716-8112** or 808/667-3200. 1021 units. $303–$770 studio; $419–$1,040 1-bedroom; $629–$1,810 2-bedroom. Extra person $89. Valet $12, self-parking $10. **Amenities:** 3 restaurants; 2 bars; babysitting; children's program; complimentary logo shopping bag; concierge; 36-hole golf course; gym; 3 outdoor pools; children's pool w/pirate ship; room service; shuttle service; spa; tennis courts; Wi-Fi (free).

Westin Maui Resort & Spa ★★ The fantasy begins in the lobby, where waterfalls spill into pools stocked with flamingos and black swans. The lavishly landscaped grounds wind around an 87,000-square-foot water wonderland with five pools and an extra-speedy 128-foot-long water slide. (I screamed the first time I flew down it.) After enjoying the pool amenities (waterfalls, aquatic basketball, volleyball), hit the beach for snorkeling, stand-up paddling, kayaking, or parasailing . . . the sky truly is the limit. Recharge at **Relish,** the poolside restaurant, but save your appetite for **Wailele,** the resort's wonderful 3-hour lūʻau experience. Take a stroll two doors down to shop 'til you drop at Whalers Village. After you've thoroughly exhausted yourself, return to your room to sink into your fabulous Heavenly Bed, a Westin trademark with no fewer than five different pillows. If you need further refreshment, hit the **Heavenly Spa** for a Hualani fruit scrub and lomilomi massage—I highly recommend it. There's also a "mind and body" studio for yoga and meditation classes, as well as a 2,000-square-foot fitness center. Forgot your workout clothes? No problem. You can borrow a set provided by New Balance.

2365 Ka'anapali Pkwy., Lahaina. www.westinmaui.com. ✆ **866/716-8112** or 808/667-2525. 759 units. $299–$939 double; from $566 suite. Children 18 and under stay free in parent's room. Extra person $89. Packages available. Daily $30 resort fee. Valet parking $15, self-parking free. **Amenities:** 3 restaurants; 3 bars; babysitting; bike rental; children's program; concierge; fitness center/yoga studio; 36-hole golf course; 5 pools; room service; shuttle service; salon; complimentary logo shopping bag; spa w/steam rooms, saunas, and co-ed lounge; tennis courts; watersports equipment rentals; Wi-Fi (free).

The Whaler on Ka'anapali Beach ★ Situated in the center of Kaʻanapali Beach next door to Whalers Village, this collection of condos feels more formal and sedate than its high-octane neighbors. Maybe it's the koi turning circles in the meditative lily pond, the manicured lawn between the two 12-story towers, or the lack of a water slide populated by stampeding kids. Decor in the individually owned units varies widely, but most boast full kitchens, upscale bathrooms, private lānais with views of Kaʻanapali's gentle waves or the emerald peaks of the West Maui Mountains. Unit no. 723, in the back corner of the north tower, is exquisite. The beachfront barbecue area is the envy of passersby on the Kaʻanapali Beach walkway.

2481 Ka'anapali Pkwy. (next to Whalers Village), Lahaina. www.astonhotels.com. ✆ **877/997-6667** or 808/924-2924. 360 units. $239–$345 studio double; $334–$430 1-bedroom (up to 4 people); $575–$899 2-bedroom (up to 6 people). Check website for specials. Parking $12 per day. **Amenities:** Concierge; fitness center; outdoor pool; salon and spa; tennis courts; Wi-Fi (free).

Moderate

Ka'anapali Beach Hotel ★ A relic from a bygone era, Kaʻanapali Beach Hotel has humble charm and authentic Hawaiian warmth. Depending on your taste, you'll find this property's giant carved tikis, whale-shape pool, and somewhat dated decor either kitschy or refreshingly unpretentious. Instead of African parrots and Asian artwork, the lobby is adorned with traditional Hawaiian hula implements and weapons—many created by the staff during their annual Makahiki celebration. Three low-rise buildings border fabulous Kaʻanapali Beach; the beachfront units are mere steps from the water. The large-ish, motel-like rooms are decorated with wicker and rattan furniture, historic photos or renderings of native flora and fauna, and Hawaiian-style bedspreads. Hula and live music create a festive atmosphere every night in the courtyard. During the day, you can snorkel out front, try stand-up paddling, or even learn to speak a little *'ōlelo Hawai'i*—the Islands' lyrical native language. The staff serenades you during a morning welcome reception and a farewell lei ceremony. Even if you don't stay here, pay a visit to the grassy lawn where a giant checkerboard has red-and-black painted coconuts for game pieces. ***Added bonus:*** no resort fee.

2525 Ka'anapali Pkwy., Lahaina. www.kbhmaui.com. ✆ **800/262-8450** or 808/661-0011. 430 units. $195–$334 double; from $311–$544 suite. Extra person $40. Packages available, as well as senior discounts. Valet parking $13; self-parking $11. **Amenities:** 2 restaurants; poolside bar; babysitting; children's program (not supervised); concierge; 36-hole golf course nearby; outdoor pool; spa and salon services; access to tennis courts; watersports equipment rentals; Wi-Fi (free).

Outrigger Maui Eldorado ★ It may have been one of Ka'anapali's first properties in the late 1960s, but this 10-acre condo complex still manages to feel new. Developed in an era when real estate was abundant and contractors built to last, each spacious, individually owned unit has a full kitchen, washer/dryer, central air-conditioning, and outstanding ocean and mountain views. This is a great choice for active families. It's set on Ka'anapali Golf Course, not on the beach, but guests have exclusive use of a beachfront pavilion on North Ka'anapali, aka Kahekili Beach. You're also within walking distance of the Fairway Shops' excellent and affordable restaurants—a real bonus in otherwise pricey Ka'anapali. ***Note:*** It's a two-level walkup without elevators. Grocery service and daily housekeeping are optional.

2661 Keka'a Dr., Lahaina. www.outrigger.com. ✆ **888/339-8585** or 808/661-0021. 204 units, 87 managed by Outrigger. $135–$199 studio double; $169–$345 1-bedroom (up to 4); $229–$509 2-bedroom (up to 6). 2-night minimum. Numerous packages available. Daily $14 resort fee; $95–175 mandatory cleaning charge. Free parking. **Amenities:** Beach pavilion; concierge; 36-hole golf course; 3 outdoor pools; Wi-Fi (free).

HONOKŌWAI, KAHANA & NĀPILI

Expensive

Kahana Sunset ★ Set in the crook of a sharp bend on Lower Honoapi'ilani Road is a series of three-story wooden condos, stair-stepping down a hill to a private Keonenui beach—a strip of golden sand all but unknown, even to locals. Decor varies dramatically in the individually owned units, many of which feature master and children's bedrooms up a short flight of stairs. All units have full kitchens with dishwashers, washer/dryers, cable TV, and expansive lānais with marvelous views. Some rooms have air-conditioning, while most rely on ceiling fans—suitable on this cooler end of the coastline. The center of the property features a small heated pool, Jacuzzi, and barbecue grills. This complex is

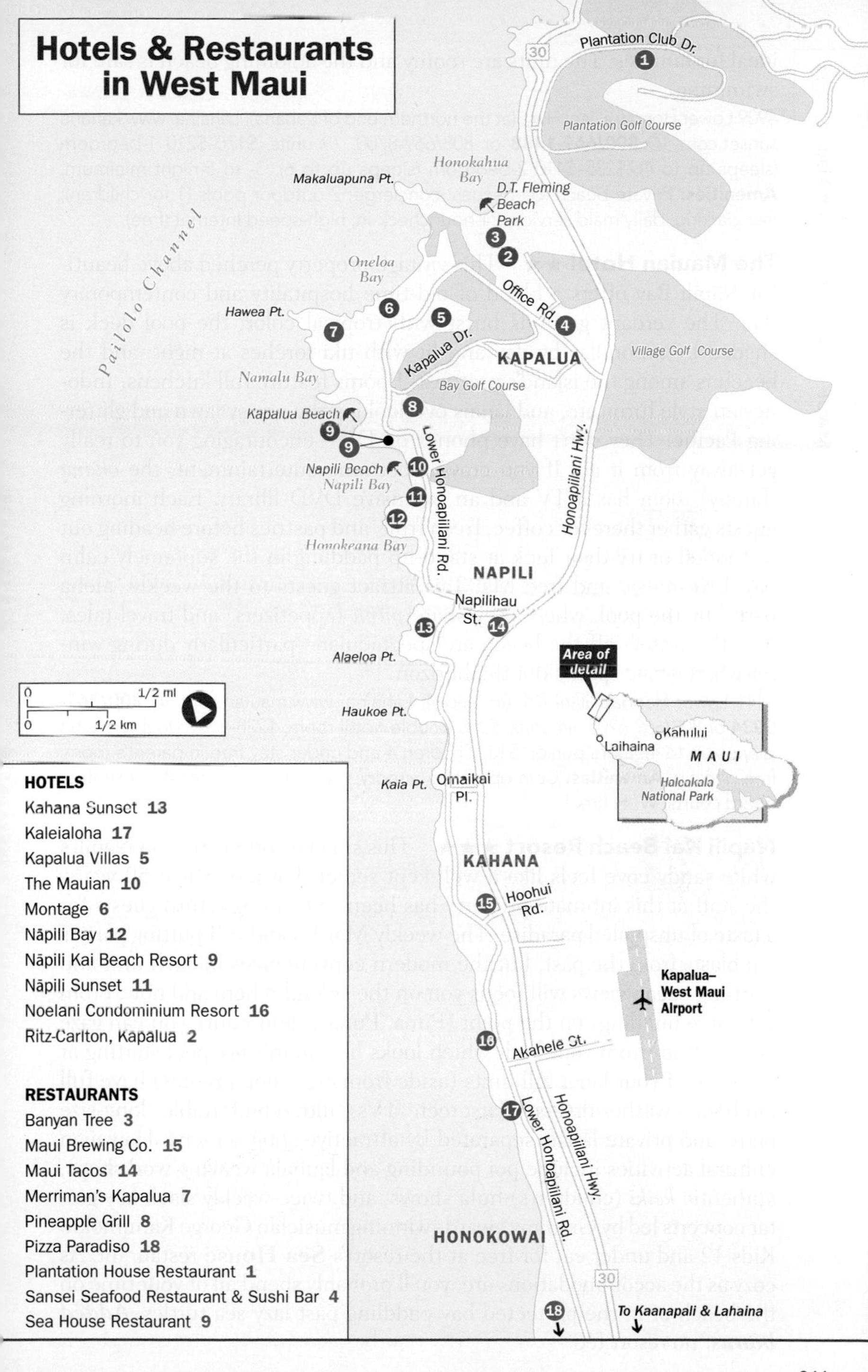

Hotels & Restaurants in West Maui
Plantation Club Dr.
Plantation Golf Course
Honokahua Bay
Makaluapuna Pt.
D.T. Fleming Beach Park
Pailolo Channel
Oneloa Bay
Office Rd.
Hawea Pt.
Kapalua Dr.
KAPALUA
Village Golf Course
Namalu Bay
Bay Golf Course
Kapalua Beach
Napili Beach
Napili Bay
Lower Honoapiilani Rd.
Honoapiilani Hwy.
Homokeana Bay
NAPILI
Napilihau St.
Alaeloa Pt.
Area of detail
Haukoe Pt.
Lahaina
Kahului
MAUI
Haleakala National Park
Kaia Pt.
Omaikai Pl.
KAHANA
Hoohui Rd.
Kapalua–West Maui Airport
Akahele St.
Lower Honoapiilani Rd.
Honoapiilani Hwy.
HONOKOWAI
To Kaanapali & Lahaina
0 1/2 mi
0 1/2 km
HOTELS
Kahana Sunset 13
Kaleialoha 17
Kapalua Villas 5
The Mauian 10
Montage 6
Nāpili Bay 12
Nāpili Kai Beach Resort 9
Nāpili Sunset 11
Noelani Condominium Resort 16
Ritz-Carlton, Kapalua 2
RESTAURANTS
Banyan Tree 3
Maui Brewing Co. 15
Maui Tacos 14
Merriman's Kapalua 7
Pineapple Grill 8
Pizza Paradiso 18
Plantation House Restaurant 1
Sansei Seafood Restaurant & Sushi Bar 4
Sea House Restaurant 9

ideal for families: The units are roomy and the adjoining beach is safe for swimming.

4909 Lower Honoapi'ilani Hwy. (at the northern end of Kahana), Lahaina. www.kahanasunset.com. ✆ **800/669-1488** or 808/669-8700. 79 units. $170–$210 1-bedroom (sleeps up to 4); $235–$410 2-bedroom (sleeps up to 6). 3- to 5-night minimum. **Amenities:** Private beach; barbecues; concierge; 2 outdoor pools (1 for children); free parking; daily maid service; 24-hour check-in; high-speed Internet (free).

The Mauian Hotel ★★ This vintage property perched above beautiful Nāpili Bay offers a blend of old-time hospitality and contemporary flair. The verdant grounds burst with tropical color; the pool deck is shaded by umbrellas by day and lit with tiki torches at night; and the beach is among the island's prettiest. Rooms feature full kitchens, Indonesian-style furniture, and lānais overlooking the grassy lawn and glittering Pacific. They don't have phones or TVs—encouraging you to really get away from it all. If you crave electronic entertainment, the *ohana* (family) room has a TV and an extensive DVD library. Each morning guests gather there for coffee, fresh fruit, and pastries before heading out to snorkel or try their luck at stand-up paddling in the supremely calm bay. Live music and free Mai Tais attract guests to the weekly "aloha party" by the pool, where they share *pūpū* (appetizers) and travel tales. Nightly sunsets off the beach are spectacular—particularly during winter when whale spouts dot the horizon.

5441 Lower Honoapi'ilani Rd. (in Nāpili), Lahaina. www.mauian.com. ✆ **800/367-5034** or 808/669-6205. 44 units. $208 double hotel room; $228–$325 double studio (sleeps up to 4). Extra person $13. Children 4 and under stay free in parent's room; free parking. **Amenities:** Coin-operated laundry; outdoor pool; oceanfront shuffleboard courts; Wi-Fi (free).

Nāpili Kai Beach Resort ★★★ This small resort nestled on Nāpili's white sandy cove feels like a well-kept secret. For more than 50 years, the staff at this intimate property has been welcoming return guests for a taste of unspoiled paradise. The weekly Mai Tai and golf putting parties are blasts from the past, but the modern conveniences in each unit and startling ocean views will focus you on the splendid here and now. From the three buildings on the point (Puna, Puna 2, and Lani), you can gaze at the ocean from your bed, which looks like an infinity pool starting at the edge of your lānai. All units (aside from eight hotel rooms) have full kitchens, washer/dryers, flatscreen TVs, ultra-comfortable king-size beds, and private lānais separated by attractive shoji screens. Hawaiian cultural activities include poi pounding and lauhala weaving workshops, authentic *keiki* (children's) hula shows, and twice-weekly slack key guitar concerts led by Grammy award–winning musician George Kahumoku. Kids 12 and under eat for free at the resort's **Sea House** restaurant. As cozy as the accommodations are, you'll probably spend all of your time on the beach or in the protected bay paddling past lazy sea turtles. ***Added bonus:*** no resort fee.

5900 Honoapi'ilani Rd. (at north end of Nāpili, next to Kapalua), Lahaina. www.napilikai.com. ✆ **800/367-5030** or 808/669-6271. 162 units. Hotel room double from $351; studio double (sleeps 3–4) from $442; 1-bedroom suite (sleeps up to 5) from $703; 2-bedroom suite (sleeps up to 7) from 1,156; 3-bedroom suite (sleeps up to 7) from 1,380. Packages available. **Amenities:** Restaurant; bar; babysitting; free children's activities at holidays; concierge; 24-hr. fitness room; 2 18-hole putting greens; discounted rates at nearby Kapalua golf courses; 4 pools; free Kapalua shuttle; tennis courts nearby (and complimentary use of tennis rackets); complimentary watersports equipment; Wi-Fi (free).

Nāpili Sunset ★ This humble property hidden down a side street consists of three buildings, two facing spectacular Nāpili Bay and one across the street. At first glance, they don't look like much, but the prime location, low prices, and friendly staff make up for the plain-Jane exterior. The one- and two-bedroom units are beachfront. Upstairs units have bathtubs, while those downstairs have direct access to the sand. Across the street, overlooking a kidney-shaped pool and gardens, the economical studios feature expansive showers and Murphy beds. All units benefit from daily maid service, full kitchens (with dishwashers), and ceiling fans (no air-conditioning). Unfortunately, bedrooms in the beachfront buildings face the road, but the ocean views from the lānais are outstanding. The strip of grassy lawn adjoining the beach is an added perk—especially when the sandy real estate is crowded. Several good restaurants are within walking distance, along with Kapalua's tennis courts and golf courses.

46 Hui Rd. (in Nāpili), Lahaina. www.napilisunset.com. ✆ **808/669-8083.** 43 units. $180 studio double; $340–$360 1 bedroom double (sleeps 5–6); $510 2-bedroom (sleeps up to 7). **Amenities:** Daily maid service; free parking; barbecues; coin-operated laundry; small outdoor pool; Wi-Fi (free).

Noelani Condominium Resort ★★ This Kahana condo is a real gem. Whether you book a studio or a three-bedroom unit, everything from the furnishings to the oceanfront pool is first class for budget prices. The only caveat: There's no sandy beach attached. Pōhaku Beach Park (good for surfing, not as great for swimming) is next door and better beaches are less than 10 minutes away. All units feature full kitchens, daily maid service, panoramic views of passing whales during winter, and spectacular sunsets year-round; one-, two-, and three-bedrooms have washer/dryers. My favorites are the Orchid building's deluxe studios, where you can see the ocean from your bed. Units in the Anthurium Building boast oceanfront lānais just 20 feet from the water (the nicest are on the ground floor), but the bedrooms face the road. Guests are invited to lei-making and Mai Tai parties in the poolside cabana and have access to a teeny-tiny gym with a million-dollar view. It doesn't have air-conditioning, but the ceiling fans and ocean breezes are adequate.

4095 Lower Honoapi'ilani Rd. (in Kahana), Lahaina. www.noelani-condo-resort.com. ✆ **800/367-6030** or 808/669-8374. 40 units. $150–$209 studio double; $185–$237

1-bedroom (sleeps up to 4); $290–$339 2-bedroom (sleeps up to 6); $345–$403 3-bedroom (sleeps up to 8). Extra person $20. Children under 18 stay free in parent's room. Packages available. Rates include continental breakfast on 1st morning. 3-night minimum. **Amenities:** Concierge; fitness center; oceanfront Jacuzzi; laundry center (for studios); 2 freshwater pools (1 heated for night swimming); Wi-Fi (free).

Inexpensive

Kaleialoha ★ This four-story condo complex is conveniently located near Honokōwai's grocery shopping, budget restaurants, and public beach park. Each one-bedroom unit comes with a fully equipped kitchen with marble countertops and dishwashers; a sofa bed in the living room; stacked washer/dryers; outdoor barbecues; and a view of Lāna'i and Moloka'i across the turquoise expanse of the Pacific. Top-floor units have the best views; bottom-floor units open onto the lawn and oceanfront pool. There's decent snorkeling beyond the rock retaining wall, but you'll have to walk a block down the road for a sandy beach. ***Tip:*** You can inspect each unit on the website.

3785 Lower Honoapi'ilani Rd. (in Honokōwai), Lahaina. www.mauicondosoceanfront.com. ✆ **800/222-8688** or 808/669-8197. 18 units. $149–$245 1-bedroom double. Extra person $10. Children 3 and under stay free in parent's room. Cleaning fee $125 for less than 7-night stay. **Amenities:** Concierge; Wi-Fi (free).

Nāpili Bay ★ This small two-story condo complex sits on the southern edge of picturesque Nāpili Bay. Fall asleep to the sound of the surf and wake to birdsong. Individually owned studio apartments are compact, with king- or queen-size beds in the oceanfront living room (rather than facing the road like so many on this strip). You'll find everything you need, including a stocked kitchen, beach and snorkeling equipment, and a lānai with front-row seats for the sunset. You won't find a pool on the property or air-conditioning in the rooms, but louvered windows and ceiling fans keep the units fairly cool—and why waste time in a pool when you're steps away from one of the island's calmest, prettiest bays?

33 Hui Dr. (off Lower Honoapi'ilani Hwy., in Nāpili), Lahaina. www.alohacondos.com. ✆ **877/877-5758.** 28 units. $149–$279 double. Cleaning fees and minimum stays may apply. **Amenities:** Wi-Fi (free).

KAPALUA

Note: You'll find the following hotels on the "Hotels & Restaurants in West Maui" map (p. 361).

Expensive

Kapalua Villas ★★★ The stately townhouses populating the oceanfront cliffs and fairways of this idyllic coast are a (relative) bargain, particularly if you're traveling with a group. You're granted signing privileges at its championship golf courses and free access to the resort's deluxe tennis complex, golf academy, and luxurious 5-acre Spa Montage Kapalua Bay, with its rainwater showers and co-ed saltwater infinity pool—a dreamy place to spend an afternoon. Several of the island's best restaurants (Sansei, Pineapple Grill, and Merriman's Kapalua) are within walking distance or a quick shuttle trip. Outrigger manages the individually owned one-, two-, and three-bedroom units, which feature upscale furnishings, full kitchens, queen-size sofa beds, and large private lānais. You'll feel like royalty—even the one-bedrooms exceed 1,200 square feet. Of the three complexes (Golf, Ridge, and Bay Villas), the Bay units are the nicest, positioned on the windswept bluff overlooking Moloka'i on the horizon. In the winter you can whale-watch without leaving your living room.

200 Village Rd., Kapalua. www.kapaluavillasmaui.com. ✆ **800/545-0018** or 808/665-9170. 1-bedroom from $169; 2-bedroom from $255; 3-bedroom from $599. Daily $25 resort fee; $130–$200 cleaning fee. Free parking. **Amenities:** Access to Kapalua Resort's 12 dining options; close to 3 excellent beaches; concierge; in-room laundry; full kitchen; privileges at Spa Montage, Kapalua golf courses and tennis courts; 9 outdoor pools; resort shuttle; Wi-Fi (free).

Montage ★★★ From the dramatic entry to the superlative spa, Montage is a full-service resort that invites families to feel luxuriously at home. Enormous residences range from 1,250 to 4,050 square feet—each with gourmet kitchens, deep soaking tubs, walk-in closets, and expansive lānais. Rooms overlook the lavish gardens, pools, and island of Moloka'i on the horizon. The elevator delivers you to your private floor, where you can store the gear you will almost certainly use at nearby Kapalua and Oneloa beaches. The open-air restaurant, **Cane and Canoe,** is great day or night, and the **Kapalua Beach Club** is a chic hangout spot with its own pool, hot tub, and comparatively cheap drinks. Kids will love the outdoor movies and games of capture the flag. Adults will adore the royal treatment in the cabanas, the convenience of everything being close at hand, and the museum-quality artwork exhibited throughout the property. Guests have free use of **Spa Montage**—a wellness wonderland with outdoor rain showers, cedar saunas, waterfall hot tubs, an oceanview yoga studio, and (best of all) a coed serenity pool where couples can lounge and order organic juices before or after their spa treatments.

1 Bay Dr., Kapalua. www.montagekapaluabay.com. ✆ **808/662-6600.** 50 units. $705–$3,685 1-bedroom; $1005–$4,950 2-bedroom; $1,305–$8,070 3-bedroom, $2,545–$10,635 4-bedroom. Daily $30 resort fee; wedding/honeymoon, golf, and other packages available. Resort fee $30; Valet parking $20. **Amenities:** 3 restaurants; 1 bar; babysitting; children's and teens programs; concierge; cultural classes; fitness classes; 3 pools; room service; in-room laundry; full kitchen; shuttle service; luxury spa w/steam rooms, saunas, whirlpools, juice bar, and co-ed pool; privileges at Kapalua golf courses and tennis courts; Wi-Fi (free).

Ritz-Carlton, Kapalua ★★★ Perched on a knoll above D. T. Fleming Beach, this resort is a complete universe, where you can while away whole weeks. The property's intimate relationship to Hawaiian culture began during construction: When the remains of hundreds of ancient

Hawaiians were unearthed, the owners agreed to shift the hotel inland to avoid disrupting the graves. Today, Native Hawaiian cultural advisor Clifford Naeole helps guide resort developments and hosts the Ritz's signature events, such as the Celebration of the Arts—a weeklong, indigenous arts and cultural festival. (The annual Wine & Food Festival is another, worth planning your vacation around.) The resplendent accommodations feature dark wood floors, plush beds, marble bathrooms, and private lānais overlooking the landscaped grounds and mostly undeveloped coast. The Ritz's Club Level offers one of the best lounges in the state, serving gourmet coffee and pastries, a lunch buffet, cookies in the afternoon, and hot appetizers and drinks at sunset. Additional amenities include several superior restaurants; a 10,000-square-foot, three-tiered pool; and the 17,500-square-foot **Waihua Spa,** with steam rooms, saunas, and whirlpools surrounded by lava-rock walls. Make sure to visit **Jean-Michel Cousteau's Ambassadors of the Environment center** and explore the captivating, educational activities for adults and kids. (You can even feed the resident pot-bellied pigs.) A bit of a hike from the resort proper, **D. T. Fleming Beach** is beautiful but tends to be windier and rougher than the bays immediately south; a 5-minute shuttle ride delivers you to Oneloa or Kapalua. The forest and coastal hiking trails offer superlative views and opportunities to see native flora and fauna.

1 Ritz-Carlton Dr., Kapalua. www.ritzcarlton.com/en/hotels/kapalua-maui. ✆ **800/262-8440** or 808/669-6200. 463 units. Double from $520; club-level double from $920; suite from $730; club-level suite from $1,390. Extra person $50 (club level $100). Daily $35 resort fee; wedding/honeymoon, golf, and other packages available. Valet parking $30; self-parking $22. **Amenities:** 4 restaurants; 4 bars; babysitting; basketball and bocce ball courts; bike rentals; children's program; club floor; concierge; cultural-history tours; 24-hr. oceanview fitness room; fitness classes; 2 championship golf courses (each w/its own pro shop) and golf academy; hiking trails; outdoor 3-tiered pool; room service; shuttle service; luxury spa w/steam rooms, saunas, and whirlpools; deluxe tennis complex; watersports equipment rentals; Wi-Fi (free).

South Maui

Two recommended booking agencies rent a host of condominiums and vacation homes throughout South Maui. **Condominium Rentals Hawai'i** (www.crhmaui.com; ✆ **800/367-5242**) offers affordable, quality properties primarily in Kīhei, with a few in Wailea and Lahaina. **Destination Resorts Hawai'i,** 34 Wailea Gateway Place, #A102, Wailea (www.drhmaui.com; ✆ **866/384-1366** or 808/891-6200), is the more upscale option, offering a wide selection of luxury rentals in Wailea and Mākena. One-bedroom units start at $159 and include many extras: a hospitality desk to assist with activity planning, $155 in dining and spa credits, a discount grocery card, free Wi-Fi and parking, and, in some cases, a free rental car! ***Tip:*** The **Polo Beach** and **Mākena Surf** units are a bit older, but nicer and closer to the beach.

Hotels & Restaurants in South Maui

HOTELS

Andaz Maui **26**
Aston Maui Hill **16**
Dreams Come True on Maui **21**
Eva Villa **22**
The Fairmont Kea Lani Maui **35**
Four Seasons Resort Maui at Wailea **32**
Grand Wailea **31**
Hotel Wailea **37**
Kealia Resort **1**
Mā'alaea Surf Resort **2**
Mana Kai Maui Resort **17**
Maui Coast Hotel **12**
Maui Kama'ole **15**
Maui Sunseeker LGBT Resort **4**
Nona Lani Cottages **3**
Pineapple Inn Maui **20**
Punahoa Beach Condominiums **11**
Tutu (Two) Mermaids on Maui B&B **18**
Wailea Beach Marriott Resort & Spa **29**
What a Wonderful World B&B **19**

RESTAURANTS

Cafe O' Lei Kihei **14**
Capische? **38**
Cow Pig Bun **8**
Fabiani's **7, 23**
Ferraro's Bar e Ristorante **33**
Gannon's **39**
Joy's Place **10**
Ka'ana Kitchen **27**
Kō **36**
Longhi's **25**
Mala Wailea **30**
Maui Tacos **13**
Monsoon India **5**
Morimoto Maui **28**
Pita Paradise **24**
Sansei Seafood Restaurant & Bar **9**
Spago **34**
Wow Wow Lemonade **6**

KĪHEI

Moderate

Aston Maui Hill ★ This stately condo complex with Mediterranean-style stucco buildings, red-tile roofs, and three-stories-tall arches marks the border between Kīhei and Wailea—an excellent spot to launch your vacation from. Managed by the respected Aston chain, Maui Hill combines the amenities of a hotel—24-hour front desk, concierge, pool, hot tub, tennis courts, putting green, and more—with the convenience of a condo. Units are spacious, with ample kitchens, air-conditioning (welcome in this climate), washer/dryers, queen-size sofa beds, and roomy lānais—most with ocean views. (For prime views, seek out units #35 and #36.) Two of South Maui's best beaches are immediately across the street; restaurants, shops, and golf courses are nearby. The management goes to lengths to make sure your stay is perfect—right up to the moment you print your boarding pass for free in the lobby. Check the website for significant discounts.

2881 S. Kīhei Rd. (across from Kama'ole Park III, btw. Keonekai St. and Kilohana Dr.), Kīhei. www.astonmauihill.com. ✆ **855/945-4044** or 808/879-6321. 140 units. $235–$425 1-bedroom; $254–$499 2-bedroom; $399–$695 3-bedroom. **Amenities:** Concierge; putting green; outdoor pool; tennis courts; Wi-Fi (free).

Eva Villa ★★ At the top of the Maui Meadows neighborhood above Wailea, Rick and Dale Pounds have done much to make their affordable bed-and-breakfast one of Maui's classiest. The hillside location offers respite from the shoreline's heat—and yet it's just a few minutes' drive to the beaches, shopping, and restaurants of both Kīhei and Wailea. The tastefully designed cottage has a decent-size kitchen and living room, smallish bedroom, washer/dryer, and a sweet outdoor shower. The poolside studio is a single, long room with a huge kitchen and barstool seating. The suite next door has two bedrooms and a kitchenette. You aren't forced to be social here; continental breakfast (fresh fruit, juice, muffins, coffee) comes stocked in your kitchen. And with just three units, the luxurious pool deck is rarely ever crowded.

815 Kumulani Dr., Kīhei. www.mauibnb.com. ✆ **808/874-6407.** 3 units. $155–$210 double. Extra person $20. Rates include continental breakfast. 5-night minimum. No credit cards. **Amenities:** Heated outdoor pool; Wi-Fi (free).

Mā'alaea Surf Resort ★ Despite its name, this little-known beachfront retreat isn't in Mā'alaea, nor is it a proper resort. Rather, it's a collection of charming condos spread out across 5 acres at the far north end of Kīhei. The four-unit townhouses with double-hipped roofs all have ocean views, big kitchens (with dishwashers), cable TV, and central air conditioning—a necessity in summer. Sugar Beach, the adjacent salt-and-pepper stretch of sand, extends 3-plus miles to Mā'alaea. Often windy, it's not the best for swimming, but it's unmatched for sunsets (and whale-watching in winter). This is a decent headquarters for adventurers who want to explore the entire island. The property is nonsmoking.

12 S. Kīhei Rd. (at N. Kīhei Rd. and Mokulele Hwy. 311), Kīhei. www.maalaeasurfresort.com. ✆ **800/423-7953** or 808/879-1267. 34 units. $220–$385 1-bedroom (sleeps up to 4); $315–$550 2-bedroom (sleeps up to 6). 5-night minimum. **Amenities:** Concierge; housekeeping 3 days a week; 2 outdoor pools; barbecues; 2 tennis courts; Wi-Fi (free).

Mana Kai Maui Resort ★ Even the views outside the elevator are astounding at this eight-story hotel/condo, which practically has its toes in the sand of beautiful Keawakapu Beach. Every unit in the 1973 building is oceanfront (though many lack views). Most, if not all, have been renovated with contemporary, island-inspired furnishings. The north-facing hotel rooms, which account for half of the units, have no lānais and are small enough to be filled by their king-size beds and kitchenettes. The one- and two-bedroom condos have full kitchens, sitting areas, and small lānais that overlook the glittering Pacific and several islands on the horizon. There's a surf shack on site, along with a gourmet grocery/deli, oceanfront restaurant, and yoga studio. ***Fun fact:*** The lobby's iconic turtle mural appears in the film *Just Go With It*.

2960 S. Kīhei Rd. (btw. Keonekai and Kilohana rds., at the Wailea end of Kīhei), Kīhei. www.manakaimaui.com. ✆ **800/525-2025** or 808/879-1561. 98 units. Rates for booking direct from hotel: $206–$263 hotel room double; $330–$562 1-bedroom (sleeps up to 4); $397–$635 2-bedroom (up to 6). Booking fee $35. Free parking. **Amenities:** Restaurant; bar; barbecues; concierge; coin-operated laundry; daily maid service; outdoor pool; watersports equipment rentals; Wi-Fi (free).

Maui Coast Hotel ★ The chief advantage of Kīhei's sole hotel is location, location, location. It's less than a block from sandy, sun-kissed Kama'ole Beach Park I and within walking distance of South Kīhei Road's bars, restaurants, and shopping. Another plus: nightly entertainment at the popular pool bar. Guest rooms are smallish, with sitting areas, huge flatscreen TVs, central air, and private garden lānais—no ocean views, though. Throughout the hotel, you'll find wonderful paintings by local artist Avi Kiriaty. Book the less-expensive "deluxe room" over the somewhat cramped "one-bedroom suite," unless you absolutely need the extra privacy. The **'ami 'ami** restaurant serves affordable local and organic dishes.

2259 S. Kīhei Rd. (across from Kama'ole Beach Park I), Kīhei. www.mauicoasthotel.com. ✆ **800/895-6284** or 808/874-6284. 265 units. $180 double; $190 suite; $200 1-bedroom (sleeps up to 4). Children 17 and under stay free in parent's room using existing bedding. Daily resort fee $25. Extra person charge $30. Packages available. **Amenities:** Restaurant; pool bar w/nightly entertainment; complimentary bicycles; concierge; rental car desk; fitness room; laundry facilities; outdoor pool (plus children's wading pool); room service; 2 lighted tennis courts; Wi-Fi (free).

Maui Kama'ole ★ Directly across from Kama'ole Beach Park III's sandy beach, enormous lawn, and playground, this comfortable condo complex is ideal for families. Convenience is key here in the center of K īhei's beach and shopping zone. Each roomy, privately owned, and furnished unit comes with an all-electric kitchen, central air, two bathrooms (even in the one-bedroom units), and two private lānais. The one-bedroom units—which can easily accommodate four—are a terrific deal, especially during low season. Ground-floor units open onto a grassy lawn. The attractively landscaped property runs perpendicular to the shoreline, and some buildings (indicated by room numbers that start with E, F, K, L, and M) are quite a trek from the beach. Families with small children should seek out units beginning with A, B, G, or H, which are nearest to the beach but off the road. C units are close to both beach and pool.

2777 S. Kīhei Rd. (btw. Keonekai and Kilohana Rds., at the Wailea end of Kīhei), Kīhei. www.mauikamaole.com. (Maui Condo and Home management site). ✆ **844/430-0606** or 808/874-5445. 316 units (not all in rental pool). $190–$339 1-bedroom (sleeps up to 4); $268–$525 2-bedroom (sleeps up to 6). $40 booking fee. **Amenities:** 2 outdoor pools; 2 tennis courts; Wi-Fi (free).

Maui Sunseeker LGBT Resort ★ Across the street from windswept Sugar Beach in North Kīhei, this cheery, adults-only boutique property welcomes all, but caters especially to gay and lesbian travelers. In 2012, Maui Sunseeker received a snazzy renovation after appearing on the reality TV show, *Hotel Impossible*. Now when you book a standard room, studio, or suite, expect a bright decor, comfy California king–size beds, air-conditioning (wall mount), and spacious ocean- or mountain-view lānais. Studios and suites have full kitchens or kitchenettes. The three penthouse suites are fabulous—especially #622, a gorgeous 3-bedroom retreat that was formerly the owner's private residence. Chat with fellow guests by the pool or in the rooftop hot tub, where you can take in the panoramic view of Mā'alaea Bay and the West Maui Mountains. Maui's best beaches are a short drive away; the owners supply beach chairs and coolers. This is a great spot to launch an adventurous vacation.

551 S. Kīhei Rd., Kīhei. www.mauisunseeker.com. ✆ **800/532-6284** or 808/879-1261. 26 units. $199 standard room; $224 studio; $269 junior suite; $289 full suite; $399–$499 penthouse suite. Extra person $45. No children allowed. **Amenities:** Concierge; 2 Jacuzzis (rooftop hot tub is clothing-optional); pool; free parking; no resort fee; Wi-Fi (free).

Inexpensive

Dreams Come True on Maui ★ After several years of vacationing on Maui, Tom Croly and Denise McKinnon moved here to open this bed-and-breakfast—a dream come true for both them and their guests. They offer a stand-alone cottage and two private suites in their house, which is centrally located in the Maui Meadows neighborhood, just a 5- to 10-minute drive from the shopping, restaurants, golf courses, and white-sand beaches of Kīhei and Wailea. Each of the colorfully decorated suites has a private entrance and lānai, kitchenette, 42-inch TV, air-conditioning, and use of laundry facilities. Continental breakfasts are offered room-service style: Choose from the menu of freshly baked pastries, tropical fruits (mangoes right off of the tree), yogurts, and pop tarts. Hang your order on your door, and in the morning, it'll be delivered at your chosen time. Rooms are a bit tight, but you're free to use the ocean-view deck, main living room, and outdoor cooking area. The cozy one-bedroom cottage has ocean views from several rooms, vaulted ceilings in the living room, wraparound decks, marble in the kitchen and bathroom, a private washer/dryer, and a computer with high-speed Internet. Tom is always on duty as a personal concierge, doling out beach equipment and suggestions for where to snorkel, shop, or eat dinner.

3259 Akala Dr., Kīhei. www.dreamscometrueonmaui.com. ✆ **877/782-9628** or 808/879-7099. 3 units. $99–$139 double (4-night minimum); $139–$199 cottage double (6-night minimum; extra person $15). Room rates include continental breakfast for the B&B guest rooms. **Amenities:** Concierge; Wi-Fi (free).

Kealia Resort ★ This oceanfront property at the northernmost end of Kīhei isn't a resort, but it *is* worth a second look. From the outside, the older building might seem shabby, but on the inside the privately owned units shine—and rates are excellent. Avoid the lower-priced studios facing noisy Kīhei Road. Instead, go for one of the oceanfront units (such as no. 203, which hangs over the pool). All have full kitchens, washer/dryers, and private lānais with truly spectacular views of 3-plus-mile-long Sugar Beach. Twice a week the management hosts social events for guests to mingle: Wednesday *pūpū* parties and Friday morning coffee-and-doughnut get-togethers. ***Tip:*** Ask for some leeway with the 10am checkout time.

191 N. Kīhei Rd. (north of Hwy. 31 at the Mā'alaea end of Kīhei), Kīhei. www.kealiaresort.com. ✆ **800/265-0686.** 51 units. $125–$140 studio double; $160–$195 1-bedroom double; $225–$260 2-bedroom (sleeps up to 4). Children 12 and under stay free in parent's room. Extra person $10. Cleaning fee $75–$125. Booking fee $25. 4- to 10-night minimum. **Amenities:** Outdoor pool; Wi-Fi (free).

Nona Lani Cottages ★ Family-owned since the 1970s, this oceanside retreat is one of North Kīhei's sweetest deals. Eight tiny, vintage cottages are tucked among the coconut palms and plumeria trees, a stone's throw from Sugar Beach. Inside is everything you'll need: a compact kitchen, a separate bedroom with a queen-size bed, air-conditioning, and a cozy lānai—not to mention new travertine tile floors and cabinetry. The three suites in the main house are stuffy; stick to the cottages. The charming grounds include a barbecue area and outdoor *hale* for weddings or parties—but no pool or spa. Your hosts, the Kong family, don't offer daily maid service, but they do make fresh flower lei—buy one and fill your entire cottage with fragrance.

455 S. Kīhei Rd. (just south of Hwy. 31), Kīhei. www.nonalanicottages.com. ✆ **800/733-2688** or 808/879-2497. 11 units. $170–$220 double. Extra person $25. 2- to 5-night minimum depending on season. Free parking. **Amenities:** Onsite wedding coordinator; Wi-Fi (free).

Pineapple Inn Maui ★★ Enjoy a resort vacation at a fraction of the price at this oasis in residential Maui Meadows, luxuriously landscaped with tall coconut palms, dinner-plated-size pink hibiscus, red gingers, a lily pond, and—best of all—a saltwater pool that's lit at night. The four guest rooms in the two-story "inn" are equally immaculate: Each has upscale furnishings, a private lānai with a serene ocean view, and a kitchenette that your hosts, Mark and Steve, stock with pastries, bagels, oatmeal, juice, and coffee upon arrival. The bright and airy cottage (two bedrooms, one bath) is one of the island's best deals. Landscaped for maximum privacy, it has a full kitchen (including a dishwasher), dark wood floors, central air, beautiful artwork, and a private barbecue area. Guests are invited to stargaze from the communal hot tub and make use of the outdoor kitchen, fully equipped with barbecue utensils. Before you head out on an adventure (shopping, beaches, restaurants, and golf are mere minutes away), you can load up your car with snorkeling equipment, beach chairs, umbrellas, boogie boards, and a cooler.

3170 Akala Dr., Kīhei. www.pineappleinnmaui.com. ✆ **877/212-MAUI** (6284) or 808/298-4403. 5 units. $159–$189 double; $215–$255 cottage for 4. 3-night minimum for rooms, 6-night minimum for cottage. Rates include breakfast. No credit cards. **Amenities:** Saltwater pool; watersports equipment; Wi-Fi (free).

Punahoa Beach Condominiums ★ This oceanfront condo complex sits on a large grassy lawn between the Charley Young surf break and Kama'ole I Beach—an ideal location for active, sun-seeking travelers. Each unit in the small four-story building boasts a lānai with a marvelous view of the Pacific and islands on the horizon. All are individually owned and decorated, so the aesthetic varies widely. (The website features photos of each.) Studios feature queen-size Murphy beds, full bathrooms, and compact, full-service kitchens. The three one-bedroom penthouses—the only units with air conditioning—are the sweetest option. Kīhei's shopping and restaurants are all within walking distance.

2142 Ili'ili Rd. (off S. Kīhei Rd., 300 ft. from Kama'ole Beach I), Kīhei. www.punahoabeach.com. ✆ **800/564-4380** or 808/879-2720. 15 units. studio double from $132; 1-bedroom double from $164; 2-bedroom double from $234; 1-bedroom penthouse from $229. $125–$150 cleaning fee. Extra person $15. 5-night minimum ($100 fee added for 3- or 4-night stays when available). **Amenities:** Wi-Fi (free).

Tutu Mermaids on Maui B&B (aka the Two Mermaids) ★ Your mermaid hosts, Juddee and Miranda, are both avid scuba divers, and the colorful decor throughout their charming B&B reflects their love of the sea. In the large, one-bedroom Ocean Ohana, the marine theme continues from the turquoise walls and dark stranded bamboo floors all the way to the kitchenette's fish-shaped cabinet knobs. This breezy, clean unit has air-conditioning, its own hot tub, and an adjoining "Surf Room" with bunk beds that's available for families. The equally stylish two-bedroom Poolside Suite opens up to the refreshing rock-lined pool. Every morning, Juddee places a deluxe continental breakfast (Greek yogurt, tropical fruits, and homemade banana bread) at your doorstep. Other amenities include Direct TV, barbecues, beach gear, and a tuned guitar in each unit for strumming island serenades. The house sits in a quiet residential cul-de-sac just a 3-minute drive (or 20-min. walk) from Kama'ole III Beach. Juddee is a licensed minister and can perform weddings. She'll also help you book massages or childcare.

2840 Umalu Place, Kīhei. www.twomermaids.com. ✆ **808/874-8687.** 2 units. $145–$230 studio double. Rates include continental breakfast. 3-night minimum. Credit cards through PayPal only. **Amenities:** Babysitting; barbecue; beach equipment; pool; Wi-Fi (free).

What a Wonderful World B&B ★ Repeat guests here adore hostess Eva Tantillo, whose years of experience in the travel industry shows in thoughtful touches around her lovely property. Every unit is lovingly furnished with hardwood floors, Hawaiian quilts, and luxurious slate showers. The Guava Suite is smallest and a little dark for my taste. The Papaya Suite, with its spacious living room and bathroom and separate bedroom, is just right. Eva serves continental breakfast on the lānai, which boasts views of the ocean, West Maui Mountains, and Haleakalā. You're also welcome to use the full kitchen or barbecue. For movie nights, the common area has a gigantic flatscreen TV and fancy popcorn maker. This elegant B&B is centrally located in a residential Kīhei neighborhood—next door to Tutu Mermaids, above—about a half-mile from Kama'ole III Beach Park and 5 minutes from Wailea's golf courses, shopping, and restaurants.

2828 Umalu Place (off Keonakai St., near Hwy. 31), Kīhei. www.amauibedandbreakfast.com. ✆ **808/879-9103.** 4 units. $90–$195 double. Children 11 and under stay free in parent's room. Rates include breakfast. No cleaning fee. **Amenities:** Beach equipment; barbecue; laundry facilities; free international calls; Wi-Fi (free).

WAILEA

Golfers should note that all Wailea resorts enjoy special privileges at the Wailea Golf Club's three 18-hole championship courses: Blue, Gold, and Emerald.

Note: You'll find the following hotels on the "Hotels & Restaurants in South Maui" map (p. 367).

Expensive

Andaz Maui at Wailea ★★★ The newest resort in Wailea opened to rave reviews—small wonder, considering its prime beachfront locale, chic decor, apothecary-style spa, and two phenomenal restaurants, including one by superstar chef Masaharu Morimoto. Foodies should look no further: Not only is the **Morimoto Maui** sushi bar a must, but the resort's other restaurant, **Ka'ana Kitchen,** might be *even better.* Before you eat, though, you'll want to freshen up in your room. Accommodations here aren't the island's largest, but they ramp up the style quotient a notch with crisp white linens, warm wood furniture, and midcentury accents. Wrap yourself in a plush robe and nosh on the complimentary minibar snacks from the sanctuary of your private lānai. Wander past the tiered infinity pools (which look best at night, when lit in a shifting palette of colors). Then hit gorgeous **Mokapu Beach** out front to snorkel, kayak, or paddle outrigger canoe. This resort is a dynamic blend of modern and ancient values. Visit with the resident artist in the lobby gallery, or learn to braid ti leaf lei and make coconut fiber cordage. Whatever you do, don't miss the **'Āwili Spa,** where you can mix your own massage oil and body scrubs. Yoga and fitness classes are complimentary. If you've got the cash, consider renting one of the resort's two-, three-, or four-bedroom villas—you'll have an entire wall that opens to the Pacific, a private plunge pool, and a Viking range to call your own.

3550 Wailea Alanui Dr., Wailea. www.maui.andaz.hyatt.com. © **808/573-1234.** 198 units. $409–$604 double; $553–$1,849 1-bedroom suite; call for villa prices. Valet parking $30. Complimentary minibar. **Amenities:** 3 restaurants, plus 24-hr. market; 3 bars; concierge; 24-hr. fitness center; use of Wailea Golf Club's 3 18-hole championship golf courses; 4 cascading infinity pools; 24-hr. room service; shuttle service; luxury spa w/steam rooms, lounge, and spa pool; watersports equipment rentals; Wi-Fi (free).

The Fairmont Kea Lani Maui ★★★ At first blush, this blinding-white complex of Arabian turrets and arches may look a tad out of place—but once you enter the orchid-filled lobby and see the big blue Pacific outside, there's no doubt you're in Hawai'i. For the price of a regular room at the neighboring luxury resorts, you get an entire suite here. Each unit in the all-suites hotel has a kitchenette with granite countertop, living room with sofa bed (great for kids), spacious bedroom, marble bathroom fit for royalty (head immediately for the deep soaking tub), and large lānai with views of the pools, lawns, and Pacific Ocean. The two- and three-bedroom beachfront villas are perfect for families or couples traveling together. Each two-story unit has a gourmet kitchen, washer/dryer, and private plunge pool just steps from the white sand. **Polo Beach** is public, but feels private and secluded. Huge murals and artifacts decorate the resort's manicured property, which is home to several good restaurants, an excellent bakery and deli, and the **Willow Stream Spa.** Escape into this heavenly retreat to experience the rain showers, steam rooms, and warm lava-stone foot beds. Youngsters will enjoy building volcanoes in the 1,500-square-foot kids' club, while the entire family can get into rhythm paddling a Hawaiian outrigger canoe.

4100 Wailea Alanui Dr., Wailea. www.fairmont.com/kealani. © **866/540-4456** or 808/875-4100. 450 units. $459–$1,049 suite (sleeps up to 4); from $1,775 villa. $35 resort fee. Valet parking $27; free self-parking. **Amenities:** 4 restaurants, plus gourmet bakery and deli; 3 bars; babysitting; children's program; year-round concierge; 24-hr. fitness center; use of Wailea Golf Club's 3 18-hole championship golf courses; 2 large pools; adults-only pool; 140-ft. water slide and swim-up bar, 24-hr. room service; luxury spa and salon; use of Wailea Tennis Center's 11 courts for special rates and pro shop; watersports equipment rentals and 1-hr. complimentary use of snorkel equipment; Wi-Fi (free).

Four Seasons Resort Maui at Wailea ★★★ Words fail to describe how luxurious you'll feel rubbing elbows with celebrities in this über-elegant yet relaxed atmosphere. Perched above Wailea Beach's golden sand, the Four Seasons Resort Maui inhabits its own world, where pool-side attendants anticipate your needs: cucumber slices for your eyes? Mango smoothie sampler? Or perhaps your sunglasses need polishing? The adults-only infinity pool with underwater music and a swim-up bar is what all pools aspire to. The roughly 600-sq.-ft. guest rooms feature dream-inducing beds, deep marble bathtubs, walk-in showers big enough for two, and furnished lānais, most with superlative ocean views. If you get stuck with a North Tower room over the parking lot, ask politely to be moved. The sublime spa offers an incredible array of body treatments ranging from traditional Hawaiian to craniosacral and Ayurvedic massage. (As nice as the spa facility is, treatments in the oceanside thatched *hale* are even more idyllic.) The resort's restaurants, **Spago, Ferraro's,** and **DUO,** are great; room service here is a must. Finally, this might be the island's most kid-friendly resort: Perks include milk and cookies on arrival, toddler-proofing for your room (everything from furniture bumpers to toilet-seat locks), *keiki* menus in all restaurants, a high-tech game room, and the unmatched Kids for all Seasons program from 9am to 5pm—complimentary, of course. No resort fee. ***Tip:*** Wedding parties should book #798 or #301—stunning suites with room for entertaining.
3900 Wailea Alanui Dr., Wailea. www.fourseasons.com/maui. ✆ **800/311-0630** or 808/874-8000. 380 units. $599–$1,059 double; $1,249–$1,329 Club Floor double; from $1,179 suite. Children 17 and under stay free in parent's room. Packages available. Valet parking $29. **Amenities:** 3 restaurants, 3 bars (w/nightly entertainment); babysitting; free use of bicycles; complimentary children's program; concierge; concierge-level rooms; putting green; use of Wailea Golf Club's 3 18-hole championship golf courses; health club featuring outdoor cardiovascular equipment (w/individual TV/VCRs); 3 outdoor pools; room service; luxury spa and salon; 2 on-site tennis courts (lit for night play); use of Wailea Tennis Center's 11 courts (3 lit for night play); watersports equipment rentals and 1-hr. free use of snorkel equipment; Wi-Fi (free; $20 for premium).

Grand Wailea ★★★ Built by a Japanese multimillionaire at the pinnacle of Hawai'i's fling with fantasy megaresorts, the Grand Wailea is wildly popular with families and corporate groups. It's the grand prize in Hawai'i vacation contests and the dream of many honeymooners. No expense was spared during construction: Some $30 million worth of original artwork decorates the grounds, much of it created expressly for the hotel by Hawai'i artists and sculptors. More than 10,000 tropical plants beautify the lobby alone, and rocks hewn from the base of Mount Fuji adorn the Japanese garden. A Hawaiian-themed restaurant floats atop a man-made lagoon, and light filters majestically through the stained-glass walls of the wedding chapel. Guest rooms, too, come with lavish accouterments, like oversize bathrooms and plush bedding. But for kids, all that matters is the resort's unrivaled pool: an aquatic playground with nine separate swimming pools connected by slides, waterfalls, caves, rapids, a Tarzan swing, a swim-up bar, a baby beach, and a water elevator that shuttles swimmers back to the top. If this doesn't sate them, an actual beach made of real golden sand awaits just past the resort hammocks. The Grand is also home to Hawai'i's largest and most resplendent spa: a 50,000-square-foot marble paradise with mineral soaking tubs, thundering waterfall showers, Japanese furo baths, Swiss jet showers, and many other luxurious features. Dining options include **Humuhumunukunukuapua'a,** the aforementioned floating restaurant where you can fish for your lobster straight from the lagoon. Minimalists may scoff, but the Grand Wailea's extravagance is worth experiencing even if you don't stay here.

3850 Wailea Alanui Dr., Wailea. www.grandwailea.com. ✆ **800/888-6100** or 808/875-1234. 780 units. $399–$1,130 double; from $1,049 suite; from $599 Napua Club Room (in Napua Tower); from $1,036 Hoolei Villas. Membership rates available. Extra person $50 ($100 in Napua Tower). Daily resort fee $30. Valet parking (only) $30. **Amenities:** 6 restaurants; 4 bars; art and garden tours; babysitting; children's program; concierge; concierge-level rooms; use of Wailea Golf Club's 3 18-hole championship golf courses; fitness center; fitness classes; 5 whirlpools (including one atop a man-made volcano); adults-only outdoor pool; 2,000-ft.-long Activity Pool, featuring a swim/ride through grottoes; room service; scuba-diving clinics; shuttle service to Wailea area; Hawai'i's largest luxury spa and salon; racquetball court; use of Wailea Tennis Center's 11 courts and pro shop; watersports equipment rentals; Wi-Fi (free).

Hotel Wailea ★★★ This stylish boutique hotel is one of a kind in Wailea. Compared with the flashier resorts at the coastline, it's small, secluded, and serene—a perfect oasis for honeymooners. The pool and cabanas are swank, with free cocktails by the fire pit from 5 to 6pm and mixology classes every Sunday morning. The verdant grounds, fruit orchard, and koi ponds have been transformed into a meditative garden. Large suites are outfitted with modern luxuries: wide-planked wood floors, Hawaiian *kapa*-inspired prints on plush king-size platform beds, super-deep soaking tubs, and daybeds on the lānai. Tidy kitchenettes feature Nespresso machines, two-burner Wolf stoves and Sub-Zero pull-out-drawer refrigerators. Room service is provided by **Capische?,** the excellent on-site restaurant. Imagine noshing on fresh burrata and toast and house-cured charcuterie while soaking in views of neighbor islands on the horizon. Hotel staff will load up a complimentary tote bag with towels and water and chauffeur you throughout Wailea in the resort's Mercedes SUV. It's a 3-minute shuttle ride to the beach, and the hotel's kiosk at Wailea Beach will supply you with umbrellas and chairs. Take advantage of the free outrigger canoe trip offered on Wednesdays. This isn't a place that nickel-and-dimes guests, and employees come to know you on a first-name basis. **Brides- and grooms-to-be, take note:** The lawn and gazebo at the hotel's entrance is a fairy-tale venue for weddings and receptions.

555 Kaukahi St., Wailea. www.hotelwailea.com. © **866/970-4167** or 808/874-0500. 72 units. $499–$799 suite. 2-person max occupancy. Daily $30 resort fee. Packages available. **Amenities:** Restaurant; 2 bars; concierge; fitness center; outdoor pool; room service; complimentary shuttle service throughout Wailea; free mixology classes and canoe trips; signing privileges at nearby Grand Wailea; spa; Wi-Fi (free).

Wailea Beach Marriott Resort & Spa ★★ Airy and comfortable, with touches of Hawaiian art throughout, this hotel fits into its sublime environment without overwhelming it. Eight buildings, all low-rise except for an eight-story tower, unfold along 22 luxurious acres of lawns and gardens punctuated by coconut palms and an exquisite infinity pool—you'll want to spend your entire vacation beneath the cabanas here. Positioned on a grassy slope between Wailea and Ulua beaches, the resort has plenty of sandy expanse to explore. Rooms have tile or wood floors, rattan furnishings, and lānais with views of the picturesque coastline. The small **Mandara Spa** offers an array of treatments, from massages to body wraps and rejuvenating facials in a very Zen atmosphere. Two things distinguish this property. First, it's probably the most affordable resort on the Wailea coast. Second, guests benefit from two fantastic restaurants, including **Mala** and **Migrant.** (Rumor has it that **Roy's** will replace Migrant this year.)

3700 Wailea Alanui Dr., Wailea. www.waileamarriott.com. © **808/879-1922.** 554 units. $199–$825 double; suite from $539; 2-bedroom from $679. Packages available. Extra person $40. Daily $30 resort fee. Valet parking $35, self-parking $25. **Amenities:** 3 restaurants; 2 bars; babysitting; concierge; use of Wailea Golf Club's 3 18-hole championship golf courses; fitness center; outdoor pools (including adults-only and 1 for kids only); room service; full-service spa w/steam rooms and whirlpools; use of Wailea Tennis Center's 11 courts and pro shop; watersports equipment rentals; Wi-Fi (free in lobby, $15–$19 in room).

Upcountry Maui

MAKAWAO

Here you'll be (relatively) close to Haleakalā National Park; Makawao is approximately 90 minutes from the entrance to the park at the 7,000-foot level (from there it's another 3,000 ft. and 45 min. to get to the top). Temperatures are 5° to 10° cooler than at the coast, and misty rain is common.

Aloha Cottage ★★ If getting away from it all is your goal, this exotic retreat in the eucalyptus forest above Makawao might be your place. On 5 luxuriously landscaped acres sits the octagonal Aloha Cottage and Thai Tree House, both reminiscent of something you'd see in Southeast Asia. The 590-square-foot cottage's interior is lavishly furnished with vaulted ceilings, teak floors, Oriental rugs, and intricate Balinese carvings. (Whenever you glance at your reflection in the magnificent bathroom mirror, you'll feel like royalty.) Both the Cottage and Tree House feature granite counters, a gas stove, and teak cabinetry that makes cooking a pleasure. Olinda Road is a winding, narrow track that ascends through the trees above Makawao—coming and going from here is an adventure unto itself. After a day of exploring Maui, it's a sweet relief to enjoy a home-cooked dinner on the lānai, soak in the outdoor tub built for two, and retire to the king-size cherrywood bed where you can stare through the skylight at the stars.

1879 Olinda Rd., Makawao. www.alohacottage.com. ✆ **888/328-3330** or 808/573-8555. 2 units. Cottage/treehouse from $239. $100 cleaning fee. Not suitable for children under 10. **Amenities:** Outdoor tub; barbecue; laundry facilities; Wi-Fi (free).

Banyan Bed & Breakfast Retreat ★ Shaded by huge monkeypod trees, this upcountry estate on meandering Baldwin Avenue has a quaint old-Hawai'i ambience. Accommodations include three suites within a beautifully restored 1927 plantation manager's house and four individual cottages. Each suite has a queen-size and a twin bed (perfect for families traveling with youngsters), a marble shower, a private entrance, a modest kitchenette, rich hardwood floors, and lovely antique furniture. The cottages feature similar amenities; some (such as Gardenia) have full kitchens and bathtubs. Each morning, Marty, the retreat's proprietor, delivers a continental breakfast to your door. Fruit trees and flowers decorate the property; hammocks and swings hang from the branches of the massive shade trees. Guests have the use of a 50-foot-long saltwater swimming pool, Jacuzzi, and 700-square-foot yoga and meditation studio equipped with yoga props and a sophisticated audio/video system. This fully handicapped-accessible retreat is ideal for groups, and the house, lavishly decorated with vintage Hawaiian furniture, can be rented as a whole. Makawao's restaurants and shops are just minutes away, and Pā'ia's beaches are less than a 15-minute drive from here.

3265 Baldwin Ave. (less than a mile below Makawao), Makawao. www.banyantreehouse.com. ✆ **808/572-9021.** 7 units. $185–$220 double room in house; $175–$220 cottage for 2. Entire estate $1300 (sleeps 14). Extra person $30, children 12 and under $15. Cleaning fee $30–$40. Rates include breakfast. **Amenities:** Babysitting; whirlpool; outdoor pool; Wi-Fi (free).

Hale Ho'okipa Inn Makawao ★★ Cherie Attix restored this historic 1924 plantation-style home to its original charm, filling it with Hawaiian artwork, antique furniture (a giant oak armoire, wrought-iron bed frame, and vintage shutters repurposed as a headboard), and a generous dose of love. It's a 5-minute walk from the shops and restaurants of Makawao, 15 minutes from beaches, and an hour's drive from the top of Haleakalā. The pretty guest rooms have separate outside entrances and private bathrooms—two with claw-foot tubs. The Kona Wing is a two-bedroom suite with use of the kitchen. In addition to a daily continental breakfast, Cherie offers guests fresh eggs from her hens. Unlike

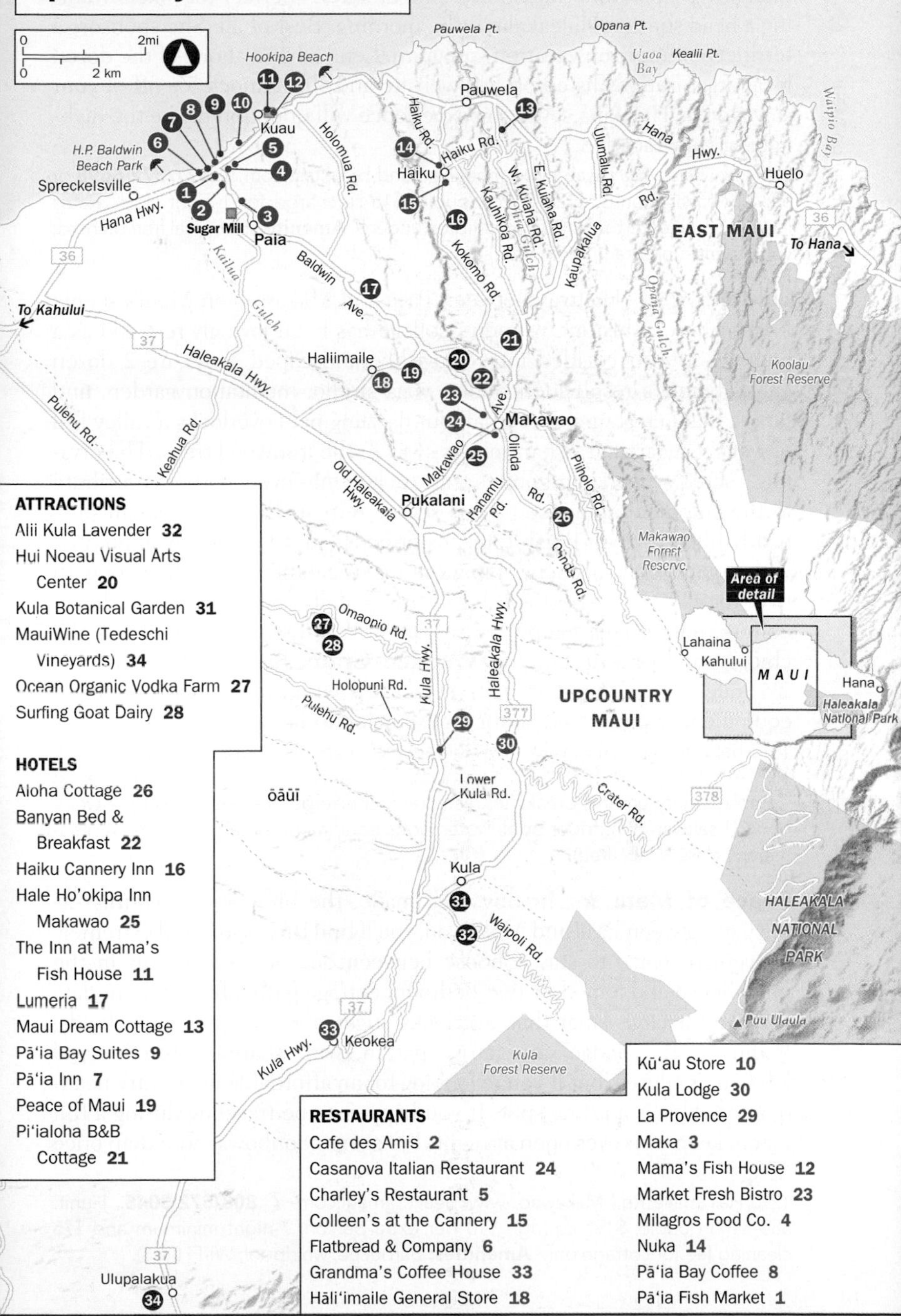

Upcountry & East Maui
PACIFIC OCEAN
0 2mi
0 2 km
Pauwela Pt.
Opana Pt.
Uaoa Bay
Kealii Pt.
Hookipa Beach
Pauwela
Kuau
H.P. Baldwin Beach Park
Spreckelsville
Hana Hwy.
Sugar Mill
Paia
Holomua Rd.
Haiku Rd.
Haiku
Ulumalu Rd.
Hana Hwy.
Huelo
Waipio Bay
E. Kuiaha Rd.
W. Kuiaha Rd.
Kauhikoa Rd.
Kokomo Rd.
Kaupakalua Rd.
EAST MAUI
To Hana
To Kahului
Kailua Gulch
Baldwin Ave.
Haleakala Hwy.
Haliimaile
Pulehu Rd.
Keahua Rd.
Makawao
Olinda Rd.
Piiholo Rd.
Koolau Forest Reserve
Old Haleakala Hwy.
Pukalani
Hanamu Rd.
Makawao Forest Reserve
Area of detail
Omaopio Rd.
Holopuni Rd.
Kula Hwy.
Haleakala Hwy.
Lahaina
Kahului
MAUI
Hana
Haleakala National Park
UPCOUNTRY MAUI
Lower Kula Rd.
Crater Rd.
Kula
Waipoli Rd.
HALEAKALA NATIONAL PARK
Puu Ulaula
Keokea
Kula Forest Reserve
Ulupalakua
ATTRACTIONS
Alii Kula Lavender 32
Hui Noeau Visual Arts Center 20
Kula Botanical Garden 31
MauiWine (Tedeschi Vineyards) 34
Ocean Organic Vodka Farm 27
Surfing Goat Dairy 28
HOTELS
Aloha Cottage 26
Banyan Bed & Breakfast 22
Haiku Cannery Inn 16
Hale Ho'okipa Inn Makawao 25
The Inn at Mama's Fish House 11
Lumeria 17
Maui Dream Cottage 13
Pā'ia Bay Suites 9
Pā'ia Inn 7
Peace of Maui 19
Pi'ialoha B&B Cottage 21
RESTAURANTS
Cafe des Amis 2
Casanova Italian Restaurant 24
Charley's Restaurant 5
Colleen's at the Cannery 15
Flatbread & Company 6
Grandma's Coffee House 33
Hāli'imaile General Store 18
Kū'au Store 10
Kula Lodge 30
La Provence 29
Maka 3
Mama's Fish House 12
Market Fresh Bistro 23
Milagros Food Co. 4
Nuka 14
Pā'ia Bay Coffee 8
Pā'ia Fish Market 1

many B&B operators, she allows 1-night stays—perfect for hikers wanting a head start on Haleakalā in the morning. Best of all: She sponsors a terrific "volunteer on vacation" program. Lend a hand at one of the dozen local organizations listed on her website and she'll knock 5% off of your stay at Hale Ho'okipa. (And the experience will undoubtedly be the highlight of your vacation.)

32 Pakani Place, Makawao. www.maui-bed-and-breakfast.com. ✆ **877/572-6698** or 808/572-6698. 4 units. $125–$198 double. $15 surcharge for 1-night stays. Rates include continental breakfast. No children under 9. **Amenities:** Tropical fruit orchard; voluntourism program; Wi-Fi (free).

Lumeria ★★ Halfway between Pā'ia and Makawao on Maui's scenic North Shore, a historic women's college has been lovingly restored as a boutique resort. Nestled into 6 lavishly landscaped acres are 2 dozen guest rooms, a resplendent lobby, yoga studio, meditation garden, and farm-to-table restaurant. A small but dazzling pool overlooks a valley full of waving sugarcane as hammocks sway in the ironwood trees. The crystals, sacred artwork, and objets d'art tucked into every corner contribute to the charmed ambience of this serene retreat. Rooms are smallish—nearly filled by their plush four-poster beds—but luxuriously appointed with organic Italian linens, Japanese tansu cabinets, and showers with river-rock floors. A stay includes access to daily yoga, meditation, horticulture, and aromatherapy classes, as well as breakfast for two at the chic, semi-private restaurant, **Wooden Crate.** Baldwin Beach is only 2½ miles away; the staff will set you up with stand-up paddleboard equipment or pack a picnic for an excursion to Hāna.

1813 Baldwin Ave., Makawao. www.lumeriamaui.com. ✆ **808/579-8877.** 25 units. $329–$459 king bed; $369–$419 two beds; $899 suite. Resort fee $25. **Amenities:** Complimentary organic breakfast; restaurant; concierge; free self-parking; 2 whirlpools (1 saltwater); outdoor pool; watersports equipment rentals; yoga and aromatherapy class; Wi-Fi (free).

Peace of Maui ★ In tiny Hāli'imaile, the blink-and-you'll-miss-it-town in between Pā'ia and Makawao, you'll find this casual and extremely convenient place to stay. Choose between one of seven rooms in the main house and a modest two-bedroom cottage with a full kitchen, daybed, and a large lānai that overlooks sugarcane and pineapple fields. Rooms in the "lodge" are fairly spartan, with shared bathroom and kitchen privileges, but if you're looking for an affordable upcountry headquarters, this is a prime spot. If you happen to be traveling during a full moon, keep your eyes open at night: I've seen moonbows more than once here.

1290 Hāli'imaile Rd., Makawao. www.peaceofmaui.com. ✆ **808/572-5045.** 1 unit. $85–$105 double; $195 cottage $10 per extra person; 7-night minimum and $75 cleaning fee for cottage only. **Amenities:** Barbecue; whirlpool; Wi-Fi (free).

East Maui: On the Road to Hāna

Note: You'll find the accommodations in this section on the "Upcountry & East Maui" map (p. 379).

PĀ'IA-KŪ'AU

Expensive

Pā'ia Inn ★★ Embedded in colorful Pā'ia town, this vibrant boutique inn offers a stylish introduction to Maui's North Shore. The inn is comprised of several vintage buildings that get progressively closer to the turquoise waters of Pā'ia Bay. The nine rooms in the main building hang right over Hāna Highway's restaurants, surf shops, and cafes. After a day of mingling with big-wave surfers, yoga teachers, and other north-shore dwellers, slip up to your soundproofed room and sink into the 500-thread-count sheets. The owner's impeccable style seeps into every corner of the inn, from the organic Malie bath products in the travertine-tiled showers to the antique Balinese drawers repurposed as sink cabinets. The one- and two-bedroom suites in the next buildings are spacious, secluded retreats where you'll feel immediately at home. My favorite, #10, has a private outdoor shower and four-poster daybed. But it can't rival the three-bedroom beach house nestled up against the golden, sandy beach. Idyllic in every way, this miniature mansion is outfitted with a Viking stove, Jacuzzi, gorgeous artwork, and huge outdoor living room. It's exclusive enough to attract celebrities, who've made it their Maui headquarters.

93 Hāna Hwy., Pā'ia. www.paiainn.com. ✆ **800/721-4000** or 808/579-6000. 17 units. $199–$259 double; $259–$450 1-bedroom suite; $499 2-bedroom suite; $999 3-bedroom beach house. **Amenities:** Beach access; concierge; laundry services; free parking; complimentary watersports equipment; Wi-Fi (free).

Moderate

Mama's Fish House Restaurant & Inn ★★ The Gaudí-esque architect responsible for Mama's Fish House also works his magic on a handful of private suites and cottages next door. In a coconut grove on a secluded north-shore beach, the Inn at Mama's features gracious accommodations with plenty of extras: daily maid service; large private lānais with barbecues; imaginative Hawaiian artwork; fresh flowers tucked into large, fluffy bath towels; terrific toiletries; free laundry; an easy stroll to what many consider to be the finest restaurant on Maui. Each unit is unique; the luxury junior suites are especially classy, with deep soaking tubs and travertine showers. One- and two-bedroom cottages sit amid the tropical garden's red ginger, while a few two-bedroom units face the ocean. Restaurant guests can stroll about the property until 10pm, but privacy is assured in your cottage's large enclosed lānai. In the morning, you'll be greeted with a tray of fresh fruit and banana bread. The inn sits on a small, sandy beach known simply as Mama's. It's better for exploring tide pools than for swimming—though Baldwin Beach is a short drive away and the thrills of Ho'okipa are right next door. Keep in mind that this is the windward side of the island—it's often windy and rainy. You'll be perfectly situated here for a trip to Hāna.

799 Poho Place (off the Hāna Hwy. in Kū'au), Pā'ia. www.mamasfishhouse.com. ✆ **800/860-HULA** or 808/579-9764. 12 units. $250 garden studio double; $300 1-bedroom (sleeps up to 4); $425 junior suites double; $350–$850 2-bedroom cottage (up to 6). **Amenities:** Beach; barbecue; free laundry; Wi-Fi (free).

Pā'ia Bay Suites ★ A 5-minute walk from Pā'ia town, this two-story beach cottage is tucked away down a tiny side street populated by surfers and roosters. You'll feel like a local within moments of moving in—especially after stocking your kitchen with fresh fish, local coffee, and other treats from nearby Mana Foods. The fenced lot offers plenty of privacy—not to mention ripe mangoes off the tree in season. The upstairs and downstairs units are rented individually, but only to a single party so you never have to share the property. The palm-fringed ocean views, hardwood floors, tasteful decor, and spa-like bathroom add to the charm of this special spot, owned by the same folks who run Ha'ikū Cannery Inn. If you're planning a "Road to Hāna" adventure, this is an excellent launching spot.

45 Loio Pl., Pā'ia. www.paiabaysuites.com (also www.vrbo.com/494898). ✆ **800/721-4000** or 808/281-3508. 2 units. $225 1-bedroom cottage. Cleaning fee: $75. **Amenities:** Close to beaches, restaurants, and shopping; barbecue; laundry facilities; outdoor shower; Wi-Fi (free).

HA'IKŪ

Inexpensive

Ha'ikū Cannery Inn ★★ This is one of my favorite B&Bs, located in the most convenient (and sunny) section of Ha'ikū's rainforest. Built in 1921 for the manager of the bygone pineapple cannery, this charming estate has been converted into a pastoral inn. Tropical fruit trees abound on the 3-acre property, alongside sweet-smelling plumeria and gingers. Guests can help themselves to papayas, avocados, bananas, and citruses. In the main house are two large, attractive guest rooms and a modest suite with a small kitchenette. The two-bedroom cottage across the lawn has a nicely stocked kitchen and a two-car garage—perfect for families or travelers needing to stow windsurfing or scuba equipment. Much of the inn's handcrafted furniture and flooring was made from eucalyptus and mango trees milled on the property. Local artists contributed the paintings decorating nearly every wall. Rates include a breakfast of fresh fruits and pastries from the local bakery, prepared by the resident innkeeper, Benni Denbeau. The long-time Maui resident has marvelous suggestions for where to go and what to do. She raised her family here;

the entire property is child-friendly. The inn is just uphill from Ha'ikū's great restaurants and grocery store.

1061 Kokomo Rd., Ha'ikū. www.haikucanneryinn.com. © **808/283-1274.** 4 units. $115–$135 double; $145 suite; $200 cottage. $120 cleaning fee for cottage only. **Amenities:** Day spa; Wi-Fi (free).

Maui Dream Cottage ★ Danielle Chomel and her husband rent out a piece of their hidden paradise in Ha'ikū. She's an expert orchid grower, and her blooms and bromeliads cover every inch of the property, from the entrance gate onwards. He's a classic car buff, and if you ask nicely he might show you his immaculate antique Porsche and Devins. Tucked in a corner of their fecund fruit orchard and garden, the two-bedroom cottage is comfortably furnished with a smallish kitchen, washer/dryer, pull-out futon bed in the living room, and a California king–size bed with Tempur-Pedic mattress in each of the cozy bedrooms. The off-the-beaten-path location is quiet and restful, offering a window into how real islanders live. It's a 3-minute walk to a great breakfast spot, but you'll have to drive 20 to 25 minutes to access Pā'ia's restaurants, shopping, and beaches.

265 W. Kuiaha Rd., Ha'ikū. www.mauidreamcottage.com. © **808/575-9079.** 1 unit, with shower only. $140 double. Extra person $15. 7-night minimum. **Amenities:** Wi-Fi (free).

Pilialoha B&B Cottage ★ In the heart of Ha'ikū, this country cottage is set on a large lot with towering eucalyptus trees and some 200 varieties of roses blooming in the garden. Tastefully appointed in green and white, the cottage has warm wood floors and is private, clean, and spacious. The kitchen and closets are extremely well equipped—you'll find everything you need here, from a rice cooker to beach towels, coolers, yoga mats, and fleece jackets for Haleakalā sunrise trips. Your hosts, Machiko and Bill, live on-site and are happy to offer sightseeing suggestions. If you mention to Machiko that you're heading up the mountain, she'll likely send you off with a thermos of coffee and her homemade bread. The cottage is minutes from the restaurants and shopping of Ha'ikū and Makawao and a short drive from Pā'ia's beaches. In the winter months when Ha'ikū weather can be cool and rainy, the gas fireplace is a welcome amenity.

2512 Kaupakalua Rd. (½-mile from Kokomo intersection), Ha'ikū. www.pilialoha.com. © **808/572-1440.** 1 unit. $165 double. Suitable for a couple only. 3-night minimum. **Amenities:** Watersports equipment; laundry facilities; Wi-Fi (free).

At the End of the Road in East Maui: Hāna

Note: You'll find Hāna accommodations on the map on p. 379.

EXPENSIVE

Travaasa Hāna ★★★ Ahhh . . . arriving at Travaasa (formerly the Hotel Hāna Maui) is like letting out a deep sigh. The atmosphere is so profoundly relaxing you'll forget everything beyond this remote seaside sanctuary. Nestled in the center of quaint Hāna town, the 66-acre resort wraps around Kauiki Head, the dramatic point where Queen Kaahumanu was born. All of the accommodations here are wonderful, but the Sea Ranch Cottages (adults only, except over the holidays) are downright heavenly. These duplex bungalows face the craggy shoreline, where horses graze above the rolling surf. Floor-to-ceiling sliding doors open to spacious lānais. Book your stay here a la carte or all-inclusive; the latter includes three meals, snacks, and a treatment in one of the planet's nicest spas. Whichever you choose, your room will be stocked with luxurious necessities: plush beds with organic linens, bamboo floors, giant soaking tubs, complimentary bottled water, Fair Trade coffee, homemade banana bread, and irresistibly scented bath products. You'll be far from shopping malls and sports bars, but exotic red-, black-, and white-sand beaches are just a short walk or shuttle ride away. The genuinely hospitable staff will set you up with numerous activities, many at no charge. Try stand-up paddling in the bay, practice your archer's aim, take a tour of a nearby tropical fruit farm, or learn to throw a traditional Hawaiian fishing net. Rooms have no TVs (the Club Room has a giant one), but there are nightly talk-story sessions around the fire. This is luxury in its purest form. ***Tip:*** Stay 3 nights and fly for free from Kahului to Hāna Airport.

5031 Hāna Hwy., Hāna. www.travaasa.com/hana. ✆ **888/820-1043.** 66 units. $350 single a la carte; $650 single inclusive; $400 double a la carte; $950 double inclusive. **Amenities:** 2 restaurants (w/Hawaiian entertainment Sun evenings); 2 bars (entertainment nightly); concierge; fitness center/fitness classes; complimentary use of the 3-hole practice golf courses (complimentary use of clubs); 2 outdoor pools; limited room service; luxury spa; tennis courts; Wi-Fi (free).

MODERATE

Bamboo Inn ★ This oceanfront "inn" is really just three exquisite suites, all with private lānais overlooking Waikaloa Beach's jet-black sand. The sumptuous accommodations include beds with ocean views, separate living rooms, and either a full kitchen or kitchenette. Naia, the largest unit, sleeps four and has a deep soaking tub on the lānai. The rooms and grounds are decorated with artifacts that your friendly and knowledgeable host, John Romain, collected during travels across Asia and Polynesia. Carved Balinese doors, Samoan tapa cloths, coconut wood floors, and a thatched-roof gazebo (where breakfast is served) add a rich and authentic elegance to a naturally lovely location. Waikaloa isn't great for swimming, but it's an incredible spot to watch the sunrise. All of Hāna is within easy walking distance.

Uakea Rd. (between Waikaloa and Keanini rds.; look for the sign), Hāna. www.bambooinn.com. ✆ **808/248-7718.** 3 units. $195–$265 double. Extra person $15. Rates include continental breakfast. 2-night minimum. **Amenities:** Beach equipment; barbecue; Wi-Fi (free, but only available in outdoor gazebo).

Hamoa Beach House Just around the bend from famed Hamoa Beach, this enormous three-bedroom, two-bathroom house is a great option for families or big parties. The rich woods, earthy tones, and rattan furnishings imbue the spacious interior of this '70s-era house with a cozy, nostalgic feeling. The living room has cathedral ceilings and two-story-tall windows that open up to the ocean. The upstairs bedrooms have vaulted ceilings, outdoor lānais, and a total of four king-size beds. A sweet little library is stocked with beach reading. Beneath the coconut palms outside, you'll find hammocks, a stone barbecue grill, a hot tub, and an outdoor shower—essentially everything you need to enjoy Hāna to the fullest.

487 Haneo'o Rd., Hāna. www.vrbo.com/242599. ✆ **808/248-8277.** 1 unit. $525–$575 house (sleeps up to 8). 3-night minimum. **Amenities:** Black-sand beach; beach equipment; barbecue; outdoor shower; whirlpool; Wi-Fi (free).

Hāna Kai Maui Resort ★★ "Condo complex" might not mesh with your idea of getting away from it all in Hāna, but Hāna Kai is truly special. Set on Hāna Bay, the individually owned units are dotingly furnished and feature many hotel-like extras, such as organic bath products and fresh tropical bouquets. Studios and one- and two-bedroom units have kitchens and private lānais—but the corner units with wraparound ocean views are worth angling for. Gorgeously appointed Ka'ahumanu (#5) has a daybed on the lānai that you may never want to leave. For couples, Popolana (#2) is small but sweet, with woven bamboo walls and a Murphy bed that no one ever puts up. And why would you? You can lie in it and stare out to sea or, at daybreak, watch the sun rise straight out of the ocean. No air-conditioning or TVs—but they're not necessary here.

1533 Uakea Rd., Hāna. www.hanakaimaui.com. ✆ **800/346-2772** or 808/248-8426. 18 units. $210–$308 studio double; $235–$325 1-bedroom (sleeps up to 4); $425–$465 2-bedroom. Extra person $15. 2-night minimum for beachfront units. Children 6 and under stay free in parent's room. **Amenities:** Black-sand beach; beach equipment; barbecue; daily housekeeping; laundry facilities; breakfast service (for a charge); ocean lānai; Wi-Fi (free).

Hāna Ocean Palms Bungalow ★ This bungalow's location—directly across from Waioka Pond—is perfect for adventurers who want to shed the trappings of multitasking modern life and dive deep into island culture. Spend your days relaxing in the hammock, jumping off the waterfall across the street, swimming at the black-sand beach, or exploring the nearby taro farm and national park trails. This rustic cabin is far from it all—stock up on groceries before heading out here. Remember, this is country living: At night the rain might rattle against the tin roof, and if a gecko or two finds its way inside, consider it good luck.

Hāna Hwy. btw. Waiohonu and St. Peter Church rds., Hāna. www.hanapalmsbungalow.com. ✆ **800/327-8097** or 808/248-8980. 1 unit. $245–$275 cottage (sleeps 4). Extra person $15. 2-night minimum. $50 cleaning fee for under 4 nights. **Amenities:** Barbecue; beach equipment; waterfall and swimming hole across street; Wi-Fi (free).

INEXPENSIVE

Hāna's Tradewind Cottages ★ On a 5-acre flower farm, nestled amid pink gingers and scarlet heliconias, you have a choice of two rentals: the Hāna Cabana or the Tradewinds Cottage. Each is sequestered in its own private corner of the farm and has a full kitchen, private hot tub, carport, and barbecue. Best for couples, the Cabana is a studio with vaulted ceilings and coconut palm–themed decor. The two-bedroom Tradewinds Cottage has a queen-size bed in one room and two twins in the other, one bathroom (with shower only), and a sizable living room and front porch. Days here are indescribably serene, and stars fill the sky at night. Guests are welcome to pick fruit from the surrounding banana and avocado trees, and you'll almost certainly want to take a box of tropical flowers home with you.

135 Alalele Place (the airport road), Hāna. www.hanamaui.net. ✆ **800/327-8097** or 808/248-8980. 2 units. $175–$195 double. Extra person $25. 2-night minimum. $50 Cleaning for under 4 nights. **Amenities:** Barbecue; whirlpool; Wi-Fi (free, but service not consistent).

Camping

Camping on Maui can be extreme (inside a volcano) or laidback (by the sea in Hāna). It can be wet, cold, and rainy, or hot, dry, and windy—often all on the same day. If you're heading for Haleakalā, remember that U.S. astronauts trained for the moon inside the volcano; pack survival gear. You'll need both a swimsuit and raincoat if you're bound for Waianapanapa. Bring your own equipment—Maui has no place that rents camping gear.

Camp Olowalu Halfway to Lahaina on the Honoapi'ilani Highway, this campground abuts one of the island's best coral reefs. It's perfect for avid snorkelers and, during the winter months, whale-watchers. (You can hear them slap their fins against the sea's surface at night—a magical experience.) Camping sites sit beneath shady *kiawe* trees—watch out for thorns—on flat, relatively soft ground. The porta-potties and outdoor showers are rustic; the campground is next to the highway and can be noisy—but for $20, you'll have the gently lapping Pacific outside your tent's door. Tentalows, the camp's newest addition, are large tents with two twin beds and private showers. They're quite close together and a distance from the beach, but still a bargain at $70 per night ($95 during holiday season). For large groups, six A-frame cabins with bathrooms, showers, and a kitchen are available. You can also rent kayaks onsite.

800 Olowalu Village Rd., Lahaina (off Honoapi'ilani Hwy.). www.campolowalu.com. ✆ **808/661-4303.** 6 cabins, 36 tent sites. Tent sites: $20 per night adults ($5 per night children 6–12). Tentalows: $75–$90 (2-night minimum). Cabins: $750–$1,100 for all 6 cabins (sleeps 36, 2-night minimum); contact camp for individual rates.

Haleakalā National Park ★★★ This stunning national park offers a variety of options for campers throughout its diverse landscape: **car camping** at Hosmer's Grove halfway up the summit or at 'Ohe'o Gulch in Kīpahulu; **pitching a tent** in the central Haleakalā wilderness; or cozying up in one of the crater's **historic cabins.** The first three are free (aside from the $25 park entrance fee). No permit is required, but there's a 3-night limit. The cabins cost a flat $75, whether you rent them for 1 or 12 people.

Hosmer Grove, located at 6,800 feet, is a small, open grassy area surrounded by forest and frequented by native Hawaiian honeycreepers. Trees protect campers from the winds, but nights still get very cold; sometimes there's even ice on the ground up here. This is an ideal spot to spend the night if you want to see the Haleakalā sunrise. Come up the day before, enjoy the park, take a day hike, and then turn in early. Facilities include a covered pavilion with picnic tables and grills, chemical toilets, and drinking water.

On the other side of the island, **'Ohe'o Campground** is in the Kī pahulu section of Haleakalā National Park. You can set up your temporary home at a first-come, first-served drive-in campground with tent sites for 100 near the ocean. ***Tip:*** Get here early in the day to snag one of the secluded oceanfront sites under a shady *hala* tree. The campground has picnic tables, barbecue grills, and chemical toilets—but no potable water, so bring your own. Bring a tent as well—it rains 75 inches a year here. Call the **Kīpahulu Ranger Station** (© **808/248-7375**) for local weather.

Inside the volcano are two **wilderness tent-camping** areas: **Hōlua,** just off the Halemau'u Trail and **Palikū,** 10 miles away, near the Kaupō Gap at the eastern end of the valley. Both are well over 6,000 feet in elevation and chilly at night. Facilities are limited to pit toilets and nonpotable catchment water. Water at Hōlua is limited, especially in summer. No open fires are allowed inside the volcano, so bring a stove if you plan to cook. Tent camping is restricted to the signed area and is not allowed in the horse pasture or the inviting grassy lawn in front of the cabins. Permits are issued at park headquarters daily from 8am to 3pm on a first-come, first-served basis on the day you plan to camp. Occupancy is limited to 25 people in each campground.

Also inside the volcano are three **wilderness cabins,** built in 1937 by the Civilian Conservation Corps. Each has 12 padded bunks (bring your own bedding), a table, chairs, cooking utensils, a two-burner propane stove, and a wood-burning stove with firewood. The cabins are spaced so that each one is a nice hike from the next: **Hōlua** cabin is 3.7 miles down the zigzagging Halemau'u Trail, **Kapalaoa** cabin is 5.5 miles down the Sliding Sands Trail, and Palikū cabin is the farthest, at 9.3 miles down Sliding Sands and across the moonscape to the crater's eastern end. In spring and summer, the endangered *'ua'u* (Hawaiian dark-rumped petrel) can be heard yipping and chortling on their way back home to their cliffside burrows. Some campers and hikers exit through the Kaupō Gap—8.6 miles to the remote Pi'ilani Highway. You can reserve cabins up to 6 months in advance on the park's reservation website (www.recreation.gov; ✆ **877/444-6777**). You're limited to 2 nights in 1 cabin and 3 nights total in the wilderness each month.

Note: All wilderness campers must watch a 10-minute orientation video at the park's visitor center.

Haleakalā National Park, at top of Crater Rd., and at Kīpahulu Visitor Center, 12 miles past Hāna on Hāna Hwy. www.nps.gov/hale. ✆ **808/572-4400.** 3 cabins, 100-plus tent sites. $75 flat rate for cabins; tent campers free (aside from $25 park entrance fee). Cabins by reservation only.

Polipoli State Park High up on the slope of Haleakalā, at 6,200 feet in elevation, this state park has extensive trails that wind through conifer forests reminiscent of the Pacific Northwest. It's frequently cold and foggy here—be prepared for extra-chilly nights! One eight-bunk cabin is available for $90; it has a cold shower and a gas stove but no electricity or drinking water (bring your own). Tent-campers can pitch on the grass nearby. Reserve on the website (or in person at the Wailuku office) and print out your permit, which must be displayed. ***Note:*** This park is only accessible by a four-wheel-drive vehicle.

9¾ miles up Waipoli Rd., off Kekaulike (Hwy 377); 4-wheel drive vehicle recommended. By reservation only c/o State Parks Division, 54 S. High St., Room 101, Wailuku. www.dlnr.hawaii.gov/dsp/camping-lodging/maui. ✆ **808/984-8109.** 1 cabin. $90 per night (sleeps up to 8). $18 for 1st tent-camper, $3 for additional campers. 5-night maximum.

Wai'ānapanapa State Park ★★ The 12 rustic cabins tucked in the *hala* (pandanus) groves of Wai'ānapanapa State Park were once the best lodging deal on Maui—but years of use have taken their toll. They've been under renovation for the last year; call before you book to check the status. In the meantime, you can still pitch a tent above the black-sand beach on Pailoa Bay. Watch the sun rise out of the ocean and beat the crowds to the freshwater cave pool. There's an on-site caretaker, along with restrooms, showers, picnic tables, shoreline hiking trails, and historic sites. Bring rain gear and mosquito protection—this is the rainforest, after all. Reserve both tent sites and cabins on the website (or in person at the Wailuku office) and print out your permit, which must be displayed.

End of Wai'ānapanapa Rd., off Hāna Hwy. By reservation only c/o State Parks Division, 54 S. High St., Room 101, Wailuku. http://dlnr.hawaii.gov/dsp/parks/maui/waianapanapa-state-park. ✆ **808/984-8109.** 10 units. $90 per cabin per night (sleeps up to 6). $18 for 1st tent-camper, $3 for additional campers. 5-night maximum.

WHERE TO EAT ON MAUI

When it comes to dining in Maui, all I can say is: Come hungry and bring a fat wallet. Dining has never been better on the Valley Isle, which is presently producing numerous enterprising and imaginative chefs. The farm-to-table concept has finally taken root on this bountiful island, where in past years up to 90% of the food had been imported. Today chefs and farmers collaborate on menus, filling plates with tender micro-greens and heirloom tomatoes picked that morning. Fishers reel in glistening ʻopakapaka (pink snapper), and ranchers offer up flavorful cuts of Maui-grown beef.

A new crop of inspired chefs is taking these ripe ingredients to new heights. At **Kaʻana Kitchen,** chef Isaac Bancaco nearly outshines his celebrity neighbor, "Iron Chef" Masaharu Morimoto (who brought his high-octane Japanese fusion cuisine to Wailea). Both are outstanding; make time for each. Up the street, chef Brian Etheredge makes traditional Italian seem brand-new again at **Capische?** On the other side of the island, at Kapalua's **Plantation House,** Jojo Vasquez adds exciting Filipino accents to his gourmet dishes. Stellar dining experiences all, with prices to match. You don't *have* to spend a fortune to eat well here—Maui does have a few budget eateries, noted below. But if you want to feast, there's never been a better time to do so on Maui.

Central Maui

Kahului and Wailuku have a few tasty finds. Minutes outside of the airport in a windy dirt lot across from Costco, you'll find an array of **food trucks** dishing out everything from pork belly sandwiches to poke (seasoned raw fish). Also, keep an eye out for celebrity chef Sheldon Simeon's **Tin Roof Maui,** scheduled to open in 2016 at 360 Papa Place, near the intersection of Dairy Road and Hāna Highway. It's sure to be delicious.

MODERATE

Bistro Casanova ★ MEDITERRANEAN Hungry and marooned in Kahului? Head to this Mediterranean bistro for sweet and savory crepes, traditional Italian pastas, or a giant bowl of paella. The casual but classy restaurant fills with business lunchers at noon. It's more relaxed at dinner (unless there's a big show at the nearby Maui Arts & Cultural Center—then it will be hopping). It offers a private room for big parties and a full bar for *pau hana* (after work) drinks.

33 Lono Ave., Kahului. www.casanovamaui.com. ✆ **808/873-3650.** Lunch main courses $9–$18; dinner main courses $14–$32. Mon–Sat 11am–9:30pm.

Marco's Grill & Deli ★ ITALIAN Located just outside the airport, Marco's offers decent Italian fare in an upscale diner with black-and-white booths and white linens on the tables. Portions tend to be huge, and everything is made in house, from the meatballs, sausages, and burgers to the sauces and salad dressing. Favorites include chicken Parmesan and vodka rigatoni.

395 Dairy Rd., Kahului. ✆ **808/877-4446.** Breakfast $6–14; lunch and dinner main courses $12–$39. Daily 7:30am–9:30pm (Sat–Sun until 1am).

A Saigon Cafe ★★ VIETNAMESE It's hard to say which is better at this beloved neighborhood restaurant—the delicious Vietnamese cuisine or the hilarious waiters who make wisecracks while taking your order. Whatever you order—the steamed ʻopakapaka with ginger and garlic, one of a dozen soups, the catfish simmering in a clay pot, or the fragrant lemongrass curry—you'll notice the freshness of the flavors. Owner Jennifer Nguyen grows many of her own vegetables and herbs and even sprouts her own mung beans. My favorites are the Buddha rolls dunked in spicy peanut sauce and the Vietnamese "burritos." You make the latter tableside—tricky at first, but fun.

1792 Main St., Wailuku. ✆ **808/243-9560.** Main courses $9–$27. Daily 10am–9:30pm (Sun until 8:30pm). Heading into Wailuku from Kahului, go over the bridge and take the 1st right onto Central Ave.; then take the 1st right on Nani St. At the next stop sign, look for the building with the neon sign that says open.

INEXPENSIVE

Down to Earth ★ ORGANIC HEALTH FOOD Stop in here for a vegetarian snack or bag full of local organic produce. During mango season, this full-service natural-foods store carries as many as three different locally grown varieties of the fruit—worth their weight in gold. The deli includes creative salads, lasagna, chili, curries, and dozens of tasty dishes—including gluten-free and vegan options. Deli attendants can whip up a faux Reuben sandwich or tasty meatless burger for you. The upstairs dining area is plain but convenient.

305 Dairy Rd., Kahului. www.downtoearth.org. ✆ **808/877-2661.** Self-serve hot buffet, salad bar, and deli; food sold by the pound; average $7–$12 for a plate; sandwiches $6–$11. Mon–Sat 7am–9pm, Sun 8am–8pm.

Sam Sato's ★ NOODLES/PLATE LUNCHES Hidden away in Wailuku's industrial area, this humble, family-owned eatery dates back to 1933. It's one of Maui's last ma-and-pa establishments, and everything on the menu is under $10. Sit at the cafeteria-like counter and strike up a conversation with your neighbor. Try your dry mein (al dente noodles served with slices of char siu pork, bean sprouts, green onions, and broth on the side) with a side order of grilled teriyaki meat sticks. On the way out, stock up on Sam Sato's other famous specialty: baked *manju,* flaky pastries filled with sweetened lima or adzuki beans.

At the Millyard, 1750 Wili Pa Loop, Wailuku. ✆ **808/244-7124.** Plate lunches $8–$9. No credit cards. Mon–Sat 7am–2pm; 7am–4pm bakery and preordered takeout items.

West Maui

LAHAINA

Expensive

The Feast at Lele ★★★ POLYNESIAN The Feast at Lele stands out from other lū'aus as the gourmand's choice. Although most lū'au seating is en masse, guests here sit at elegant tables in the sand facing a cirque-inspired stage. As the sun dips into the sea behind you, chanting dancers regale you with stories of Polynesia. You'll progress from Hawai'i to New Zealand, Tahiti, and Samoa, feasting on each island nation's culinary specialties in turn. During the opening hula, you'll sample Hawaiian fish with mango sauce and *imu*-roasted kalua pig. While watching the exciting Maori *haka,* you'll eat New Zealand sea bean and duck salad. Pace yourself; each of the four savory courses includes three dishes and then there's dessert, accompanied by a fantastic fire knife dance! The swish of *ti*-leaf skirts and the beat of the drums enhances the meal's flavors; it's a sensory experience even for the most jaded lū'au-goer.

505 Front St., Lahaina. www.feastatlele.com. ✆ **866/244-5353** or 808/667-5353. Reservations required. Set 5-course menu (includes all beverages) $125 adults, $94 children 2–12. Apr 1–Sept 30 daily 6:30–9:30pm; Oct 1–Mar 31 daily 5:30–8:30pm.

Gerard's ★★★ FRENCH Chef Gerard Reversade has called Hawai'i home for nearly 4 decades, but his French accent hasn't lost one cédille. His charming residence-turned-restaurant beneath the Plantation Inn in Lahaina is equally authentic. I never would've imagined that a simple chilled cucumber soup could be transcendent—but this one is, its delicacy amplified by goat cheese and fresh dill. The roasted 'opakapaka served with fennel fondue and spiked with hints of orange and ginger is stellar, as is the grilled Hawaiian filet with salsify au gratin. Chef Reversade is every bit as much of a baker as a chef, and the savory dishes that incorporate pastry—such as the Hāmākua mushroom appetizer—are delights. The dessert menu has a half-dozen excellent offerings, including a marvelous *millefeuille* and chocolate mousse with pistachio ice cream.

At the Plantation Inn, 174 Lahainaluna Rd., Lahaina. www.gerardsmaui.com. ✆ **808/661-8939.** Reservations recommended. Main courses $39–$60. Daily 6–9pm.

Lahaina Grill ★★ NEW AMERICAN For more than 2 decades, this classy restaurant has been collecting accolades for its perfectly executed island cuisine, gracious service, and great wine list. The striking decor—splashy artwork by local painter Jan Kasprzycki, pressed-tin ceilings, and warm lighting—creates an appealing atmosphere. The bar, despite lacking an ocean view, is among the busiest in town and often features special pricing. The menu hasn't strayed much over the years; fans will still find their favorites: the zesty "toy box" heirloom-tomato salad served in a martini glass, the aromatic Kona coffee–roasted rack of lamb, and the divinely rich seared ahi with foie gras, truffle oil, and fig compote. If you're planning a special event or a large party, you can book one of two private rooms and design your own menu with the chef.

127 Lahainaluna Rd., Lahaina. http://lahainagrill.com. © **808/667-5117.** Reservations required. Main courses $33–$87. Daily 5:30–9 or 10pm. Bar daily 6–10pm (closing earlier on slow nights).

Pacific'O Restaurant ★★ CONTEMPORARY PACIFIC RIM You can't get any closer to the ocean than these tables overlooking the beach at 505 Front Street. Start with flash-fried oysters and wakame seaweed salad or lobster ravioli. Move on to saffron beet risotto studded with seared shrimp and chunks of seafood. Vegetarians will delight in the Portobello mushrooms with quinoa and cilantro pesto. (The kitchen sources ingredients from its own O'o Farm up in Kula.) This is a superb and relatively affordable lunch spot. Indulge in ginger-crusted fish or Kalbi beef tacos and glass of spicy Syrah while watching the ships sail by.

505 Front St., Lahaina. www.pacificomaui.com. © **808/667-4341.** Reservations recommended. Main courses $13–$16 lunch, $27–$42 dinner. Daily 11:30am–3:30pm and 5:30–9:30pm.

Moderate

Fleetwood's on Front Street ★ AMERICAN Rock and Roll Hall of Famer Mick Fleetwood ventured into the restaurant business with commendable results. His snazzy eatery occupies the top two floors of a lovingly restored three-story building on Front Street. For dinner, choose from locally grown salads, fresh fish entrees, or a Harley-Davidson Hog burger—hold the Harley. I find the food a little lackluster, but the atmosphere is outstanding. The dining room's cozy booths and wraparound bar evoke an older, more sophisticated era. But the real draw is the rooftop dining—plus the live entertainment. ***Tip:*** Nightly at 6pm, local musicians offer a short, free performance, ranging from bagpipes to Hawaiian chanting. Mick and his celebrity friends often pop in to play a set. When it rains, the upstairs seating is closed.

744 Front St., Lahaina. www.fleetwoodsonfrontst.com. © **808/669-6425.** Reservations recommended. Main courses $18–$45. Daily 5–10pm.

Frida's Mexican Beach House ★ MEXICAN Mark Ellman owns three restaurants in a row on the beautiful strip fronting Mala Wharf. Frida's, his latest, features Latin-inspired cuisine in a breezy dining room accented with pretty Mexican tiles and wrought-iron chandeliers. Sip one of 40 tequilas at the open-air bar. Lamb-shoulder tacos with tomatillos and guajillos and whole grilled fish with San Marzano tomatoes are tasty, especially on the romantic oceanfront lānai.

1287 Front St., Lahaina. www.fridasmaui.com. © **808/661-1287.** Reservations recommended. Main courses $17–$38. Daily 11am–9:30pm.

Honu ★★ PIZZA/SEAFOOD Snag an oceanfront table where the gentle tide nearly tickles your toes and spy on the green sea turtles for whom this restaurant is named. Honu's diverse menu is guaranteed to

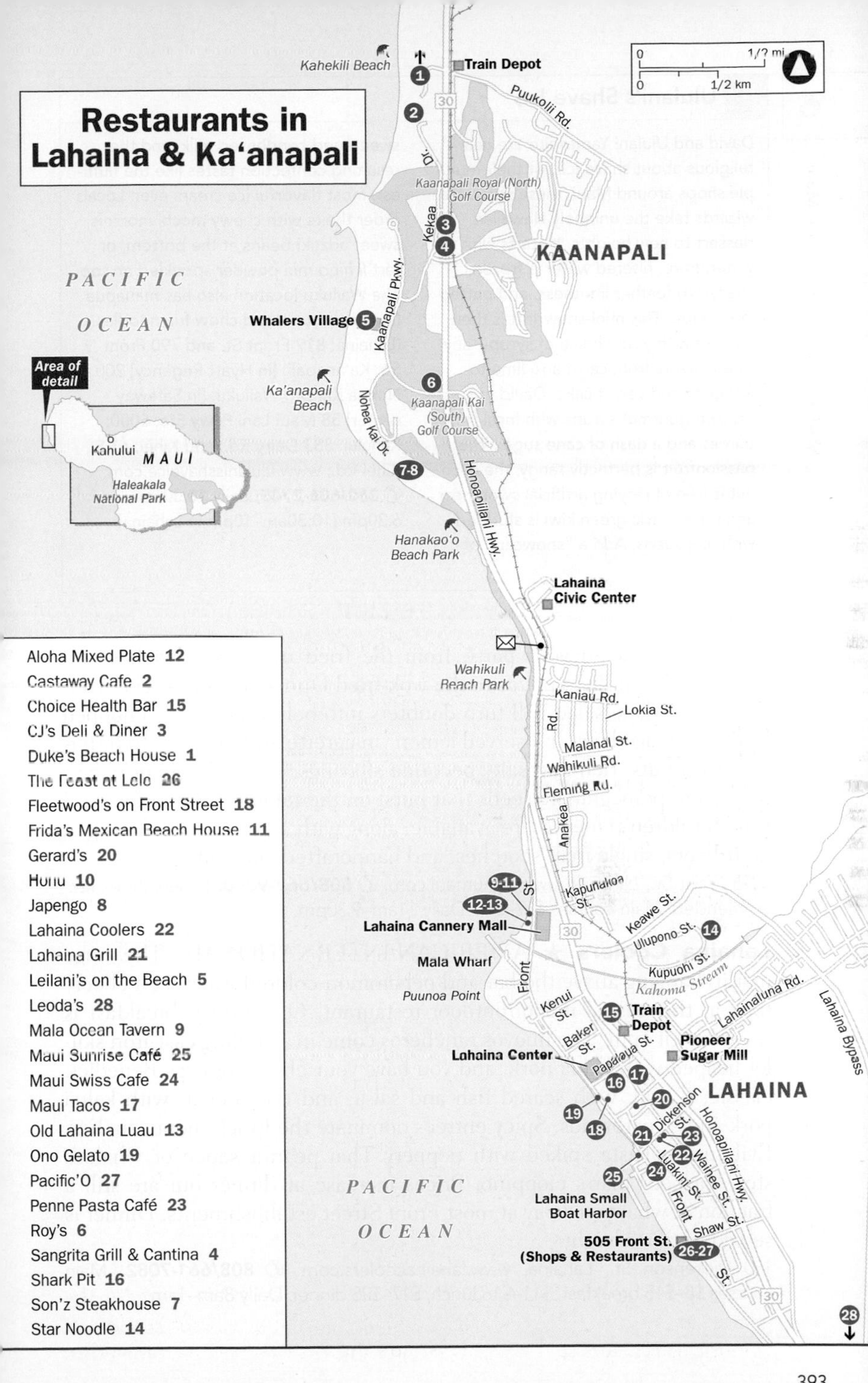
Restaurants in Lahaina & Ka'anapali
PACIFIC OCEAN
Area of detail
Kahului
MAUI
Haleakala National Park
Kahekili Beach
Train Depot
Puukolii Rd.
Kaanapali Royal (North) Golf Course
Kekaa Dr.
KAANAPALI
Whalers Village
Kaanapali Pkwy.
Ka'anapali Beach
Kaanapali Kai (South) Golf Course
Nohea Kai Dr.
Honoapiilani Hwy.
Hanakao'o Beach Park
Lahaina Civic Center
Wahikuli Beach Park
Kaniau Rd.
Lokia St.
Malanai St.
Wahikuli Rd.
Fleming Rd.
Anakea Rd.
Kapunakea St.
Keawe St.
Ulupono St.
Kupuohi St.
Kahoma Stream
Lahaina Cannery Mall
Mala Wharf
Puunoa Point
Front St.
Kenui St.
Baker St.
Papalaua St.
Train Depot
Pioneer Sugar Mill
Lahainaluna Rd.
Lahaina Bypass
Lahaina Center
LAHAINA
Dickenson St.
Luakini St.
Wainee St.
Front St.
Shaw St.
Lahaina Small Boat Harbor
505 Front St. (Shops & Restaurants)
PACIFIC OCEAN
0 1/2 mi
0 1/2 km
Aloha Mixed Plate 12
Castaway Cafe 2
Choice Health Bar 15
CJ's Deli & Diner 3
Duke's Beach House 1
The Feast at Lele 26
Fleetwood's on Front Street 18
Frida's Mexican Beach House 11
Gerard's 20
Honu 10
Japengo 8
Lahaina Coolers 22
Lahaina Grill 21
Leilani's on the Beach 5
Leoda's 28
Mala Ocean Tavern 9
Maui Sunrise Café 25
Maui Swiss Cafe 24
Maui Tacos 17
Old Lahaina Luau 13
Ono Gelato 19
Pacific'O 27
Penne Pasta Café 23
Roy's 6
Sangrita Grill & Cantina 4
Shark Pit 16
Son'z Steakhouse 7
Star Noodle 14

Ululani's Shave Ice

David and Ululani Yamashiro are near-religious about shave ice. At their multiple shops around Maui, these shave-ice wizards take the uniquely Hawaiian dessert to new heights. It starts with the water: Pure, filtered water is frozen, shaved to feather lightness, and patted into shape. This mini-snowdrift is then doused with your choice of syrup—any three flavors from calamansi lime to lychee to red velvet cake. David makes his own gourmet syrups with local fruit purees and a dash of cane sugar. The passionfruit is perfectly tangy, the coconut is free of cloying artificial sweetness, and the electric green kiwi is studded with real seeds. Add a "snowcap" of sweetened condensed milk, and the resulting confection tastes like the fluffiest, most flavorful ice cream ever. Locals order theirs with chewy mochi morsels, sweet adzuki beans at the bottom, or tart *li hing mui* powder sprinkled on top. The Wailuku location also has *manapua* (steamed buns) and chow fun noodles (Lahaina: 819 Front St. and 790 Front St.; Ka'anapali: [in Hyatt Regency] 200 Nohea Kai Dr.; Wailuku: [in Safeway center] 58 Maui Lani Pkwy Ste. 5000; Kahului: 333 Dairy Rd.; and Kīhei: 61 S. Kīhei Rd.; www.ululanisshaveice.com; ✆ **360/606-2745;** daily 10:30am–6:30pm [10:30am–10pm in Lahaina]).

please someone in your party, from the fried oyster sandwiches and authentic Neapolitan pizzas to the wok-fried Dungeness crab. The Middle Eastern kale salad will turn doubters into believers: Finely chopped kale is massaged with preserved lemon vinaigrette and tossed with bittersweet walnuts, rich and salty pecorino shavings, sweet slivers of chewy dates, and pomegranate seeds that burst on the tongue. Gluten-free and *keiki* (children's) menus are available, along with an extensive offering of draft beers, single malt scotches, and handcrafted cocktails.

1295 Front St., Lahaina. www.honumaui.com. ✆ **808/667-9390.** Reservations recommended. Main courses $17–$48. Daily 11am–9:30pm.

Lahaina Coolers ★ AMERICAN/INTERNATIONAL The huge marlin hanging above the bar and persimmon-colored walls set a cheery tone at this casual indoor/outdoor restaurant. On Sunday, breakfast is served until 1pm. The huevos rancheros come in a sizzling cast-iron skillet heaped with kalua pork, and you have your choice of eggs Benedict: classic; Cajun, with seared fish and salsa; and the "Local" with kalua pork and sweetbreads. Spicy entrees dominate the lunch menu, such as Evil Jungle Pasta spiked with peppery Thai peanut sauce or whaler's stew—a poor man's cioppino. Prices increase at dinner but are still a fraction of what you'd pay at most Front Street establishments. Dinner is served until midnight.

180 Dickenson St., Lahaina. www.lahainacoolers.com. ✆ **808/661-7082.** Main courses $8–$15 breakfast, $11–$16 lunch, $17–$28 dinner. Daily 8am–1am.

Mala Ocean Tavern ★★ AMERICAN/INTERNATIONAL This tiny tavern overlooking Mala Wharf in Lahaina is as perfect as can be. It's brighter and classier than "tavern" suggests, and the oceanfront seating lets diners peer down on sea turtles foraging in the surf. The bartenders know their business, and the complimentary edamame guacamole alerts your taste buds that something delicious is about to happen. The menu offers health-conscious and hedonistic options, from the *gado gado* (a vegan Indonesian rice dish heaped with sugar-snap peas and coconut peanut sauce) to the insanely rich and delicious adult mac and cheese (an oven-baked medley of three cheeses and Hāmākua mushrooms). The weekend brunch is among the island's tastiest, with local organic eggs served in Benedicts, chilaquiles, and huevos rancheros.

1307 Front St., Lahaina. www.malaoceantavern.com. ✆ **808/667-9394.** Main courses $12–$27 lunch, $18–$42 dinner; brunch $8–$15. Mon–Fri 11am–9:30pm; Sat–Sun 9am–9:30pm.

Star Noodle ★★ NOODLES/FUSION This hip noodle house at the top of Lahaina's industrial park offers a deceivingly simple menu of noodles and share plates. The hapa ramen, with its smoky pork and spicy miso broth, is guaranteed to be unlike any you've had before. Each dish is a gourmet twist on a local favorite; the Lahaina fried soup isn't soup at all but thick and chewy house-made noodles tossed with ground pork and bean sprouts. The 'ahi avo is a divine mix of fresh red tuna and buttery avocado swimming in a pool of lemon-pressed olive oil and spiked with sambal. With its long communal table, Shepard Fairey artwork, and glamorous washrooms, this casual eatery has an urban feel. From the window seats you can catch a hint of an ocean view—just enough to remind you that you're still in Hawai'i.

286 Kupuohi St., Lahaina. www.starnoodle.com. ✆ **808/667-5400.** Main courses $7–$30. Daily 10:30am–10pm.

Inexpensive

Aloha Mixed Plate ★ PLATE LUNCHES/BEACHSIDE GRILL Right on the ocean, in the midst of tourist-heavy Lahaina, this local favorite dishes out budget-friendly breakfasts and island-style plate lunches: fresh-made chow mein, teriyaki chicken, and Korean kalbi ribs with the proverbial two-scoops-rice and macaroni salad. If you have a hankering for a loco moco (hamburger, rice, and an egg ladled with gravy), this is your spot. It's also a sweet hideaway at happy hour (3–6pm). Toss out your dietary restrictions, order the furikake garlic fries, coconut prawns, and a few Maui microbrews. The banana caramel cheesecake lumpia is out of this world.

1285 Front St., Lahaina. www.alohamixedplate.com. ✆ **808/661-3322.** Main courses $6–$14. Daily 8am–10pm.

Choice Health Bar/Garden Sushi ★★ GOURMET DELI/CAFE This health-conscious juice bar and cafe is where the beautiful people in Lahaina come to fuel up. After a taxing morning of sunbathing or paddling past sea turtles, re-energize here with a sunrise acai bowl drizzled in honey or a "macca-chino"—a frothy blend of banana, cacao, and shijilat. What, you've never heard of shijilat? Don't worry; the friendly chefs behind the counter will give you the lowdown on this Ayurvedic superfood and all of the other exotic treats on the menu. Daily lunch specials include wholesome soups and savory rawviolis—a colorful raw reinvention of the Italian pasta. The plate lunches are an edible rainbow of scrumptious kale salad, coconut-garlic quinoa, and ruby red beet soup, with a bonus dessert. For dinner: A vegetarian sushi chef sets up shop, turning out wildly inventive veggie rolls and nigiri that are delicious works of art.

1087 Limahana Place (off of Honoapi'ilani Hwy.), Lahaina. www.choicehealthbar.com. ✆ **808/661-7711.** Breakfast and lunch main courses $6–$12; dinner $12–$14. Mon–Sat 8am–4pm, 6–9pm.

Leoda's ★★ SANDWICHES/BAKERY Who would have thought—a pie place in tiny Olowalu? As you approach the counter, you'll see why the line stretches to the door: a glass case full of banana and coconut pies slathered in fresh whipped cream. The savory pies are just okay. But the sweet pies—especially the chocolate macadamia nut praline—are intergalactic. For breakfast, Leoda's serves an outstanding seared 'ahi Benedict with pesto, watercress, avocado, and eggs raised nearby. For lunch, the Ham'n sandwich is a hot and juicy mess of duroc ham, island pesto, melted Jarlsberg cheese, and apricot-tomato jam on buttered rye bread. The seasonal fried Brussels sprout salad is sinfully delicious. Leoda's belongs to the Star Noodle, Old Lahaina Lū'au, and Aloha Mixed Plate restaurant family—a crew that knows how to please. The eatery's bright decor pays homage to Maui's bygone plantation days.

820 Olowalu Village Rd. (off of Honoapi'ilani Hwy), Lahaina. www.leodas.com. ✆ **808/662-3600.** Breakfast items $3–$19; lunch and dinner items $4–$16. Daily 7am–8pm.

Maui Sunrise Café ★ CAFE For a bargain lunch or breakfast, follow the surfers to this hole-in-the-wall cafe located just off Front Street. (The address says Front St., but it's really off of Market, across from the library.) The kitchen turns out tasty breakfast burritos, a lox Benedict with home-fried potatoes, and decent sandwiches. Service can be slow, but the prices can't be beat in this neighborhood. Eat in the covered patio out back or take it to go and picnic in the adjoining park.

693A Front St., Lahaina. ✆ **808/661-8558.** Breakfast items under $11; lunch items $7–$12. No credit cards. Daily 7am–4pm.

Maui Swiss Café ★ SANDWICHES This cafe boldly announces itself with flamingo-pink fringed umbrellas over its sidewalk seating. Inside is a selection of crepes, sandwiches, and ice creams, along with 12 Internet stations—perfect for printing out your flight's boarding pass. The affordable and tasty crepes all come with side salads and sour cream. The signature melted sandwiches—such as the BBQ roast beef—come with Dijon mustard and cream cheese.

640 Front St., Lahaina. www.swisscafe.net. ✆ **808/661-6776.** Sandwiches and crepes $8–$13. Daily 8am–8pm.

Ono Gelato ★ CAFE/ICE CREAM Who doesn't want to hang out on a picnic bench perched over the Lahaina surf while eating creamy gelato? This classy creamery uses locally sourced *lilikoi* (Hawaiian passionfruit), mango, and coffee to craft rich and flavorful scoops of Italian gelato and sorbets. The coffee bar opens for breakfast, and the baristas make a mean *affogato*—gelato drowned in two shots of espresso. The back patio is the best spot to chill in town—and it has free Wi-Fi.

815 Front St., Lahaina. ✆ **808/495-0203.** Most items under $7. Daily 8am–10pm.

Penne Pasta Café ★ ITALIAN/MEDITERRANEAN With outdoor seating on a Lahaina side street, this casual spot features delicious Italian and Mediterranean cuisine. Order at the counter, and the manager delivers your pasta, pizza, or salad Niçoise to your table. It's a sit-down meal at takeout prices. The penne puttanesca, baked penne with braised beef, and lamb osso buco (the Wednesday night special) are wonderful. Try the oven-roasted butternut squash simmered in almonds and sage.

180 Dickenson St., Lahaina. ✆ **808/661-6633.** Main courses $9–$18. Daily 11am–9:30pm.

Shark Pit ★ MEXICAN/ECLECTIC This beloved food truck has found a brick-and-mortar home in downtown Lahaina. Come here for taco plates featuring delicious "funked-up fish," kalbi ground beef, and kimchi shrimp fillings. The burger menu has some tasty fusion options, too: egg-wrapped meat jun with spicy pickled cabbage and gochujang aioli on a taro brioche bun. The Brussels sprouts Caesar is a sweet and salty medley tossed with bacon and chili croutons. The owner cares about every dish; he cooks nightly and will do his best to impress you.

170 Papalaua St., Unit 4, Lahaina. ✆ **808/662-3663.** Main courses $9–$18. Daily 11am–3pm and 6–10pm.

KA'ANAPALI

Expensive

Japengo ★★ SUSHI/PACIFIC RIM The open-air dining room hanging over the Hyatt pool is divided into multiple private nooks, evoking the feel of a Japanese teahouse. Meander inside for superb Japanese-influenced entrees and inspired sushi, sashimi, and hand rolls. Look around for signs of *tengu,* a long-nosed mythological trickster and the restaurant's mascot. Depending on what the fishermen reeled in that day, the *moriawase,* or chef's platter, may include achingly red tuna, translucent slivers of Big Island *hirame* (flounder), poached local abalone, creamy wedges of *uni* (sea urchin), or raw New Caledonia prawn. The sushi wizards at the bar beautifully garnish this bounty with nests of peppery daikon and aromatic shiso leaves. Delicious vegetable sides—kabocha pumpkin, asparagus in Thai chili sauce, and lavender-honey corn—originate on nearby Simpli-Fresh farm.

At the Hyatt Regency Maui Resort, 200 Nohea Kai Dr., Ka'anapali. www.maui.hyatt.com. ✆ **808/661-1234.** Main courses $24–$54. Daily 5–10pm.

Roy's ★ HAWAI'I REGIONAL CUISINE Roy Yamaguchi, the James Beard award–winning chef and one of the pioneers of Hawai'i Regional Cuisine, owns eponymous restaurants all over the world. At his Maui kitchen, executive chef Ryan Fergussen sends out perfect braised ribs with Dijon crust, crab-stuffed mahimahi, and rich misoyaki butterfish. The restaurant serves lunch from 11am to 2pm and a bar menu from 2 to 5pm, which features the "canoe for two," an appetizer platter of 'ahi poke, pork lumpia, chicken potstickers, Szechuan short ribs, and skewered shrimp. Hallelujah for the bartender who created the "Skinny Colada," a cocktail that delivers the flavor of a piña colada without the overwhelming milky cream. ***Tip:*** Two words: chocolate soufflé. This signature dessert is so tantalizing I sometimes call in an order to eat at the bar. It takes 20 minutes to prepare, so let your waiter know you want it in advance. And when it arrives, wait a moment for it to cool—don't burn your tongue on the hot lava chocolate!

2290 Ka'anapali Pkwy., Ka'anapali. www.roysrestaurant.com. ✆ **808/669-6999.** Lunch main courses $18–$32; dinner main courses $27–$50. Daily 11am–10pm.

Son'z Steakhouse ★ STEAKHOUSE Descend a palatial staircase for dinner at Son'z, where tables overlook a lagoon with white and black swans swimming by. This is classy digs for a steakhouse; imagine Ruth's Chris with extra flavor and a fairy-tale atmosphere. Chef Geno Sarmiento knows how to prepare protein; his filet is on point with "Mauishire" sauce, as is the New Zealand rack of lamb with fig sauce and kohlrabi potato puree. Sides are generally sold separately; choose from grilled asparagus, truffle mac and cheese, or the loaded baked potato: a decadent spud cooked low and slow (200° for 4 hr.) and sinfully stuffed with mascarpone, bacon bits, truffle butter, chives, and Parmesan. Finish with Portuguese sweet bread French toast, vanilla gelato, and sweetly tart local bananas set aflame, Foster's style.

At the Hyatt Regency Maui Resort, 200 Nohea Kai Dr., Ka'anapali. www.sonzrestaurant.com. ✆ **808/667-4506.** Main courses $30–$57. Daily 5:30–9:30pm.

Moderate

Duke's Beach House ★ PACIFIC RIM There are few more beautiful places to enjoy breakfast than here, facing Kahekili Beach. This restaurant mimics an open-air plantation home, decorated with memorabilia chronicling the life of Duke Kahanamoku, the famous Hawaiian surfer and Ambassador of Aloha. It's part of the TS Restaurants family, which includes Kimo's, Hula Grill, and Leilani's on Maui, Keoki's on Kaua'i, and Duke's in Waikīkī—among others. The menu reflects much of what you'll find at the other locales: "onolicious" French toast made with Moloka'i sweet bread, various omelets, and steel-cut oats for breakfast; coconut shrimp and burgers for lunch; macadamia-nut-crusted fish and steak for dinner; and the signature hula pie for dessert. What sets this restaurant apart is its gracious sea-breeze-kissed locale and the kitchen's commitment to serving locally raised beef, eggs, and vegetables. Add to that live music during the "aloha hour" daily from 3 to 5pm. At Honua Kai Resort & Spa, 130 Kai Malina Pkwy., North Ka'anapali Beach. www.dukesmaui.com. ✆ **808/662-2900.** Breakfast items $5–$15, lunch main courses $10–$15; dinner main courses $18–$44. Daily 7:30am–9:30pm.

Leilani's on the Beach ★★ STEAK/SEAFOOD When Chef Ryan Luckey took over the kitchen at Leilani's, everything on the menu rose three or four points in deliciousness. He amped up the offerings from generic surf-and-turf to include filet mignon with black truffle butter and sesame-crusted 'ahi steak with coconut and citrus jasmine rise. The Surfing Goat cheese plate includes a trio of delectable local cheeses, served with taro crisps and lavosh. The **Beachside Grill**—the tables underneath the colorful umbrellas that bank right up to Ka'anapali Beach—features a separate, more casual menu. Here you can people-watch while snacking on Cajun-rubbed fish tacos or a kalua pork Cuban and tossing back a Ka'anapali cosmo. Leilani's belongs to the TS Restaurant family, so you can get the trademark Hula Pie—but I prefer the passionfruit Pono Pie made with breadfruit and without refined sugar. At Whalers Village, 2435 Ka'anapali Pkwy., Ka'anapali. www.leilanis.com. ✆ **808/661-4495.** Reservations suggested for dinner. Beachside Grill lunch and dinner main courses $12–$18; Leilani's dinner main courses $23–$33. Beachside Grill daily 11am–11pm. Leilani's daily 5–9:30pm.

Sangrita Grill & Cantina ★ MEXICAN This popular cantina pays homage to Mexico's most inventive gourmet cuisine. The owner, Paris Nabavi, imports ingredients from Oaxaca and serves chorizo with house-made cheese. The rotisserie chicken is mouthwateringly delicious, as are the "kick ass" pork carnitas braised in duck fat. The deli case by the door is stocked with take-away salsas, slaws, and other savory items. The a la carte entrée portions are somewhat small, but everything on the menu is fresh, from the house-made corn-and-flour tortilla chips to the guacamoles, one of which combines chunks of chipotle-spiced pineapple with ripe local avocado and pumpkin seeds. The bar features a tequila shrine with 30 premium tequila and mescal varieties—perfect for mixing with the restaurant's namesake, sangrita.

At the Fairway Shops at Ka'anapali, 2580 Keka'a Dr. (just off the Honoapi'ilani Hwy.), Ka'anapali. www.sangritagrill.com. ✆ **808/662-6000.** Main courses $12–$26. Mon–Sat 11am–10pm. Sun 11am–9:30pm.

Inexpensive

Castaway Café ★ AMERICAN Hidden away in the Aston Maui Ka'anapali Villas, this little cafe sits right on Kahekili Beach—privvy to perfect views and salty breezes. Chef Lyndon Honda and the Cohn Restaurant group recently breathed new life into this local favorite, which has long been famous for its Saturday-night prime rib special. New menu items include a savory guava barbecue beef sandwich with carmelized Maui onions on ciabatta and a fancy burger topped with merlot-poached pears, melted brie, and arugula. Breakfast is extra-relaxing here, and so is Happy Hour, now with live entertainment.

In the Aston Maui Ka'anapali Villas, 45 Kai Ala Dr., Ka'anapali. www.castawaycafe.com. ✆ **808/661-9091.** Main courses: $7–$12 breakfast; $10–$16 lunch; $24–$38 dinner. Daily 7:30am–9pm.

CJ's Deli & Diner ★ AMERICAN/DELI Need a break from resort prices? Head to this happening eatery just off of Honoapi'ilani Highway in Ka'anapali. Prices are so low you won't believe you're still on Maui. The atmosphere is colorful and slightly chaotic, with a huge billboard menu that spans the back wall, shelves stuffed with souvenirs and brochures, and a . . . basketball hoop? Practice your free throws while debating over breakfast options: spinach-stuffed omelet, smoked salmon bagel, or French toast made with Hawaiian sweet bread. Lunch ranges from grilled panini sandwiches to fish and chips, mochiko chicken, and barbecue ribs. Kids can order happy-face pancakes and squid-eyes soup—just joking. If you're heading out to Hāna or up to Haleakalā, stop by for a box lunch. Toppings are packed separately so sandwiches don't get soggy. You can even order online for a to-go pickup.

At the Fairway Shops at Ka'anapali, 2580 Keka'a Dr. (just off the Honoapi'ilani Hwy.), Ka'anapali. www.cjsmaui.com. ✆ **808/667-0968.** Breakfast items $5–$10; lunch items $8–$19; Hāna Lunch Box and Air Travel Lunch Box $12 each. Daily 7am–8pm.

HONOKŌWAI, KAHANA & NĀPILI

Note: You'll find the restaurants in this section on the "Hotels & Restaurants in West Maui" map (p. 361).

Moderate

Maui Brewing Co. ★ BREWPUB The island's only microbrewery offers beer flights at the bar, excellent pub fare—much of it beer-battered—and ice cream floats made with coconut porter instead of root beer! (The brewery makes a fine root beer, too.) You can try limited-release brews here, along with the company's standards: Bikini Blonde

Ale, Big Swell IPA, Mana Wheat, and the aforementioned rich and chocolatey coconut porter. Note the cute lamps made from miniature kegs. This eco-friendly, community-minded business regularly donates a portion of its sales to the Maui Forest Bird Recovery Project. Also in Kīhei at 605 Lipoa Pkwy. (✆ **808/213-3002**).

At the Kahana Gateway Shopping Center, 4405 Honoapi'ilani Hwy. www.mauibrewingco.com. ✆ **808/669-3474.** Main courses $12–$25. Daily 11am–10pm.

Sea House Restaurant ★ PACIFIC RIM Old-fashioned and a bit dated, this oceanfront restaurant at the Nāpili Kai Beach Resort is a throwback to earlier days. But the view here can't be beat. Breakfast is lovely under the umbrellas outside, overlooking serene Nāpili Bay. The oven-baked Crater pancake is a special treat, made with custard batter. Sunset is a good time to come, too. Sit at the **Whale Watcher's Bar** and order classic cocktails and poke nachos.

At the Nāpili Kai Beach Resort, 5900 Honoapi'ilani Hwy. www.napilikai.com. ✆ **808/669-1500.** Main courses $7–$12 breakfast, $10–$16 lunch, $24–$38 dinner, appetizer menu $3–$6 served 2–5pm. Daily 7am–9pm.

Inexpensive

Maui Tacos ★ MEXICAN Many years ago, Mark Ellman launched this restaurant chain, dedicated to Mexican food with "Mauitude." Now it has locations as far away as Minnesota. Ellman has since moved on, but his successor's healthful take on fast food is still worth a try. Menu choices include fish tacos, chimichangas, and "surf burritos," loaded with charbroiled chicken or slow-cooked Hawaiian pork, black beans, rice, and salsa. Other locations are at Lahaina Square, Lahaina (✆ **808/661-8883**); Kama'ole Beach Center, Kīhei (✆ **808/879-5005**); Pi'ilani Village, Kīhei (✆ **808/875-9340**); and Ka'ahumanu Center, Kahului (✆ **808/871-7726**).

At Nāpili Plaza, 5095 Nāpili Hau St., Lahaina. ✆ **808/665-0222.** All items $5–$12. Mon–Sat 9am–9pm; Sun 9am–8pm.

Pizza Paradiso Mediterranean Grill ★ ITALIAN/MEDITERRANEAN The pledge on the wall at this Honokōwai hot spot—to use organic, local ingredients wherever possible and treat employees like family—gives a hint to the quality of food here. The large ish menu includes gourmet and gluten-free pizzas with terrific toppings (barbecue chicken, smoked Gouda, cilantro), chicken shawarma, lamb gyros, kabobs, pastas, and more. The kitchen makes its own meatballs, out of grass-fed Maui Cattle Company beef, and its own sauces and dressings. But save room for dessert. The tiramisu is an award winner, and the locally made coconut gelato should be.

At the Honokōwai Marketplace, 3350 Lower Honoapi'ilani Rd., Ka'anapali. www.pizzaparadiso.com. ✆ **808/667-2929.** Pastas $9–$11; pizzas $16–$27. Daily 10am–9pm.

KAPALUA

Note: You'll find the restaurants in this section on the "Hotels & Restaurants in West Maui" map (p. 361).

Expensive

Banyan Tree ★★ PACIFIC RIM At the edge of the pool at the Ritz-Carlton, Kapalua, this elegant dining room serves beautifully prepared dishes, many inspired by local farms. Fat Hāmākua mushrooms and crispy baby parsnip accompany the Kula corn and farro risotto. Succulent braised short ribs come in a pool of creamy kabocha pumpkin. The bouillabaisse features a lemongrass-scented Kona lobster broth with prawns, scallops, octopus, and island snapper. The "garden to glass" cocktail menu is especially inspired, with muddled herbs and eclectic combinations. My favorite is the Aloha E Ka La—a tantalizing mix of fresh-squeezed grapefruit juice, peach vodka, dry rosé, honey syrup, orange bitters, and crushed sage leaves. For a little bit of drama at dessert, order the flaming crème brûlée.

At the Ritz-Carlton, Kapalua Resort 1 Ritz-Carlton Dr., Lahaina. www.ritzcarlton.com/kapalua. ✆ **808/665-7096.** Reservations recommended. Dinner main courses $29–$65. Tues–Sat 5:30–9:30pm.

Merriman's Kapalua ★★ PACIFIC RIM Merriman's Kapalua sits on a rocky point jutting out into the Pacific, overlooking picturesque Kapalua Bay and the island of Moloka'i in the distance. As you might have guessed, it belongs to Peter Merriman, a James Beard award–winning chef who helped launch the Hawai'i Regional Cuisine movement in the 1990s and has restaurants on the Big Island and Kaua'i. He continues to champion the farm-to-table concept here, serving Keahole lobster with crispy pumpkin polenta and collards grown down the road. Sautéed taro cakes come with plump and meaty Hāmākua mushrooms. For the full Merriman's experience, order the "Pupu Taster," an entree sampler that includes the lobster, kalua pig, crispy Hawai'i Island goat cheese, and fresh 'ahi poke. Book a reservation just before sunset to soak in the sensational scenery. If twilight tables are booked, come anyway and enjoy a handcrafted Mai Tai with *lilikoi* foam on the large patio out on the point. It's an exceedingly romantic spot; don't be surprised if you see a "Just Maui'd" couple stroll by or witness a neighboring diner propose.

One Bay Club Place, Kapalua Resort, Kapalua. www.merrimanshawaii.com. ✆ **808/669-6400.** Reservations recommended. Dinner main courses $24–$62. Daily 5:30–9pm. Point Bar menu daily 3–9pm.

Moderate

Pineapple Grill ★★ PACIFIC RIM This gracious dining room on the Bay golf course offers views of the azure Pacific in one direction and the misty West Maui Mountains in the other. The menu has some real winners; my favorites are the braised short ribs and the pistachio-encrusted 'ahi with coconut-scented forbidden black rice. The wine program is inspired; the glass-enclosed cellar is huge, and on Wednesday select bottles are 50% off and glasses are discounted 25%. The signature dessert is irresistible: moist pineapple upside-down cake with Hāna Bay dark-rum sauce and macadamia nut ice cream. For late risers (or those who simply crave Belgian waffles or crispy masa huevos rancheros with braised pork chili verde), brunch is served on weekends until 2:00pm.

At the Kapalua Golf Club Bay Course, 200 Kapalua Dr., Kapalua. www.pineapplekapalua.com. ✆ **808/669-9600.** Reservations recommended for dinner. Main courses $14–$20 breakfast and lunch, $19–$60 dinner. Daily 8am–9:30pm.

Plantation House Restaurant ★★ PACIFIC RIM A dramatic destination for breakfast, lunch, or dinner, the Plantation House sits amid lush golf greens. Make sure to arrive early enough to enjoy the panoramic ocean views. Chef Jojo Vasquez's menu features simple yet sophisticated preparations that draw on an international culinary vocabulary. His *kampachi* tartare, lightly dressed in dashi soy and decorated with a spicy nasturtium flower, is bright and fresh. The *monchong* (pomfret), served in tamarind coriander broth, is a perfect balance of sweet, sour, and salty flavors. At breakfast, enjoy a bowl of flawlessly ripe tropical fruit or choose from "Six Degrees of Benediction," a half-dozen Benedicts made with such delicacies as lox, roasted Maui vegetables (superb), or seared ahi and wasabi hollandaise. On Friday nights, the chef and his wife team up to present "Beats and Eats," specialty cocktails and appetizers served with DJ Eliza's smooth tunes.

At the Kapalua Golf Club Plantation Course, 2000 Plantation Club Dr., Kapalua. www.cohnrestaurants.com/plantationhouse. ✆ **808/669-6299.** Reservations recommended. Main courses $9–$19 breakfast, $11–$20 lunch, $29–$47 dinner. Daily 8am–9pm.

Sansei Seafood Restaurant & Sushi Bar ★★ PACIFIC RIM/SUSHI With its creative take on sushi (think foie gras nigiri and "Pink Cadillac" rolls with eel, shrimp, *tamago,* and veggies wrapped in light pink rice paper), Sansei's menu scores higher with adventurous diners than with purists. But expertly sliced sashimi platters and straightforward gobo rolls will accommodate even the pickiest sushi snobs. Small and big plates are meant for sharing, though you'll fight over the last bites of misoyaki butterfish. The Dungeness crab ramen ranks as my favorite—I like to inhale the fragrant truffle broth flecked with cilantro, Thai basil, and jalapeños. For dessert, most people go for tempura-fried ice cream or the Granny Smith apple tart with homemade caramel sauce. ***Tip:*** On Thursday and Friday nights, a rousing karaoke session erupts at the bar from 10pm to 1am and sushi is 50% off. At the second location in Kīhei Town Center, Kīhei (✆ **808/879-0004**), sushi is 50% off on Sunday and Monday from 5 to 6:30pm.

600 Office Rd., Kapalua Resort, Kapalua. www.sanseihawaii.com. ✆ **808/669-6286.** Reservations recommended. Main courses $16–$43. Daily 5:30–10pm.

South Maui

KĪHEI/MĀ'ALAEA

Note: You'll find the Kīhei restaurants in this section on the "Hotels & Restaurants in South Maui" map (p. 367).

Moderate

Cafe O'Lei Kīhei ★ STEAK/SEAFOOD Over the years, chefs Michael and Dana Pastula have opened multiple Cafe O'Lei restaurants across Maui. Every one has been a winner, and this one is nicest of all. The open, airy dining room is casual and inviting, with hardwood floors, tables separated by sheer curtains, a big circular bar in the center of the restaurant, and a sushi bar and brick oven in back. The food is delicious and a bargain to boot. Call ahead for a midday table—locals flood this place during their lunch break. For dinner, the Maui onion soup (baked in the wood-burning oven) is a savory treat with fresh thyme and brandy. The *togarashi* (chili) and sesame-seared 'ahi with ginger butter sauce and wasabi aioli over steamed rice is as good as you'll find at fancier restaurants, here for nearly half the price. This is a great place to bring a group—the diverse menu offers something for everyone, from prime rib to sushi and even pizza with gluten-free crusts.

2439 S. Kīhei Rd., Kīhei. www.cafeoleirestaurants.com. ✆ **808/891-1368.** Reservations recommended. Main courses $7–$13 lunch, $15–$27 dinner. Daily 10:30am–3:30pm and 4:30–9:30pm.

Cow Pig Bun ★★ AMERICAN The anonymous entryway through the black glass building at the Maui Tech Park should tip you off: This is something different for Maui. For starters, it's open long after most island residents have knocked off for the day. This hole-in-the-wall hosts late-night "knife fights," during which local celebrity chefs battle for the CPB crown. It's crazy, decadent fun, worth postponing bedtime for. From lunchtime onward, this eatery supports the gluttonous celebration of pork, beef, bourbon, and beer. Indulgent burgers are served on brioche buns and topped with bacon jam, bourbon pickled veggies, or Sriracha aioli. The pork belly banh mi comes with foie gras butter. The Brussels sprouts and mac and cheese both have devout fans—maybe something to do with bacon?

In the Kīhei Tech Park., 535 Lipoa Pkwy., Ste. 100, Kīhei. www.cowpigbun.com. ✆ **808/875-8100.** Main courses $15–$24. Daily 11am–2am.

Monsoon India ★ INDIAN If there's one thing Maui could use more of, it's Indian flavors. Thank goodness for Monsoon India, a humble restaurant at the north edge of Kīhei—without it, we'd have to board a plane to enjoy piping-hot naan bread and crisp papadum. The chicken korma here is creamy and fragrant, the chana masala spicy and satisfying. Even the simple dal curry is delightful. With tables that overlook Mā'alaea Bay, this serene spot is lovely just before sunset—particularly during winter when whales are jumping. ***Note:*** The open-air dining room is closed when it rains.

In the Menehune Shores Bldg., 760 S. Kīhei Rd., Kīhei. www.monsoonindiamaui.com. ✆ **808/875-6666.** Main courses $15–$28. Daily 5–9pm; Wed–Sun 11:30am–2pm.

Pita Paradise ★ GREEK/MEDITERRANEAN For fresh, flavorful Greek food cooked to order and served with creamy tzatziki sauce and rice pilaf, head to this oasis in Wailea. Owner Johnny Arabatzis, Jr., catches his own fish, which he prepares with dill scallionaise and roasted red peppers. The roasted lamb shank with gnocchi and fennel puree is a delight, if a bit heavy. A trickling fountain serenades the tables in the courtyard, which sometimes hosts musicians and belly dancers. The baklava ice cream cake is exquisite—though definitely enough to share.

34 Wailea Gateway Center. www.pitaparadisehawaii.com. ✆ **808/879-7177.** Lunch main courses $8–$15; dinner main courses $16–$30. Daily 11am–9:30pm.

Inexpensive

Joy's Place ★ HEALTHY DELI Nourish yourself with nutritious, delicious meals at this small cafe, where the emphasis is on healthful living. For breakfast, rev your engine with an acai bowl or a still-warm spelt muffin. Soups are made daily, and the sandwiches are huge, with thick slices of nitrate-free turkey piled onto sprouted grain bread—or, if you prefer, packed into a collard-green wrap. Most ingredients are organic.

In the Island Surf Bldg., 1993 S. Kīhei Rd. (entrance on Auhana St.), Kīhei. www.joysplacemauihawaii.com. ✆ **808/879-9258.** All items under $12. Mon–Sat 7:30am–4pm.

WowWow Lemomande ★ CAFE/JUICE BAR The cashiers at this permanent lemonade stand are a testament to their product: sweet, wholesome, and helpful. Choose from an array of fresh-squeezed lime- and lemonades made with local honey, strawberry, *lilikoi,* watermelon, mint, and basil. Purchase a custom Mason jar (complete with cozy and reusable straw), and your future drinks are discounted. Trust us, you'll want to return as often as possible. The açai and pitaya bowls are enormous and generously loaded with goodies: coconut custard, cacao, bee pollen, taro, and apple bananas. Smoothies have similar ingredients, blended with sprouted almond or coconut milk.

1279 S. Kīhei Rd. (in Azeka's II), Kīhei. www.wowwowhawaiianlemonade.com. ✆ **808/344-0319.** All items under $12. Daily 7:30am–4pm.

WAILEA

Note: You'll find the restaurants in this section on the "Hotels & Restaurants in South Maui" map (p. 367).

Expensive

Capische? ★★★ FRENCH/ITALIAN Capische? is an intimate, sensual destination, whether you dine in the torch-lit garden surrounded by fresh herbs or up on the lānai soaking in the sunset. Chef/owner Brian

Etheredge harvests produce from an on-site garden and offers a 100%-organic tasting menu. The kitchen cures its charcuterie from locally raised Berkshire pigs, just as Italian chefs have done for generations. The Caesar crudo tops a few seared romaine leaves with Kona kampachi dressed in abalone vinaigrette, garlic aioli, and a sprinkling of black salt. It's phenomenal, and it's just the start. Hand-cut pasta, risotto, and gnocchi are paired with such rich and expertly prepared entrees as aromatic braised lamb shank or aged ribeye. The cioppino is a revelatory mix of lobster, shrimp, and clams steeped in a saffron broth so tantalizing you'll want to drink it straight from the bowl.

At the Hotel Wailea, 555 Kaukahi St., Wailea. www.capische.com. © **808/879-2224.** Reservations recommended. Main courses $35–$55. Mon–Sat 5:30–9:30pm.

Ferraro's Bar e Ristorante ★★ ITALIAN The stunning location—overlooking Wailea Beach with an unobstructed view of the West Maui Mountains—sets the stage for a romantic (if pricey) repast, whether you dine beneath sun-splashed umbrellas by day or the starry sky at night. For lunch, indulge your inner celebrity: Sip a Prosecco or blueberry mojito and snack on a lobster sandwich or roasted pear and Gorgonzola pizza pulled from the wood-burning oven. As the sun sinks into the Pacific, the atmosphere transforms. Live classical music casts a spell over the terraced dining area. The breadbaskets are sumptuous, freshly baked with flecks of olive. You have your choice of two sea salts to season your meal, should you so desire. The entrees are not particularly adventurous—braised veal shank osso buco with saffron risotto, and striped seabass with roasted potatoes and lemon butter sauce—but they are delivered in flawless fashion. The desserts, which change often, are creative and worth every calorie.

At the Four Seasons Resort Maui at Wailea, 3900 Wailea Alanui Dr., Wailea. www.fourseasons.com/maui. © **808/874-8000.** Reservations recommended. Main courses $19–$28 lunch, $34–$52 dinner. Daily 11:30am–9pm (beverages served from 11am).

Ka'ana Kitchen ★★★ HAWAI'I REGIONAL CUISINE You can hardly tell where the dining room ends and the kitchen begins in this bright, open restaurant. Sit ringside where you can watch chef Isaac Bancaco in action. Start off with a hand-mixed cocktail and the grilled octopus: fat chunks of tender meat tossed with frisée, watercress, and goat cheese. The 'ahi tataki is edible artwork: ruby-red tuna, heirloom tomato, and fresh burratta decorated with black salt and nasturtium petals. Don't be thrown by Bancaco's grid menu. Treat it like a gourmet bingo card; every combo is a winner. Breakfasts here are among the island's best, with local poached eggs, Moloka'i sweet potatoes, and creative bento boxes packed with fried rice and pickled vegetables. The $45 buffet grants you access to the kitchen's novel chilled countertops, which are stocked with every delicacy and fresh juice you could imagine.

At the Andaz Maui, 3550 Wailea Alanui Dr., Wailea. www.maui.andaz.hyatt.com. ✆ **808/573-1234.** $47 breakfast buffet, main courses $19–$29, $17–$56 dinner. Daily 6:30–11am and 5:30–9pm.

KŌ ★★ GOURMET PLANTATION CUISINE *Kō* is Hawaiian for sugarcane, and this restaurant revives the melting pot of Maui's bygone plantation days. Chef Tylun Pang takes the ethnic foods of the islands' Japanese, Filipino, Chinese, Portuguese, and Korean immigrants and presents them in gourmet fashion. The "'ahi on the rock" appetizer is my favorite: large squares of seasoned ruby-red tuna delivered with a hot *ishiyaki* stone. Sear the 'ahi on the rock to your desired temperature, and then submerge it in an orange-ginger miso sauce. The paella, fat chunks of lobster, shrimp, scallops, and chorizo simmered in a rich saffron broth, is also fantastic. If dishes sound unfamiliar, let your waiter guide you. On Sunday, a special Hawaiian *luulau* is served: Fresh fish, shellfish, and bok choy are wrapped in ti leaves and steamed. Served with jasmine rice, it's a marvelous re-creation of a traditional island meal. Monthly wine-makers' dinners here are special treats; check the website for dates. At lunchtime, you can order small portions of many of the dinner entrees, as well as 'ahi sandwiches and *paniolo* burgers.

Fairmont Kea Lani Maui, 4100 Wailea Alanui Dr., Wailea. www.korestaurant.com. ✆ **808/875-4100.** Reservations recommended. Main courses $14–$28 lunch, $28–$58 dinner. Lunch 11:30am–2:30pm, dinner 5–9pm.

Longhi's ★ ITALIAN After a tough day sunbathing or shopping, head to the bar at Longhi's for an elegant *pau hana* (finish work) martini. The breezy restaurant with its trademark black-and-white-checkered floor is a great backdrop for breakfast, too. Luxurious lobster eggs Benedict is certainly worth waking up for, served on thick slices of grilled Italian bread. If an omelet is more your style, you can get that with lobster too, along with spinach and fresh mozzarella. At lunch and dinner, standard Italian fare is served: eggplant Parmesan, pasta Bolognese, and fresh fish. The restaurant's most coveted item isn't even on the menu: the cheesy jalapeño pizza bread. It's served free with dinner, but you should ask for a few slices, even at breakfast.

At the Shops at Wailea, 3750 Wailea Alanui Dr., Wailea. www.longhis.com. ✆ **808/891-8883.** Breakfast items $10–$21; lunch items $11–$38; dinner main courses $29–$120. Mon–Fri 8am–10pm; Sat–Sun 7:30am–10pm.

Mala Wailea ★★ HAWAI'I REGIONAL CUISINE/SEAFOOD This Wailea resort restaurant doesn't have the intimacy of its cousin, Mala Ocean Tavern in Lahaina (p. 395), but it's still a delicious destination with a nearly identical menu. Beloved chef/restaurateur Mark Ellman knows how to craft locally sourced dishes that are both health conscious and full of flavor. (One of the pioneers of Hawai'i Regional Cuisine, he also owns **Honu** [p. 392], and **Frida's** [p. 392].) Specials include the wonderful fried Tamashiro tofu with coconut peanut sauce and Thai basil, and a moist panko-crusted snapper with Moloka'i sweet potato mash. There's an entire menu of gluten-free and vegan items. If that doesn't apply to you, I recommend the insanely rich mac and cheese. In the a.m., don't miss the killer French toast drizzled with house-made caramel sauce and tropical fruit—it's the breakfast version of Ellman's legendary Caramel Miranda dessert.

Wailea Beach Marriott Resort & Spa, 3700 Wailea Alanui Dr., Wailea. www.malawailea.com. ✆ **808/875-9394.** Reservations recommended. Breakfast buffet $29, main courses $14–$25; dinner main courses $14–$55. Daily 6:30–11am and 5:30–9:30pm; bar until 10pm.

Morimoto Maui ★★★ JAPANESE/PERUVIAN Iron Chef Masaharu Morimoto's poolside restaurant is sedate and spare, directing all of the attention to the culinary fireworks. The immaculate kitchen houses a space-age freezer full of fish bought at auction, and a rice polisher that ensures that every grain is perfect. The tasting menu starts with Morimoto-san's signature appetizer, the toro tartare. Balanced on ice, it's edible artwork. A tilted rectangle offers up a delectable smear of minced Kindai bluefin tuna, accented by colorful stripes of condiments: black nori paste, creamy green avocado, wasabi, crème fraîche, Maui onion, and tiny yellow rice crackers. A chilled Japanese mountain peach serves as a palate cleanser. The chef's tribute to Maui features locally caught 'opakapaka (pink snapper) in Thai curry with *pohole* fern, plump mussels, and sushi rice, topped with grilled bananas that balance the curry's heat. Everything is indulgent here: A *chawanmushi* (Japanese custard) is flavored with foie gras and topped with slivered duck breast; spicy Spanish octopus comes in Morimoto's angry sauce; and an amazing crispy, salty, fatty seared pork is amplified by sweet *poha* berry and applesauce. For dessert, the resourceful pastry chef uses leftover rice shavings to create an earthy panna cotta paired with miso butterscotch ice cream and crowned with a wee wasabi sprout. The incredibly decadent lunch features flatbreads, sushi, Asian-inspired sandwiches, and many of the items served at dinner.

At the Andaz Maui, 3550 Wailea Alanui Dr., Wailea. www.maui.andaz.hyatt.com. ✆ **808/573-1234.** Main courses $18–$39 lunch, $36–$150 dinner. Daily 11:30am–9pm.

Spago ★★★ ASIAN FUSION/NEW AMERICAN Wolfgang Puck is Spago's celebrity chef/owner, but the magic in this kitchen belongs to Cameron Lewark. At the gorgeous restaurant tucked into the posh lobby of the Four Seasons, Lewark dazzles diners with dishes that are flavorful but light—not burdened by heavy sauces. If he tried to remove the 'ahi sesame-miso cones from the menu, fans would probably riot. This appetizer is perfection: bright red. spicy 'ahi spooned into a crunchy, sweet, and nutty cone and topped with flying fish roe. His Thai seafood curry with kaffir lime and green papaya salad is a gourmet version of the traditional staple—and it excels on every level. The Chinois lamb chops are worth the steep price tag. During truffle season, fragrant shavings of black or white truffles can be added to your dish. If you're a vegetarian, this is heaven. Chef Lewark is masterful at preparing vegetables in unexpected and wonderful ways—consider his foamy tomato "cappuccino" or the sesame-miso cones with hearts of palm standing in for 'ahi. Seating hangs over the elegant pool with Pacific views, and the bartenders pour handcrafted libations with clever names: Pavlov's Dog, Tainted Love, and Rolling Fog Over Mount Fuji.

At the Four Seasons Resort Maui at Wailea, 3900 Wailea Alanui Dr., Wailea. www.fourseasons.com/maui. ✆ **808/879-2999.** Reservations required. Main courses $39–$135. Daily 6–9:30pm. Bar with appetizers daily 6–11pm.

Moderate

Fabiani's ★ ITALIAN At the top of tony Wailea, this little bistro serves the most affordable breakfast, lunch, and dinner in the neighborhood. Come here early in your stay because you'll want to return. The Italian-born chef turns out tasty pastas and pizzas for literally half the price of spots down the road. Sate your hunger with chef Lorenzo's meat lasagna—a rich medley of Italian sausage, ground beef, pork, marinara, and béchamel sauce. Make your own thin-crust Italian-style pizza with an array of gourmet toppings—a selection you won't find elsewhere on island—including mascarpone, Kalamata olives, shrimp, and pancetta. The bakery offers tempting French macaroons: pistachio and caramel sea salt, among others. A second location is in Kīhei (95 E. Lipoa St., #101; ✆ **808/874-0888**).

In the Wailea Gateway Plaza, 34 Wailea Gateway Place, #A101, Wailea. www.fabianis.com. ✆ **808/874-1234.** Main courses $12–$29. Daily 8am–9pm.

Gannon's ★ HAWAI'I REGIONAL CUISINE/AMERICAN Set up above the Mākena and Wailea coastline, this clubhouse on the Wailea Gold golf course has spectacular views in every direction. Award-winning chef Bev Gannon—the culinary force behind Hāli'imaile General Store (p. 410)—has brought her gourmet-style comfort food to Wailea. The restaurant opens at 8:30am for continental breakfast, but the kitchen doesn't get cranking until 10:30am, when you can dine on crab-cake eggs Benedict or a fancy loco moco with Kobe beef, kimchi, and crispy Maui onions. At night, when the view isn't a lure, it's fun to sit at the sparkly **Red Bar.** Dig into ginger hoisin barbecue ribs or an 'ahi tempura roll. The raw bar features flash-cured hamachi with honey yuzu vinaigrette—yum. Handcrafted cocktails include the refreshing Wailea Spritz (Aperol and Prosecco with a dash of passionfruit puree) or the Road to Hana (Maui vodka with orchid guava liqueur and ginger syrup).

At the Wailea Gold Golf Course, 100 Wailea Golf Club Dr., Wailea. www.gannonsrestaurant.com. ✆ **808/875-8080.** Reservations recommended for dinner. Main courses $14–$24 brunch, $26–$70 dinner. Daily 8:30am–9pm.

Upcountry Maui

Note: You'll find the restaurants in this section on the "Upcountry & East Maui" map (p. 379).

HĀLI'IMAILE (ON THE WAY TO UPCOUNTRY MAUI)

Moderate

Hāli'imaile General Store ★★ HAWAI'I REGIONAL/AMERICAN Three decades ago Bev Gannon, one of the pioneering chefs of Hawai'i Regional Cuisine, brought her gourmet comfort food to this renovated plantation store in rural Hāli'imaile. It was a gamble then; now it's one of the island's most beloved restaurants. Menu items reflect island cuisine with hints of Texas, from which Gannon hails. The Asian duck tostada, for example, pairs shredded duck with ginger chili dressing, jicama, and toasted macadamia nuts in a crispy lumpia shell. The warm goat cheese tart comes with slivered poached pears, fennel, and pine nuts. Sauces can be rich (and too many at one time hard to digest), so it's best to stick to one or two items rather than ordering a bunch to share. That rule does not apply to the sashimi Napoleon, however. The creamy wasabi vinaigrette that the waiter pours atop your stack of 'ahi tartare, smoked salmon, and wonton chips *is* rich, but worth the indulgence. Sound ricochets in this vintage camp store, with its polished wooden floors, high ceilings, and open kitchen. It's quieter in the back room, which is worth exploring anyway for its rotating exhibit of paintings by top local artists. Vegetarians: Ask for the extensive veggie menu.

900 Hāli'imaile Rd., Hāli'imaile. www.hgsmaui.com. ✆ **808/572-2666.** Reservations recommended. Main courses $16–$26 lunch, $20–$46 dinner. Mon–Fri 11am–2:30pm; daily 5:30–9pm.

MAKAWAO & PUKALANI

Moderate

Market Fresh Bistro ★ HAWAIIAN/MEDITERRANEAN At this off-the-beaten-path bistro, chef Justin Pardo steadfastly adheres to the locavore ethic: Nearly everything he serves is grown within a few miles of the kitchen. Because of this, the menu changes daily. Salads are exceptional here, with slivered rainbow radishes, heirloom carrots, and greens picked literally that morning. Past entrees have included Kupa'a Farm taro-crusted fish with asparagus in fennel-saffron tomato jus, and lamb ragout atop 2-inch-wide pasta ribbons. Breakfasts in the shaded courtyard will transport you to the French countryside: Thick slices of wheat toast slathered in house-made *lilikoi* (passionfruit) jam accompany omelets stuffed with goat cheese, mushroom, and pesto. The high-quality ingredients are fresh off the farm, and you can taste it. The front of the house is managed by Pardo's sister and brother-in-law, who are alternately gracious and aloof—stay on their good side if you can. On

Thursday night, the team serves prix-fixe farm dinners, seven courses for $75 (more with wine pairing).

3620 Baldwin Ave., Makawao. www.marketfreshbistro.com. ✆ **808/572-4877.** Reservations recommended for dinner. Breakfast $10–$13; lunch $10–$15; dinner $28–$34. Tues–Sat 9–11am; Tues–Sat 11:30am–3pm; Sun 9am–2pm; Thursday prix-fixe 6–8:30pm.

Inexpensive

Casanova Italian Restaurant & Deli ★ ITALIAN On the corner of Baldwin and Makawao avenues, this upcountry institution serves wonderful Italian fare at a sit-down restaurant and an attached cozy deli. The deli serves simple breakfasts (omelets with fresh mozzarella, and buttermilk muffins and bagels loaded with lox and capers) and terrific sandwiches for lunch. Try the New York meatball on a baguette, or the goat cheese and eggplant on focaccia. The deli's outdoor barstool seating makes a great perch for observing the Makawao traffic—always entertaining. The restaurant proper opens for lunch and serves a range of pastas and pizzas baked in a brick oven, and tables are set with white linens. At dinner, snack on freshly baked focaccia with olive oil and balsamic vinegar while waiting for your entree; the truffle ravioli with sage sauce is a favorite of mine. Pizza is served until at least 10pm, and on many nights of the week the dance floor erupts to the sounds of live salsa or reggae music or visiting DJs—dinner earns you free admission. Check the website for the entertainment calendar.

1188 Makawao Ave., Makawao. www.casanovamaui.com. ✆ **808/572-0220.** Reservations recommended for dinner. Lunch items $9–$18; dinner main courses $14–$44. Mon–Sat 11:30am–2pm; daily 5:30–9pm. Dancing Wed and Fri–Sat 10pm–1:30am. Deli Mon–Sat 7:30am–5:30pm; Sun 8:30am–5:30pm.

KULA

Moderate

Kula Lodge ★ HAWAI'I REGIONAL/AMERICAN The Kula Lodge's restaurant is best at breakfast, when the prices are lower and the views through the picture windows have an eye-popping intensity. The million-dollar vista spans the flanks of Haleakalā, all of Central Maui, the emerald-green West Maui Mountains, and the Pacific Ocean on two coasts. The kitchen turns out decent eggs Benedicts, including one topped with fresh fish and a veggie version crowned with spinach, tomatoes, and feta cheese. The buttermilk pancakes with macadamia nuts are tasty, but avoid the bland loco moco (hamburger, rice, and a fried egg slathered in listless brown gravy). For dinner, your best bet is pizza baked in the brick oven outdoors (if it's fired up). Try the upcountry vegetable pie with San Marzano tomato sauce, smoked mozzarella, and herb-roasted veggies.

15200 Haleakalā Hwy. (Hwy. 377), Kula. www.kulalodge.com. ✆ **808/878-2517.** Main courses $9–$20 breakfast, $11–$28 lunch, $14–$42 dinner. Daily 7am–9pm.

Inexpensive

Grandma's Coffee House ★ COFFEEHOUSE/AMERICAN Alfred Franco's grandmother started growing and roasting coffee in remote and charming Kēōkea back in 1918. Five generations later, this family-run cafe is still fueled by homegrown Haleakalā beans and frequented by local *paniolo* (cowboys). Line up at the busy counter for espresso, home-baked pastries, hot oatmeal, scrambled eggs, or, on Sundays, eggs Benedict served on a cornmeal waffle. Rotating lunch specials include spinach lasagna, teriyaki chicken, and beef stew. Sit out on the scenic lānai where the air is always the perfect temperature and listen to a Hawaiian guitarist serenade his bygone sweethearts. Pick up a few lemon squares and a slice of pumpkin bread to go.

At the end of Hwy. 37, Kēōkea (about 6 miles before the Tedeschi Vineyards in 'Ulupalakua). www.grandmascoffee.com. ✆ **808/878-2140.** Most items under $10. Daily 7am–5pm.

La Provence ★★ BAKERY/FRENCH/PIZZA Hidden away up in Kula is a family-owned French bakery that's worth driving across the island for. Every item on the menu and stashed in the bakery case is exquisite. Get there early (well before noon) or risk arriving as the last almond croissants and mango blueberry scones walk out the door. Dine in the garden courtyard beside cyclists who've worked up appetites circumnavigating the island. The crepes, filled with Kula vegetables and goat cheese or salmon and spinach, have a secret addictive ingredient: béchamel sauce. On Sunday, eggs Benedict is served with perfect roasted potatoes and wild greens drizzled in a transcendent *lilikoi* balsamic dressing. For lunch, try the marvelous duck confit salad or roast chicken sandwich with melted Brie cheese. They're still ironing out the kinks of dinner service in their newly renovated space next door—but the exquisite filet mignon in puff pastry and lamb chops with peppercorn sauce are worth the gamble. Bring cash; there isn't an ATM for miles and they don't take credit cards.

3158 Lower Kula Hwy., Kula. ✆ **808/878-1313.** Breakfast $12–$13; lunch $12–$17; dinner $26–$32. Cash or check only. Wed–Sun 7am–2pm and 6–9pm.

East Maui

Note: You'll find the restaurants in this section on the "Upcountry & East Maui" map (p. 379).

PĀ'IA

Moderate

Charley's Restaurant ★ AMERICAN/MEXICAN Named after Charley P. Woofer—a spotted Great Dane—this North Shore institution serves food and music to the masses. This downtown Pā'ia hangout does double duty as a power-breakfast fuel station for windsurfers and an after-dark saloon with live music and DJs. It's also a decent place to grab a bite before heading out to Hāna. For breakfast, you'll find standards: omelets, pancakes, biscuits and gravy. Lunch is half-pound burgers (made from locally raised beef), fish and chicken sandwiches, Philly cheesesteaks, salads, and pizza. Dinner is grilled fish and steak—hearty, but nothing exciting.

142 Hāna Hwy., Pā'ia. www.charleysmaui.com. ✆ **808/579-8085.** Breakfast items $10–$16; lunch items $11–$12; dinner main courses $11–$22. Daily 7am–10pm; food served at the bar until 10pm.

Flatbread & Company ★★ PIZZA This family-friendly Pā'ia outpost embraces a locavore philosophy. The hand-colored menus highlight the best Maui farmers have to offer, particularly where the inventive daily *carne* and veggie specials are concerned. You can watch the chefs hand-toss organic dough, dress it with high-quality toppings—local goat cheese, macadamia-nut pesto, slow-roasted kalua pork, or homemade, nitrate-free sausage—and shovel it into the wood-burning furnace that serves as the restaurant's magical hearth. Salads come sprinkled with grated green papaya and dressing so delicious that everyone clamors for the recipe. Tuesdays are charity night: $3.50 of each flatbread sold benefits a local cause.

71 Baldwin Ave., Pa'ia. www.flatbreadcompany.com. ✆ **808/579-9999.** Reservations recommended. Entrees $15–$23. Daily 11am–10pm.

Milagros Food Company ★ SOUTHWESTERN/SEAFOOD You'll have a prime view of the Pā'ia action from the lānai of this corner restaurant. The kitchen turns out Tex-Mex dishes with Maui flair, such as blackened mahimahi tacos with salsa, cheese, fresh guacamole, and sweet chili sauce (sounds strange perhaps, but tastes great). You can also order Anaheim chili enchiladas, fajitas with sautéed vegetables finished in achiote glaze, a variety of burgers, and giant salads. The bar pours an assortment of fine tequilas, offering several flights so that you can compare flavors and no fewer than 10 different margaritas. Don Julio Reposado in a classic margarita on the rocks, please! The restaurant is sometimes open for breakfast; call ahead.

3 Baldwin Ave., Pa'ia. www.milagrosfoodcompany.com. ✆ **808/579-8755.** Main courses $12–$20. Daily 8am–10pm.

Inexpensive

Cafe des Amis ★★ CREPES/MEDITERRANEAN/INDIAN This sweet, eclectic restaurant serves crepes, curries, and Mediterranean platters that are fresh, tasty, and easy on the wallet. Crepes come with organic local greens and a dollop of sour cream. The breakfast crepe with Gruyère and ham is perfect any time of day, as is the Italian lentil crepe with pesto and mozzarella. The curries aren't exactly Indian, but they are delicious. Wraps come with cucumber raita; bowls with mango and tomato chutneys. Ask for the extra-hot habañero chutney on the side. The coconut shrimp curry is a fragrant blend of ginger, garlic, cinnamon, cilantro, and Bengal spices; the slow-cooked organic chicken curry has a creamy, tomato-y base. For dessert, sweet crepes are stuffed with melted Nutella or bananas and chocolate. The best espresso in Pā'ia is found here, along with some stiff *lilikoi* margaritas. Musicians often play beneath the twinkling lights in the courtyard seating area.

42 Baldwin Ave., Pa'ia. www.cdamaui.com. ✆ **808/579-6323.** All-day menu items: crepes $9–$12; main courses $15–$21. Daily 8:30am–8:30pm.

Maka ★★ VEGAN/JUICE BAR All of the North Shore's beautiful people eat or work at Maka, Pā'ia's vegan, gluten-free cafe—a gourmet offshoot of Mana Foods grocery store down the street. The clean, bright atmosphere is matched by the menu: fuchsia dragonfruit juices, jade green seaweed salads, and purple sweet-potato chili bowls. Everything is good, particularly the katsu tempeh sandwich served on a warm buckwheat waffle slathered with sun-dried tomato paste. A small kale Caesar salad accompanies sandwiches and wraps, which, under $10 apiece, are some of the best deals on the island. The dessert case yields treasures: feather-light *lilikoi* pies and cacao truffles studded with almonds and dehydrated strawberries. Naturally, kombucha is on tap.

115 Baldwin Ave., Pa'ia. www.makabymana.com. ✆ **808/579-9125.** Breakfast items $5–$8; lunch and dinner items $8–$14. Tues–Sun 10am–8pm.

Pā'ia Bay Coffee ★★ CAFE Tucked behind the San Lorenzo swimsuit shop, this garden coffee shop is Pā'ia's best-kept secret. Pop in for an expertly brewed espresso and a fresh-baked croissant or slice of banana bread and you'll see locals networking in shady corners over cappuccinos. The menu is a bit more sophisticated than that of your typical cafe. In addition to the standard bagel and lox, the kitchen turns out organic scrambled eggs and sandwiches garnished with brie, sliced green apple, microgreens, tomato, and black-pepper herb mayo. The vegan bagel is delicious—topped with roasted red peppers, local avocado, tomato, and pesto. The baristas are genuinely friendly and make everything with care here.

115 Hāna Hwy., Pa'ia. www.paiabaycoffee.com. ✆ **808/579-9125.** All items under $11. Daily 7am–5:30pm.

Pā'ia Fish Market ★ SEAFOOD At the corner of Baldwin Avenue and Hāna Highway in Pā'ia, this busy fish market must maintain its own fleet of fishing boats. How else to explain how the cooks can dish out filet after giant fresh filet for little more than it would cost to buy the same at the grocery? There's only one thing to order here: a fish sandwich. A giant slab of perfectly grilled 'ahi, opah, or 'opakapaka laid out on a bun with coleslaw and grated cheese is extra satisfying after a briny day at the beach.

110 Hāna Hwy., Pa'ia. www.paiafishmarket.com. ✆ **808/579-3111.** Lunch and dinner plates $10–$21. Daily 11am–9:30pm.

HA'IKŪ

Moderate

Colleen's at the Cannery ★ ECLECTIC This go-to spot for Ha'ikū residents serves an excellent breakfast, lunch, and dinner in a casual yet classy setting. Slide into a booth beside world-famous surfers, yoga teachers, and inspirational speakers: Maui's local celebrities. Wake up with an omelet stuffed with portobello mushroom and goat cheese, accompanied by organic chai or a spicy Bloody Mary, depending on your mood. For lunch, the roasted eggplant sandwich is served warm, with sun-dried tomatoes, carrots, and melted Muenster cheese. Hearty burgers are made from Maui Cattle Company beef, and pizzas are loaded with creative toppings. For dinner, the local fish specials are spot-on, rivaling some of the island's pricier restaurants—but service can be frustratingly inattentive here. The dessert case contains some treasures, including extra-rich espresso brownies and sweetly tart *lilikoi* (passionfruit) bars.

At the Ha'iku Cannery Marketplace, 810 Ha'iku Rd., Ha'iku. www.colleensinhaiku.com. ✆ **808/575-9211.** Reservations not accepted. Breakfast $8–$15; lunch $8–15; dinner main courses $9–$30. Daily 6am–10pm.

Nuka ★★ SUSHI Sushi chef Hiro Takanashi smiles from behind the bar as he turns out beautiful specialty rolls loaded with sprouts, pea shoots, avocado, and glistening red tuna. The garden-fresh ingredients served at this compact sushi restaurant reflect its rural Ha'ikū address, but its stylish decor suggests somewhere more cosmopolitan. Start with a side of house pickles or *kinpira gobo*—a salty, sweet, and sour mix of slivered burdock root. Then proceed to the sushi menu for excellent nigiri, sashimi, and rolls. Not up for sushi? The wonderful Nuka bowls—your choice of protein piled atop fresh herbs, crushed peanuts, sesame lime dressing, rice, and veggies—are deeply nourishing. For dessert, try the house-made black sesame ice cream. ***Tip:*** Nuka doesn't take reservations and is often packed; plan to eat early (before 6pm) or late (after 7:30pm) to avoid crowds.

780 Ha'iku Rd., Ha'iku. www.nukamaui.com. ✆ **808/575-2939.** Reservations not accepted. Dinner $8–$38. Daily 4:30–10pm.

ON THE ROAD TO HĀNA

Expensive

Mama's Fish House ★★★ SEAFOOD Overlooking idyllic Kū'au Cove on Maui's North Shore, this island institution is the realization of a South Pacific fantasy. Though pricey, a meal at Mama's is a complete experience. Recapture the grace of early Hawai'i when feasts lasted for days beneath the swaying palms. Wander through the landscaped grounds down to the restaurant, where smiling servers wear Polynesian prints and flowers behind their ears. The dining room features curved *lauhala*-lined ceilings, lavish arrangements of tropical flowers, and windows open wide to let the ocean breeze in. Every nook and cranny is decorated with some fanciful artifact of salt-kissed adventure. Start your repast with the coconut ceviche or the marvelous beef Polynesian—a garlicky mix of seared-steak morsels, tomatoes, and onion served in a papaya half. The menu lists the names of the anglers who reeled in the day's catch; you can order ono "caught by Keith Nakamura along the 40-fathom ledge near Hāna" or deepwater 'ahi seared with coconut and lime. As a finale, the Tahitian Pearl dessert is almost too stunning to eat: a shiny chocolate ganache sphere filled with *lilikoi* crème, set in an edible pastry clamshell. Everything is perfect, from the refreshing, umbrella-topped cocktails to the almond-scented hand towels passed out before dessert. As a parting shot, squares of creamy coconut *haupia* are delivered with your bill.

799 Poho Place, just off the Hāna Hwy., Kū'au. www.mamasfishhouse.com. ✆ **808/579-8488.** Reservations recommended for lunch, required for dinner. Main courses: $26–$48 lunch; $28–$62 dinner. Daily 11am–3pm and 4:15–9pm (last seating).

Inexpensive

Kū'au Store ★★ DELI This is one of my favorite spots on the North Shore for breakfast or lunch to go. The handsome convenience store and deli offers gourmet breakfast paninis, smoothies with all kinds of extras, fresh juices, kombucha on tap, shoyu chicken plate lunches, and pulled pork sandwiches. Inside the deli case you'll find quinoa salads and four types of *poke* (seasoned raw fish). The store is decorated with vintage maps of Maui. The espresso counter is built out of repurposed wood from the mart that was here before. The logo hats behind the register make great souvenirs. For an easy entrance and exit, park on the side street under the fantastic mural featuring surfers, sharks, and owls.

701 Hāna Hwy., Pā'ia. www.kuaustore.com. ✆ **808/579-8844.** Deli items $5–$10. Daily 6:30am–7pm.

HĀNA

Expensive

The Preserve Kitchen + Bar ★ HĀNA FUSION Breakfasts are luxurious here, where you can sip locally grown coffee while watching the *'iwa* (frigate birds) circle Kau'iki Hill. All day long the menu showcases Hāna-grown ingredients: The baby beet salad is a lavish affair with crunchy green beans and creamy goat cheese, and blanched *pohole* ferns decorate the 'ahi and Kona kampachi sashimi. For dinner, the togarashi seared scallops and the chimichurri Hāmākua mushrooms are irresistible. Hāna's only fine-dining restaurant has always struggled to assert itself; starting fresh with a new concept and chef, it might finally succeed.

At Travaasa Hāna, 5031 Hāna Hwy., Hāna. www.travaasa.com/hana. ✆ **808/248-8211.** Main courses: $12–$28 breakfast; $17–$32 lunch; $30–$50 dinner. Daily 7:30am–9pm.

Moderate

Hāna Ranch Restaurant ★ AMERICAN Dining options are slim in Hāna after 3pm, so you might find yourself hungry with nowhere else to eat. The ranch restaurant serves diner fare for slightly more than you'd pay elsewhere on Maui; adjust your expectations accordingly and you'll be satisfied. The service is friendly (if slow) and the portions are large. The seared 'ahi and coconut shrimp are better bets than the pasta.
2 Mill St. (off Hāna Hwy.), Hāna. ✆ **808/270-5280.** Lunch items $6–$17; dinner main courses $15–$35. Daily 11am–8:30pm.

Inexpensive

Barefoot Café ★ SNACKSHOP/CAFE Place your order for simple homespun fare at the window and eat at picnic tables facing picturesque Hāna Bay. This is the spot for an unpretentious East Maui breakfast: Choose from Benedicts, fried rice, eggs, and fresh baked goods. Although lunch and dinner (kalbi beef, saimin) are less inspired, this is still an affordable alternative to the neighboring resort restaurants. Cash only.
1632 Keawa Pl., Hāna. ✆ **808/446-5732.** Breakfast items $5–$10; lunch and dinner items $4–$8. Cash only. Daily 7–10am and 11am–8pm.

Hāna Farms ★★ CAFE/PIZZA/FARM STAND Just before Hāna proper, a series of thatched huts offers a bounty of locally grown treats. Baskets overflow with every variety of tropical fruit, Maui-grown coffee, and fresh-squeezed juices and ginger sodas (just the ticket if the drive has made you queasy). Stock up on coconut candy, hot sauce, *lilikoi* jam, and banana butter to slather on top of your choice of six banana breads. Everything is grown on the nearby farm, which is mostly organic. On Friday and Saturdays nights, the friendly, hip farm workers fire up the clay oven and bake gourmet pizzas with hilarious names (such as Porky Pine). It's the tastiest meal in town—but expect to wait an hour for your pie. To-go orders are beautifully wrapped in banana leaves.
2190 Hāna Hwy., Hāna. www.hanafarmsonline.com. ✆ **808/248-7553.** Snack items $3–$13; dinner main courses $13–$19. Farm stand Daily 7am–sunset. Dinner Fri–Sat 4–8pm.

MAUI SHOPPING

Maui's best shopping is found in the small, independent boutiques and galleries scattered around the island—particularly in Makawao and Pā'ia. (If you're in the market for a bikini, there's no better spot than the intersection of Baldwin Ave. and Hāna Hwy. on Maui's North Shore.) The two upscale resort shopping malls, the **Shops at Wailea** in South Maui and **Whalers Village** in Ka'anapali, have everything from Louis Vuitton to Gap—plus a handful of local designers to boot. If you're looking for that perfect souvenir, consider visiting one of Maui's farms (or farmer's markets), most of which offer fantastic value-added products. Take home Ka'anapali coffee, Kula lavender spice rub, Ocean Vodka (p. 323), Maui Gold pineapple, and other tasty treats that can be shipped worldwide.

Central Maui

KAHULUI

Kahului's shopping is concentrated in two malls. The **Maui Mall,** 70 E. Ka'ahumanu Ave. (www.mauimall.com; © **808/877-8952**), is home to **Whole Foods, Longs Drugs, T.J. Maxx,** and **Tasaka Guri Guri** (the decades-old purveyor of inimitable icy treats that are neither ice cream nor shave ice, but something in between) and Kahului's largest movie theater, a 12-screen megaplex that features mainly current releases.

Queen Ka'ahumanu Center, 275 Ka'ahumanu Ave. (www.queenkaahumanucenter.com; © **808/877-3369**), a 7-minute drive from the Kahului Airport, offers two levels of shops, restaurants, and theaters. It covers the bases, from arts and crafts to **Macy's** and everything in between: a thriving food court and mall standards like **Sears, Sunglass Hut,** and **Local Motion** (surf and beach wear). The **Maui Friends of the Library** (www.mfol.org; © **808/877-2509**) runs a new and used bookstore that is an excellent source for Hawai'i reading material. Like Tasaka Guri Guri, **Camellia Seed Shop** (© **808/877-5714**) is a throwback to plantation days when locals enjoyed strange sweet-and-sour treats made from pickled plum seeds. Give them a try!

Maui Swap Meet ★ For just 50¢, you're granted admission to a colorful maze of booths and tables occupying the Maui Community College's parking lot every Saturday from 7am to 1pm. Vendors come from across the island to lay out their treasures: fresh fruits and vegetables from Kula and Ke'anae, orchids, jewelry, ceramics, clothing, household items, homemade jams, and baked goods. It's fun to stroll around and "talk story" with the farmers, artists, and crafters. At Maui Community College in an area bounded by Kahului Beach Rd. and Wahine Pio Ave. (access via Wahine Pio Ave.). © **808/244-3100.**

WAILUKU

Wailuku's vintage architecture, antiques shops, and mom-and-pop eateries imbue the town with charm. You won't find any plastic aloha in Wailuku; in fact, this is the best place to buy authentic souvenirs.

Bailey House Museum Shop The small gift shop at the entrance of this wonderful museum offers a treasure trove of authoritative Hawaiiana, from hand-sewn feather hatbands to traditional Hawaiian games, music, and limited-edition books. Make sure to stroll through the gracious gardens and view Edward Bailey's paintings of early Maui. At the very least, take time to appreciate the massive koa outrigger canoe displayed outside. Bailey House Museum, 2375-A Main St. www.mauimuseum.org. © **808/244-3326.**

Bird of Paradise Unique Antiques Come here for old Matson liner menus, vintage aloha shirts, silk kimonos, and anything nostalgic that happens to be Hawaiian. Owner Joe Myhand collects everything from 1940s rattan furniture to Depression-era glass and lilting Hawaiian music on vinyl or cassette. 56 N. Market St. © **808/242-7699.**

Native Intelligence ★★★ This wonderful shop feels like a museum or gallery—only you can take the marvelous artifacts home with you. From the rich monkeypod wood floors to the collection of finely woven *lauhala* hats, shopping here is a feast for the senses. The store's owners are committed to supporting indigenous Hawaiian artisans, who come here both to shop and stock the shelves with artwork of the highest craftsmanship. Browse the truly Hawaiian keepsakes and gifts: locally designed Kealopiko clothing silkscreened with Hawaiian proverbs, *kukui* nut spinning tops, soaps scented with native herbs, and *lei o manu*—fierce war clubs fringed with shark teeth. You can also buy bags of fresh poi and the island's most precious leis, made of feathers, shells, or fragrant flowers. 1980 Market St., #2. www.native-intel.com. © **808/242-2421.**

Central Maui Edibles

Maui's produce has long been a source of local pride. You'll find fresh Maui-grown fruit, vegetables, flowers, and plants at the **Ohana Farmer's Market** at Queen Ka'ahumanu Shopping Center (© **808/877-3369**), every Tuesday, Wednesday, and Friday from 8am to 4pm.

In the northern section of Wailuku, **Takamiya Market,** 359 N. Market St. (© **808/244-3404**), is much loved by local folks and visitors with adventurous palates. People often drive all the way from Kīhei to stock up on picnic fare and mouthwatering ethnic foods for sunset gatherings. Unpretentious home-cooked foods from East and West are prepared daily and served on plastic-foam plates. The chilled-fish counter has fresh sashimi and poke, and prepared foods include shoyu chicken, fried squid, kalua pork, Chinese noodles, fiddlehead ferns, and Western comfort foods such as cornbread and potato salad.

West Maui

LAHAINA

Lahaina's merchants and art galleries go all out from 7 to 10pm every Friday, when **Art Night ★** brings an extra measure of hospitality and community spirit. The Art Night openings are usually marked with live entertainment and refreshments, plus a livelier-than-usual street scene. A free walking map of participating galleries is available at the **Lahaina Visitor Center** in the Old Lahaina Courthouse, 648 Wharf St. #101, Lahaina (www.visitlahaina.com; © **808/667-9175**).

Across from the seawall on Front Street, you'll find the **Outlets of Maui,** 900 Front St. (www.theoutletsofmaui.com; © **808/667-9216**). There's plenty of free validated parking and easy access to more than two dozen outlet shops, including **Calvin Klein, Coach, Banana Republic, Adidas, Kay Jewelers,** and more. **Ruth's Chris Steak House** serves its famed cuts of beef here, and the **Hard Rock Cafe** serves lunch and dinner with live music most nights.

At the northern end of Lahaina town, what was formerly a big, belching pineapple cannery is now a maze of shops and restaurants known as the **Lahaina Cannery Mall,** 1221 Honoapi'ilani Hwy. (www.lahainacannerymall.com; ✆ **808/661-5304**). Inside the air-conditioned building there's a **Longs Drugs** and a 24-hour **Safeway** for groceries. **Footprints Maui** may surprise you with its shoe selection—everything from Cole Haan sophisticates to inexpensive sandals. In the food court, try **Ba-Le French Sandwich and Bakery** for great banh mi and croissant sandwiches, while **L&L Drive-Inn** sells plate lunches. At **Lulu's Lahaina Surf Club & Grill,** you can get a frosty beer and watch big-wave surfers on the multiple flatscreen TVs.

Lahaina Arts Society Galleries ★ Since 1967, the Lahaina Arts Society has been promoting the excellent work of local artists. The society's two galleries inhabit the Old Lahaina Courthouse, the historic building that sits between Lahaina harbor and the giant banyan tree in the center of town. In addition to hosting changing monthly exhibits, the galleries are jam-packed with paintings, photography, ceramics, jewelry, and more. The artists host "Art in the Park" fairs several times each

Traditional crafts for sale at the Baldwin Home Museum in Lahaina.

month in the shade of the sprawling banyan tree (check the website for dates). 648 Wharf St. www.lahaina-arts.com. ✆ **808/661-0111.**

Lahaina Galleries ★ Sea creatures sculpted from bronze and wood greet you at the entrance of this Front Street haven for art. Whether you fancy Robert Bissell's whimsical portraits of elephants swarmed by monarch butterflies, Guy Buffet's Parisian cafe scenes, or Dario Campanile's provocative still lifes, this gallery has an artist and aesthetic for you. The knowledgeable staff is helpful and not prone to the high-pressured sales pitches of some nearby galleries. Also at the **Shops at Wailea** (3750 Wailea Alanui; ✆ **808/874-8583**). 828 Front St. www.lahainagalleries.com. ✆ **808/661-6284.**

Maui Hands ★★ This artists' collective has several consignment shops/galleries around the island, each teeming with handcrafted treasures by local artisans. You'll find Ni'ihau shell necklaces, vivid paintings of local beaches and tropical flowers, carved koa bowls and rocking chairs, screen-printed textiles, and one-of-a-kind souvenirs for every budget. The artists are on hand and happy to discuss their work. www.mauihands.com. Lahain: 612 Front St. ✆ **808/677-9898.** Pā'ia: 84 Hāna Hwy. ✆ **808/579-9245.** Makawao: 1169 Makawao. ✆ **808/572-2008.** Ka'anapali: In the Hyatt Regency, 200 Nohea Kai Dr., Ka'anapali. ✆ **808/667-7997.**

KA'ANAPALI

WHALERS VILLAGE This Ka'anapali Beach landmark offers everything from **Louis Vuitton** to **Tommy Bahama** and **Sephora,** with a few local designers in the mix. Find classy aloha wear at **Tory Richard** (✆ **808/667-7762**) and matching mother-daughter batik clothing at **Blue Ginger** (✆ **808/667-5793**). The **Sandal Tree** (✆ **808/667-5330**) has one of the best shoe selections on the island—including fashionable Olukai sandals with arch support. The **Totally Hawaiian Gift Gallery** (www.totallyhawaiian.com; ✆ **808/667-4070**) carries Ni'ihau shell jewelry, Norfolk pine bowls, and Hawaiian quilt kits. **Na Hoku** jewlers (www.nahoku.com; ✆ **808/667-5411**) offers stellar island-inspired sparkles and watches.

In contrast to most Maui shops, stores here remain open until 10pm. The complex is also home to the **Whalers Village Museum** (p. 305). Although under renovation at press time, its interactive exhibits and 40-foot sperm-whale skeleton are worth investigation. Parking at Whalers Village is unfortunately expensive; be sure to get validation. 2435 Ka'anapali Pkwy. www.whalersvillage.com. ✆ **808/661-4567.**

HONOKŌWAI, KAHANA & NĀPILI

Those driving north of Ka'anapali toward Kapalua will notice the **Honokō wai Marketplace,** on Lower Honoapi'ilani Road, only minutes before the Kapalua Airport. It houses restaurants and coffee shops, a dry cleaner, the flagship **Times Supermarket,** and a few clothing stores.

KAPALUA

Village Galleries ★ This well-regarded gallery showcases the finest regional artists in a small space inside the Ritz-Carlton lobby. View Pegge Hopper's iconic Hawaiian women, George Allan's luminous oil landscapes, and Betty Hay Freeland's colorful local scenes. Three-dimensional pieces include gemstone-quality Ni'ihau shell leis, hand-blown glass sculptures, and delicately turned bowls of Norfolk pine. The Ritz-Carlton's monthly artist-in-residence program features the gallery's artists in hands-on workshops (free, including materials). It has two additional locations in Lahaina, one at 120 Dickenson St. (✆ **808/661-4402**) and another in the Baldwin House's Master Reading Room at the corner of Dickenson and Front St. (✆ **808/661-5199**). At the Ritz-Carlton Kapalua, 1 Ritz-Carlton Dr. www.villagegalleriesmaui.com. ✆ **808/669-1800.**

South Maui

KĪHEI

Kīhei is one long stretch of strip malls. Most of the shopping is concentrated in the **Azeka Place Shopping Center** on South Kīhei Road. Across the street, **Azeka Place II** houses several prominent attractions, including a cluster of specialty shops with everything from children's clothes to shoes, sunglasses, and swimwear.

WAILEA

Shops at Wailea ★ This elegant high-end mall mainly features luxury brands (**Prada, Bottega Veneta, Tiffany & Co., Gucci**), but some unique gems are hidden amid the complex's 50-odd shops. **Martin & MacArthur** (✆ **808/891-8844**) sells luminous, curly koa bowls and keepsake boxes—or you could bring home a beautiful handmade Hawaiian musical instrument from **Mele 'Ukulele** (www.meleukulele.com; ✆ **808/879-6353**). When Paris Hilton shops for bling on Maui, she heads to **Maui Enchantress** (www.mauienchantress.com; ✆ **808/891-6360**), a pinker-than-thou boutique brimming with Swarovski crystal–studded slippers, glitter powder, fringed tank tops, and shell-encrusted silver mirrors. The mall is home to several good restaurants, and the **Island Gourmet Markets** offer affordable options for breakfast and lunch: everything from pastries to sushi, burgers, sandwiches, and gelato. 3750 Wailea Alanui. www.theshopsatwailea.com. ✆ **808/891-6770.**

Upcountry Maui

Hot Island Glassblowing Studio & Gallery ★ Watch glass blowers transform molten glass into artwork in this Makawao Courtyard studio. If you didn't witness it happening, you might not believe that the kaleidoscopic vases and charismatic marine animals were truly made out of the fragile, fiery-hot medium. Several artists show their work here; prices range from under $20 for pretty plumeria dishes to over $4,000 for stunning sculptural pieces. In the middle range are luminescent jellyfish floating in glass. 3620 Baldwin Ave. www.hotislandglass.com. © **808/572-4527.**

The Mercantile ★ Every texture in this boutique is sumptuous, from the cashmere sweaters to tooled leather belts. In addition to upscale men and women's clothing, you'll find Kiehl's cosmetics, Jurlique organic body products, eye-catching jewelry, and an assortment of French soaps and luxurious linens. 3673 Baldwin Ave. © **808/572-1407.**

Viewpoints Gallery ★★ This handsome gallery located in Makawao Courtyard features the museum-quality work of 40 established Maui artists. The front half is dedicated to revolving solo shows and invitational exhibits—including the annual Malama Wao Akua show, which celebrates native Hawaiian flora and fauna. The gallery's back half features works by collective artists: luminous oils by George Allan, breathtakingly realistic pastels by Kit Gentry, and ceramic tea sets brimming with personality by Christina Cowan. 3620 Baldwin Ave. www.viewpointsgallerymaui.com. © **808/572-5979.**

FRESH FLOWERS IN KULA

Like anthuriums on the Big Island, proteas are a Maui trademark and an abundant crop on Haleakalā's rich volcanic slopes. They also travel well, dry beautifully, and can be shipped worldwide with ease. **Proteas of Hawai'i,** 15200 Haleakalā Hwy., Kula (www.proteasofhawaii.com; © **808/878-2533,** ext. 210), located next door to the Kula Lodge, is a reliable source of this exotic flower.

UPCOUNTRY EDIBLES

Working folks in Makawao pick up spaghetti and lasagna, sandwiches, salads, and changing specials from the **Rodeo General Store,** 3661 Baldwin Ave. (© **808/572-1868**). At the back of the store, a superior wine selection is housed in its own temperature-controlled cave.

For nearly a century, the hard-working Komoda family has been satisfying Maui's sweet tooth. Untold numbers have creaked over the wooden floors to pick up a box of famous cream puffs at **T. Komoda Store and Bakery,** 3674 Baldwin Ave. (© **808/572-7261**). The coveted pastries (filled with vanilla or mocha cream) are just the beginning. Stick donuts encrusted with macadamia nuts, Chantilly cakes, fruit pies, and butter rolls keep loyal customers coming back. Old-timers know to arrive before noon or miss out. Bring cash and note the odd business hours (Mon, Tues, Thurs, Fri 7am–5pm and Sat 7am–2pm).

East Maui

PĀ'IA

Mana Foods ★★ The state's best health-food store hides behind an unimposing dark-green facade. Shopping at Mana Foods is an adventure, to be sure—parking can be a nuisance, and the narrow aisles inside are crammed with *nuevo* hippies, yoga instructors, and wild-haired children. Don't let this dissuade you. Though compact, this store has a better natural-foods selection than you'll find in most big cities—at great prices, too. The deli holds delicious fresh-made sushi, soups, salads, hot entrees, and raw desserts. The produce shelves are worthy of worship: pyramids of ripe avocados, local asparagus, and more tropical fruits than you have names for. Ask the stocker for a sample of rambutan or rolinia. Hit up the health and beauty room for locally made soaps and hard-to-find essential oils. 49 Baldwin Ave. www.manafoodsmaui.com. ✆ **808/579-8078.**

Maui Crafts Guild ★★ On the corner of Hāna Highway and Baldwin Avenue, this artists' collective features distinctive, high-quality crafts. For over 3 decades, the guild's dozen or so artists have been fashioning exquisite works out of ceramic, glass, wood, mixed media, and natural fibers. The fluid, evocative stained-glass pieces by Joshua Lee Cox and the whimsical ceramics by Arabella Ark are particularly wonderful—and well worth the trouble of shipping home. 120 Hāna Hwy. www.mauicraftsguild.com. ✆ **808/579-9697.**

Pearl ★ This chic housewares shop supplies everything necessary for beach cottage living: Turkish spa towels, vintage hardware, embroidered cover-ups, and Indonesian furnishings. Stylish shop owner Malia Vandervoort collects treasures from around the globe that match her soulful, simple aesthetic. Among her best-selling items, Annie Fischer's hand-painted, made-in-Maui pillows capture the hypnotic colors of Baldwin Beach just down the road. 285 Hāna Hwy. www.pearlbutik.com. ✆ **808/579-8899.**

King protea.

Tamara Catz ★★★ Visiting fashionistas, take note: A stop at local designer Tamara Catz's flagship store is de rigueur. The adorable boutique is small but stocked with wardrobe essentials. Designed on Maui, the filmy cotton slips, silk maxi-dresses,

> **Maui's North Shore Is Bikini Central**
>
> Pā'ia has no fewer than six boutiques dedicated to Maui's sun-kissed beach uniform, the bikini. And that's not all; many of the other shops lining Baldwin Avenue and Hāna Highway also sell swimwear. Head to this north-shore beach town for everything from Brazilian thongs to full-figured, mix-and-match-your-own suits. The best of the bunch are **Maui Girl,** 12 Baldwin Ave. (www.maui-girl.com; ✆ **808/579-9266;** daily 9am–6pm), a cheery beach shack that has outfitted more than one *Sports Illustrated* cover model; and **Le Tarte,** 24 Baldwin Ave. (www.letarteswimwear.com; ✆ **808/579-6022;** daily 10am–6pm), an ultra-chic boutique with embroidered beach cover-ups so pretty you'll want to wear them out. Maui Girl and Le Tarte are both owned by local designers, as are two other great spots to shop for suits: **Wings Hawai'i,** 69 Hāna Hwy. (www.wingshawaii.com; ✆ **808/579-3110**), and **Tamara Catz,** 83 Hāna Hwy. (www.tamaracatz.com; ✆ **808/579-9184**). At the intersection of Baldwin and Hāna Highway, **San Lorenzo,** 115 Hāna Hwy. (www.sanlorenzobikinis.com; ✆ **808/873-7972**) sells skimpy, ultra-feminine suits for ladies who want to show off a little sun-kissed skin.

and pantsuits hand-embroidered with birds and flowers capture the relaxed elegance and heat of the tropics. One half of the shop is devoted to Catz's dreamy bridal collection, with ultra-romantic, no-fuss gowns that can easily transition from barefoot vows on the beach to dancing the night away. The jewelry case has tempting pieces studded with crystals, shells, and coral. 83 Hāna Hwy. www.tamaracatz.com. ✆ **808/579-9184.**

HĀNA

Hāna Coast Gallery ★★★ Hidden away in the posh Travaasa Hāna resort, this critically acclaimed, 3,000-square-foot gallery is an cultural experience to savor. You won't find pandering sunsets or jumping dolphins here. Known for its quality curatorship and commitment to Hawaiian culture, this art haven is almost entirely devoted to Hawai'i artists. Among the stellar Maui artists represented are *plein air* painter Michael Clements, master carver Keola Sequeira, and Melissa Chimera, whose massive botanical canvases feature endemic Hawaiian flowers. If you're considering buying a koa wood bowl or piece of furniture, look here first; you'd be hard-pressed to find a better selection under one roof. At the Travaasa Hāna. www.hanacoast.com. ✆ **808/248-8636.**

Hasegawa General Store Since 1910, this family-run mercantile has been serving the Hāna community. This humble, tin-roofed grocery store has just about anything you might need. Harkening back to the days when stores like these were islanders' sole shopping outlet, the aisles are packed with books and music, fishing poles, Hāna-grown coffee, diapers, fridge magnets, garden tools, fresh vegetables, dry goods, and ice cream. Don't leave without a Hasegawa T-shirt or baseball cap to prove you were here. 5165 Hāna Hwy. ✆ **808/248-8231.**

MAUI NIGHTLIFE

Maui tends to turn out the lights at 10pm; nightlife options on this island are limited, but you'll find a few gems listed below.

Many lobby lounges in the major hotels offer Hawaiian music, soft jazz, or hula shows beginning at sunset. If **Hapa, Amy Hanaiali'i,** or **Keali'i Reichel** are playing anywhere on their native island, don't miss them; they're among the finest Hawaiian musicians around today. **Willie K** (Maui's answer to Jimi Hendrix) performs a weekly dinner show at **Mulligan's on the Blue,** 100 Kaukahi St., Wailea (www.mulligansontheblue.com; ✆ **808/874-1131** [restaurant] and ✆ **808/280-8288** [show reservations]).

West Maui

Make time to see **'Ulalena ★★**, Maui Theatre, 878 Front St., Lahaina (www.ulalena.com; ✆ **808/856-7900**), a Cirque du Soleil–style entertainment that weaves Hawaiian mythology with drama, dance, and state-of-the-art multimedia capabilities in a multimillion-dollar theater. It's interactive; dancers stream down the aisles and musicians play from surprising corners. The story unfolds so seamlessly that at the end you'll be shocked to realize that not a single word of dialogue was spoken. Performances are given Tuesday through Saturday. Tickets are $60 to $80 for adults, $30 to $50 for children 6 to 12.

A very different type of live entertainment, **Warren & Annabelle's,** 900 Front St., Lahaina (www.warrenandannabelles.com; ✆ **808/667-6244**), is a magic/comedy cocktail show with illusionist Warren Gibson and "Annabelle," an 1800s-era ghost who plays the grand piano (even taking requests from the audience) as Warren dazzles with his sleight-of-hand magic. Appetizers, desserts, and cocktails are available (as a package or a la carte). Check-in is at 5 and 7:30pm. The show-only price is $67; the show plus gourmet appetizers and dessert costs $109. You must be 21 to attend.

Slack key guitar masters are showcased every Wednesday and Thursday night at the Nāpili Kai Beach Resort's indoor amphitheater, thanks to the **Masters of Hawaiian Slack Key Guitar Series ★★** (www.slackkey.com; ✆ **888/669-3858**). The intimate shows present a side of Hawai'i that few visitors get to see. Host George Kahumoku, Jr., introduces a new slack key master every week. Not only is there incredible Hawaiian music and singing, but George and his guest also "talk story" about old Hawai'i, music, and local culture. Not to be missed.

At **Cheeseburger in Paradise,** 811 Front St., Lahaina (www.cheeseburgernation.com; ✆ **808/661-4855**), at the corner of Front and Lahainaluna streets, loud, live, and lively tropical rock blasts into the streets and out to sea nightly from 4:30 to 10pm.

Other venues for music in west Maui include the following:

LŪ'AU, MAUI STYLE

Most of the larger hotels in Maui's major resorts offer lū'au on a regular basis. You'll pay about $80 to $120 to attend one, but don't expect it to be a home-grown affair prepared in the traditional Hawaiian way. There are, however, commercial lū'au that capture the romance and spirit of the lū'au with quality food and entertainment.

Maui's best choice is indisputably the nightly **Old Lahaina Lū'au ★★★** (www.oldlahainaluau.com; ✆ **800/248-5828** or 808/667-1998). Located just ocean-side of the Lahaina Cannery, the Old Lahaina Lū'au maintains its high standards in food and entertainment—and enjoys an oceanfront setting that is peerless. Local craftspeople display their wares only a few feet from the ocean. Seating is provided on *lauhala* mats for those who wish to dine as the traditional Hawaiians did, but there are tables for everyone else. There's no fire dancing in the 3-hour program, but you won't miss it (for that, go to the **Feast at Lele;** p. 391). This lū'au offers a healthy balance of entertainment, showmanship, authentic high-quality food, educational value, and sheer romantic beauty. (No watered-down Mai Tais either; these are the real thing.)

The lū'au begins at sunset and features Tahitian and Hawaiian entertainment, including powerful hula *kahiko* (ancient hula), hula *auana* (modern hula), and an intelligent narrative on the dance's rocky course of survival into modern times. The food, served from an open-air thatched structure, is as much Pacific Rim as authentically Hawaiian: *imu*-roasted kalua pig, baked mahimahi in Maui onion cream sauce, guava chicken, teriyaki sirloin steak, lomi salmon, poi, dried fish, poke, Hawaiian sweet potato, sautéed vegetables, seafood salad, and taro leaves with coconut milk. The cost is $115 for adults, $78 for children 12 and under.

For information on all of Maui's lū'au, go to **www.mauihawaiiluau.com**.

- **Hula Grill,** in Whalers Village, Ka'anapali (www.hulagrillkaanapali.com; ✆ **808/667-6636**), has live music (usually Hawaiian) every day from 11am to 9pm.
- **Kimo's,** 845 Front St., Lahaina (www.kimosmaui.com; ✆ **808/661-4811**), has live musicians every night at various times; call for details.
- **Pioneer Inn,** 658 Wharf St., Lahaina (www.pioneerinn-maui.com; ✆ **808/661-3636**), offers a variety of live music Tuesday and Thursday nights 5:30 to 8pm.
- **Sansei Seafood Restaurant & Sushi Bar,** 600 Office Rd., Kapalua (www.sanseihawaii.com; ✆ **808/669-6286**), has karaoke Thursday and Friday from 10pm to 1am—during which time you can enjoy 50% off sushi and appetizers.
- **Sea House Restaurant,** at the Nāpili Kai Beach Resort, Nāpili (www.napilikai.com; ✆ **808/669-1500**), has live music nightly from 7 to 9pm.

South Maui

The Kīhei, Wailea, and Mā'alaea areas in south Maui also feature music in a variety of locations:

- **Kahale's Beach Club,** 36 Keala Place, Kīhei (© **808/875-7711**), is a bit of a dive bar but has a potpourri of rock music nightly.
- **Haui's Life's a Beach,** 1913 S. Kīhei Rd., Kīhei (www.mauibars.com; © **808/891-8010**), has live music nightly and karaoke; call for times.
- **Mulligan's on the Blue,** 100 Kaukahi St., Wailea (www.mulligansontheblue.com; © **808/874-1131**), offers rollicking Irish music on Sunday, a Wednesday dinner show with local legend Willie K, and other entertainers during the week.
- **Sansei Seafood Restaurant & Sushi Bar,** in Kīhei Town Center, 1881 South Kīhei Rd., Kīhei (www.sanseihawaii.com; © **808/879-0004**), has karaoke Thursday through Saturday from 10pm to 1am—during which time you can enjoy 50% off sushi and appetizers.
- **South Shore Tiki Lounge,** 1913 S. Kīhei Rd., Kīhei (www.southshoretikilounge.com; © **808/874-6444**), has dancing nightly from 10pm to 1:30am.

Upcountry Maui

Upcountry in Makawao, the party never ends at **Casanova,** 1188 Makawao Ave. (www.casanovamaui.com; © **808/572-0220**), the popular Italian restaurant. If a big-name Mainland band is resting up on Maui

Hula dancers at the Old Lahaina Lū'au.

following a sold-out concert on O'ahu, you may find its members setting up for an impromptu night here. DJs take over on Wednesday (ladies' night); on Friday and Saturday, live music starts between 9 and 10pm and continues to 1:30am. Expect blues, rock 'n' roll, reggae, jazz, and Hawaiian. Elvin Bishop, the local duo Hapa, Los Lobos, and others have taken Casanova's stage. The cover is usually $10 to $20.

Central Maui & Pā'ia

The island's most prestigious entertainment venue is the $32-million **Maui Arts & Cultural Center** in Kahului (www.mauiarts.org; © **808/242-7469**). The center is as precious to Maui as the Met is to New York, with a visual arts gallery, outdoor amphitheater, rehearsal space, a 300-seat theater for experimental performances, and a 1,200-seat main theater. Check the website for schedules and buy your tickets in advance.

The **Kahului Ale House,** 355 E. Kamehameha Ave., Kahului (www.kahuluialehouse.com; © **808/877-0001**), has live music or a DJ most nights. In Waikapū, the **Mill House** at the Maui Tropical Plantation, 1670 Honoapi'ilani Hwy. (www.mauitropicalplantation.com; © **808/270-0333**) is a dynamic venue for outdoor movies, parties, and live entertainment. Check the website for upcoming events.

In Pā'ia, **Charley's Restaurant,** 142 Hāna Hwy. (www.charleysmaui.com; © **808/579-8085**), features an eclectic selection of music, from country to reggae to rock 'n' roll Thursday through Saturday.

7

MOLOKA'I

by Jeanne Cooper

"Don't try to change Moloka'i. Let Moloka'i change you" is the mantra on this least developed of the major Hawaiian islands. No luxury hotels, no stoplights, and "no hurry" are points of pride for locals, nearly half of whom are of Native Hawaiian descent. The island welcomes adventure travelers, spiritual pilgrims, and all who appreciate its untrammeled beauty and unrushed ways.

Known as "the child of the moon" in Native Hawaiian lore, Moloka'i remains a place apart, luminous yet largely inaccessible to the casual visitor. Tourism, and modern conveniences in general, have only a small footprint here, and although the island is just 38 miles long by 10 miles wide, it takes time to see what it has to offer. As the sign at the airport reads: aloha, slow down, this is molokai.

Patience and planning do reward travelers with a compass of superlatives. The world's tallest sea cliffs stand on the North Shore; on the South Shore, historic fish ponds line the state's longest fringing reef. The island's most ancient settlement sits within gorgeous Hālawa Valley on the East End, while the West End offers one of the most impressive sandy beaches in Hawai'i, the more than 2-mile-long (and often empty) Pāpohaku.

The percentage of people with Native Hawaiian blood is also higher on Moloka'i than on the other major islands. Many have maintained or revived Hawaiian traditions such as growing taro, managing fish ponds, and staging games for Makahiki, the winter festival. "Sustainability" isn't a buzzword but a centuries-old way of life that eyes modern innovations with caution—and many on island are fierce in opposition to growth.

Residents and visitors alike take inspiration from the stories of Father Damien and others who cared for the suffering exiles of Kalaupapa. Once a natural prison for those diagnosed with leprosy, the remote North Shore peninsula is now a national historical park with very limited access but profound appeal—much like Moloka'i itself.

FACING PAGE: **Moloka'i coastline.**

ESSENTIALS

Note: The use of Hawaiian spellings in business names below reflects the owners' usage; some use "Molokai" and "Moloka'i" interchangeably.

Arriving

BY PLANE Unless you're flying to the island as part of a Kalaupapa charter tour, you'll arrive in **Ho'olehua** (airport code: MKK), which many just call the Moloka'i Airport. It's about 7½ miles from the center of Kaunakakai town. ***Note:*** If you're connecting from the Mainland, try to arrange your connecting flight so that you arrive during the day, even it means spending a night (or more) on another island first. You'll appreciate the aerial sightseeing on the interisland flights (flying time: 25–35 min.) as well as easier navigation once on land.

'Ohana by Hawaiian (www.hawaiianairlines.com/ohana; **© 800/367-5320**), a Hawaiian Airlines subsidiary launched in spring 2014, flies three to four times a day between Ho'olehua and Honolulu on 48-passenger, twin-engine turboprops. It also flies one to two times a day from Kahului, Maui, and has a daily morning flight from Lāna'i.

The visuals are even more impressive from the single-engine, nine-seat aircraft of **Mokulele Airlines** (www.mokuleleairlines.com; **© 866/260-7070** or 808/270-8767 outside the U.S.). It provides nonstop service 9 to 10 times a day from Honolulu, with most flights on Friday and Sunday, and two to three times a day from the West Oahu airport of Kalaeloa (Barbers Point) near the Ko Olina Resort. Mokulele also flies to Moloka'i nonstop from two airports on Maui: six to seven times a day from Kahului, and once a day from Kapalua. ***Note:*** At check-in, you'll be asked to stand on a scale with any carry-on luggage. Only the agent is able to see the results, but those who weigh more than 350 pounds are not allowed to board. Keep your shoes on—there are no security screenings.

Mokulele also offers "adventure tours" to Kalaupapa National Historical Park from Honolulu, Kahului, Kapalua, and Kona (Big Island) in partnership with **Damien Tours**—the only way visitors, who must be at least 16 years old, are allowed inside the national historical park. (Don't book Kalaupapa flights independently.)

Makani Kai Air (www.makanikaiair.com; **© 808/834-1111**) also flies nine-seaters to Moloka'i, departing from its private terminal on the perimeter of the Honolulu airport (Mokulele operates from the more centrally located commuter terminal and 'Ohana by Hawaiian from the main interisland terminal). Makani Kai flies six times a day between Honolulu and Ho'olehua and, in conjunction with Damien Tours, offers scheduled service to Kalaupapa from Honolulu and "topside" Moloka'i (as islanders call Ho'olehua and basically anywhere but Kalaupapa). Chartered flights to Ho'olehua and Kalaupapa tours are also available from other islands.

Moloka‘i

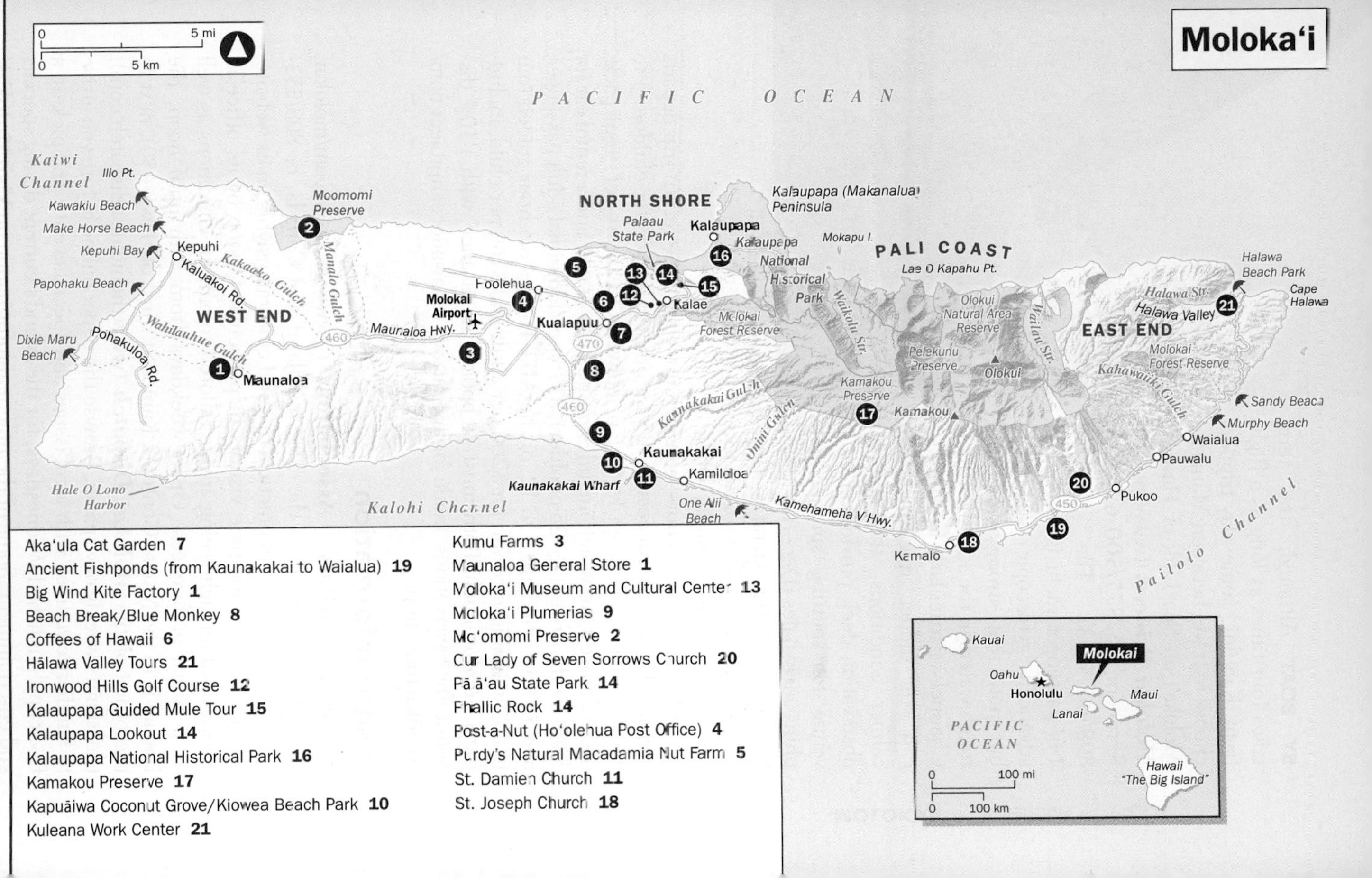

Aka‘ula Cat Garden **7**
Ancient Fishponds (from Kaunakakai to Waialua) **19**
Big Wind Kite Factory **1**
Beach Break/Blue Monkey **8**
Coffees of Hawaii **6**
Hālawa Valley Tours **21**
Ironwood Hills Golf Course **12**
Kalaupapa Guided Mule Tour **15**
Kalaupapa Lookout **14**
Kalaupapa National Historical Park **16**
Kamakou Preserve **17**
Kapuāiwa Coconut Grove/Kiowea Beach Park **10**
Kuleana Work Center **21**
Kumu Farms **3**
Maunaloa General Store **1**
Moloka‘i Museum and Cultural Center **13**
Moloka‘i Plumerias **9**
Mo‘omomi Preserve **2**
Our Lady of Seven Sorrows Church **20**
Pālā‘au State Park **14**
Phallic Rock **14**
Post-a-Nut (Ho‘olehua Post Office) **4**
Purdy's Natural Macadamia Nut Farm **5**
St. Damien Church **11**
St. Joseph Church **18**

Coastline of Moloka'i.

BY BOAT Although the ferry takes four times as long as a flight from Kahului, some day-trippers choose to travel between Maui and Moloka'i on Sea Link of Hawaii's ***Molokai Princess*** (www.molokaiferry.com; ✆ **877/500-6284** or 808/667-5553). The 100-foot, 149-passenger yacht is fitted with advanced gyroscopic stabilizers, but note that strong winds and rough waters in the 15-mile Pailolo Channel—particularly in winter—can still induce queasiness. In calmer conditions, the open-air observation deck provides a great venue for spotting spinner dolphins and whales (Dec–Apr for the latter). The ferry operates Tuesdays, Thursdays, Fridays, and Saturdays, departing Lahaina, Maui, at 6am and arriving 2 hours later at Kaunakakai; the return trip departs at 5pm. The round-trip costs $125 for adults and $63 for children 4 to 12. Most day-trippers opt for one of Hawaii Ocean Project's tour packages: **Cruise/Car,** which includes round-trip passage and a rental car for $260 for the driver (age 25 or older), $125 per additional adult passenger, and $63 per child age 4 to 12; or the **Ali'i Tour,** a 6½-hour guided tour in an air-conditioned van for $260 per adult and $160 per child, including a stop for lunch. Both must be booked in advance, with a 10% discount for reservations made online at www.hawaiioceanproject.com/MolokaiTours.php.

Visitor Information

Moloka'i Visitors Association (www.gohawaii.com/molokai; ✆ **800/800-6367** from the U.S. mainland and Canada, or 808/553-3876) offers a wealth of practical tips and cultural insights on its website, and encourages first-time visitors in particular to stop by its office in Kaunakakai for sightseeing advice tailored to current conditions as well as personal preferences. Open weekdays from 9am until noon, the bureau is in the Moore Center, 2 Kamoi St. (just off Hwy. 450), next to the office of the ***Molokai Dispatch*** (www.themolokaidispatch.com), the island's weekly newspaper. Browse the paper online before you arrive to familiarize yourself with local issues and special events, and pick up a free copy, published Wednesdays, for the island's current dining specials and entertainment. Some of the practical information on **VisitMolokai.**

com (slogan: "Everything About Molokai, By Folks Who Live on Molokai") is outdated, but the website still has a useful events calendar, sightseeing tips, photos, and insights. These sources all maintain Facebook pages, too.

The Island in Brief

KAUNAKAKAI ★

If any place on Moloka'i can be described as "bustling," this centrally located, usually sunny town on the south side would be it. Nearly every restaurant, store, and community facility on the island lies within a few blocks of one another, with only a sprinkling of modern edifices to spoil the illusion that you're in the Old West; the state's longest pier serves the ferry, fishing boats, outrigger canoes, and kids enjoying a dip in the ocean. Other than Saturday mornings, when it seems as if the entire town (pop. 3,500) turns out for the farmer's market, it's easy to find a parking space among the pickup trucks.

CENTRAL UPLANDS & NORTH SHORE ★★

Upland from Kaunakakai, Hawaiian homesteaders in **Ho'olehua** tend small plots near the state's largest producer of organic papaya and the main airport. In the nearby plantation town of **Kualapu'u,** the espresso bar at Coffees of Hawaii perks up hikers and mule riders returning from **Kalaupapa National Historical Park ★★★** on the North Shore's isolated peninsula, where generations of people diagnosed with leprosy (now called Hansen's disease) were exiled. The forest grows denser and the air cooler as Kala'e Highway (Hwy. 470) passes the island's lone golf course and ends at **Pālā'au State Park ★★**, known for its phallic rock and dramatic overlook of Kalaupapa, some 1,700 feet below. To the east stand the world's tallest sea cliffs, 3,600 to 3,900 feet, which bracket the North Shore's secluded beaches, waterfalls, and lush valleys, all virtually inaccessible. Fishing charters, helicopter tours from Maui, and, in summer, a strenuous kayak trip can bring them within closer view.

THE WEST END ★

Moloka'i Ranch (www.molokairanch.com) owns most of the rugged, often arid West End of the island, famous for the nearly 3-mile-long **Pāpōhaku Beach ★★★**—and not much else since the ranch infamously shut down in 2008, closing its lodge, beach camp, movie theater, and golf course, among other facilities. In 2012, the ranch reintroduced cattle and announced intentions to "revitalize" its hospitality operations, but in the meantime, the plantation-era village of **Maunaloa** at the end of the Maunaloa Highway (Hwy. 460) remains a virtual ghost town, and the decaying buildings of Kaluako'i Hotel (closed in 2001), above **Kepuhi Beach ★★**, look like a set from *Lost*. Summer is the best time to explore the shoreline here, although the crash of winter waves

Hālawa Valley.

provides a convenient sleep aid for inhabitants of the three still-open condo developments on the overgrown **Kaluakoʻi** resort. Look out for axis deer when driving here at night; wild turkeys rule the roost by day.

THE EAST END ★★★

From Kaunakakai, the two-lane King Kamehameha V Highway (Hwy. 450) heads 27 miles east through lush greenery to **Hālawa Valley,** a culturally significant as well as beautiful enclave, open only for guided tours except for the twin-coved **Hālawa Beach Park ★★**. Before the road makes its final dip to the valley, pull over for a distant view of 500-foot **Hīpuapua Falls** and 250-foot, two-tiered **Moʻoula Falls** (also known as Moaʻula Falls). Before you arrive, though, you'll pass pocket beaches, historic fish ponds, two churches built by Father Damien, and the entrance to **Puʻu O Hoku,** a working cattle ranch that also serves as a reserve for nēnē, the endangered state bird. Blink along the way and you'll miss the region's one condo resort and single grocery/dining outlet. All the greenery indicates you're on the rainier half of the island, with more frequent showers January through March, but be careful: The sun still blazes here, too.

GETTING AROUND

Getting around Molokaʻi isn't easy without a rental car, which you need to reserve as early as possible. During special events and holiday weekends (see "When to Go," in chapter 3), rental agencies simply run out of vehicles. Stay alert to invasive axis deer darting onto the highway, especially at night.

BY CAR The international chain **Alamo Rent a Car** (www.alamo.com; ✆ **888/826-6893**) has both an office and cars at the airport in Hoʻolehua. The office of **Molokai Car Rental** (www.molokaicars.com;

✆ **808/336-0670**) may be in Kaunakakai, where owner Amanda Schonely also sells her unique shell-decorated caps and island jewelry, but she's happy to leave a serviceable car (or minivan) for you at the airport or ferry dock, with the keys inside. If you're renting for a week or longer, consider reserving a similarly lightly used but perfectly adequate car, van, or SUV from **Mobettah Car Rentals** (www.mobettahcarrentals.com; ✆ **808/213-5365**). The company will drop vehicles off at the airport, or you can pick up your rental car at its office 2 miles west on the Maunaloa Highway.

BY TAXI Per state law, taxis charge $3 a mile plus a "drop charge" of $3.50, or about $32 from the airport to the Hotel Moloka'i in Kaunakakai and $42 to a West End condo. Try to arrange rides a day or two in advance, either with the friendly folks at **Hele Mai Taxi** (www.molokaitaxi.com; ✆ **808/336-0967**) or **Midnight Taxi** (✆ **808/658-1410**).

BY BUS The nonprofit **Maui Economic Opportunity, Inc.** (www.meoinc.org; ✆ **808/877-7651**) provides free daytime shuttle bus service between Kaunakakai and the East End, Ho'olehua/Kualapu'u, and Maunaloa/Kaluako'i, running six times daily Monday to Friday and once on Saturdays. It's designed for rural residents but open to all, if you're feeling adventurous, check out the online schedule (click "Programs & Services," and then follow the drop-down links, starting with "Transportation").

[FastFACTS] MOLOKA'I

Note: All addresses are in Kaunakakai unless otherwise noted.

ATMs/Banks Both **Bank of Hawaii,** 20 Ala Malama St. (www.boh.com; ✆ **808/553-3273**), and **American Savings Bank,** 40 Ala Malama St. (www.asbhawaii.com; ✆ **808/553-8391**), have 24-hour ATMs.

Cellphones The island has a few cellphone towers, but the signal can be weak, especially outside of Kaunakakai and Ho'olehua.

Dentists/Doctors The **Molokai Community Health Center,** 30 Oki Place (www.molokaichc.org; ✆ **808/553-5038**), provides dental and medical services from 8am to 5pm weekdays.

Emergencies Call ✆ **911** in life-threatening circumstances. Otherwise, contact the **police** at ✆ **808/553-5355** or the **fire department** at ✆ **808/553-5601.**

Hospital **Molokai General Hospital,** 280 Home'olu Place (www.molokaigeneralhospital.org; ✆ **808/553-5331**), has 15 beds, a 24-hour emergency room open daily, and an outpatient clinic open 7am to 6pm weekdays.

Internet Access **Hotel Moloka'i,** most vacation rentals, and a handful of restaurants offer free, if not necessarily reliable, Wi-Fi. See listings under "Where to Stay" and "Where to Eat," below.

Pharmacy The only pharmacy, **Molokai Drugs,** 28 Kamoi St. (www.molokaidrugs.com; ✆ **808/553-5790**), is open 8:45am to 5:45pm Monday to Friday and 8am to 2pm Saturday.

Post Office The **central office** at 120 Ala Malama is open Monday to Friday 9am to 3:30pm and Saturday 9 to 11am. The **Ho'olehua branch,** just off Farrington Avenue (Hwy. 480) at 69-2 Pu'upe'elua Ave., offers the popular "Post-a-Nut" service (p. 440); it's open weekdays 8:30am to noon and 12:30 to 4pm.

EXPLORING MOLOKA'I

Note: You'll find the following attractions on the "Moloka'i" map, on p. 433.

Attractions & Points of Interest

Most of Moloka'i's attractions are of the natural variety, but a few man-made sights are worth adding to your itinerary. For the quaint churches related to St. Damien, see "The Saints of Moloka'i," p. 442.

KAUNAKAKAI

Molokai Plumerias ★★ FARM Hundreds of plumeria trees produce fragrant yellow and pink blooms virtually year-round here, just off the main highway between the airport and town. Make a weekday appointment for an informative blossom-gathering tour ($25) that ends with a lesson on how to string your own lei. Tours (Tues and Thurs by request) with the genial co-owner, artist, and former pro surfer Jaia Waits include a private showing of his art and Hawaiian crafts.

1342 Maunaloa Hwy. (Hwy. 460), 2½ miles west of Kaunakakai. www.molokaiplumerias.com. ✆ **808/553-3391.** Tours $25 (Mon–Fri by appointment).

CENTRAL UPLANDS & NORTH SHORE

Aka'ula Cat Garden ★ ANIMAL SHETER You're bound to see homeless (not necessarily feral) cats on the island, but thanks to this indoor-outdoor shelter—the only animal sanctuary on the island, and welcoming to visitors—more of the island's felines stand a chance of finding homes. Founder Carol Gartland enlists the help of students at neighboring Aka'ula School to care for the cats, and will even pay the costs of flying a kitty home with you, should you be so smitten.

Next to Aka'ula School, 900 Kala'e Hwy. (Hwy. 470), just south of Farrington Rd., Kualapu'u. www.akaulacatgarden.com. ✆ **808/658-0398.** Open by appointment.

Coffees of Hawaii ★ FARM Prolonged drought and the economic downturn forced this farm to sell most of its former pineapple land, discontinue tours, and lease its espresso bar/cafe to the folks running the nearby mule ride. Prices of its estate coffee beans have also risen sharply since a new partner joined the

Coffees of Hawaii.

A HIKE BACK IN history

"There are things on Moloka'i, sacred things, that you may not be able to see or hear, but they are there," says Pilipo Solatorio, who was born and raised in **Hālawa Valley.** "As Hawaiians, we respect these things."

Solatorio and his family are among the few who allow visitors into the emerald East End valley, offering **cultural waterfall tours ★★★** Monday to Saturday by reservation only. After welcoming visitors with traditional chants and the sharing of inhaled breath, foreheads pressed together, "Uncle" Pilipo relates the history of the area before son Greg guides the group along the rocky trail, which crosses two shallow streams. Greg also notes ancient sites, taro terraces, and native and invasive species along the path (1.7 miles each way). If conditions permit, visitors may swim in the pool below the 250-foot, double-tiered Mo'o'ula Falls, which the Solatorios explain is named after its legendary resident *mo'o*, or lizard.

Uncle Pilipo, who can recall the 1946 tsunami that barreled into the ancient settlement when he was 6 years old, feels that learning about the history and culture of Moloka'i is part of the secret to appreciating the island. "To see the real Moloka'i, you need to understand and know things so that you are *pono,* you are right with the land, and don't disrespect the culture," he says.

Book at least several days in advance. **Moloka'i Outdoors** (www.molokai-outdoors.com; ✆ **877/553-4477** or 808/553-4477) offers online bookings for $75 adults, $45 children 6 to 12. Or take your chances with leaving a phone message for the Solatorios (www.halawavalleymolokai.com; ✆ **808/551-5538** or 808/551-1055), giving your name, telephone number, the number of people in your party (minimum of two), and requested date of visit; the cash-only price is $60 adults, $35 children. Wear a swimsuit under your clothes and wear shoes that can get wet; bring a backpack with insect repellent, sunscreen, water, a rain poncho, a towel, lunch, and a camera.

operation a couple of years ago. Still, many visitors enjoy browsing the attractive plantation store, sipping an iced coffee, or eating lunch on the roomy porch, within view of 115 acres of coffee trees. Don't miss the weekly Hawaiian music jam by *kūpuna* (seniors) on the porch, from 10am to noon Tuesday.

1630 Farrington Ave. (Hwy. 480), off Highway 470, Kualapu'u. www.coffeesofhawaii.com. ✆ **877/322-3276** or 808/567-9490. Espresso bar Mon–Fri 7am–5pm, Sat 8am–8pm, Sun 8am–5pm; gift shop Mon–Sat 9am–4pm.

Molokai Museum and Cultural Center ★ MUSEUM/HISTORIC SITE Halfway between Coffees of Hawaii and the Kalaupapa Overlook, this small museum on the site of a restored sugar mill has a large gift shop of local arts and crafts (look for *liliko'i* butter) and eclectic exhibits from petroglyphs to plantation-era furnishings. Lining the walls are the poignant stories and photos of Kalaupapa residents, including a granddaughter of mill founder Rudolph W. Meyer, a German surveyor who married Kalama, a Hawaiian chieftess. Kalaupapa's historic buildings are the subject of one of two 10-minute videos shown on a TV; the

Post-a-Nut sign.

other focuses on the ingenuity of the mill, built in 1878. Walk a few yards uphill from the museum (the Meyers' former home) to see the barnlike mill and outdoor pit where circling mules once powered cane-crushing machinery.
West side of Kala'e Hwy. (Hwy. 470), near mile marker 4 (just past turnoff for the Ironwood Hills Golf Course), Kala'e. Admission $5 adults, $1 children and students. Mon–Sat 10am–2pm.

Post-a-Nut ★ ICON Moloka'i postmaster Gary Lam will help you say "Aloha" with a Moloka'i coconut. Just write a message on the coconut with a felt-tip pen, and he'll send it via U.S. mail. Coconuts are free, but postage averages $10 to $15 for a smaller, Mainland-bound coconut. Gary mails out about 3,000 per year, usually decorated with colorful stamps.
Ho'olehua Post Office, 69-2 Pu'upe'elua Ave. (Hwy. 480), near Maunaloa Hwy. (Hwy. 460). ✆ **808/567-6144.** Mon–Fri 8:30am–noon and 12:30–4:30pm.

Purdy's All-Natural Macadamia Nut Farm ★★ FARM Hawaiian homesteaders Kammy and Tuddie Purdy (who after 25 years has his patter down pat) offer free tours in the shade of their orchard, first planted in the 1920s. Tours include samples of delicious raw nuts and macadamia blossom honey; they'll ship products home for you, of course.
Lihi Pali Ave., above Moloka'i High School, Ho'olehua. www.molokai-aloha.com/macnuts. ✆ **808/567-6601.** Mon–Fri 9:30am–3:30pm and Sat 10am–2pm, Sunday and holidays by appointment.

EAST END

Ancient Fish Ponds ★ HISTORIC SITE The rock walls of dozens of ancient fish ponds—a pinnacle of Pacific aquaculture—can be seen for miles along the shoreline from the highway between Kaunakakai and the East End. The U-shaped lava rock and coral walls contain sluices that allowed smaller fish to enter and trapped them as they grew larger. Some are still in use today; join volunteers with **Ka Honua Momona** (www.kahonuamomona.org; ✆ **808/553-8353**) in restoring the 15th-century **Ali'i Fish Pond,** a half-mile west of One Ali'i Beach Park (p. 446) and once reserved for kings, and **Kalokoel'i Pond,** another 3½ miles east, generally on the third Saturday of each month.

Kuleana Work Center ★ FARM The Pruet family grows a brilliantly hued mosaic of organic heliconia and ginger in Hālawa Valley. Although drop-in visits are theoretically possible, it's best to make an appointment at least several days in advance via e-mail with Kalani Pruet (kuleanaworkcenter@yahoo.com), who can whip up a fresh fruit smoothie, show you around the farm, and lead you on a waterfall hike while sharing some of the area's history.
Hālawa Valley, east end of Hwy. 450. www.molokaiflowers.com. Tues–Sat 10am–4pm; Sun by appointment. Smoothies by donation. Waterfall tour $40 adults ($75 couple), $20 children 17 and younger.

Parks & Preserves

For information on the relatively inaccessible Kamakou and Mo'omomi preserves, managed by the Nature Conservancy, see "Fragile Beauties," p. 451.

Kapuāiwa Coconut Grove ★ HISTORIC SITE Planted in the 1860s by King Kamehameha V (born Prince of Kapuaiwa), what remains of this royal grove of 1,000 coconut trees (some sadly now frondless) on 10 oceanfront acres is off-limits to visitors, for safety and preservation reasons, but still presents a side-of-the-road photo op. (***Note:*** At press time, the adjacent **Kiowea Beach Park** and picnic area with restrooms also remained closed for remodeling.) Across the highway stands Church Row: seven churches, each of a different denomination—clear evidence of the missionary impact on Hawaii.
Ocean side of Maunaloa Hwy. (Hwy. 460), 1 mile west of Kaunakakai.

CENTRAL UPLANDS & NORTH SHORE

Kalaupapa National Historical Park ★★★ HISTORIC SITE Only 100 people a day, age 16 and older, may visit this isolated peninsula below the North Shore's soaring sea cliffs, and then only by reservation with **Damien Tours** (see "Organized Tours" on p. 444). Visitors must arrive on foot, by mule, or by plane—there's no road, and access by water is not allowed—but the trek is well worth the effort. The area formally known as the Makanalua Peninsula was once home to the Native Hawaiian enclaves of Kalawao and Kalaupapa, on either side of 443-foot Kauhakō Crater. Residents had to abandon their homes after King Kamehameha V signed the Act to Prevent the Spread of Leprosy in 1865, which ultimately exiled some 8,000 people with the dreaded disease. The exiles' suffering was particularly acute before the arrival of

THE saints OF MOLOKA'I

Tiny Moloka'i can claim two saints canonized by the Roman Catholic church in recent years, both revered for years of devotion to the outcasts of Kalaupapa (see "Kalaupapa National Historical Park," below). Born in Belgium as Joseph de Veuster, **Father Damien** moved to Hawai'i in 1864, building churches around the islands until 1873, when he answered a call to serve in the infamous leper colony (a now-discouraged term). He tended the sick, rebuilt St. Philomena's church, and pleaded with church and state officials for better care for the exiles, the earliest of whom had been thrown overboard and left to fend for themselves. Damien ultimately died of Hansen's disease, as leprosy is now known, in Kalaupapa in 1889. Caring for him at the end was **Mother Marianne,** who came to Hawai'i with a group of nuns from New York in 1883. She spent 30 years serving the Kalaupapa community, before dying in 1918 at age 80, without contracting Hansen's disease. (It's only communicable to a small percentage of people.)

You'll see many images of both saints in Kalaupapa as well as "topside," which has three churches worth peeking into. Under the angled red roofs of Kaunakakai's modernist, concrete **St. Damien Church** ★ (115 Ala Malama St.) stands a life-size wooden sculpture of the eponymous saint, canonized in 2009. Turn around to see the large banners bearing his photograph and one of Marianne, canonized in 2012; on the wall outside are four mosaics depicting scenes from Damien's life. Next door, the parish office offers exhibits on both saints (open Tues–Fri 9am–noon).

Ten miles east of Kaunakakai, on the ocean side of Highway 450, **St. Joseph** ★★ is a diminutive wood-frame church built by Damien in 1876. A lava-rock statue of the sainted Belgian priest stands in the little cemetery by the newer, 7-foot marble sculpture of Brother Dutton, a Civil War veteran and former alcoholic inspired by Damien to serve at Kalaupapa for 45 years, until his death in 1931. Four miles east, set back from the large cross on the mountain side of the highway, is the larger but still picturesque **Our Lady of Seven Sorrows** ★, the first church Damien built outside Kalaupapa. Inside both East End churches hang colorful iconic portraits of the saints by local artist Linda Johnston.

now-canonized Father Damien (see "The Saints of Moloka'i," above) in 1873. Damien who worked tirelessly on their behalf until his death from the disease in 1889. Only a handful of elderly patients, free to come and go since the 1960s, still live on site, but many buildings and ruins remain from more populous times; the park service is kept busy restoring many of them. Intrepid visitors can take the **Kalaupapa Guided Mule Tour** ★★★, a once-in-a-lifetime ride down and around the 26 switchbacks on the narrow, 2.9-mile **Kalaupapa Trail** ★★★. By the time the mules get to No. 4, riders may start to enjoy the views. Hikers (Damien Tours reservations required) must watch their footing on the knee-pounding descent, which takes 60 to 90 minutes; it's 90 to 120 minutes back up. The Damien Tours bus picks up passengers from arriving prop planes at the tiny airport, near the Pacific's tallest lighthouse, before retrieving riders and hikers near the beach at the trail's end.

Kalaupapa. www.nps.gov/kala. ✆ **808/567-6802.** Access restricted to ages 16 and older on guided tours only, Mon–Sat. **Kalaupapa Guided Mule Tour** (www.muleride.com; ✆ **800/567-7550** or 808/567-6088) starts at mule barn near mile marker 5 on Kala'e Hwy. (Hwy. 470), Kala'e, at 8am Mon–Sat, returning 3pm). Riders must weigh under 250 pounds with "good height to weight distribution." $199, includes lunch, tour, and certificate. Reservations required; accepted up to 4 months in advance (a year for groups of 6 or more). **Kalaupapa Trail** starts just north of mule barn, on east side of Kala'e Hwy. (behind gate marked "No Trespassing"). Mule Tours hiking package with tour and lunch, $69. Permit and tour only, $50 from Damien Tours (✆ **808/567-6171)** or Moloka'i Outdoors (www.molokai-outdoors.com; ✆ **877/553-4477** or 808/553-4477). **Makani Kai** (www.makanikaiair.com; ✆ **808/834-1111**) offers air/tour/lunch packages from Ho'olehua, $249 fly in/fly out, $149 hike in/fly out; from Honolulu, $315 and $249, respectively; from Kapalua, Maui, $399 fly in/fly out only. **Mokulele Airlines** (www.mokuleleairlines.com; ✆ **866/260-7070** or 808/426-7070) also has packages with Damien Tours from Oahu (Honolulu, Kalaeloa), Maui (Kahului, Kapalua), Big Island (Kona) and Ho'olehua; prices ranges from $230 to $395.

Pālā'au State Park ★★ PARK This 234-acre forest park literally puts visitors between a rock and a hard place. From the parking lot, go left on the short but steep dirt trail through an ironwood grove to the **Phallic Rock** ★; go right on the paved path, and the **Kalaupapa**

St. Joseph Catholic Church.

Moloka'i mules at the ready for guided tours.

Lookout ★★★ offers a panoramic view of the peninsula that was once a place of exile (see "Kalaupapa National Historical Park," above). Interpretive signs identify the sights some 1,700 feet below and briefly relate the tragic history that also spawned inspirational stories. As for that unmistakably shaped 6-foot boulder, one legend holds that it's the fertility demigod Nānāhoa, turned to stone after he threw his wife over a cliff during an argument about his roving eye. It's also believed that a woman wishing to become pregnant need only spend the night nearby. (But please treat this cultural site with respect, as signs urge.) ***Note:*** There are restrooms near the overlook and at a small pavilion on the left before the parking lot, but no potable water. Tent camping allowed with state permit (see "Camping," p. 455).

At the end of Kala'e Hwy. (Hwy. 470), Pālā'au. www.hawaiistateparks.org. ✆ **808/567-6923.** Free admission.

Organized Tours

Although Moloka'i attracts (and rewards) independent travelers, a few group tours are absolute musts for those who are able—they're the only way to see the island's most awe-inspiring sights up close.

DAMIEN TOURS Run by the family of a former Kalaupapa resident with Hansen's disease (aka leprosy), **Damien Tours ★★★** (✆ **808/567-6171**) provides the required permit to explore the haunting and inspiring sights of Kalaupapa as part of its guided bus tour. Those able to descend the treacherous sea cliffs by foot, mule, or air are met at 10am (Mon–Sat) for the approximately 4-hour tour, which protects the privacy of the few remaining residents while visiting numerous sites. Stops include the original graves of Father Damien and Mother Marianne (see "The Saints of Moloka'i," above); St. Philomena Church, where the Belgian priest carved holes in the floor so patients could discreetly spit during services; a snack shop and bookstore (bring cash; no large bills); and a small museum with heart-rending photos and artifacts, such as a spoon reshaped for a disfigured hand. Lunch is an oceanside picnic on the cooler Kalawao side of the peninsula. Restricted to ages 16 and older, the tour costs $50, with limited spaces. ***Note:*** All tours must be booked in advance, which is easier to do through the "topside" outfitters listed in "Kalaupapa National Historical Park," p. 441.

HĀLAWA VALLEY TOURS On the East End, a guided tour or authorized escort is required to go beyond Hālawa Beach Park into breathtakingly beautiful Haālawa Valley, home to the island's earliest settlement and 250-foot Mo'o'ula Falls. **Pilipo Solatorio**'s 4-hour, culturally focused tours are the most renowned ($75 adults, $45 children when booked through Moloka'i Outdoors; see "A Hike Back in History" on p. 439 for details). **Kalani Pruet** will pair Hālawa Valley tours ($40 adults, $20 children) with a visit to his flower farm (www.molokaiflowers.com; Tues–Sat 10am–4pm, Sun by appointment; e-mail him several days in advance at kuleanaworkcenter@yahoo.com). ***Note:*** Since the valley is privately owned, trespassers may be prosecuted, and almost certainly hassled, if caught.

WHALE-WATCHING TOURS If you're on island December through March, don't miss the chance to watch humpback whales from Alaska frolic in island waters, often with clingy calves in tow, or boisterous pods of males competing for a female's attention. Though you may spot whales spouting or breaching from the shore, a whale-watching cruise from Kaunakakai skirts the fringing reef to provide front-row seats. Veteran outfitter **Molokai Fish & Dive** (www.molokaifishanddive.com; © **808/553-5926**) offers 2- to 3-hour tours for $79 on its comfortable 31-foot power catamaran

Hālawa Falls in Hālawa Valley.

or 38-foot, two-level dive boat. **Molokai Ocean Tours** (www.molokaioceantours.com; © **808/553-3290**) also leads humpback-spotting hunts on its 40- and 30-foot power catamarans for $75.

VAN TOURS If your time on the island is tight—as on a day trip from Maui or O'ahu—I also recommend a van tour with an affable local guide. On Tuesday, Thursday, and Saturday, **Moloka'i Outdoors** (www.molokai-outdoors.com; © **877/553-4477** or 808/553-4477) offers the 7- to 8-hour **Island Tour** ($151), covering Hālawa Valley Lookout on the East End to Pāpōhaku Beach on the West End, with lunch included at oceanfront Hale Kealoha at Hotel Moloka'i. **Hawaii Ocean Project** (www.hawaiioceanproject.com; © **808/667-6165**) operates the 6-hour **Ali'i Tour** ($260), which includes basic continental breakfast, sandwich lunch, and round-trip ferry passage from Maui (2 hr. each way, departing Lahaina at 6am and returning at 5pm); it's offered Tuesday, Thursday, Friday, and Saturday.

Molokai Ocean Tours (molokaioceantours.com; © **808/553-3290**) provides a rare glimpse of natural and historic sites in the nearly inaccessible upland forest on its 6-hour **Mountain Cultural Tour** ($175, including lunch). The expert local guide uses a four-wheel-drive (4WD) vehicle (four guests maximum) to explore Moloka'i Forest Reserve, home to the dramatic Waikolu Canyon Overlook and a massive ship-size pit dug during the early-19th-century sandalwood trade, among other places of note.

BEACHES

Because of the South Shore's extensive shallows, hemmed by a fringing reef and fish ponds, and the general inaccessibility of the North Shore, the best Moloka'i beaches for visitors are on the East or West Ends. There are no lifeguards; on weekdays, you may even be the sole person on the sand. So enter the water only in calm conditions, and even then be cautious: If you get into trouble, help may take longer to arrive than you need. ***Note:*** You'll find relevant sites on the "Moloka'i" map on p. 433.

Kaunakakai

Local kids swim off the wharf, but if you just want to dip your feet in the water, head 3 miles east along the Kamehameha V Highway to the sandy shore of **One Ali'i Beach Park ★**. Pronounced *"o-nay ah-lee-ee,"* it has a thin strip of golden *one* (sand) once reserved for the *ali'i* (high chiefs). Although the water is too shallow and murky for swimming, the spacious park draws many families on weekends. Facilities include outdoor showers, picnic areas, and restrooms; tent camping allowed with permit (see "Camping" on p. 455).

Kūmimi Beach.

East End

At mile marker 20, palm-fringed **Kūmimi Beach ★★**, also known as Murphy or 20-Mile Beach, provides a small, shaded park with picnic tables, white sand, and good swimming, snorkeling, and diving in calm conditions. Look for **Sandy Beach ★★** between mile markers 21 and 22—the last beach before you head uphill en route to lush Hālawa Valley. It has no facilities, just winsome views of Maui and Lāna'i and generally safe swimming; stay out of high surf.

At the narrow end of the winding highway, 28 miles east of Kaunakakai, lie the twin coves of **Hālawa Beach Park ★★**, one with gray sand and the other more rocky. Neither is safe for swimming—avoid in winter or after heavy rains—but both destination and journey are memorable. Look back into Hālawa Valley (accessible only via cultural tours; see p. 445) for distant waterfall views. A picnic pavilion has restrooms, a shower, and water tap; it's 100 yards from the shore, across from **Ierusalema Hou,** a tiny, green church built in 1948.

West End

Much of the shoreline here is for sightseeing only, thanks to dangerous currents and fierce surf, especially in winter, but solitude, sunsets, and clear-day vistas of Diamond Head on O'ahu across the 26-mile Kaiwi Channel make it worth the trek. From Kaunakakai, take Maunaloa Highway (Hwy. 460) almost 15 miles west, turn right on Kaluako'i Road, and drive 4½ miles until you see the sign on your right pointing to Ke Nani Kai; turn right for public beach access parking at the end of the road. Walk past the eerily decaying, closed hotel to gold-sand **Kepuhi Beach ★★**, and watch surfers navigate the rocky break. A 15-minute walk north along the bluff leads to the Po¯haku Ma¯uliuli cinder cone, which shares its name with two sandy coves better known as **Make Horse Beach ★**, pronounced *"mah-kay"* and meaning "dead horse" (don't ask). You can snorkel and explore the tide pools in calm conditions, but do keep an eye on the waves. Hiking several miles north on a rugged dirt road leads to the white crescent of **Kawākiu Beach ★**, the original launch site of the Moloka'i to O'ahu outrigger canoe race. It's relatively safe in summer, but be wary whenever surf is up.

Continue on Kaluako'i Road 2 miles south from the resort to the parking lot for **Pāpōhaku Beach Park ★★★**, where the light-blond sand is more than 2 miles long and 300 feet wide. Enjoy strolling the broad expanse, but beware the water's voracious rip currents. County facilities—restrooms, water, picnic, and campsites (see "Camping," on p. 455)—are at the northern end, a third of a mile past the intersection with Pā Loa Loop Road (a shortcut back to upper Kaluako'i Rd.). Don't miss cozy **Dixie Maru Beach ★★** (formerly Kapukahehu, but renamed after a Japanese shipwreck), which offers the most protected waters and is popular with families in summer. From the Pāpōhaku parking lot, follow Kaluako'i Road 1¾ miles south to the T at Pōhakuloa Road; turn right and head another 1¾ miles until the road ends at a small unpaved parking lot, with a short downhill path to the beach.

WATERSPORTS

The miles-long, untrammeled South Shore reef is home to curious turtles and Hawaiian monk seals, billowing eagle and manta rays, and giant bouquets of colorful fish, but because it lies a half-mile or more offshore, it's easiest to explore via watercraft of some kind. Surfers, stand-up paddleboarders, and boogie boarders can find waves to entertain themselves, just as sport fishers have numerous near-shore and deep-sea options; since conditions are variable by day as well as by season, consult one of the Kaunakakai-based outfitters below before venturing out.

Diving, Fishing & Snorkeling

Molokai Fish & Dive, 61 Ala Malama St. (www.molokaifishanddive.com; ✆ **808/553-5926**), carefully selects the day's best sites for its **snorkel tours** ($79 standard, $99 with handheld "sea rocket" propulsion) and two-tank **scuba dives** ($145). Owner, captain, and certified dive master Tim Forsberg runs tours from one of two Coast Guard–inspected boats: the comfy, 38-foot Delta dive boat *Coral Princess* and the twin-hulled, 31-foot power catamaran *Ama Lua*. When conditions permit, he also offers three-tank dives ($295) along the remote North Shore. Half-day **deep-sea fishing charters** start at $695, while groups of up to six may also charter the new 42-foot sailing cruiser, *Maka Pueo,* for 2- to 3-hour sunset cruises ($395). All kinds of dive and fishing gear, along with snacks and gifts, are for rent or sale at the downtown headquarters.

Among several other charter operators, Captain Tim Brunnert of **Captain's Gig Charters** (www.molokaifishingcharters.com; ✆ **808/552-0390**) books **sport-fishing, snorkel, sunset,** and **sightseeing**

Stand-up paddleboarder in Moloka'i.

cruises; he's also a certified dive master. Contact him directly for current rates.

Molokai Ocean Tours, 40 Ala Malama St., above American Savings Bank (www.molokaioceantours.com; © **808/553-3290**), uses its two six-passenger power catamarans to offer 3-hour **troll fishing** ($190 for the first two people, $75 per additional person) and a half-day **deep-sea fishing charter** ($625). Its **snorkel tours** ($75 adults, $60 children 10 and younger) include a **SNUBA** option that allows up to two people at a time to dive 30 feet, using hoses connected to a special mouthpiece.

For **whale-watching tours** (Dec–Apr), see "Organized Tours" on p. 444.

Paddling

Moloka'i Outdoors (www.molokai-outdoors.com; © **877/553-4477** or 808/553-4477) leads **kayak and stand-up-paddleboard reef tours** from 5 to 14 miles ($52–$68 adult, $27–$33 ages 4–12); owner and former world champion windsurfer Clare Seeger Mawae occasionally guides the tours. Her company also rents kayaks ($42), snorkel sets and boogie boards ($7), and stand-up paddleboards ($27–$42); in summer, experienced paddlers can arrange a North Shore kayak excursion that starts in Hālawa Valley, with pickup by boat. Her office is at the Hotel Moloka'i (see p. 452).

The ancient sport of **outrigger canoe paddling** is available to anyone age 10 and up at 7:15am every Thursday morning (except major holidays or in bad weather) at Kaunakakai Wharf. The $25 cash donation for the 1-hour paddle helps buy canoes for the youth teams of community-based **Wa'akapaemua Canoe Club** (© **808/553-3999**); custom bookings are available for parties of four or more. E-mail lfoster@heartof-hawaii.com for details.

Surfing & Bodyboarding

Conveniently located between the airport and Kaunakakai at the corner of highways 460 and 470 (Holomua Junction), you'll spot **Beach Break** (www.bigwindkites.com/beachbreak; ✆ **808/567-6091**) by its rainbow fence made of surfboards. Inside, owner, photographer, and avid surfer Zach Socher rents surfboards ($24–$30 daily/$120–$150 weekly), bodyboards ($10/$35), and fins ($5/$21), among other beach gear for rent or sale. Check out the bright array of bikinis, boardshorts, "slippahs," T's and sarongs, too. Socher dispenses free coffee and advice on surf spots during store hours, Monday through Saturday 10am to 4pm.

OTHER OUTDOOR ACTIVITIES

Biking

Moloka'i is a great place to see by bicycle, with lightly used roads and, on the East End, inviting places to pull over for a quick dip. **Molokai Bicycle,** 80 Mohala St., Kaunakakai (www.mauimolokaibicycle.com; ✆ **800/709-2453,** 808/553-3931), offers mountain, road, and hybrid bike rentals for $25 to $32 a day, or $95 to $130 a week, including helmet and lock; add a trailer for $12 a day, $60 a week. Because owner Phillip Kikukawa is a schoolteacher, the store is open only Wednesday 3 to 6pm and Saturday 9am to 2pm; call to set up an appointment for other hours. Dropoff and pickup in or near Kaunakakai is free, with charges for airport runs ($20 each way) and Kaluako'i Resort and Wavecrest condos ($25 each way).

Golf

The high elevation will help keep you cool at **Ironwood Hills Golf Course** (✆ **808/567-6000**), at least if you opt for a motorized cart. Built in 1929 by the Del Monte Plantation for its executives, the nine-hole, undulating course with uneven fairways lies a half-mile down an unpaved road off Highway 470 in Kala'e, between Coffees of Hawaii in Kualapu'u and the Kalaupapa Lookout. It's lovingly maintained by PGA pro Darrell Rego. Gorgeous mountain and ocean views, some now filtered by tree growth, also compensate for the challenging course. Greens fees are $36 for 9 holes, including cart; club rentals are $10. Pick up a logo cap in the pro shop trailer.

Hiking

With most land privately held, the only real hiking opportunities on Moloka'i are the Kalaupapa Trail (permit required; see p. 442), Hālawa Valley by guided tour (see p. 445), or in two hard-to-access Nature

FRAGILE BEAUTIES: HIKING MOLOKA'I'S nature reserves

For spectacularly unique views of Moloka'i, the Nature Conservancy of Hawaii offers **monthly guided hikes ★★★** March through October into two of the island's most fragile landscapes: the windswept dunes in the 920-acre **Mo'omomi Preserve** on the northwest shore, and the cloud-ringed forest of the island's highest mountain, part of the 2,774-acre **Kamakou Preserve** on the island's East End.

Just 8½ miles northwest of Ho'olehua, Mo'omomi is the most intact beach and sand dune area in the main Hawaiian islands, harboring rare native plants, nesting green sea turtles, and fossils of now-extinct flightless birds.

Towering over the island's eastern half, 4,970-foot Kamakou provides 60% of the fresh water on Moloka'i and shelter for endangered or threatened native species. The Pēpē'opae Trail boardwalk (3 miles round-trip) meanders through a bog with miniature trees and other delicate greenery that evolved over millennia; it leads to a view of pristine Pelekunu Valley on the North Shore.

Hikes are free (donations welcome), but the number of participants is limited. Book in advance; exact dates (usually Sat) are listed on the conservancy website (www.nature.org/hawaii). To check availability, e-mail hike_molokai@tnc.org, or call the field office (✆ **808/553-5236;** weekdays 8am–3pm).

It's also possible to access the preserves on your own, but you'll need a rugged four-wheel-drive (4WD) vehicle, dry roads, and clear weather. Check in first at the field office, just north of Kaunakakai in Moloka'i Industrial Park, 23 Pueo Place, off 'Ūlili Street near Highway 460. Ask for directions and current road conditions; in the case of Mo'omomi, you'll also need to get a pass for the locked gate. Clean your shoes and gear before visiting the preserves to avoid bringing in invasive species—and drive cautiously—a tow job from these remote areas can easily cost $1,000.

Conservancy preserves (see "Fragile Beauties," above). Molokai Ocean Tours' 6-hour **Mountain Cultural Tour** (p. 446) includes some hiking in the Moloka'i Forest Reserve.

WHERE TO STAY ON MOLOKA'I

With only one hotel (offering just 40 rooms for the general public) on the island, the majority of the island's approximately 58,000 annual visitors tend to stay in one of a very mixed bag of five condo developments. All have individually owned and decorated units that vary widely in taste and quality, leaning heavy on the rattan. (Don't expect air-conditioning or elevators in the two- and three-story buildings either.)

Moloka'i also offers a similar patchwork of mostly unassuming vacation rental cottages and basic B&Bs. Unfortunately, nearly all of these are unlicensed. Maui County doesn't make it easy—or inexpensive—to get permits, but out of respect for guest welfare as well as local concerns, the recommendations below include only licensed accommodations. (A licensed property lists the permit number on its website; rental cottages must also have a sign with the number.)

Offering the most choices on the island, as well as excellent customer service, **Molokai Vacation Properties** (www.molokai-vacation-rental.net; ✆ **800/367-2984** or 808/553-8334) represents only licensed houses and condos, most of them oceanfront and all guaranteed to be clean and fully equipped. Although you can book online, it's best to contact the office directly to find the most suitable unit for your needs. You'll find more (not necessarily licensed) properties online at VRBO.com and other rental websites.

Note: Taxes of 13.416% are added to hotel and vacation rental bills. Parking is free. Unless noted, cleaning fees refer to one-time charges.

Kaunakakai

Note: Some travelers may appreciate the convenience of a condo at **Molokai Shores,** 1 mile east of town, with many units managed by Molokai Vacation Properties (see above) or **Castle Resorts** (www.castleresorts.com; ✆ **877/367-1912**). I find the complex lacks the resort ambience and privacy found on the East and West End, while the compact units (510–663 sq. ft.) can be noisy; caveat emptor.

MODERATE

Hotel Moloka'i ★ The free earplugs on the nightstands give away the downside of this retro collection of Polynesian-style A-frames and a single-story wing: Some rooms suffer from highway and/or parking-lot noise, while the buzz at the popular **Hale Kealoha** bar (open until 10pm, with live music Fri 4–6pm) may disturb guests in others. Also, as with most lodgings on the South Side, the beach isn't good for swimming. The upside: You can easily enjoy views of Lāna'i from the pool or hammocks, the staff is friendly, and the remodeled rooms are literally cooler than before, thanks to big ceiling fans (a few even have air-conditioning units). All have microwaves, mini-fridges, and coffeemakers, but since most are a petite 228 square feet, it's better to spring for one of the deluxe second-floor rooms (432 sq. ft.) with kitchenette, including a two-burner stove and dishes. Families can take advantage of suites with a king-size bed downstairs and twin beds in a loft. Bonus: The onsite **Hale Kealoha** restaurant, which debuted in late 2015, is a more-than-worthy successor to the long-closed Hula Shores; breakfast, lunch, and dinner offer tasty, locally sourced options.

1300 Kamehameha V Hwy. (Hwy. 450), 2 miles east of Kaunakakai. www.hotelmolokai.com. ✆ **877/553-5347** or 808/553-5347. 40 units (14 timeshares). $179–$269 double. Daily resort fee $5 (includes Wi-Fi, snorkel and beach gear, DVD library). Rollaway $25 (not permitted in all rooms); crib free. **Amenities:** Restaurant; bar; coin laundry, gift shop; pool; activity desk; Wi-Fi (included in resort fee).

Hotels & Restaurants on Moloka'i

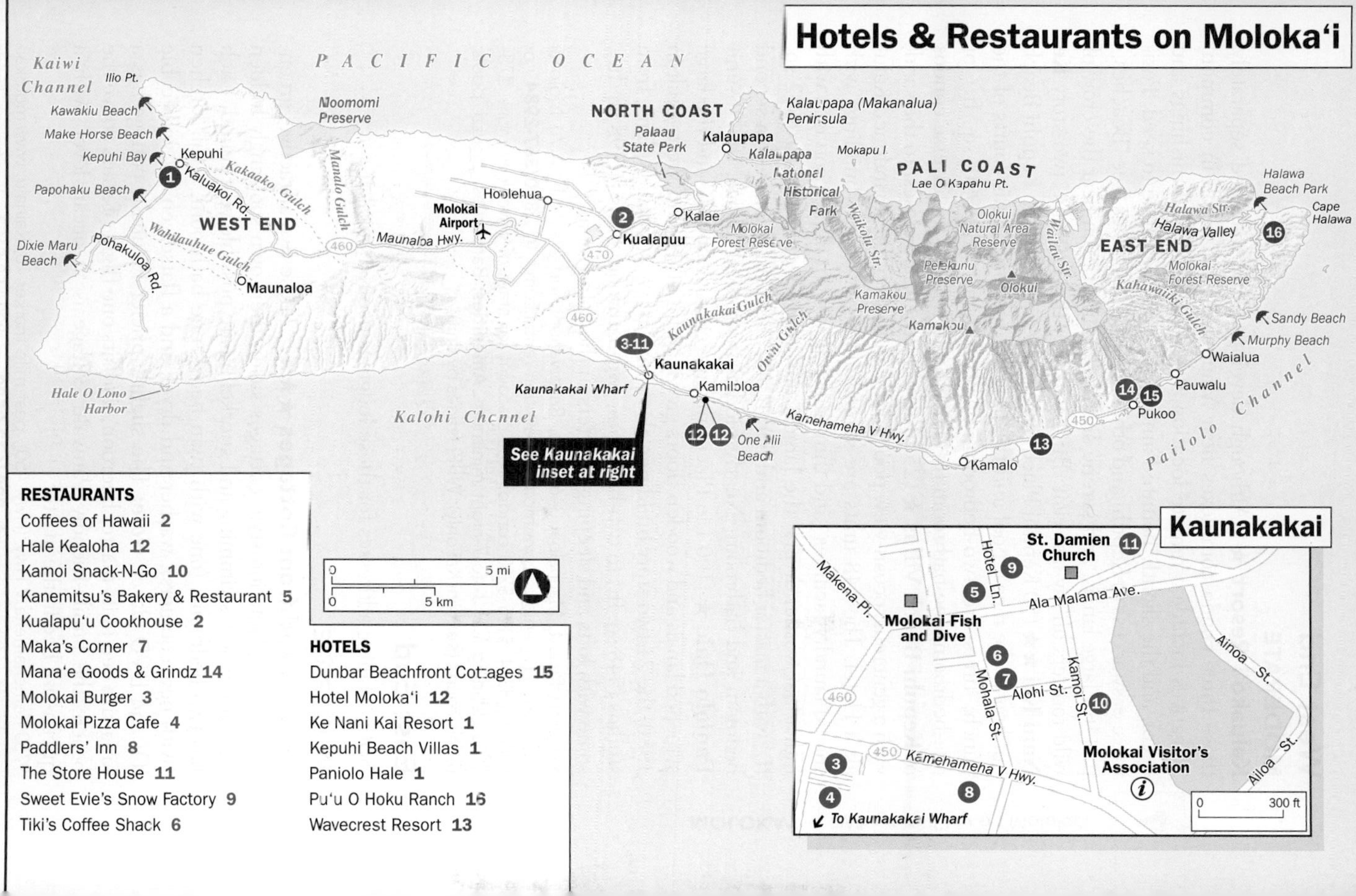

RESTAURANTS

Coffees of Hawaii 2
Hale Kealoha 12
Kamoi Snack-N-Go 10
Kanemitsu's Bakery & Restaurant 5
Kualapu'u Cookhouse 2
Maka's Corner 7
Mana'e Goods & Grindz 14
Molokai Burger 3
Molokai Pizza Cafe 4
Paddlers' Inn 8
The Store House 11
Sweet Evie's Snow Factory 9
Tiki's Coffee Shack 6

HOTELS

Dunbar Beachfront Cottages 15
Hotel Moloka'i 12
Ke Nani Kai Resort 1
Kepuhi Beach Villas 1
Paniolo Hale 1
Pu'u O Hoku Ranch 16
Wavecrest Resort 13

Kaunakakai

West End

MODERATE

Kaluako'i Resort ★ Although developed and managed separately, these three condo complexes near Maunaloa have much in common. Negatives include a remote location, varying quality of furnishings and decor, and the slightly haunted ambience of an area gone to seed. Positives: easy access to Kepuhi and other West End beaches (see "Beaches," p. 446), large lanais, and serene silence—I didn't even hear the crow of wild roosters on my last visit. Built in 1983, the 120-unit, two-story **Ke Nani Kai ★★** (50 Kepuhi Place) is set back farthest from Kepuhi Beach but boasts the nicest pool and the only hot tub and tennis courts of the bunch; units are two-bedroom, two-bathroom (880–990 sq. ft.) or one-bedroom, one-bathroom (680 ft.). Built in 1978, the diverse condos of **Kepuhi Beach Villas ★** (255 Kepuhi Beach) are closest to the sand, with a generous, ocean-view pool on the grounds of the abandoned Kaluako'i Hotel. The 148 units are spread among two-story buildings with shared laundry facilities (and thin walls), and eight duplex cottages with individual washer/dryers; the largest units have a ground floor (642 sq. ft.) with a master bedroom and bathroom, and a small loft with a second bedroom and bathroom. Nearly hidden in tropical foliage, the 78-unit **Paniolo Hale ★** (100 Lio Place) means "cowboy house," and the large screened lanais and wooden floors give it a hint of the Old West. Built in 1980, the 21 two-story buildings also come in a host of floor plans, from studios (548 sq. ft.) to two-bedroom, two-bathroom units (1,398 sq. ft.), some with lofts and sleeping quarters in the living room.

Kaluako'i Resort, Maunaloa. 346 units. Reservations for select units c/o Molokai Vacation Properties: www.molokai-vacation-rental.com. ✆ **800/367-2984** or 808/553-8334. $125–$250 condo; 10% discount for stays of a week or more. $75–$100 cleaning fee. 3- to 7-night minimum. **Amenities:** Barbecues; Jacuzzi; pools; tennis courts (Ke Nani Kai only); Wi-Fi (varies by unit).

East End

Note: Mailing addresses for these lodgings use Kaunakakai.

MODERATE

Dunbar Beachfront Cottages ★★★ These two attractive, green-and-white, plantation-style cottages sit on their own soothingly hidden beaches, where swimming and snorkeling are possible year-round. Each has two bedrooms (one with twin beds), one bathroom, a full kitchen (with new counters), washer and dryer, and a flatscreen TV with cable TV and DVD player. ***Note:*** The slightly pricier Pu'unana cottage has a king-size bed in its master bedroom and sits one flight of stairs above the beach; the family-friendly Pauwalu cottage is at ocean level, with a queen-size bed in the master.

9750 Kamehameha V Hwy. (Hwy. 450), past mile marker 18, Kainalu. www.molokai-beachfront-cottages.com. ✆ **800/673-0520** or 808/558-8153. 2 cottages (each sleeps up to 4). $190. $85 cleaning fee. 3-night minimum. No credit cards. **Amenities:** Wi-Fi (free).

Pu'u O Hoku Ranch ★★★ Its name means "hill of stars," which accurately describes this 14,000-acre retreat on a cloudless night. You'll stay in one of three 1930s-era cottages, thoughtfully decorated with Hawaiian and Balinese furnishings. Sitting well above the ocean, the four-bedroom, three-bathroom **Grove Cottage** is in a field closer to the cattle ranch operations, while the two-bedroom, two-bathroom **Sunrise Cottage** has a more secluded feel. The one-bedroom, one-bathroom **Sugar Mill Cottage,** named for the nearby remains of a mill, hides just above **Kūmimi Beach ★★** (p. 447). Only ranch guests have access to its numerous hiking trails, which pass ocean bluffs, an ancient grove, and a nursery for nēnē. ***Note:*** Groups (a minimum of 14 people) can also book the handsome 11-room hunting-style **lodge,** which comes with a private pool, yoga deck, and fireplace as well as three meals a day featuring the ranch's organic meat and produce ($185 per person, 4-night minimum).

Main entrance off Kamehameha V Hwy. (Hwy. 450) at mile marker 25. www.puuohoku.com. ✆ **808/558-8109.** 3 cottage units. $200–$300 double, seventh night free. Extra person $30. $100–$150 refundable cleaning fee (charged at check-in). 2-night minimum. **Amenities:** Store (9am–5pm weekdays); Wi-Fi (free at select hotspots).

Wavecrest Resort ★ Your best lodging bet in this complex of three three-story buildings on 6 green acres halfway to Hālawa Valley from Kaunakakai is Building A, the closest to the ocean. Top floors offer the best views of Maui, Lāna'i, and uninhabited Kaho'olawe, but keep in mind that the resort has no elevators (or air-conditioning). Bedroom windows face walkways above the parking lot, so you may hear conversations as well as crowing roosters. As with other West End condos, units are individually owned and decorated; you'll want to scrutinize photos and amenity lists closely. The gated pool and cabana with barbecues are well maintained, and the front desk has free tennis equipment to use on its two courts.

7148 Kamehameha V Hwy. (Hwy. 450), 13 miles east of Kaunakakai. 128 total units. Reservations for select units c/o Molokai Vacation Properties: www.molokai-vacation-rental.com. ✆ **800/367-2984** or 808/553-8334. $105–$165 condo; 10% discount for stays of a week or more. $75–$100 cleaning fee. 3- to 7-night minimum. **Amenities:** Barbecues; coin laundry; pool; tennis courts; Wi-Fi (varies by unit).

Camping

All campgrounds are for tents only, and permits for county and state sites must be purchased in advance. You'll have to bring your own equipment or plan to buy it on the island, as there are no rentals.

County Campgrounds ★ The family-friendly **One Ali'i Beach Park** (p. 446) provides restrooms, barbecues, outdoor showers, drinking water, picnic tables, and electricity; **Pāpōhaku Beach Park ★★** (p. 448) has the same, minus electricity. ***Note:*** The no camping signs near the Pāpōhaku parking lot apply only to the lawn to the right of the restrooms.

Permits $10 adults, $6 minors Mon–Thurs, $20 adults, $12 minors Fri–Sun and holidays (discounts for state residents). 3-night maximum. Available in person 8am–1pm and 2:30–4pm weekdays at the Maui County parks office, Mitchell Pauole Community Center, 90 Ainoa St., Kaunakakai, 96748. ✆ **808/553-3204**. To purchase by mail, download the form at www.co.maui.hi.us/index.aspx?NID=409 and mail to the parks office with check and self-addressed, stamped envelope.

State Campgrounds ★ The state manages two campgrounds at high, often misty elevations: **Pālā'au State Park ★★** (p. 443) and the remote **Waikolu Overlook** in the Moloka'i Forest Reserve. Both have restroom and picnic facilities, but no drinking water or barbecues. ***Note:*** Waikolu requires a four-wheel-drive (4WD) to drive 10 miles up mostly unpaved Maunahui Road starting from its unmarked intersection with Maunaloa Highway (Hwy. 460) near mile marker 4; do not attempt in muddy or rainy conditions. If the area is not covered in clouds, you'll be rewarded with views of the pristine Waikolu Valley and the Pacific, and be that much closer to the **Kamakou Preserve ★★** (p. 451).

Permits $18 per campsite (up to 6 persons), $3 per additional person (kids 2 and under free). 5-night maximum. Available online at https://camping.ehawaii.gov.

WHERE TO EAT ON MOLOKA'I

Note: You'll find the restaurants noted below on the "Hotels & Restaurants on Moloka'i" map on p. 453. Unless noted, they're open Monday through Saturday; most only accept cash and offer counter service.

Kaunakakai

Those looking for fine dining on Moloka'i will be disappointed, but if you just want something fresh and hearty to eat, Kaunakakai has more than a week's worth of options, all inexpensive and most with counter service. Dinner options are fewer than lunch and breakfast. **Paddlers' Inn** (see "Nightlife," below), which has an eclectic menu and free Wi-Fi, is one of only two restaurants serving alcohol (including draft beer), which explains its popularity. The other is **Hale Kealoha ★★★**, opened in late 2015 at Hotel Moloka'i (p. 452) after extensive remodeling of the former, fire-damaged Hula Shores. The new owners, who run a beloved restaurant by the same name on O'ahu, have created a locally sourced and Hawaiian-inspired menu that finally lives up to the oceanfront setting. Try one of the hearty omelets at breakfast, the island veggie burger or grilled fish sandwich at lunch, or a playful seafood bucket at dinner; entrees run $14 to $22, with large portions.

Other dinner choices include **Maka's Corner ★**, 35 Mohala St. (✆ **808/553-8058**), which serves rib-sticking, local-style plate lunches (try the mahimahi) and satisfying burgers. It has a handful of outdoor tables with counter service for breakfast, lunch, and dinner weekdays

GROCERIES, MARKETS & Edibles

Kaunakakai has an impressive (for its size) array of family-run general stores, groceries, and convenience shops. Sunday and evening hours are limited, though, with one exception: The surprisingly gourmet **Molokai Minimart,** 35 Mohala St. (✆ **808/553-4447**), is open until 11pm daily. Organic devotees and vegetarians will appreciate the mini Whole Foods vibe of **Simply Natural** (✆ **808/560-0010**), which also has a few lunch items; it's at 145 Pū'ali Place, next to Store House Deli (which also has some healthy to-go food items). **Molokai Wines N Spirits,** 77 Ala Malama (✆ **808/553-5009**), stocks cheeses, crackers, and snacks, along with an excellent array of alcoholic beverages; it's open 9am to 7pm weekdays, till 7:30pm weekends.

For produce, hit the **Saturday morning farmer's market** in Kaunakakai (8am–noon) or head to the **Kumu Farms farmstand,** Hua 'Ai Road, 1 mile south of Highway 460, near the airport (✆ **808/351-3326**). Famed for luscious papayas, the farmstand also sells organic produce, herbs, pesto, banana bread, and other treats. It's open Tuesday through Friday 9am to 4pm.

Outside of Kaunakakai, grocery shopping is very limited. On the West End, the **Maunaloa General Store,** 200 Maunaloa Hwy., Maunaloa (✆ **808/552-2346),** has the best selection and occasional plate lunches for sale; it's open Monday to Saturday 9am to 6pm, Sunday 9am to noon. Beachgoers in search of refreshments will be glad to know that **A Touch of Molokai,** inside the otherwise-empty Kaluako'i Hotel, is open 9 to 5 daily (✆ **808/552-0133**), with snacks, sodas, and microwaveable fare. On the East End, the "Goods" (convenience store) half of **Mana'e Goods & Grindz,** 8615 Kamehameha V Hwy., Pūko'o, near mile marker 16 (✆ **808/558-8498**), is open weekdays 8am to 6pm (until 5pm weekends). In the central uplands, **Kualapu'u Market,** 311 Farrington Rd. (Hwy. 480) at Uwao Street, Kualapu'u (✆ **808/567-6243**), is handy for picking up a ready-to-grill steak (Mon–Sat 8:30am–6pm; closed Sun).

(breakfast and lunch only weekends). Locals often suggest **Moloka'i Pizza Cafe ★**, 15 Kaunakakai Place, off Wharf Road (✆ **808/553-3288**), perhaps because it's the only place to get a pizza, and it stays open late (until 11pm Fri–Sat, otherwise 10pm). I prefer the cleaner, brighter setting and fresh food at **Molokai Burger ★★**, on the corner of Hwy. 450 and Ala Malama (www.molokaiburger.com; ✆ **808/553-3533**), which prepares its burgers with island-raised beef and also offers dinner plates ($14) such as salmon, fried chicken, or kalbi ribs. It's open until 9pm (closed Sun), with egg dishes and pancakes available 7 to 10:30am Saturday and free Wi-Fi.

For breakfast and lunch, other appealing choices are found at **Tiki's Coffee Shack ★**, 35 Mohala St. (✆ **808/553-5488**), which provides free Wi-Fi along with savory panini, sandwiches, baked goodies, espresso, and bubble drinks. It's also open for breakfast; order the kale smoothie if it's available. The quaint **Store House ★**, 145 Pū'ali St. (✆ **808/553-5222**), has a surprising array of tropical lemonades, pastries, salads, sandwiches (check the specials), and smoothies.

THE hot bread RUN

When people on Moloka'i mention "hot bread," they're talking about the signature item of **Kanemitsu's Bakery** (see below), an iconic island experience. First, you have to find the Kaunakakai bakery's back door: From Ala Malama, head up the Hotel Street alley and turn left at the white awning; walk 10 yards past a few benches and turn left again; the window counter is just ahead. You can order loaves of hot (or warm) white bread and a few select pastries from 8pm to around 11pm nightly except Monday. Ask for butter, jelly, cinnamon, or cream cheese ($7 for two fillings, $8 for the works; cash only); the bakers will cut the hot loaves down the middle and slather on fillings so they melt in the bread—perfect for dessert, breakfast, and several snacks.

Sweets lovers have many temptations. At **Kamoi Snack-n-Go ★**, 28 Kamoi St. (✆ **808/553-3742**), choose from more than 31 flavors of Dave's Hawaiian Ice Cream from Honolulu, including local favorites such as *kulolo* (taro-coconut custard), *haupia* (coconut pudding), and *ube* (purple yam). For a creamy spin on shave ice, visit **Sweet Evie's Snow Factory ★** in the cottage complex behind Home Town deli at 108 Ala Malama (✆ **808/553-4567**); if you can't choose from one of 50 luscious combinations of fluffy shaved ice cream and tropical toppings, try one of the dessert crepes. Or go on a post-dinner "hot bread run" (see above box) to **Kanemitsu's Bakery ★**, 79 Ala Malama (✆ **808/553-5585**). The bakery churns out pies, pastries, and cookies as well as sweet and savory breads; during breakfast and lunch hours, the restaurant side serves typical American fare with local touches such as kimchi fried rice with eggs ($9) and local organic papaya (for just $1).

Elsewhere on the Island

Outside of Kaunakakai, the **Kualapu'u Cookhouse ★**, Farrington Road and Uwao Street, Kualapu'u (✆ **808/567-9655**), serves a near-gourmet dinner, with entrees ($11–$33) such as spicy crusted ahi with lime cilantro sauce and a Thursday prime-rib special that's a local favorite. Breakfast and lunch menus are less ambitious but still tasty; sit amid cheery plantation-style decor inside or at covered picnic tables outside. The espresso bar at **Coffees of Hawaii,** 1630 Farrington Ave., Kualapu'u (✆ **808/567-9499**), offers a few inexpensive breakfast and lunch items with its caffeinated beverages and smoothies 7am to 4pm Monday through Saturday; it also has a small but welcome stand at the airport. On the East End, the takeout counter at **Mana'e Goods & Grindz,** 8615 Kamehameha V Hwy., Pūko'o, near mile marker 16 (© **808/558-8498**), is the area's lone dining option, which may make its burgers and lunch plates taste a bit better than they really are. For food on the West End, see "Groceries, Markets & Edibles," above.

MOLOKA'I SHOPPING

Gifts & Souvenirs

KAUNAKAKAI

Shoppers of every stripe will want to schedule a trip to the bustling **Saturday morning farmer's market** (8am–noon) in downtown Kaunakakai; among the couple of aunties sitting on the sidewalk with fresh papaya and other produce, you'll find a dozen or more vendors of island arts and crafts, vintage and new clothing, handmade soaps, and specialty foods such as local vanilla extract.

Other troves are less visible. Behind **Imports Gift Shop,** itself fine for inexpensive souvenirs, the **Warehouse** at 82 Ala Malama (www.molokaiartgallery.com; © **808/553-5734**) brims with a wide selection of oil paintings, giclee prints, watercolors, and carvings by local artists. Inside the office for **Molokai Ocean Tours,** 40 Ala Malama (www.molokaioceantours.com; © **808/553-8391**), you'll find Tula's pretty sterling silver and 14-karat gold jewelry, created by two Moloka'i sisters with local shells and sea glass.

Several gift shops are destinations in their own right. In Kaunakakai, the delightfully eclectic **Kalele Bookstore & Divine Expressions,** 64 Ala Malama (www.molokaispirit.com; © **808/553-5112**), offers a variety of Moloka'i-made arts and crafts, including wooden bowls, feather lei, and earrings made with *kapa* (traditional bark fabric); owner Teri Waros also dispenses free coffee and sightseeing advice. The artist cooperative **Molokai Art From the Heart,** also at 64 Ala Malama (http://molokaigallery.com; © **808/553-8018**), features the works of some 150 artists, virtually all from Moloka'i. Decorated with vintage finds, the **Attic Boutique,** 145 Pū'ali St., specializes in handmade jewelry and casual women's wear with a delicate flair (© **808/553-5222**). **Something For Everybody,** 40 Ala Malama, lives up to its name, especially if you want locally

The Perfect Moloka'i Souvenir

Found in nearly every Moloka'i store, the dozen varieties of local sea salts from **Pacifica Hawaii** (www.pacificahawaii.com) make ideal gifts. Salt master Nancy Gove evaporates seawater in elevated pans at the front of her home in Kaunakakai and then infuses colors and flavors via ingredients such as local clay *('alaea)*, Kaua'i-made rum, and Maui sugar. To see how she does it, call © **808/553-8484** and set up a tour ($13), which lasts an hour or so.

designed apparel, jewelry, or accessories (www.allthingsmolokai.com; © **808/553-3299**).

ELSEWHERE ON THE ISLAND

The **Beach Break** sporting goods store at the junction of highways 460 and 470 in Kualapu'u (© **808/567-6091**) also boasts 'ukuleles, cards, books, children's items, home decor, women's clothing in natural fabrics, and large-format prints of owner Zach Socher's impressive photos from around the island. Two miles uphill, **Denise's Gifts,** inside Molokai Furniture at the intersection of Hwy. 470 and Farrington Road (Hwy. 480), offers bargain-priced *lauhala* (woven) boxes, straw fedoras, woven ornaments, shell and pearl jewelry, and children's aloha wear (www.molokaifurniture.com; © **808/567-6083**).

Zach Socher's parents, Jonathan and Daphne, own the equally intriguing **Big Wind Kite Factory & Plantation Gallery,** 120 Maunaloa Hwy., Maunaloa (http://bigwindkites.com; © **808/552-2364**), chock-full of Balinese furnishings, stone and shell jewelry, Kalaupapa memoirs, and other books on Moloka'i. Test-fly one of the handmade Big Wind kites at the nearby park.

MOLOKA'I NIGHTLIFE

The few choices for evening entertainment at least mean a lively crowd is guaranteed wherever you go. On Thursdays, live Hawaiian music as well as prime rib draw patrons to **Kualapu'u Cookhouse** (p. 458). The parking lot at Hotel Moloka'i (p. 452) starts filling up by 3:30pm for Aloha Friday at **Hale Kealoha,** its oceanfront/poolside bar and restaurant. From 4 to 6pm, "old-style" recording artist Lono plays slack key guitar and leads a group of 'uke-strumming aunties and uncles known as Nā Kūpuna (the elders) in American and Hawaiian standards. Lono hoped to relaunch his Saturday-night concerts sometime in 2016, with even more live music planned by the restaurant's new owners.

For sale at press time, cavernous **Paddlers' Inn,** on the ocean side of Highway 450 at Mohala Street (http://molokaipaddlersinn.com; © **808/553-3300**), offers predominantly local acts onstage most nights and Sunday afternoons, when Nā 'Ohana Aloha plays Hawaiian music at 3pm. For the later shows, you'll hear classic and contemporary Hawaiian music, country, even jazz, usually 6:30 to 8:30pm; some nights, a disco DJ or karaoke will keep the party going till midnight. There's also a big-screen TV tuned to pro sports, with food and drink specials during football season.

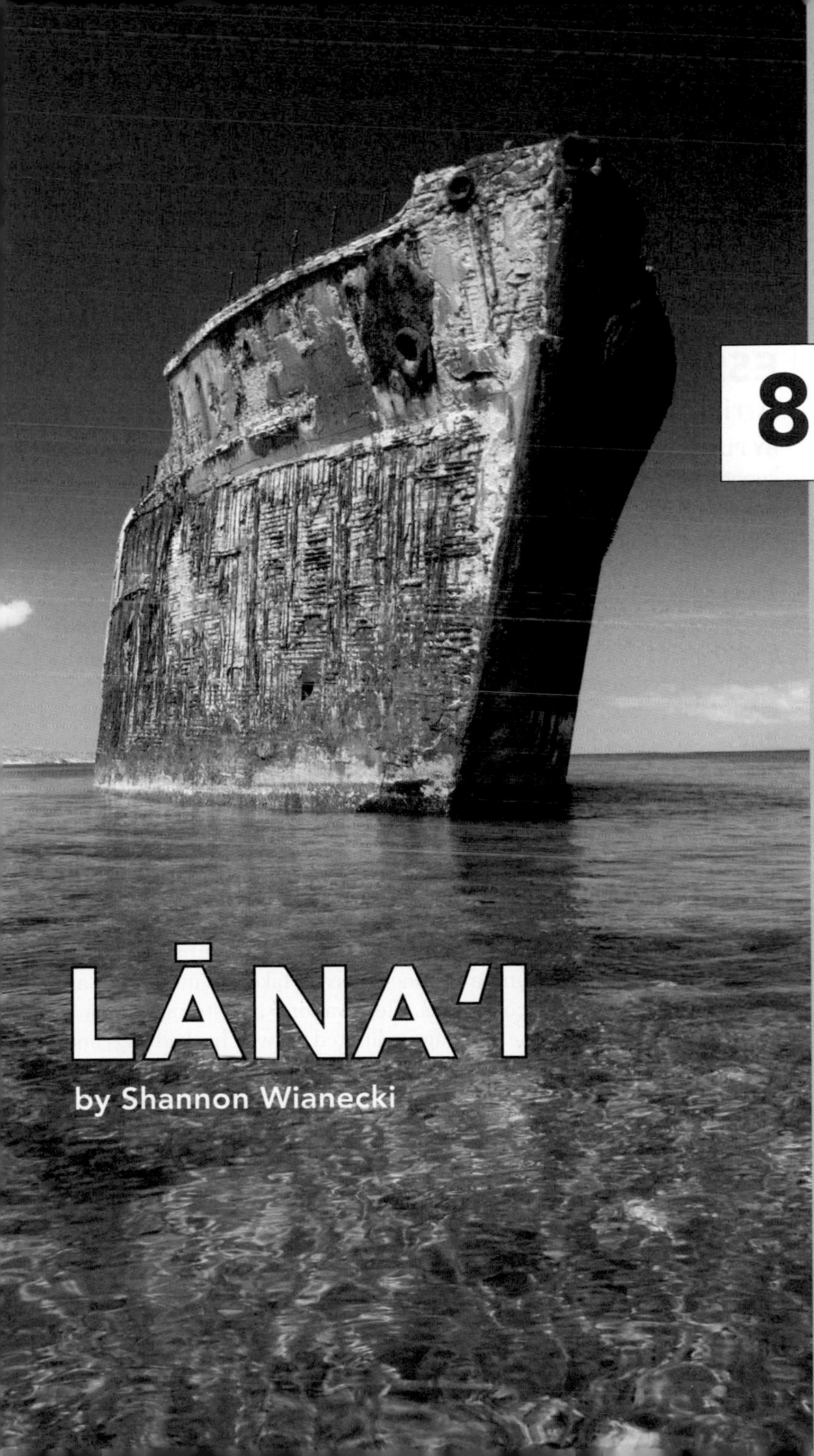

8

LĀNA'I

by Shannon Wianecki

Lāna'i is deliciously remote: The island's tiny airport doesn't accommodate direct flights from the Mainland and its closest neighbor is a 45-minute ferry ride away. It's almost as if this quiet, gentle oasis—known for both its small-town feel and celebrity appeal—demands that visitors go to great lengths to get here in order to better appreciate it.

ESSENTIALS

Arriving

BY PLANE If you're coming from outside Hawai'i, you'll have to make a connection on O'ahu (Honolulu/HNL) or Maui (Kahului/OGG or Kapalua/JHM), where you can catch a blink-and-you'll-miss-it flight to Lāna'i's airport. You'll touch down in Palawai Basin, once the world's largest pineapple plantation; it's about 10 minutes by car to Lāna'i City and 25 minutes to Mānele Bay.

Hawaiian Airlines (www.hawaiianairlines.com; © **800/367-5320**) operates 'Ohana by Hawaiian, a fleet of pretty turboprop planes that fly direct from Honolulu to Lāna'i. The small commuter airlines, **Island Air** (www.islandair.com; © **800/652-6541**) and **Mokulele Airlines** (www.mokuleleairlines.com; © **866/260-7070**), have both recently suspended general flights to Lāna'i, but double-check to see if service has been reinstated. Mokulele Airlines offers charter flights to the island on nine-passenger Cessna Grand Caravan planes.

BY BOAT A round-trip on **Expeditions Lahaina/Lāna'i Passenger Ferry** (http://go-lanai.com; © **800/695-2624**) takes you between Maui and Lāna'i for $30 adults and $20 children each way. The ferry runs five times a day, 365 days a year, between Lahaina (on Maui) and Lāna'i's Mānele Bay harbor. The 9-mile channel crossing takes 45 minutes to an hour, depending on sea conditions. Reservations are strongly recommended; call or book online. Baggage is limited to two checked bags and one carry-on. ***Bonus:*** During the winter months, taking the ferry amounts to a free whale-watch.

Visitor Information

Lāna'i Visitors Bureau, 1727 Wili Pa Loop, Wailuku, Maui 96793 (www.gohawaii.com/lanai; © **800/947-4774** or 808/565-7600), and the **Hawai'i Visitors & Convention Bureau** (www.gohawaii.com; © **800/GO-HAWAII** or 808/923-1811) provide brochures, maps, and island guides.

PREVIOUS PAGE: **Shipwreck on the coast of Lāna'i.**

Lāna'i

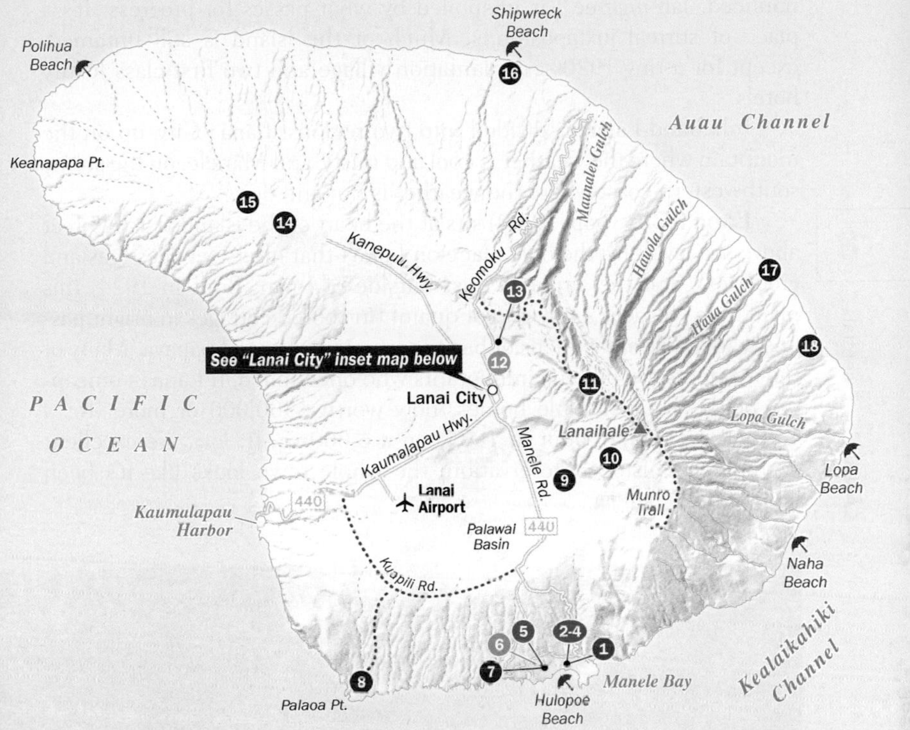

Shipwreck Beach
Polihua Beach
Keanapapa Pt.
Auau Channel
Maunalei Gulch
Hauola Gulch
Haua Gulch
Kanepuu Hwy.
Keomoku Rd.
See "Lanai City" inset map below
Lanai City
PACIFIC OCEAN
Kaumalapau Hwy.
Manele Rd.
Lanaihale
Lopa Gulch
Lopa Beach
Munro Trail
Lanai Airport
Kaumalapau Harbor
440
Palawai Basin
Kuapili Rd.
Naha Beach
Kealaikahiki Channel
Manele Bay
Hulopoe Beach
Palaoa Pt.

0
2 mi
0
2 km

Ilima Ave.
Jacaranda St.
Sixth St.
Nani St.
Houston St.
Gay St.
Seventh St.
Dole Park
Lanai Ave.
Eighth St.
Koali St.
Kiele St.
Fraser Ave.
Gay St.
Houston St.
Ninth St.
Ilima Ave.
Lāna'i City

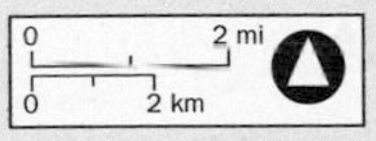

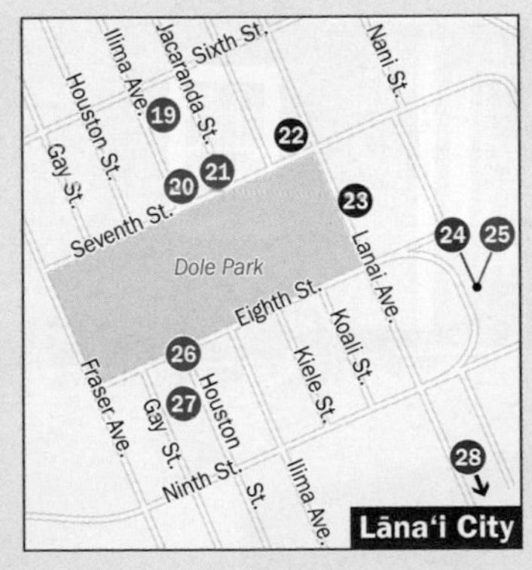

ATTRACTIONS
Hale Keaka **22**
Halepaloa (Club Lanai) **18**
Kānepu'u Preserve **14**
Kapiha'a Trail **7**
Kaunolu Village **8**
Keahiakawelo (Garden of the Gods) **15**
Keōmoku Village **17**
Kukui Point Petroglyphs **16**
Lāna'i Culture & Heritage Center **23**
Lāna'ihale **10**
Luahiwa Petroglyph Field **9**
Munro Trail **11**

GOLF COURSES
Cavendish Golf Course **12**
The Challenge at Mānele **6**

HOTELS
Dreams Come True **28**
Four Seasons Resort Lāna'i at Mānele Bay **1**
Four Seasons Resort Lāna'i, The Lodge at Koele **13**
Hotel Lāna'i **24**

RESTAURANTS
Blue Ginger Cafe **20**
Canoes Lanai **21**
Coffee Works **19**
Lanai City Grille **25**
Lanai 'Ohana Poke Market **27**
Malibu Farms **4**
Nobu Lāna'i **2**
One Forty **3**
Pele's Other Garden **26**
Views **5**

The Island in Brief

With barely 30 miles of paved road and not a single stoplight, Lāna'i (pronounced "lah-*nigh*-ee") is unspoiled by what passes for progress. It's a place of surreal juxtapositions. Much of the island is still untamed, except for a tiny 1920s-era plantation village and two first-class luxury hotels.

Inhabited Lāna'i is divided into two regions: Lāna'i City, up on the mountain where the weather is cool and misty, and Mānele, on the sunny southwestern coast where the weather is hot and dry.

Lāna'i City (pop. 3,200) sits at the heart of the island at 1,645 feet above sea level. It's the only place on Lāna'i that offers services (gas and groceries), and the airport is just outside of town. Built in 1924, this plantation village is a tidy grid of quaint tin-roofed cottages in bright pastels, with backyard gardens of banana, passionfruit, and papaya. Many of the residents are Filipino immigrants who once toiled in Lāna'i's pineapple fields. Their humble homes, now worth $500,000 or more (for a 1,500-sq.-ft. home, built in 1935, on a 6,000-sq.-ft. lot), are excellent examples of historic preservation; the whole town looks like it's been kept under a bell jar.

Plantation houses in Lāna'i.

Vintage shot of Lāna'i pineapple fields.

Around **Dole Park,** a charming village square lined with towering Norfolk and Cook pines, plantation buildings house general stores, a post office (where people stop to chat), two banks, a half-dozen restaurants, an art gallery, an art center, a few boutiques, and a coffee shop that easily outshines any Starbucks. The historic one-room police station displays a "jail" consisting of three padlocked, outhouse-size cells as a throwback to earlier times. The new station—a block away, with regulation-size jail cells—probably sees just as little action.

Just up the road from Dole Park is the **Lodge at Ko'ele** (owned by Larry Ellison, managed by the Four Seasons, and closed at the time of publication). The stately resort stands alone on a knoll overlooking pastures and the sea at the edge of a pine forest, like a grand European manor.

Mānele is directly downhill—comprised of Mānele Bay (with its small boat harbor), Hulopo'e Beach, and the island's other bastion of extravagance, the **Four Seasons Resort Lāna'i.** You'll see more of "typical" Hawai'i here—sandy beach, swaying palms, and superlative sunsets.

With a population of just over 3,000, everybody knows everybody here. The minute you arrive on island, you'll feel the small-town coziness. People wave to passing cars, residents stop to talk with friends, and fishing and gardening are considered top priorities in life. Leaving the keys in your car's ignition is standard practice.

ghosts **TO GOLF COURSES**

Lāna'i hasn't always been so welcoming. Early Hawaiians believed the island was haunted by Pahulu (the god of nightmares) and spirits so wily and vicious that no human could survive here. But many have, for the past 1,000 years. Remnants of ancient Hawaiian villages, temples, fishponds, and petroglyphs decorate the Lāna'i landscape. King Kamehameha spent his summers here at a cliffside palace overlooking the sunny southern coast.

The island's arid terrain was once native forest—patches of which persist on the 3,379-foot summit of **Lāna'ihale**—along with native birds, insects, and jewel-like tree snails. But the 1800s brought foreign ambitions and foreign strife to Hawai'i: Disease took more than half of her native people, and Western commerce supplanted the islanders' subsistence culture. Exotic pests such as rats, mosquitos, and feral goats and cattle decimated the native ecosystem and the island's watershed. Various entrepreneurs tried to make their fortune here, farming sugarcane, cotton, sisal, or sugar beets. All failed, mostly for lack of water.

Jim Dole was the first to have real commercial success here. In 1921, he bought the island for $1.1 million. He built Lāna'i City, blasted out a harbor, and turned the island into a fancy fruit plantation. For 70 years, the island was essentially one big pineapple patch. Acres of prickly fields surrounded a tiny grid of workers' homes. Life continued pretty much unchanged into the 1980s.

Ultimately, cheaper pineapple production in Asia brought an end to Lāna'i's heyday. In 1985, self-made billionaire David Murdock acquired the island in a merger (well, 98% of it anyway; the remaining 2% is owned by the government or longtime Lāna'i families). Murdock built two grand hotels, and almost overnight the plain, red-dirt pineapple plantation became one of the world's top travel destinations. Murdock's grand maneuver to replace agriculture with tourism never proved quite lucrative enough, however. In 2010, after years of six-figure losses, he sold his share of the island to the third-richest person in the United States, Larry Ellison.

The software tycoon made important moves to endear himself to the tiny, tight-knit community. He reopened the movie theater and the public swimming pool, closed for a decade. He built ball courts so that student athletes finally had somewhere to practice. He formed Pulama Lāna'i, a company tasked with directing the island's future, and hired a Lāna'i native to run its chief operating office. Mr. Ellison's ambitious plans include everything from sustainable agriculture to a third über-exclusive resort at Halepalaoa on Lāna'i's pristine eastern shore. Longtime residents (who've lived through several island makeovers) remain optimistic but cautious.

Visitors will find an island still in flux. At press time, the Lodge Ko'ele was closed for renovation, and several of the island's popular activities—shooting clays, sailing excursions—were temporarily on hold. But Lāna'i has plenty of charms to capture a traveler's imagination, from wild dolphins jumping at Hulopo'e Beach to hidden *heiau* (temples) that seem to vibrate with power.

GETTING AROUND

It's entirely possible to enjoy Lāna'i without getting behind the wheel. Lāna'i City is easily walkable and if you're staying at the Four Seasons you'll hardly want to stray from the luxurious property. But if you plan to explore the island's remote shores or forested summit (which I highly recommend), you'll need a four-wheel-drive (4WD) vehicle for at least a day or two.

The island has very little infrastructure, so you'll need to plan your transportation in advance. **Rabaca's Limousine Service** (© **808/565-6670**) will retrieve you from the airport or harbor for $10 per person. Guests at the **Four Seasons Lāna'i** (© **808/565-2000**) have the option of taking a luxury shuttle bus ($20 per person) or a private SUV ($85 per vehicle, limit four passengers). If you're camping at Hulopo'e Beach, you can walk over from the harbor.

Dollar Rent A Car at **Lāna'i Plantation Store/Lāna'i City Service,** 1036 Lāna'i Ave. (www.dollarlanai.com; © **800/533-7808**), rents standard cars, minivans, and 4WD jeeps. Expect to pay $139 (plus taxes) per day. Make sure to reserve your ride far in advance; cars are in short supply here. On top of that, gas is expensive on Lāna'i—upward of $5 a gallon—and off-road vehicles get lousy mileage. Spending $40 to $50 per day on gas isn't unheard of.

Tip: Rent only for the day (or days) you want to explore the island's hinterlands. Keep in mind that rainy weather makes many roads impassable. Check with the Dollar office to see which roads are open—and whether renting that day is worth your money.

With all of that in mind, if you'd rather leave the driving to someone else, **Rabaca's Limousine Service** (see above) is a terrific option for a short romp around the island. Knowledgeable local drivers will navigate the wild roads for you, visiting Shipwreck Beach, Keahiakawelo, and even Keōmoku Village in roomy Suburbans. Three-and-a-half-hour trips are $75 per person (minimum two guests). Or book the "4x4 Trekker Tour" package from **Expeditions,** which includes ferry travel to Lāna'i (www.go-lanai.com; © **808/565-6670;** from $181).

Whether or not you rent a car, sooner or later you'll find yourself at the **Lāna'i Plantation Store,** 1036 Lāna'i Ave. (© **808/565-7227**). Get directions, maps, and all the local gossip at this all-in-one grocery, gas station, rental-car agency, and souvenir shop. It's also a good place to fill your water jugs: A reverse-osmosis water dispenser is just out front.

[Fast FACTS] LĀNA'I

Note: Lāna'i is part of Maui County.

Emergencies In case of **emergencies,** call the police, fire department, or ambulance services at ✆ **911,** or the **Poison Control Center** at ✆ **800/222-1222.** For non-emergencies, call the **police** at ✆ **808/565-6428.**

Doctors & Dentists For over-the-counter prescriptions and vaccines, head to **Rainbow Pharmacy** right in Dole Park (431 7th St., Lāna'i City; ✆ **808/565-9332**). For emergency dental care, call **Hawaii Dental Clinic** (www.hawaiidentalclinic.com; ✆ **808/565-6418**). If you need a doctor, contact the **Straub Lāna'i Family Health Center** (✆ **808/565-6423**) or the **Lāna'i Community Hospital** (✆ **808/565-8450**).

Weather For both land and sea conditions, visit the **National Weather Service** website (www.prh.noaa.gov) and type Lāna'i, Hawai'i, in the search box.

EXPLORING LĀNA'I

You'll need an off-road vehicle to reach the sights listed below. Four-wheel-drive rentals on Lāna'i are expensive—but worth it for a day or two of adventure. For details on vehicle rentals, see "Getting Around," above.

Your first stop on Lāna'i (perhaps after baptizing yourself at Hulopo'e Beach) should be the **Lāna'i Culture & Heritage Center ★★,** 730 Lāna'i Ave. (www.lanaichc.org; ✆ **808/565-7177**), located in the heart of town. Orient yourself to the island's cultural and natural history at this tiny, well-curated museum. Learn how indigenous Hawaiians navigated thousands of miles of Pacific Ocean, see relics of the Dole plantation years, and get directions to the island's petroglyph fields. Even better, ask the docents to recount local legends passed down in their families. A visit is guaranteed to make your explorations of Lāna'i that much richer.

The Lāna'i Culture & Heritage Center partnered with Pulama Lāna'i to create a great new tool for exploring the island: the **Lāna'i Guide** app (available for free on iTunes). The GPS-enabled app directs you to historic sites and shares old photos, aerial videos, and chants.

Note: You'll find the following attractions on the "Lāna'i" map on p. 463.

Kānepu'u Preserve

This ancient grove on Lāna'i's western plateau is the island's last remaining dryland forest, containing 48 native species. A self-guided hike allows visitors to see the rare trees and shrubs that once covered the dry lowlands of all the main Hawaiian Islands. Elsewhere these species have succumbed to axis deer, agriculture, or "progress." The botanical marvels growing within this protected reserve include *olopua* (Hawaiian olive), *lama* (Hawaiian ebony), *ma'u hau hele* (a Hawaiian hibiscus), and *nānuū* (Hawaiian gardenia). Kānepu'u is easily reached via four-wheel-drive vehicle. Drive west from Koele Lodge on Polihua Road; in about 1¾ miles, you'll see the fenced area on the left.

Keahiakawelo (Garden of the Gods) ★★★

A four-wheel-drive dirt road leads out of Lāna'i City, through fallow pineapple fields, past the Kānepu'u Preserve (see above) to Keahiakawelo. This rugged, beautiful place is punctuated by boulders strewn by volcanic forces and sculpted by the elements into varying shapes and colors—brilliant reds, oranges, ochers, and yellows.

Modern visitors nicknamed this otherworldly landscape "the Garden of the Gods," but its ancient Hawaiian name, Ke-ahi-a-kawelo, means "the fire of Kawelo." According to legend, it's the site of a sorcerers' battle. Kawelo, a powerful *kahuna* (priest) noticed that the people and animals of Lāna'i were falling ill. He traced their sickness to smoke coming from the neighboring island of Moloka'i. There, an ill-intentioned priest, Lanikaula, sat chanting over a fire. Kawelo started a fire of his own, here at Keahiakawelo, and tossed some of Lanikaula's excrement into the flames. The smoke turned purple, Lanikaula perished, and health and prosperity returned to Lāna'i.

Take the dusty, bumpy drive out to Keahiakewalo early in the morning or just before sunset, when the light casts eerie shadows on the mysterious lava formations. Drive west from Kō'ele Lodge on Polihua Road; in about 2 miles, you'll see a hand-painted sign pointing left down a one-lane, red-dirt road through a *kiawe* forest to the large stone sign. Don't stack rocks or otherwise disturb this interesting site; leave everything as you found it.

Garden of the Gods.

Luahiwa Petroglyph Field ★★

Lāna'i is second only to the Big Island in its wealth of prehistoric rock art, but you'll have to search a little to find it. Some of the best examples are on the outskirts of Lāna'i City, on a hillside site known as Luahiwa Petroglyph Field. The characters incised on 13 boulders in this grassy 3-acre knoll include a running man, a canoe, turtles, and curly-tailed dogs (a latter-day wag put a leash on one).

To get here, take Mānele Road from Lāna'i City towards Hulopo'e Beach. About 2 miles out of town, you'll see a pumphouse on the left. Look up on the hillside for a cluster of dark boulders—the petroglyphs are there, but you'll have to zigzag to get to them. Two dirt roads lead off of Mānele Road, on either side of the pumphouse. Take the first one, which leads straight toward the hillside. After about 1 mile, you'll come to a fork. Head right. Drive for another ½ mile. At the first V in the road, take a sharp left and double back the way you came, this time on an upper road. After about ¼ mile; you'll come to the large cluster of boulders on the right. It's just a short walk up the cliffs (wear walking or hiking shoes) to the petroglyphs. Exit the same way you came. Go between 3pm and sunset for ideal viewing and photo ops. Don't touch the petroglyphs or climb on the rocks; these cultural resources are very fragile.

off the tourist trail: EASTSIDE LĀNA'I

If you've got good weather and a trusty 4×4 vehicle, go find adventure on Lāna'i's untamed east side. Bring snacks and extra water; there are no facilities out here and cell service is scarce. But once you've made it to the shoreline, you're likely to have a wide stretch of sand all to yourself. Follow Keomoku Road for 8 miles to the coast. Here the road turns to dirt, mud, or sand; proceed with caution. Head left to find **Shipwreck Beach** and the **Kukui Point petroglyphs** (p. 475).

Venture right to explore a string of empty beaches and abandoned villages, including **Keōmoku**—about 5¾ miles down the rough-and-tumble dirt road. This former ranching and fishing community of 2,000 was home to the first non-Hawaiian settlement on Lāna'i. A ghost town since the mid-1950s, it dried up after droughts killed off the Maunalei Sugar Company. Check out **Ka Lanakila,** the sweetly restored church that dates back to 1903.

Continue another 2 miles to the deserted remains of **Club Lāna'i.** A lonely pier stretches into the Pacific from a golden-sand beach populated by coconut palms, a few gazebos, and an empty bar floating in a lagoon. You can pretend you're on the set of *Gilligan's Island* here. This secluded area's Hawaiian name, **Halepaloa,** means "whale ivory house." Historians speculate that the teeth and bones of a sperm whale—rare in these waters—once washed ashore here. If you have time, press on to **Lopa Beach** (good for surfing, not for swimming). The road ends at **Naha Beach** with its ancient fishponds. Return the way you came and take any trash with you.

Tide pool at Kaunolu Village site.

Munro Trail ★

In the first golden rays of dawn, when owls swoop silently over the abandoned pineapple fields, take a peek at **Mount Lāna'ihale,** the 3,370-foot summit of Lāna'i. If it's clear, hop into a 4×4 and head for the Munro Trail, the narrow, winding ridge trail that runs across Lāna'i's razorback spine to its peak. From here, you may get a rare treat: On a clear day, you can see most of the main islands in the Hawaiian chain.

But if it's raining, forget it. On rainy days, the Munro Trail becomes slick and boggy with major washouts. Rainy-day excursions often end with a rental jeep on the hook of the island's lone tow truck—and a $250 tow charge. You could even slide off into a major gulch and never be found, so don't try it. But in late August and September, when trade winds stop blowing and the air over the islands stalls in what's called a *kona* condition, Mount Lāna'ihale's suddenly visible summit becomes an irresistible attraction.

Look for a red-dirt road off Mānele Road (Hwy. 440), about 5 miles south of Lāna'i City; turn left and head up the ridgeline. No sign marks the peak, so you'll have to keep an eye out. Look for a wide spot in the road and a clearing that falls sharply to the sea. From here you can see Kaho'olawe, Maui, the Big Island of Hawai'i, and Molokini's tiny crescent. Even the summits show. You can also see the silver domes of Space City on Haleakalā in Maui; Pu'u Moa'ulanui, the tongue-twisting summit of Kaho'olawe; and, looming above the clouds, Mauna Kea on the Big Island. At another clearing farther along the thickly forested ridge, all of Moloka'i, including the 4,961-foot summit of Kamakou and the faint

Ka Lanakila church.

outline of O'ahu (more than 30 miles across the sea), are visible. Once you could see all five islands in a single glance, but now a thriving pine forest blocks the view. For details on hiking the trail, see "Hiking" on p. 479.

Kaunolu Village ★★

Out on Lāna'i's nearly vertical, Gibraltar-like sea cliffs is an old royal compound and fishing village. Now a national historic landmark and one of Hawai'i's most treasured ruins, it's believed to have been inhabited by King Kamehameha the Great and hundreds of his closest followers about 200 years ago.

It's a hot, dry, dusty, slow-going 3-mile 4×4 drive from Lāna'i City to Kaunolu, but the mini-expedition is worth it. Take plenty of water, don a hat for protection against the sun, and wear sturdy shoes. New signs explain the sacred site's importance. Ruins of 86 house platforms and 35 stone shelters have been identified on both sides of Kaunolu Gulch. The residential complex also includes the **Halulu Heiau temple,** named after a mythical man-eating bird. The king's royal retreat is thought to have stood on the eastern edge of Kaunolu Gulch, overlooking the rocky shore facing **Kahekili's Leap.** Chiefs leapt from the 62-foot-high perch as a show of bravado. Nearby are **burial caves,** a **fishing shrine,** a **lookout tower,** and warriorlike stick figures—**petroglyphs**—carved on boulders. Just offshore stands the telltale fin of little **Shark Island,** a popular dive spot that teems with bright tropical fish and, frequently, sharks.

From Lāna'i City, take Kaumalapau Highway past the airport. Look for a carved boulder on the left side of the road. Turn left onto a dirt road (Kaupili Rd.) and drive east until you see another carved boulder. Turn right, toward the ocean. ***Tip:*** On your way out, turn right to continue on Kaupili Road. It meets with Hulopo'e Drive, a shortcut to Mānele Bay.

BEACHES

If you like big, wide, empty, gold-sand beaches and crystal-clear, cobalt-blue water full of bright tropical fish—and who doesn't?—go to Lāna'i. With 18 miles of sandy shoreline, Lāna'i has some of Hawai'i's least crowded and most interesting beaches.

Hulopo'e Beach ★★★

Hulopo'e is one of the loveliest beaches in all of Hawai'i. Palm-fringed golden sand is bordered by black-lava fingers, which protect swimmers from ocean currents. The bay at the foot of the Four Seasons Resort Lāna'i at Mānele Bay is a protected marine preserve, with schools of colorful fish, spinner dolphins, and humpback whales that cruise by in winter and often stop to put on a show. The water is perfect for snorkeling, swimming, or just lolling about; the water temperature is usually in the

Hulopo'e Beach.

Polihua Beach.

mid-70s (mid-20s Celsius). Swells kick up slightly in winter. Hulopo'e is also Lāna'i's premier beach park, with a grassy lawn, picnic tables, barbecue grills, restrooms, showers, and ample parking. You can camp here, too.

HULOPO'E'S TIDE POOLS ★★ Some of the best **tide pools** in Hawai'i are found along the south shore of Hulopo'e Bay. These submerged pockets of lava rock are full of strange creatures such as asteroids (sea stars) and holothurians (sea cucumbers), not to mention spaghetti worms, barber pole shrimp, and Hawai'i's favorite local delicacy, the *opihi,* a tasty morsel also known as the limpet. Youngsters enjoy swimming in the enlarged tide pool at the eastern edge of the bay. ***A few tips:*** When you explore tide pools, do so at low tide. Never turn your back on the waves. Wear tennis shoes or reef walkers, as wet rocks are slippery. Collecting specimens in this marine preserve is forbidden, so don't take any souvenirs home.

Polihua Beach ★

So many sea turtles once hauled themselves out of the water to lay their eggs in the deep sand on Lāna'i's northwestern shore that Hawaiians named the beach here Polihua, or "egg nest." The endangered green sea turtles are making a comeback, but they're seldom seen here now. You're more likely to spot an offshore whale (in season) or the perennial flotsam that washes up onto this deserted beach at the end of Polihua Road, a 4-mile jeep trail. When it isn't windy, this huge, empty stretch is ideal for beachcombing, fishing, or indulging fantasies of being marooned on a desert island. When the wind *is* blowing, beware—you'll be sandblasted. There are no facilities except fishermen's huts and driftwood shelters. Bring water and sunscreen. Strong currents and undertow make the water unsafe for swimming.

Shipwreck Beach ★★

This 8-mile-long windswept strand on Lāna'i's northeastern shore—named for the rusty ship *Liberty* stuck on the coral reef—is a sailor's nightmare and a beachcomber's dream. The strong currents yield all sorts of sea debris, from Japanese hand-blown-glass fish floats and rare pelagic paper nautilus shells to lots of junk. This is also a great place to spot whales from December to April, when Pacific humpbacks cruise in from Alaska. The road to the beach is paved most of the way, but you really need a four-wheel-drive to get down here. At the end of the road, you'll find a trail that goes about 200 yards inland to the **Kukui Point petroglyphs;** follow the stacked rock *ahu* (altars). Respect this historic site by not adding anything to it or taking anything away. Most important, *do not* touch the petroglyphs.

WATERSPORTS

Because Lāna'i lacks major development, it has Hawai'i's best water clarity. It also has low rainfall and runoff, and its coast is washed clean daily by the strong sea currents. But these currents also pose a threat to swimmers, and there are few good surf breaks. Most of the aquatic adventures—swimming, snorkeling, scuba diving—are centered on the somewhat protected South Shore, around Hulopo'e Bay.

The main watersports outfitter is **Trilogy Excursions ★★★** (Lāna'i-based trips: www.scubalanai.com; Maui-to-Lāna'i trips: www.sailtrilogy.com; © **808/874-5649**). This Maui-based company has built a well-deserved reputation as the leader in sailing/snorkeling cruises in Hawai'i. Trilogy's superb crew offers daylong snorkeling trips from Maui to Lāna'i, plus a few Lāna'i-based excursions. The latter are ideal: less crowded, less expensive, and less time spent en route, all of which adds up to more fun.

Trips with Trilogy—along with most other island activities—can be booked at the **Four Seasons Lāna'i Island Adventure Center** (1 Mānele Bay Rd., Lāna'i City; © **808/565-2072**).

Sailing & Snorkeling

Trilogy Excursions (see above) offers wonderfully uncrowded snorkel sailing trips on board its luxury catamarans and 32-foot, jet-drive rigid aluminum inflatable vessel. Cruises along Lāna'i's protected coastline sail past hundreds of spinner dolphins and into some of the best snorkeling sites in the world ($250 adults, 25% off for teens 13–18, and 50% off for children 3–12). Breakfast and lunch are included, along with sodas,

Convict Tang in Hulopo'e Bay.

snorkel gear, and instruction. Mondays and Thursdays only. Book at the **Four Seasons Lāna'i Island Adventure Center** (✆ **808/565-2072**).

If you just want to snorkel on your own, **Hulopo'e Beach** is Lāna'i's best snorkeling spot. Fish are abundant in the marine-life conservation area. Try the lava-rock points at either end of the beach and around the lava pools.

Scuba Diving

Two of Hawai'i's best-known dive spots are found in Lāna'i's clear waters, just off the south shore: **Cathedrals I** and **II,** so named because the sun lights up an underwater grotto like a magnificent church. In the past, **Trilogy Excursions** (see above) offered regular boat dives here; currently only **chartered trips** are available. For $4,750, you and five friends will have a decked-out catamaran to yourselves for two-tank dives, plus food and beverages. Trilogy also offers **shore dives** right off of Hulopo'e Beach for just $149; beginners can try an introductory dive for $189.

Sport Fishing

Spinning Dolphin Charters of Lāna'i (www.sportfishinglanai.com; ✆ **808/565-7676**) offers sport-fishing expeditions on *Fish-n-Chips,* a 36-foot Twin-V boat. It costs $700 for 4 hours for six passengers ($110 for each additional hour), or you can share a boat for $150 each for 4 hours.

Surfing/Stand-up Paddleboarding (SUP)

If you've ever wanted to learn how to surf, let instructor and surfing champion Nick Palumbo take you on a four-wheel-drive surfing safari to a secluded surf spot on the island's rugged eastside. He'll have you up and riding the waves in no time. His **Lāna'i Surf School & Surf Safari** ★★ (www.lanaisurfsafari.com; © **808/649-0739**) offers 5-hour surf safaris, which include four-wheel-drive transportation to Lopa Beach, refreshments, and "a really good time." The adventures cost $200 per person, minimum of two guests. He also offers stand-up paddleboarding (SUP) lessons at Hulopo'e Beach, two hours for $100.

Whale-Watching

During whale season (Dec–Mar), Hawaiian humpback whales put on impressive shows, breaching, slapping their pectoral fins, and singing complex melodies underwater. You can view them from just about any spot on Lāna'i, particularly on the eastside, looking toward Maui.

If you want to witness whales or simply watch the sunset while out on the water, contact **Trilogy Excursions** (see above) for a 2-hour chartered sail aboard a catamaran. Cruise past sea cliffs and unspoiled coastline while watching spinner dolphins and flying fish dart ahead of the bow. You'll arrive at Pu'u Pehe, Sweetheart Rock, just in time for the best sunset shots. The captain and crew are certified naturalists who make each trip educational. The boat is yours for $2,667, inclusive of snacks and beverages. The company currently only offers private charters for whale-watching—though it has offered group sails in the past and will likely do so again. **Spinning Dolphin Charters of Lāna'i** (see above) also offers private charters.

OTHER OUTDOOR ACTIVITIES

The **Four Seasons Lāna'i** operates the **Island Adventure Center,** 1 Mānele Bay Rd., Lāna'i City (© **808/565-2072**), where resort guests and the general public can book an assortment of activities: golf, utility task vehicle (UTV) tours, horseback rides, sunset sails, and more. Located next door to the resort's tennis courts, the center is open from 6am to 6pm.

Biking

Lāna'i Cycles (www.lanaicycles.com; © **808/563-0535**) offers terrific, 3½-hour guided tours of off-the-beaten-path locales. Start your adventure in the misty clouds above Lāna'i City. Hop on a specialized Sirrus multiuse bike and coast 7 miles down to the island's scenic east coast. A support vehicle will shuttle you back up to town, where you can fuel up on smoothies or coffee before taking off again, this time down to Kuamalapau Harbor. Tours cost $180 and are small and personalized.

Golf

Note that as we went to press, Jack Nicklaus was (still) redesigning **The Experience at Kō'ele** (www.fourseasons.com/lanai) golf course. We can't wait to see how he improves on the existing 18th hole, a par-5 grand finale featuring waterfalls that flow into a lake.

Cavendish Golf Course ★ This quirky par-36, 9-hole public course lacks not only a clubhouse and club pros, but also tee times, scorecards, and club rentals. To play, just show up, put a donation into the little wooden box next to the first tee, and hit away. The 3,071-yard, E. B. Cavendish–designed course was built by the Dole plantation in 1947 for its employees. The greens are a bit bumpy, but the views of Lāna'i are great and the temperatures usually quite mild.

Off of Kauna'oa Dr., next to the Lodge at Ko'ele, Lāna'i City. ✆ **808/565-7300.** Greens fees by donation.

The Challenge at Mānele ★★★ Designed by Jack Nicklaus, this target-style, desert-links course, is one of the most challenging courses in the state. Check out some of the course rules: no retrieving golf balls from the 150-foot cliffs on the ocean holes 12, 13, or 17, and all whales, axis deer, and other wild animals are considered immovable obstructions. That's just a hint of the unique experience you'll have on this starkly beautiful oceanfront course, which is routed among lava outcroppings, archaeological sites, and *kiawe* groves. The five sets of staggered tees pose a challenge to everyone from the casual golfer to the pro. Want an even bigger challenge? Swap your golf cart for a golfboard—an electric vehicle that maneuvers like a skateboard and carries your clubs. Facilities include a clubhouse, pro shop, rentals, practice area, lockers, and showers.

Next to the Four Seasons Resort Lāna'i at Mānele Bay. www.fourseasons.com/lanai. ✆ **800/321-4666** or 808/565-2222. Greens fees $295 ($250 for guests).

Horseback Riding

Get a taste of the *paniolo* (cowboy) life on a horseback tour. Sign up for an upland trail ride at the **Four Seasons Lāna'i Island Adventure Center,** 1 Mānele Bay Rd., Lāna'i City (✆ **808/565-2072**), where you'll catch a shuttle up to Kō'ele and meet your steed. On horseback, you'll meander through guava groves and past ironwood trees; catch glimpses of spotted deer, wild turkeys, and quail; and end with panoramic views of Maui and Lāna'i. The trails are dusty and rain is frequent; wear clothes you don't mind getting dirty and bring a light jacket. Long pants and closed-toe shoes are required. Daily tours start at 9:30am and 2pm, last 1½ hours, and cost $150 per person.

Hiking

KŌ'ELE NATURE HIKE The leisurely 2-hour self-guided **Kō'ele Nature Hike** starts by the reflecting pool in the backyard of the Lodge at Kō'ele and takes you on a 5-mile loop through Norfolk Island pines, into Hulopo'e Valley, past wild ginger, and up to Koloiki Ridge, with its panoramic view of Maunalei Valley and the islands of Moloka'i and Maui in the distance. You're welcome to take the hike even if you're not a guest at the lodge. Go in the morning; by afternoon, the clouds usually roll in, marring visibility at the top and increasing your chance of being caught in a downpour. The path isn't clearly marked, so ask the concierge at the Four Seasons (www.fourseasons.com/lanai; ✆ **808/565-2000**) for a free map, or sign up for one of the resort's guided hikes. It's considered moderate, with some uphill and downhill hiking.

MUNRO TRAIL This tough, 11-mile (round-trip) uphill climb through groves of Norfolk pines is a lung-buster, but if you reach the top, you'll be rewarded with a breathtaking view of Moloka'i, Maui, Kaho'olawe, the peaks of the Big Island, and—on a really clear day—O'ahu in the distance. Figure on 7 hours. The trail begins at Lāna'i Cemetery (interesting in its own right) along Keomoku Road (Hwy. 44) and follows Lāna'i's

Maunalei Gulch.

ancient caldera rim, ending up at the island's highest point, **Lāna'ihale.** Go in the morning for the best visibility. After 4 miles, you'll get a view of Lāna'i City. The weary retrace their steps from here, while the more determined go the last 1.25 miles to the top. Diehards head down Lāna'i's steep south-crater rim to join the highway to Mānele Bay. For more details on the Munro Trail—including four-wheel-driving it to the top—see "Munro Trail" (p. 471).

KAPIHA'A TRAIL An old fisherman's trail snakes along the scenic coastline, starting at Mānele Bay. This easy hike will expose you to Lāna'i's unique geography and many unusual native Hawaiian coastal plants. The back-and-forth trek takes around 90 minutes. Venture out on your own or, if you're a hotel guest at the Four Seasons Resort Lāna'i, arrange a complimentary guided hike through the concierge (www.fourseasons.com/lanai; © **808/565-2000;** $10 donations accepted). You can also download an informative brochure from the **Lāna'i Visitor Center website** (www.lanaichc.org/kapihaa.html).

Tennis

Public courts, lit for night play, are available in Lāna'i City at no charge; call © **808/565-6979** for reservations. If you're staying at the Four Seasons, you can take advantage of the six Premiere Cushion outdoor hard courts for free, with complimentary use of Prince rackets, balls, and bottled water—even shoes if you need.

UTV Tours

For a unique view of the island, book a 2-hour UTV tour at the **Four Seasons Lāna'i Island Adventure Center** (1 Mānele Bay Rd., Lāna'i City © **808/565-2072**). You can pretend you're Mad Max or Furiosa as you slide on your sleek helmet, balaclava, and goggles, and mount your Polaris Razor 1000. (The off-road suspension is so smooth you'll hardly notice the boulders.) Local guides will chauffeur you into the forested uplands above Palawai Basin where you'll explore an ancient agricultural temple, view petroglyphs, and dodge spotted deer. Wear clothes you're willing to sacrifice to Lāna'i's red dirt (long pants and closed-toe shoes are required) and bring a jacket (rain is frequent). Tours leave twice daily at 9am and 1:30pm and cost $150 per person.

WHERE TO STAY ON LĀNA'I

Accommodations on Lāna'i are limited: You can go for broke at one (or both) of the luxurious Four Seasons properties, book a plantation-style room at the Hotel Lāna'i, or camp under the stars at Hulopo'e Beach Park. When you stay with the Four Seasons, you're greeted at the airport or ferry with chilled towels and shuttled off in style. Later, if you move from one resort to the other, the staff will pack and deliver your luggage for you.

Expensive

Four Seasons Resort Lāna'i, The Lodge at Kō'ele *Note:* **At press time, the property was closed due to construction and slated to reopen by January 2017.** This elegant retreat sits against Lāna'ihale, the island's tallest peak, in the cool mist of the mountains. On 21 immaculately landscaped acres, it resembles a grand country estate, complete with croquet lawns, gazebos, orchid greenhouse, reflecting pond, and Chinese pagoda. Inside, the Great Hall's beamed ceilings and enormous stone fireplaces evoke the atmosphere of a storied hunter's lodge. Leather couches invite lounging around the fireplaces—coveted spots during the nightly live music sessions.

At 1,700 feet above sea level, temperatures can drop into the 50s—especially during winter. Never fear, the rooms have heat as well as air-conditioning, extra blankets are in the closet, and the cooler climate just makes everything cozier. This isn't your stereotypical Hawaiian vacation; people come to Kō'ele to play golf on one of the world's most scenic courses, explore the hinterlands on horseback, hike up into the forested hillside, or simply put their feet up on the foyer's comfy rattan chairs and disappear into a novel.

1 Keōmoku Hwy., Lana'i City. www.fourseasons.com/lanai. © **800/321-4666** or 808/565-4000. 100 units. Call for current rates. Free parking. **Amenities:** 3 restaurants; bar; babysitting; bike rentals; children's program; concierge; croquet; fitness room; golf; self-guided hike; Jacuzzi; outdoor pool; room service; spa treatments; tennis courts; watersports equipment; Wi-Fi (free).

Four Seasons Resort Lāna'i at Mānele Bay ★★★ A conch shell's trumpeting call announces your arrival at this oceanfront retreat, where everyone magically knows your name—even the computer screen in your bathroom mirror. Every inch of this opulent oasis reflects the latest in tech-savvy luxury, from the wristband room keys to the Toto toilets. Service is impeccable: The concierge texts you when dolphins or whales appear in the bay. Beach attendants set up umbrellas in the sand for you, spritz you with Evian, and deliver smoothie samples.

Guest rooms are large and luxurious, with blackout shades that you can control with a flick of your hand. Suites have Japanese cedar tubs and views that stretch on forever. The resort's two wings overlook Hulopo'e Beach and are lushly landscaped with waterfalls, koi-filled lotus ponds, and artwork tucked into every corner. Rare Polynesian artifacts purchased from the Bishop Museum decorate the main lobby's lower level, which is home to two fantastic restaurants: **Nobu Lāna'i ★★★** and **One Forty ★★★**. Other amenities sprinkled around the property include a first-rate adventure center, shuffleboard tables in the chic sports bar, and an exercise room with a view so grand you'll forget you're burning calories on a stationary cycle. Inspired by indigenous healing traditions, the resort's spa offers traditional *lomi lomi* Hawaiian massages, taro body wraps, facials, and salon services in serene treatment rooms. Guests have free access to the spa facility's saunas and steam rooms. The "Kids for All Seasons" child-care programs activities are excellent, but you'll probably have trouble pulling your youngsters away from the beach and tide pools.

1 Mānele Bay Rd., Lāna'i City. www.fourseasons.com/lanai. ✆ **800/321-4666** or 808/565-2000. 21 units, 25 suites. $1,075–$4,925 double; $1,875–$21,000 suite. Numerous packages available. **Amenities:** 5 restaurants; bar with live music; babysitting; children's program; concierge; fitness center w/classes; golf at Jack Nicklaus–designed Challenge at Mānele; whirlpools; 2 pools; room service; full spa; tennis courts; watersports equipment; Wi-Fi (free or premium for $20 per day).

Moderate

Hotel Lāna'i ★ This boutique hotel in the heart of town is perfect for families and other vacationers who can't afford to spend a small fortune but still want to experience Lāna'i. If you're looking for the old-time aloha that the island is famous for, this is your place. Built in the 1920s, it has retained its quaint, plantation-era character.

That character comes at a price: Guest rooms are small and noise travels. But the comfy beds come with Hawaiian quilts, and the ceiling fans do a more than adequate job in the cooler climate. The popular Lāna'i units are slightly larger and share a furnished deck that faces Dole Park. The one-bedroom cottage costs slightly more than those rooms and boasts the added amenities of a private yard, living room with TV, and a bathtub. All of Lāna'i City is within walking distance. The in-house restaurant, **Lāna'i City Grille,** is excellent. This social spot is where visitors might mingle with locals in the bar, talking or playing the 'ukulele long into the night. Although it lacks the luxury of the nearby resorts, Hotel Lāna'i offers an authentic, unpretentious peek into the island's Hawaiian heart.

828 Lāna'i Ave., Lāna'i City. www.hotellanai.com. ✆ **800/795-7211** or 808/565-7211. 10 units, 1 cottage. $174–$304 double; $254–$279 cottage, $55 for child. Rates include continental breakfast. Free parking. **Amenities:** Restaurant; bar; access to golf courses on the island; complimentary beach equipment; nearby tennis courts; Wi-Fi (free).

Inexpensive

Dreams Come True ★ Susan and Michael Hunter have operated this bed-and-breakfast in the heart of Lāna'i City for 30-plus years. The nicely renovated 1925 plantation house is roomy and quaint, with four bedrooms, four bathrooms, and a backyard orchard of papaya, banana, and avocado trees. Among the many perks: marble bathrooms, fresh *lilikoi* juice served with the delicious breakfast each morning, and private four-wheel-drive rentals—a real bonus on this car-deficient island!

1168 Lāna'i Ave., Lāna'i City. ✆ **808/565-6961** or 808/565-7211. 4 rooms, or entire house. $141 double; $564 entire house. Rates include continental breakfast. **Amenities:** Car rental; concierge; laundry; barbecue; Wi-Fi (free).

Camping at Hulopo'e Beach Park ★★★

There is only one legal place to camp on Lāna'i, but it's a beauty. **Hulopo'e Beach Park (© 808/215-1107)** has eight campsites on the shady grass lawn fronting this idyllic white-sand beach. Each site accommodates up to five people. Facilities include restrooms, showers, barbecues, and picnic tables. Email info@lanaibeachpark.com 72 hours in advance to request a permit. You'll pay a $30 registration fee, plus a charge of $15 per person per night. Payment is by credit card only. Permits are issued in person, first-come, first-served, for 3 nights max, major holidays excluded.

WHERE TO EAT ON LĀNA'I

Lana'i offers dining experiences on two ends of the spectrum, from humble ma-and-pa eateries to world-class culinary adventures. The posh resort restaurants require deep pockets, and Lāna'i City has only a handful of other options.

Note: You'll find the restaurants reviewed in this chapter on the "Lāna'i" map on p. 463.

Expensive

Nobu Lāna'i ★★★ JAPANESE What does Lāna'i have in common with New York, Milan, Budapest, and Mexico City? All have a Nobu restaurant—a measure of how fun a place is, according to pop star Madonna. The best way to experience this epicurean phenomenon is to order the *omakase*—the chef's tasting menu—for $120. Every dish is as delicious as it is artful: the smoked Wagyu gyoza with jalapeño miso, the immaculate plates of nigiri sushi, and the ahi avocado salad with greens grown at Alberta's farm up the road. Vegetarian? Nobu has a sophisticated menu just for you, featuring fusion tacos and tofu *tobanyaki anticucho*—a melting pot of Japanese and Peruvian flavors. The wine and cocktail list is top-notch, including exclusive Hokusetu sake and a sassy caipirinha with Pisco, fresh lime, ginger beer, and sprigs of shiso. Request a sake tasting, and the resident sake master will teach you the subtleties of a dry *onigorishi* and a dynamic *daiginjo*.

At the Four Seasons Resort Lāna'i, 1 Mānele Bay Rd., Lāna'i City. www.fourseasons.com/lanai. © **808/565-2832.** Main courses $12–$58; multicourse tasting menu $120. Daily 6–9pm.

One Forty ★★★ BREAKFAST/STEAK & SEAFOOD This breakfast buffet is probably the best in the state. Weeks later I'm still fantasizing about my One Forty breakfast overlooking sparkling Mānele Bay. Imagine: a cornucopia of ripe tropical fruit, "make-your-own" omelet and smoothie stations, artisan cheese, charcuterie, four types of sausages, brioche French toast, eggs any which way, and a malasada machine. Not just lox but house-cured *ono* with toasted bagels—now *that* is what I call breakfast. Dinner is also stellar. The pan-seared kampachi with forbidden rice, bok choy, and chimichurri sauce is perfectly on point, as is the 20-ounce bone-in ribeye (it should be, for a staggering $95). Order the chocolate soufflé early; it takes 20 minutes to bake and is worth every second of the wait.

At the Four Seasons Resort Lāna'i, 1 Mānele Bay Rd., Lāna'i City. www.fourseasons.com/lanai. ✆ **808/565-2290.** Breakfast main courses $12–$24; buffet $52; dinner $32–$95. Daily 6:30–10am and 6–9pm.

Moderate

Lāna'i City Grille ★★ HAWAI'I REGIONAL/COUNTRY This Lāna'i mainstay has three comfortable dining areas to choose from: the bright and lovely dining room, the bar with large-screen TVs and couch-like chairs, and the outdoor patio where Hawaiian musicians croon under the stars. The menu ranges from trendy American comfort food (chicken and waffles, adult mac and cheese, sliders) to local specialties (pan-seared fish over garlicky bok choy, braised short ribs). The service is on point and the food is fresh—if a bit pricier than it would be on another island. Bring a jacket if you want to sit outside by the fire pits and soak up the friendly Lāna'i ambiance and fantastic live music.

At the Hotel Lāna'i, 828 Lāna'i Ave., Lāna'i City. www.hotellanai.com. ✆ **808/565-7211.** Main courses $18–$36. Wed–Sat 5–9pm; Sun 8am–1pm.

Malibu Farms ★ AMERICAN Breakfast and lunch are glamorous affairs by the Four Seasons pool. Start your day with fresh-pressed juice and quinoa oatmeal while scanning Hulopo'e Bay for dolphins. For lunch, indulge in a burger with bacon marmalade. At dusk, pull up a seat at the bar for a craft cocktail and watch the sun melt into the sea.

At the Four Seasons Resort Lāna'i, 1 Mānele Bay Rd., Lāna'i City. www.fourseasons.com/lanai. ✆ **808/565-2290.** Breakfast and lunch main courses $18–$26. Daily 8am–7pm.

Views ★★ PACIFIC RIM Take a stroll or hop the shuttle to the Challenge at Mānele's clubhouse, the island's best spot for lunch, where the idyllic view of Pu'u Pehe and Hulopo'e Beach is even better than at the resort proper—if you can fathom that. Sip a Lāna'i Mule (vodka with ginger beer and calamansi lime juice), nosh on a prawn B.L.T. (pita stuffed with fat prawns, Creole aioli, and caramelized onions), and crown your meal with a decadent ice cream sandwich. My fave: the gingersnap cookie loaded with pineapple coconut ice cream.

At the Challenge at Mānele Golf Course, 1 Mānele Bay Rd., Lāna'i City. www.fourseasons.com/lanai. ✆ **808/565-2230.** Main courses $19–$34. Daily 11am–6pm.

Inexpensive

Blue Ginger Cafe ★ COFFEE SHOP With its cheery curtains and oilcloth-covered tables, this humble eatery welcomes residents and locals alike in for eggs and Spam (yes, Spam is a beloved breakfast meat in Hawai'i), adequate bowls of saimin, epic plates of fried rice, fried chicken katsu, and decent egg/tuna/chicken salad sandwiches on homemade bread. The kitchen staff bakes all of its own breads and pastries, so burgers and sandwiches taste especially fresh. Hot out of the oven, the blueberry turnovers, cinnamon buns, and cookies are legendary. 409 Seventh St. (at Ilima St.), Lāna'i City. www.bluegingercafelanai.com. ✆ **808/565-6363.** Breakfast and lunch items under $17; dinner main courses under $18. Cash only. Thurs–Mon 6am–8pm; Tues–Wed 6am–2pm.

Canoes Lāna'i ★ LOCAL "Lāna'i's oldest eating establishment" opened in 1926 as a soda fountain. The Tanigawa family took it over in the 1950s and began selling their secret-recipe hamburgers, still on the menu. Today's favorites are *furikaki* chicken served with (of course) two scoops of rice and macaroni salad, and the Tanigawa loco moco: a monster pile of rice topped with that famous burger, a fried egg, and a slather of gravy. 419 Seventh St., Lāna'i City. www.facebook.com/Canoes-Lanai-Restaurant-278954825810. ✆ **808/565-6537.** Breakfast items under $14; sandwiches $5–$8; burgers $3–$6. Cash only. Mon–Fri 6:30am–1pm; Fri–Sat 6:30am–8pm.

Coffee Works ★ COFFEEHOUSE A biscuit's toss from Dole Park, this cozy coffeehouse churns out excellent espresso drinks, amply loaded lox and bagels, açai bowls, ice cream, crepes, and sandwiches. The renovated plantation home is the perfect place to fuel up in the morning. It's also Lāna'i City's local watering hole—expect to see your waiter from dinner last night chatting away with the shuttle driver on the wide wooden deck. As you wait for your cappuccino, browse the gift items opposite the counter: T-shirts to prove you were here, tea infusers and pots, and island coffee beans. 604 Ilima St., Lāna'i City. www.coffeeworkshawaii.com. ✆ **808/565-6962.** Most items under $15. Mon–Fri 7am–3pm; Sat 8am–3pm.

Lāna'i 'Ohana Poke Market ★ LOCAL/SEAFOOD On a side street off of Dole Park, a takeout window offers fresh, affordable seafood. Poke (raw, seasoned fish) is a local comfort food, and this spot does it right. The sushi poke bowl is my favorite—sushi rice heaped with fresh ahi, *masago* (flying fish roe), nori, chili aioli, and crunchy puffed rice. So *ono* (delicious)! The deluxe poke bowl comes with two pieces of teriyaki steak and mac salad. Try the *limu kohu* poke—the native seaweed is mineral-y and potent, a fine complement to the rich fish. Come early; the *furikake* (seasoned) poke and coconut shrimp bowls run out quickly. 834-A Gay St., Lāna'i City. ✆ **808/565-6537.** Lunch items $8–$11. Cash only. Mon–Thurs 10:30am–4pm; Fri 10:30am–8pm.

Pele's Other Garden ★ DELI/BISTRO The checkered floor and vanity license plates decorating the walls set an upbeat tone at this casual bistro. For lunch, dig into an avocado and feta wrap or an Italian hoagie.

Cheese lovers will swoon over the thin-crusted four-cheese pizza—a gooey medley of mozzarella, Parmesan, feta, and provolone. During happy hour, nosh on onion rings and coconut shrimp at one of Lāna'i City's only bars. Enjoy cocktails, wine by the glass, or one of the dozen brews on tap. The atmosphere grows slightly more romantic after sundown, with white linens on the tables and twinkle lights over the outdoor seating.

811 Houston St., Lāna'i City. www.pelesothergarden.com. © **808/565-9628.** Main courses $9–$13 lunch, $17–$20 dinner; pizza from $9. Mon–Fri 11am–3pm; Mon–Sat 5–8pm; bar menu Mon–Sat 4:30–6:30pm.

LĀNA'I SHOPPING

Lāna'i has limited shopping, but you can find some glittering gems here. A stroll around Dole Park will yield original artwork, clothing, and souvenirs, and the Four Seasons has excellent boutiques. Just remember that groceries are delivered only once a week (Wed is barge day)—so plan your shopping accordingly.

Art

Lāna'i Art Center ★★ Established in 1989, the Lāna'i Art Center showcases works by Lāna'i residents, including evocative watercolor paintings of local landmarks, silk-screened clothing, and necklaces made of polished shells and bone. Often, the artists are at work in back. Check out the center's reasonably priced workshops, where local and visiting artists offer instruction on everything from *raku* (Japanese pottery) to silk-printing, quilting, lei-making, felting, and *gyotaku* (printing a real fish on your own T-shirt). 339 Seventh St., Lāna'i City. www.lanaiart.org. © **808/565-7503.**

Mike Carroll Gallery ★★ Oil painter Mike Carroll left a successful 22-year career as a professional artist in Chicago for a distinctly slower pace on Lāna'i. His gorgeous, color-saturated interpretations of local life and landscapes fill the walls of his eponymous gallery, which also sells original work by top Maui and Lāna'i artists, prints, and locally made, one-of-a-kind jewelry. 443 Seventh St., Lāna'i City. www.mikecarrollgallery.com. © **808/565-7122.**

Edibles & Grocery Staples

Pine Isle Market ★ This family-run grocery, three doors down from Richard's, carries everything that its competition doesn't. A visit to both will net you a fine haul. Pine Isle specializes in locally caught fresh fish, but you can also find ice cream, canned goods, fresh herbs, toys, diapers, paint, and other essentials. Take a spin through the fishing section to ogle every imaginable lure. The Hondas, who've operated the shop for 6 decades, still observe the "plantation days" tradition of closing for lunch on Tuesdays and Thursdays. 356 Eighth St., Lāna'i City. © **808/565-6488.**

Richard's Market ★★ Since 1946, this family grocery has been the go-to for dry goods, frozen meats and vegetables, liquor, paper products, cosmetics, utensils, and other miscellany. It got a major makeover, courtesy of Larry Ellison and Pulama Lāna'i. Now the inside resembles a miniature Whole Foods with an array of fancy chocolates and fine wines, mixed in with aloha shirts, fold-up *lauhala* mats, and Filipino staples such as tapioca pearls. Don't faint when you see that milk costs $9 a gallon; that's the price of paradise. Even still, the spiffy new shelves are often empty by the weekend. The fish counter in back sells no fewer than eight types of poke (raw seasoned fish) and super-tasty cone sushi topped with your choice of poke for just $2.99. Open until 10pm. 434 Eighth St., Lāna'i City. ✆ **808/565-3780.**

Saturday Market ★ From 8am to noon-ish each Saturday, the southeast corner of Dole Park turns into a farmer's market. Lana'i residents bring their homegrown fruits and vegetables, freshly baked pastries, plate lunches, and handicrafts to sell. The best lunches sell out quickly—if you want one of Juanita's scrumptious pork flautas with a dollop of hot sauce, get here early. Other treats include fresh pressed juices from the bygone 'Anuenue Juice Bar and fantastic Thai summer rolls.

Gifts & Souvenirs

The Local Gentry ★★ Jenna (Gentry) Majkus manages to outfit her small but wonderful boutique with every wardrobe essential, from fancy lingerie to stylish chapeaux, for the whole family. Browse the selection of OluKai sandals, Kahala aloha shirts, handmade onesies, and (best of all) T-shirts with Lāna'i-inspired silkscreens, including What Happens on Lāna'i Everybody Knows. 363 Seventh St., Lāna'i City. ✆ **808/565-9130.**

Makamae/Pilina ★★ Just try to resist this resort shop's bona-fide (read: top-dollar) treasures, including delicately wrapped freshwater pearl and diamond bead necklaces by Jordan Alexander, the cutest-ever bikinis and beach cover-ups by Hawai'i's own Letarte, and slinky dresses and housewares by Missoni (yes, you can fit that throw pillow in your suitcase). Slip into a pair of Jimmy Choo sandals and wear them out to dinner at Nobu. Four Seasons Resort Lāna'i, 1 Mānele Bay Rd. ✆ **808/565-2093.**

Rainbow Pharmacy ★ Like so many island institutions, this pharmacy plays dual roles. It's not just a place to fill your prescription or stock up on earplugs and sunburn gel; you'll also find quality locally made souvenirs here (including Cory Labang's coin purses and clutches made with vintage Hawaiian fabric). From the counter in back, you can order an assortment of medicinal Chinese teas and—unpredictably—shave ice. 431 Seventh St., Lāna'i City. ✆ **808/565-9332.**

The Local Gentry.

LĀNA'I NIGHTLIFE

The Hotel Lāna'i and two Four Seasons resorts have been the island's mainstays for nightlife—but since all three locations have undergone management changes and/or renovations, I can't promise who's playing what music where.

Several nights a week, local musicians get together for jams at the **Lāna'i City Grille ★** at the Hotel Lāna'i, 828 Lāna'i Ave. (www.hotellanai.com; ✆ **800/795-7211** or 808/565-7211). No trip to the island is complete without an evening spent here, enjoying Hawaiian harmonies under the stars alongside the locals and day-trip golfers. Bring a jacket if you plan to sit outside; the fire pits are cozy, but not quite enough to keep you warm. Before sunset, head to **Kailani** at the **Four Seasons Resort Lāna'i,** 1 Mānele Bay Rd. (www.fourseasons.com/lanai; ✆ **808/565-2093**), for Hawaiian music and light jazz; after dark, you can play pool in the **Sports Bar.**

A major addition to Lāna'i's nightlife is the newly renovated Lāna'i Theater, renamed **Hale Keaka ★** (456 Seventh St., Lāna'i City; ✆ **808/565-7500**). Built in 1926, this iconic landmark shared films, live plays, and musical performances with the island community for 80 years. The $4-million renovation kept the vintage feel but added air-conditioning, digital sound, two stages and screens, cushy seats, and a green room for entertainers. Two films—an adult and a children's selection—rotate out each week. The box office opens 1 hour prior to the start of each movie. And because it's Lāna'i, you'll find *furikake* and shoyu among the complimentary popcorn condiments.

9

KAUA'I

by Jeanne Cooper

Time has been kind to Kaua'i, the oldest and northernmost of the Hawaiian Islands. Millions of years of erosion have carved fluted ridges, emerald valleys, and glistening waterfalls into the flanks of Wai'ale'ale, the extinct volcano at the center of this near-circular isle. Similar eons have created a ring of enticing sandy beaches and coral reefs. Its wild beauty sometimes translates to rough seas and slippery trails, but with a little caution anyone can safely revel in the natural grandeur of Kaua'i.

ESSENTIALS

Arriving

BY PLANE A number of North American airlines offer regularly scheduled, nonstop service to Kaua'i's main airport in Līhu'e (airport code: LIH) from the Mainland, nearly all from the West Coast. (***Note:*** From Los Angeles, flights generally take about 5½ hours heading to Kaua'i, but only 4½ hours on the return due to prevailing winds.)

United Airlines (www.united.com; ✆ **800/225-5825**) flies nonstop to Kaua'i daily from Los Angeles and San Francisco; **Delta Airlines** (www.delta.com; ✆ **800/221-1212**) offers the same from Los Angeles. **American Airlines** (www.aa.com; ✆ **800/433-7300**) has nonstop services from Los Angeles and Phoenix, and also code-shares on some routes of **Alaska Airlines** (www.alaska.com), which flies nonstop to Līhu'e several times a week from San Jose, Oakland, and San Diego in California, as well as Portland and Seattle in the Pacific Northwest.

Other carriers' service varies by season. **WestJet** (www.westjet.com; ✆ **888/937-8538**) offers nonstop flights between Vancouver and Līhu'e from November to May, with most departures from December to March. From mid-June through Sept. 5, **Hawaiian Airlines** (www.hawaiianairlines.com; ✆ **800/367-5320**) flies nonstop daily to Līhu'e from Los Angeles and Oakland; otherwise, Hawaiian offers nonstops three to four times weekly from L.A. and, from May 27 to mid-June, thrice weekly from Oakland.

You can also travel to Līhu'e via O'ahu and Maui. **Hawaiian Airlines** (see above) flies nonstop to Kaua'i up to 23 times a day from Honolulu and 4 times a day from Kahului, Maui. The Honolulu route lasts about 35 minutes; the Maui route, about 10 minutes more, both using Boeing 717s that seat around 120. **Island Air** (www.islandair.com;

PREVIOUS PAGE: **Waipo'o Falls.**

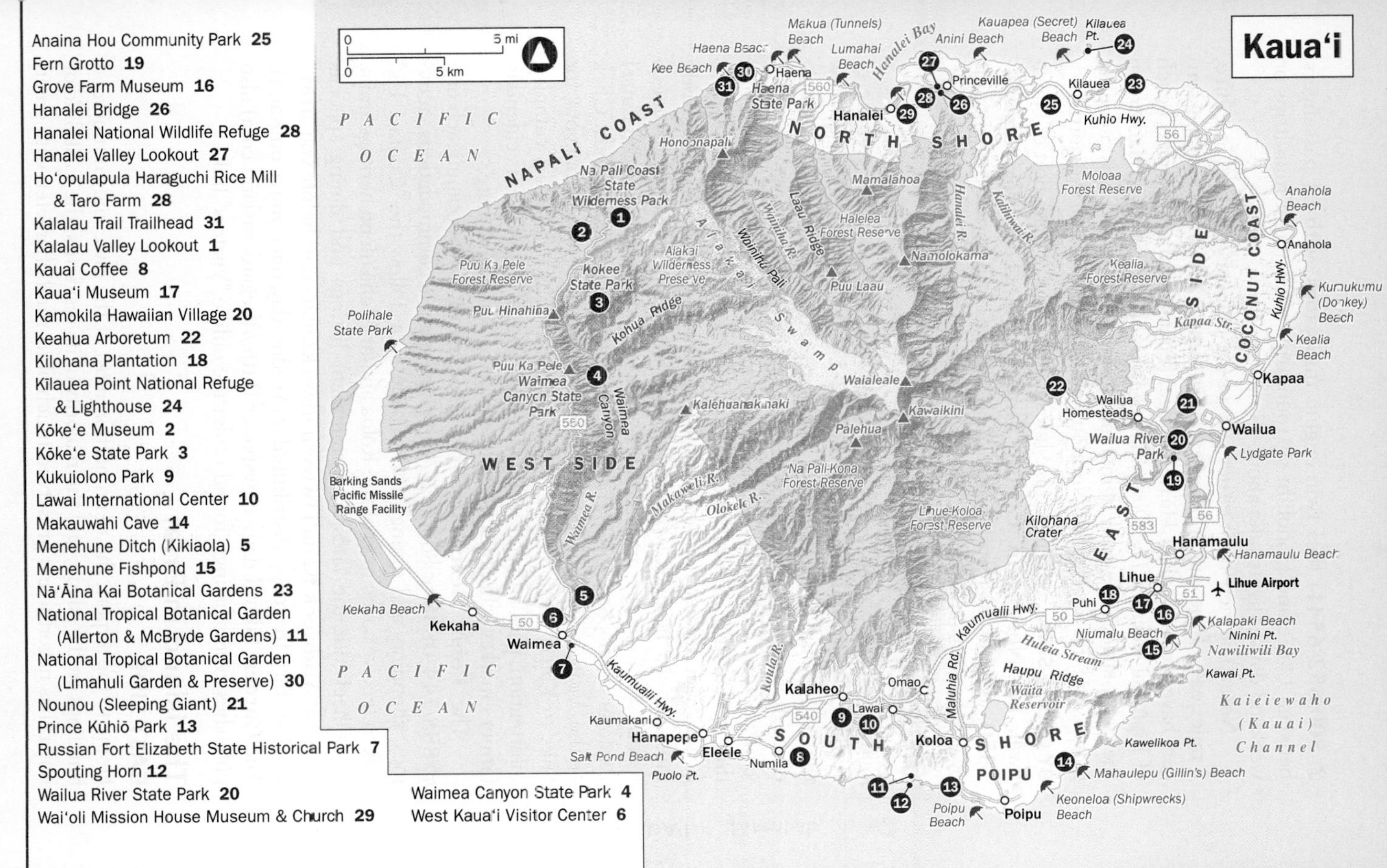
Kaua'i
Anaina Hou Community Park 25
Fern Grotto 19
Grove Farm Museum 16
Hanalei Bridge 26
Hanalei National Wildlife Refuge 28
Hanalei Valley Lookout 27
Ho'opulapula Haraguchi Rice Mill & Taro Farm 28
Kalalau Trail Trailhead 31
Kalalau Valley Lookout 1
Kauai Coffee 8
Kaua'i Museum 17
Kamokila Hawaiian Village 20
Keahua Arboretum 22
Kilohana Plantation 18
Kīlauea Point National Refuge & Lighthouse 24
Kōke'e Museum 2
Kōke'e State Park 3
Kukuiolono Park 9
Lawai International Center 10
Makauwahi Cave 14
Menehune Ditch (Kikiaola) 5
Menehune Fishpond 15
Nā'Āina Kai Botanical Gardens 23
National Tropical Botanical Garden (Allerton & McBryde Gardens) 11
National Tropical Botanical Garden (Limahuli Garden & Preserve) 30
Nounou (Sleeping Giant) 21
Prince Kūhiō Park 13
Russian Fort Elizabeth State Historical Park 7
Spouting Horn 12
Wailua River State Park 20
Wai'oli Mission House Museum & Church 29
Waimea Canyon State Park 4
West Kaua'i Visitor Center 6
0 5 mi
0 5 km
PACIFIC OCEAN
NAPALI COAST
NORTH SHORE
COCONUT COAST
EAST SIDE
SOUTH SHORE
WEST SIDE
Na Pali Coast State Wilderness Park
Kokee State Park
Waimea Canyon State Park
Waimea Canyon
Alakai Wilderness Preserve
Alakai Swamp
Hanalei
Hanalei Bay
Princeville
Kilauea
Kilauea Pt.
Kuhio Hwy.
Anahola
Kapaa
Wailua
Wailua Homesteads
Wailua River Park
Lydgate Park
Lihue
Lihue Airport
Hanamaulu
Hanamaulu Beach
Puhi
Kilohana Crater
Kalapaki Beach
Ninini Pt.
Nawiliwili Bay
Niumalu Beach
Kawai Pt.
Kaieiewaho (Kauai) Channel
Huleia Stream
Haupu Ridge
Waita Reservoir
Kaumualii Hwy.
Maluhia Rd.
Koloa
Omao
Lawai
Kalaheo
Poipu
Poipu Beach
Keoneloa (Shipwrecks) Beach
Mahaulepu (Gillin's) Beach
Kawelikoa Pt.
Numila
Eleele
Hanapepe
Salt Pond Beach
Puolo Pt.
Kaumakani
Waimea
Kekaha
Kekaha Beach
Barking Sands Pacific Missile Range Facility
Polihale State Park
Puu Ka Pele Forest Reserve
Puu Hinahina
Puu Ka Pele
Kohua Ridge
Kalehuanakinaki
Waimea R.
Makaweli R.
Olokele R.
Koula R.
Na Pali-Kona Forest Reserve
Lihue-Koloa Forest Reserve
Waialeale
Kawaikini
Palehua
Wainiha Pali
Wainiha R.
Laau Ridge
Puu Laau
Halelea Forest Reserve
Mamalahoa
Namolokama
Hanalei R.
Kalihiwai R.
Moloaa Forest Reserve
Kealia Forest Reserve
Kapaa Str.
Honopu napali
Kee Beach
Haena Beach
Haena
Haena State Park
Makua (Tunnels) Beach
Lumahai Beach
Anini Beach
Kauapea (Secret) Beach
Anahola Beach
Kumukumu (Donkey) Beach
Kealia Beach

✆ **800/652-6541**) flies twin-engine turboprops, with 64 passengers, between Līhu‘e and Honolulu six roundtrips a day (eight roundtrips on weekend days); flights take about 45 minutes.

Note: The view from either side of the plane as you land in Līhu‘e, 2 miles east of the center of town, is arresting. On the left side, passengers have a close look at Hā‘upu Ridge, separating the unspoiled beach of Kīpū Kai (seen in *The Descendants*) from busy Nāwiliwili Harbor; on the right, shades of green demarcate former sugarcane fields, coconut groves, and the ridgeline of Nounou ("Sleeping Giant") to the north.

BY CRUISE SHIP Several cruise lines call in Kaua‘i's main port of Nāwiliwili, but **Norwegian Cruise Lines** (www.ncl.com; ✆ **866/234-7350**) is unusual in offering weekly Hawai‘i itineraries that include overnight stays on Kaua‘i and Maui, allowing for multiple excursions.

Visitor Information

Before your trip begins, visit www.gohawaii.com/kauai, the website of **Kaua‘i Visitors Bureau** (✆ **800/262-1400**), and download or view the free "Kaua‘i Official Travel Planner." (***Note:*** The bureau's Līhu‘e office in Watumull Plaza, 4334 Rice St., Suite 101, is not the most convenient area for drop-bys, but it's open 8am–3pm weekdays.) Before and during your trip, consult the authoritative **Kaua‘i Explorer** website (www.kauaiexplorer.com) for detailed descriptions of 18 of the island's most popular beaches (with or without lifeguards), plus a daily ocean report, surf forecasts, and safety tips. Hikers will also want to read Kaua‘i Explorer's notes on 10 island trails, from easy to super-strenuous. Click on the "Visitors" link of **Kaua‘i County**'s homepage (www.kauai.gov), for links to Kaua‘i Explorer, the Visitors Bureau, bus schedules, camping information, park and golf facility listings, a festival and events calendar, farmer's market schedules, recycling drop-off sites, and more.

The **Poipu Beach Resort Association** (www.poipubeach.org; ✆ **888/744-0888** or 808/742-7444) highlights accommodations, activities, shopping, and dining in the Po‘ipū area; follow the "Contact Us" link to receive a free map of the Kōloa and/or Māhā‘ulepū heritage trails.

Check out the latest entertainment listings and dining specials online at **Midweek Kaua‘i** (www.midweekkauai.com) before you arrive, and look for a free copy, distributed on Wednesday, once you're on Kaua‘i. The **Garden Island** daily newspaper (http://thegardenisland.com) also publishes events listings, found under the online "Visitors" link.

The Island in Brief

EAST SIDE

Home to the airport, the main harbor, most of the civic and commercial buildings on the island, and the majority of its residents, the East Side of Kaua‘i has nevertheless preserved much of its rural character, with green

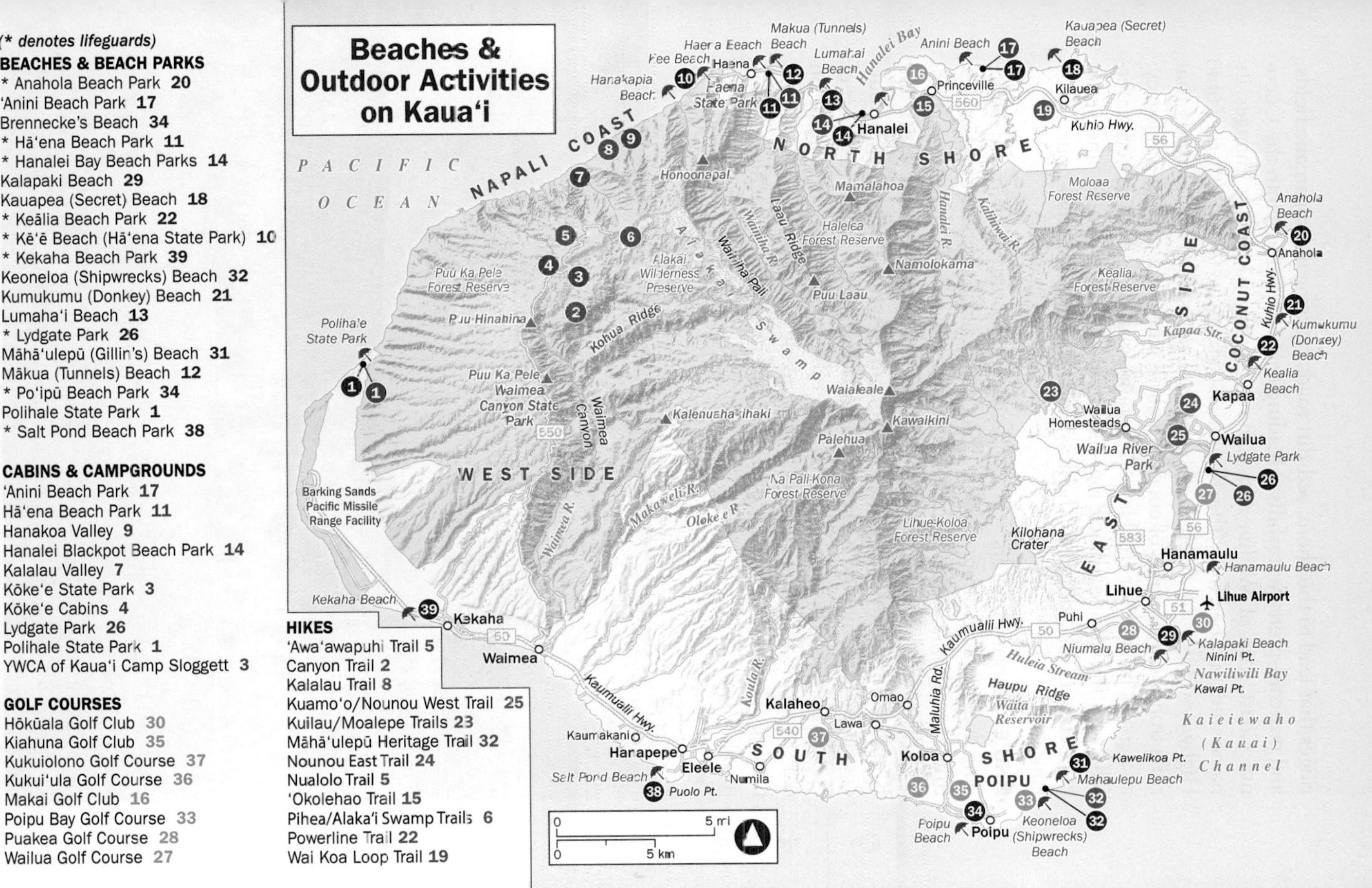

Beaches & Outdoor Activities on Kaua'i
(* denotes lifeguards)
BEACHES & BEACH PARKS
* Anahola Beach Park 20
'Anini Beach Park 17
Brennecke's Beach 34
* Hā'ena Beach Park 11
* Hanalei Bay Beach Parks 14
Kalapaki Beach 29
Kauapea (Secret) Beach 18
* Keālia Beach Park 22
* Kē'ē Beach (Hā'ena State Park) 10
* Kekaha Beach Park 39
Keoneloa (Shipwrecks) Beach 32
Kumukumu (Donkey) Beach 21
Lumaha'i Beach 13
* Lydgate Park 26
Māhā'ulepū (Gillin's) Beach 31
Mākua (Tunnels) Beach 12
* Po'ipū Beach Park 34
Polihale State Park 1
* Salt Pond Beach Park 38
CABINS & CAMPGROUNDS
'Anini Beach Park 17
Hā'ena Beach Park 11
Hanakoa Valley 9
Hanalei Blackpot Beach Park 14
Kalalau Valley 7
Kōke'e State Park 3
Kōke'e Cabins 4
Lydgate Park 26
Polihale State Park 1
YWCA of Kaua'i Camp Sloggett 3
GOLF COURSES
Hōkūala Golf Club 30
Kiahuna Golf Club 35
Kukuiolono Golf Course 37
Kukui'ula Golf Course 36
Makai Golf Club 16
Poipu Bay Golf Course 33
Puakea Golf Course 28
Wailua Golf Course 27
HIKES
'Awa'awapuhi Trail 5
Canyon Trail 2
Kalalau Trail 8
Kuamo'o/Nounou West Trail 25
Kuilau/Moalepe Trails 23
Māhā'ulepū Heritage Trail 32
Nounou East Trail 24
Nualolo Trail 5
'Okolehao Trail 15
Pihea/Alaka'i Swamp Trails 6
Powerline Trail 22
Wai Koa Loop Trail 19
PACIFIC OCEAN
NAPALI COAST
NORTH SHORE
COCONUT COAST
EAST SIDE
SOUTH SHORE
WEST SIDE
POIPU
Hanalei Bay
Princeville
Kilauea
Hanalei
Anahola
Kapaa
Wailua
Lihue
Lihue Airport
Hanamaulu
Puhi
Koloa
Poipu
Kalaheo
Lawa
Omao
Eleele
Hanapepe
Kaumakani
Numila
Waimea
Kekaha
Waimea Canyon
Alakai Swamp
Waialeale
Kawaikini
Kalalau Trail
Nawiliwili Bay
Kaieiewaho (Kauai) Channel
Kaumualii Hwy.
Kuhio Hwy.
Maluhia Rd.
Barking Sands Pacific Missile Range Facility
0 5 mi
0 5 km

ridges that lead to the shore, red-dirt roads crossing old sugarcane fields, and postcard-pretty waterfalls. Heading east from Līhu'e into the Coconut Coast strip of Wailua and Kapa'a, the main highway changes its name and number from the Kaumuali'i Highway (Hwy. 50) to Kūhiō Highway (Hwy. 56). More noticeable are the steady trade winds that riffle fronds of hundreds of coconut palms, part of the area's royal legacy; a long and broad river (by Hawai'i standards) and easily accessed waterfalls; and the chock-a-block low-rise condos, budget hotels, and shopping centers, all adding to the East Side's significant rush-hour traffic jams.

LĪHU'E Bargain hunters will appreciate the county seat's many shopping, lodging, and dining options, but Līhu'e also boasts cultural assets, from the exhibits at the **Kaua'i Museum ★★** to hula shows, concerts, and festivals at the **Kaua'i War Memorial Convention Hall** and **Kaua'i Community College's Performing Arts Center.** Nearby outdoor attractions include **Kalapaki Beach ★★**, next to the cruise port of Nāwiliwili; ATV, ziplining, hiking, and tubing excursions, the latter on old sugarcane irrigation flumes; and kayaking on Hulē'ia River past the historic **Menehune Fish Pond,** an ancient feat of aquaculture, now privately owned.

Nāpali Coast cliffs.

MOA BETTER: chickens & roosters

One of the first things visitors notice about Kaua'i is the unusually large number of wild chickens. Mostly rural, Kaua'i has always had plenty of poultry, including the colorful jungle fowl known as *moa*, but after Hurricane 'Iniki blew through the island in 1992, they soon were everywhere, reproducing quickly and, in the case of roosters, crowing night and day. Although resorts work tirelessly to trap or shoo them away, it's impossible to ensure you'll never be awakened by a rooster; if you're staying outside a resort, it's pretty much guaranteed you will be. Light sleepers should bring earplugs; some hotels provide them on demand.

WAILUA **Wailua Falls ★** (seen in the opening credits of *Fantasy Island*), the twin cascades of **'Ōpaeka'a Falls ★★**, and a riverboat cruise to **Fern Grotto ★★** are highlights of this former royal compound, which includes remains of stone-walled heiau (places of worship), birthstones, and other ancient sites. Kayakers flock to Wailua River, which also offers wakeboarding and water-skiing opportunities; the municipal **Wailua Golf Course ★★** is routinely ranked as one of the top in the state; and hikers can choose from three trail heads to ascend Nounou (Sleeping Giant) mountain. Highway 56 also passes by the decaying structures of the Coco Palms resort, featured in Elvis Presley's *Blue Hawaii,* closed after being damaged by Hurricane 'Iniki in 1992, and still awaiting restoration at press time. The family-friendly destination of **Lydgate Park ★** connects with one leg of the popular **Ke Ala Hele Makalae coastal path ★★**.

KAPA'A The modern condos, motels, and shopping strips of Wailua and Waipouli along the Kūhiō Highway eventually segue into **Old Kapa'a Town,** where funky boutiques and cafes share plantation era buildings with mom-and-pop groceries and restaurants. There are sandy beaches here, but they're hidden from the highway until the road rises past **Keālia Beach Park ★**, a boogie-boarding destination and northern terminus of the coastal bike path.

ANAHOLA Just before the East Side becomes the North Shore, the highway dips and passes through this predominantly Native Hawaiian community near Kalalea Mountain, more widely known as **King Kong Mountain,** or just Kong, for its famous profile. Farm stands, a convenience store with homemade goodies, and the roadside **Duane's Ono**

Char-Burger ★★ can supply provisions for a weekday picnic at **Anahola Beach Park ★**; weekends draw local crowds. (Give the poles and nets of local fishermen a wide berth.)

NORTH SHORE

On a sunny day, there may be no more beautiful place on earth than North Shore Kaua'i. It's not half-bad even on a rainy day (more frequent in winter) when waterfalls almost magically appear on verdant mountains; once the showers stop, rainbows soar over farms, taro patches, and long, curving beaches. The speed limit, and pace of life, slow down dramatically as the Kūhiō Highway traverses a series of one-lane bridges, climaxing at a suitably show-stopping beach and the trailhead for the breathtaking **Nāpali Coast.** Two quaint towns—one home to a lighthouse and a seabird preserve—plus the island's most luxurious resort provide ample lodging, dining, and shopping options to match the natural wonders. But it's far enough from the South Shore (minimum 1½ hr. away) that day-trippers may wish they had relocated for a night or two.

KĪLAUEA A right turn going north on Kūhiō Highway brings you to this village of quaint stone buildings and the plantation-vintage **Kong Lung Historic Market Center ★**, a cozy den of cafes, crafts makers, and boutiques. Kīlauea Road heads *makai* (seaward) to **Kīlauea Point National Wildlife Refuge ★★★**, a sanctuary for nēnē (the gooselike state bird) and other endangered species, and home to the stubby, red-topped **Kīlauea Lighthouse,** built in 1913. Shortly before the preserve is the turnoff for scenic but not-so-secret **Kauapea (Secret) Beach ★★**, a 15-minute hike from a dirt parking lot. Actor Ben Stiller owns a home on the cliffs here; numerous farms, the island's only mini-golf course, and the extensive **Nā 'Āina Kai Botanical Gardens ★★** are the immediate area's other claims to fame. Two miles north, a 5-minute detour off the highway leads to **'Anini Beach ★★★**, where a 2-mile fringing reef—the longest on Kaua'i—creates a shallow, pondlike setting for swimmers, snorkelers, and (when conditions permit) windsurfers.

Kīlauea Lighthouse.

PRINCEVILLE This 11,000-acre resort and residential development is home to two 18-hole golf courses, steep trails to pocket beaches, and gorgeous views of crescent-shaped Hanalei Bay and iconic **Makana,** the mountain that portrayed Bali Hai in *South Pacific*. The **Princeville Shopping Center** holds a few bargain eateries as well as supplies for those staying in one of the many condo or timeshare units; money is generally no object for guests at the **St. Regis Princeville ★★**, the island's most luxurious hotel (formerly the Princeville Hotel), with elevator service to the beach below. Just before the highway drops into Hanalei Valley, a vista point offers a photo-worthy panorama of the Hanalei River winding through wetland taro patches under towering green peaks.

HANALEI Waiting to cross the first of nine one-lane bridges on the northern stretch of the Kūhiō Highway (now Hwy. 560) is a good introduction to the hang-loose ethos of the last real town before road's end. The fringing green mountains share their hue with the 1912 **Wai'oli Hui'ia Church ★** and other vintage wooden buildings, some of which house unique shops and moderately priced restaurants. Nearby, the beaches along 2-mile-long, half-moon **Hanalei Bay ★★★** attract surfers year-round; during the calmer summer conditions, children splash in the water while parents lounge on the sand (a la *The Descendants*). Three county beach parks offer various facilities, including several lifeguard stations; the southernmost **Black Pot Beach Park ★★**, renowned for its 300-foot-long pier, allows camping on weekends and holidays.

HĀ'ENA Homes modest and grand hide in the lush greenery of Hā'ena on either side of the Kūhiō Highway as it undulates past rugged coves, tranquil beaches, and immense caves, finally dead-ending at **Kē'ē Beach ★★★**, gateway to the Nāpali Coast and a popular destination for snorkelers (when the surf permits) and campers. **Limahuli Garden and Preserve ★★**, the northern outpost of the National Tropical Botanical Garden, explains Hā'ena's legends, rich cultural heritage, and ecological significance to visitors able to navigate its steep terraces in the shadow of Mount Makana. Food trucks at **Hā'ena Beach Park ★★★** supplement the meager if popular dining options, such as Mediterranean Gourmet at the **Hanalei Colony Resort ★★** (p. 568), the only North Shore resort with rooms on the sand.

NĀPALI COAST ★★★ Often written as Nā Pali ("the cliffs"), this dramatically crenellated region that bridges the North Shore and West Side begins not far from where the road ends. Hardy (and some foolhardy) hikers will cross five valleys as they follow the narrow, 11-mile Kalalau Trail to its end at beautiful **Kalalau Valley,** with tempting detours to waterfalls along the way. The less ambitious (or more sensible) will attempt shorter stretches, such as the 2-mile hike to Hanakāpī'ai Beach. In summer, physically fit kayakers can spend a day exploring Nāpali's pristine reefs, sea caves, and hidden coves, which also come into view on

Hanalei.

catamaran and motorized raft tours (almost all departing from the West Side); helicopter tours from Līhu'e, Port Allen, or Princeville offer the quickest if most expensive way to explore Nāpali's stunning topography (see "Organized Tours," p. 523).

SOUTH SHORE

After a short drive west from Līhu'e on Kaumuali'i Highway, a well-marked left turn leads to a mile-long **tree tunnel** of eucalyptus trees, planted in 1911. The well-shaded Maluhia Road is ironically the primary entrance to the sunniest of Kaua'i resort areas, Po'ipū. The South Shore also generally has the calmest ocean conditions in winter. Among outdoor attractions are the geyser-like **Spouting Horn ★★**, the McBryde and Allerton gardens at the **National Tropical Botanical Garden ★★**, family-friendly **Po'ipū Beach Park ★★★**, and other sandy beaches, including those in rugged **Māhā'ulepū ★★**. Pocket coves, surf breaks, and dive sites also make the area ideal for watersports. The only downside: The North Shore is at least 1½ hours away.

PO'IPŪ Three of the best hotels on Kaua'i—the lavish **Grand Hyatt Kauai Resort & Spa ★★★**, the family-friendly **Sheraton Kauai Resort ★★★**, and the luxury boutique **Ko'a Kea Hotel & Resort ★★★**—punctuate the many low-rise condos and vacation homes in the master-planned **Po'ipū Beach Resort.** Landlubbers can enjoy tennis, 36 holes of golf, and numerous options for dining and shopping, including those at the **Shops at Kukui'ula** just outside the resort proper.

KŌLOA Before the Kōloa Bypass Road (Ala Kinoiki) was built, nearly every South Shore beachgoer drove through Hawaii's oldest sugar plantation town, founded in 1835. If you're staying elsewhere, it would be a shame not to visit at least once, to browse the shops and restaurants in quaint storefronts under towering monkeypod trees. Historical plaques on each building give glimpses into the lives of the predominantly Japanese-American families who created the first businesses there. Those staying in South Shore condos may find themselves making multiple trips, especially to stock up on produce at the "sunshine market" at noon Mondays, to buy fresh seafood from the **Koloa Fish Market ★,** or to purchase other groceries from two local supermarkets; several food trucks also hang out here.

KALĀHEO & LĀWA'I These more residential communities on either side of the main highway are just a 15-minute drive to Po'ipū Beach Park. On the way, you'll pass through the green fields of rural 'Ōma'o along Kōloa Road (Hwy. 530). Visitors en route to or from Waimea Canyon often refuel at the locally oriented restaurants here; others find lodgings in the relatively inexpensive (but often unlicensed) bed-and-breakfasts. (Keep in mind higher elevations are mistier, with wild chickens roaming even more freely than on the resorts below.) Savvy golfers savor the views and discount fees at upcountry **Kukuiolono Golf Course ★★**. On the west edge of Kalāheo, look for the turnoff for **Kauai Coffee ★★**, whose 3,100 acres produce a dizzying variety of coffees, with free samples at the visitor center.

Kōloa eucalyptus tree tunnel.

WEST SIDE

This arid region may have the fewest lodgings, destination restaurants, or swimmable beaches, but the twin draws of **Waimea Canyon State Park ★★★** (rightly hailed as the "Grand Canyon of the Pacific") and the **Kalalau Overlook ★★★** in Kōke'e State Park make up for the long drive (80 min. to the latter from Po'ipū). Most Nāpali snorkel tours are also based here, not to mention two swinging bridges, a weekly art festival, and other good excuses to pull over. Those who can manage the bumpy, unpaved 5-mile road to **Polihale State Park ★★** are rewarded with views of Ni'ihau and Nāpali, as well as a 17-mile stretch of sand (including the restricted-access **Barking Sands Beach** on the Pacific Missile Range Facility).

'ELE'ELE & PORT ALLEN The main highway from Kalāheo passes by 'Ele'ele's plantation homes and several miles of coffee trees before the intersection with Waialo Road. Turn *makai* (seaward) and the road deadends a few blocks later at Port Allen, the island's second largest commercial harbor; nearly all boat tours launch from here. Although the area is fairly industrial—and its once-vaunted "Glass Beach" by the oil tanks no longer has enough polished sea glass left to recommend it—the affordable dining and shopping options in Port Allen and adjacent **'Ele'ele Shopping Center** are worth exploring post-snorkel or pre-sunset cruise.

NI'IHAU Just 17 miles across the Kaulakahi Channel from the West Side of Kaua'i lies the arid island of Ni'ihau (pronounced "nee-ee-how"), nicknamed "The Forbidden Island." Casual visitors are not allowed on this privately owned isle, once a cattle and sheep ranch that now supports fewer than 200 full-time residents, all living in the single town of Pu'uwai, and nearly all Native Hawaiians. Nonresidents can visit on hunting safaris (starting at $1,750) and half-day helicopter tours ($385 per person, five-person minimum) departing from the West Side. Helicopter tours include lunch and several hours of beach time. You're more likely to see the endangered Hawaiian monk seal than Niihauans, which is how they like it; see **www.niihau.us** for safari and tour details.

HANAPĒPĒ An easy detour off Kaumuali'i Highway, Hanapēpē looks like an Old West town, with more than 2 dozen art galleries and quaint stores, plus a couple of cafes, behind rustic wooden facades that inspired Disney's *Lilo & Stitch.* Musicians, food trucks, and other vendors truly animate the quiet town during the Friday night festival and artwalk from 6 to 9pm. The other daytime attraction is the **swinging footbridge ★** over Hanapēpē River (rebuilt after 1992's Hurricane 'Iniki, and marked by a large sign off Hanapēpē Rd.). Across the highway, family-friendly **Salt Pond Beach ★★** is named for the traditional Hawaiian salt pans in the red dirt, which gives the salt *('alae)* its distinctive color and flavor.

WAIMEA Hawaii's modern history officially begins here with the landing of British explorer Capt. James Cook on Jan. 20, 1778, 2 days after

Hanapēpē swinging footbridge.

his ships sailed past O'ahu. Despite Cook's orders to the contrary, his sailors quickly mingled with native women, introducing venereal disease to a long-isolated population. Foreigners kept coming to this enclave at the mouth of the Waimea ("reddish-water") River, including a German doctor who tried to claim Kaua'i for Russia in 1815, and American missionaries in 1820. Today Waimea is attuned to its more recent history of plantation and *paniolo* (cowboy) culture, as well as its Native Hawaiian roots, all of which can be explored at the **West Kaua'i Visitor Center ★**. Waimea Canyon and Kōke'e State Park hikers flock to Waimea's shave ice stands and budget dining choices in the late afternoon, while locals seek out **Waimea Theater,** one of the island's few places to catch a movie or concert.

KEKAHA Travelers heading to or from Waimea Canyon may be tempted to go via Kōke'e Road (Hwy. 55) in Kekaha as a change of pace from Waimea Canyon Road. Don't bother. There's not much to see in this former sugar town, whose mill operated for 122 years before shutting down in 2000, other than **Kekaha Beach Park,** a long, narrow strand with often-rough waters. You do have to pass through Kekaha on the way to **Polihale State Park ★★★**; if the latter's access road is impassable, stop by Kekaha for a striking view of **Ni'ihau,** 17 miles offshore.

GETTING AROUND

Unless you're on a fairly leisurely schedule, you'll need a car or other motorized vehicle to see and do everything on Kaua'i, which has one major road—one lane in each direction in most places—that rings the island except along the Nāpali Coast. During rush hour, from about 6 to 9am and 3 to 6pm, the road between Līhu'e and Kapa'a—the central business district—can turn into a giant parking lot, even with a third, "contra-flow" lane whose direction is determined by time of day. Bypass roads in Kīpū (when heading north from Po'ipū) and Kapa'a (when heading south) can alleviate some of the stress, but plan accordingly.

Note: The top speed is 50mph, with many slower sections in residential and business areas. Addresses in this chapter will use Kaumuali'i Highway for Hwy. 50 and Kūhiō Highway for Hwy. 56/560, following local convention. Some addresses use a single number before a dash, which simply indicates one of five island divisions. Since highway addresses can be hard to spot (if marked at all), directions may be given with mile marker numbers, cross streets, and/or the descriptors *mauka* (toward the mountains) and *makai* (toward the sea).

The official mailing address of sites in and around Poʻipū Beach is Kōloa, which GPS devices may require. This chapter lists them as "Poʻipū" to distinguish them from Old Kōloa Town and environs. Also, the spelling of Hawaiian words in business names reflects their preferences.

BY CAR All of the major car-rental agencies are represented on Kauaʻi. At the airport baggage claim, cross the street to catch one of the frequent shuttle vans to the rental lots. **Avis** (www.avis.com; ✆ **800/230-4898**) also rents cars from the Grand Hyatt Kauai and the Princeville Airport. Be sure to book early for peak periods. **Discount Hawaii Car Rental** (www.discounthawaiicarrental.com; ✆ **800/292-1939**) may have cheaper options for last-minute bookings; it also offers free pickup for cruise passengers.

BY MOTORCYCLE, MOPED, OR SCOOTER Riders 21 and older with a heavyweight motorcycle license can rent a "hog" from **Kauai Harley-Davidson** (www.kauaiharley.com; ✆ **888/690-6233** or 808/212-9469) outside Līhuʻe. Rates start at $179 for 24 hours, with unlimited mileage. **Kauai Mopeds** (www.kauai-mopeds.com; ✆ **808/652-7407**) in Līhuʻe offers two-person scooters with similar age and license restrictions; daily rates start at $75 for models with a top speed of 52mph, and $110 for those reaching 75mph. For cruising back roads (directions provided), those 18 or older with a driver's license can rent a single-person moped with a top speed of 30mph for $65 a day.

BY TAXI OR SHUTTLE Set by the county, taxi meter rates start at $3, with an additional $3 per mile; it's about $50 to Poʻipū and $90 to Princeville from the airport, plus 40¢ per item of luggage, and $4 per bulky item. You can also arrange private tours by taxi starting at $120 for 2 hours. Call **Kauai Taxi Company** (www.kauaitaxico.com; ✆ **808/246-9554**) for taxi, limousine, or airport shuttle service. From the airport, solo travelers will find it cheaper ($42 to Poʻipū, $72 to Princeville) to take the shared-ride **SpeediShuttle** (www.speedishuttle.com; ✆ **877/242-5777**), but be aware it may make multiple stops. **Pono Express** (http://ponoexpress.com; ✆ **800/258-6880**) offers private airport shuttles and sightseeing tours in vans accommodating one to 14 passengers; rate is by vehicle or by hour. Once in Poʻipū, book a free ride on the **Aloha Spirit Shuttle** (✆ **808/651-9945**); the 12-person open-air tram—a former Disneyland people-mover—shuttles locals and visitors around resorts and restaurants from 5 to 10pm daily.

BY BUS **Kaua'i Bus** (www.kauai.gov/transportation; ✆ **808/246-8110**) continues to expand bus service between Kekaha and Hanalei daily, including stops near several Po'ipū and Līhu'e hotels, the central Kapa'a hotel corridor, the Princeville Shopping Center, and Hanalei. ***Note:*** There's also an airport stop, but suitcases, large backpacks, and surfboards are not allowed on the bus. The white-and-green buses, which have small bike racks in front, run more or less hourly from 5:30am to 10:30pm weekdays, and 6:30am to 6pm on weekends and holidays. The fare (exact change only) is $2 for adults and $1 for seniors, 60 and older, and children, 7 to 18.

BY BIKE Due to narrow (or nonexistent) shoulders along much of the main highway, relying on bicycles for transportation is generally unsafe. For recreational routes, see "Biking," p. 546.

[Fast FACTS] KAUA'I

Dentists Emergency dental care is available from **Dr. Mark A. Baird,** 4–9768 Kūhiō Hwy. (at Keaka Rd.), Kapa'a (✆ **808/822-9393**) and **Dr. Terry Allen,** 4366 Kukui Grove St., Ste. 24, Līhu'e (www.lihue-dental.com; ✆ **808/378-4754** Tues–Thurs 9am–5pm and Mon and Fri 9am–6pm; after hours, ✆ **808/651-8404**).

Doctors Walk-ins are accepted from 8am to 7pm daily (except Jan. 1, Thanksgiving, and Dec. 25) at the **Kauai Urgent Care Clinic** (✆ **808/245-1532**), 4484 Pahe'e St., Līhu'e. The non-urgent-care **Kauai Medical Clinic** (✆ **808/245-1500**), part of the Wilcox Memorial Hospital complex at 3-3420 Kūhiō Hwy., Līhu'e (*makai* side, at 'Ehiku St.), is open for appointments 8am to 5pm weekdays and 8am to noon Saturday. Kauai Medical Clinic also has branches, with varying hours, in **Kōloa,** 5371 Kōloa Rd. (✆ **808/742-1621**); **Kapa'a,** 4-1105 Kūhiō Hwy., *mauka* side, in the Kapa'a Shopping Center (✆ **808/822-3431**); and **'Ele'ele,** 4392 Waialo Rd. (✆ **808/335-0499**). **Hale Lea Medicine,** 2460 Oka St. (at Kīlauea Rd.), in Kīlauea (✆ **808/828-2885**), serves the North Shore, with appointments offered 9am to 5pm weekdays and 9am to 1pm Saturday.

Emergencies Dial ✆ **911** for police, fire, or ambulance service.

Hospitals **Wilcox Memorial Hospital,** 3-3420 Kūhiō Hwy. (*makai* side, at Ehiku St.), Līhu'e (✆ **808/245-1100**), has emergency services (✆ **808/245-1010**) available 24 hours a day, as do the smaller **Mahelona Memorial Hospital,** 4800 Kawaihau Rd., Kapa'a (✆ **808/823-4166**), and **Kaua'i Veterans Memorial Hospital,** 4643 Waimea Canyon Dr., Waimea (✆ **808/338-9431**).

Internet Access Numerous cafes (including three **Starbucks** outlets in Po'ipū, Līhu'e, and Kapa'a; www.starbucks.com) offer free Wi-Fi hotspots; many hotels offer free Wi-Fi in public areas and, if not free, for a fee in rooms. All Hawai'i public libraries have free Wi-Fi but require a library card ($10 nonresidents, good for 3 months). Local branches are in Hanapēpē, Kapa'a, Kōloa, Līhu'e, Princeville, and Waimea; all are closed Sunday. For details on locations, hours, and reserving a personal computer with Wi-Fi, see http://librarieshawaii.org (click on "Services").

Police For non-emergencies, call ✆ **808/241-1711.**

Post Office The **main** post office is at 4441 Rice St., Līhu'e, open 8am to 4pm weekdays and 9am to 1pm Saturday; hours vary at the 14 other offices across the island. To find the one nearest you, visit www.usps.com or call ✆ **800/275-8777.**

Weather For current weather conditions and forecasts, call the National Weather Service at ✆ **808/245-6001.** For the daily ocean report, including surf advisories, visit **www.kauaiexplorer.com/ocean_report**.

EXPLORING KAUA'I

Attractions & Points of Interest

EAST SIDE

Fern Grotto ★★ NATURAL ATTRACTION The journey as much as the destination has kept this tourist attraction popular since 1946, when the Smith family first began offering boat trips 2 miles up the Wailua River to this lava-rock cave with lush ferns hanging from its roof. The open-air barge cruises past royal and sacred sites of antiquity, noted by a guide, until it arrives at a landing that's a short walk from the grotto. Although you can no longer enter the cave, an observation deck provides a decent view, as well as the stage for a musician and hula dancer to perform the "Hawaiian Wedding Song" (made famous by Elvis Presley's

Fern Grotto.

1961 film *Blue Hawaii,* filmed nearby at the Coco Palms.) The tour, a total of 80 minutes, includes music and hula on the return trip down Hawaii's longest river (see "Wailua River State Park," below.) ***Note:*** Kayakers may visit Fern Grotto on their own, as long as their arrival or departure doesn't overlap with those of the tour boats; see "Kayaking" on p. 537 for rental information. **Kamokila Hawaiian Village** (see below), across the river from the grotto, also offers guided outrigger canoe tours and kayak rentals.

2 miles inland from Wailua Marina State Park, south side of Wailua River off Kūhiō Hwy. **Smith's Motor Boats** (www.smithskauai.com; ✆ **808/821-6895**) tours depart at 9:30 and 11am, and 2 and 3:30pm. $20 adults, $10 children 3 to 12 (book online for 10% off). Free shuttle from Wailua area.

Grove Farm Museum ★ HISTORIC SITE/MUSEUM AOL cofounder Steve Case may own Grove Farm now, but little else has changed at the 100-acre homestead of George N. Wilcox. The son of missionaries in Hanalei, Wilcox bought the original 900-acre Grove Farm from a German immigrant in 1864 and turned it into a successful sugar plantation. Two-hour guided tours start at the original plantation office and include the two-story main home, still furnished with vintage decor and Hawaiiana, plus extensive gardens and intriguing outbuildings, such as a Japanese teahouse built in 1898. ***Note:*** Tours may be canceled on rainy days. Contact the museum about its free rides on restored, plantation-era steam trains near the old Līhu'e Sugar Mill, usually offered the second Thursday of each month.

4050 Nāwiliwili Rd. (Hwy. 58), at Pīkaka St., Līhu'e. http://grovefarm.org. ✆ **808/245-3202.** Admission $20 adults, $10 children 11 and under. Open only for guided tours Mon and Wed–Thurs at 10am and 1pm; reservations required.

Kamokila Hawaiian Village ★ CULTURAL ATTRACTION This family-run 4-acre compound of thatched huts and other replica structures, opened in 1979 on the site of an ancient village, always looks in need of more upkeep. Nevertheless, it serves as a pleasantly low-key introduction to traditional Hawaiian culture, especially for families. Peacocks and wild chickens roam around huts designated for healing, sleeping, eating, birthing, and more, all part of a self-guided tour, with displays inside some huts. You're also welcome to sample fruit hanging from the many labeled trees, including mountain apple, guava, and mango. A stand-in for an African village in the 1995 movie *Outbreak,* Kamokila is known as having the fastest (and cheapest) access for paddling to **Uluwehi (Secret) Falls ★★**, **Fern Grotto ★★**, and several swimming holes.

Off Kuamo'o Rd. (Hwy. 580), Kapa'a. Look for sign across from 'Ōpaeka'a Falls, 2 miles inland from Kūhiō Hwy.; entrance road is steep. http://villagekauai.com. ✆ **808/823-0559.** Admission $5 adults, $3 children 3–12. Daily canoe and kayak rentals $35 adults, $30 children 3–12. Guided outrigger canoe rides: **Secret Falls** $30 adults, $20 children 3–12; **swimming hole** $20 adults, $15 children 3–12; **Fern Grotto** $20 adults, $15 children 3–12. Daily 9am–5pm.

Kaua'i Museum ★★ MUSEUM Though admission has jumped to $15, that fee allows you to return within a week—and you may well want to, in order to absorb more of the fascinating geological and cultural history of Kaua'i and Ni'ihau. Visitors enter through the Wilcox Building, the former county library built in 1924 with a Greco-Roman facade on its lava rock exterior. Pass through the small gift shop with an extensive book selection into the Heritage Gallery, where koa wood-lined cases brim with exquisite Ni'ihau shell lei, feather work, and other items that once belonged to royalty. Also on display are some of the hundreds of Western and Hawaiian artifacts recovered from *Ha'aheo O Hawai'i* ("Pride of Hawai'i"), King Kamehameha II's luxurious barge, which sank off the North Shore in 1824. Another room holds beautifully carved wooden bowls (*'umeke*) and other handsome koa pieces, while a theater has continuous screenings of *The Hawaiians,* a sobering (if somewhat dated) hour-long documentary on Hawaiian history.

The adjacent Rice Building, a two-story lava rock structure opened in 1960, tells "The Story of Kaua'i." The main floor's exhibits focus on the island's volcanic origins through the arrival of Polynesian voyagers and the beginning of Western contact, including the whalers and missionaries who quickly followed in Capt. Cook's wake. Rare artifacts include a torn piece of a Ni'ihau *makaloa* mat, a highly prized bed covering and art form that was essentially abandoned in the late 19th century. On the second floor, the story shifts to that of the plantation era, when waves of immigrants fomented the complex stew known as "local" culture, and continues through World War II.

4428 Rice St., Līhu'e. www.kauaimuseum.org. ✆ **808/245-6931.** Admission $15 adults, $12 seniors, $10 students 13–17, $3 children 7–12, free. Guided tours Mon, Tues, and Thurs 10:30am free with admission. Check "Events" listings online for frequent crafts workshops and festivals.

Keahua Arboretum ★ GARDEN Part of the vast Līhu'e–Kōloa Forest Reserve, this grove of rainbow eucalyptus (named for its colorful bark), monkeypod, and mango trees may not be well maintained from an arborist's standpoint, but it's a nifty, family-friendly place to picnic and dip in a cool stream, particularly after a hike on the nearby **Kuilau Trail** (p. 552). A short loop trail leads to a "swimming hole" with a rope swing; be sure to wear mosquito repellent. Facilities include picnic tables, pavilions, and composting toilets. Part of the fun is getting here: The main parking area and picnic tables are across a spillway at the paved end of Kuamo'o Road, about 5 miles inland from 'Ōpaeka'a Falls. (Please use good judgment when deciding if it's safe to ford the stream.) This is also where adventurers will find the trail head for the 13-mile **Powerline Trail** (p. 552), which ends near Princeville, and the extremely rugged, unpaved Wailua Forestry Management Road, the start of much more challenging treks to the *Jurassic Park* gates (just poles now) and the "Blue Hole" inside Wai'ale'ale.

End of Kuamo'o Rd., Kapa'a. 7 miles inland from intersection with Kūhiō Hwy., Wailua. www.dlnr.hawaii.gov/forestry/frs/reserves/kauai/lihue-koloa. ✆ **808/274-3433.** Free admission. Daily during daylight hours.

Kilohana Plantation ★★ FARM/ATTRACTIONS Longtime Kaua'i visitors might remember this 105-acre portion of a former sugar plantation for the unique shops tucked into a handsome 1930s mansion, its lū'au, or the courtyard Gaylord's restaurant, named for original owner Gaylord Wilcox. Although all of those elements are still there, so many changes have happened in recent years that few should skip a visit here. In addition to sampling the wares of the **Mahikō Lounge,** the 2013 conversion of the mansion's former living room (see "Kaua'i Nightlife," p. 599), tipplers ages 21 and up can create their own mini Mai Tai around a gleaming wood bar in the **Kōloa Rum Co.**'s tasting room (www.koloarum.com; ✆ **808/246-8900**). There's a 16-person maximum for the free half-hour tasting (see website for hours), while an all-ages store sells the locally made spirits and non-alcoholic gifts.

The first new railroad to open on the island in almost 100 years, the **Kauai Plantation Railway** (www.kauaiplantationrailway.com; ✆ **808/245-7245**) uses a restored diesel locomotive to pull open-sided cars with trolley-style bench seats around a 2½-mile track. The train passes by Kilohana's gardens growing 50 varieties of fruit and vegetables and through flowering fields and forest on a 40-minute narrated tour that

Kilohana Plantation.

includes a stop to feed goats, sheep, and wild pigs (watch your hands). It departs five times daily between 10am and 2pm, with a 5:30pm trip on Tuesday and Friday. Tickets are $18 for adults and $14 for kids 3 to 12; if booking by phone, request the Web discount of 15%. On weekdays, you can also combine a train ride that starts at 9:30am with an easy hike, lunch, and orchard tour that costs $75 for adults and $65 for kids 3 to 12 (ask for the 15% Web discount when reserving.)

On Tuesday and Friday, the railway offers an "express train" package with **Lū'au Kalamakū** (www.luaukalamaku.com; © **808/833-3000**), a theatrical-style show with dinner buffet in a specially-built theater-in-the-round near the Wilcox mansion. The train-lū'au package is $113 for adults and $83 for teens 13 to 18, and $59 kids 3 to 12 (ask for Web discount of 10% when reserving). For the lū'au only, it's $95 for adults, $65 for teens, and $45 for children.

3-2087 Kaumuali'i Hwy., Līhu'e, just north of Kaua'i Community College and a half-mile south of Kukui Grove Shopping Center. www.kilohanakauai.com. © **808/245-5608.** Mansion opens at 10:30am daily; restaurant, lounge, and shop hours vary.

Lydgate Park ★ PARK This is one of the rare beach parks in Hawai'i where the facilities almost outshine the beach. In front of the Hilton Garden Inn Kauai Wailua Bay, **Lydgate Beach** ★ (p. 528) offers two rock-walled ponds for safe swimming and snorkeling. But many families also gravitate to the 58-acre, half-mile-long park for the immense **Kamalani Playground,** a sprawling wooden fantasy fortress decorated with ocean-themed ceramics. Stroller pushers, joggers, and cyclists also pick up the 2.5-mile southern leg of the **Ke Ala Hele Makalae coastal path** here; Lydgate's northern end is next to **Hikinaakalā Heiau,** part of Wailua River State Park (below). Facilities include picnic tables, restrooms, showers, pavilions, and campgrounds.

Leho Dr. at Nalu Rd., Wailua. From intersection of Kūhiō Hwy. and Hwy. 51 outside of Līhu'e, head 2½ miles north to Leho Dr. and turn right. Turn right again on Nalu Rd. and follow to parking areas. Free admission. Daily during daylight hours.

Wailua River State Park ★★ PARK/HISTORIC SITE Ancients called the Wailua River "the river of the great sacred spirit." Seven temples once stood along this 20-mile river, Hawaii's longest, fed by the some 450 inches of rain that fall annually on Wai'ale'ale at the island's center. The entire district from the river mouth to the summit of Wai'ale'ale was once royal land, originally claimed by Puna, a Tahitian priest said to have arrived in one of the first double-hulled voyaging canoes to come to Hawaii.

Cultural highlights include the remains of four major temples; royal birthing stones, used to support female *ali'i* in labor; a stone bell used to announce such births; and the ancient stone carvings known as petroglyphs, found on boulders near the mouth of the Wailua River when currents wash away enough sand. Many sites have **Wailua Heritage Trail** markers; go to www.wailuaheritagetrail.org for map and details.

The **Hawai'i State Parks website** (http://dlnr.hawaii.gov/dsp) also has downloadable brochures on two *heiau* (temples) that each enclosed an acre of land: Just north of Lydgate Park, next to the mouth of the Wailua River, **Hikinaakalā Heiau** once hosted sunrise ceremonies; its name means "rising of the sun." Now reduced to its foundation stones, it's part of a sacred oceanfront complex that also appears to have been a place of refuge *(pu'uhonua)*. Two miles up Kuamo'o Road (Hwy. 580) from the main highway, **Poli'ahu Heiau** shares its name with the goddess of snow (admittedly a weather phenomenon more common to the Big Island). The 5×5-feet lava rock walls—attributed to *menehune,* and most likely erected by the 1600s—may have surrounded a *luakini,* used for human sacrifice. (Please don't stand on the rock walls, enter the center of the heiau, or leave "offerings," which are al considered disrespectful.)

Across the road from Poli'ahu is an ample parking lot and sidewalk leading to the overlook of 40-foot-wide, 151-foot-tall **'Ōpaeka'a Falls ★★**. Named for the "rolling shrimp" that were once abundant here, this twin cascade glistens under the Makaleha ridge—but don't be tempted to try to find a way to swim beneath it. The danger keep out signs and wire fencing are there because two hikers fell to their deaths from the steep, slippery hillside in 2006.

You're allowed to wade at the base of the 100-foot **Uluwehi Falls ★★,** widely known as Secret Falls, but first you'll need to paddle a kayak several miles to the narrow right fork of the Wailua River, and then hike about 30 to 45 minutes on a trail with a stream crossing. Many kayak rental companies offer guided tours here (see "Kayaking," p. 537)

Also part of the state park, but at the end of Mā'alo Road (Hwy. 583), 4 miles inland from the main highway in Kapaia, is equally scenic **Wailua Falls ★.** Pictured in the opening credits of *Fantasy Island,* this double-barreled waterfall drops at least 80 feet (some say 113) into a large pool. Go early to avoid crowds and enjoy the morning light. ***Note:*** The state has also installed fencing here to block attempts at a hazardous descent.

'Ōpaeka'a Falls and **Poli'ahu Heiau:** Off Kuamo'o Rd., 2 miles inland from intersection with Kūhiō Hwy. just north of Wailua River Bridge. **Hikinaakalā Heiau:** South side of Wailua River mouth; access from Lydgate Park (p. 508). **Wailua Falls:** end of Mā'alo Rd. (Hwy. 583), 4 miles north (inland) of intersection with Kūhiō Hwy. in Kapaia, near Līhu'e. http://dlnr.hawaii.gov/dsp/parks/kauai. ✆ **808/274-3444.** Free admission. Daily during daylight hours.

NORTH SHORE

Anaina Hou Community Park ★ GARDEN/ATTRACTIONS Anywhere else, a mini-golf park might be easily dismissed as a tourist trap. On Kaua'i, it's a wonderful introduction for families to the Garden Island's tropical flora and cultural history, and just one of several visitor attractions in this inviting park. The well-landscaped, 18-hole **Kauai Mini Golf & Botanical Gardens** (www.kauaiminigolf.com;

© **808/828-2118**) showcases native species, Polynesian introductions, plantation crops, Japanese and Chinese gardens, and modern plantings; take a free tour 9:30am Friday. Open daily, the mini golf course is quite popular on weekends. For a more natural experience, walk or bike along the park's 5-mile **Wai Koa Loop Trail.** This unpaved, rolling path starts in a forest of albizia and Cook Island pines and passes through a working farm and mahogany orchard before reaching the Kalihiwai Lagoon reservoirs and stone dam lookout. The trail is open during daylight hours and access is free, but because it crosses private property, you're asked to sign a waiver at the **Namahana Cafe,** a pleasant cafe and gift shop where you can also rent a mountain bike. Donated by the founder of E-Trade and his wife, Bill and Joan Porter, the 500-acre community park also offers a playground, skateboard ramps, dog park, and farmer's markets (see p. 598).

5-2723 Kūhiō Hwy., Kīlauea. Heading north from Līhu'e, pass the Shell station at the Kolo Rd. turnoff to Kīlauea; the entrance is 500 yards farther on the left at the Kauai Mini Golf sign. www.anainahou.org. © **808/828-2118. Anaina Hou Community Park:** Free admission. **Kauai Mini Golf:** Daily 8am–8pm (last golfers start at 7pm); admission $18 ages 11 and up, $10 children 5–10, free for children 4 and under. **Wai Koa Loop Trail:** Free admission.

Hā'ena State Park ★★ NATURAL ATTRACTIONS Besides snorkeling at pretty **Kē'ē Beach ★★★** (p. 530), in the shadow of jutting Makana (Bali Hai) mountain, or camping, the main allure of this state park is that it's at the end of the road, the perfect place to witness sunset after a leisurely drive to the North Shore. It's also the start of the 11-mile **Kalalau Trail** (p. 552), meaning its large parking area can still fill up quickly—if so, just turn around and you'll find overflow parking farther away. At the western end of Kē'ē Beach, an uphill path leads to an ancient hula platform and temple *(heiau),* where hula *hālau* (schools) still conduct formal ceremonies; please be respectful by wearing a coverup over your bathing suit before hiking here, and leave any offerings undisturbed. Before the road's end, you'll also want to stop for a look at two **wet caves,** former sea caves left high but not dry when the ocean receded; chilly water percolates into them from a spring that's affected by the nearby tides. The larger **Waikanaloa** is just off the road, with parking in front. From there it's a short, uphill walk to the craggier **Waikapala'e,** seen as the entrance to the Fountain of Youth in *Pirates of the Caribbean: On Stranger Tides.* Note that swimming is not allowed—nor considered safe.

Northern end of Kūhiō Hwy., Hā'ena. http://dlnr.hawaii.gov/dsp/parks/kauai. © **808/274-3444.** Free admission. Daily during daylight hours.

Ho'opulapula Haraguchi Rice Mill & Taro Farm ★★ FARM/MUSEUM Many of the green taro patches seen from the Hanalei Valley Overlook belong to the 30-acre **Haraguchi Farm,** where fifth-generation farmer Lyndsey Haraguchi-Nakayama, family members, and other laborers tend Hawaii's revered staple by hand. When the Haraguchis bought the farm in 1924, the wetlands were rice paddies, planted by Chinese immigrants in the 1800s. With the purchase came a wooden rice mill that stayed in operation until 1960 and is the only such structure left in the state. Restored several times after fire and hurricanes, the **Hoʻopulapula Haraguchi Rice Mill** is now a nonprofit "agrarian museum" and, like the farm, is open to visitors only as part of a weekly guided tour. Adults will appreciate hearing Haraguchi-Nakayama's stories from the family's rice-growing days, when children would be tasked with keeping grain-hungry birds away; she'll also point out the endangered birds in this corner of the **Hanalei National Wildlife Refuge.** Once you've begun to appreciate the hard work of cultivating *kalo,* as the Hawaiians call taro, it's time to sample fluffy, freshly pounded taro rolled in coconut. The 3.5-hour tour begins at the family's roadside stand in Hanalei with a taro smoothie and ends there with a tasty lunch; a small gift shop is nearby.

Check in at Hanalei Taro & Juice stand, 5-5070 Kūhiō Hwy., Hanalei, 1¼ miles west of Hanalei Bridge. www.haraguchiricemill.org. ✆ **808/651-3399.** Tours $87 adults, $52 children 5–12; Wed. 9:45am by reservation only.

Kīlauea Point National Wildlife Refuge & Lighthouse ★★★

NATURE PRESERVE/LIGHTHOUSE Two miles north of the historic town of Kīlauea is a 200-acre headland habitat—the island's only wildlife refuge open to the public—that includes cliffs, two rocky wave-lashed bays, and a tiny islet serving as a jumping-off spot for seabirds. You can easily spot red-footed boobies, which nest in trees and shrubs, and wedge-tailed shearwaters, which burrow in nests along the cliffs between March and November (they spend winters at sea). Scan the skies for the great frigatebird, which has a 7-foot wingspan, and the red-tailed tropicbird, which performs aerial acrobatics during the breeding season of March through August. Endangered nēnē, the native goose reintroduced to Kauaʻi in 1982, often stroll close to visitors, but please don't feed them. Mounted telescopes and loaner binoculars may bring into view the area's marine life, from spinner dolphins, Hawaiian monk seals, and green sea turtles year-round to humpback whales in winter. Still, the primary draw for many of the refuge's half-million annual visitors is the **Kīlauea Point Lighthouse** (www.kilauealighthouse.org), built in 1913 and listed on the National Register of Historic Places. The 52-foot-tall white lighthouse wears a jaunty red cap above its 7,000-pound Fresnel lens, whose beam could be seen from 20 miles away before it was deactivated in 1976. Docents offer free tours of the beacon, officially renamed the Daniel K. Inouye Lighthouse in 2013, in memory of the state's late senator.

End of Kīlauea Rd., Kīlauea. www.fws.gov/refuge/kilauea_point. ✆ **808/828-1413.** Admission $5 ages 16 and up; free for ages 15 and under. Tues–Sat 10am–4pm. Heading north on Kūhiō Hwy., turn right on Kolo Rd., just past mile marker 23, then left on Kīlauea Rd., and follow 2 miles to entrance.

Limahuli Garden and Preserve ★★ GARDEN Beyond Hanalei and the last wooden bridge, there's a mighty cleft in the coastal range where ancestral Hawaiians lived in what can only be called paradise. Carved by a waterfall stream known as Limahuli, the lush valley sits at the foot of steepled cliffs that Hollywood portrayed as Bali Hai in *South Pacific*. This small, almost secret garden, part of the National Tropical Botanical Garden, is ecotourism at its best. Here botanists hope to save endangered native plants, some of which grow in the 1,000-acre Limahuli Preserve behind the garden, an area that is off-limits to visitors. The self-guided tour encourages visitors to walk slowly up and down the .75-mile loop trail (resting places provided) to view indigenous and "canoe" plants, which are identified in Hawaiian and English, as well as plantation-era imported flowers and fruits. From taro to sugarcane, the plants brought over in Polynesians' voyaging canoes (hence their nickname) tell the story of the people who cultivated them for food, medicine, clothing, shelter, and decoration. The tour booklet also shares some of the fascinating legends inspired by the area's dramatically perched rocks and Makana mountain, where men once hurled firebrands *('oahi)* that floated far out to sea. You'll learn even more on the daily 2½-hour guided tour, if you reserve well in advance; a new weekly family tour, for parties with at least one child age 12 or younger, treats the garden as an outdoor classroom and lasts 1½ to 2 hours.

5-8291 Kūhiō Hwy., Hā'ena, ½-mile after mile marker 9. www.ntbg.org/gardens/limahuli.php. ✆ **808/826-1053.** Self-guided tour $20 adults, $10 college students with ID, free for children 18 and younger with paying adult; Tues–Sat 9:30am–4pm. Guided tour $40 adults, $20 college students with ID, free for children 10–18 with paying adult (younger not recommended); Tues–Sat 10am by reservation only. Family guided tour $30 adults, $20 college students, $5 ages 4 to 18, free for ages 3 and under. Credit card required for all guided tours.

Nā 'Āina Kai Botanical Gardens & Sculpture Park ★★ GARDEN Off the North Shore's beaten path, this magical garden and hardwood plantation covers 240 acres, sprinkled with 70 life-size (some larger-than-life-size) whimsical bronze statues. It's the place for avid gardeners, as well as people who think they don't like botanical gardens. It has something for everyone: a poinciana maze, an orchid house, a lagoon with spouting fountains, a Japanese teahouse, a streamside path to a hidden beach—even re-creations of traditional Navajo and Hawaiian compounds. A host of different tours is available, from 1½ hours ($35) to 5 hours ($85) long, ranging from casual, guided strolls and rides in small covered trams to treks from one end of the gardens to the ocean. Currently, these tours are open only to adults and children 13 and older. Younger kids are invited on tours of the wonderful "Under the Rainbow" garden, featuring a gecko hedge maze, a tropical jungle gym, a pint-size railroad, a treehouse in a rubber tree, and a 16-foot-tall Jack-and-the-Beanstalk giant with a 33-foot wading pool below. The 2-hour tour is $35

Nā 'Āina Kai Botanical Gardens.

for adults and $20 for kids 13 and under, and includes the maze and koi pond in the formal gardens. ***Tip:*** Most tours are limited to eight or nine guests, and the gardens are closed weekends and Monday, so book a tour before you arrive. Families should note the last Saturday of each month is usually Keiki (Children's) Day, when the children's garden is open from 9am to noon for just $10.

4101 Wailapa Rd., Kīlauea. www.naainakai.org. ✆ **808/828-0525.** Tours Tues Fri; most tours start at 9 or 9:30am, with some repeated at 1 or 1:30pm; $35–$85. Dec–Apr bird watching tours, 8:30am Wed; $60. Reservations strongly recommended. From Līhu'e, drive north on Kūhiō Hwy. past mile marker 21 and turn right on Wailapa; from Princeville, drive south 6½ miles and take the 2nd left past mile marker 22 onto Wailapa. At road's end, drive through iron gates to visitor center on the right.

Nāpali Coast State Wilderness Park ★★★ PARK This 15-mile-long crown of serrated ridges and lush valleys is the most impressive of Kaua'i's natural features—and also its most inaccessible. Only hardy, well-equipped hikers should attempt the full length of the 11-mile **Kalalau Trail,** which begins at Kē'ē Beach and plunges up and down before ending at **Kalalau Valley.** The area's last Hawaiian community lived in this 3-mile-wide, 3-mile-deep valley until the early 1900s. The valley, which can also be viewed from an overlook in Kōke'e State Park ★★★ (p. 518), is the setting for Jack London's 1912 short story "Koolau the Leper," based on a true tale of a man who hid from authorities determined to exile him to Moloka'i. (Today the bohemian squatters bedevil rangers and others determined to protect the valley's cultural treasures.) Most visitors just huff and puff 4 miles round-trip from Kē'ē Beach to

Wai'oli Hui'ia Church.

scenic but unswimmable **Hanakāpi'ai Beach,** or make it a daylong adventure by adding a 4-mile, boulder-hopping slog to Hanakāpi'ai Falls (see "Hiking," p. 551).

In late spring and summer, kayakers may explore the sea caves and oceanside waterfalls of Nāpali, but landing is only allowed at Kalalau and **Miloli'i beaches;** Kalalau requires a camping permit, while Miloli'i allows day use (see "Kayaking," p. 537). **Nualolo Kai,** the lower, seaside portion of another valley, has many archaeological sites, some under restoration, but only motorized raft (Zodiac) tours may land here (see "Boat & Raft [Zodiac] Tours," p. 535.) The natural arch at **Honopū Beach** is a highlight of the snorkel cruises passing by, but may be examined closely only by the few capable of swimming here from Kalalau or a moored kayak—a dicey proposition much of the year.

The easiest, and most expensive, way to survey Nāpali's stunning land- and seascape is by helicopter (see "Helicopter Tours," p. 523). However you experience it, though, you'll understand why Nāpali remains the star of countless calendars, postcards, and screen savers.

Btw. Kē'ē Beach and Polihale State Park. http://dlnr.hawaii.gov/dsp/parks/kauai/napali-coast-state-wilderness-park. © **808/274-3444.**

Wai'oli Mission House Museum and Church ★ HISTORIC SITE/MUSEUM Many visitors passing through Hanalei pull over for a photo of **Wai'oli Hui'ia Church** (www.hanaleichurch.org; © **808/826-6253**), a 1912 American Gothic wooden church with a steep roof, forest-green walls, and belfry reflecting the shape and hues of the mountains behind it. Nearby is the timber-and-plaster **Mission Hall,** built in 1841 and the oldest surviving church building on Kaua'i. Hidden by a grove of trees behind it is the two-story **Mission House,** erected in 1837 by the area's first missionaries, who traveled from Waimea via outrigger canoe. Teachers Abner and Lucy Wilcox and their four sons moved to this two-story, surprisingly airy home in 1846; four more sons were born here while the Wilcoxes instructed native students in English and the newly transliterated Hawaiian language. The homespun Americana—well-thumbed Bibles, braided rugs, and a spinning wheel—is complemented by Hawaiian elements such as 'ōhi'a wood floors, a lava rock chimney, and lanais. Restored in 1921, the house is open for first-come, first-served guided tours by 3 days a week; you'll leave your shoes on the lanai, and stay about 30 minutes.

5-5363 Kūhiō Hwy., Hanalei. Heading north from Hanalei Bridge, pass Waioli Huiia Church and turn left on the dirt road just before Hanalei School. A dirt parking area is about 150 hundred yards (137 meters) on the left, with a footpath to the house. www.grovefarm.org/waiolimissionhouse. ✆ **808/245-3202.** Requested donation $10 adults, $5 children 5–12. Tours on demand Tues, Thurs, and Sat 9am–3pm.

SOUTH SHORE

Kauai Coffee ★★ FARM Some 4 million coffee trees grow on 3,100 acres of former sugarcane fields from Lāwa'i Valley to 'Ele'ele, making Kauai Coffee the largest producer of coffee in Hawaii—and the United States. Kona coffee fans might sniff at the fact that the beans are machine-harvested, but it's surprisingly sustainable for such massive production, with 2,500 miles of drip-irrigation tubes, water recycling, cherry-pulp mulching, and other practices. You can learn all about the coffee-growing and roasting process on a free short, self-guided or guided tour, or from a video and displays in the free tasting area behind the gift shop on a covered porch. Let's face it; everyone heads to the latter first: How better to determine the difference between coffee varietals such as Blue Mountain, yellow catuai, or red catuai beans in an equally wide array of roasts and blends? A small snack bar in the tasting room helps take the edge off all that caffeine.

870 Halewili Rd. (Hwy. 540), Kalāheo. www.kauaicoffee.com. ✆ **808/335-0813.** Free admission. Daily 9am–5pm. Free guided tours daily 10am, noon, and 2 and 4pm. From westbound Kaumuali'i Hwy., drive through Kalāheo and look for Hwy. 540 on left just outside of town. From that intersection, it's 2½ miles to the visitor center. Hwy. 540 rejoins Kaumuali'i Hwy. another 1½ miles west.

Kukuiolono Park ★ HISTORIC SITE/GARDEN Hawaiians once lit signal fires atop this Kalāheo hillside, perhaps to aid seafarers or warn of invaders. Most visitors are still in the dark about this unusual park, created by pineapple magnate Walter McBryde and then bequeathed to the public after his death in 1930. A mile off the main highway, the recently renovated park includes the 9-hole **Kukuiolono Golf Course ★★** (p. 550); lively clubhouse restaurant, **Birdie's;** a Japanese garden, where you might see weddings being held; a collection of intriguing Hawaiian lava rock artifacts; and several miles of jogging paths. A meditation pavilion and stone benches also provide excuses to enjoy the views.

854 Pu'u Rd., Kalāheo. ✆ **808/332-9151.** Free admission. Gates open daily 7am–6pm. From Līhu'e, take Kaumuali'i Hwy. west into Kalāheo, turn left on Pāpālina Rd., and drive mostly uphill for about a mile; look for sign at right—entrance has huge iron gates and stone pillars—and continue uphill to park.

Lawai International Center ★★ BUDDHIST SHRINE/HISTORIC SITE Although you'll hear some noise from the unseen highway, the serenity of this historic 32-acre valley, open only on free guided tours, is unshakable, especially once you ascend the former Hawaiian *heiau* (temple) to the new **Hall of Compassion,** a gleaming wooden structure in the style of a 13th-century Buddhist shrine. You're expected to keep silent there and on the hillside path marked by 88 diminutive Shingon Buddhist shrines, a replica of a 900-mile temple route in Shikoku, Japan. Built in 1904 by young plantation workers from Japan, the shrines beckoned pilgrims for decades until the local cannery closed, workers moved away, and the site became overgrown. An all-volunteer, nondenominational effort has led to their restoration; you'll hear that inspiring story over a cup of tea and cookies first before heading up the steep hill (walking staffs included).

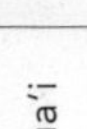

End of Wāwae Rd., off Kaumuali'i Hwy., *makai* side, Lāwa'i. From Līhu'e, turn left onto Wāwae just west of stoplight at Kōloa Rd. www.lawaicenter.org. ✆ **808/639-4300.** Tours by reservation at 10am, noon, and 2pm the 2nd and last Sun of each month, and by appt. Free admission; donations welcomed.

Makauwahi Cave Reserve ★★ ARCHAEOLOGICAL SITE The Pacific's greatest cache of fossils, including those of enormous, long-extinct waterfowl, may lie in the depths of the largest limestone cave in Hawai'i. Exposed by a sinkhole thousands of years ago, the cave is managed by paleoarchaeologists and conservationists David and Lida Pigott Burney, who have opened it for fascinating docent-led tours 4 days a week. After a slow, bumpy ride through former cane fields near the Grand Hyatt Kauai, a short walk takes you to the small entrance to the cave—stay hunched until you see sky overhead. Non-native tortoises, abandoned as house pets, help keep the vegetation down; visit their sanctuary outside the cave, where the Burneys are restoring native plants. Admission is free, but please donate toward upkeep and research. ***Tip:*** Rough roads may make it easier to park near the arena at CJM Stables (see p. 555) and follow signposts north to the cave.

Near Māhā'ulepū (Gillin's) Beach, Māhā'ulepū. From Po'ipū, take Po'ipū Rd. east past the Grand Hyatt Kauai onto dirt road. Follow 2 miles to crossroads, turn right, and turn right again just past green gate and shack. Follow farm road along edge of field and park on left just past signpost 18. Then hike trail over footbridge, turn right, and head to signpost 15; cave entrance is small hole. Tortoise rescue is to left of parking area. http://cavereserve.org. ✆ **808/634-0605** or 808/212-1710. Tours 10am–2pm Wed and Fri–Sun. Free admission; donations welcomed.

Allerton Garden.

National Tropical Botanical Garden ★★★ HISTORIC SITE/ GARDEN Formerly owned by the McBryde Sugar Company, which bought the land from Queen Emma in 1886, this lush swath of Lāwa'i Valley contains three separate gardens worth visiting, as well as the headquarters and research facilities of the National Tropical Botanical Garden. The 186-acre **McBryde Garden,** open for self-guided tours, boasts the largest collection of rare and endangered Hawaiian plants in the world, plus numerous varieties of palms, fruit trees, heliconias, orchids, and other colorful flowers. Its Spice of Life trail, which includes cacao and allspice trees, meanders past picturesque Maidenhair Falls. The accessible Diversity Trail follows a 450-million-year timeline as it passes through a misty tunnel and ends at a pavilion with restrooms and cafe. You'll want to allow at least 90 minutes to explore this garden; note that most of the trails are unpaved.

Open only to guided tours, the captivating formal gardens of adjacent **Allerton Garden** are the legacy of wealthy Chicagoan Robert Allerton and his companion John Gregg, whom Allerton later adopted. Allerton bought the land from McBryde in 1938 and with Gregg designed a series of elegant outdoor "rooms," where fountains and European statuary bracket plants collected from Southeast Asia and the Pacific. Garden tours last about 2½ hours; 3-hour sunset tours begin in the afternoon and end with a peek inside the oceanfront Allerton estate (normally off-limits), plus appetizers and drinks on the lanai.

Both the Allerton and McBryde garden tours require a tram ride down to the valley, and reservations (by credit card) are required. It's free, however, to tour the well-labeled **Southshore Visitors Center Garden,** where the trams depart. Its several acres include separate areas for ornamental flowers and trees, plants evocative of a plantation-era home garden, Hawaiian native plants, and the profusion of color and textures known as the Gates Garden at the entrance.

NTBG Southshore Visitors Center, 4425 Lāwa'i Rd. (across the street from Spouting Horn), Po'ipū. www.ntbg.org. ✆ **808/742-2623. Visitors Center Garden:** Self-guided tours daily 8:30am–5pm; free admission. **McBryde Garden:** Self-guided tours daily 9:30am–5pm; admission $30 adults, $15 children 6–12, free for children 5 and under. Trams leave hourly on the half-hour, last tram 3:30pm. **Allerton Garden:** Guided tours daily 9 and 10am, and 1, 2, and 3pm; admission $50 adults, $25 children 6–12, free for children 5 and under. Sunset tours (hours vary), $95 adults, $45 children 6–12, free for children 5 and under. All tours require reservations and check-in 30 min. in advance.

Spouting Horn ★★ NATURAL ATTRACTION The Hawaiian equivalent to Old Faithful—at least in regularity, if not temperature—is an impressive plume of seawater that jettisons anywhere from 10 to 50 or so feet into the air above the rocky shoreline (fenced for safety reasons). The spout comes from the force of ocean swells funneling waves through a lava tube, with the most spectacular displays in winter and other high-surf days. The *whoosh* of the spraying water is often followed by a load moaning sound, created by air being pushed through another nearby hole. There's an ample parking lot (as well as restrooms) on the site, but if you spot tour buses, don't try to compete with the crowds for a Spouting Horn photo. Instead, browse the vendors of arts, crafts, and jewelry (from $5 bangles to Ni'ihau shell leis costing hundreds of dollars) under the tents along the bluff, or watch the wild chickens put on a show until the buses pull out 15 to 20 minutes later. Keep an eye out for whales December through April.

Ocean side of Lāwa'i Rd., Po'ipū, 2 miles west of the traffic circle with Po'ipū Rd. Free admission. Daily during daylight hours.

WEST SIDE

Kōke'e State Park ★★★ PARK It's only 16 miles from Waimea to Kōke'e, but the two feel worlds apart: With 4,345 acres of rainforest, Kōke'e is another climate zone altogether, where the breeze has a bite and trees look quite continental. This is a cloud forest on the edge of the Alaka'i Swamp, the largest swamp in Hawaii, on the summit plateau of Kaua'i. Days are cool and wet, with intermittent bright sunshine, not unlike Seattle on a good day. Bring your sweater, and, if you're staying over, be sure you know how to light a fire (overnight lows dip into the 40s/single-digit Celsius).

Although invasive foreign plants such as strawberry guava, kahili ginger, and Australian tree ferns have crowded out native plants, the forest still holds many treasures, including several species that only grow on Kaua'i: mokihana trees, whose anise-scented green berries adorn the

A prince OF A PRINCE

With his name gracing half of the main Kaua'i highway as well as a popular beach and busy avenue in Waikīkī, you could say **Prince Jonah Kūhiō Kalanianaole** is all over the map, just as he was in life. The nephew and adopted son of King David Kalākaua and Queen Kapi'olani, Prince Kūhiō studied in California and England before the American-backed overthrow of the monarchy in 1893. He spent a year in prison after being arrested in 1895 for plotting to restore the kingdom and later fought with the British in the Boer War. In 1903, he was elected as a territorial delegate to the U.S. Congress, where he served until his death in 1922, at age 50.

Along the way, Prince Kūhiō founded the first Hawaiian Civic Club, restored the Royal Order of Kamehameha, created the Hawaiian Home Lands Commission (which awards long-term leases to Native Hawaiians), established national parks on Maui and the island of Hawai'i, opened his Waikīkī beachfront to the public, and popularized outrigger canoe racing—just to name a few of the reasons "the people's prince" is so revered. His March 26 birthday is a state holiday, which his home island of Kaua'i marks with 2 weeks of **festivities** (see www.kauaifestivals.com).

His birthplace in Po'ipū is part of **Prince Kūhiō Park,** a small, grassy compound off Lāwa'i Road, not far from where surfers navigate "PK's," a break also named for the prince. The park holds the foundations of the family home, a fish pond that's still connected by a culvert to the sea, the remains of a *heiau* (shrine), and a monument that still receives floral tributes. ***Note:*** It's considered disrespectful to sit on the rock walls, as tempting as it might be to picnic or don snorkel gear there.

island's signature lei; iliau, a spiky plant similar to Maui's silversword; and the endangered white hibiscus, one of the few of its kind to have a fragrance.

Before exploring the area, though, be sure to stop by the **Kōke'e Natural History Museum ★★** (www.kokee.org; **© 808/335-9975;** daily 9am–4:30pm). It's right next to the restaurant/gift shop of the Lodge at Kōke'e, in the meadow off Kōke'e Road (Hwy. 550), 5 miles past the first official Waimea Canyon lookout. Admission is free, but it deserves at least the $1 donation requested per person. The museum shop has great trail information as well as local books and maps, including the official park trail map. A .1-mile nature walk with labeled plants starts just behind the museum.

Another 2.7 miles up the road from Kōke'e Lodge is **Kalalau Overlook ★★★**, the spectacular climax of your drive through Waimea Canyon and Kōke'e—unless the gate is open to the Pu'u O Kila Lookout 1 mile farther, the true end of the road. The latter lookout is usually closed in inclement weather, which is frequent: Nearby Wai'ale'ale is playing catch for clouds that have crossed thousands of miles of ocean. The view from Kalalau Overlook can be Brigadoon-like, too, but when the mists part, it's breathtaking. Shadows dance cross the green cliffs dappled with

View from Kalalau Overlook.

red and orange, white tropicbirds soar over a valley almost 4,000 feet below, and the turquoise sea sparkles on the horizon. Just below the railing, look for the fluffy red *'apapane* honeycreepers darting among the scarlet-tufted 'ōhi'a lehua trees. Mornings tend to offer the clearest views.

With so many trails to hike up here, including the boardwalk through the Alaka'i Swamp (p. 555), some choose to stay overnight, either by pitching a tent in one of several campsites (by permit only) or opting for one of the cabins run by West Kauai Lodging or the YWCA's Camp Sloggett (see p. 577). You'll need to plan carefully, though, when it comes to food and drink: The lodge's restaurant (see p. 592) is open only from 9am to 2:30pm, with takeout till 3pm, but I've found it closes early when business is slow. In the late afternoon, your best hope may be a snack vendor at a Waimea Canyon overlook; otherwise, it's a winding 15-mile drive down to Waimea.

Kōke'e Rd., 7 miles north of its merge with Waimea Canyon Rd. (Hwy. 550). http://dlnr.hawaii.gov/dsp/parks/kauai/kokee-state-park. ✆ **808/274-3444.** Free admission. Daily during daylight hours.

Russian Fort Elizabeth State Historical Park ★ HISTORIC SITE To the list of those who tried to conquer Hawaii, add the Russians. In 1815, a German doctor tried to claim Kaua'i for Russia. He even supervised the construction of this fort in Waimea, named for the wife of Czar Alexander I (spelled "Elisabeth" on some signage), but he and his handful of Russian companions were expelled by Kamehameha I a couple of years later. Only the walls remain today, built with stacked lava rocks in the shape of a star. If the grounds have been recently mowed, you can easily follow a path around the fort's perimeter to the oceanside entrance to the interior; see the interpretive sign by the parking lot. The site also provides panoramic views of the west bank of the Waimea River, where Captain Cook landed, and the island of Ni'ihau. ***Note:*** Tidy restrooms and a picnic table make this a convenient pit stop.

Ocean side of Kaumuali'i Hwy., Waimea, just after mile marker 22, east of Waimea River. http://dlnr.hawaii.gov/dsp/parks/kauai/russian-fort-elizabeth-state-historical-park. ✆ **808/274-3444.** Free admission. Daily during daylight hours.

Waimea Canyon State Park ★★★ PARK/NATURAL ATTRACTION Often called the Grand Canyon of the Pacific—an analogy attributed to Mark Twain, although there's no record he ever visited—Waimea Canyon is indeed spectacular, albeit on a smaller scale. A mile wide, 3,600 feet deep, and 14 miles long, depending on whom you ask, this counterpart to Arizona's icon deserves accolades for its beauty alone. A jumble of red-orange pyramids, striped with gray bands of volcanic rock and stubbled with green and gold vegetation, Waimea Canyon was formed by a series of prehistoric lava flows, earthquakes, and erosion from wind and water, including the narrow Waimea River, still carving its way to the sea. You can stop by the road and look at the canyon, hike into it, admire it from a downhill bicycle tour, or swoop through it in a heli-

Russian Fort.

copter. (For more information, see "Organized Tours" and "Other Outdoor Activities," below.)

By car, there are two ways to visit Waimea Canyon and reach Kōke'e State Park, 15 miles up from Waimea. From the main road of Kaumuali'i Highway, it's best to head up Waimea Canyon Drive (Hwy. 550) in Waimea town. You can also pass through Waimea and turn up Kōke'e Road (Hwy. 55) at Kekaha, but it's steeper—one reason the twice-daily downhill bike tours prefer that route—and its vistas, though lovely, are not as eye-popping as those along Waimea Canyon Drive, the narrower rim road. The two routes merge about 7 miles up from the highway and continue as Kōke'e Road.

The first good vantage point is **Waimea Canyon Lookout,** between mile markers 10 and 11 on Kōke'e Road; there's a long, gently graded, paved path for those who can't handle the stairs to the observation area. Far across the canyon, two-tiered **Waipo'o Falls** cascades 800 feet; you might spot a nimble mountain goat clambering on the precipices just below. From here, it's about another 5 miles to Kōke'e. A few more informal and formal lookout points along the way also offer noteworthy views. **Pu'u Ka Pele Lookout,** between mile markers 12 and 13, reveals the multiple ribbons of water coursing through Waipoo Falls. **Pu'u Hinahina Lookout,** between mile markers 13 and 14, actually has two different

Waimea Canyon.

vista points, one with a sweeping view of the canyon down to the Pacific, and another of Ni'ihau, lying 17 miles west.

Waimea Canyon Drive and Kōke'e Road, Waimea. http://dlnr.hawaii.gov/dsp/parks/kauai/waimea-canyon-state-park. ✆ **808/274-3444.** Free admission. Daily during daylight hours.

West Kauai Visitor Center ★ MUSEUM/ATTRACTION Although its hours are limited, this center's two free weekly activities and the small but well-curated cultural exhibitions merit a stop here before or after your Waimea Canyon expedition. The **"Keepers of the Culture"** displays include vintage photos, artifacts, and panels on Waimea's natural and cultural history, from traditional Hawaiian practices such as salt-making and herbal medicine to the arrival of Captain Cook, the sugar plantation era, *paniolo* (cowboy) culture, and the modern Pacific Missile Range Facility. Kids will more likely enjoy the **lei-making class,** which takes place at 9:30am Friday from March to mid-November (when fresh blossoms are available); admission is by donation, but you need to reserve by phone no later than noon the Thursday before. On Monday, a free **guided walking tour** of historic Waimea Town explores its ancient Hawaiian roots and modern history with stops at the Captain Cook monument, missionary churches, and picturesque Waimea Pier. It starts at 9:30am and lasts about 3 hours; reservations are required by 4pm the Friday before.

9565 Kaumuali'i Hwy. (*mauka* side) at Waimea Canyon Rd., Waimea. Parking is at rear of building, with lot entrance only from Kaumuali'i Hwy. www.westkauaivisitorcenter.org. ✆ **808/338-1332.** Free admission. Mon–Fri 10am to 4pm.

Organized Tours

Farms, gardens, historic houses, and other points of interest that may be open only to guided tours are listed under "Attractions & Points of Interest," earlier. For boat, kayak, bicycle, hiking, and similar tours, see listings under "Other Outdoor Activities."

HELICOPTER TOURS ★★★

If you forgo touring Kaua'i by helicopter, you'll miss seeing the vast majority of its untouched ridgelines, emerald valleys, and exhilarating waterfalls. Yes, the rides are expensive ($200–$300 per person), but you'll take home memories—not to mention photos, videos, and/or a professional DVD—of the thrilling ride over Waimea Canyon, into Kalalau Valley on Kaua'i's wild Nāpali Coast, and across the green crater of Wai'ale'ale, laced with ribbons of water.

Most flights depart from Līhu'e, last about 55 to 75 minutes, and, regardless of advertising, offer essentially the same experience: narrated flights, noise-canceling headphones with two-way communication, and multicamera videos of your ride or a pre-taped version (often a better souvenir). The risks are also about the same—the last crash involving a sightseeing helicopter over Kaua'i was in 2007, with many thousands of flights safely flown since. (If your pilot chooses to bypass Wai'ale'ale due to bad weather, appreciate his or her caution.) So how to distinguish among the half-dozen major operators?

Given the noise inflicted on residents, wildlife, and tranquility-seeking hikers by flights that hover as low as 500 feet, I recommend touring with the most eco-friendly of the bunch, and most luxurious: **Blue Hawaiian ★★★** (www.bluehawaiian.com; © **800/745-2583** or 808/245-5800). Its American Eurocopter Eco-Star choppers have a unique tail design that reduces noise and fuel use, while the roomy interior has six business-class-style leather seats with premium views. The best seats are the two next to the pilot, but the raised row of rear seats won't disappoint (keep in mind seating is usually determined by weight distribution.) The 55-minute "Eco Adventure" ride from Līhu'e costs $247 ($217 when booked online at least 5 days in advance), which also makes Blue Hawaiian the best value.

For those staying on the North Shore, it may be more convenient to do a tour with **Sunshine Helicopters ★★** (www.sunshinehelicopters.com; © **866/501-7738** or 808/270-3999). Its 40- to 50-minute flights

Nāpali Coast viewed from helicopter.

HOLLYWOOD loves KAUA'I

More than 50 major Hollywood productions have been shot on Kaua'i since the studios discovered the island's spectacular natural beauty. Two of the most recent star turns were in 2015's *Jurassic World* (an update of 1993's *Jurassic Park*) and 2011's ***The Descendants.*** The latter includes several scenes in Hanalei and at the breathtaking overlook of Kīpu Kai. You can visit a number of Kaua'i locations that made it to the silver screen—including the settings of such TV classics as *Fantasy Island* and *Gilligan's Island*—on the **Hawaii Movie Tour** from Roberts Hawaii (www.robertshawaii.com/island/kauai; ✆ **800/831-5541**). Offered daily except Sunday, the narrated minibus tour features singalongs and video clips that play between sightseeing stops. You'll likely see more of Kaua'i on this 6-hour tour, which includes exclusive access to the shuttered Coco Palms resort, than you could on your own. Tickets are $114 for adults and $61 for children 4 to 11 (free for younger, if seated on an adult's lap); prices include lunch at Wahooo Seafood Grill and pickup/drop-off ($10 extra for Princeville lodgings). ***Tip:*** Book online for discounted fares—$103 adults, $55 children—and reserve early.

from Princeville Airport are in quiet, roomy Whisper Star models, similar in design to Blue Hawaiian's Eco-Stars (it flies different craft out of Līhu'e). Tours cost $289 for open seating, $364 if you want to reserve an even roomier "first class" seat in the front row; it's $249 and $324, respectively, if you book online, with an extra $10 off on flights before 8:30am or after 2pm.

Although its aircraft are not as quiet as those of Blue Hawaiian and Sunshine, two other companies have unique itineraries deserving of consideration. **Island Helicopters** (www.islandhelicopters.com; ✆ **800/829-5999** or 808/245-8588) has exclusive rights to land at remote 350-foot Manawaiopuna Falls, nicknamed "Jurassic Falls" for its movie cameo. During your 25 minutes on the ground, you'll hear about the geological history and rare native plants in this area of Hanapēpē Valley, which like Ni'ihau is owned by the Robinson family. In part due to landing fees and fuel costs, the 75- to 85-minute **Jurassic Falls Tour ★** costs $329 (plus 4% if using a credit card); it leaves from Līhu'e Airport. **Safari Helicopters** (www.safarihelicopters.com; ✆ **800/326-3356** or 808/246-0136) offers the 90-minute **Kaua'i Refuge Eco-Tour ★★,** which includes a 30- to 40-minute stopover at an otherwise inaccessible Robinson-owned site overlooking vast Olokele Canyon; Keith Robinson is occasionally on hand to explain his efforts to preserve rare, endemic plants here (which your landing fees subsidize). The tour costs $304 ($274 booked online) and departs from Līhu'e. ***Note:*** For Ni'ihau helicopter tours, see p. 523.

BEACHES

Note: You'll find relevant sites on the "Kaua'i" map, p. 491.

Kaua'i's nearly 70 beaches include some of the most beautiful in the world, and all are open to the public, as required by state law. They are also in the middle of the vast, powerful Pacific, where currents and surf patterns are often quite different than those of Mainland beaches. The North Shore sees the highest surf in winter (Oct–Apr), thanks to swells originating in the Arctic that can also wrap around the West Side and turn the East Side's waters rough. In summer, Antarctic storms can send large swells to the South Shore that wrap around the West Side and churn up the East Side.

The good news is there's almost always a swimmable beach somewhere: You just need to know where to look. Start by asking your hotel concierge or checking the daily ocean report at **Kauaiexplorer.com** to find out current conditions. Nine beaches—all of them county or state parks—have lifeguards, who are keen to clue you in on safety.

Below are highlights of the Garden Isle's more accessible beaches. For detailed listings, including maps and videos, of virtually all strands and coves, see **www.kauaibeachscoop.com**.

East Side

ANAHOLA BEACH ★

Anahola is part of the Hawaiian Home Lands federal program, meaning that much of the land here is reserved for long-term leases by Native Hawaiians; you'll pass their modest homes on the road to this secluded, mostly reef-protected golden strand. The 1½-acre **Anahola Beach Park** on the south end feels like the neighborhood's back yard, particularly on weekends, with kids learning to surf or bodyboarding, a hula class on the grass, and picnickers. It's better to explore here during the

Safe Swimming on Kaua'i

"When in doubt, don't go out" is the mantra of local authorities, who repeat this and other important safety tips in public service announcements. That refers to going into unsafe waters, walking on slippery rocks and ledges that may be hit by high surf, or other heedless acts, such as disregarding beach closed signs in winter. Many of the unguarded beaches have waters that should only be enjoyed from the sand or during calm conditions, which can change rapidly; large waves may come in sets as much as 20 minutes apart. Although you might see locals seemingly ignoring the warning signs that note hazards such as strong currents, steep drop-offs, dangerous shorebreak, and the like, keep in mind they've had years to acclimatize. Don't be afraid to ask for their advice, though, since they'll tailor it for newcomers. By all means, *do* go out to Kaua'i's beaches; just use prudence before going in or near the water.

DEADLY BEAUTY: QUEEN'S BATH

With so many lovely places to hike, swim, or snorkel in relative safety on Kaua'i, it's hard to understand why so many visitors put themselves in jeopardy at Queen's Bath, an oceanfront "pond" in the lava rocks below the Princeville cliffs, where 29 recorded drownings and numerous injuries have occurred. The site is most dangerous from October to April, but even on seemingly calm summer days, rogue waves can knock the unwary off ledges or surge across the pond and pull swimmers into the open ocean, where they can drown long before help arrives. Others receive broken limbs by falling on the steep, rough trail—which is extremely slippery when wet—or while trying to enter the rocky pond. Unlike the many blithe reviewers on TripAdvisor who happened to experience tranquil conditions, I cannot in good conscience direct visitors here. If nothing else will dissuade you, know that parking is tight and illegally parked cars can and will be booted.

week when you might share it with just a few fishermen and campers (who may also be locals). There are sandy-bottomed pockets for swimming and reefy areas for snorkeling, safe except in high surf. The Anahola River, usually shallow enough to walk across, bisects the beach. Facilities include picnic tables, restrooms, campsites, and lifeguards.

From Kūhiō Hwy. heading north, turn right on Anahola Rd. (between mile markers 13 and 14) and head ¾-mile to the beach park. You can also park north of the Anahola River by taking a right on Aliomanu Rd. ½-mile past Anahola Rd., just after Duane's Ono Char-Burger (p. 586).

KUMUKUMU (DONKEY) BEACH ★★

When the only way to reach this beach was by a downhill hike through sugarcane fields near a donkey pasture, nude sunbathers took full advantage of its seclusion. Now it's bordered by large luxury estates and the **Ke Ala Hele Makalae** coastal path, connecting it to Keālia Beach, 1.5 miles south; the 10-minute walk down to the ocean is mostly paved, and even starts at a parking lot with restrooms. So keep your clothes on, but do enjoy the soft golden sand at this tree-lined beach, also known as Palikū ("vertical cliff") and Kuna Bay. The water is too rough for swimming or snorkeling, but you may see advanced surfers and bodyboarders here. The north side has a shallow cove that's safe for wading in calm conditions.

From Kapa'a, take Kūhiō Hwy. north past mile marker 11; parking is on right, marked by sign with two hiking figures on it. Footpath to beach starts near parking lot entrance.

KALAPAKI BEACH ★★

This quarter-mile-long swath of golden sand may seem like a private beach, given all the lounge chairs on its border with the Kaua'i Marriott Resort, which towers behind. But there's generally plenty of room to find your own space to sunbathe, while the jetty stretching across much of Kalapaki Bay offers a protected place to swim or paddle; body-surfing and surfing are also possible at a small break. The view of the mossy-green Hā'upu Ridge rising out of Nāwiliwili Bay is entrancing, as is watching massive cruise ships and Matson barges angle their way in and out of the nearby harbor. The water is a little murkier here, due to stream runoff. Facilities include restrooms and showers, with numerous shops and restaurants within a short walk.

From Līhu'e Airport, turn left onto Hwy. 51, then turn left on Rice St, and look for the Kaua'i Marriott Resort entrance on the left. Free beach access parking is in the upper lot, past the hotel's porte-cochère.

KEĀLIA BEACH ★

Only very experienced surfers and bodyboarders should try their skill on the usually powerful waves here, but everyone else can enjoy the show from the broad golden sand, a picnic table, or the nearby coastal multi-use path. The lifeguards can advise you if it's calm enough to go for a swim and where to do it. When the wind is up, which is often, you might see kite flyers. The 66-acre **Keālia Beach Park** is just off the main highway, often with food trucks and coconut vendors in the parking lot, making it a convenient place for an impromptu break. Facilities include restrooms and picnic shelters.

Off Kūhiō Hwy. in Kapa'a, just north of Kapa'a River and Mā'ilihuna Road.

LYDGATE BEACH ★

Part of the family oasis of 58-acre **Lydgate Park ★** (p. 508) on the south side of the Wailua River mouth, Lydgate Beach has two rock-walled ponds that create the safest swimming and best snorkeling on the East Side—unless storms have pushed branches and other debris into the pond, which can take several days to clear. Families also gravitate here for the immense wooden play structure known as the **Kamalani Playground** and access to a 2.5-mile stretch of the **Ke Ala Hele Makalae coastal path,** suitable for strollers and bikes. Facilities include a pavilion, restrooms, outdoor showers, picnic tables, barbecue grills, lifeguards, campsites, and parking.

Leho Dr. at Nalu Rd., Wailua. From the intersection of Kūhiō Hwy. and Hwy. 51 outside of Līhu'e, head 2½ miles north to Leho Dr. and turn right, just before the Hilton Garden Inn Kauai Wailua Bay. Turn right again on Nalu Rd. and follow to parking areas.

North Shore

'ANINI BEACH ★★★

'Anini is the safest beach on Kaua'i for swimming and windsurfing, thanks to one of the longest, widest fringing reefs on the island, among the very largest in all of Hawaii. With shallow water 4 to 5 feet deep, it's also a good snorkel spot for beginners (although the coral and varieties of

'Anini Beach.

fish are sparse closer to shore). In summer months, divers are attracted to the 60-foot dropoff near the channel in the northwest corner of the nearly 3-mile-long reef. In winter, this channel creates a very dangerous rip current, although the near-shore waters generally stay calm; it can be fun to watch breakers pounding the distant reef from the bath-like lagoon. The well-shaded, sinuous beach is very narrow in places, so just keep walking if you'd like more privacy. The 13-acre **'Anini Beach Park** on the southwestern end has restrooms, picnic facilities, a boat-launch ramp, campsites, and often a food truck or two.

From Līhu'e, follow Kūhiō Hwy. past Kīlauea to the 2nd Kalihiwai Rd. exit on right (the 1st Kalihiwai Rd. dead-ends at Kalihiwai Beach). Head downhill ½-mile to a left on 'Anini Rd.

HANALEI BEACH ★★★

Easily one of the most majestic settings in Hawai'i, and unbelievably just a few blocks from the main road, Hanalei Beach is a gorgeous half-moon of golden-white sand, 2 miles long and 125 feet wide. Hanalei means "lei-shaped," and like a lei, the curving, ironwood-fringed sands adorn Hanalei Bay, the largest inlet on Kaua'i. While the cliffside St. Regis Princeville dominates the eastern vista, the view west is lush and green; behind you, emerald peaks streaked with waterfalls rise to 4,000 feet. Renowned for experts-only big surf in winter (Sept–May), Hanalei attracts attract beginners and old hands with steady, gentler waves the rest of the year. In summer, much of the bay turns into a virtual lake. The county manages three different beach parks here, two with lifeguards.

Black Pot Beach Park, near the historic, 300-foot-long pier, is particularly good for swimming, snorkeling, surfing, and fishing, while you'll also see kayakers and stand-up paddleboarders coming in from the mouth of the Hanalei River—note that it can be difficult to find parking on weekends and during holiday periods. Facilities include restrooms, showers, picnic tables, and campsites. **Hanalei Pavilion Beach Park,** in the center of the bay, has wide-open swimming (in calm weather), surfing, and boogie-boarding under the watchful eye of lifeguards; facilities include restrooms, showers, and pavilions. "Pine Trees" is the widely used moniker for **Wai'oli Beach Park,** shaded by ironwood trees towards the western edge of the bay. It's another popular surf spot—champions Andy and Bruce Irons grew up riding the waves here and started the children's Pine Trees Classic held here every April. Check with lifeguards in winter about possible strong currents; facilities include showers and restrooms.

From Princeville heading north on Kūhiō Hwy., enter Hanalei and turn right at Aku Rd. just after Tahiti Nui; then right on Weke Rd. Hanalei Pavilion Beach Park will be on your left; the road dead-ends at parking lot for Black Pot Beach Park. For Wai'oli Beach Park (Pine Trees), take Aku Rd. to a left on Weke Rd.; then right on He'e Rd.

KAUAPEA (SECRET) BEACH ★★

Not exactly secret, but still wonderfully secluded, this long, broad stretch of light sand below forested bluffs lies snugly between rocky points, with only a few cliff-top homes and Kīlauea Point Lighthouse to the east providing signs of civilization. Although strong currents and high surf, especially in winter, make the water unsafe, tide pools at the west end invite exploration when the surf is low, creating beguiling mini-lagoons; a small artesian waterfall to the east is perfect for washing off salt water. ***Note:*** Despite its reputation as a safe haven for nudists (who hang out at the more remote eastern end), Kaua'i County does occasionally enforce the "no public nudity" law here. And as with all destinations where your car will be out of sight for extended periods, be sure to take your valuables with you. It's a 15-minute walk downhill to the beach.

Heading north on Kūhiō Hwy., pass Kīlauea and take 1st Kalihiwai Rd. turnoff on right. Drive about 50 yards, then turn right on unmarked dirt road on right, and follow to parking area. Trail at end of lot leads downhill to beach, about a 15-min. walk.

KĒ'Ē BEACH ★★★

The road ends here at this iconic tropical beach, hugged by swaying palms and sheltering ironwoods, its pale dunes sloping into a cozy lagoon brimming with a kaleidoscope of reef fish. You could feel like a sardine during the peak summer period when the ocean is at its most tranquil and the parking lot is full by 9am. To be fair, many cars are for hikers tackling all or part of the 11-mile **Kalalau Trail** (p. 552), whose trail head is just before the beach, and some belong to campers. Kē'ē (pronounced *"kay-eh"*) is also subject to high surf in winter when rogue waves can grab unwitting spectators from the shoreline and dangerous currents form in a channel on the reef's western edge. It's best to avoid the channel year-round, and always check with the lifeguards about the safest areas for swimming or snorkeling. Part of **Hā'ena State Park** (p. 510), Kē'ē has restrooms and showers in the woodsy area east of the parking lot. This is also a spectacular place to observe sunset, but you won't be alone in that endeavor either.

From Hanalei, take Kūhiō Hwy. northwest about 7½ miles to the road's end.

LUMAHA'I BEACH ★

Between lush tropical jungle of pandanus and ironwood trees and the brilliant blue ocean lie two crescents of inviting golden-sand beach, separated by a rocky outcropping. Here is Kaua'i at its most captivating—and where you must exercise the most caution. Locals have nicknamed it "Luma-die," reflecting the sad tally of those drowned or seriously injured here. With no reef protection and a steeply sloping shore, the undertow and shorebreak are exceptionally strong, while the rocky ledges that seemingly invite exploration are often slapped by huge waves that knock sightseers into the tumbling surf and sharp rocks. Flash floods can also make the Lumaha'i River, which enters the ocean from the western beach, turn from a wading pool into a raging torrent. Plus, it has neither lifeguards nor facilities; parking is in a bumpy, unpaved area or along the narrow highway. So why would one even go here? When summer brings more tranquil surf, it's a gorgeous setting to stretch out on the sand—not too close to the shorebreak—and soak in the untamed beauty. ***Note:*** The eastern beach, reached by a short, steep trail from the highway, is where Mitzi Gaynor sang "I'm Gonna Wash That Man Right Outta My Hair" in *South Pacific*.

From Hanalei, follow Kūhiō Hwy. about 2½ miles west. Look for pull-off on ocean side, near mile marker 4, for trail leading to eastern beach. For western beach, continue west (downhill) to larger, unpaved parking area on *makai* side by mile marker 5.

MĀKUA (TUNNELS) BEACH ★★★ & HĀ'ENA BEACH ★★★

Mākua Beach earned the nickname of "Tunnels" from the labyrinth of lava tubes that wind through its inner and outer reef, making this the island's premiere snorkeling and diving site. The reefs mean the water is safe to enter nearly year-round. But as fascinating as the rainbow of tropical fish and the underwater tunnels, arches, and channels may be, they're more than matched by the beauty of what's above water. The last pinnacle in a row of velvety green mountains, Makana (Bali Hai) rises over the western end of a golden curved beach with a fringe of ironwood trees. The only problem: Where to park? The handful of spots on dirt access roads fills up first thing, and residents vigilantly enforce "no parking" zones.

Fortunately, a quarter-mile up the sand is **Hā'ena Beach Park,** a county facility with plenty of parking—plus restrooms, showers, picnic tables, campsites, and lifeguards. During calm conditions, most frequent in summer, Hā'ena Beach offers good swimming and some snorkeling, though not as enticing as at Mākua. Winter brings enormous waves, rip currents, and a strong shorebreak: time to leave the water to the expert local surfers. Do walk across the road for a gander at **Maniniholo Dry Cave,** another former sea cave (see "Hā'ena State Park," p. 510), but in this case, it's one where you can walk for yards and yards inside before it gets too dark and low (watch your noggin).

From Hanalei, Mākua (Tunnels) is just after mile marker 8 on Kūhiō Hwy., but not visible from the road. Continue ½-mile to Hā'ena Beach Park and parking lot on right.

South Shore

MĀHĀ'ULEPŪ BEACHES ★★

Not far from the well-groomed resorts of Po'ipū is a magical place to leave the crowds—and maybe the last few centuries—behind. To reach the three different beaches of Māhā'ulepū, framed by lithified sand dunes, former sugarcane fields, and the bold Hā'upu ridge, you'll have to drive at least 3 miles on an uneven dirt road through private land (gates close at 6pm) or hike the fascinating Māhā'ulepū Heritage Trail (p. 554). The first tawny strand is **Māhā'ulepū Beach,** nicknamed Gillin's Beach after the former Grove Farm manager whose house is the only modern structure you'll see for miles; the house is available for rent starting at $3,450 a week (www.gillinbeachhouse.com). Windsurfing is popular here, yet the strong currents prevent swimming or snorkeling. Around the point is **Kawailoa Bay,** also a windsurfing destination, with a rockier shoreline great for beachcombing and fishing. Wedged between dramatically carved ledges, **Hā'ula Beach** is a picturesque pocket of sand with a rocky cove, best for solitude. ***Note:*** The coastline here can be very windy and subject to high surf in summer.

By car: From Po'ipū Rd. in front of Grand Hyatt Kauai, continue on unpaved road 3 miles east, past the golf course and stables. Turn right at the T intersection, go 1 mile to big sand dune, turn left, and drive ½-mile to a small lot under the trees to reach **Māhā'ulepū Beach.** You can continue on dirt road (high-clearance four-wheel-drive recommended) another ¼-mile to **Kawailoa Bay,** and then another ½-mile to short trail to **Hā'ula Beach. By foot:** Follow Māhā'ulepū Heritage Trail (www.hikemahaulepu.org) 2 miles from east end of Keoneloa (Shipwrecks) Beach; public access parking is just east of Grand Hyatt Kauai on 'Ainakō St.

PO'IPŪ BEACH ★★★

A perennial "best beach" winner, the long swath of Po'ipū is actually two beaches in one, divided by a tombolo, or sandbar point. On the left, a lava-rock jetty protects a sandy-bottom pool that's perfect for children most of the year; on the right, the open bay attracts swimmers, snorkelers, and surfers. (If the waves are up, check with the lifeguards for the

Māhā'ulepū Beach.

safest place to swim.) The sandy area is not especially large, but the 5½-acre **Po'ipū Beach Park** offers a spacious lawn for kids to run around in, plus picnic shelters, play structures, restrooms, and showers. There are plenty of palm trees, but not much shade; bring a beach umbrella to stay cool. Given the resorts and condos nearby, Po'ipū understandably stays busy year-round, and on New Year's Eve, it becomes Kaua'i's version of Times Square with a fireworks celebration. ***Note:*** A short walk east is **Brennecke's Beach,** a sandy cove beloved by bodysurfers and boogie-boarders; be forewarned that waves can be large, especially in summer, and the rocky sides are always hazardous. Injuries do occur at Brennecke's, which has no lifeguard.

From Kōloa, follow Po'ipū Rd. south to traffic circle and then east to a right turn on Ho'owili Rd. Parking is on the left at intersection with Ho'ōne Rd.

KEONELOA (SHIPWRECKS) BEACH ★

Makawehi Point, a lithified sand dune, juts out from the eastern end of this beach, whose Hawaiian name means "the long sand." Harrison Ford and Anne Heche jumped off Makawehi in *Six Days, Seven Nights* (don't try it yourself), while bodysurfers and boogie-boarders find the roiling waters equally exhilarating. Novices should enjoy their antics from the shore or follow the ironwood trees to the path to the top of Makawehi Point, which is also the start of the **Māhā'ulepū Heritage Trail** (p. 554). A paved beach path in front of the Grand Hyatt Kauai leads west past tide pools to the blustery point at Makahū'ena, perfect for photographing Makawehi Point. Restrooms and showers are by the small parking lot on 'Ainakō Street.

Public access from 'Ainakō St., off Po'ipū Rd., just east of Grand Hyatt Kauai.

West Side

SALT POND BEACH ★★

You'll see Hawai'i's only salt ponds still in production across from Salt Pond Beach, just outside Hanapēpē. Generations of Hawaiians have carefully tended the beds in which the sun turns seawater into salt crystals, *pa'akai*. Tinged with red clay, *'alae,* the salt is used as a health remedy as well as for seasoning food and drying fish. Although the salt ponds are off-limits to visitors, 6-acre **Salt Pond Beach Park** is a great place to explore, offering a curved reddish-gold beach between two rocky points, a protective reef that creates lagoon-like conditions for swimming and snorkeling (talk to the lifeguard first if waves are up), tide pools, and a natural wading pool for kids. Locals flock here on weekends for individual recreation and large family gatherings. Facilities include showers, restrooms, a campground, and picnic areas.

From Līhu'e, take Kaumuali'i Hwy. to Hanapēpē, cross Hanapēpē Bridge, and look for Lele Rd. on left (½-mile ahead). Turn left and follow Lele Rd. to a right turn on Lokokai Rd. Salt Pond Beach parking lot is 1 mile ahead.

POLIHALE BEACH ★★

This mini-Sahara on the western end of the island is Hawai'i's biggest beach: 17 miles long and as wide as three football fields in places. This

Polihale State Park.

is a wonderful place to get away from it all, but don't forget your flip-flops—the midday sand is hotter than a lava flow. The pale golden sands wrap around Kaua'i's northwestern shore from Kekaha plantation town, just beyond Waimea, to where the ridges of Nāpali begin. For military reasons, access is highly restricted for a 7-mile stretch along the southeastern end near the Pacific Missile Range Facility, including the famed **Barking Sands Beach,** known to Hawaiians as Nohili. You'll still have miles of sand to explore in 140-acre **Polihale State Park,** provided you (or your car) can handle the 5-mile, often very rutted dirt road leading there. (Avoid driving on the car-trapping sand, too.) The sheer expanse, plus views of Ni'ihau and the first stark cliffs of Nāpali, make the arduous trek worth it for many. Although strong rip currents and a heavy shorebreak make the water dangerous, especially in winter, **Queen's Pond,** a small, shallow, sandy bottom inlet, is generally protected from the surf in summer. The park has restrooms, showers, picnic tables, campsites, and drinking water (usually), but no lifeguards or any other facilities nearby, so plan accordingly. As in all remote areas, don't leave any valuables in your car.

From Kekaha, follow Kaumuali'i Hwy. 7 miles northwest past Pacific Missile Range Facility to fork at Kao Rd., bear right, and look for sign on left to Polihale. Follow dirt road 5 miles to main parking area, bearing right at forks.

WATERSPORTS

Several outfitters on Kaua'i not only offer equipment rentals and tours, but also give out expert information on weather forecasts, sea and trail conditions, and other important matters for adventurers. Brothers Micco and Chino Godinez at **Kayak Kaua'i** (www.kayakkauai.com; **© 888/596-3853** or 808/826-9844) are experts on paddling Kaua'i's rivers and coastline (as well as hiking and camping), offering guided tours and equipment rentals at their store in the Wailua River Marina. You can also learn about ocean and reef conditions and recommended boat operators at **Snorkel Bob's** (www.snorkelbob.com), with two locations in Kapa'a and Po'ipū (see "Snorkeling," later). ***Note:*** Expect to tip $10 to $20 for the crew or guides on any tours.

Boat & Raft (Zodiac) Tours

One of Hawaii's most spectacular natural attractions is Kaua'i's **Nāpali Coast.** Unless you're willing to make an arduous 22-mile round-trip hike (see "Hiking" on p. 551), there are only two ways to see it: by helicopter (see "Helicopter Tours" on p. 523) or by water. Cruising to Nāpali may involve a well-equipped yacht under full sail, a speedy powerboat, or for the very adventurous, a Zodiac inflatable raft, in which you may explore Nāpali's sea caves or even land at one of Nāpali's pristine valleys—be prepared to hang on for dear life (it can reach speeds of 60 miles an hour) and get very wet.

You're almost guaranteed daily sightings of pods of spinner dolphins on morning cruises, as well as Pacific humpback whales during their annual visit from December to early April. In season, both sailing and powerboats combine **whale-watching** with their regular adventures. **Sunset cruises,** with cocktails and/or dinner, are another way to get out on the water and appreciate Kaua'i's coastline from a different angle.

Note: In addition to Captain Andy's (details below), only two other companies have permits to land at Nualolo Kai, home to the ruins of an 800-year-old Hawaiian village below an elevated Nāpali valley: **Na Pali Explorer** (http://napaliexplorer.com; ✆ **808/338-9999**), which departs from Kekaha ($149), and **Kauai Sea Tours** (www.kauaiseatours.com; ✆ **800/733-7997** or 808/826-7254), leaving from Port Allen ($159); book online for $10 off. All trips are on rigid-hull inflatables, which, unlike larger boats, can pass through the reef opening; landings take place April through October, conditions permitting.

Captain Andy's Sailing Adventures ★ Captain Andy has been sailing to Nāpali since 1980, with a fleet that now includes two sleek 55-foot custom catamarans, the *Spirit of Kauai* and *Akialoa;* two luxurious 65-foot catamarans, the *Southern Star* and the *Northern Star;* and the zippy 24-foot Zodiac, which holds about a dozen thrillseekers. The 5½-hour **Nāpali catamaran cruise** costs $149 for adults and $109 for children 2 to 12, and it includes a continental breakfast, a deli-style lunch, snorkeling, and drinks; aboard the *Southern Star* ($169 adults, $119 children), a barbecue lunch replaces the deli fare. A 4-hour Nāpali Coast dinner cruise—which sails around the South Shore when Nāpali's waters are too rough, most often in winter—costs $119 for adults and $89 for children ($149/$109 on the *Southern Star*), with no snorkeling; all Nāpali catamaran cruises leave from Port Allen. The 2-hour **Po'ipū cocktail sunset sail** aboard the *Spirit of Kauai* or *Akialoa,* including drinks and pupu (appetizers), is $79 for adults and $59 for children; it sails Saturday only, from Kukui'ula Small Boat Harbor near Po'ipū. **Nāpali Zodiac cruises** depart from Kikiaola Small Boat Harbor in Kekaha; the 4-hour version ($139 adults, $119 children 5–12) includes snorkeling and snacks, while the 6-hour version ($159/$119) adds a landing at Nualolo Kai (depending on conditions) and expands snacks to a picnic lunch. ***Tip:*** Book online for a $10-per-person discount.
www.napali.com. ✆ **800/535-0830** or 808/335-6833.

Holo Holo Charters ★★★ Port Allen is the point of departure for Holo Holo's two gleaming catamarans. The 50-foot *Leila,* licensed for 45 passengers but limited to just 37, serves Holo Holo's 5-hour, year-round **Nāpali snorkel sails:** They're $149 adults and $109 children 6 to 12, including a continental breakfast and deli lunch, and post-snorkel beer and wine. The 65-foot *Holo Holo* power catamaran, the island's largest, was built specifically to handle the channel crossing between Kaua'i and

Ni'ihau, where passengers snorkel after Nāpali sightseeing on 7-hour trips, also with two meals and post-snorkel libations ($205 adults, $139 children 6–12). The 3½-hour **Nāpali sunset cruise** ($119 adults, $99 children 5–12), also aboard the *Holo Holo,* offers heavy appetizers, cocktails, and, at sunset, a champagne toast. The **2-hour Kaua'i sunset cruise** ($108) aboard the *Leila* serves the same fare but heads south to Po'ipū. Holo Holo also runs Nāpali snorkel tours from Hanalei on comfortable inflatable "rafts," really speedboats with fiberglass hulls, twin motors, stadium seats, and a freshwater shower. The 4-hour trip, including drinks and lunch, costs $189 for ages 6 and older (younger not allowed). ***Tip:*** Book online at least 1 day in advance for $15 to $20 off per person.
www.holoholokauaiboattours.com. ✆ **800/848-6130** or 808/335-0815.

Liko Kauai & Makana Charters ★ Born and raised on Kaua'i, in a Native Hawaiian family with roots on Niihau, Captain Liko Ho'okano offers more than just a typical cruise; this is a 5-hour combination Nāpali Coast tour/snorkel/cultural history class/seasonal whale-watching extravaganza with lunch. It all happens on the new 49-foot *Na Pali Kai III* power catamaran, limited to 32 passengers and narrow enough to go in the sea caves normally only visited by inflatable craft. The tours cost $140 for adults (pregnant women not allowed) and $95 for children 4 to 12. Boats depart twice daily from Kikiaola Small Boat Harbor in Kekaha; check in at 4516 Alawai Rd., Waimea (from Kaumuali'i Hwy., turn right at Alawai just west of the Waimea River).
www.tournapali.com. ✆ **808/338-9980.**

Bodysurfing & Boogie Boarding

The best places for beginners' bodysurfing and boogie boarding are **Kalapaki Beach** and **Po'ipū Beach;** only the more advanced should test the more powerful shorebreaks at **Keālia, Shipwrecks (Keoneloa),** and **Brennecke's** beaches (see "Beaches," p. 526.) Boogie-board rentals are widely available at surf shops (see "Surfing," p. 544) and beachfront activity desks. On the South Shore, **Nukumoi Surf Shop** (www.nukumoi.com; ✆ **808/742-8019**), right across from Brennecke's Beach at 2100 Ho'ōne Rd., Po'ipū, has the best rates and selections ($6 a day; $20 a week). On the North Shore, **Hanalei Surf Co.** (www.hanaleisurf.com; ✆ **808/826-9000**), rents boogie boards for $5 a day, $20 a week, or $7 with fins, $22 weekly (3- and 5-day discounts also available); it's in Hanalei Center (the old Hanalei School Building), 5-5161 Kūhiō Hwy., *mauka* side, Hanalei.

Kayaking

With Hawaii's only navigable river (some would say rivers), numerous bays, and the stunning Nāpali Coast, Kaua'i is made for kayaking. The

Boogie boarding the Kaua'i surf.

most popular kayaking route is up the Wailua River to Uluwehi (Secret) Falls (limited to permitted kayaks Mon–Sat), but you can also explore the Hulē'ia and Hanalei rivers as they wind through wildlife reserves, go whale-watching in winter along the South Shore, or test your mettle in summer with an ultrastrenuous, 17-mile paddle from Hanalei to Polihale.

Kayak Kaua'i (www.kayakkauai.com; ✆ **888/596-3853** or 808/826-9844), the premiere outfitter for all kinds of paddling, offers a range of rentals and tours from its store in Wailua River Marina, 3-5971 Kūhiō Hwy., Kapa'a (just south of the Wailua River Bridge, *mauka* side). River kayak rental starts at $29 for a one-person kayak and $54 for a two-person kayak per day ($64 for Wailua River-permitted double kayaks), including paddles, life preservers, back rests, and car racks. Twice-daily, 5-hour guided Wailua River tours with a Secret Falls hike/swim and picnic lunch cost $85 for adults and $60 for children under 12; a 3-hour version that skips the waterfall hike but adds a swimming hole is $55 for adults and $45 for children. The 5-hour Blue Lagoon tour from the Hanalei River mouth includes a shuttle to/from the Wailua River Marina, snorkeling, bird-watching, and beach time; it's $95 for adults and $85 for children.

Kayak Kaua'i's Nāpali tours ($240, including lunch), offered April through September, are only for the very fit who also aren't prone to seasickness; the 12-hour tour requires 5 to 6 hours of paddling, often through large ocean swells, in two-person kayaks. Co-owner Micco Godinez calls it "the Everest of sea kayaking." Trips depart Hā'ena Beach and end at Polihale, with lunch and a rest stop at Miloli'i Beach, with shuttle to/from Wailua. Guided tours to Kalalau and Miloli'i for those with camping permits (see "Camping & Cabins," p. 576) are also available, starting at $159 a day (two-person minimum), as are 90-minute "Kayak School" sessions on the Wailua River ($75).

Headquartered in Po'ipū, **Outfitters Kauai** (www.outfitterskauai.com; ✆ **888/742-9887** or 808/742-9667) offers a similar variety of well-organized tours, from a Wailua kayak/waterfall hike ($108 adults, $88 children 5–14, including lunch) to a summer Nāpali adventure ($238 ages 15 and older only) and a winter whale-watching paddle from Po'ipū to Port Allen ($158 adults, $128 children 10–14). The kid-friendly Hidden Valley Falls tour heads 2 miles downwind on the Hulē'ia River and includes a short hike to a swimming hole and a picnic by a small waterfall, with the bonus of a motorized canoe ride back; it's $118 for adults and $68 for children 3 to 14.

Family-owned **Kayak Hanalei** (www.kayakhanalei.com; ✆ **808/826-1881**) offers relaxed, informative guided tours of Hanalei River, with snorkeling in Hanalei Bay, at 8:30am weekdays for $106 adults, $96 children 5 to 12. Daily rentals start at $27 half-day for a single kayak to $81 full-day for a triple, all gear included. No hauling is required; you launch under the colorful "Dock Dynasty" sign behind the store, 5-5070A Kūhiō Hwy., Hanalei (*makai* side, behind Hanalei Taro & Juice Co.).

Sailing

Kalapaki Bay and Nāwiliwili Harbor provide a well-protected if bustling place to learn to sail or, with sufficient experience, take a spin around the harbor yourself. In addition to surfing and stand-up paddleboarding lessons and rentals, **Kauai Beach Boys** (www.kauaibeachboys.com; ✆ **808/246-6333**) offers 1-hour rides with an instructor ($39) and sailing lessons for $140 an hour on its two-person, 18-foot Hobie Tandem Island boat and six-person, 16-foot Hobie Getaway boat; skilled sailors can tool around Kalapaki Bay on their own for $95 an hour ($75 per additional hour, up to $195 a day) or go out on the ocean with an instructor.

Scuba Diving

Diving, like all watersports on Kaua'i, is dictated by the weather. In winter, when heavy swells and high winds hit the island, it's generally limited to the more protected South Shore. Probably the best-known site along the South Shore is **Caverns,** located off the Po'ipū Beach resort area. This site consists of a series of lava tubes interconnected by a chain of archways. A constant parade of fish streams by (even shy lionfish are spotted lurking in crevices), brightly hued Hawaiian lobsters hide in the lava's tiny holes, and turtles sometimes swim past.

In summer, the magnificent North Shore opens up, and you can take a boat dive locally known as the **Oceanarium,** northwest of Hanalei

Bay, where you'll find a kaleidoscopic marine world in a horseshoe-shaped cove. From the rare (long-handed spiny lobsters) to the more common (ta'ape, conger eels, and nudibranchs), the resident population is one of the more diverse on the island. The topography, which features pinnacles, ridges, and archways, is covered with cup corals, black-coral trees, and nooks and crannies enough for a dozen dives.

Because the best dives on Kaua'i are offshore, including the crystal-clear waters off Nāpali and Niihau, I recommend booking a dive with **Bubbles Below Scuba Charters** (www.bubblesbelowkauai.com; ✆ **808/332-7333**), specializing in highly personalized small-group dives with an emphasis on marine biology. Based in Port Allen, the 36-foot *Kaimanu* is a custom-built Radon dive boat that comes complete with a hot shower, accommodating up to eight passengers; the 31-foot, catamaran-hulled *Dive Rocket,* also custom-built, takes just six. Standard two-tank boat dives cost $135 (if booked directly); it's $245 for the two-tank dive along the Mana Crack, an 11-mile submerged barrier reef, as well as a Nāpali cruise. Bubbles Below also offers a three-tank trip, for experienced divers only, to more challenging locations such as the "forbidden" island of Niihau, 90 minutes by boat from Kaua'i, and its nearby islets of Lehua and Kaula; locations vary by time of year and conditions ($345). You should also be willing to share water space with the resident sharks. The all-day, three-tank trip costs $345 (booked directly), including tanks, weights, dive computer, lunch, drinks, and marine guide. Ride-alongs for nondivers and crustacean-focused twilight/night dives, as well as bottles of Nitrox, are also available.

On the South Shore, the highly regarded **Fathom Five Adventures** (www.fathomfive.com; ✆ **800/972-3078** or 808/742-6991) offers customized boat dives for up to six passengers, starting at $140 for a two-tank dive up to $377 for a three-tank Ni'ihau dive ($43 more for gear rental.)

GREAT SHORE DIVES Spectacular shoreline dive sites on the North Shore include beautiful **Kē'ē Beach,** where the road ends and the drop-off near the reef begs for underwater exploration (check with lifeguards first). **Cannons,** east of Hā'ena Beach Park, has lots of vibrant marine life in its sloping offshore reef. Another good bet is the intricate underwater topography off **Mākua Beach,** widely known as Tunnels. The wide reef here makes for some fabulous snorkeling and diving, especially during the calm summer months. (See "Beaches" on p. 526 for location details.)

On the South Shore, head to the right of the tombolo (sand bar) splitting **Po'ipū Beach** if you want to catch a glimpse of sea turtles; it's officially known as Nukumoi Point but nicknamed Tortugas (Spanish for "turtle"). The former boat launch at **Kōloa Landing** has a horseshoe-shaped reef that's teeming with tropical fish. It's off Ho'onani Road, about a quarter-mile south of Lāwa'i Road near the Po'ipū traffic circle.

Sea turtles in Kaua'i waters.

Sheraton Caverns, located off the Sheraton Kauai, is also popular—its three large underwater lava tubes are usually filled with marine life.

If you want a guided shore dive, **Fathom Five Adventures** (see above) will take you out daily for $75 for one tank and $90 for two tanks at Kōloa Landing. Spring through fall, it also offers weekday, two-dive shore dives at Tunnels/Mākua for $115, with the same rate for a one-tank night dive.

Snorkeling

You can buy snorkel gear at any number of stores on the island, but with luggage fees going up, I find it easier just to rent. **Kauai Bound** (www.kauaiboundstore.com; ✆ **808/320-3779**) provides top-quality snorkel sets, including carrying bags, fish ID card, and no-fog drops, for $7.50 a day or $28 a week (child's version $5 daily, $20 weekly) at its store in Anchor Cove Shopping Center, 3366 Wa'apā Rd., Līhu'e, open 8am to 5pm daily. You can also rent pro-level underwater cameras ($20–$30 a day), camera accessories, and other outdoor gear here.

Robert Wintner, the quirky founder of the statewide chain **Snorkel Bob's** (www.snorkelbob.com; ✆ **800/262-7725**), is a tireless advocate for reef protection, funding campaigns for more legislation through the Snorkel Bob Foundation. His two stores here rent a great variety of snorkel gear ($35 a week for adult sets, $22 for child sets), with the convenience factor of 24-hour and interisland drop-offs, plus discounts on reputable snorkeling cruises. The East Side location (✆ **808/823-9433**) is at 4-734 Kūhiō Hwy., Kapa'a, just north of Coconut Marketplace, while the South Shore outlet (✆ **808/742-2206**) is at 3236 Po'ipū Rd., just south of Old Kōloa Town.

In general, North Shore snorkeling sites are safest in summer and South Shore sites in winter, but all are subject to changing conditions; check daily ocean reports such as those on **Kauaiexplorer.com** before venturing out. See "Boat & Raft (Zodiac) Tours" for snorkel cruises to the reefs off Nāpali and Ni'ihau. The following shoreline recommendations apply in times of low surf (see "Beaches" on p. 526 for more detailed descriptions):

EAST SIDE The two rock-walled ponds at **Lydgate Park** south of the Wailua River are great for novices and children, if it hasn't rained heavily.

NORTH SHORE **Kē'ē Beach,** located at the end of Kūhiō Hwy., and **Mākua (Tunnels) Beach,** about a mile before in Hā'ena, offer the greatest variety of fish. **'Anini Beach,** located off the northern Kalihiwai Road, between Kūhiō Hwy. mile markers 25 and 26, south of Princeville, has the most protected waters; avoid the channel in the reef in winter or strong surf.

SOUTH SHORE The right side of the tombolo, the narrow strip of sand dividing **Po'ipū Beach** into two coves, has good snorkeling but can be crowded. You can also follow the beach path west past the Waiohai Marriott to the pocket cove in front of Ko'a Kea Hotel. A boat ramp leads into the rocky cove of **Kōloa Landing** (see "Scuba Diving," above), where on clear days you'll spot large corals, turtles, and plenty of reef fish. (***Note:*** Rain brings in stream runoff, which turns the water murky.) Tour groups often visit rock-studded **Lāwa'i Beach** off Lāwa'i Road, next to the Beach House Restaurant; watch out for sea urchins as you swim among parrotfish, Moorish idols, and other reef fish.

WEST SIDE **Salt Pond Beach,** off Kaumuali'i Hwy. near Hanapēpē, has good snorkeling amid hundreds of tropical fish around two rocky points.

Sport Fishing

DEEP-SEA FISHING Kaua'i's fishing fleet is smaller than others in the islands, but the fish are still out there, and relatively close to shore. All you need to bring is your lunch (no bananas, per local superstition) and your luck. **Sportfish Hawaii** (www.sportfishhawaii.com; ✆ **877/388-1376** or 808/396-2607), which inspects and books boats on all the islands, has prices starting at $675 for a 4-hour exclusive charter (six passengers maximum), up to $1,440 for 8 hours. Rates may be better, though, booking directly through local operators such as Captain Lance Keener at **Ohana Fishing Charters** (www.fishingcharterskauai.com; ✆ **800/713-4682**); excursions on the wide and stable 30-foot *Ho'o*

Maika'i out of Kapa'a start at $140 per person for a 4-hour shared trip up to $1,250 for a private 8-hour trip (up to six passengers).

Captain Harry Shigekane of **Happy Hunter Sport Fishing** (www.happyhuntersportfishing.com; ✆ **808/639-4351**) offers 4-hour shared charters for $200 per person aboard his 41-foot Pacifica, the *Happy Hunter II,* out of Nāwiliwili Small Boat Harbor. Private tours run $700 to $1,300.

FRESHWATER FISHING Freshwater fishing is big on Kaua'i, thanks to dozens of reservoirs full of largemouth, smallmouth, and peacock bass (also known as *tucunare*). The **Pu'u Lua Reservoir,** in Kōke'e State Park, also has rainbow trout and is stocked by the state every year, but has a limited season, in recent years mid-June to late September.

Sportfish Hawaii (www.sportfishhawaii.com; ✆ **877/388-1376** or 808/396-2607) offers guided bass-fishing trips starting at $265 for one or two people for a half-day and $375 for one person for a full day, beginning at 6:30am in Kapa'a.

Whatever your catch, you're required to first have a **Hawai'i Freshwater Fishing License,** available online through the **State Department of Land and Natural Resources** (http://freshwater.ehawaii.gov) or through fishing-supply stores such as **Wal-Mart,** 3–3300 Kūhiō Hwy., Līhu'e (✆ **808/246-1599**), or **Waipouli Variety,** 4–911 1-A Kūhiō Hwy., Kapa'a (✆ **808/822-1014**). A 7-day nonresident license is $10 (plus a $1 convenience fee if purchased online).

Stand-Up Paddleboarding (SUP)

Like everywhere else in Hawaii, stand-up paddleboarding (SUP) has taken off on Kaua'i. It's easily learned when the ocean is calm, and still easier than traditional surfing if waves are involved. Lessons and equipment are generally available at all beachfront activity desks and the island's surf shops (see "Surfing," below), while Kaua'i's numerous rivers provide even more opportunities to practice. Kaua'i native and pro surfer Chava Greenlee runs **Aloha Stand Up Paddle Lessons** (www.alohasuplessonskauai.com; ✆ **808/639-8614**) at Kalapaki Beach, where he first learned to stand-up paddle; the bay offers a large, lagoon-like section ideal for beginners, plus a small surf break for more advanced paddlers. He and his fellow instructors (all licensed lifeguards) also teach SUP in Po'ipū, just south of the Sheraton Kauai. Two-hour group lessons (eight-person maximum) cost $75 and include 30 minutes on land and 90 minutes on water, both with instructor; sessions are offered four times a day, with private lessons $150 per person. Walk-ups are welcome, but reservations are recommended.

Kauai Beach Boys (www.kauaibeachboys.com) gives 90-minute lessons three times a day on the beach at Kalapaki (✆ **808/246-6333**) and Po'ipū (✆ 808/742-4442); the $79 fee includes a rash guard, which also helps prevent sunburn. Once you've got the hang of it, **Nukumoi**

Surf Shop, across from Brennecke's Beach (www.nukumoi.com; © **808/742-8019**), will rent you boards with paddles and wheels (for easy transport) for $20 an hour, $60 for a full day, $80 overnight, or $250 a week.

In Hanalei, launch directly into the river and head to the bay from **Kayak Hanalei** (www.kayakhanalei.com; © **808/826-1881**), 5-5070A Kūhiō Hwy., *makai* side, behind Hanalei Taro & Juice. Rental boards are $43 daily, $32 half-day, offered daily; 90-minute lessons are available Monday through Saturday, with group classes starting at $91 for ages 8 and up. Private sessions for ages 5 and up cost $139.

Outfitters Kauai (www.outfitterskauai.com; © **808/742-9667**) combines a SUP lesson with a 2-mile, downwind paddle on the Hulē'ia River and hike to a swimming hole; a motorized outrigger brings you back up the river. The half-day trip starts at 7:45am and costs $128 for adults and $98 for kids 12 to 14.

Surfing

With the global expansion in surfing's popularity, the most accessible breaks around the island have plenty of contenders. Practice patience and courtesy when lining up to catch a wave, and ask for advice from local surf shops before heading out on your own. **Hanalei Bay**'s winter surf is the most popular on the island, but it's for experts only. **Kalapaki and Po'ipū beaches** are excellent spots to learn to surf; the waves are generally smaller, and—best of all—nobody laughs when you wipe out. Go to **Kaua'i Explorer Ocean Report** (www.kauaiexplorer.com/ocean_report) or call the **Weather Service** (© **808/245-3564**) to find out where the surf's up.

Pro surfer and Garden Island native Chava Greenlee runs **Aloha Surf Lessons** (www.alohasurflessonskauai.com; © **808/639-8614**) at both Kalapaki and Po'ipū, just south of the Sheraton Kauai. Group lessons, offered four times a day, cost $75 and include a short briefing on land, an hour in the water with an instructor, and 30 minutes to surf on your own; private lessons cost $300, but you can include up to four people if you choose. Rates include a rash guard and reef walkers. Reservations are recommended. ***Note:*** "All-girl" lessons with a female instructor may also be arranged in advance.

If you want to keep practicing, in Po'ipū it's easy to rent from **Nukumoi Surf Shop** (www.nukumoi.com; © **808/742-8019**), right across from Brennecke's Beach at 2100 Ho'ōne Rd. Nukumoi charges $6 an hour, $25 a day, or $75 a week for soft boards; the hard (epoxy) boards, for experienced surfers, cost $8 an hour, $30 a day, or $90 a week. Keep surfing at either Kalapaki or Po'ipū with a rental from **Kauai Beach Boys** (www.kauaibeachboys.com, © **808/246-6333**) for $15 an hour, $25 a day.

Surfing near Po'ipū Beach.

If you're staying on the North Shore, consider a lesson from **Hawaiian Surfing Adventures** (www.hawaiiansurfingadventures.com; ✆ **808/482-0749**), which offers smaller group lessons (maximum of four students) that include 90 minutes of instruction, up to an hour of practice, and soft boards for $65; it's $150 for a private class ($100 for ages 12 and younger). The exact surf spot in Hanalei will vary by conditions; check-in for lessons is at the **Hawaiian Beach Boys Surf Shop,** 5-5134 Kūhiō Hwy. (*makai* side, just before Aku Rd. when heading north). Daily rentals start at $20 for soft boards and $25 for the expert epoxy boards, with discounts for longer periods; rent for the same rates at **Hanalei Surf Co.** (www.hanaleisurf.com/rentals; ✆ **808/826-9000**), 5–5161 Kūhiō Hwy. (*mauka* side, in Hanalei Center), Hanalei.

Tubing

Back in the days of the sugar plantations, local kids would grab inner tubes and jump in the irrigation ditches crisscrossing the cane fields for an exciting ride. Today you can enjoy this (formerly illegal) activity by "tubing" the flumes and ditches of the old Līhu'e Plantation with **Kaua'i Backcountry Adventures** (www.kauaibackcountry.com; ✆ **888/270-0555** or 808/245-2506). Passengers are taken in four-wheel-drive (4WD) vehicles high into the mountains above Līhu'e to look at vistas generally off-limits to the public. At the flumes, you will be outfitted with a giant tube, gloves, and headlamp (for the long passageways through the tunnels, hand-dug circa 1870). All you do is jump in the water, and the gentle flow will carry you through forests, into tunnels, and finally to a mountain swimming hole, where a picnic lunch is served. The 3-hour tours are $106, open to ages 5 and up (minimum height 43 in., maximum weight 300 pounds). Swimming is not necessary—all you do is relax and drift downstream—but do wear a hat, swimsuit, sunscreen, and shoes that can get wet, and bring a towel, change of clothing, and insect repellent. Tours are offered at 8, 9 and 10am, noon, and 1 and 2pm. ***Tip:*** The water is always cool, so starting midday, when it's warmer, might be more pleasant.

Windsurfing & Kite Surfing

With a long, fringing reef protecting shallow waters, the North Shore's 'Anini Beach is one of the safest places for beginners to learn windsurfing. Lessons and equipment rental are available at **Windsurf Kauai** (www.windsurf-kauai.com; ✆ **808/828-6838**). Owner Celeste Harzel has been teaching windsurfing on 'Anini Beach for decades, with special equipment to help beginners learn the sport; she and fellow teacher Lani White offer novice and refresher classes at 10am and 1pm on weekdays and advanced classes by request. A 2-hour lesson is $100 and includes equipment and instruction. Competent windsurfers may rent the equipment for $25 an hour.

Serious windsurfers and kitesurfers (that is, those who travel with their own gear) will want to check out **Hā'ena Beach Park** and **Mākua (Tunnels) Beach** on the North Shore, and the **Māhā'ulepū** coastline (including Māhā'ulepū/Gillin's Beach and Kawailoa Bay) on the South Shore. See "Beaches," p. 526, for details.

OTHER OUTDOOR ACTIVITIES

Biking

Although the main highway has few stretches truly safe for cycling, there are several great places on Kaua'i for two-wheeling. The **Po'ipū** area has wide, flat paved roads and several dirt cane roads (especially around Māhā'ulepū), while the **East Side** has two completed legs of the **Ke Ala Hele Makalae** multi-use trail (www.kauaipath.org/kauaicoastalpath), eventually intended to extend from Anahola to the airport in Līhu'e. For now, the 2.5-mile Lydgate Park loop connects it with Wailua Beach, while another 4.1-mile leg in Kapa'a links Lihi Park to 'Āhihi Point, just past Kumukumu (Donkey) Beach, 1.5 miles north of Keālia Beach Park. Mountain bikers can also ride the scenic 5-mile **Wai Koa Loop Trail** at the Anaina Hou Community Park (p. 509) in Kīlauea, or attempt more challenging trails in actual mountains, if it's not too muddy.

Several places rent mountain bikes, road bikes, and beach cruisers, including helmets and locks, with sizeable discounts for multiday rentals. In Po'ipū, **Outfitters Kauai** (www.outfitterskauai.com; ✆ **888/742-9887** or 808/742-9667) charges $25 a day for hybrid bikes and $35 to

$45 for Kona-brand utility, off-road, and road bikes; reservations are recommended. The shop is at 2827 Po'ipū Rd., Po'ipū, in the Kukui'ula Market strip, across from the fire station; look for the yellow mini-submarine out front. Outfitters Kauai also leads twice-daily, 4½-hour **downhill Waimea Canyon bicycle tours** ($108 adults, $88 kids 12 to 14) that follow the Kōke'e Road spur to Kekaha. Some find the experience memorable, but I think there are better places on Kaua'i to cycle, and certainly better ways to see the canyon.

Kapa'a has choices for both adventurers itching to explore the single-track trails in the mountains and vacationers just wanting to pedal the coastal path for a couple of hours. **Kauai Cycle** (www.kauaicycle.com; ✆ **808/821-2115**) offers cruisers for $20 a day but specializes in road and mountain bikes for $30 a day ($45 full-suspension), with maps and advice customized to abilities and current trail conditions. No reservations are needed; just walk in to its store and repair shop, which also sells clothing and gear, at 4-934 Kūhiō Hwy., Kapa'a, north of Ala Road, *makai* side (across from Taco Bell). Families in particular will want to take note of the shiny Trek beach cruisers, tandems, and trailers from **Coconut Coasters** (www.coconutcoasters.com; ✆ **808/822-7368**) at 4-1586 Kūhiō Hwy., Kapa'a, just north of Kou Street on the ocean side. Half-day rentals start at $18; reservations are recommended.

On the North Shore, **Pedal 'n Paddle** in Hanalei (www.pedalnpaddle.com; ✆ **808/826-9069**) rents beach cruisers for $15 a day and hybrids for $20; it's in the Ching Young Village Shopping Center, 5-5190 Kūhiō Hwy., *makai* side, just past Aku Road. In Kīlauea, the rental mountain bikes from **Namahana Cafe** (www.namahanacafe.org/bike rentals; ✆ **808/828-2118**) in Anaina Hou Community Park can be used on the Wai Koa Loop Trail or taken elsewhere; the rate is $25 for 1 to 6 hours and $35 for 24 hours (discounts for longer rentals).

Birding

Kaua'i provides more than 80 species of birds—not counting the "wild" chickens seen at every roadside attraction. Coastal and lowland areas, including the wildlife refuges at Kīlauea Point (p. 511) and along the Hanalei River, are home to introduced species and endangered native waterfowl and migratory shorebirds; the cooler uplands of Kōke'e State Park shelter native woodland species, who were able to escape mosquito-borne diseases that killed off lowland natives. David Kuhn of **Terran Tours** (✆ **808/335-0398**) leads custom bird-watching excursions that spot some of Hawaii's rarest birds, using a four-wheel-drive (4WD) vehicle to access remote areas. Rate start at $300 for a half-day, with longer periods available; e-mail info@soundshawaiian.com for details.

Many pairs of endangered nēnē, the endemic state bird, call Princeville's **Makai Golf Club** home, as do nesting Laysan albatross in winter; for $50 a cart, you can ogle them, their carefully marked nests,

Red-crested cardinal.

and spectacular scenery on a self-guided **sunset golf cart tour** (www.makaigolf.com; © **808/826-1863**).

Golf

It's no wonder that Kaua'i's exceptional beauty has inspired some exceptionally beautiful links. More surprising is the presence of two lovely, inexpensive public courses: the 9-hole **Kukuiolono** on the South Shore, and the even more impressive 18-hole **Wailua Golf Course** on the East Side; see details below.

Value-seekers who don't mind occasionally playing next to a Costco and suburban homes—amid panoramas of several soaring green ridges—will appreciate **Puakea** (www.puakeagolf.com; © **808/245-8756**), part of AOL founder Steve Case's Grove Farm portfolio. Greens fees for 18 holes are $105, $65 after 11am, and $45 after 3pm; it's $45 for 9 holes anytime. It's centrally located, at 4150 Nuhou St., off Nāwiliwili Road, Līhu'e. ***Note:*** Greens fees in this section include cart rentals unless stated otherwise.

To play the newest course on the Garden Island, you'll need to be a guest in one of the $1,000-plus-a-night Club Cottages and Club Villas at Kukui'ula (www.parrishkauai.com/kukuiula; © **800/325-5701**). Along with members of **Kukui'ula** (www.kukuiula.com; © **855/742-0234**), guests also have exclusive access to Tom Weiskopf's rolling 18-hole course through gardens, orchards, and South Shore grasslands. Wherever you play, money can't buy your way out of dealing with trade winds, so start early for best scores.

EAST SIDE

Hōkūala Golf Club ★★ The former Kaua'i Lagoons Golf Club is now part of the new Timbers Resort development, Hōkūala, which will eventually include private homes, a boutique hotel, and retail center. Jack Nicklaus originally designed the 18-hole, oceanfront Kiele Course (since renamed the **Ocean Course**) in the late 1980s, returning in 2011 to create even more spectacularly sited links with views of Ninini Point Lighthouse, Kalapaki Bay, and Hā'upu Mountain. ***Note:*** Timbers planned to close the front 9 holes for renovations for much of 2016 and reopen them by late fall 2016. Facilities (also subject to renovation or relocation) include a driving range, snack bar, pro shop, practice greens, clubhouse, and club and shoe rental.

3351 Ho'olaulea Way, Līhu'e, next to Marriott's Kauai Lagoons–Kalanipu'u and Kaua'i Marriott Resort. www.hokualakauai.com/golf. ✆ **808/241-6000.** Greens fees $205, $135 after noon; nine holes $105.

Wailua Golf Course ★★ Highly rated by both *Golf Digest* and the Golf Channel, this coconut palm–dotted, largely seafront course in windy Wailua has hosted three U.S. amateur championships. Spread along the *makai* (ocean) side of the main highway, the first 9 holes were built in the 1930s; the late Kaua'i golf legend Toyo Shirai designed the second 9 in 1961. Nonresident rates start at just $48 (plus $20 for a cart) for 18 holes. Facilities include the **Over Par** snack bar/restaurant and bar, a locker room with showers, driving range, practice greens, and club rentals.

3-5350 Kūhiō Hwy. (Hwy. 56), Wailua, 3 miles north of Līhu'e airport. www.kauai.gov/golf. ✆ **808/241-6666.** Greens fees $48 weekdays, $60 weekends/holidays, half-price after 2pm or for back 9 only in morning. Motorized cart $20 ($11 for 9 holes), pull cart $7 ($5 for 9 holes).

NORTH SHORE

Makai Golf Club ★★★ This gem of a course—the first on the island to be designed by Robert Trent Jones, Jr.—has extra luster now that the nearby Prince Course has gone private. It's already gained favor with nongolfers by offering self-guided **sunset golf cart tours** ($50 per cart; ✆ **808/826-1863**), with a map to memorable vistas, flora, and fauna (including nesting Laysan albatross in winter), plus **sunrise yoga** on the 7th hole at 7:30am Monday and Wednesday ($15; cash only). For golfers, it's worth noting that Jones returned in 2009 to remake the 27 holes he created here in 1971. The resulting 18-hole championship Makai Course winds around ocean bluffs and tropical forest with compelling sea and mountain views, including Mount Makana. There's a "time par" of 4 hours, 18 minutes, here, to keep golfers on track (otherwise they might be gawking at the scenery all day). Sadly, the family-friendly 9-hole Woods Course is in rough shape, and likely not worth taking a swing at. Other facilities include a clubhouse, a pro shop, practice facilities, the

Makai Grill restaurant, and club rentals. ***Note:*** "Dynamic" pricing means greens fees vary by time, season, and demand, but all guests of a Kaua'i hotel are eligible for a maximum $205 rate.

4080 Lei O Papa Rd., Princeville. www.makaigolf.com. ✆ **808/826-1912.** Greens fees $205 if staying in local hotel, $275 otherwise; check online for discounts. Mahalo Mixer at 4pm Mon includes full swing clinic, several holes on the front 9, sparkling wine toast at sunset, and commemorative glasses for $99 a couple. Nonrenovated Woods Course, $55 for adults; $28 for juniors 16–17 and children 6–15 unaccompanied by adult; free for children 6–15 with paying adult. From Līhu'e, take Kūhiō Hwy. to the Princeville main entrance, turn right, go 1 mile and course is on the left.

SOUTH SHORE

Kiahuna Golf Club ★ This par-70, 6,353-yard course designed by Robert Trent Jones, Jr., is a veritable wildlife sanctuary, where black-crowned night herons, Hawaiian stilts, and moorhens fish along Waikomo Stream, and outcroppings of lava tubes by the second fairway hold rare blind spiders. Keep your eyes peeled for remains of a stone-walled *heiau* (temple) and a Portuguese home from the early 1800s, whose former inhabitants lie in a nearby crypt—and watch out for the mango tree on the par 4, 440-yard hole 6. Facilities include a driving range, practice greens, club rentals, and a restaurant, **Joe's on the Green,** popular with locals.

2545 Kiahuna Plantation Dr. (off Po'ipū Rd.), Kōloa. www.kiahunagolf.com. ✆ **808/742-9595.** Greens fees $95, $60 for 9 holes or after 3pm. $47 for juniors 17 and under with paying adult.

Kukuiolono Golf Course ★★ Although not on a resort, this 9-hole hilltop course has unbeatable views to match an unbeatable price: $9 for all day, plus $9 for an optional cart. The course is part of woodsy **Kukuiolono Park** (p. 515), which includes a Japanese garden and Hawaiian rock artifacts; both the garden and the course were developed by pineapple tycoon Walter McBryde, who bequeathed it to the public in 1930. The course is well maintained, given the price, with relatively few fairway hazards (barring a wild pig now and then). Facilities include a driving range, practice greens, club rental, and **Birdies** restaurant in the clubhouse.

Kukuiolono Park, 854 Puu Rd., Kalāheo. ✆ **808/332-9151.** Greens fees $9 per day, optional cart rental $9; cash only. From Līhu'e, take Kaumuali'i Hwy. west into Kalā heo, turn left on Pāpālina Rd., and drive uphill for nearly a mile. Look for sign at right; the entrance has huge iron gates and stone pillars.

Poipu Bay Golf Course ★★ This 7,123-yard, par-72 course with a links-style layout was, for years, the home of the PGA Grand Slam of Golf. Designed by Robert Trent Jones, Jr., the challenging course features undulating greens and water hazards on 8 of the holes. The par-4 16th hole has the coastline weaving along the entire left side. The most striking hole is the 201-yard par-3 on the 17th, which has an elevated tee next to an ancient *heiau* (place of worship) and a Hawaiian rock wall along the fairway. Facilities include a restaurant, lounge, locker room, pro shop, club and shoe rentals, and practice facilities (off grass).

2250 'Ainakō St. (off Po'ipū Rd., across from the Grand Hyatt Kauai), Po'ipū. www.poipubaygolf.com. ✆ **808/742-8711.** Greens fees (includes $5 resort fee): $255 before noon ($185 for Grand Hyatt guests); $175 after 11am; $140 after 1pm (18 holes not guaranteed). Nine holes at 7am, $99.

Hiking

As beautiful as Kaua'i's drive-up beaches and waterfalls are, some of the island's most arresting sights aren't reachable by the road: You've got to hoof it. Highlights are listed below; for descriptions of the 34 trails in Kaua'i's state parks and forestry reserves, check out **Nā Ala Hele Trail & Access System** (http://hawaiitrails.ehawaii.gov; ✆ **808/274-3433**).

Note: When heavy rains fall on Kaua'i, normally placid rivers and streams overflow, causing flash floods on some roads and trails. Check the weather forecast, especially November through March, and avoid dry streambeds, which flood quickly. Always bring more drinking water than you think you need, too; stream water is unsafe to drink, due to the risk of leptospirosis.

For guided hikes, Micco Godinez of **Kayak Kaua'i** (www.kayakkauai.com; ✆ **888/596-3853** or 808/826-9844) is just as expert on land as he is at sea. He and his savvy guides lead regular trips (with shuttles

Hiking the Kalalau Trail.

from the Wailua River Marina) to Waipo'o Falls through Kōke'e/Waimea Canyon ($126), Nāpali's Hanakāpi'ai Beach ($126) and Hanakāpi'ai Falls ($168), Kapa'a's Sleeping Giant ($81) and Kuilau Ridge ($85), and the 'Awa'awapuhi/Nualolo loop trail ($231), an impressive 11-mile loop starting in Kōke'e and leading to dazzling overlooks of Nāpali. Departing from Po'ipū Beach Park, naturalists with **Kauai Nature Tours** (www.kauainaturetours.com; ✆ **888/233-8365** or 808/742-8305) lead a similar variety of day hikes, focusing on Kaua'i's unique geology, environment, and culture; they're $135 to $165 adults and $100 to $135 for children 7 to 12, including lunch.

The Kaua'i chapter of the **Sierra Club** (http://sierraclubkauai.org) offers four to seven different guided hikes around the island each month, varying from easy 2-milers to 7-mile-plus treks for serious hikers only; they may include service work such as beach cleanups and trail clearing. Listings on the online "outings calendar" include descriptions and local phone contacts; requested donation per hike is $5 adults and $1 for children under 18 and Sierra Club members.

EAST SIDE

The dappled green wooded ridges of the Līhu'e-Kōloa and Nounou (Sleeping Giant) forest reserves provide the best hiking opportunities here. From Kuamo'o Road (Hwy. 580) past 'Ōpaeka'a Falls, you can park at the trailhead for the easy, 2-mile **Kuamo'o Trail,** which connects with the steeper, 1.5-mile **Nounou West Trail;** both have picnic shelters. Stay on Kuamo'o Road till just before the Keahua Arboretum to pick up the scenic, 2.1-mile **Kuilau Trail,** often used by horses, which can be linked with the more rugged, 2.5-mile **Moalepe Trail,** ending at the top of Olohena Road in Kapa'a. In the arboretum, you'll find the trail head for the challenging **Powerline Trail,** an unmaintained path that follows electric lines all the way to Princeville's Kapaka Street, on the *mauka* side of Kūhiō Highway; avoid if it's been raining (the mud can suck your sneakers off, or worse.). A steady climb, but worth the vista at the top, is the 2-mile **Nounou East Trail,** which takes you 960 feet up a mountain known as Sleeping Giant (which does look like a giant lying down); the trail ends at a picnic shelter on his "chest," and connects with the west leg about 1.5 miles in. The east trailhead, which has parking, is on Hale'ilio Road in Kapa'a; turn inland just past mile marker 6 on Kūhiō Highway and head 1¼ miles uphill.

NORTH SHORE

Traversing Kaua'i's amazingly beautiful Nāpali Coast, the 11-mile (one-way) **Kalalau Trail** is the definition of breathtaking: Not only is the scenery magnificent, but even serious hikers will huff and puff over its extremely strenuous up-and-down route, made even trickier to negotiate by winter rains. It's on every serious hiker's bucket list, and a destination

WATERFALL ADVENTURE: rappelling

Gain a unique perspective of two hidden waterfalls—by walking down them. Technically, you're rappelling on the 30- and 60-foot cataracts, with help from guide Charlie Cobb-Adams of **Island Adventures** (www.islandadventureskauai.com; ✆ **808/246-6333**). A Native Hawaiian nicknamed "Hawaiian Dundee," Cobb-Adams leads a practice session on a 25-foot wall before a 15-minute hike near the Hulē'ia National Wildlife Refuge to the otherwise off-limits falls. The 5.5-hour tour ($180 adults, $158 children 6 to 17, including lunch) departs from Līhu'e at 8:30am Monday, Wednesday, and Saturday; tours with kayaking (same length and cost) depart at 8:30am Tuesday and 11am Friday.

for seemingly every young backpacking bohemian on the island. That's one reason a camping permit ($20 per night; http://camping.chawaii.gov) is required for those heading beyond Hanakāpi'ai Beach; the permits often sell out up to a year in advance (see "Camping & Cabins," p. 576).

People in good but not great physical shape can still tackle the 2-mile stretch from the trail head at Kē'ē Beach to Hanakāpi'ai, which starts with a mile-long climb; the reward of Nāpali vistas starts about a half-mile in. You'll see the occasional barefoot local surfer on the first 2 miles, but wear sturdy shoes (preferably hiking boots) and a hat, and carry plenty of water. The trail can be very narrow and slippery in places; don't bring children who might need to be carried. At Hanakāpi'ai Beach, sandy in summer and mostly rocks in winter, strong currents have swept more than 80 visitors to their deaths over the years; best just to admire the view. Those able to rock-hop can clamber another 2 miles inland to the 120-foot Hanakāpi'ai Falls, but only when it has not been raining heavily. Allow 3 to 4 hours for the round-trip trek to the beach, and 7 to 8 hours with the falls added in.

Nearly as beautiful, but much less demanding and much less crowded, is the 2.5-mile **'Ōkolehao Trail** in Hanalei, which climbs 1,232 feet to a ridge overlooking Hanalei Bay and the verdant valley. It starts at a marked parking area off 'Ōhiki Road, heading inland from Kūhiō Hwy.; take an immediate left just past the Hanalei Bridge and look for the parking lot on the left and the trailhead across a small bridge to the right. Be sure to brake for nēnē (geese).

If you don't mind paying for the privilege, **Princeville Ranch Adventures** (www.princevilleranch.com; ✆ 808/826-7669) leads guided hikes on private land along the five tiers of **Kalihiwai Falls**. The 4.5-hour tour ($99) involves 3 hours of hiking, with swimming below an 80-foot cascade and an uphill climb to a point with sweeping North Shore views; it's open to ages 5 and up.

SOUTH SHORE

At the end of Keoneloa (Shipwrecks) Beach, in front of the Grand Hyatt Kaua'i, the limestone headland of Makawehi Point marks the start of the **Māhā'ulepū Heritage Trail** (www.hikemahaulepu.org), an easy coastal walk—after the first few minutes uphill—along lithified sand dunes, pinnacles, craggy coves, and ancient Hawaiian rock structures. Inland lie the green swath of Poipu Bay Golf Course and the Hā'upu summit. Keep a safe distance from the fragile edges of cliffs, and give the green sea turtles and endangered Hawaiian monk seals a wide berth, too. It's 1.5 miles to the overlook of Māhā'ulepū (Gillin's) Beach, but you can keep on another 2 miles to windy Hā'ula Beach.

WEST SIDE

Some of Hawaii's best hikes are found among the 45 miles of maintained trails in **Kōke'e State Park** (p. 518), 4,345 acres of rainforest with striking views of the Nāpali Coast from up to 4,000 feet above, and the drier but no less dazzling **Waimea Canyon State Park** (p. 521). Pick up a trail map and tips at the **Kōke'e Museum** (www.kokee.org; ✆ **808/335-9975**), which also describes a number of trails in the two parks on its website.

The best way to experience the bold colors and stark formations of Waimea Canyon is on the **Canyon Trail,** which starts after a .8-mile forested walk down and up unpaved Halemanu Road, off Kōke'e Road (Hwy. 550) between mile markers 14 and 15. From there, it's another mile to a small waterfall pool, lined with yellow ginger, that lies above the main cascade of 800-foot **Waipo'o Falls;** you won't be able to see the latter, but you can hear it and gaze far across the canyon to try to spot the lookout points you passed on the way up. On the way back, check out the short spur called the **Cliff Trail** for more vistas. (***Note:*** Families can hike this trail, but be mindful of the steep dropoffs.)

Two more challenging hikes beckon in dry conditions. The 6.2-mile round-trip **'Awa'awapuhi Trail** takes at least 3 hours—1 hour down, 2 hours coming back up, depending on your fitness level—but it offers a jaw-dropping overlook for two Nāpali valleys: 'Awa'awapuhi (named for the wild ginger blossom) and Nualolo. Usually well maintained, it drops about 1,600 feet through native forests to a thin precipice with a guardrail at the overlook. (***Note:*** The **Nualolo Cliff Trail** that connects with the even more strenuous 8-mile **Nualolo Trail** remained closed at press time due to significant erosion.) The trail head is just past mile marker 17 on Kōke'e Road at a clearing on the left.

Slippery mud can make the **Pihea Trail** impassable, but when the red clay is firm beneath your feet, it's another must-do for fit hikers. Starting at the end of the Pu'u O Kila Lookout at the end of Kōke'e Road (Hwy. 550), the trail provides fantastic views of Kalalau Valley and the distant ocean before turning into a boardwalk through a bog that connects with the **Alaka'i Swamp Trail,** which you'll want to follow to its end at the Kilohana Overlook; if it's not socked in with fog, you'll have an impressive view of Wainiha Valley and the North Shore. The Pihea-Alaka'i Swamp round-trip route is 8.6 miles; allow at least 4 hours and be prepared for drizzle or rain.

Horseback Riding

Ride a horse across the wide-open pastures of a working ranch under volcanic peaks and rein up near a waterfall pool, or explore a pristine shoreline hidden by former sugarcane field: You'll see parts of Kaua'i many have missed, while helping keep its treasured *paniolo* (cowboy) culture alive. Pack a pair of jeans or long pants and closed-toe shoes.

CJM Country Stables ★★ A trail ride through the rugged Māhā'ulepū region, passing through former plantation fields and natural landscape to the untrammeled sandy beaches under the shadow of Hā'upu Ridge, may well be the highlight of your trip. CJM's standard rides both include 2 hours of riding, but the **Secret Beach Picnic Ride** ($140) adds an hour for lunch and beach exploration; reserve early. Private rides, which allow paces faster than a walk, are also available. ***Note:*** CJM also hosts rodeos throughout the year that are open to the public (see www.kauaifestivals.com and www.koloaplantationdays.com for details).

Off Po'ipū Rd., Po'ipū. From Grand Hyatt Kauai, head 1½ miles east on unpaved Po'ipū Rd. and turn right at sign for stables. www.cjmstables.com. ✆ **808/742-6096. 2-hr. Māhā'ulepū Beach Ride:** $110; Mon–Sat 9:30am and 2pm. **3-hr Secret Beach Picnic Ride:** $140; Wed and Fri 1pm. Private rides from $140 per hour.

Princeville Ranch Adventures ★★ There's no nose-to-tail riding at this working North Shore ranch, owned by descendants of the area's first missionaries. Instead, horses amble across wide-open pastures with mountain and ocean views as you learn about Kaua'i's *paniolo* (cowboy) history and distinctive landscape. The **"ride n' glide"** option ($145) takes you to a secluded valley that you traverse via ziplines (see "Ziplining," p. 557), while the **Waterfall Picnic Ride** ($135) leads to a short (but steep) hike down to a trail leading to a swimming pool at the base of an 80-foot waterfall; after a picnic lunch, you'll climb out via a 10-foot rock wall. Both rides last 3 hours, with 90 minutes in the saddle. Less exertion is required on the 2-hour **Paniolo Ride** ($99) through pastures and the occasional herd of cattle. ***Note:*** Tours go out rain or shine, just like the cowboys.

Check in *makai* side of Kūhiō Hwy., just north of mile marker 27, Princeville. www.princevilleranch.com. ✆ **888/955-7669** or 808/826-7669. Booking by phone required. **Ride N' Glide:** $145; Mon–Sat 1:30pm; ages 10 and older. **Waterfall Picnic Ride:** $135; Mon–Sat 9am, noon, and 1pm (8am June–Aug); ages 8 and older. **Paniolo Ride:** $99; Mon–Sat 10am; ages 8 and older. Rental shoes $5.

Seeing Kaua'i on horseback.

Silver Falls Ranch Stables ★★ The wide falls here may not be as impressive as the taller ones on Princeville Ranch, but the swimming hole is equally refreshing and the scenery just as stimulating. The 300-acre ranch in Kalihiwai Valley features an 80-acre tropical garden and close-up views of the 2,800-foot-tall Makaleha Range. The 2-hour **Silver Falls Ride** ($115) includes a barbecue picnic that's a cut above the usual sandwich fare, plus a dip in the waterfall pool, while the 90-minute **Hawaiian Discovery Ride** ($99) follows flower-lined streams through the garden, home to more than 150 species of palms. Combine the two itineraries on the 3-hour **Tropical Trail Adventure** ($139).

Note that **Esprit de Corps Riding Academy** (www.kauaihorses.com; ✆ **808/822-4688**), also operates out of Silver Falls Ranch, with private rides for advanced riders ($99–$139).

Kamo'okoa Rd., Kīlauea. From Līhu'e, take Kūhiō Hwy. north past mile marker 24 to a left turn on Kāhiliholo Rd. at Kalihiwai Ridge sign; follow 2¼ miles to a left on Kamo'okoa Rd. www.silverfallsranch.com. ✆ **808/828-6718. Discovery Ride:** $99. **Silver Falls Ride:** $119. **Tropical Trails:** $139. All rides offered 3 times daily 9am–3:30pm June–Aug, twice daily Sept–May.

Tennis

Public tennis courts are managed by the **Kaua'i County Parks and Recreation Department** (www.kauai.gov/parks; ✆ **808/241-4460**). Its webpage lists the 24 public tennis courts around the island, 20 of which are lighted and all of which are free. ***Note:*** Lights are shut off Sept. 15–Dec. 15 to protect endangered shearwater fledglings, which may be misdirected by them. Other courts open to the public include those of **Hanalei Bay Resort,** Princeville (www.hanaleibayresort.com; ✆ **808/821-8225**), which has eight courts available for $15 per person per day; the resort also offers private lessons, daily clinics, and a pro shop. Also in Princeville, the **Makai Club** (www.makaigolf.com; ✆ **808/826-1912**) charges $15 per player for 90 minutes on one of its four courts, with private lessons available.

The South Shore is brimming with resort courts—including **Sheraton Kauai, Grand Hyatt Kauai, Poipu Kai Resort, Nihi Kai Villas,** and **Kukui'ula**—but they're restricted to overnight guests. Guests in **Kiahuna Plantation** units managed by Castle Resorts (see p. 573) have access to the otherwise members-only four tennis courts and other facilities at the **Poipu Beach Athletic Club;** so do guests in rentals of **Great Vacation Retreats** (www.alohagvr.com; ✆ **866/541-1033**) for a $100 weekly fee per property. On the East Side, the **Hōkūala Golf Course** was offering public access at press time to its four courts for $20 (1 hour free for **Marriott's Kaua'i Lagoons–Kalanipu'u** guests), subject to change due to renovations.

Ziplining

Kaua'i apparently has Costa Rica to thank for its profusion of ziplines, the metal cable-and-pulley systems that allow harness-wearing riders to "zip" over valleys, forests, and other beautiful but inaccessible areas. After reading about Costa Rica's rainforest canopy tours, Outfitters Kauai co-founder Rick Haviland was inspired to build the Garden Isle's first zipline on Kōke'e Ranch in 2003. Others soon followed, with ever longer, higher, and faster options. It may seem like a splurge, but keep in mind that ziplines not only offer an exhilarating rush and breathtaking views; they also help keep the verdant landscape gloriously undeveloped.

Be sure to book ahead, especially for families or groups—because of the time spent on harness safety checks, tour sizes are limited—and read the fine print about height, age, and/or weight restrictions. Tours usually go out rain or shine, except in the most severe weather. Plan to tip your guides ($10–$20 per rider).

SOUTH SHORE Opened in 2012, **Koloa Zipline** (www.koloazipline.com; ✆ **877/707-7088** or 808/742-2894) has an eight-line course ($139) in Kōloa that includes a 2,500-foot zip—Kaua'i's longest—over the Waitā Reservoir. For just $10 more, the Flyin' Kaua'ian harness option allows you to soar like a superhero over most of the lines on the 3½- to 4-hour tour. Check in at the office at 3477-A Weliweli Rd., Kōloa, in the Kauai ATV office behind the Old Kōloa Town shops. Kauai's newest, **Skyline Eco Adventures** (www.zipline.com; ✆ **888/864-6947** or 808/878-8400) opened its eight-line course above Po'ipū in 2013 and shares a different legend of Kaua'i for each of the progressively longer, faster lines on the 2½- to 3-hour tour. The cost is $140 for eight zips, $100 for five (with 50% off for one child or teen for each paid adult, and

ESPECIALLY FOR kids

Climbing the Wooden Jungle Gyms at Kamalani Playground (p. 508) Located in Lydgate Park, Wailua, this unique playground has a maze of jungle gyms for kids of all ages, including an actual labyrinth. Spend an afternoon whipping down slides, exploring caves, hanging from bars, and climbing all over.

Exploring a Magical World (p. 512) **Nā 'Āina Kai Botanical Gardens** sits on some 240 acres, sprinkled with around 70 life-size (or larger-than-life-size) whimsical bronze statues, hidden off the beaten path of the North Shore. The tropical children's garden features a gecko maze, a tropical jungle gym, a treehouse in a rubber tree, and a 16-foot-tall Jack-and-the-Beanstalk giant with a 33-foot wading pool below. Family tours take place Tuesday through Friday; book well in advance.

Riding an Open-Sided Train (p. 507) The **Kauai Plantation Railway** at Kilohana Plantation is a trip back in time (albeit on new tracks and replica cars) to the sugarcane era, with younger kids exhilarated just by the ride. Parents can justify it as an informal botany class, since passengers learn about the orchards, gardens, and forests they pass along the 2½-mile journey. Children of all ages will enjoy the stop to feed goats, chickens, and wild pigs (as long as they watch their fingers).

10% online discount for everyone else); check in at the office at Shops at Kukui'ula, 2829 Ala Kalanikaumaka St., Po'ipū.

EAST SIDE **Outfitters Kauai** (www.outfitterskauai.com; ✆ **888/742-9887** or 808/742-9667) updated its original zipline course on 4,000-acre Kōke'e Ranch in 2012; the nine-line course includes suspension bridges, tandem lines, and a "zippel" (a zipline/rappelling combo) over picturesque streams and waterfalls. The full-length, 6-hour course, **Zipline Trek Nui Nui Loa,** costs $158 for adults and $138 for children 7 to 14; the six-line, 4-hour **Lele 'Eono** option is $123 for adults and $113 for children 7 to 14. My favorite, the all-day **Kīpuū Zipline Safari** ($188 adults, $148 children 3–14), includes two of the course's longest ziplines and a water zipline over a swimming hole, plus kayaking the Hulē'ia River, hiking, swimming, and lunch. Check in at the Po'ipū office, 2827 Po'ipū Rd., across from the fire station, or at the Outfitters Kayak Shack in Nāwiliwili Small Boat Harbor at Wilcox and Niumalu roads, Līhu'e.

Kaua'i Backcountry Adventures (www.kauaibackcountry.com; © **888/270-0555** or 800/245-2506) is the only outfitter with excursions through 17,000 acres of former sugarcane fields above Līhu'e. In addition to its unique tubing ride (see "Tubing," p. 545), the company has a seven-line zip course leading from the lush mountainside to a bamboo grove, where you can take a dip in a swimming hole (book the 9am tour for the warmest swimming weather). The 3-hour tour costs $125; a 5-hour tour with a side trip to multitiered Hali'i Falls for a picnic and swim is $169. Check in at the office at 3-4131 Kūhiō Hwy., Hanamā'ulu, between Hanamā'ulu Road and Laulima Street.

The ecology-focused **Just Live! Zipline Tours** (www.ziplinetourskauai.com; © **808/482-1295**) offers three tours ranging from 2½ to 4½ hours ($79–$125). All glide over forest canopy in multiple shades of green, and the longest includes a 60-foot rock climbing wall and 100-foot rappelling tower. The online-only Early Bird Special offers $20 to $30 off tours with 7 and 7:45am check-ins, held at the office/outdoor gear store in Anchor Cove Shopping Center, 3416 Rice St., Līhu'e, between Kalapaki Beach and Nāwiliwili Harbor.

NORTH SHORE If you just want to zip nine lines over a verdant valley, then take the 3½-hour Zip Express Tour ($125) at **Princeville Ranch Adventures** (www.princevilleranch.com; © **888/955-7669** or 808/826-7669). But it would be a shame, particularly in summer, to miss the chance to swim in a waterfall pool offered by the 4½-hour **Zip N' Dip** ($145, including picnic lunch). The company also pairs ziplines with its popular horseback rides and kayak/hike excursions (3 and 4½ hours, respectively; $145). ***Note:*** The latter Jungle Valley Adventure is unique in that it allows children as young as 5 and weighing as little as 50 pounds to zip on the two 400-foot-plus lines included on the tour ($99 ages 5 to 11).

WHERE TO STAY ON KAUA'I

To avoid long drives, it pays to base your lodgings on the kind of vacation you envision, and consider dividing your time among locations. The island's East Side makes the most sense for those planning to divide their time equally among island sights; however, the best resorts for families and winter weather are on the South Shore. The most gorgeous scenery and best summertime ocean conditions are on the North Shore. If you're planning more than a day of hiking in Waimea Canyon or Kōke'e, or just want to experience the low-key island lifestyle, the West Side will definitely suit.

Taxes of 13.42% are added to all hotel bills. Parking is free, and pools are outdoors unless otherwise noted. Parking, Internet, and resort fees where applicable are charged daily; "cleaning" fees refer to one-time charges for cleaning after your stay, not daily housekeeping—the latter often available for an additional fee for condos and other vacation rentals.

East Side

Convenient to all parts of the island (except during rush hour), Līhu'e and the Coconut Coast have the greatest number of budget motels, affordable beachfront condos, and moderately priced hotel rooms, along with a couple of posh resorts. Bed-and-breakfasts and vacation rentals in rural and residential areas such as Anahola and upcountry Kapa'a are outside the official "visitor destination area" and may not be licensed, although many have paid taxes and operated without complaints for years.

In addition to the properties below, consider renting a one- or two-bedroom oceanfront condo at one of two complexes in Kapa'a. At the 84-unit **Kapa'a Shores ★**, 4-900 Kūhiō Hwy., the nine condos managed by Garden Island Properties (www.kauaiproperties.com; ✆ **800/801-0378** or 808/822-4871) run from $800 a week for a one-bedroom, one-bath unit to $1,050 for a two-bedroom, two-bath unit (plus $100–$130 cleaning and $25–$50 reservation fees). At the more upscale **Lae Nani ★★**, 410 Papaloa Rd. (off Kūhiō Hwy.), Outrigger (www.outrigger.com/laenani; ✆ **866/956-4262** or 808/823-1401) manages about a quarter of the 83 spacious units ($159–$349 nightly; cleaning fees $150–$195); the beach here offers a rock-walled swimming area perfect for children.

If you prefer something more private, check out the two elegantly furnished (and licensed) cottages in a leafy setting known as **17 Palms Kauai Vacation Cottages ★** (www.17palmskauai.com; ✆ **888/725-6799**), a block away from Wailua's beaches. Rates for the one-bedroom, one-bathroom Hale Iki (sleeps two adults, plus a small child) start at $189 a night, plus $110 cleaning; the two-bedroom, one-bathroom Meli Meli (sleeps four adults, plus a small child) starts at $239 plus $145 cleaning. Tucked off busy Kuamo'o Road, with easy access to the Wailua River, the pleasant Kapa'a compound known as the **Fern Grotto Inn ★** (www.ferngrottoinn.com; ✆ **808/821-9836**) comprises five quaint cottages (most sleeping just two), for $175 to $225 a night, plus $100 to $125 cleaning, and one three-bedroom house (up to six adults) for $300 nightly and $250 cleaning.

EXPENSIVE

Kaua'i Marriott Resort ★★★ This 10-story, multiwing hotel—the tallest on Kaua'i since opening in 1986—may be what prompted the

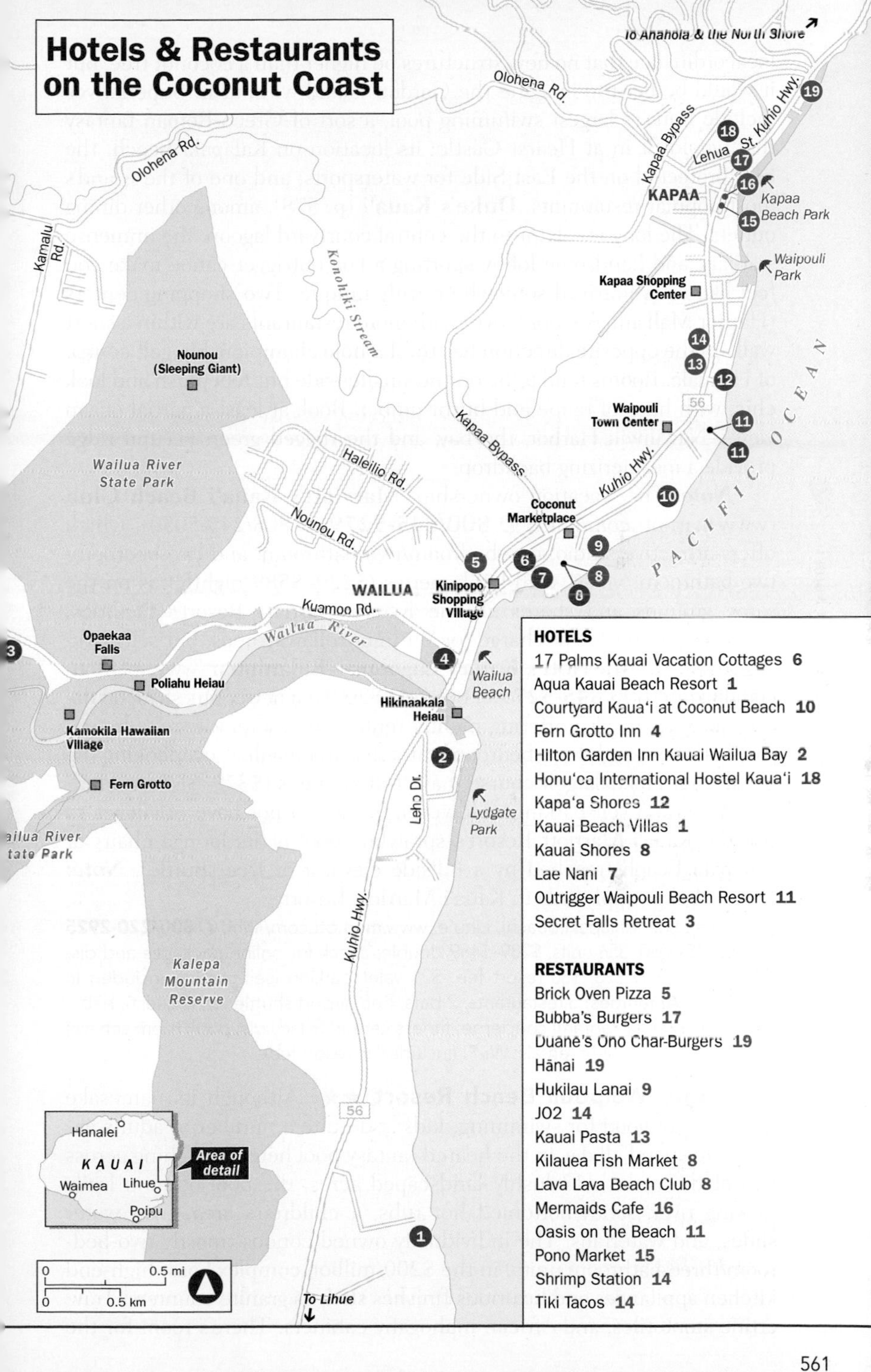

Hotels & Restaurants on the Coconut Coast
To Anahola & the North Shore
Olohena Rd.
Olohena Rd.
Kamalu Rd.
Konohiki Stream
Kapaa Bypass
St. Kuhio Hwy.
Lehua
KAPAA
Kapaa Beach Park
Waipouli Park
Kapaa Shopping Center
Nounou (Sleeping Giant)
Waipouli Town Center
Kapaa Bypass
Haleilio Rd.
Kuhio Hwy.
Wailua River State Park
PACIFIC OCEAN
Nounou Rd.
Coconut Marketplace
WAILUA
Kinipopo Shopping Village
Kuamoo Rd.
Wailua River
Opaekaa Falls
Poliahu Heiau
Wailua Beach
Hikinaakala Heiau
Kamokila Hawaiian Village
Fern Grotto
Leho Dr.
Lydgate Park
ailua River
tate Park
Kuhio Hwy.
Kalepa Mountain Reserve
Hanalei
KAUAI
Waimea
Lihue
Poipu
Area of detail
0.5 mi
0.5 km
To Lihue
HOTELS
17 Palms Kauai Vacation Cottages 6
Aqua Kauai Beach Resort 1
Courtyard Kaua'i at Coconut Beach 10
Fern Grotto Inn 4
Hilton Garden Inn Kauai Wailua Bay 2
Honu'ea International Hostel Kaua'i 18
Kapa'a Shores 12
Kauai Beach Villas 1
Kauai Shores 8
Lae Nani 7
Outrigger Waipouli Beach Resort 11
Secret Falls Retreat 3
RESTAURANTS
Brick Oven Pizza 5
Bubba's Burgers 17
Duane's Ono Char-Burgers 19
Hānai 19
Hukilau Lanai 9
JO2 14
Kauai Pasta 13
Kilauea Fish Market 8
Lava Lava Beach Club 8
Mermaids Cafe 16
Oasis on the Beach 11
Pono Market 15
Shrimp Station 14
Tiki Tacos 14

local ordinance that no new structures be higher than a coconut tree, but it would be hard to imagine the Garden Island without it. Superlatives include Kaua'i's largest swimming pool, a sort of Greco-Roman fantasy that would fit in at Hearst Castle; its location on Kalapaki Beach, the best protected on the East Side for watersports; and one of the island's most popular restaurants, **Duke's Kaua'i** (p. 578), among other dining outlets. The long escalator to the central courtyard lagoon, the immense statuary, and handsome lobby sporting a koa outrigger canoe make you feel like you've arrived somewhere truly unique. Two shopping centers (Harbor Mall and Anchor Cove) with more restaurants are within a short walk; in the opposite direction lies the 18-hole championship golf course of Hōkūala. Rooms tend to be on the smaller side but feel plush and look chic, with hues of taupe and burnt umber. Book at least a partial ocean view—Nāwiliwili Harbor, the bay, and the rugged green Hā'upu ridge provide a mesmerizing backdrop.

Note: The "vacation ownership" **Marriott's Kaua'i Beach Club** (www.marriott.com/lihka; ✆ **800/845-5279** or 808/245-5050), which offers attractive studio, one-bedroom/two-bathroom, and two-bedroom/two-bathroom "villas" with kitchenettes ($229–$589 nightly), is on the same grounds and shares all the Kaua'i Marriott Resort's facilities. There's no resort fee or charge for Wi-Fi or rollaway beds, but self-parking costs $18. **Marriott's Kaua'i Lagoons—Kalanipu'u** (www.marriott.com/lihkn; ✆ **800/845-5279** or 808/632-8200) is a newer timeshare on the 800-acre resort, also offering nightly rentals. Its roomier two-bedroom/two-bathroom and three-bedroom/three-bathroom villas, overlooking the oceanfront Hōkūala golf course, have full kitchens ($379–$679, including Wi-Fi and self-parking). However, guests do not have privileges to use the Kaua'i Marriott Resort's sprawling pool or its lounge chairs at Kalapaki Beach (reached by a hillside elevator or free shuttle). ***Note:*** Details below apply only to Kaua'i Marriott Resort.

3610 Rice St. (at Kalapaki Beach), Līhu'e. www.marriott.com/lihhi. ✆ **800/220-2925** or 808/245-5050. 356 units. $289–$489 double; check for online packages and discounts. Rollaway $25. $30 resort fee. $21 valet parking (self-parking included in resort fee). **Amenities:** 5 restaurants; 2 bars; free airport shuttle (on request); babysitting; children's program; concierge; fitness center; 5 Jacuzzis; pool; room service; watersports equipment rentals; Wi-Fi (included in resort fee).

Outrigger Waipouli Beach Resort ★★ Although its namesake beach is not good for swimming, kids and quite a number of adults are happy to spend all day in the heated fantasy pool here. Stretching across two of the resort's 13 lushly landscaped acres, the pool offers a lazily flowing river, sandy-bottomed hot tubs, a children's area, twin water slides, and waterfalls. The individually owned condos (mostly two-bedroom/three-bathroom units) in the $200-million complex boast high-end kitchen appliances and luxurious finishes such as granite counters, Travertine stone tiles, and African mahogany cabinets. There's room for the

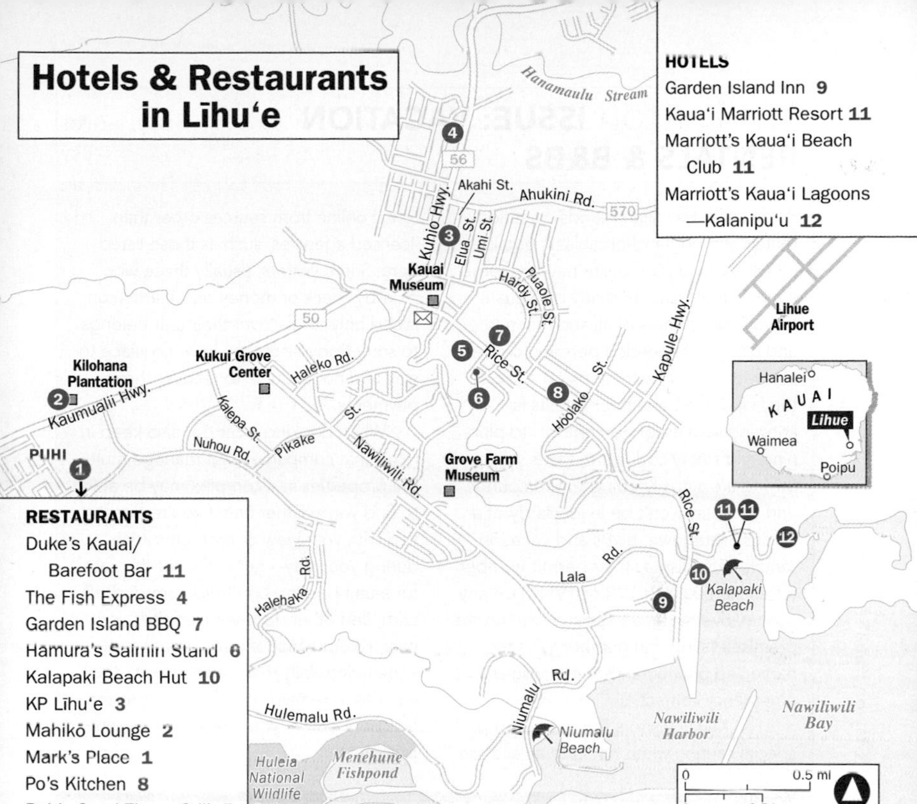

whole family, too: Most of the two-bedroom units are 1,300 square feet, while a few corner penthouses are 1,800 square feet; all units have washer/dryers and central A/C. The resort lies conveniently across the street from a Safeway grocery store and close to other shops and restaurants—but you'll want to avoid the cheaper units facing the parking lot due to noise. Outrigger manages the most units here and operates the front desk, but be sure to compare rates (which vary widely by view) and cleaning fees with those of independently rented condos.

4–820 Kūhiō Hwy., Kapa'a. www.outrigger.com. ✆ **877/418-0711** or 808/823-1401. 196 units. From $165 studio; $225–$295 1-bedroom/2-bath for 4; $255–$385 2-bedroom/3-bath for 6. Cleaning fee $120–$220. Resort fee $15. 2-night minimum. **Amenities:** Oasis on the Beach restaurant (p. 582); business center; fitness center; pool; day spa; 3 outdoor whirlpools; Wi-Fi (included in resort fee).

MODERATE

Aqua Kauai Beach Resort ★★ Less than 5 minutes from the airport, but hidden from the highway by a long, palm-lined drive, this is the jewel in the crown of Aqua Hotels and Resorts' 15 moderately priced hotels in the islands, thanks to its beautifully sculpted saltwater

hot-button ISSUE: VACATION RENTALS & B&BS

As on other Hawaiian Islands, vacation rentals and bed-and-breakfasts outside of areas zoned for tourism have become a hot-button issue for many on Kaua'i. Since 2008, owners of all such rentals and B&Bs have needed permits to operate, with special restrictions on agricultural land; the benefit for guests is knowing your lodgings conform to planning and safety codes, the taxes you're paying are actually going to the county, and your stay won't be in jeopardy of a surprise shutdown. B&Bs and vacation rentals must display their permit number (often starting with TVR or TVNC) on any online advertising, and post a sign on the premises listing that number, plus the name and phone number of an on-island emergency contact.

The Kaua'i Visitors Bureau also urges special caution when booking a vacation rental online from sources other than licensed agencies, such as those listed here. Some visitors, usually those who paid by check or money order, arrive on island only to discover their unit belongs to somebody else; they have no place to stay and no recourse to recover their payments.

When booking a condo, also keep in mind that companies that manage multiple properties in a complex may be able to find you another unit if you're dissatisfied with your view or problems arise during your stay—generally not the case for a unit booked on VRBO.com, AirBnB.com, and other do-it-yourself sites. However, some management companies are eliminating daily maid service and other niceties to remain competitive; read the fine print before you arrive to know what to expect.

pools—four in all, with adult and children's options, a 75-foot lava-tube water slide, whirlpools, waterfalls, and a sandy-bottomed beachfront lagoon. Decorated in a Balinese wood/Hawaiian plantation motif, rooms in the hotel itself are not particularly commodious, and some "mountain view" (odd-numbered rooms) units overlook parking lots, where wild chickens like to congregate. No matter: If you're not lingering by the pool, you can be walking for miles along the windswept beach (not recommended for swimming), which passes by the budget-friendly Wailua Golf Course, or indulging in a spa treatment.

Note: Aqua's hotel rates listed below reflect typical availability online; rack rates are higher. A number of hotel rooms are also individually owned "condos"; you'll find lower daily rates when booking through an owner, but you'll pay an extra $80 in resort/cleaning fees, with maid service upon request ($15–$30 daily). The 25-acre resort is also home to the **Kauai Beach Villas,** one- and two-bedroom condos operated as timeshares or privately owned rentals, all with access to the hotel facilities. **Kauai Vacation Rentals** (www.kauaivacationrentals.com; **© 800/367-5025** or 808/245-8841) manages the majority of the non-timeshare units, with daily rates and cleaning fees starting at $165 and

$110, respectively, plus a $35 reservation fee. Details below apply only to the Aqua Kauai Beach Resort hotel.

4331 Kaua'i Beach Dr., Līhu'e. From the airport, drive 2½ miles northeast on Hwy. 51 to Kūhiō Hwy. and turn right on Kaua'i Beach Dr. www.kauaibeachresorthawaii.com. ✆ **866/536-7976** or 808/245-1955. 350 units. $179–$259 double; $329–$540 suite. Check for online specials. Extra person $45. Rollaway $20. Resort fee $22. **Amenities:** 2 restaurants; cafe; lounge; poolside bar; free airport/shopping/golf shuttle; babysitting; concierge; fitness center; 2 Jacuzzis; laundry facilities; 4 pools; rental cars; room service; Hawaiian Rainforest Spa & Salon; Wi-Fi (included in resort fee).

Courtyard Kaua'i at Coconut Beach ★ This centrally located Marriott hotel wins the most raves for its oceanfront courtyard and pool, with fire pits, fountains, and a large whirlpool spa. A well-manicured lawn separates the hotel from golden-sand Makaīwa Beach, which is too reefy to do much swimming in, but just the ticket for long walks. Rooms, most of which are just 320 square feet, have lanais with cinnamon wood shutters (to match the dark-veneered, Hawaiian-style decor), and two-thirds have at least partial ocean views. If you want more space, book the executive oceanfront rooms, 528 square feet, with rates starting at $359. The $20 resort fee is more comprehensive than most and includes self-parking (plus first night of valet parking), Wi-Fi, two complimentary Mai Tais, yoga classes, and beach-gear rentals, among other perks.

650 Aleka Loop, Kapa'a. www.courtyardkauai.com. ✆ **877/997-6667** or 808/822-3455. 311 units. $159–$209 standard double, $359 executive room. Check for online packages. Extra person $25. Children 17 and under stay free in parent's room. Resort fee $20. Valet parking $5 after 1st free night. **Amenities:** Restaurant; bar; business center; fitness center; Jacuzzi; pool; room service; spa; basketball/tennis court; Wi-Fi (included in resort fee).

INEXPENSIVE

Young backpackers and adventurous adults on a shoestring budget should consider **Honu'ea International Hostel Kaua'i** (www.kauaihostel.com; ✆ **808/823-6142**) in historic Kapa'a. Bunks in the three, 10-bed single-sex and co-ed dorm rooms (one bathroom per dorm) start at $30 per person, including taxes; the two deluxe private rooms, which share a bathroom, have the nicest setting, in the main house, for $75 a night (single or double occupancy, taxes included).

Garden Island Inn ★★ Thrifty travelers will love this cheerily renovated, well-maintained motel within a short walk of Kalapaki Beach, shops, and restaurants, while families will appreciate the large suites (with up to one king-size bed with three twin beds) and extra guest fees of just $10 per person. It's easy to make breakfast on the cheap, too, thanks to the mini-fridge, microwave, wet bar, and kitchenware, plus standard coffeemaker—the front desk even offers free coffee and pie. Other freebies include parking, Wi-Fi, and use of beach gear, not to mention happily given advice. Hanalei artist Camile Fontaine's bright, island-inspired murals and paintings make this a welcome antidote to neutral, cookie-cutter resort decor, while owners Lis and Steve Layne work tirelessly to improve their guests' comfort, even providing DVDs of movies made on Kaua'i to watch on flatscreen TVs. One caveat: Use earplugs to offset street noise. The inn also manages two two-bedroom condos ($179; sleep six) nearby at the hilltop Banyan Harbor, which boasts an oceanview pool and tennis courts.

3445 Wilcox Rd. (across the street from Kalapaki Beach, near Nāwiliwili Harbor), Līhu'e. www.gardenislandinn.com. ✆ **800/648-0154** or 808/245-7227. 21 units. $113–$169 double. Extra person $10. **Amenities:** Free use of watersports equipment and beach gear; Wi-Fi (free).

Hilton Garden Inn Kauai Wailua Bay ★★ Formerly the Aston Aloha Beach Resort, this 10-acre property has a great location for families: next to the protected swimming/snorkeling ponds of Lydgate Beach, the fanciful Kamalani Playground, and historic Hawaiian sites by the Wailua River. Under new management, the "refreshed" rooms, suites, and cottages now have crisp white bedding, contemporary lighting, and splashes of orchid and gold in cushions, artwork, and ottomans to offset the sand-hued carpets and sofa beds. All units come with mini-fridges, microwaves, and Keurig coffeemakers; some oceanview rooms and all cottages (which are closest to Kamalani Playground) include lanais. ***Note:*** Wi-Fi and parking are free (no resort fee), making rates a bargain.

3–5920 Kūhiō Hwy., Kapa'a. www.hiltongardeninn.com. ✆ **808/823-6000.** 216 units. $129–$159 double, $149–$189 oceanview; $189–$219 oceanview junior suite with sofa bed; $239–$269 1-bedroom cottage; check online discounts and packages. Extra person $30. Children 18 and under stay free in parent's room. **Amenities:** Restaurant; bar; business center; fitness room; Jacuzzi; coin laundry; 2 pools; Wi-Fi (free).

Kauai Shores ★★ Now managed by Aqua Hotels, this recently renovated beachfront bargain features small but functional rooms with slightly quirky, Ikea-style furnishings (curvy mirrors, square lamps), bright blue geometric-patterned rugs, and very compact bathrooms. No need to hole up in your room, though: The oceanview pool is especially inviting, while the oceanfront **Lava Lava Beach Club** (p. 581) serves three meals daily, with a full bar, indoor/outdoor seating, and nightly live entertainment. Swimming isn't safe here, but the rock-walled pool in front of neighboring Lae Nani is good for children, and the Lydgate Beach ponds are just a short drive away. Yoga fans can take a free class on the oceanfront lawn three mornings a week. ***Note:*** Request a second-floor room for more privacy (if you can carry your own bags) and a room not adjacent to the parking lot.

420 Papaloa Rd. (off Kūhiō Hwy.), Kapa'a. www.kauaishoreshotel.com. ✆ **855/309-5483** or 808/822-4951. 206 rooms. $119–$145 double; studio suite with kitchenette $165. Check for online discounts. Extra person $25. $15 resort fee (includes Wi-Fi, DVDs, PlayStation, and more). **Amenities:** 2 pools; barbecue grills; business center; coin laundry; restaurant; Wi-Fi (free).

North Shore

Despite this magical region's popularity with visitors, only Princeville is officially one of Kaua'i County's "visitor destination areas"; it's important to be aware that many rural bed-and-breakfasts and vacation rentals here are unlicensed. In 2014, the state abruptly shut down one longtime Hanalei B&B for building and operating in a conservation district; unhappy neighbors of unlicensed rentals may report them to authorities. If you're not staying in one of the few hotels, I recommend booking through one of the following agencies, which manage only licensed properties.

Founded in 1978, **Kauai Vacation Rentals** (www.kauaivacationrentals.com; © **800/367-5025** or 808/245-8841) manages well-maintained homes and condos across the island, with the majority (96 at press time) on the North Shore. Most have a 3- to 5-night minimum that expands to 1 week or 2 weeks from December 15 to January 6, when rates also rise. You can search online listings by location, size, view, and amenities such as air-conditioning (not so common where trade winds blow), a swimming pool, and high-speed Internet access (increasingly more common); agents can also help you find the perfect match. In **Hā'ena,** for one example, the standard rate for a one-bedroom, one-bathroom garden-view cottage that's a short walk to Mākua (Tunnels) Beach is $235 a night or $1,410 a week; for an oceanview, two-bedroom, one-and-a-half-bathroom cottage right on **'Anini Beach,** it's $360 a night or $1,800 a week—a good deal if you're splitting the expenses with another couple. For all rentals, you'll also pay a $35 reservation fee and one-time cleaning fee, anywhere from $90 for a studio condo to as high as $565 for a five-bedroom house.

Parrish Collection Kaua'i (www.parrishkauai.com; © **800/325-5701** or 808/742-2000), which has made a name for itself with high-quality Po'ipū vacation rentals (see "Finding a Perfect Place in Po'ipū," p. 571), also represents 14 homes and cottages from Kīlauea to Hā'ena and 53 properties (nearly all condos) in Princeville. Many of the latter are in the **Hanalei Bay Resort ★★,** which has spectacular views rivaling those of the St. Regis, air-conditioning in units, and a recently redone fantasy pool with waterfalls, slides, and so forth; rates start at $125 a night (5-night minimum, plus daily $18 resort fee) for a gardenview studio. If you can forgo an ocean view, Parrish's best values are in the **Plantation at Princeville ★,** roomy two- and three-bedroom air-conditioned units in a complex built in 2004 with a pool, spa, barbecues, and fitness center; rates start at $130 for a two-bedroom, two-bathroom unit. Not included in the rates are the $50 "processing" fee per booking and cleaning fees, starting at $100 for a studio and increasing by size.

Coldwell Banker Bali Hai Realty (www.balihai.com; © **808/826-8000**) manages about 80 luxury vacation rentals, all of them licensed; expect a 7-night minimum June 1 to August 31 and

December 15 to January 5, otherwise 4 to 5 nights. Its Princeville properties include 11 units at the desirable **Pali Ke Kua ★** and **Pu'u Poa ★★** complexes, less than a half-mile from each other on the bluff above Hideaways Beach. At Pali Ke Kua, nightly rates start as low as $135 for a two-bedroom, two-bathroom mountainview unit, and $195 for a two-bedroom with an ocean view. Its lowest rate at Pu'u Poa is $290 a night for a two-bedroom, two-bathroom oceanview unit (ideal for couples to share). For condo bookings, Bali Hai charges a reservation fee of $25 to $50 and a cleaning fee of $150 to $200.

A frequent resource for Hollywood film crews, Mike Lyons of **Kauai Style Vacation Rentals** (www.kauaistyleconcierge.com; ✆ **808/482-1572**) specializes in licensed properties on the North Shore; you won't find listings on his site because he prefers to work with clients individually. A passionate surfer, Lyons also enjoys escorting guests on ocean and trail adventures and can arrange private chefs and other services.

EXPENSIVE

Hanalei Colony Resort ★★ With two bedrooms (separated by louvered wooden doors), one-and-a-half to two bathrooms, full kitchens, and living rooms, these 48 individually owned, updated condos are perfect for families—or anyone who can appreciate being as few as 10 feet from the beach in the shadow of green peaks near the end of the road. It has no TVs, phones, or entertainment systems, although free Wi-Fi means guests don't disconnect quite as much as they used to. The beach is generally not safe for swimming, but you're less than a mile from Mākua (Tunnels) Beach, and the barbecue area by the small pool boasts lush landscaping and a koi pond. The resort runs a 13-passenger shuttle to Hanalei and beaches during the day, at no cost; in the evening, the shuttle takes guests to and from dining and entertainment destinations in Hanalei and Princeville for a $10 charge per unit. The independently run Ayurvedic-themed **Hanalei Day Spa** and the award-winning **Mediterranean Gourmet** (p. 583) restaurant are also on-site. Check online for romance and activity packages.

5–7130 Kūhiō Hwy. (*makai* side), Hā'ena, about 5 miles west of Hanalei. www.hcr.com. ✆ **800/628-3004** or 808/826-6235. 48 units. $289–$489 2-bedroom apt for 4. 2-night minimum; 7th night free. **Amenities:** Restaurant; coffee bar/art gallery; free weekly continental breakfast; babysitting; barbecues; concierge; Jacuzzi; coin laundry; pool; day spa; Wi-Fi (free).

St. Regis Princeville ★★ The state's first and only St. Regis—a brand renowned for its opulence and service—opened in 2009, following a multimillion-dollar transformation of the Princeville Hotel. The dramatic cliffside layout didn't change: You enter on the ninth floor, with a dazzling panorama of Hanalei Bay and Makana (the "Bali Hai" mountain) across the airy lobby and an elevator to take you down to the narrow but pleasant sandy beach and 5,000-square-foot infinity pool. The spacious (540 sq. ft. and up) rooms still feature extra-large bedroom windows as well as "magic" bathroom windows, which toggle between clear and opaque. A welcome sheen of sophisticated Hawaiiana replaced the formerly palatial European decor, however, typified by the 11,000-square-foot **Halele'a Spa,** which combines traditional Hawaiian healing practices and local botanicals with Western treatments. Among the many lavish amenities are goose-down comforters, 42- and 52-inch flatscreen TVs, and, in junior suites on up, personal butler service.

5520 Ka Haku Rd., Princeville. www.stregisprinceville.com. © **877/787-3447** or 808/826-9644. 252 units. $480–$725 double; $875–$1,025 jr. suite (820 sq. ft.); $1,750 St. Regis suite (1,200 sq. ft.); $3,525–$4,525 larger suites (1,800–2,400 sq. ft.). Extra person $100. Children 17 and under stay free in parent's room. Parking (valet only) $32. **Amenities:** 3 restaurants; 3 bars; children's program; concierge; weekly Polynesian dinner show ($135 adults, $68 ages 3 to12); fitness center; Makai Club golf and tennis access; Jacuzzis; pool; room service; spa; watersports equipment rentals; Wi-Fi (free).

Westin Princeville Ocean Villas ★★★ A superb "vacation ownership" property that nonetheless offers nightly rentals, this 18½-acre bluffside resort is a winner with families and couples seeking condo-style units with resort furnishings and amenities. Besides Westin's justly famed "Heavenly Beds," the roomy studios and one-bedroom suites (which can be combined into two-bedroom units) have immaculate, well-stocked kitchens, washer/dryers, and huge bathrooms with separate glass showers and deep whirlpool tubs. Playful statuary and fountains mark the centrally located children's pool next to the main pool; adults will appreciate the quieter, bluff-side plunge pools. The indoor-outdoor **Nanea Restaurant and Bar,** one of the better hotel restaurants on Kaua'i, has substantial discounts for children 11 and younger, and the on-site deli has a tempting array of farm-fresh items. ***Note:*** Since the nearby unmaintained trail to 'Anini Beach is steep and often muddy, most guests opt to take the free shuttle to the St. Regis Princeville, where they walk down nearly 200 steps to Pu'u Poa Beach, or drive themselves to 'Anini or another beach.

3838 Wyllie Rd., Princeville. www.westinprinceville.com. © **808/827-8700.** 346 units. From $335 studio (sleeps 2); $470 1-bedroom (sleeps 4); $785 2-bedroom (sleeps 8). $13 parking. **Amenities:** 2 restaurants; bar; deli/store; barbecues; children's program; concierge; fitness room w/steam room and sauna, plus use of Makai Club Lap Pool and Fitness Center, 1 mile away; golf at Makai Club; 4 pools; free resort shuttle; Wi-Fi (free).

MODERATE

The best values on the North Shore can be found among Princeville's many condo complexes, which vary widely in age and amenities; check the listings of the brokers mentioned above. I recommend either the dramatically perched **Hanalei Bay Resort ★★** (www.hanaleibayresort.com; © **877/344-0688**) or the residential-style **Cliffs at Princeville ★★** (www.cliffsatprinceville.com; © **808/826-6129**); both participate in timeshare and vacation rental programs but also offer direct bookings. At the 22-acre Hanalei Bay Resort, just west of the St. Regis and known for its fantasy pool, rates start at $219 a night, plus a $19 daily resort fee, for a studio unit (512 sq. ft.) with kitchen, lanai, and pull-out sofa bed. At the posher, more tranquil Cliffs on the northern edge of the Princeville bluff, one-bedroom, two-bathroom units (sleeping four) with full kitchen, living room, and two lanais start at $227 ($268 for loft units that sleep six), plus a weekly resort fee of $75. ***Note:*** The three-story Cliffs has no elevators or A/C; it does have two tennis courts, playground, pool, hot tub, and a putting green.

South Shore

The most popular place to stay year-round, the resort area of Po'ipū Beach is definitely a "visitor destination area," with hundreds of rental condos, cottages, and houses vying with Kaua'i's best luxury resorts for families and a romantic boutique hotel. Upcountry Lāwa'i and Kalāheo brim with more modest, not necessarily licensed, bed-and-breakfasts and vacation homes.

EXPENSIVE

Grand Hyatt Kauai Resort & Spa ★★★ The island's largest hotel aims to have one of the smallest carbon footprints. Its 602 luxurious rooms feature not only pillow-top beds and Toto toilets, but also eco-friendly elements such as recycled-yarn carpets and plush robes made from recycled plastic bottles. Grass-covered roofs and solar panels reduce emissions, a hydroponic garden grows produce for its dining outlets (such as the thatched-roof **Tidepools** restaurant), and used cooking oil becomes biodiesel fuel. But that's just green icing on the cake of this sprawling, family-embracing resort where the elaborate, multitiered fantasy pool and saltwater lagoon more than compensate for the rough waters of Keoneloa (Shipwrecks) Beach. The 45,000-square-foot indoor/outdoor **Anara Spa** and adjacent **Poipu Bay Golf Course** offer excellent adult diversions, as do the fire pits overlooking the pool by Dondero's Italian restaurant. To feel even more virtuous about splurging on a stay, check out the hotel's volunteer programs with the National Tropical Botanical Garden and Kauai Humane Society, among others. ***Tip:*** Sign up for the Hyatt Gold Passport loyalty program to receive discounts of $65 to $80 off nightly standard rates.

1571 Po'ipū Rd., Po'ipū. www.grandhyattkauai.com. ✆ **800/554-9288** or 808/742-1234. 602 units. $429–$599 double; from $699 Grand Club; from $959 suite. $30 resort fee includes self-parking, Wi-Fi, fitness classes, and more. Children 17 and under stay free in parent's room. Packages available. Valet parking $15. **Amenities:** 5 restaurants; 5 bars; babysitting; bike and car rentals; children's program; club lounge; concierge; fitness center; golf course and clubhouse; 3 Jacuzzis; 1½-acre saltwater swimming lagoon; lū'au; 2 nonchlorinated pools connected by river pool; room service; spa; 2 tennis courts; watersports equipment rentals; Wi-Fi (included in resort fee.)

FINDING A PERFECT PLACE in Po'ipū

The best way to find a high-quality, licensed vacation rental in Po'ipū is through **Parrish Collection Kaua'i** (www.parrishkauai.com; ✆ **800/325-5701** or 808/742-2000). Parrish manages more than 200 units for 20 different island-wide condo developments, plus dozens of vacation houses ranging from quaint cottages to elite resort homes; about three-quarters are in Po'ipū, in a wide range of prices. The company sets resort-like standards for decor and maintenance, classifying its lodgings into four categories ("premium plus" is the highest, for new or completely renovated units), sending linens out for professional laundering, and providing signature bathroom amenities. At Parrish's flagship **Waikomo Stream Villas ★** and **Nihi Kai Villas ★★** in Po'ipū, where the company manages about half the condos (75 in total), there's even concierge service—with no kickbacks for referrals, according to owner J. P. Parrish. "Our guides know the island really well and have no agenda; we only recommend what works and has good customer service," he notes.

Each well-equipped rental offers a full kitchen, washer/dryer, TV/DVD, phone, and free Wi-Fi; condo rates in the introductory Value Collection start as low as $100 a night; you'll pay cleaning but not resort or parking fees. At Nihi Kai Villas, which has a heated pool (a rarity here) and large floor plans, off-peak nightly rates start at $225 for a two-bedroom condo (sleeps six), plus $166 cleaning; at Waikomo Stream Villas, a one-bedroom condo (sleeps four) starts at $100 a night, plus $125 cleaning.

Parrish, which also rents vacation cottages and sumptuous multimillion-dollar ocean estates, is the exclusive agent for the villas, cottages, and bungalows at heavenly **Kukui'ula ★★★**; renters gain access to Kukui'ula's private, ultra-posh spa, golf course, and clubhouse dining (see http://kukuiula.com for details.)

There's a 3- to 5-night minimum for condos, a 7-night minimum for houses, and no minimum at Kukui'ula cottages, except during winter holidays. For 5-night or longer stays, inquire about the **Frommer's Preferred Guest Discount,** good for 5% to 10% off; if a better deal is available, agents will let you know. The company also offers a price-match guarantee.

Ko'a Kea Hotel & Resort ★★★ If everything seems to run like clockwork at this oceanfront jewel box, hidden between the sprawling Kiahuna Plantation Resort and the densely built Marriott Waiohai Beach Club, chalk it up to general manager Chris Steuri, whose Swiss family has been in the hotel business for generations. He oversaw the years-long, multimillion-dollar transformation of the Poipu Beach Hotel, dormant since 1992's Hurricane 'Iniki, into a posh boutique inn with arguably the island's best hotel restaurant, **Red Salt** (p. 588), as well as a small but expertly staffed spa. *Ko'a kea* means "white coral," which inspires the white and coral accents in the sleek, modern decor; all rooms feature lanais, many with views of the rocky coast (a short walk from sandy beaches). Steuri's European flair shows in the Nespresso espresso machines and L'Occitane bath products, but his staff resounds with pure

Hawaiian aloha. ***Note:*** At prices this steep, the "garden view" will disappoint—best to spring for at least a partial ocean view.

2251 Po'ipū Rd., Po'ipū. www.koakea.com. ✆ **888/898-8958** or 808/828-8888. 121 units. $379–$499 gardenview double; $379–$729 oceanview or oceanfront double; from $979 suite. Packages available. $26 resort fee includes valet parking, Wi-Fi, fitness center, and more. **Amenities:** Restaurant; 2 bars; concierge; fitness room; Jacuzzi; pool; room service; spa; watersports equipment rentals; Wi-Fi (included in resort fee).

Poipu Kapili Resort ★★ All of the 60 upscale, individually owned and furnished condos overlook the waves crashing on the rocky shoreline just across the little-traveled street. Floor plans start at 1,200 square feet for a one-bedroom unit with one-and-a-half to two bathrooms, all on the ground floor with pool and ocean views; the larger two-bedroom units come with either three bathrooms in two-level townhomes with ground-level entries or with two bathrooms in third-floor penthouses accessed by an elevator. The layouts are especially appealing to families, but couples will appreciate the high priority the management places on maintaining a tranquil atmosphere, especially around the central pool area; cooks should take note of the spacious kitchens and free herb garden. Friday mornings there's a free social with juice, coffee, and pastries by the pool.

2221 Kapili Rd., Po'ipū. www.poipukapili.com. ✆ **800/443-7714** or 808/742-6449. 60 units. $255–$320 1-bedroom (sleeps up to 4); $385–$550 2-bedroom (up to 6); $485–$525 2-bedroom penthouse. Check online for longer-stay discounts and specials. **Amenities:** Barbecue area; saltwater pool; 2 tennis courts; coin laundry (washer/dryer in all 2-bedroom units, some 1 bedrooms); Wi-Fi (free).

Sheraton Kauai Resort ★★★ Thanks to a $16-million remodel, this appealingly low-key resort now lives up to its ideal beachfront location, where the western horizon sees a riot of color at sunset and rainbows arc over a rocky point after the occasional shower. The expanded oceanfront pool—with rock-lined whirlpool and luxurious bungalows and cabanas (for rent)—provides a much more inviting place for a dip, conveniently making the traditional pool in the garden wing a quieter oasis. Nights here are livelier, too, thanks to large fire pits in the oceanview courtyard and the tasty libations and wine-tasting social hours at **RumFire Poipu Beach,** the resort's ambitious, island-inspired restaurant/lounge with walls of glass. ***Tip:*** Ask for a room on the ocean side, even if gardenview, to avoid having to frequently cross the street; oceanside rooms seem larger, too.

2440 Ho'onani Rd., Po'ipū. www.sheraton-kauai.com. ✆ **866/716-8109** or 808/742-1661. 391 units. $259–$749 double (prepaid as low as $199–$259); $689–$1,299 suite. $31 resort fee includes self-parking (and first night valet parking), Wi-Fi, use of fitness center, bicycles, bottled water, and more. Extra person $70. Valet parking free for first night, additional nights $10. **Amenities:** 3 restaurants; bar; babysitting; concierge; free computer use; cultural lessons, fitness room; Jacuzzi; lū'au; 2 pools; room service; spa services; watersports equipment rentals; nightly torchlighting; Wi-Fi (included in resort fee).

MODERATE

Besides the listings below, the 35-acre, green-lawned **Kiahuna Plantation Resort ★★,** on the sandy beach next to the Sheraton, is also worth considering, although its 333 individually furnished, one- and two-bedroom condos vary widely in taste; they also rely on ceiling fans (and trade winds) for cooling, and there's no elevator in the three-story buildings. **Outrigger** (www.outrigger.com; ✆ **808/742-6411**) manages more than half of the units, but only those rented from **Castle Resorts** (www.castleresorts.com; ✆ **800/367-5004** or 808/545-5310) receive daily housekeeping and access to the tennis courts and resort-style pool of the Poipu Beach Athletic Club across the street. Outrigger's nightly one-bedroom rates start at $149 gardenview and $219 oceanview, plus $150 cleaning, while Castle's equivalent units start at $191 and $259, respectively, plus $50 to $120 cleaning (depending on length of stay). Both Outrigger and Castle include free Wi-Fi and parking in their rates.

Among other options outside of Po'ipū, **Kauai Banyan Inn ★** (www.kauaibanyan.com; ✆ **888/786-3855**) in rural Lāwa'i offers six airy suites and a cottage, all with gleaming wood floors, Hawaiian quilts, and kitchenettes or full kitchens. Co-owners Lorna and John Hoff, who live on the 11-acre compound that they helped build, were in the process of being licensed at press time; bed-and-breakfast rates previously ranged from $155 to $230 per night, plus $45 cleaning.

Kauai Cove ★★ Honeymooners and other romance seekers find a serene oasis on a quiet lane just a few houses up from the snorkeling cove of Kōloa Landing and a short walk to a sandier cove known as Baby Beach. The bright cottage provides a four-poster canopy queen-size bed under high vaulted ceilings, private bamboo-walled lanai with barbecue grill, flatscreen TV with DVD player, and full kitchen. Since it can get hot in Po'ipū, the wall-unit A/C (along with ceiling fan) is a nice touch. Helpful owners E. J. and Diane Olsson live nearby in Poipu Kai, where they also rent out an attractive studio and one-bedroom suite.

2672 Pu'uholo Rd., Po'ipū. www.kauaicove.com. ✆ **800/624-9945** or 808/742-2562. Cottage: $149–$229 double, cleaning $75. Studio: $129–$159 double, cleaning $60. 1-bedroom: $169–$239 double, cleaning $90. **Amenities:** Barbecue grill, beach gear, use of Poipu Kai pool and hot tub, Wi-Fi (free).

Poipu Plantation B&B Inn and Vacation Rentals ★★★ This ultratranquil compound almost defies description. It comprises four adults-only, bed-and-breakfast suites of various sizes in a lovingly restored 1938 plantation house; seven vacation rental units in three modern cottage-style wings behind the B&B; and a one-bedroom condo across the street at the 35-unit Sunset Kahili complex. The B&B suites, fully renovated in 2013, feature handsome hardwood floors, sturdy vintage furnishings, bright tropical art, and (thankfully) modern bathrooms; the 700-square-foot Ali'i Suite also includes a wet bar, two-person whirlpool tub, and private lanai. The one- and two-bedroom cottage units on the foliage-rich 1-acre lot have less character but offer more space (plus full kitchens); some have ocean views across the rooftops of Sunset Kahili, where the neatly maintained oceanview condos have use of a small pool (but no A/C). Innkeepers Chris and Javed Moore and their friendly staff delight in offering travel tips. ***Note:*** When comparing rates, consider that the units here have no cleaning, resort, parking, or Wi-Fi fees; plus, breakfasts for the B&B units include Kaua'i coffee, hot entrees, and fresh island fruit and juice.

1792 Pe'e Rd., Po'ipū. www.poipubeach.com. © **800/643-0263** or 808/742-6757. 12 units. Inn suites: $145–$300, including breakfast and daily housekeeping; adults only (2 maximum); 3-night minimum (7 for winter holidays). Rental units: $135–$210 1-bedroom (sleeps up to 3); $165–$235 2-bedroom (sleeps up to 5). Condo: $145–$265 (sleeps up to 3); additional person $20. **Amenities:** Use of beach gear; laundry facilities; Wi-Fi (free).

INEXPENSIVE

In pricey Po'ipū, staying anywhere for $150 a night—especially if fees and taxes are included—can be a real challenge. **Kauai Vacation Rentals** (www.kauaivacationrentals.com; © **800/367-5025** or 808/245-8841), located in the well-kept **Prince Kūhiō ★★** complex across from Lāwa'i Beach, manages 10 garden- and oceanview studios that cost about $140 a night (5-night minimum), even with taxes, reservation and cleaning fees rolled in. It also has eight one-bedroom/one-bathroom units (some sleeping four) that cost, all told, about $175 a night. During spring and fall, **Suite Paradise** (www.suite-paradise.com; © **800/367-8020**) frequently has gardenview one-bedroom/one-bathroom units in the **Kahala ★** condominium on the 70-acre, verdant Poipu Kai resort for $145 to $155 a night, all inclusive.

Marjorie's Kauai Inn ★ In keeping with its hilltop pastoral setting in Lāwa'i, this three-room bed-and-breakfast prides itself on green touches: energy-efficient appliances, eco-friendly cleaning products, and local organic produce (some of it grown on site) on the lavish breakfast buffet. You're more likely to notice the sweeping valley views from your private lanais. All rooms have private entrances and kitchenettes, while Sunset View, the largest, boasts its own hot tub in a gazebo and a fold-out couch for extra guests. Any guest can use the 50-foot-long saltwater pool and hot tub, down a long flight of stairs (this isn't the best place for young children.) Rooms include TV with cable and DVD player, but guests are encouraged to explore the island with a booklet of helpful suggestions and free use of bikes, a surfboard, a kayak, and beach gear.

Off Ha'ilima Rd., Lāwa'i. www.marjorieskauaiinn.com. © **800/717-8838** or 808/332-8838. 3 units. $200–$240 double, including continental breakfast. Extra person $20. **Amenities:** Barbecue; complimentary use of bikes, kayak, and beach gear; Jacuzzi; laundry facilities; pool; Wi-Fi (free).

West Side

EXPENSIVE

Waimea Plantation Cottages ★★★ Serenity now: That's what you'll find at this 30-acre oceanfront enclave of restored vintage cottages, spread among large lawns dotted with coconut palms, banyan trees, and tropical flowers. The black-sand beach is not good for swimming (there's a small pool for that), but it offers intriguing driftwood for beachcombers and mesmerizing sunset views; claim a hammock or a lounge chair. The charmingly rustic but airy cottages feature full kitchens, lanais, and modern perks such as Wi-Fi, A/C (window units), and flatscreen TVs. The one- and two-bedroom units (594–726 sq. ft.) have one bathroom, while the three-bedroom versions (1,088 sq. ft.) offer two baths, perfect for families. Owned by the heirs of Norwegian immigrant Hans Peter Faye, who ran a sugar plantation, it's now managed by Coast Hotels, which has poured money into tasteful upgrades. The property also includes the four-bedroom, three-bathroom Jean Faye House and five-bedroom Manager's House, both oceanfront (1,250 and 4,240 sq. ft., respectively), as well as the five-bedroom, five-bathroom Kruse House (4,020 sq. ft.), which offers A/C in all the bedrooms and a kitchenette in the master suite. A new restaurant was expected to open by 2017. ***Tip:*** Gardenview units have lower rates.

9400 Kaumuali'i Hwy. (*makai* side, west of Huaka'i Rd.), Waimea. www.coasthotels.com. ✆ **808/338-1625.** 56 units. $188–$286 1-bedroom double; $205–$346 2-bedroom (sleeps up to 4); $262–$569 3-bedroom (up to 5); from $515 4-bedroom (up to 8); from $633 5-bedroom (up to 10). $25 resort fee. Children 17 and under stay free in parent's room. Check for online specials. **Amenities:** Bar and restaurant (by 2017); gift shop; laundry; pool; Wi-Fi (included in resort fee).

MODERATE

The West Inn ★ The closest thing the West Side has to a Holiday Inn Express, the West Inn offers clean, neutral-toned rooms with bright accents and stone counters. One two-story wing of medium-size rooms is just off the highway across from Waimea Theater; some second-story rooms have an ocean view over corrugated metal roofs from the long, shared lanai, and all units have refrigerators, microwaves, A/C, coffeemakers, and cable TV. Another wing of one- and two-bedroom suites, designed for longer stays with full kitchens and living rooms, is tucked off to the side, with a small barbecue area between the wings. ***Note:*** There's no elevator; call ahead to arrange check-ins after 6pm.

9690 Kaumuali'i Hwy. (*makai* side at Pōkole Rd.), Waimea. http://thewestinn.com. ✆ **808/338-1107.** 20 units. $198 king or double. 3-night minimum for larger rooms: $269 king, $305 1-bedroom suite, $359 2-bedroom suite. $30 extra person. **Amenities:** Barbecue grills, coin laundry, Wi-Fi (free).

INEXPENSIVE

Inn Waimea/West Kaua'i Lodging ★★ If you're looking for accommodations with both character and modern conveniences, check out the small lodge and four vacation rentals managed by West Kaua'i Lodging. A former parsonage that's also known as Halepule ("House of Prayer"), **Inn Waimea** is a Craftsman-style cottage in the center of quaint Waimea, with simple, tropical-tinged, plantation-era decor in its four wood-paneled suites, all but one with a separate living area. Updated in 2013 and under new management, the suites now offer flatscreen TVs, Wi-Fi, and (in some rooms) air-conditioning, as well as private bathrooms with pedestal sinks, coffeemakers, mini-fridges, and ceiling fans. West Kaua'i Lodging also manages three moderately priced two-bedroom cottages in Waimea (owned by the Faye family, which has deep roots on the island), plus the newly built three-bedroom, four-bathroom **Hale Lā** beach house in Kekaha, all with full kitchen and laundry facilities. The plantation-style **Beach Cottage,** which includes a claw-foot tub, bamboo furniture, and sunset views over the ocean and Waimea Pier, is closest to the inn. The homey, Craftsman-inspired **Ishihara Cottage,** which features exotic hardwoods and an eat-in kitchen, and the tree-shaded **Pali Cottage,** with vintage furnishings and an enclosed lanai, are above town, with sweeping views of ridges and the distant sea. ***Note:*** Manager Patrick McLean, who owns Hale Lā, is a former Kaua'i bed-and-breakfast pro who loves to help visitors plan where to eat, when to take a boat tour, you name it. He is now also managing—and upgrading—the cabins in Kōke'e State Park (see "Camping & Cabins," below.)

4469 Halepule Rd. (off Kaumuali'i Hwy.), Waimea. www.westkauailodging.com. ✆ **808/652-6852.** Inn (4 units) $135–$150 ($25 for 3rd person). 3 cottages (sleep 4–6) $179–$195, plus $95–$125 cleaning fee. Hale Lā beach house (sleeps 8) $395, plus $250 cleaning. **Amenities:** Wi-Fi (free).

Camping & Cabins

Kaua'i offers tent camping in seven county-run beach parks and, for extremely hardy and self-sufficient types, several state-managed, back-country areas of the **Nāpali Coast** and **Waimea Canyon.** Tents and simple cabins are also available in the cooler elevations of **Kōke'e State Park,** and minimal campgrounds at **Polihale State Park;** you have to be hardy and well equipped for the rugged conditions in the latter.

All camping requires permits, which must be purchased in advance, and camping in vehicles is not allowed.

County campsites, often busy with local families on weekends, close one day each week for maintenance. The most recommended for visitors, both for scenery and relative safety, are at **Hā'ena, Hanalei Blackpot, 'Anini,** and **Lydgate** beach parks. Go to **www.kauai.gov/camping** for schedules, downloadable mail-in permit applications, hours, and addresses for the neighborhood centers where permits are issued in person. Permits for nonresidents cost $3 per adult (free for children 17 and under, with adult), except for Lydgate, which is $25 per site.

For camping in state parks and forest reserves, the **Department of Land & Natural Resources** (http://camping.ehawaii.gov; ✆ **808/274-3444**) prefers to issue online permits; its office in Līhu'e, 3060 'Eiwa St., Suite 306, is also open 8am to 3:30pm weekdays. **Nāpali Coast State Wilderness Park** allows camping at two sites along the 11-mile Kalalau Trail—Hanakoa Valley, 6 miles in, and Kalalau Valley, at trail's end—for a maximum of 5 nights (no more than 1 consecutive night at Hanakoa). Camping is also permitted at Miloli'i, for a maximum of 3 nights; it's reached only by kayak or authorized boats mid-May through early September. There's no drinking water, trash must be packed out, and composting toilets are not always in good repair, yet permits ($20 per night) often sell out a year in advance. (***Note:*** Rangers conduct periodic permit checks here, so make sure yours is handy.)

Permits for primitive campsites in eight backcountry areas of Waimea Canyon and nearby wilderness preserves cost $18 per night, with a 5-night maximum; see http://camping.ehawaii.gov for detailed descriptions.

In **Kōke'e State Park,** which gets quite chilly on winter nights, **West Kauai Lodging** (www.westkauailodging.com; ✆ **808/652-6852**) now manages 11 cabins ($59–$119 a night, 2-night minimum) that sleep two to six people and come with fully equipped kitchens and linens. Be sure to book well in advance. Less than a mile away, down a dirt road, the YWCA of Kaua'i's **Camp Sloggett** (www.campingkauai.com; ✆ **808/245-5959**) allows tent camping in its large forest clearing for $15 per tent per night, with toilets and hot showers available; there's also a four-person cottage ($120–$150). Groups may rent its bunkhouse ($160–$200) or lodge ($200–$225), both of which sleep up to 15.

If you need gear, **Just Live** (www.ziplinetourskauai.com; ✆ **808/482-1295**) sells and rents top brands of tents, camping stoves, sleep sacks, and more in the Anchor Cove Shopping Center, 3416 Rice St., Līhu'e. **Kayak Kaua'i** (www.kayakkauai.com; ✆ **888/596-3853** or 808/826-9844) offers rentals, supplies, and even car and bag storage at its Wailua River Marina shop, 3-5971 Kūhiō Hwy., Kapa'a. **Pedal 'n Paddle** (www.pedalnpaddle.com; ✆ **808/826-9069**) sells hiking boots, freeze-dried food, and other necessities and rents tents, backpacks, and sleeping bags; it's in Ching Young Village, 5-5190 Kūhiō Hwy., Hanalei.

WHERE TO EAT ON KAUA'I

Thanks to a proliferation of hamburger joints, plate-lunch counters, and food trucks, you'll find affordable choices (by local standards) in every town. Even in pricey Princeville, the shopping center food court offers a few tasty bargains. At the gourmet end of the spectrum, Kaua'i's very expensive restaurants—both on and off the resorts—provide excellent service along with more complex but reliably executed dishes. And nearly every establishment trumpets its Kaua'i-grown ingredients, which help keep the Garden Island green and the flavors fresh.

The challenge is finding exceptional quality in the moderate to expensive range. Costs are indeed higher here, and service is often slower; it's best not to arrive anywhere—even at one of the many food trucks—in a state of starvation. Patience and pleasantness on your part, however, will usually be rewarded. During peak holiday and summer seasons, avoid stress by booking online with **Open Table** (www.opentable.com), currently available for 33 restaurants and dinner shows. The listings below, not all of which are on Open Table, will note where reservations are recommended.

For those with access to a kitchen (or even just a mini-fridge), check out "Kauai Farmer's Markets" (p. 598). You're guaranteed farm-to-table cuisine at a good price—and at your own pace.

East Side

At press time, fans of former Red Salt executive chef Adam Watten were eagerly awaiting the opening of his new, locally sourced **Hānai** (www.hanaikauai.com) in Kapa'a at 4-1543 Kūhiō Hwy, after a year of well-received pop-ups in other locales. ***Note:*** The restaurants in this section are on either the "Hotels & Restaurants on the Coconut Coast" map (p. 561) or the "Hotels & Restaurants in Līhu'e" map (p. 563).

EXPENSIVE

Duke's Kaua'i ★ STEAK/SEAFOOD The view of Kalapaki Beach, an indoor waterfall, koi pond, and a lively beachfront bar have as much, if not more, to do with the popularity of this outpost of the California–Hawai'i TS Restaurants chain as do the fresh seafood, vast salad bar, and belt-straining Hula Pie (a macadamia-nut ice cream confection built for sharing). The downstairs **Barefoot Bar**'s lunch and dinner menu offers the best values, with burgers, hearty salads, and flatbread pizzas, but the dinner-only upstairs dining room shows local flair with Lāwa'i mushroom gnocchi, seared ahi with papaya mustard sauce, and Kunana Dairy goat cheese atop grilled New York steak—among other tasty but less ambitious dishes such as shrimp scampi and macnut-crusted mahimahi. A trip to the island's biggest salad bar costs $3 with any entree upstairs or $18 as a stand-alone meal. ***Note:*** The Barefoot Bar offers live music 4 to 6pm daily except Tuesday, and 8:30 to 10:30pm Friday and Saturday nights.

At west end of Kaua'i Marriott Resort, 3610 Rice St., Līhu'e (valet parking at restaurant or self-parking in hotel lot). www.dukeskauai.com. ✆ **808/246-9599.** Reservations recommended for dinner. Main courses $12–$20 lunch and dinner in bar; dinner $25–$35 in dining room. $4–$5 taco specials in bar Tues 4–6pm. Bar daily 11am–11pm; dining room daily 5–10pm.

Hukilau Lanai ★★ SEAFOOD/ISLAND FARM Although his restaurant is hidden inside the nondescript Kauai Coast Resort at the Beachboy, off the main highway in Kapa'a, chef/owner Ron Miller has inspired diners to find their way here in droves since 2002. The lure: a hearty menu that's virtually all locally sourced—from Kaua'i whenever possible, and other islands when not—as well as expertly prepared and presented. Four to six seafood specials, incorporating local produce, are offered nightly; try the coffee-spiced candied ahi, or the hebi (short-billed spearfish) when available. The mushroom meatloaf also packs a savory punch, thanks to grass-fed beef from local Sanchez Ranch and Big Island mushrooms. Value-conscious diners should try the $32 five-course tasting menu ($50 with wine pairings) offered from 5 to 5:45pm. Reservations are strongly recommended, especially for oceanview seating; the less-scenic lobby bar has nightly music. ***Note:*** An extensive gluten-free menu includes variants of the five-course tasting menus.

In the Kauai Coast Resort at the Beachboy, 520 Aleka Loop, Kapa'a. www.hukilaukauai.com. ✆ **808/822-0600.** Reservations recommended. Main courses $18–$32. Tues–Sun 5–9pm; poolside happy hour daily 3–5pm.

JO2 ★★★ ASIAN/FRENCH Foodies will want to check out chef Jean-Marie Josselin's recent triumphant return to Kapa'a, in a strip mall not unlike the one where he first gained renown with A Pacific Cafe. A Hawai'i Regional Cuisine co-founder and six-time nominee for a James Beard Foundation Award, Josselin reestablished himself on Kaua'i in 2010 with Josselin's Tapas Bar & Grill (now Tapas@Kukui'ula; see p. 588), leaving it behind in 2015 to focus on JO2, his island-sourced, "natural cuisine" restaurant with Asian-influenced dishes prepared using classic French techniques. The tiny but chic dining room has a neutral palette that makes the artful presentations of brightly hued greens, sauces, and glazes pop. Among the small plates, try the seared tuna belly bibimbap or crispy duck salad with persimmon; for larger dishes, seared Hokkaido scallops or the Hunan-style rack of lamb with chipotle blueberry sauce (serves two). Save room for the yuzu lemon cheesecake or local banana cream pie with roasted banana gelato.

4-971 Kūhiō Hwy., Kapa'a. www.jotwo.com. ✆ **808/212-1627.** Reservations recommended. Main courses $29–$35; small plates $10–$19. Daily 5–9pm.

MODERATE

Kauai Pasta/KP Lihue ★ ITALIAN The owners' marital split has led to a breakup of the two Kauai Pasta locations, but fortunately you don't have to choose which one to remain loyal to. Although the Līhu'e site has changed its name to KP Lihue, both have kept essentially the same menus, emphasizing homemade pasta standards, such as chicken parm and fettuccine Alfredo, and meat specials, such as ossobuco or *sous vide* pork. The larger Kapa'a locale also offers $10 lunch specials, a late-night lounge with its own menu (try the truffled prawn "ramen" with

PLATE LUNCH, BENTO & poke

If you haven't yet tried the Hawai'i staples of plate lunch, bento, or poke (see p. 142), Kaua'i is a good place to start.

EAST SIDE In Kapa'a, the indispensable **Pono Market,** 4–1300 Kūhiō Hwy., Kapa'a (✆ **808/822-4581**), has enticing counters of sashimi, poke, sushi, and a diverse assortment of takeout fare. The roast pork and the potato-macaroni salad are top sellers, but it's also known for plate lunches, including pork and chicken *laulau* (steamed in ti leaves), plus flaky *manju* (sweet potato and other fillings in baked crust). It's on the *makai* side of the highway, between Īnia and Kauwila streets, open Monday to Saturday 6am to 4pm. Kapa'a also has a branch of **Kilauea Fish Market** (see "North Shore," below) at 440 Aleka Pl. (✆ **808/822-3474**).

In Līhu'e, **Po's Kitchen,** 4100 Rice St. (✆ **808/246-8617**), packs a lot of goodies in its deluxe bentos ($8.50), including shrimp tempura, chicken katsu, chow fun noodles, spaghetti mac salad, hot dog, ham, and rice balls. It's hidden behind Ace Hardware and open Monday to Saturday from 6am to 2pm (cash only). One block away, **Garden Island BBQ,** 4252 Rice St. (www.gardenislandbbq.com; ✆ **808/245-8868**), is the place for Chinese plate lunches, as well as soups and noodle dishes; it's open Monday to Saturday 10am to 9pm. Across the highway from Wal-Mart, **the Fish Express,** 3343 Kūhiō Hwy. (✆ **808/245-9918**), draws crowds for its wide assortment of poke (the ahi with spicy crab in a light mayo sauce is a favorite), pork laulau, Spam musubi, bentos, and plate lunches, including lighter entree options such as Cajun blackened ahi and smoked fish. The downside: no seating. It's open Monday to Saturday from 10am to 5pm.

Mark's Place, in Puhi Industrial Park at 1610 Haleukana St., Līhu'e (www.marksplacekauai.com; ✆ **808/245-2722**), fashions daily salad and entree specials with a California-healthy bent: shrimp and grilled-vegetable quinoa salad, say, or cornmeal-crusted mahi with chipotle aioli. But it also serves island standards such as Korean-style chicken, beef stew, and chicken katsu and is famed for its baked goods, including butter mochi and bread pudding. It's open weekdays from 10am to 8pm, with a handful of picnic tables for seating.

NORTH SHORE Everything is pricier on the North Shore, and ahi poke and plate lunches are no exception at **Kīlauea Fish Market,** 4270 Kīlauea Rd.

angel hair pasta), and, at dinner, *pizzetta* choices such as rosemary grilled chicken with Gorgonzola. Portions are generous at both sites, but plan to order at least one of the tasty sides to share—I recommend the truffle Parmesan fries with a variety of dipping sauces. The *keiki* (kids') menus are a good deal too, from $5 pastas to $10 for grilled shrimp with mashed potatoes and vegetable.

Kauai Pasta, 4-939 Kūhiō Hwy., Kapa'a (*mauka* side, north of Taco Bell.) www.kauaipasta.com. ✆ **808/822-7447.** Main courses $12–$26 lunch, $13–$28 dinner. Restaurant daily 11am–9pm; lounge Sun–Thur 11am–10pm, Fri–Sat 11am–10pm, happy hour daily 3–5pm. Dinner reservations recommended. **KP Lihue:** 3-3142 Kūhiō Hwy., Līhu'e (btw. Poinciana and Hardy sts. in the Garden Island Publishing building).

(enter from Keneke St. across the street from Kong Lung Market), Kīlauea (✆ **808/828-6244**). At $29 a pound, skip the poke and opt for Korean BBQ or grilled teri chicken plates ($11–$12); the burrito-like ahi wrap ($11) is a messy but filling alternative. It's open Monday to Saturday from 11am to 8pm, with outdoor seating only. Locals head to **Village Snack Shop and Bakery**, across from Puka Dog inside Hanalei's Ching Young Village, 5-5190 Kūhiō Hwy. (✆ **808/826-6841**), for loco moco (eggs, meat, and gravy on rice) at breakfast and chili pepper chicken at lunch; everyone loves the chocolate *haupia* (coconut cream) pies, malasadas (doughnut holes), and other pastries, which sell out quickly. It's open 6:30am to 4pm Monday to Saturday, 6:30am to 3pm Sunday (kitchen closes an hour earlier). Near the end of the road in Wainiha, **Sushigirl Kauai,** 5-6607 Kūhiō Hwy. (www.sushigirlkauai.fish; ✆ **808/827-8171**), offers gluten-free takeout, from ahi poke bowls with rice, local organic greens, or quinoa ($12) to huge seafood and veggie sushi rolls ($12–$15). It's open 11am to 7pm daily.

SOUTH SHORE The **Koloa Fish Market,** 5482 Kōloa Rd. (✆ **808/742-6199**) in Old Town Kōloa, is a tiny corner store with two stools on the veranda. Grab some excellent fresh poke, plate lunches, or seared ahi to go, and don't forgo decadent desserts such as Okinawan sweet potato haupia pie on macadamia nut crust. You can also pick up raw seafood to grill. It's open weekdays from 10am to 6pm and Saturday from 10am to 5pm. Down the road is **Sueoka's Snack Shop** (✆ **808/742-1112**), the cash-only window counter of Sueoka grocery store, 5392 Kōloa Rd. (www.sueokastore.com; ✆ **808/742-1611**). It offers a wide selection of meat-based lunch plates, such as shoyu chicken or kalua pork for just $6.25. It's open Tuesday to Sunday 8:30am to 3pm.

WEST SIDE **Ishihara Market,** 9894 Kaumuali'i Hwy., Waimea (✆ **808/338-1751**), a block past the bridge on the *makai* side, is well worth a stop heading to or from Waimea Canyon. A local favorite founded in 1934, the family-run Ishihara's deli counter stocks an impressive variety of fresh poke (including hamachi, baby octopus, salmon, and cooked lobster) and has a grill making plate lunches Tuesday to Saturday. The grocery store is open Sunday to Thursday 6am to 7:30pm and Friday and Saturday 6am to 8pm.

www.kplihue.com. ✆ **808/245-2227.** 11am–9pm daily. Main courses lunch $13–$24, dinner $13–$30.

Lava Lava Beach Club ★★ AMERICAN/ISLAND It took more than a year to mount this bright jewel in the crown of the recently renovated Kauai Shores hotel, but look at the result. Besides the island's only "toes-in-the-sand" dining area on comfy wicker sofas facing Wailua Bay, Lava Lava Beach Club offers plenty of other oceanview indoor and outdoor seating, a full bar with zippy tropical cocktails and a dozen beers (seven local), and attentive staff serving American and island-flavored specialties, including a burger made from local beef and Portuguese

sausage ($17), from 7am to 10pm. The fact that prices border on the expensive ($22 for a lunch salad with five shrimp) is the only bummer at this otherwise beachy-keen hideaway, which also hosts live music nightly.
At Kauai Shores hotel, 420 Papaloa Rd., Kapa'a (off Kūhiō Hwy., *makai* side, south of Coconut Marketplace). www.lavalavabeachclub.com. ✆ **808/822-7447.** Main courses $12–$15 breakfast, $15–$26 lunch, $16–$36 dinner. Daily breakfast 7–10am, lunch 11am–2pm, happy hour 3–5pm, dinner 5–9pm, bar menu 8–10pm. Lunch and dinner reservations recommended. Free valet parking (required).

Oasis on the Beach ★ SEAFOOD/ISLAND FARM Though not actually on the sand, the open-air, oceanfront setting at the Waipouli Beach Resort is still memorable, as are the daily fresh-catch (grilled or pan-seared) and curry specials, the grilled kale salad with whipped Brie, and braised short ribs with bacon-truffle fried rice. Chef de cuisine Sean Smull proudly notes that 90% of ingredients come from Kaua'i. Presentation wins points, too: Witness the pretty flower of blackberry syrup in the pineapple martini. Luckily, half portions of many dinner entrees make sharing a breeze; the handsome canoe bar and sounds of ocean surf also make the occasional wait worthwhile. Save room for the apple banana spring roll with salted caramel ice cream. Wednesdays are an ideal time to discover this culinary oasis, with live music and a special "chef's choice" menu from 4 to 6pm. ***Note:*** Brunch entrees are tasty but petite, especially by local standards.
In the Waipouli Beach Resort, 4-820 Kūhiō Hwy., Kapa'a (across from Safeway). www.oasiskauai.com. ✆ **808/822-9332.** Reservations recommended. Main courses $13–$16 lunch, $16–$33 dinner, $11–$17 brunch. Mon–Sat 11:30am–3pm and 4–9pm; Sun brunch 10am–2pm; dinner 4–9pm.

INEXPENSIVE

In addition to these listings, and the many in "Plate Lunch, Bento & Poke" (p. 580), check out these two Kapa'a food counters with limited seating: **Shrimp Station ★** (details on p. 592) and **Tiki Tacos ★★,** 4–961 Kūhiō Hwy., *mauka* side, in the Waipouli Complex. Billed as "Mexican food with a Hawaiian heart," the latter features tacos ($6–$8) with island fish, kalua pork, and other fillings on large handmade tortillas. It's open 11am to 8:30pm daily.

Hamura's Saimin Stand ★★★ JAPANESE NOODLES Honored by the James Beard Foundation in 2006 as one of "America's Classics," this hole in the wall has been satisfying local palates since 1951. Visitors have also now caught on to the appeal of saimin: large bowls of ramen noodles in salty broth with green onion, cabbage, and slices of fish cake, hard-boiled eggs, and pork, for starters. Here the housemade noodles are served al dente, and sometimes brusquely; figure out what you're going to order before seating yourself at one of the U-shaped counters. The "special regular" includes wontons and diced ham; top off any dish with a barbecued chicken skewer. If your appetite isn't large, order a to-go slice of the ultra-fluffy *liliko'i* (passionfruit) chiffon pie, just as renowned as the saimin. Shave ice is also delicious, but its separate counter isn't always open. ***Note:*** There's often a line inside and out; it moves fast, so stay put.

2956 Kress St., Līhu'e (1 block west of Rice St. in small blue building on left; park farther down the street). ✆ **808/245-3271.** All items under $10. No credit cards. Mon–Thurs 10am–10:30pm; Fri–Sat 10am–midnight; Sun 10am–9:30pm.

North Shore

Note: The restaurants in this section are on the "Hotels & Restaurants on Kaua'i's North Shore" map (p. 585). Also see the listings for family-friendly **Tahiti Nui** and **Tiki Iniki** in "Kaua'i Nightlife," p. 599.

EXPENSIVE

Bar Acuda ★★★ TAPAS Named one of *Food & Wine* magazine's "Top 10 New American Chefs" in 1996, when he was still working in San Francisco, chef/owner Jim Moffatt later decided to embrace a low-key lifestyle in Hanalei. But he hasn't relaxed his standards for expertly prepared food, in this case tapas—small plates inspired by several Mediterranean cuisines—enjoyed here on the torch-lit veranda or in the sleek, warm-toned dining room. Given Bar Acuda's deliciously warm, crusty bread, ordering one hearty and one light dish per person, plus a shared starter of spiced olives or crostini, should suffice for a couple. But ask the server for help in ordering the right amount—some dishes, such as the wonderful seared single scallop on mashed potatoes, aren't really suitable for sharing. The menu changes to reflect seasonal tastes and availability but usually includes a seared fresh fish and grilled beef skewers. An excellent finish is locally roasted coffee ice cream with caramel sauce and chocolate cookie. Note that this is a more smartly dressed crowd than just about anywhere else in Hanalei.

In Hanalei Center, 5-5161 Kūhiō Hwy., Hanalei. www.restaurantbaracuda.com. ✆ **808/826-7081.** Reservations recommended. Hearty tapas $9–$16. Daily 5:30–9:30pm (bar open till 10pm).

Mediterranean Gourmet ★★ MEDITERRANEAN Imad and Yarrow Beydoun's unlikely but delightful oasis between Hanalei and the end of the road provides a welcome respite from the usual macnut-crusted mahimahi. At lunch, add fresh grilled fish to one of several generous salads featuring locally grown greens, or try the housemade falafel. Meat-and-potato lovers can chow down on the well-spiced beef and lamb gyros wrapped in fluffy pita. At dinner, seafood paella or rosemary rack of lamb for two can make a special occasion that much more special, although the classic chicken shishkabobs are no slouch. Imad, the Lebanese-born chef, and his wife, Yarrow, a Hanalei native, opened the restaurant in 2006 and, for years, offered weekly belly dancing as well as a lū'au before closing for renovations in 2015. At press time, belly dancing was off the menu, but the Tuesday night lū'au ($74 adults, $38 children) was due to return. Reserve early to enjoy dinner at Sunday, or the lū'au, when it resumes.

Hanalei Colony Resort, 5–7132 Kūhiō Hwy., Hā'ena. www.kauaimedgourmet.com. ✆ **808/826-9875.** Dinner reservations recommended. Main courses $12–$18 lunch, $17–$37 dinner. Tues–Sun noon to 8:30pm. Happy hour 3–6pm. Live music Tues–Wed and Fri–Sun.

MODERATE

The Bistro ★★★ CONTEMPORARY AMERICAN/ISLAND FARM John-Paul Gordon is yet another Kaua'i chef taking inspiration from the bounty of local fields and fishing grounds, with an admirably inventive palate and a well-practiced eye for presentation. Although his menu is largely seasonal, the "fish rockets" starter of seared ahi in lumpia wrappers with wasabi aioli is a signature dish; rich cuts of grass-fed beef from Medeiros Farms with mashed potatoes are also standards. If you crave something lighter, order the curly kale salad with local goat cheese and almonds or the grilled fresh catch, perhaps with a baby spinach ragu. Lunch includes simpler but satisfying options such as a Kaua'i beef burger and barbecued pork sandwich. The wine list is reasonably priced; ask about the $5 daily special, which you can pair with live music Thursday and Saturday. In 2015, the owners opened **Palate Wine Bar** (www.palatewinebar.net; ✆ **808/212-1974**) a few doors down at 2474 Keneke St. The wine bar serves flatbreads ($15–$16) and a few main courses ($18–$29) from 4 to 10pm daily, with quality wine and beer starting at $8 a glass.

In Kong Lung Historic Market Center, 2484 Keneke St., Kīlauea. http://lighthousebistro.com. ✆ **808/828-0480.** Reservations recommended for parties of 6 or more. Lunch $10–$17; dinner main courses $15–$26. Daily noon–2:30pm and 5:30–9pm. Bar noon–9pm. Happy hour 4–6pm.

Hanalei Gourmet ★ AMERICAN This casual, decidedly nongourmet spot offers the best values (by local standards) at lunch, with a variety of burgers and ample sandwiches on freshly baked bread starting at $8; order the latter to go from the deli. The market-priced beer-battered fish and chips, accompanied by a suitably tart Asian slaw and soy wasabi sauce, is also notable. (If you want a half papaya, though, skip the $7 version here and walk a few steps to Harvest Market or across the street to the Big Save grocery.) Dinner has rather higher aspirations, not always met, as well as higher prices, but you can still order from much of the lunch menu. The atmosphere tends to be lively if not downright noisy, thanks to wooden floors, the popular bar, TV, and occasional live music, which draws an enthusiastic local crowd. Service is laidback but friendly.

In Hanalei Center, 5–5161 Kūhiō Hwy., *mauka* side, Hanalei. www.hanaleigourmet.com. ✆ **808/826-2524.** Main courses $8–$13 lunch, $10–$29 dinner. Daily deli 8am–10:30pm; restaurant 11am–9:30pm; bar 11am–10:30pm.

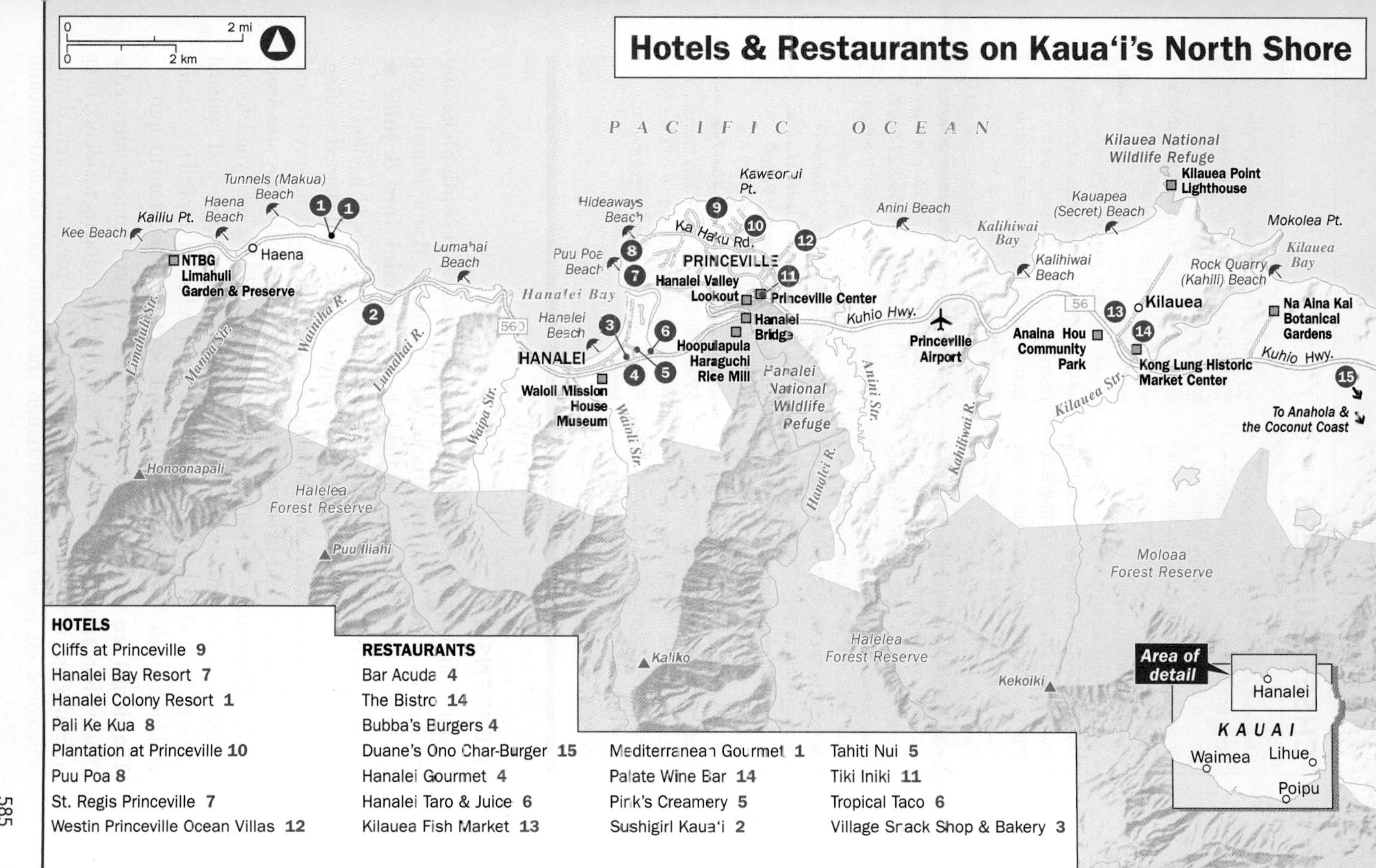
Hotels & Restaurants on Kaua'i's North Shore
0
2 mi
0
2 km
PACIFIC OCEAN
Kilauea National Wildlife Refuge
Kilauea Point Lighthouse
Kaweonui Pt.
Tunnels (Makua) Beach
Haena Beach
Kailiu Pt.
Kee Beach
NTBG Limahuli Garden & Preserve
Haena
Hideaways Beach
Ka Haku Rd.
Anini Beach
Kalihiwai Bay
Kauapea (Secret) Beach
Mokolea Pt.
Kilauea Bay
Rock Quarry (Kahili) Beach
Lumahai Beach
Puu Poa Beach
PRINCEVILLE
Hanalei Valley Lookout
Princeville Center
Hanalei Bay
Kalihiwai Beach
Kilauea
Na Aina Kai Botanical Gardens
Hanalei Beach
Hanalei Bridge
Hoopulapula Haraguchi Rice Mill
Kuhio Hwy.
Princeville Airport
Anaina Hou Community Park
Kong Lung Historic Market Center
HANALEI
Waioli Mission House Museum
Hanalei National Wildlife Refuge
Anini Str.
Kilauea Str.
To Anahola & the Coconut Coast
Limahuli Str.
Manoa Str.
Wainiha R.
Lumahai R.
Waipa Str.
Waioli Str.
Hanalei R.
Kalihiwai R.
Honoonapali
Halelea Forest Reserve
Puu Iliahi
Moloaa Forest Reserve
Kaliko
Kekoiki
Area of detail
Hanalei
KAUAI
Waimea
Lihue
Poipu
HOTELS
Cliffs at Princeville 9
Hanalei Bay Resort 7
Hanalei Colony Resort 1
Pali Ke Kua 8
Plantation at Princeville 10
Puu Poa 8
St. Regis Princeville 7
Westin Princeville Ocean Villas 12
RESTAURANTS
Bar Acuda 4
The Bistro 14
Bubba's Burgers 4
Duane's Ono Char-Burger 15
Hanalei Gourmet 4
Hanalei Taro & Juice 6
Kilauea Fish Market 13
Mediterranean Gourmet 1
Palate Wine Bar 14
Pink's Creamery 5
Sushigirl Kaua'i 2
Tahiti Nui 5
Tiki Iniki 11
Tropical Taco 6
Village Snack Shop & Bakery 3

CHEESEBURGERS in paradise

Delicious as Hawaii's fresh seafood is, sometimes what you're really looking for—in the words of Jimmy Buffett—is a cheeseburger in paradise. Luckily, Kaua'i boasts several inexpensive burger joints that are bound to satisfy.

The first thing to know about **Duane's Ono Char-Burger,** 4-4350 Kūhiō Hwy., *makai* side, Anahola (✆ **808/822-9181**), is that its burgers ($5–$8) are not made of the fish called ono (wahoo); they're just *'ono* ("delicious" in Hawaiian.) The second thing to know is that waits can be long at this red roadside stand, opened in 1973, where wild chickens, cats, and birds are ready to share your meal with you. Duane's is open Monday to Saturday 10am to 6pm and Sunday 11am to 6pm. The founders of Duane's also run **Kalapaki Beach Hut,** 3474 Rice St., Līhu'e, near the west end of Kalapaki Beach (www.kalapakibeachhut.com; ✆ **808/246-6330**). The two-story oceanview "hut" offers grass-fed Kaua'i beef burgers ($7–$10), a unique taro burger ($9) made from organic taro grown nearby, and a shave ice stand.

Famed for its sassy slogans ("We Cheat Tourists, Drunks & Attorneys," among them) as much as for burgers ($4–$7) made from Kaua'i beef, **Bubba's** (www.bubbaburger.com) claims to have been around since 1936. It's certainly had time to develop a loyal following even while charging $1 for lettuce and tomato. Hearty appetites will want to try the Coors-spiked chili that comes on the open-face Slopper ($6) and with the Hubba Bubba ($7), in which it's poured over rice, a burger patty, and a grilled hot dog. The oldest Bubba's is in **Kapa'a** (4-1421 Kūhiō Hwy.; ✆ **808/823-0069**), where the deck has a view of the ocean across Kapa'a Beach Park. Bubba's other two locations are in **Hanalei** (5-5161 Kūhiō Hwy. in Hanalei Center; ✆ **808/826-7839**) and in **Po'ipū** at the Shops at Kukui'ula (2829 Ala Kalanikamauka, Po'ipū; ✆ **808/742-6900**). All three are open daily from 10:30am to 8pm, although the Kukui'ula closing time may vary depending on business.

INEXPENSIVE

Beside plate lunches (see above), the best bargains in North Shore dining usually come from food trucks, often found at 'Anini, Hanalei, and Hā'ena beach parks, but with fickle hours. **Hanalei Taro & Juice ★** (✆ **808/826-1059;** www.hanaleitaro.com), *makai* side of Kūhiō Hwy. a mile west of the Hanalei Bridge, has reliable hours and shaded seating. It's open daily 11am to 3pm, with most items under $10; be sure to sample the banana-bread-like taro butter mochi. Nearby, the tiny storefront **Pink's Creamery ★,** 4489 Aku Rd., is as justifiably renowned for its grilled-cheese sandwiches on sweet bread with pineapple and optional kalua pork ($7–$9, including chips) as it is for delicious tropical ice creams and housemade frozen yogurt and sorbets; it's open daily 11am to 9pm.

Tropical Taco ★ MEXICAN SEAFOOD Roger Kennedy operated a North Shore taco wagon for 20-odd years before taking up residence over a decade ago in this cottage-style building with a pleasant porch; dishes still come on paper plates. Although the menu has local/sustainable touches—the fresh seafood comes from North Shore fishermen, the lettuce mix is organic, and the fish and chips come with taro fries—the focus here is on satisfying hefty appetites. You might opt for the grilled fish special in soft corn tacos or as a crispy tostada rather than the gut-busting, deep-fried Fat Jack beef or veggie burrito, and be aware that any extras (cheese, sour cream, avocado) drive up prices quickly. ***Note:*** Hanalei has few places that are open for breakfast, so it's worth the occasional wait for your choice of one of four scrambled-egg burritos (try the taro and cheese).

5–5088 Kūhiō Hwy. (*makai* side, parking in rear), Hanalei. http://tropicaltaco.com. ✆ **808/827-8226.** Most items $13–$15, breakfast $7–$8. No credit cards. Mon–Fri 8am–8pm; Sat–Sun 11am–5pm.

South Shore

Note: You'll find the restaurants in this section on the "Hotels & Restaurants on Kaua'i's South Shore" map (p. 589).

EXPENSIVE

In addition to the choices here, see the listing for **Keoki's Paradise ★,** a perennial tourist favorite for its tropical landscaping and fresh seafood (dinner main courses $30–$35), under "Kaua'i Nightlife," p. 599.

The Beach House ★★★ HAWAI'I REGIONAL Call it dinner and a show: As sunset approaches, diners at this beloved oceanfront restaurant start leaping from their tables to pose for pictures on the grass-covered promontory, while nearby surfers try to catch one last wave. The genial waiters are as used to cameras being thrust upon them as they are reciting specials featuring local ingredients—a staple here long before "farm to table" became a catchphrase. But there are other good reasons to dine here, whether you're splurging on dinner or sampling the more affordable lunch. Among them: the sherry-finished corn chowder, brimming with crab and fresh fish; the house ceviche of fish, prawns, and scallops in a citrus-*lilikoi* marinade, served in a half coconut; and the grilled fresh catch with citrus brodo, Parmesan polenta, and candied fennel. Desserts are less memorable than the well-crafted cocktails, also served with pupu in the lounge.

5022 Lāwa'i Rd., Kōloa. www.the-beach-house.com. ✆ **808/742-1424.** Reservations recommended. Main courses $9–$19 lunch, $20–$48 dinner. Lunch daily 11am–3pm; light fare daily 3–5:30pm; dinner daily 5:30–10pm mid-Sept to mid-Mar (6–9pm mid-Mar to mid-Sept); lounge daily 11am–10pm.

Eating House 1849 ★★★ GOURMET PLANTATION Hawai'i Regional Cuisine co-founder Roy Yamaguchi surprised many in 2015 when he announced he was closing his upscale Roy's, a fixture of Poipu Shopping Village for 2 decades, in order to open this more casual concept inspired by the multicultural plantation era (and named for the islands' first restaurant, founded in Honolulu in 1849). The throngs now ascending the stairs to the second-story, open-walled dining room in the

Shops at Kukui'ula may only be surprised by the noise. Yamaguchi's culinary finesse and local beef, fish, and produce ensure excellent preparations of "humble" fare such as Portuguese bean and kale soup, pork and shrimp potstickers, the Hapa burger made of grass-fed Kaua'i beef and wild boar, and *kamameshi* (hot-pot rice bowl) with chicken, butterfish, salmon, or Hawaiian opah (moonfish). ***Note:*** Most main courses are in the $18 to $24 range.

In the Shops at Kukui'ula, 2829 Ala Kalanikaumaka St., Po'ipū. www.eatinghouse1849.com. ✆ **808/742-5000.** Reservations recommended. Main courses $13–$42. Daily 5–9:30pm.

Red Salt ★★ HAWAI'I REGIONAL One of the best hotel restaurants on Kaua'i, this is also one of the smallest and hardest to find, tucked inside the discreetly located **Ko'a Kea Hotel & Resort** (p. 571). Although rivals offer more dramatic ocean views in plusher settings, Red Salt has consistently executed elegantly presented dishes from a menu first designed by El Bulli–trained chef Ronnie Sanchez in 2009 and expanded by later chefs. Under new ownership in early 2016, the restaurant was still serving favorites such as pan-roasted chicken and lobster saffron ravioli, with a cloud of candlelit cotton candy (in varying flavors) for a dramatic if sugary finish. ***Note:*** On most nights the adjacent lounge serves exquisite sashimi and sushi, along with small plates such as kalua pork potstickers and crab cakes. Breakfast and poolside lunch items are less adventurous but no less carefully prepared; try the lemon pineapple souffle pancakes.

In Ko'a Kea Hotel & Resort, 2251 Po'ipū Rd., Po'ipū. www.koakea.com. ✆ **808/828-8888.** Dinner reservations recommended. Valet parking. Main courses $14–$17 breakfast, $10–$21 lunch, $25–$69 dinner (most $33–$39). Daily breakfast 6:30–11am, lunch (poolside) 11am–6pm, dinner 6–10pm; sushi lounge Tues–Sat 5:30–9pm.

Tapas@Kukui'ula ★★★ ASIAN FUSION Yup, this is the former Josselin's Tapas Bar & Grill, which chef/owner Jean-Marie Josselin left in late 2015 to focus on his newer JO2 restaurant (see p. 579). Executive chef Kristen Yanagawa, a rising star trained on Kaua'i, puts more of an emphasis on Asian-inspired dishes than Mediterranean and relies exclusively on local produce. Standouts include Okinawan sweet potato and kabocha pumpkin tortellini (the size of large ravioli) in a miso brown-butter vinaigrette, Kaua'i shrimp tempura dynamite (with fish roe), and crab-crusted monchong with Israeli couscous; plan on a return visit to sample more. ***Note:*** Many of the artfully presented "tapas" are fairly substantial, so ask your server for input on portions. Happily, Yanagawa has kept Josselin's tradition of concocting sangria tableside, including lychee, mango, and classic versions.

In the Shops at Kukui'ula, 2829 Ala Kalanikaumaka St., Po'ipū. www.josselinstapas.com. ✆ **808/742-7117.** $11–$36. Daily 5:30–9pm (bar till 11pm Fri–Sat). Happy hour daily 5:30–6:30pm. Late-night happy hour & live music and DJs Fri–Sat 10pm–closing.

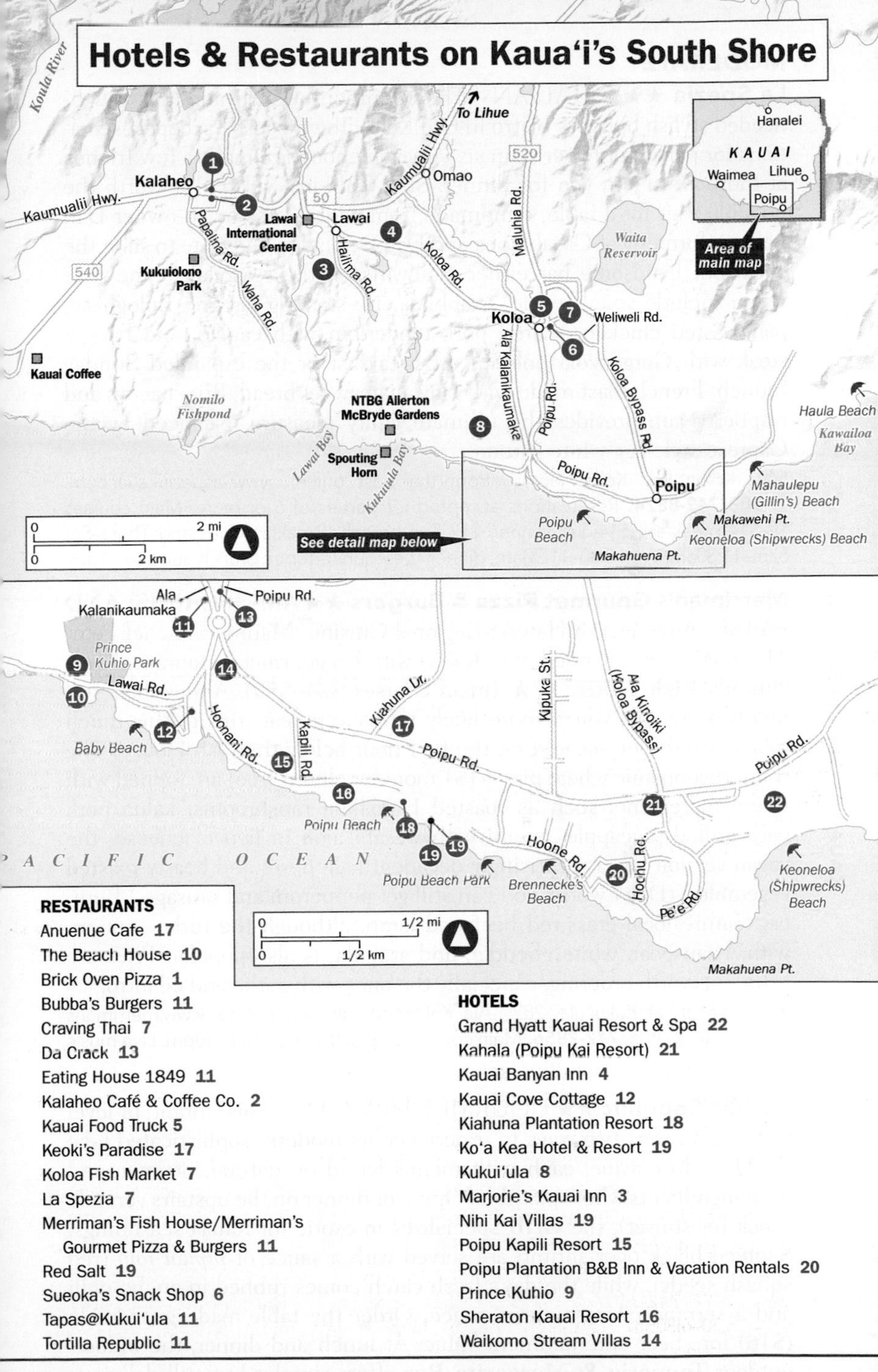
Hotels & Restaurants on Kaua'i's South Shore
Koula River
To Lihue
Kaumualii Hwy.
520
Omao
Kalaheo
Kaumualii Hwy.
50
Lawai International Center
Lawai
Papalina Rd.
Hailima Rd.
Koloa Rd.
Maluhia Rd.
Waita Reservoir
540
Kukuiolono Park
Waha Rd.
Koloa
Weliweli Rd.
Ala Kalanikaumaka
Poipu Rd.
Koloa Bypass Rd.
Kauai Coffee
Nomilo Fishpond
NTBG Allerton McBryde Gardens
Spouting Horn
Lawai Bay
Kukuiula Bay
Poipu Rd.
Poipu
Poipu Beach
Makahuena Pt.
Haula Beach
Kawailoa Bay
Mahaulepu (Gillin's) Beach
Makawehi Pt.
Keoneloa (Shipwrecks) Beach
Hanalei
KAUAI
Waimea
Lihue
Poipu
Area of main map
0
2 mi
2 km
See detail map below
Ala Kalanikaumaka
Poipu Rd.
Prince Kuhio Park
Lawai Rd.
Baby Beach
Hoonani Rd.
Kapili Rd.
Kiahuna Dr.
Kipuka St.
Ala Kinoiki (Koloa Bypass)
Poipu Rd.
Poipu Rd.
Poipu Beach
Hoone Rd.
Hochu Rd.
Pe'e Rd.
PACIFIC OCEAN
Poipu Beach Park
Brennecke's Beach
Keoneloa (Shipwrecks) Beach
Makahuena Pt.
1/2 mi
1/2 km
RESTAURANTS
Anuenue Cafe 17
The Beach House 10
Brick Oven Pizza 1
Bubba's Burgers 11
Craving Thai 7
Da Crack 13
Eating House 1849 11
Kalaheo Café & Coffee Co. 2
Kauai Food Truck 5
Keoki's Paradise 17
Koloa Fish Market 7
La Spezia 7
Merriman's Fish House/Merriman's Gourmet Pizza & Burgers 11
Red Salt 19
Sueoka's Snack Shop 6
Tapas@Kukui'ula 11
Tortilla Republic 11
HOTELS
Grand Hyatt Kauai Resort & Spa 22
Kahala (Poipu Kai Resort) 21
Kauai Banyan Inn 4
Kauai Cove Cottage 12
Kiahuna Plantation Resort 18
Ko'a Kea Hotel & Resort 19
Kukui'ula 8
Marjorie's Kauai Inn 3
Nihi Kai Villas 19
Poipu Kapili Resort 15
Poipu Plantation B&B Inn & Vacation Rentals 20
Prince Kuhio 9
Sheraton Kauai Resort 16
Waikomo Stream Villas 14

MODERATE

La Spezia ★★★ ITALIAN The definition of charming, this much-needed stylish but cozy bistro in Old Kōloa Town doesn't accept reservations for parties of fewer than six—reason enough to make a few friends at the pool to join you for dinner. Still, walk-ins will find it worth the possible wait for a table, handmade from wine crates by co-owner Dan Seltzer (formerly of Casablanca and Dali Deli); don't hesitate to sit at the small but handsome bar either. Stalwarts on the seasonal, home-style menu include spicy veggie arrabbiata, rib-sticking lasagne Bolognese, pan-roasted chicken, seared pork tenderloin with capers, and hanger steak with Gorgonzola polenta. At breakfast or the expanded Sunday brunch, French toast made with Hawaiian sweet bread, Brie, bacon, and raspberry jam provides the ultimate guilty pleasure, balanced by the Caprese-style egg-white frittata.

5492 Kōloa Rd., Kōloa (across from the post office). www.laspeziakauai.com. ✆ **808/742-8824.** Reservations accepted for parties of 6 or more. Main courses $9–$14 breakfast, $14–$24 dinner, $12 Sun brunch. Breakfast Tues and Thurs–Sat 8am–11:30am, Wed 8:30–11:30am; dinner Tues–Sun 5–10pm; brunch Sun 8am–1pm.

Merriman's Gourmet Pizza & Burgers ★★ AMERICAN/ISLAND FARM A pioneer in Hawai'i Regional Cuisine, Maui-based chef Peter Merriman first expanded onto Kaua'i with his gourmet restaurant, **Merriman's Fish House ★★** (main courses $24–$59). Although it still merits a splurge, you're more likely to make repeat trips to this much more casual spot, located on the first floor below the Fish House. The thin-crust organic wheat pizzas ($1 more for gluten-free) are topped with island ingredients such as roasted Hāmākua mushrooms, kalua pork with grilled pineapple, or ahi with wasabi aioli in lieu of cheese; the vegan version has a surprisingly decadent kale pesto and hearty roasted vegetables. (Don't worry; you can still get pepperoni and sausage.) Burgers feature local grass-fed beef and lamb, although the turkey option, with Asian pear, white cheddar, and arugula, is also popular. Fries are extra but worth ordering, especially the ones with garlic and cilantro.

In the Shops at Kukui'ula, 2829 Ala Kalanikaumaka St., Po'ipū. www.merrimanshawaii.com. ✆ **808/742-2856.** Main courses $13–$20. Daily 11am–10pm. Live music Wed and Sun.

Tortilla Republic ★★ GOURMET MEXICAN This vibrant, bi-level restaurant offers two ways to experience its modern, sophisticated take on Mexican cuisine, each with menus based on natural, organic, and local ingredients where possible. Open for dinner on the upstairs veranda (book for sunset), the **Grill** specializes in exotic-for-Kaua'i seasonings: Sautéed black tiger shrimp are served with a sauce of *pipián rojo* (red squash seeds), while the day's fresh catch comes rubbed in ancho chili and a serrano cilantro citrus sauce. Order the table-made guacamole ($16) for sheer entertainment value. At lunch and dinner, the indoor/outdoor **Taqueria & Margarita Bar** offers simpler but still delicious dishes, including a trio of guajillo-rubbed grilled fish tacos. For weekend brunch, it steps it up a notch with dishes such as seared ahi hash and fresh corn and blueberry pancakes.

In the Shops at Kukui'ula, 2829 Ala Kalanikaumaka St., Po'ipū. http://tortillarepublic.com/hawaii. © **808/742-8884.** Dinner/brunch reservations recommended. **Grill:** Main courses $18–$32; Mon–Sat 5:30–9pm. **Taqueria:** Main courses $10–$15 brunch, $11–$15 lunch and dinner; Mon–Thur 11am–9pm, Fri 11am–10pm, Sat–Sun 9am–10pm. Happy hour daily 3–5pm.

INEXPENSIVE

In addition to the listings below, consider the food trucks in Old Town Kōloa, including **Kauai Food Truck ★**, serving hearty local fare in Knudsen Park across from Sueoka Market (www.facebook.com/kauaifoodtruck), and **Craving Thai ★,** dishing out noodles and curries at 3477 Weliweli Rd., next to Koloa Zipline (www.cravingthaikauai.com; © **808/634-9959**).

In the Kukui'ula strip mall north of the Po'ipū roundabout, **Da Crack ★** (© **808/742-9505**) is a takeout window where a line often forms for fish tacos with wasabi cream and the massive but relatively healthful burritos (vegan beans, brown rice).

Anuenue Cafe ★ (www.anuenuecafe.com; © **808/295-0109**) in Poipu Shopping Village opens daily at 6am, serving locally sourced omelets, pancakes, and burritos till 12:30pm, with salads, pastries, and prepared foods available till 1 or 2pm, depending on the surf.

Brick Oven Pizza ★ PIZZA There's nothing particularly gourmet about these pizzas, made with a hand-tossed, medium-thin, chewy crust (white with garlic butter, wheat, or, for $4 more, gluten-free) and the usual toppings, plus Portuguese sausage. Still, this local favorite is relatively easy on the budget the 12-slice pizzas are genuinely large, and there's a bountiful, all-you-can-eat buffet from 5 to 9pm Monday and Thursday ($17 adults, $13 children 4–12). Pastas, subs, and salads are basic but well priced. For island flavors, order the kimchi tofu or guava-glazed smoked pork appetizers at the bar, which has a surprisingly broad beer list. ***Note:*** Order takeout from here or the Kapa'a location through **Delivery Kaua'i** (www.deliverykauai.com; © **808/755-5377**).

2–2555 Kaumuali'i Hwy., Kalāheo (*mauka* side, across the street from Kalaheo Cafe & Coffee Co.). www.brickovenpizzahi.com. © **808/332-8561.** Kapa'a: 4-4361 Kūhiō Hwy. (*mauka* side, across from Kinipopo Shopping Village). © **808/823-8561.** Sandwiches $10–$11; medium (10-slice) pizzas $17–$25. Wed–Mon 11am–9pm; buffet Mon and Thur 5–9pm.

Kalaheo Café & Coffee Co. ★★ BAKERY CAFE/ISLAND FARM Whether you just grab a freshly baked cookie and cup of Kaua'i coffee to go or make a full meal of it, you'll quickly discover why visitors and locals jockey for parking spots at this casual restaurant and bakery. Early hours and hearty breakfasts (including convenient wraps to go) make it a popular stop for folks on the way to snorkel cruises or Waimea

Canyon. About a 15-minute drive from Po'ipū, the plantation-style cafe also offers a great alternative to high-priced resort dining. Greens grown nearby dominate the extensive salad list, while the rustic housemade buns pair nicely with grass-fed Kaua'i beef, veggie, or turkey burgers, among other plump sandwiches. Dinner is on the pricier side, but fresh seafood such as blackened ahi with kale Caesar and the salt-rubbed prime rib shine.

2–2560 Kaumuali'i Hwy., Kalāheo (*makai* side, across the street from Brick Oven Pizza). www.kalaheo.com. ✆ **808/332-5858.** Breakfast $5–$13; lunch $7–$15; dinner main courses $13–$30. Mon–Sat 6:30–11:30am and 11am–2:30pm; Tues–Thurs 5–8:30pm; Fri–Sat 5–9pm; Sun 6:30am–2pm.

West Side

With fewer hotels or residents who can afford pricey dining, the West Side offers mostly unassuming food options with limited hours (typically closed Sun) and inconsistent quality. This explains why many visitors just stop in Waimea for shave ice—try **Jo-Jo's Shave Ice ★** at 9691 Kaumuali'i Hwy., *makai* side, across from the high school (✆ **808/635-7615**)—or for luscious Roselani ice cream and tropical shakes at **Super Duper ★,** 9889 Waimea Rd. (✆ **808/338-1590**). Those heading up to Waimea Canyon or Kōke'e State Park can hit the **Lodge at Kōke'e ★,** 9400 Kaumuali'i Hwy. (✆ **808/335-6061**), for inexpensive local-style breakfast and lunch entrees ($4–$12); hikers will appreciate hearty Portuguese bean soup or chili, or a pick-me-up slice of *liliko'i* chiffon pie.

INEXPENSIVE

For casual breakfast and lunch ($7–$12), or just killer coconut handheld pies ($5), pop into **Gina's at Yumi's ★,** 9734 Kaumuali'i Hwy., *mauka* side by the theater (✆ **808/338-1731**). For lunch or early dinner, shrimp platters ($13) star at **The Shrimp Station ★,** 9652 Kaumuali'i Hwy., *makai side* at Mākeke Rd. (www.theshrimpstation.com; ✆ **808/338-1242**). If you don't want to get your hands messy peeling shrimp, order the chopped shrimp on large flour tacos, a fried shrimp burger, or the fried coconut shrimp plate with a zesty papaya ginger tartar sauce. The open-air picnic tables and trash cans do attract flies, so consider making yours a to-go order to eat at the beach. It's open daily 11am to 5pm, as is the Kapa'a location at 4-985 Kūhiō Hwy., Kapa'a (*mauka* side at Keaka Rd.; ✆ **808/821-0192**). **Ishihara Market ★★** (see "Plate Lunch, Bento & Poke," p. 580) also has good picnic fare.

MODERATE

Kaua'i Island Brewery & Grill ★★ BREWPUB The owners and brewmaster of the former Waimea Brewing Company opened this snazzier industrial/loft-style microbrewery and restaurant in Port Allen in 2012. The house *liliko'i* ale flavors the batter on fish and chips, but I prefer the silken ahi poke with seaweed salad or the ahi corn chowder. If

the ample appetizers don't fill you up, the burgers, sandwiches, and beef and seafood platters certainly will. The brewery has up to 10 house beers on tap. The open-air mezzanine provides an angled view of sunset over the harbor—and it can be mobbed when snorkel boats return midafternoon. Five 55-inch flatscreen TVs draw crowds for sports events.
4350 Waialo Rd., Port Allen. www.kauaiislandbrewing.com. © **808/335-0006.** Main courses $12–$25. Daily 11am–10pm. Happy hour 3:30–5:30 daily.

Wrangler's Steakhouse ★ STEAK/SEAFOOD Like a steer in a rodeo, service here can be poky or lightning fast, but as the only full-service restaurant in town, it's often worth it even if you have to sit a spell. At lunch, skip the time-warp salad bar with green Jell-O and tiny plates in favor of sandwiches or platters with fresh fish, Ni'ihau free-range lamb, or Makaweli (Kaua'i) grass-fed beef. Tempura shrimp, teriyaki beef, and rice come in the plantation-style lunchbox known as a kau kau tin. Dinner prices rise enough to consider driving to the South Shore instead. Also owned by the Faye family, the cozy, even more informal **Saddle Room ★★** next door serves similar burgers and fish sandwiches, but with a more ambitious, locally sourced cocktail menu, such as the Polihale Sunset with Kaua'i tangerines and pineapple vodka, and intriguing specials such as *'opihi* (limpet) poke or corned-beef patties with *'ulu* (breadfruit). Alas, it's only open a few nights for dinner and Sunday brunch (see hours below); don't miss the Bloody Mary with peppered bacon.
9852 Kaumuali'i Hwy., Waimea (*makai* side at Halepule Rd.). © **808/338-1218. Wrangler's:** Main courses $10–$14 lunch, $18–$34 dinner. Mon–Thurs 11am–8:30pm; Fri 11am–9pm; Sat 5–9pm. **Saddle Room:** Burgers and small plates $7–$17. Thurs 4–9pm; Fri 4–10pm; Sat 11am–10pm; Sun 11am–4pm.

KAUA'I SHOPPING

Kaua'i has more than a dozen open-air shopping centers and historic districts well suited to browsing, so souvenir and gift hunters are unlikely to leave the island empty-handed—though often it's with items made elsewhere. To find something unique to the Garden Isle, just look for the purple **Kaua'i made** logo. The image of a *ho'okupu,* the ti-leaf wrapping for special presents, means the county certifies that these handicrafts and food items were made on the island using local materials where possible, and in relatively small batches. Search for stores or purveyors by type of product or region at **http://kauaimade.net**.

Below are some of the island's more distinctive shopping stops.

East Side

LĪHU'E

The island's largest mall, **Kukui Grove Shopping Center,** 3-2600 Kaumuali'i Hwy., *makai* side at Nāwiliwili Road (www.kukuigrovecenter.com), attracts locals with department stores such as **Macy's** and **Sears;**

visitors on a tight schedule or budget should browse the competitively priced, locally made foodstuffs (coffees, jams, cookies, and the like) at **Longs Drugs** (© **808/245-7785**). The mall's family-run **Déjà Vu Surf Hawaii** (www.dejavusurf.com; © **808/245-2174**) has a large selection of local and national brands.

Anchor Cove (3416 Rice St.) and **Harbor Mall** (3501 Rice St.), two small shopping centers near Nāwiliwili Harbor, mostly offer typical T-shirts, aloha wear, and souvenirs. One exception is Harbor Mall's **Beachrail Lines** (© **808/245-6732**), which sells vintage toys, kites, Kala ʻukuleles, miniature trains—even Hawaiian-themed metal soldiers. Fans of tropical-print fabrics, batiks, Hawaiian quilts, and aloha wear will want to seek out **Kapaia Stitchery,** 3-3351 Kūhiō Hwy., *mauka* side at Laukini Road (www.kapaia-stitchery.com; © **808/245-2281**).

The 1930s mansion at **Kilohana Plantation,** 3-2087 Kaumualiʻi Hwy. (*mauka* side, next to Kauaʻi Community College; http://kilohanakauai.com/wp), provides a handsome setting for a half-dozen boutiques selling locally made, Hawaiian-inspired artwork, jewelry, clothing, and vintage Hawaiiana. Don't miss the handmade guava and sea salt caramels at **Kauaʻi Sweet Shoppe** (www.kauaisweetshoppe.com; © **808/245-8458**) or the stand-alone **Kōloa Rum Co.** (www.koloarum.com; © **808/246-8900**), which carries five kinds of locally made rum, rum-based treats, and nonalcoholic goodies.

COCONUT COAST

At press time, **Coconut MarketPlace,** 4-484 Kūhiō Hwy., Kapaʻa (*makai* side at Aleka Loop; www.coconutmarketplace.com), remained under renovation, but it's still a haven for low-cost souvenirs. One of the MarketPlace shops, **Auntie Lynda's Treasures** (www.hawaiianjewelryandgift.com; © **808/821-1780**) has a very eclectic collection of woodcarvings, jewelry, and tchotchkes—the staff is happy to chat, too. In Wailua, **Pagoda,** 4-369 Kūhiō Hwy. (*makai* side, across from Kintaro; © **808/821-2172**), ably fills its niche with Chinese antiques and curios, Hawaiiana, Asian-inspired decor, candles, soaps, and other gifts.

The historic (and hippie) district of Kapaʻa offers an intriguing mix of shops, cafes, and galleries. **Hula Girl,** 4-1340 Kūhiō Hwy. (*makai* side at Kauwila St.; www.ilovehulagirl.com; © **808/822-1950**), not only sells women's resort wear (much of it made in Hawaiʻi), but also aloha shirts, boardshorts, and other menswear, plus tiki-style barware, island-made soaps, and accessories. Natural fibers rule the day at **Island Hemp & Cotton,** 4–1373 Kūhiō Hwy. (*mauka* side at Huluʻili St.; www.islandhemp.com; © **808/821-0225**), where the stylish men's and women's clothing lines also include linen, silk, and bamboo creations, which can be paired with long flowery scarves, beaded purses, and leather bracelets.

Hanalei Center shops, in Hanalei.

North Shore

KĪLAUEA

On the way to Kauapea (Secret) Beach and the lighthouse, **Kong Lung Historic Market Center,** at the corner of Keneke Street and Kīlauea Road (http://konglungkauai.com), deserves its own slot on the itinerary, with a bakery, bistro, and a half-dozen chic shops in vintage buildings with historical markers. Of the stores, the flagship **Kong Lung Trading** (www.konglung.com; ✆ **808/828-1822**) is a showcase for Asian-themed ceramics, jewelry, books, and home accessories, including sake sets and hand-turned Hawaiian wood bowls. Souvenir seekers can find less pricey options at the factory store of **Island Soap & Candle Works** (www.islandsoap.com; ✆ **808/828-1955**), renowned for its Surfer's Salve, tropical soaps, and soy candles in coconut shells.

PRINCEVILLE

Although the two-level **Princeville Center,** off Kūhiō Highway past the main Princeville entrance (www.princevillecenter.com), is mostly known for its inexpensive dining and resident-focused businesses, the **Hawaiian Music Store** kiosk (no phone) outside Foodland grocery has good deals on a large selection of CDs. **Magic Dragon Toy & Art Supply** (✆ **808/826-9144**) has an array of rainy-day entertainment for kids.

HANALEI

As you enter Hanalei, look for **Ola's Hanalei,** 5-5016 Kūhiō Hwy., *makai* side, next to Dolphin restaurant (http://olashanalei.com; ✆ **808/826-6937**). Opened in 1982 by award-winning artist Doug Britt and wife Sharon, this compact gallery features Doug's whimsical paintings, wooden toy boats, and furniture made from *objets trouvés,* plus engaging jewelry, glassware, koa boxes, and other works by Hawai'i and Mainland artisans. The new **Hanalei Land Company** complex at 5-5070 Kūhiō Hwy., *makai* side by Hanalei Taro & Juice Co., hosts **Mālie Organics Lifestyle Boutique** (www.malie.com), offering the Kaua'i company's signature line of bath and beauty products based on distillations of island plants, including the native *maile* vine (not to be confused with *mālie,* which means "calm" or "serene").

The center of town reveals more of Hanalei's bohemian side, with two eclectic shopping and dining complexes in historic buildings facing each other on Kūhiō Highway. In the two-story rabbit warren of **Ching Young Village Shopping Center** (www.chingyoungvillage.com), **Divine Planet** (www.divine-planet.com; © **808/826-8970**) brims with beads, star-shaped lanterns, silver jewelry from Thailand and India, and Balinese quilts. **On the Road to Hanalei** (© **808/826-7360**) also stocks unique gifts, from colorful pareos and clever figurines of Kaua'i roosters to Japanese pottery and African masks.

Across the street, the old Hanalei Schoolhouse is now the **Hanalei Center,** with two true gems tucked out of view: **Yellowfish Trading Company** (© **808/826-1227**) and **Havaiki Oceanic and Tribal Art** (www.havaikiart.com; © **808/826-7606**). At Yellowfish, retro hula girl lamps, vintage textiles and pottery, and collectible Hawaiiana mingle with reproduction signs, painted guitars, and other beach-shack musts, with ever-changing inventory. The owners of Havaiki have sailed across the Pacific many times to obtain their museum-quality collection of gleaming wood bowls and fishhooks, exotic masks, shell jewelry, and intricately carved weapons and paddles; they also sell CDs, handmade cards, and other less expensive but tasteful gifts.

South Shore

KŌLOA

Between the tree tunnel road and beaches of Po'ipū, **Old Kōloa Town** (www.oldkoloa.com) has the usual tourist tees and trinkets, but also two sources of well-made local items and the island's best wine shop. The factory store of **Island Soap & Candle Works** (© **808/742-1945**) is similar to the one in Kīlauea (see website above), while the **Koa Store** (www.thekoastore.com; © **808/742-1214**) showcases boxes, picture frames, and other small pieces by local woodworkers. **The Wine Shop** (www.thewineshopkauai.com; © **808/742-7305**) lives up to its name but also sells high-quality, locally made treats such as Monkeypod Jam's tropical curds and Hula Baby biscotti.

PO'IPŪ

Poipu Shopping Village, 2360 Kiahuna Plantation Dr. (www.poipushoppingvillage.com), is home to a couple of independent clothing

Fruit for sale at roadside shack.

boutiques as well as local branches of Hawai'i resort and surfwear chains. But the newer **Shops at Kukui'ula,** just off the Po'ipū Road roundabout (www.kukuiula.com), has even more intriguing—and often expensive—options spread among plantation-style cottages and flowering hibiscus. **Palm Palm** (www.palmpalmkauai.com; **© 808/742-1131**) prides itself on exclusive, limited-edition collections of items like Hawaiian scrimshaw and glassware etched with tropical images, as well as women's designer clothing and gifts. Amid all the high-end chic, surfers will feel right at home in **Poipu Surf** (www.poipusurf.com; **© 808/742-8797**) and **Quiksilver** (run by Déjà Vu Surf Hawaii; www.dejavusurf.com; **© 808/742-8088**).

KALĀHEO

Flavored with guava, Kona coffee, macadamia nuts, and other tropical ingredients, the crisp butter cookies of the **Kauai Kookie Kompany** are ubiquitous in Hawai'i, but even better than a trip to the factory store in Hanapēpē (1-3529 Kaumuali'i Hwy., *makai* side) is a stop at the **Kauai Kookie Bakery & Kitchen** complex in Kalāheo, 2-2436 Kaumuali'i Hwy., *makai* side (**© 808/332-0821**). One storefront is a small cafe selling specialty baked goods as well as a variety of "kookies"; the other is a vast space with even more fresh treats to consume on the spot or buy as *omiyage* (food gifts), a Japanese-inspired local tradition.

kaua'i FARMER'S MARKETS

Even if you're not staying in a place with a kitchen, a trip to one of the county-sponsored **Sunshine Markets** is a fun glimpse into island life, with shoppers queued up before the official start—listen for a yell or car honk—to buy fresh produce at rock-bottom prices. Markets end in 2 hours at the latest; arrive in time for the start, especially in Kōloa and Kapa'a. The best Sunshine Markets for visitors include

- **Monday:** noon, **Kōloa Ball Park,** off Maluhia Rd., on the left heading toward Old Town Kōloa.
- **Tuesday:** 3pm, **Kalāheo Neighborhood Center,** Pāpālina Rd. off Kaumuali'i Hwy. (*makai* side).
- **Wednesday:** 3pm, **Kapa'a New Town Park,** Kahau St. at Olohena Rd.
- **Thursday:** 4:30pm, **Kīlauea Neighborhood Center,** Keneke St. off Kīlauea (Lighthouse) Rd.
- **Friday:** 3pm, **Vidinha Stadium parking lot,** Ho'olako Rd. (off Hwy. 51), Līhu'e.

For the best selection of organic produce, visit North Shore farmer's markets. In **Kīlauea**, that includes the Sunshine Market (above) and the privately run **Namahana Farmer's Market** (www.anainahou.org; ✆ **808/828-2118**) at Anaina Hou Community Park in Kīlauea (*mauka* side of Kūhiō Hwy., next to the mini-golf; Sat 9am–1pm and Mon 2pm–dusk).

In Hanalei, the popular **Waipā Farmer's Market** (www.waipafoundation.org; ✆ **808/826-9969**) takes place every Tuesday at 2pm in a field just west of Hanalei, *mauka* side of Kūhiō Hwy., between the Wai'oli and Waipā one-lane bridges. Some vendors also sell baked goods, jewelry, and other crafts, as they do from 9:30am to noon Saturday at Hanalei's **Hale Halawai** ballpark (www.halehalawai.org; ✆ **808/826-1011**), Kūhiō Hwy., *mauka* side at Mahimahi Rd., next to the green church.

West Side

HANAPĒPĒ

Known for its Friday-night festival (see "Kaua'i Nightlife," p. 599), the historic town center of Hanapēpē and its dozen-plus art galleries are just as pleasant to peruse by day, especially the cheery paintings at the **Bright Side Gallery,** 3890 Hanapēpē Rd. (www.thebrightsidegallery.com; ✆ **808/634-8671**), and the playful tiles and other ceramics of **Banana Patch Studio,** 3865 Hanapēpē Rd. (www.bananapatchstudio.com; ✆ **808/335-5944**). The courtyard passage next to Little Fish Coffee leads to **MoonBow Magic Gift Gallery,** 3900 Hanapēpē Rd. (www.moonbowmagic.com; ✆ **808/335-5890**), which stocks an amazing potpourri of colorful gifts and baubles (such as beaded geckos and Kaua'i chickens), Ni'ihau shells, and other jewelry.

If the door is open, the store is open at tiny **Taro Ko Chips Factory,** 3940 Hanapēpē Rd. (✆ **808/335-5586**), where dry-land taro farmer Dale Nagamine slices and fries his harvest—along with potatoes, purple sweet potatoes, and breadfruit—into delectable chips for $5 a bag (cash only). The wares of **Aloha Spice Company,** 3857 Hanapēpē Rd. (www.alohaspice.com; ✆ **808/335-5960**), include grill-ready seasonings with a base of Hawaiian sea salt, and Hawaiian cane sugar infused with hibiscus, vanilla, or *liliko'i*. Pop into **Talk Story Bookstore,** 3785 Hanapēpē Rd. (www.talkstorybookstore.com; ✆ **808/335-6469**), for the island's biggest trove of new, used, and out-of-print books, plus vintage music and locally made gifts; the lounging cat is a bonus.

PORT ALLEN

Chocolate fiends need to try the luscious handmade truffles, fudge, and "opihi" (chocolate-covered shortbread, caramel, and macadamia nuts in the shape of a shell) at **Kauai Chocolate Company** in nearby Port Allen, 4341 Waialo Rd. (www.kauaichocolate.us; ✆ **808/335-0448**).

WAIMEA

The new owners of **Collectibles and Fine Junque Spice of Life,** 9821 Kaumuali'i Hwy. (*mauka* side, next to the fire station), have added North Shore honey, nursery plants, and solar-powered camping provisions such as solar flashlights to the bounty of vintage Hawaiiana, antiques, and ephemera. Like Kauai Kookies, the passionfruit (*liliko'i*) products of **Aunty Lilikoi**—including jelly, butter, wasabi mustard, and salad dressing—are increasingly found around the state, but the factory store at 9875 Waimea Rd., across from the Captain Cook statue (www.auntylilikoi.com; ✆ **808/338-1296**), offers shipping and in-store-only delicious baked goods, such as scones, bars, and fudge.

Heading upcountry, pop into the gift shops of the **Kōke'e Museum** (www.kokee.org; ✆ **808/335-9975**) and **Kōke'e Lodge** (www.kokeelodge.com; ✆ **808/335-6061**), the former for Kaua'i- and nature-themed books, maps, and DVDs, and the latter for a judicious array of souvenirs, island foods, and locally made crafts.

KAUA'I NIGHTLIFE

Local nightlife is more suited to moonlight strolls than late-night partying, but if you're simply searching for live Hawaiian music, you're in luck. Most nights virtually every hotel lounge presents a slack key guitarist singing Hawaiian *mele,* while many off-resort restaurants offer live Hawaiian music and other genres Thursday to Saturday.

Of the resort nightspots, **Duke's Barefoot Bar** (www.dukeskauai.com; ✆ **808/246-9599**), inside the Kaua'i Marriott Resort, has long drawn a crowd of visitors and locals, especially at *pau hana* (end of work) on Friday. The downstairs bar has live Hawaiian music Thursday through Monday 4 to 6pm, and Thursday through Sunday 8:30 to 10:30pm.

The view isn't as memorable, but the pupu are tastier and the music more varied in the lounge of **Hukilau Lanai** (www.hukilaukauai.com; ✆ **808/822-0600**) inside the Kaua'i Coast Resort at the Beachboy, 520

Aleka Loop, Kapa'a; top musicians playing Hawaiian, jazz, country, and blues perform Tuesday through Saturday from 6 to 9pm. The Grand Hyatt (www.grandhyattkauai.com; ✆ **808/741-1234**) presents live jazz and pop 8 to 11pm nightly at **Stevenson's Library,** a book-lined lounge and sushi bar; the Hyatt's **Seaview Terrace** offers nightly Hawaiian music from 6 to 9pm, along with gorgeous sunset views.

You'll meet more locals—and pay a good deal less for your drinks—by leaving the resorts. Here are highlights from around the island:

EAST SIDE A combination sports bar, sushi bar, family restaurant, and nightclub, **Rob's Good Times Grill,** in the Rice Shopping Center, 4303 Rice St., Līhu'e (www.kauaisportsbarandgrill.com; ✆ **808/246-0311**), bustles with live music, karaoke, swing and salsa dancing, and DJs for club dancing; check online for the current schedule. **Mahikō Lounge,** the vintage living room of the Kilohana Plantation mansion, *mauka* side of Kaumuali'i Hwy. in Līhu'e (http://kilohanakauai.com/wp; ✆ **808/245-5608**), makes artisan cocktails with fresh-crushed sugarcane and has live music (Fri–Sun) and $5 happy-hour specials (Mon–Sat 4–5:30pm) from Gaylord's. Old Kapa'a Town throws a party the first Saturday of the month with an **Art Walk** that includes live entertainment, sidewalk vendors, and extended shopping hours 5 to 9pm.

Tahiti Nui.

NORTH SHORE **Tiki Iniki** (www.tikiiniki.com; ✆ **808/431-4242**), tucked behind Ace Hardware in the Princeville Center, is a cheeky tiki bar/restaurant that Michele Rundgren and her rock-musician husband, Todd, opened in 2013. Nightly cocktail specials and theme nights keep it hopping; table reservations are recommended. Opened in 1963, **Tahiti Nui,** 5-5134 Kūhiō Hwy., Hanalei (www.thenui.com; ✆ **808/826-6277**), is pretty much as it appears in *The Descendants:* a down-home, family-friendly restaurant with live Hawaiian music nightly. Live music cranks up at **Hanalei Gourmet,** in the Old Hanalei Schoolhouse, 5–5161 Kūhiō Hwy. (✆ **808/826-2524**), at 6pm Sunday and 8pm Wednesday.

SOUTH SHORE **Keoki's Paradise,** a popular restaurant in Poipu Shopping Village (www.keokisparadise.com; ✆ **808/742-7534**), offers live music in its tropical bar most nights and dance music Thursday to Saturday. **The Shops at Kukui'ula** (http://theshopsatkukuiula.com) hosts a *kani kapila* (jam) at 6:30pm on Friday, plus live music and sidewalk vendors at the **Kukui'ula Art Walk** (second Sat of month; 6–9pm). In the same shopping center, **Tapas@Kukui'ula** (see p. 588) starts late (10pm Fri and Sat), with live music, DJs, and drink specials.

WEST SIDE **Kaua'i Island Brewery & Grill,** 4350 Waialo Rd., Port Allen (www.kauaiislandbrewing.com;✆ **808/335-0006**), boasts three pinball machines (a big deal here) and five big high-def TVs for sports events. It also hosts frequent open-mic nights.

The *tūtuū kāne* (granddaddy) of local art events is **Hanapēpē Friday Night Festival and Art Walk** (www.hanapepe.org), every Friday from 6 to 9pm along Hanapēpē Road, featuring food trucks and live music on the street and in shops and galleries.

PLANNING YOUR TRIP TO HAWAI'I

10

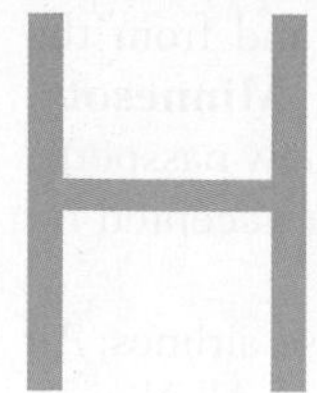awai'i is rich in natural and cultural wonders, and each island has something unique to offer. With so much vying for your attention, planning a trip can be bewildering. Here we've compiled everything you need to know before escaping to the islands.

The first thing to do: **Decide where you want to go.** Read through each chapter to see which islands fit the profile and offer the activities you're looking for. We strongly recommend that you limit your island-hopping to one island per week. If you decide to visit more than one in a week, be warned: You could spend much of your precious vacation time in airports and checking in and out of hotels. Not much fun!

Our second tip is to **fly directly to the island of your choice;** doing so can save you a 2-hour layover in Honolulu and another plane ride. O'ahu, the Big Island, Maui, and Kaua'i now all receive direct flights from the Mainland.

So let's get on with the process of planning your trip. For pertinent facts and on-the-ground resources in Hawai'i, turn to "Fast Facts: Hawai'i," at the end of this chapter on p. 610.

GETTING THERE

By Plane

Most major U.S. and many international carriers fly to **Honolulu International Airport** (HNL) on O'ahu. Some also offer direct flights to **Kahului Airport** (OGG) on Maui, **Līhu'e Airport** (LIH) on Kaua'i, and **Kona International Airport** (KOA) and **Hilo Airport** (ITO) on the Big Island. If you can fly directly to the island of your choice, you'll be spared a 2-hour layover in Honolulu and another plane ride. If you're heading to **Moloka'i Airport** (MKK) or **Lāna'i Airport** (LNY), you'll have the easiest connections if you fly into Honolulu or Kahului. See island chapters for detailed information on direct flights to each island.

Hawaiian Airlines offers flights from more mainland U.S. gateways than any other airline. Hawaiian's easy-to-navigate website makes finding the cheapest fares a cinch. Its closest competitor, price-wise, is **Virgin America Airlines,** which flies nonstop from San Francisco and Los Angeles. **Alaska Airlines** offers daily nonstop flights from West Coast cities, including Anchorage, Seattle, Portland, and Oakland. From points farther east, **United, American, Continental,** and **Delta** all fly to Hawai'i with nonstop service to Honolulu and most neighbor islands. If you're having difficulty finding an affordable fare, try routing your

FACING PAGE: **Hawaiian sunset.**

flight through Las Vegas. It's a huge hub for traffic to and from the islands. ***NOTE:* Residents of New York, Louisiana, Minnesota, New Hampshire, and American Samoa** will need to show passports; driver's licenses from these states/territories are no longer accepted for air travel.

For travel from beyond the U.S. mainland, check these airlines: Air Canada, Air New Zealand, Qantas Airways, Japan Air Lines, All Nippon Airways (ANA), the Taiwan-based China Airlines, Korean Air, and Philippine Airlines. Hawaiian Airlines also flies nonstop to Australia, American Samoa, Philippines, Tahiti, South Korea, and Japan.

ARRIVING AT THE AIRPORT

IMMIGRATION & CUSTOMS CLEARANCE International visitors arriving by air should cultivate patience and resignation before setting foot on U.S. soil. U.S. airports have considerable security practices in place. Clearing Customs and Immigration can take as long as 2 hours.

AGRICULTURAL SCREENING AT AIRPORTS At Honolulu International and the neighbor-island airports, baggage and passengers bound for the Mainland must be screened by agriculture officials. Officials will confiscate fresh local produce (avocados, bananas, and mangoes) in the name of fruit-fly control. Pineapples, coconuts, and papayas inspected and certified for export; boxed flowers; leis without seeds; and processed foods (macadamia nuts, coffee, jams, dried fruit, and the like) will pass.

GETTING AROUND HAWAI'I

For additional advice on travel within each island, see "Getting Around" in the individual island chapters.

Interisland Flights

The major interisland carriers have cut way back on the number of interisland flights. Airlines suggest showing up at least 90 minutes before your flight. This is especially true on O'ahu and during holidays. You can get by with 60 minutes at the neighbor-island airports.

Hawai'i has one major interisland carrier, **Hawaiian Airlines** (www.hawaiianair.com; ✆ **800/367-5320**), and two commuter airlines, **Island Air** (www.islandair.com; ✆ **800/323-3345**) and **Mokulele Airlines** (www.mokuleleairlines.com; ✆ **866/260-7070**). The commuter flights service the neighbor islands' more remote airports and tend to be on small planes; you'll board from the tarmac and weight restrictions apply.

By Shuttle

Roberts Hawai'i Express Shuttle (www.robertshawaii.com; ✆ **800/831-5541** or 808/539-9400), offers curb-to-curb shuttle service to and from the airports on O'ahu, Hawai'i, Maui, and Kaua'i. Booking is a breeze on their new website.

By Bus

Public transit is spotty—O'ahu has an adequate public transportation service, but even so, it's set up for residents, not tourists carrying coolers and beach toys (all carry-ons must fit on your lap or under the bus seat). **TheBus** (www.thebus.org; ✆ **808/848-5555**) delivers you to destinations around the island for $2.50. If you're traveling on a shoestring and have the patience of a saint, this could be a transportation option for you. Bus nos. 19 and 20 travel regularly between the airport and Waikīkī; the trip takes about an hour.

The neighbor-island buses are even less visitor-friendly. One-way rides cost $2. The **Kaua'i Bus** (www.kauai.gov/bus; ✆ **808/246-8110**) stops at Līhu'e Airport twice every hour, but connections to towns outside of Līhu'e are few and far between. On the Valley Isle, the **Maui Bus** (www.mauicounty.gov—hover over the "Services" option and then choose "Bus Service Information"; ✆ **808/871-4838**) picks up at Kahului Airport every 90 minutes and delivers riders to a transfer station at Queen Ka'ahumanu Mall. The **Hele-On Bus** (www.heleonbus.org; ✆ **808/961-8744**) on Hawai'i Island visits the Hilo Airport every 90 minutes and Kona Airport once a day.

By Car

Bottom line: rent a car. You will need your own wheels to get around the islands, especially if you plan to explore outside your resort—and you absolutely should. As discussed above, public transit is unreliable, and taxis are obscenely expensive.

That said, Hawai'i has some of the priciest car-rental rates in the country. The most expensive is the island of Lāna'i, where four-wheel-drive (4WD) vehicles cost a small fortune. Rental cars are often at a premium on Kaua'i, Moloka'i, and Lāna'i and may be sold out on any island over holiday weekends, so be sure to book well ahead. In fact, we recommend reserving your car as soon as you book your airfare.

To rent a car in Hawai'i, you must be at least 25 years of age and have a valid driver's license and credit card. ***Note:*** If you're visiting from abroad and plan to rent a car in the United States, keep in mind that foreign driver's licenses are usually recognized in the U.S., but you should get an international one if your home license is not in English.

At Honolulu International Airport and most neighbor-island airports, you'll find many major car-rental agencies, including **Alamo, Avis, Budget, Dollar, Enterprise, Hertz, National,** and **Thrifty.** Most of the islands have independent rental companies that

Stay off the Cellphone

Talking on a cellphone while driving in Hawaii is a big no-no. Fines start at $297 and increase in school or construction zones. Save yourself the money; if you *have* to take a photo of that rainbow, pull over.

A Weeklong Cruise Through the Islands

If you're looking for a taste of several islands in 7 days, consider **Norwegian Cruise Line** (www.ncl.com; © **866/234-7350**), the only cruise line that operates year-round in Hawai'i. NCL's 2,240-passenger ship *Pride of America* circles Hawai'i, stopping on four islands: the Big Island, Maui, Kaua'i, and O'ahu.

operate outside of the airport, often for cheaper rates; check individual island chapters. If you're traveling with windsurfing or other sports gear on Maui, check out **Al West's Surf Vans** (www.mauivans.com; © **808/877-0090**).

GASOLINE Gas prices in Hawai'i, always much higher than on the U.S. mainland, vary from island to island. Expect to pay around $4 a gallon, and as much as $5 a gallon on Lāna'i and Moloka'i. Check www.gasbuddy.com to find the cheapest gas in your area.

INSURANCE Hawai'i is a no-fault state, which means that if you don't have collision-damage insurance, you are required to pay for all damages before you leave the state, whether or not the accident was your fault. Your personal car insurance may provide rental-car coverage; check before you leave home. Bring your insurance identification card if you decline the optional insurance, which usually costs from $9 to $45 a day. Obtain the name of your company's local claim representative before you go. Some credit card companies also provide collision-damage insurance for their customers; check with yours before you rent.

DRIVING RULES Hawai'i state law mandates that all car passengers must wear a **seat belt** and all infants must be strapped into a car seat. You'll pay a $92 fine if you don't buckle up. **Pedestrians** always have the right of way, even if they're not in the crosswalk. You can turn **right on red** after a full and complete stop, unless otherwise posted. Hand-held cellphones and electronic devices are prohibited while driving.

ROAD MAPS The best and most detailed maps for activities are published by **Franko Maps** (www.frankosmaps.com); they feature a host of island maps, plus a terrific "Hawaiian Reef Creatures Guide" for snorkelers curious about those fish they spot underwater. Free road maps are published by ***This Week*** magazine, a visitor publication available on O'ahu, the Big Island, Maui, and Kaua'i.

Another good source is the **University of Hawai'i Press maps,** which include a detailed network of island roads, large-scale insets of towns, historical and contemporary points of interest, parks, beaches, and hiking trails. If you can't find them in a bookstore near you, contact **University of Hawai'i Press,** 2840 Kolowalu St., Honolulu, HI 96822 (www.uhpress.hawaii.edu; © **888/UH-PRESS** [847-7377]). For topographic maps of the islands, go to the **U.S. Geological Survey** site (https://pubs.er.usgs.gov).

SPECIAL-INTEREST TRIPS & TOURS

This section presents an overview of special-interest trips, tours, and outdoor excursions in Hawai'i. See individual island chapters for detailed information on the best local outfitters and tour-guide operators—as well as tips for exploring on your own. Each island chapter discusses the best spots to set out on your own, from the top offshore snorkel and dive spots to great daylong hikes, as well as the federal, state, and county agencies that can help you with hikes on public property. We also list references for spotting birds, plants, and sea life. Always use the resources available to inquire about weather, trail, or surf conditions; water availability; and other conditions before you take off on your adventure.

Air Tours

Nothing beats getting a bird's-eye view of Hawai'i. Some of the islands' most stunning scenery can't be seen any other way. You'll have your choice of aircraft here: **helicopter, small fixed-wing plane,** or, on O'ahu, **seaplane.** For wide open spaces such as the lava fields of Hawai'i Volcanoes National Park, a fixed-wing plane is the safest and most affordable option. But for exploring tight canyons and valleys, helicopters have an advantage: They can hover. Only a helicopter can bring you face to face with waterfalls in remote places like Mount Wai'ale'ale on Kaua'i and Maui's little-known Wall of Tears, up near the summit of Pu'u Kukui.

Today's pilots are part Hawaiian historian, part DJ, part amusement-ride operator, and part tour guide, sharing anecdotes about Hawai'i's flora, fauna, history, and culture. Top trips include:

- **Nāpali Coast,** Kaua'i, where you soar over the painted landscape of Waimea Canyon, known as the "Grand Canyon of the Pacific," and visit the cascading falls of Mount Wai'ale'ale, one of the wettest spots on Earth.
- **Haleakalā National Park and West Maui,** where you skirt the edges of Haleakalā's otherworldly crater before plunging into the deep, pristine valleys of the West Maui Mountains.
- **Hawai'i Volcanoes National Park** on the Big Island, where you stare into the molten core of a live volcano and watch lava spill into the sea.

Farm Tours

Overalls and garden spades might not be the first images that come to mind when planning your Hawai'i vacation, but a tour of a lush and bountiful island farm should be on your itinerary. Agritourism has become an important new income stream for Hawai'i farmers, who often struggle with the rising costs of doing business in paradise. Farm tours benefit everyone: The farmer gets extra cash, visitors gain an intimate understanding of where and how their food is produced, and fertile farmlands stay in production—preserving Hawai'i's rural heritage. There are so many diverse and inspiring farms to choose from: **100-year-old Kona coffee farms,** bean-to-bar **chocolate plantations, orchid nurseries,** an award-winning **goat dairy,** and even a **vodka farm!**

With its massive cattle ranches, tropical flower nurseries, and coffee-covered hillsides, the Big Island is the agricultural heart of Hawai'i. But each of the islands has farms worth visiting. Many agri-tours include sumptuous tasting sessions, fascinating historical accounts, and tips for growing your own food at home. See each island's "Exploring" section for details on visiting local farms.

On the Big Island, **Hawai'i Forest & Trail** (www.hawaii-forest.com; ✆ **808/331-8505**) visits tropical fruit and coffee farms as part of their whole-day tours. Individual coffee growers open their orchards up as well (see page 185).

Maui Country Farm Tours (www.mauicountryfarmtours.com; ✆ **808/283-9131**) offers a gorgeous overview of agriculture on the Valley Isle, traveling through working sugar and pineapple plantations and stopping at a lavender farm, goat dairy, and vodka distillery.

National Parks

Hawai'i boasts some of the oldest national parks in the system—and the only one with an erupting volcano. If you plan on visiting both Maui and Hawai'i islands, purchase a tri-park pass for $50. It allows unlimited access for 1 year to Haleakalā National Park (both the summit and Kīpahulu), Hawai'i Volcanoes National Park, and Pu'uhonua o Hōnaunau National Historical Park. Even if you visit only two of these parks, it pays for itself.

Volunteer Vacations & Ecotourism

If you're looking to swap sunbathing for something more memorable on your next trip to Hawai'i, consider volunteering while on vacation. Rewards include new friends and access to spectacular wilderness areas that are otherwise off-limits.

Check out the **Hawai'i Ecotourism Association** (www.hawaiiecotourism.org; ✆ **808/235-5431**), a comprehensive site that lists ecotourism volunteer opportunities, such as seabird habitat restoration. Local ecotourism opportunities are also discussed in the individual island chapters.

The **Surfrider Foundation** organizes beach and reef cleanups and has several active chapters throughout the islands: O'ahu (https://oahu.surfrider.org); Maui (https://maui.surfrider.org); Kaua'i (https://kauai.surfrider.org); and, on the Big Island, Kona (https://kona.surfrider.org) and Hilo (https://hilo.surfrider.org). And what could be more exciting than keeping watch over nesting sea turtles? Contact the **University of Hawai'i Sea Grant College Program** (© **808/956-7031**) and the **Hawai'i Wildlife Fund** (www.wildhawaii.org; © **808/280-8124**) to see if they need help monitoring marine life.

For a truly novel experience, sign up on the waitlist to volunteer with **Kaho'olawe Island Restoration Commission** (www.kahoolawe.hawaii.gov/volunteer.shtml; © **808/243-5020**). You'll travel by boat from Maui to Kaho'olawe, an uninhabited island that the U.S. military used as target practice for decades. Plant by plant, volunteers bring life back to the barren island, once a significant site for Hawaiian navigators. A week here is a cultural immersion unlike any other.

A great alternative to hiring a private guide is taking a trip with the **Nature Conservancy** or the **Sierra Club.** Both organizations offer guided hikes in preserves and special areas during the year, as well as day- to week-long volunteer work trips to restore habitats and trails, and root out invasive plants. It's a chance to see the "real" Hawai'i—including wilderness areas that are ordinarily off-limits.

The Sierra Club offers half- or all-day hikes to beautiful, remote spots on O'ahu, Kaua'i, the Big Island, and Maui. Knowledgeable volunteers lead the trips and share a wealth of cultural and botanical information. Hikes are classified as easy, moderate, or strenuous; some (but not all) incorporate a few hours of volunteer work. Donations of $3 for Sierra Club members and $5 for nonmembers (bring exact change) are recommended. Contact the **Hawai'i Chapter of the Sierra Club** (www.sierraclubhawaii.com; © **808/538-6616** on O'ahu).

All Nature Conservancy hikes and work trips are free (donations appreciated). However, you must reserve a spot. The hikes are offered once a month on Maui and Moloka'i, and occasionally on O'ahu. Contact the **Nature Conservancy of Hawai'i** (www.nature.org/hawaii; © **808/537-4508** on O'ahu; © **808/572-7849** on Maui; © **808/553-5236** on Moloka'i; and © **808/587-6257** on Kaua'i).

Watersports Excursions

The same Pacific Ocean surrounds all of the Hawaiian Islands, but the varying topography of each shoreline makes certain spots superior for watersports. If **surfing** is your passion, head to O'ahu. You'll find gentle waves at Waikīkī and adrenaline-laced action on the famed North Shore. Maui has plenty of surf breaks, too; plus, it's the birthplace of **windsurfing** and a top **kitesurfing** destination. Beginners and pros alike will find perfect conditions for catching air off of Maui's swells.

Kayaking is excellent statewide, particularly on Kaua'i, where you can take the adventurous Nāpali Coast challenge, and on Moloka'i, where you can lazily paddle downwind past ancient fishponds.

Sport fishing fans should head to the Big Island's Kona Coast where billfish tournaments have reeled in monster Pacific blue marlins.

The deep blue Kona waters are also home to giant manta rays, and **scuba diving** among these gentle creatures is a magical experience. Scuba diving is also spectacular off Lānaʻi, where ethereal caverns have formed in the reefs, and on Maui, on the back wall of Molokini Crater.

All of the islands have great **snorkeling** spots, but Maui's two harbors offer the widest range of snorkeling and diving boat tours. Book a half-day cruise out to Molokini or an all-day adventure over to Lānaʻi.

During the winter months, from November to April, **whale-watching** tours launch from every island, but the marine mammals seem to favor Maui's Māʻalaea Bay. **Dolphin-spotting** is most reliable on Lānaʻi at Mānele Bay and on Hawaiʻi at Kealakekua Bay, where the charismatic spinner dolphins come to rest.

Go to each island's "Watersports" sections for detailed information on watersports outfitters and tour providers.

[FastFACTS] HAWAI'I

Area Codes Hawai'i's area code is 808; it applies to all islands. Use the area code when calling from one island to another; there is a long-distance charge.

Customs For details regarding U.S. Customs and Border Protection, consult your nearest U.S. embassy or consulate, or U.S. Customs (www.cbp.gov). You cannot take home fresh fruit, plants, or seeds (including some leis) unless they are inspected and sealed. You cannot seal and pack them yourself. For information on what you're allowed to bring home, contact one of the following agencies:

U.S. Citizens: U.S. Customs & Border Protection (CBP), 1300 Pennsylvania Ave., NW, Washington, DC 20229 (www.cbp.gov; ✆ **877/CBP-5511**).

Canadian Citizens: Canada Border Services Agency (www.cbsa-asfc.gc.ca; ✆ **800/461-9999** in Canada, or 204/983-3500).

U.K. Citizens: HM Customs & Excise (www.hmce.gov.uk; ✆ **0845/010-9000** in the U.K., or 020/8929-0152).

Australian Citizens: Australian Customs Service (www.customs.gov.au; ✆ **1300/363-263**).

New Zealand Citizens: New Zealand Customs, The Customhouse, 17–21 Whitmore St., Box 2218, Wellington (www.customs.govt.nz; ✆ **64/9-927-8036** outside of NZ, or 0800/428-786).

Electricity Like Canada, the United States uses 110 to 120 volts AC (60 cycles), compared to 220 to 240 volts AC (50 cycles) in most of Europe, Australia, and New Zealand. Downward converters that change 220–240 volts to 110–120 volts are hard to find in the U.S., so bring one with you if you're traveling to Hawai'i from abroad.

Embassies & Consulates All embassies are in the nation's capital, Washington, D.C. Some consulates are in major U.S. cities, and most nations have a mission to the United Nations in New York City. If your country isn't listed below, check **www.embassy.org/embassies**.

The embassy of **Australia** is at 1601 Massachusetts Ave. NW, Washington, DC 20036 (www.usa.embassy.gov.au; ✆ **202/797-3000**). Consulates are in New York, Honolulu, Houston, Los Angeles, Denver, Atlanta, Chicago, and San Francisco.

The embassy of **Canada** is at 501 Pennsylvania Ave. NW, Washington, DC 20001 (http://can-am.gc.ca/offices-bureaux/index.aspx; ✆ **202/682-1740**). Other Canadian consulates are in Chicago, Detroit, and San Diego. See website for full listing.

The embassy of **Ireland** is at 2234 Massachusetts Ave. NW, Washington, DC 20008 (www.embassyofireland.org; ✆ **202/462-3939**). Irish consulates are in Boston, Chicago, New York, San Francisco, and other cities. See website for full listing.

The embassy of **New Zealand** is at 37 Observatory Circle NW, Washington, DC 20008 (www.nzembassy.com; ✆ **202/328-4800**). A New Zealand consulate is in Los Angeles.

The embassy of the **United Kingdom** is at 3100 Massachusetts Ave. NW, Washington, DC 20008 (www.gov.uk/government/world/usa; ✆ **202/588-6500**). Other British consulates are in Atlanta, Boston, Chicago, Cleveland, Houston, Los Angeles, New York, San Francisco, and Seattle.

Family Travel With beaches to build castles on, water to splash in, and amazing sights to see, Hawai'i is paradise for children. Take a look at "The Best of Hawai'i for Kids," in chapter 1.

The larger hotels and resorts offer supervised programs for children and can refer you to qualified babysitters. By state law, hotels can accept only children ages 5 to 12 in supervised activities programs but can often accommodate younger kids by hiring babysitters to watch over them. Contact **People Attentive to Children (PATCH)** for referrals to babysitters who have taken a training course in childcare. On O'ahu, call ✆ **808/839-1988;** on the Big Island, call ✆ **808/283-3471** in Kona or ✆ **808/961-3169** in Hilo; on Maui, call ✆ **808/242-4672;** on Kaua'i, call ✆ **808/246-0622;** on Moloka'i and Lāna'i, call ✆ **800/498-4145;** or visit www.patchhawaii.org. The **Nanny Connection** (www.thenannyconnection.com; ✆ **808/875-4777**) on Maui is a reputable business that sends Mary Poppins–esque nannies to resorts and beaches to watch children ($19 per hour and up, depending on the number of children and holiday hours). Tutoring services are also available.

Baby's Away (www.babysaway.com) rents cribs, strollers, highchairs, playpens, infant seats, and the like on O'ahu (✆ **800/496-6386** or 808/99-7749), the Big Island (✆ **800/996-9030** or 808/756-5800), and Maui (✆ **800/942-9030** or 808/631-8618). The staff will deliver whatever you need to wherever you're staying and pick it up when you're done.

Gay & Lesbian Travelers Hawai'i welcomes all people with aloha. The number of gay- or lesbian-specific accommodations on the islands is limited, but most properties welcome gays and lesbians as they would any traveler. Since 1990, the state's capital has hosted the **Honolulu Pride Parade and Celebration.** Register to participate at www.honolulupride.org.

Gay Hawai'i (www.gayhawaii.com) and **Pride Guide Hawai'i** (www.gogayhawaii.com) are websites with gay and lesbian news, blogs, business recommendations, and other information for the entire state. Also check out the website for **Out in Hawai'i** (www.outinhawaii.com), which calls itself "Queer Resources and Information for the State of Hawai'i," with vacation ideas, a calendar of events, information on Hawai'i, and even a chat room.

Health **Mosquitoes** Mosquito-borne diseases are rare in Hawai'i, though an outbreak of dengue fever did affect Hawai'i Island in 2016. The Hawai'i State Health Department recommends travelers a) choose lodging with screens or sleep under a mosquito net; b) cover up in long sleeves and pants; and c) use EPA-registered insect repellent. For more info, visit the Centers for Disease Control and Prevention website at **www.cdc.gov/features/StopMosquitoes**.

Centipedes, Scorpions, & Other Critters Although insects can get a little close for comfort in Hawai'i (expect to see ants, cockroaches, and other critters indoors, even in posh hotels), few cause serious trouble. Giant centipedes—as long as 8 inches—are occasionally seen; scorpions are rare. Around Hilo on the Big Island, little red fire ants can rain down from trees and sting unsuspecting passersby. If you're stung or bitten by an insect and experience extreme pain, swelling, nausea, or any other severe reaction, seek medical help immediately. Geckos—the little lizards circling your porch light—are harmless and considered good luck in Hawaiian homes. Yes, even *inside* homes.

Hiking Safety Before you set out on a hike, let someone know where you're heading and when you plan to return; too many hikers spend cold nights in the wilderness because they don't take this simple precaution. It's always a good idea to hike with a pal. Select your route based on your own fitness level. Check weather conditions with the **National Weather Service** (www.prh.noaa.gov/hnl; ✆ **808/973-5286** on O'ahu), even if it looks sunny: The weather here ranges from blistering hot to freezing cold and can change in a matter of hours or miles. Do *not* hike if rain or a storm is predicted; flash floods are common in Hawai'i and have resulted in many preventable deaths. Plan to finish your hike at least an hour before sunset; because Hawai'i is so close to the equator, it does not have a twilight period, and thus it gets dark quickly after the sun sets. Wear sturdy shoes, a hat, clothes to protect you from the sun and from getting scratches, and high-SPF sunscreen on all exposed areas. Take plenty of water, basic first aid, a snack, and a bag to pack out what you pack in. Watch your step. Loose lava rocks are famous for twisting ankles. Don't rely on cellphones; service isn't available in many remote places.

Vog When molten lava from Kīlau'ea pours into the ocean, gases are released, resulting in a brownish, volcanic haze that hovers at the horizon. Some people claim that exposure to the smog-like air causes headaches and bronchial ailments. To date, there's no evidence that vog causes lingering damage to healthy individuals. Vog primarily affects the Big Island—Kona, in particular—but is often felt as far away as Maui and O'ahu. You can minimize the effects of vog by closing your windows and using an air conditioner indoors. The University of Hawai'i recommends draping a floor fan with a wet cloth saturated in a thin paste of baking soda and water, which captures and neutralizes the sulfur compounds. Cleansing your sinuses with a neti pot and saltwater also helps. ***Word of caution:*** If you're pregnant or have heart or breathing problems, avoid exposure to the sulfuric fumes in and around Hawai'i Volcanoes National Park.

Ocean Safety The range of watersports available here is astounding—this is a prime water playground with conditions for every age and ability. But the ocean is also an untamed wilderness; don't expect a calm swimming pool. Many people who visit Hawai'i underestimate the power of the ocean. With just a few precautions, your Pacific experience can be a safe and happy one. Before jumping in, familiarize yourself with your equipment. If you're snorkeling, make sure you feel at ease breathing and clearing water from the snorkel. Take a moment to watch where others are swimming. Observe weather conditions, swells, and possible riptides. If you get caught in big surf, dive underneath each wave until the swell subsides. Never turn your back to the ocean; rogue waves catch even experienced water folk unaware. Be realistic about your fitness—more than one visitor has ended his or her vacation with a heart attack in the water. Don't go out alone, or during a storm.

Note that sharks are not a big problem in Hawai'i; in fact, local divers look forward to seeing them. Only 2 of the 40 shark species present in Hawaiian waters are known to bite humans, and then usually it's by accident. But here are the general rules for avoiding sharks: Don't swim at dusk or in murky water—sharks may mistake you for one of their usual meals. It should be obvious not to swim where there are bloody fish in the water, as sharks become aggressive around blood.

Seasickness The waters in Hawai'i range from calm as glass (off the Kona Coast on the Big Island) to downright turbulent (in storm conditions) and usually fall somewhere in between. In general, expect rougher conditions in winter than in summer and on windward coastlines versus calm, leeward coastlines. If you've never been out on a boat, or if you've been seasick in the past, you might want to heed the following suggestions:

- The day before you go out on the boat, avoid alcohol, caffeine, citrus and other acidic juices, and greasy, spicy, or hard-to-digest foods.
- Get a good night's sleep the night before.
- Take or use whatever seasickness prevention works best for you—medication, an acupressure wristband, ginger tea or capsules, or any combination. But do it ***before* you board;** once you set sail, it's generally too late.
- While you're on the boat, stay as low and as near the center of the boat as possible. Avoid the fumes (especially if it's a diesel boat); stay out in the fresh air and watch the horizon. Do not read.
- If you start to feel queasy, drink clear fluids like water, and eat something bland, such as a soda cracker.

Stings The most common stings in Hawai'i come from **jellyfish,** particularly Portuguese man-of-war and box jellyfish. Since the poisons they inject are very different, you'll need to treat each type of sting differently.

A bluish-purple floating bubble with a long tail, the **Portuguese man-of-war** is responsible for some 6,500 stings a year on O'ahu alone. Although painful and a nuisance, these stings are rarely harmful; fewer than 1 in 1,000 requires medical treatment. The best prevention is to watch for these floating bubbles as you snorkel (look for the hanging tentacles below the surface). Get out of the water if anyone near you spots these jellyfish. Reactions to stings range from mild burning and reddening to severe welts and blisters. Most jellyfish stings disappear by themselves within 15 to 20 minutes if you do nothing at all to treat them. *All Stings Considered: First Aid and Medical Treatment of Hawai'i's Marine Injuries,* by Craig Thomas, M.D., and Susan Scott (University of Hawai'i Press, 1997), recommends the following treatment: First, pick off any visible tentacles with a gloved hand or a stick; then, rinse the sting with salt- or fresh water, and apply ice to prevent swelling. Avoid applying vinegar, baking soda, or urine to the wound, which may actually cause further damage. See a doctor if pain persists or a rash or other symptoms develop.

Transparent, square-shaped **box jellyfish** are nearly impossible to see in the water. Fortunately, they seem to follow a monthly cycle: 8 to 10 days after the full moon, they appear in the waters on the leeward side of each island and hang around for about 3 days. Also, they seem to sting more in the morning, when they're on or near the surface. The stings from a box jellyfish can cause hive-like welts, blisters, and pain lasting from 10 minutes to 8 hours. *All Stings Considered* recommends the following treatment: First, pour regular household vinegar on the sting; this will stop additional burning. Do not rub the area. Pick off any vinegar-soaked tentacles with a stick and apply an ice pack. Seek medical treatment if you experience shortness of breath, weakness, palpitations, or any other severe symptoms.

Punctures Most sea-related punctures come from stepping on or brushing against the needle-like spines of sea urchins (known locally as *wana*). Be careful when you're in the water; don't put your foot down (even if you are wearing booties or fins) if you can't clearly see the bottom. Waves can push you into *wana* in a surge zone in shallow water. The spines can even puncture a wet suit. A sea urchin puncture can result in burning, aching, swelling, and discoloration (black or purple) around the area where the spines entered your skin. The best thing to do is to pull out any protruding spines. The body will absorb the spines within 24 hours to 3 weeks, or the remainder of the spines will work themselves out. Again, contrary to popular thought, urinating or pouring vinegar on the embedded spines will not help.

Cuts Stay out of the ocean if you have an open cut, wound, or new tattoo. The high level of bacteria present in the water means that even small wounds can become infected. Staphylococcus, or "staph," infections start out as swollen, pinkish skin tissue around the wound that spreads and grows rather than dries and heals. Scrub any cuts well with fresh water and avoid the ocean until they heal. Consult a doctor if your wound shows signs of infection.

Also see "Fast Facts" in the individual island chapters for listings of local **doctors, dentists, hospitals,** and **emergency numbers.**

Internet & Wi-Fi On every island, branches of the **Hawaii State Public Library System** have free computers with Internet access. To find your closest library, check **www.librarieshawaii.org/sitemap.htm**. There is no charge for use of the computers, but you must have a Hawai'i library card, which is free to Hawai'i residents and members of the military. Visitors can visit any branch to purchase a $10 visitor card that is good for 3 months.

If you have your own laptop, every **Starbucks** in Hawai'i has Wi-Fi. For a list of locations, go to **www.starbucks.com/retail/find/default.aspx**. Many, if not most, **hotel lobbies** have free Wi-Fi. **Whole Foods** is another reliable option.

Most interisland airports have **Internet kiosks** that provide basic Web access for a per-minute fee that's usually higher than cybercafe prices. The **Honolulu International Airport** (http://hawaii.gov/hnl) provides **Wi-Fi access** for a fee through Shaka Net. Check out copy shops like **FedEx Office,** which offers computer stations with fully loaded software (as well as Wi-Fi).

Mail At press time, domestic postage rates were 33¢ for a postcard and 49¢ for a letter. For international mail, a first-class postcard or letter up to 1 ounce costs $1.15. For more information go to **www.usps.com**.

If you aren't sure what your address will be in the United States, mail can be sent to you, in your name, c/o General Delivery at the main post office of the city or region where you expect to be. (Call ✆ **800/275-8777** for information on the nearest post office.) The addressee must pick up mail in person and must produce proof of identity (driver's license, passport, and the like). Most post offices will hold mail for up to 1 month and are open Monday to Friday from 9am to 4pm, and Saturday from 9am to noon.

Always include zip codes when mailing items in the U.S. If you don't know your zip code, visit www.usps.com/zip4.

Medical Requirements Unless you're arriving from an area known to be suffering from an epidemic (particularly cholera or yellow fever), inoculations or vaccinations are not required for entry into the United States.

Mobile Phones Cellphone coverage is decent throughout Hawai'i but tends to be inconsistent in the more remote and mountainous regions of the Islands. AT&T and Verizon tend to get the best reception.

If you are traveling from outside of the U.S., you may want to purchase an international SIM card for your cellphone or buy a prepaid cellphone with local service.

Do *not* use your cellphone while you are driving. Strict laws and heavy fines ($297 and up) are diligently enforced.

Money & Costs Frommer's lists exact prices in the local currency. The currency conversions quoted below were correct at press time. However, rates fluctuate, so before departing, consult a currency exchange website such as www.oanda.com or www.xe.com/currencyconverter to check up-to-the-minute rates.

THE VALUE OF US$ VS. OTHER POPULAR CURRENCIES

US$	Can$	UK£	Euro (€)	Aus$	NZ$
1	C$1.30	£.69	€.88	A$1.31	NZ$1.45

ATMs (cashpoints) are everywhere in Hawai'i—at banks, supermarkets, Long's Drugs, and Honolulu International Airport, as well as in some resorts and shopping centers. The **Cirrus** (www.mastercard.com; ✆ **800/424-7787**) and **PLUS** (www.visa.com; ✆ **800/843-7587**) networks span the country; you can find them even in remote regions. Go to your bank card's website to find ATM locations at your destination. Find out your daily withdrawal limit before you depart.

Note: Many banks impose a fee every time you use a card at another bank's ATM, and that fee is often higher for international transactions (up to $5 or more) than for domestic ones (rarely more than $2.50). In addition, the bank from which you withdraw cash is likely to charge its own fee. Visitors from outside the U.S. should also find out whether their bank assesses a 1 to 3% fee on charges incurred abroad.

Credit cards are accepted everywhere except TheBus (on O'ahu), most taxicabs (all islands), and some small restaurants and B&B accommodations.

Packing Tips

Hawai'i is very informal. Shorts, T-shirts, and sandals will get you by at most restaurants and attractions; a casual dress or a polo shirt and long pants are fine even in the most expensive places. (Restaurants in the Halekulani on O'ahu and the Big Island's Mauna Kea Beach Hotel require men to wear long-sleeved collared shirts.) Aloha wear is acceptable everywhere, so you may want to plan on buying an aloha shirt or a Hawaiian-style dress while you're in the islands. If you plan on hiking, horseback riding, or ziplining, bring close-toed shoes; they're required.

The tropical sun poses the greatest threat to anyone who ventures into the great outdoors, so pack **sun protection:** a good pair of sunglasses, strong sunscreen, a light hat, and a water bottle. Dehydration is common in the tropics.

One last thing: **It can get really cold in Hawai'i.** If you plan to see the sunrise from the top of Maui's Haleakalā Crater, venture into the Big Island's Hawai'i Volcanoes National Park, or spend time in Koke'e State Park on Kaua'i, bring a warm jacket. Temperatures "upcountry" (higher up the mountain) can sink to 40°F (4°C), even in summer when it's 80°F (27°C) at the beach. Bring a windbreaker, sweater, or light jacket. And if you'll be in Hawai'i between November and March, toss some **rain gear** into your suitcase, too.

Passports

Virtually every air traveler entering the U.S. is required to show a passport. All persons, including U.S. citizens, traveling by air between the United States and Canada, Mexico, Central and South America, the Caribbean, and Bermuda are required to present a valid passport. ***Note:*** U.S. and Canadian citizens entering the U.S. at land and sea ports of entry from within the western hemisphere must now also present a passport or other documents compliant with the Western Hemisphere Travel Initiative (WHTI; check www.getyouhome.gov for details). Children 15 and under may continue entering with only a U.S. birth certificate, or other proof of U.S. citizenship. Residents of New York, Louisiana, Minnesota, New Hampshire, and American Samoa will need to show passports as well; drivers licenses are no longer accepted from these states/territories.

Australia Australian Passport Information Service (www.passports.gov.au; ✆ **131-232** in Australia).

Canada **Passport Office,** Department of Foreign Affairs and International Trade, Ottawa, ON K1A 0G3 (www.ppt.gc.ca; ✆ **800/567-6868**).

WHAT THINGS COST IN HAWAI'I	US$
Hamburger	6.00–19.00
Movie ticket (adult/child)	11.00/7.50
Taxi from Honolulu Airport to Waikīkī	35.00–40.00
Entry to Bishop Museum (adult/child)	23.00/15.00
Entry to Wet 'n' Wild (adult/child)	50.00/38.00
Entry to Honolulu Zoo (adult/child)	14.00/6.00
Entry to Maui Ocean Center (adult/child)	28.00/20.00
Old Lahaina Lū'au (adult/child)	115.00/78.00
Entry to Hawai'i Volcanoes National Park (car)	15.00
Moderately priced three-course dinner without alcohol	70.00
20-ounce soft drink at convenience store	2.50
16-ounce apple juice	3.50
Cup of coffee	3.00
Moderately priced Waikīkī hotel room (double)	165.00–225.00

Ireland **Passport Office,** Setanta Centre, Molesworth Street, Dublin 2 (www.foreignaffairs.gov.ie; ✆ **01/671-1633**).

New Zealand **Passports Office,** Department of Internal Affairs, 47 Boulcott St., Wellington, 6011 (www.passports.govt.nz; ✆ **0800/225-050** in New Zealand or 04/474-8100).

United Kingdom Visit your nearest passport office, major post office, or travel agency, or contact the **Identity and Passport Service (IPS),** 89 Eccleston Sq., London, SW1V 1PN (www.ips.gov.uk; ✆ **0300/222-0000**).

United States To find your regional passport office, check the U.S. State Department website (http://travel.state.gov) or call the **National Passport Information Center** (✆ **877/487-2778**) for automated information.

Safety Although tourist areas are generally safe, visitors should always stay alert, even in laidback Hawai'i (and especially in Waikīkī). If you're in doubt about which neighborhoods are safe, the island tourist office can advise you. Avoid deserted areas, especially at night. Don't go into any city park at night unless there's an event that attracts crowds—for example, the Waikīkī Shell concerts in Kapi'olani Park. Generally speaking, you can feel safe in areas where there are many people and lots of open establishments.

Avoid carrying valuables with you on the street, and don't display expensive cameras or electronic equipment. Hold on to your purse, and place your billfold in an inside pocket. In theaters, restaurants, and other public places, keep your possessions in sight. Remember also that hotels are open to the public and that security may not be able to screen everyone entering, particularly in large properties. Always lock your room door—don't assume that once inside your hotel you're automatically safe.

Burglaries of tourists' rental cars in hotel parking structures and at beach or hiking parking lots have become more common. Park in well-lit and well-traveled areas, if possible. Never leave any packages or valuables visible in the car. If someone attempts to rob you or steal your car, do not try to resist the thief or carjacker—report the incident to the police department immediately. Ask your rental car agent about specific spots to avoid on each island, and get written directions or a map with the route to your destination clearly marked.

Generally, Hawai'i has the same laws as the mainland United States. Nudity is illegal in Hawai'i. There are *no* legal nude beaches (we don't care what you have read). If you are nude on a beach (or anywhere) in Hawai'i, you can be arrested.

Senior Travel Discounts for seniors are available at almost all of Hawai'i's major attractions and occasionally at hotels and restaurants. The Outrigger hotel chain, for instance, offers travelers ages 50 and older a 20% discount on regular published rates—and an additional 5% off for members of AARP. Always ask when making hotel reservations or buying tickets. And always carry identification with proof of your age—it can really pay off.

Smoking Smokers will be hard-pressed to find places to light up. It's against the law to smoke in public buildings (including airports, malls, stores, buses, movie theaters, banks, convention facilities, and all government buildings and facilities). There is no smoking in restaurants, bars, and nightclubs. Neither can you smoke at public beaches or parks. Essentially, you'll be relegated to the tiny smoking section on the edge of your hotel property. More hotels and resorts are becoming nonsmoking, even in public areas, and most B&Bs prohibit smoking indoors. Smoking is prohibited within 20 feet of a doorway, window, or ventilation intake (so no hanging around outside a bar to smoke—you must go 20 ft. away). Smoking **marijuana** is illegal; if you attempt to buy it or light up, you can be arrested.

Taxes The United States has no value-added tax (VAT) or other indirect tax at the national level. Every state, county, and city may levy its own local tax on all purchases, including hotel and restaurant checks and airline tickets. These taxes will not appear on price tags.

Hawai'i state general excise tax is 4.166%, which applies to all items purchased (including hotel rooms). The county of O'ahu levies an additional 0.546% tax. On top of that, the state's transient Accommodation Tax (TAT) is 9.25%. These taxes, combined with various resort fees, can add up to 17% to 18% of your room rate. Budget accordingly.

Telephones All calls on-island are local calls; calls from one island to another via a landline are long distance and you must dial 1, then the Hawai'i area code (808), and then the phone number. Convenience stores sell **prepaid calling cards** in denominations up to $50. You are unlikely to see a public pay phone, however. Those at airports now accept American Express, MasterCard, and Visa. **Local calls** made from most pay phones cost 50¢. Most long-distance and international calls can be dialed directly from any phone. **To make calls within the United States and to Canada,** dial 1, followed by the area code and the seven-digit number. **For other international calls,** dial 011, followed by the country code, city code, and the number you are calling.

Calls to area codes **800, 888, 877,** and **866** are toll-free. However, calls to area codes **700** and **900** (chat lines, bulletin boards, "dating" services, and so on) can be expensive—charges of 95¢ to $3 or more per minute. Some numbers have minimum charges that can run $15 or more.

For **reversed-charge or collect calls,** and for person-to-person calls, dial the number 0, then the area code and number; an operator will come on the line, and you should specify whether you are calling collect, person-to-person, or both. If your operator-assisted call is international, ask for the overseas operator.

For **directory assistance** ("Information"), dial 411 for local numbers and national numbers in the U.S. and Canada. For dedicated long-distance information, dial 1, then the appropriate area code plus 555-1212.

Time The continental United States is divided into **four time zones:** Eastern Standard Time (EST), Central Standard Time (CST), Mountain Standard Time (MST), and Pacific Standard Time (PST). Alaska and Hawai'i have their own zones. For example, when it's 7am in Honolulu (HST), it's 9am in Los Angeles (PST), 10am in Denver (MST), 11am in Chicago (CST), noon in New York City (EST), 5pm in London (GMT), and 2am the next day in Sydney.

Daylight saving time, in effect in most of the United States from 2am on the second Sunday in March to 2am on the first Sunday in November, is not observed in Hawai'i, Arizona, the U.S. Virgin Islands, and Puerto Rico. Daylight saving time moves the clock 1 hour ahead of standard time.

Tipping Tips are a major part of certain workers' income, and gratuities are the standard way of showing appreciation for services provided. (Tipping is certainly not compulsory if the service is poor!) In hotels, tip **bellhops** at least $2 per bag ($3–$5 if you have a lot of luggage) and tip the **housekeepers** $2 per person per day (more if you've left a disaster area for him or her to clean up). Tip the **doorman** or **concierge** only if he or she has provided you with some specific service (for example, calling a cab for you or obtaining difficult-to-get theater tickets). Tip the **valet-parking attendant** $2 to $5 every time you get your car.

In restaurants, bars, and nightclubs, tip **service staff** and **bartenders** 18% to 20% of the check, and tip **valet-parking attendants** $2 per vehicle.

As for other service personnel, tip **cab drivers** 15% of the fare; tip **skycaps** at airports at least $2 per bag ($3–$5 if you have a lot of luggage); and tip **hairdressers** and **barbers** 18% to 20%.

Toilets You won't find public toilets or "restrooms" on the streets in Hawai'i, but they can be found in hotel lobbies, restaurants, museums, department stores, railway and bus stations, service stations, and at most beaches. Large hotels and fast-food restaurants are often the best bet for clean facilities. Restaurants and bars in heavily visited areas may reserve their restrooms for patrons.

Travelers with Disabilities Travelers with disabilities are made to feel very welcome in Hawai'i. There are more than 2,000 ramped curbs in O'ahu alone, many hotels are equipped with wheelchair-accessible rooms and pools, and tour companies provide many special services. Beach wheelchairs are available at one beach on Maui (Kamaole I; ask lifeguard) and six beaches on O'ahu. Contact the **City and County of Honolulu Department of Parks and Recreation** (www.honolulu.gov/parks/dprbeachaccess; ✆ **808/768-3027**) for locations.

For tips on accessible travel in Hawai'i, go to the **Hawai'i Tourism Authority** website (www.gohawaii.com/oahu/about/travel-tips/special-needs). The **Statewide Independent Living Council of Hawaii,** 841 Bishop St., Honolulu, HI 96813 (www.hisilc.org; ✆ **808/585-7452**), can provide additional resources about accessibility throughout the Islands.

Access Aloha Travel (www.accessalohatravel.com; ✆ **800/480-1143**) specializes in accommodating travelers with disabilities. Agents book cruises, tours, rental vans (available on Maui and O'ahu only), accommodations, and airfare (as part of a package only). On Maui and Kaua'i, **Gammie Homecare** (www.gammie.com; Maui: ✆ **808/877-4032;** Kaua'i: ✆ **808/632-2333**) rents everything from motorized scooters to shower chairs.

Visas The U.S. State Department has a **Visa Waiver Program (VWP)** allowing citizens of the following countries to enter the United States without a visa for stays of up to 90 days: Andorra, Australia, Austria, Belgium, Brunei, Chile, the Czech Republic, Denmark, Estonia, Finland, France, Germany, Greece, Hungary, Iceland, Ireland, Italy, Japan, Latvia, Liechtenstein, Lithuania, Luxembourg, Malta, Monaco, the Netherlands, New Zealand,

Norway, Portugal, San Marino, Singapore, Slovakia, Slovenia, South Korea, Spain, Sweden, Switzerland, Taiwan, and the United Kingdom. (***Note:*** This list was accurate at press time; for the most up-to-date list of countries in the VWP, consult http://usvisas.state.gov.) Even though a visa isn't necessary, in an effort to help U.S. officials check travelers against terror watch lists before they arrive at U.S. borders, visitors from VWP countries must register online through the Electronic System for Travel Authorization (ESTA) before boarding a plane or a boat to the U.S. Travelers must complete an electronic application providing basic personal and travel eligibility information. The Department of Homeland Security recommends filling out the form at least 3 days before traveling. Authorizations will be valid for up to 2 years or until the traveler's passport expires, whichever comes first. Currently, there is a US$14 fee for the online application. Existing ESTA registrations remain valid through their expiration dates. ***Note:*** Any passport issued on or after October 26, 2006, by a VWP country must be an **e-Passport** for VWP travelers to be eligible to enter the U.S. without a visa. Citizens of these nations also need to present a round-trip air or cruise ticket upon arrival. E-Passports contain computer chips capable of storing biometric information, such as the required digital photograph of the holder. If your passport doesn't have this feature, you can still travel without a visa if the valid passport was issued before October 26, 2005, and includes a machine-readable zone; or if the valid passport was issued between October 26, 2005, and October 25, 2006, and includes a digital photograph. For more information, go to **http://usvisas.state.gov**. Canadian citizens may enter the United States without a visa but will need to show a passport and proof of residence.

Citizens of all other countries must have (1) a valid passport that expires at least 6 months later than the scheduled end of their visit to the U.S., and (2) a tourist visa. For information about U.S. visas, go to **http://usvisas.state.gov**. Or go to one of the following:

Australian citizens can obtain up-to-date visa information from the **U.S. Embassy Canberra,** Moonah Place, Yarralumla, ACT 2600 (✆ **02/6214-5600**) or by checking the U.S. Diplomatic Mission's website at http://canberra.usembassy.gov/visas.html.

British subjects can obtain up-to-date visa information by calling the **U.S. Embassy Visa Information Line** (✆ **09042-450-100** from within the U.K. at £1.20 per min.; or ✆ **866/382-3589** from within the U.S. at a flat rate of $16, payable by credit card only) or by visiting the American Embassy London's website at http://london.usembassy.gov/visas.html.

Irish citizens can obtain up-to-date visa information through the **U.S. Embassy Dublin,** 42 Elgin Rd., Ballsbridge, Dublin 4 (http://dublin.usembassy.gov; ✆ **1580-47-VISA** [8472] from within the Republic of Ireland at €2.40 per min.).

Citizens of **New Zealand** can obtain up-to-date visa information by contacting the **U.S. Embassy New Zealand,** 29 Fitzherbert Terrace, Thorndon, Wellington (http://newzealand.usembassy.gov; ✆ **644/462-6000**).

Water Generally the water in your hotel or at public drinking fountains is safe to drink (depending on the island, it may have more chlorine than you like).

Index

A

B

C

L

O

P

PHOTO CREDITS

p. i: © Hawaii Tourism Authority (HTA) / Dana Edmunds; p. iii: © Eric Baker; p. 1: © Vibrant Image Studio; p. 2: © norinori303; p. 4: © Deborah Kolb; p. 5: © Peter Zurek; p. 7: © Aaron D. Feen; p. 8: © tdlucas5000; p. 9: © bonnieshappell; p. 11: © PKMousie; p. 14: © Eric Baker; p. 17: © Vacclav / Shutterstock.com; p. 18: © Jeff Whyte / Shutterstock.com; p. 21: © Robert Linsdell; p. 22: © Marisa Estivill; p. 24: © Peter Liu; p. 25: © mutrock; p. 30: © jshyun; p. 31: © Frederique Lavoipierre; p. 34: © Nina B; p. 35: © Deborah Kolb; p. 38, left: © Wallyg; p. 38, right: © Patpayne79; p. 40: By unknown photographer more than 70 years ago [Public domain], via Wikimedia Commons; p. 43: © Boykov / Shutterstock.com; p. 44: © davidkosmos; p. 45: © emilychang; p. 46: © Courtesy Fox Searchlight Pictures; p. 56: © IZO / Shutterstock.com; p. 60: © Ami Parikh; p. 66: © Takayuki Nakamura; p. 71: © sandwichgirl; p. 76: © jikido; p. 77: © wallyg; p. 81: © antxoa; p. 82: © Ryan Siphers; p. 86: © James Crawford; p. 88: © cleanfotos; p. 96: © Courtesy of the Polynesian Cultural Center; p. 99: © Hawaii Tourism Japan (HTJ); p. 104: © Jeff Whyte / Shutterstock.com; p. 107: © Ryan Siphers; p. 110: © cdelacy; p. 112: © Juan Oliphant; p. 115: © lauraslens; p. 121: © Courtesy of Pearl Country Club; p. 123: © Jeff Whyte / Shutterstock.com; p. 157: © TerriJane01; p. 158: © Hartphotography | Dreamstime.com; p. 161: © Ryan Siphers; p. 165: © jon_gilbert; p. 169: © George Burba; p. 171: © Francesco Carucci; p. 172: © aquatic creature; p. 174: © Tomas Banik; p. 176: © U.S. Pacific Fleet; p. 178: © Marty Wakat; p. 182: © jeff speigner; p. 184: © Vacclav; p. 187: © JoePhilipson; p. 188: © Joy Prescott; p. 191: © Marisa Estivill; p. 192: © Stubblefield Photography; p. 193: © www.sandatlas.org; p. 194: © Maridav; p. 195: © Marisa Estivill; p. 196: © Panachai Cherdchucheep; p. 197: © Irina Mos; p. 202: © Nemo's great uncle; p. 203: © Peter Baer; p. 209: © Radoslaw Lecyk; p. 211: © Nickolay Stanev; p. 218: © SYLVIO MICHEL; p. 219: © Alberto Loyo; p. 221: © Kanaka Menehune; p. 223: © Pat McGrath; p. 225: © Radoslaw Lecyk; p. 226: © Vilainecrevette; p. 236: © Fabien Monteil; p. 242: © rocketvox_; p. 246: © forty42two; p. 248: © yliu711; p. 285: © Bonita R. Cheshier; p. 290: © Max Earey / Shutterstock.com; p. 294: © emmett anderson; p. 297: © Peter Liu; p. 298: © Leslie Ray Ware; p. 303: © Sarah Fields Photography; p. 305: © Chad Goddard; p. 306: © Jon Konrath; p. 309: © Kristina D.C. Hoeppner; p. 312: © Robert Cicchetti; p. 314: © Doug Oglesby; p. 315: © Max Earey / Shutterstock.com; p. 317: © David Casteel; p. 320: © Marisa Estivill; p. 323: © Bienchen-s; p. 326: © Eric Broder Van Dyke; p. 327: © Darren J. Bradley; p. 328: © idreamphoto; p. 329: © James Brennan; p. 332: © Ocean Image Photography; p. 337: © Dudarev Mikhail; p. 345: © Andrei Stanescu; p. 346: © Bruce Irschick; p. 350: © Madbuster75; p. 420: © Allie_Caulfield; p. 424: © Shulevskyy Volodymyr; p. 428: © Hiroyuki Saita / Shutterstock.com; p. 430: © Eugene Kalenkovich; p. 434: © munnecket; p. 436: © Karl Keller; p. 438: © jshyun; p. 440: © jshyun; p. 443: © mutrock; p. 444: © lauraslens; p. 445: © Mike Brake; p. 447: © Mike Brake; p. 449: © GROGL; p. 458: © valdezign; p. 461: © Blaiz; p. 464: © Dlabajdesign; p. 465: By Christian Hedemann (1852–1932) [Public domain], via Wikimedia Commons; p. 469: © Joe West / Shutterstock.com; p. 471: © Joe West; p. 472: © Joe West; p. 473: © lauraslens; p. 474: © Joe West; p. 476: © Darren J. Bradley; p. 479: © Joe West; p. 488: © Atelier Teee; p. 489: © David P. Smith; p. 494: © Sarah Fields Photography; p. 495: © Dan Schreiber; p. 496: © Nickolay Stanev; p. 498: © Steve Heap; p. 499: © Mike Peters; p. 501: © Steve Heap; p. 504: © Cloudia Spinner; p. 507: © Selbe B; p. 513: © pdxjeff; p. 514: © Steve Heap; p. 517: © Bonita R. Cheshier; p. 520: © Marisa Estivill; p. 521: © MNStudio; p. 522: © Sarah Fields Photography; p. 524: © MNStudio; p. 529: © Barbara Eads; p. 533: © Nina B; p. 534: © Nickolay Stanev; p. 538: © Alex Pix; p. 541: © Slateterreno; p. 545: © Crashworks; p. 548: © Nina B; p. 551: © lauraslens; p. 556: © Christian Kieffer; p. 558: © MukYJ; p. 595: © Hawaii Tourism Authority (HTA) / Tor Johnson; p. 597: © Scottt13; p. 600: © Katy Kristin; p. 602: © Mr Doomits